D1146038

AN APPROACH TO SHAKESPEARE

AN APPROACH TO SHAKESPEARE

D. A. TRAVERSI

THIRD EDITION
REVISED AND EXPANDED

NORTHWEST MISSOURI STATE
UNIVERSITY LIBRARY
MARYVILLE, MISSOURI 64468

NORTHWEST MISSOURI
STATE COLLEGE LIBRARY
MARYVILLE, MISSOURI

DOUBLEDAY & COMPANY, INC.
GARDEN CITY, NEW YORK

121482

Portions of the Third Edition of AN APPROACH TO SHAKESPEARE were originally published as AN APPROACH TO SHAKESPEARE by Sands and Company, Ltd. in 1938. The Doubleday edition is published by arrangement with Sands and Company, Ltd.

Library of Congress Catalog Card Number 68–17782
Copyright © 1956 by Doubleday & Company, Inc.
Copyright © 1960, 1969 by Derek A. Traversi
All Rights Reserved
Printed in the United States of America

822.33
DT78
1969

AUTHOR'S NOTE

The present study is conceived as an expansion of my earlier book, originally published under the same title as long ago as 1938, and reissued in a considerably longer form in 1956. It has long been apparent to me that this study suffered, even in its more extended form, by being concentrated almost exclusively on the later stages of Shakespeare's dramatic career. I hope that the new book, which deals with every undoubted play in the canon, may go some way toward correcting the balance.

The book is divided into two parts. The first aims at tracing Shakespeare's growing grasp of the full possibilities of his various forms, poetical and dramatic, and discusses in the process a number of undoubted masterpieces. The second part is almost entirely concerned with masterpieces and is on that account more compressed in its treatment of them: but here too it is my hope that something like a continuous argument emerges, though not of the kind that forces the uniformity of a thesis upon material inexhaustibly rich and suggestive in its implications.

There has been, inevitably, some overlap with previous publications. In the first part, Chapter IV on the sonnets reproduces, with some amendment, what I first wrote in 1938, and Chapter VII on the later series of English history plays largely sums up the argument of my book *Shakespeare: From "Richard II" to "Henry V,"* first published in 1957 by the Stanford University Press in the United States and by Messrs. Hollis and Carter in England. Chapter III on the early comedies also owes a good deal to an essay on the same plays published in the *Writers and Their Work* series (Longman's and the British Council) in 1960. Eleven plays, however, are studied for the first time and I hope that the argument as a whole will throw some light on the development of the dramatist's art in its earlier stages.

In the second part the original essay has been largely rewritten to take into account changes of view or emphasis in the intervening years. I have added completely fresh studies of six plays—*All's Well*, *Timon of Athens*, *Julius Caesar*, *Pericles*, *Cymbeline*, and *The*

Tempest—and have drawn heavily, in the relevant chapters, on my two books on *The Last Phase* (1954) and *The Roman Plays* (1963), both issued in the United States and in England by the publishers named above. Permission to make use of this material is in each case gratefully acknowledged.

The first part of the book, which includes the greater part of the entirely new material, was conceived and largely written during a semester spent in the autumn and early winter of 1965–66 as Visiting Professor at Swarthmore College, Pennsylvania. I am conscious of a great debt of gratitude to my colleagues and friends there; and also to my seminar students in discussion with whom not a few of the points here made were formulated or clarified. The views expressed are, of course, entirely my own, but without these advantages the book might well not have been written.

DEREK TRAVERSI

Rome, December 1967.

CONTENTS

Introduction

It is perhaps worth recalling at the outset of this study that its origins lie in a very short and perhaps rather dogmatic essay originally published thirty years ago and entitled, like the present volume, *An Approach to Shakespeare*. The point of departure for this essay was an assertion that the great nineteenth-century tradition of Shakespearean study—running from Coleridge and Goethe to Bradley's *Shakespearean Tragedy*[1]—had reached "something like the limits of its usefulness." Little more, it was suggested, remained to be discovered in that particular direction; nor, at the time of writing, were the assumptions which this school of criticism had taken for granted entirely acceptable. More particularly, the Victorian insistence upon *character*, when carried to the point of excluding other aspects of an essentially *dramatic* action, had its foundation in the subjectivism of Romantic thought. *Hamlet* the tragedy—to take the stock example—became, when considered in the light of this tradition, a fruitful mirror for the dissatisfactions of the romantic self, and even the greatest students of the plays—who gave us a great deal that was very valuable—found it difficult to avoid confusing Shakespeare's aims with their own often quite different concerns. Above all—and to this we shall return—this type of criticism found its theatrical counterpart in a conception of the stage, and of the dramatic action as a whole, which tended to distort Shakespeare's intentions and even to make some of the greatest plays[2] almost impossible to represent.

This, however, as the introduction to the 1938 essay also suggested, was not the whole of the story.

> We all know that to discuss Hamlet's life *outside* the limits of the play, to attempt to deduce the manner of his upbringing in order to explain his subsequent behavior, is an illegitimate extension of the critic's proper function. Nor can we share the confidence with which some writers fathered their own philosophies on to Shakespeare's work. But, although we are certain that the old outlook was

> incomplete and sometimes misleading—just as we know that the sumptuous and realistic productions, which were its theatrical equivalent, were not the last word in the production of the plays—we are far less sure what is to replace them.

The essay went on to say that many valuable lines of approach had been opened out since the beginning of the century; we might now add, thirty years later, that many more have become available. Among these is a notable advance in our knowledge of the Elizabethan background of thought in cosmology, psychology, rhetoric, and in ideas on literature in general and drama in particular, which has the negative virtue of discouraging us from reading the plays too directly in the light of subsequent experience. Side by side with this, and largely complementary to it, is the remarkable growth in our understanding of Elizabethan stage conditions and of their relevance for a proper understanding of the plays; already in 1938, it was possible to mention the pioneer work of Granville-Barker,[3] and a great deal has been accomplished in this direction in subsequent years. Finally, the introduction to the original essay mentioned the rise of a double-edged approach to the plays in the kind of *interpretation* proposed by Professor Wilson Knight, still a relatively new development in the thirties.

Each of these "approaches," however, though important and fruitful, brought with it its accompanying dangers. The increased modern interest in Elizabethan thought and knowledge has led us back, truly and significantly, to the contemporary setting of the plays and so has helped, among other things, to avoid the nineteenth-century errors of misplaced emphasis; but—it must be added—the criticism that has followed from this approach tends to ignore the element of essential *discontinuity* which separates a genius from the commonplaces of his age. A writer of Shakespeare's stature is of his time in the ideas he uses, and we shall always be unwise to forget this; but he uses these ideas in ways of his own, which are not necessarily those of his time alone. Shakespeare's plays on English history, for example, lean heavily upon contemporary notions concerning such subjects as monarchy, its origins, its role, and its justification; but to interpret the series of chronicles from *Richard II* to *Henry V* as no more than exercises in Tudor patriotic propaganda is, in my submission, seriously to underestimate their originality. What truly emerges from these plays—as I shall seek to show[4]—is a thoroughly personal vision, increasingly tragic in its final implications, of man as a political being; so that, properly read, they speak to us not less than they did to the late sixteenth century, and speak moreover in ways that very few minds of that age—with the possible exception of Machiavelli—would have fully understood. To compare Shakespeare, as a mature dramatist, to almost any other Elizabethan writer is to be made aware of the degree to which he evades, escapes from the current Elizabethan limitations. Such a writer, in other words, and to adapt a critical commonplace, both is of his time and transcends it. The scholar is by the very nature of his task inclined to stress those aspects of a Shakespeare that relate him to his own times. In the process of so doing he helps to save us from committing fundamental errors of appreciation; but the critic—if I may be allowed, *for my present purpose alone,* to separate him from the scholar—is there to redress a necessary balance, the failure to appreciate which will prevent a response to his subject's true originality.

Something of the same kind, though to a lesser degree, can be said of an "approach" too exclusively limited to a knowledge of the theater and, more particularly, of contemporary stage conditions. As I suggested in 1938, Granville-Barker's very considerable contribution to our understanding of Shakespeare as a working dramatist was to some extent limited by the tendency to rest on established judgments where both poetry and the definition of character were concerned. He stressed, in the body of his work, an important truth, and one that his immediate predecessors had tended to neglect; but it was possibly too much to expect that he should also transform our understanding of other and not less important aspects of Shakespeare's work to correspond to that truth and to produce a new vision in its totality. His Hamlet and his Othello, were, in other words, still close to those proposed by Bradley, though our view of the stage on which these characters appeared was revivified, largely transformed, by the line of study which he did so much to originate.

The third of our new lines of "approach," as seen thirty years ago, was that which led finally to the methods of "interpretation" largely associated with the work of Wilson Knight. The effect of these methods was to move away from the more traditional readings in terms of character or "philosophic" content to another, by which a given play was regarded, to use Wilson Knight's own phrase, as "an expanded metaphor." In the light of this contention the critic's task became very largely that of tracing in the plays significant threads and patterns of imagery within a "spacial unity," recurrent themes through whose study and correlation the full "meaning" of the work as a whole was to emerge. This line of approach can be associated, on a more academic level, with that of Professor Caroline Spurgeon, who—in a pioneer study published at this time[5]—card-indexed and catalogued Shakespeare's images, following up the repetition of particular images in a given play, and who even claimed as a result to be able to tell us something about the writer's own tastes and prejudices. Because, for example, the dramatist can be shown repeatedly to associate spaniels with cloying flattery, and because this association tends to produce in his poetry a sense of almost physical revulsion, we are asked to conclude that Shakespeare the man—that dim and unsatisfactory abstraction—felt a particular dislike for this species of dog, and perhaps for dogs in general. Whether this deplorably un-English trait contributes anything to an appreciation of his work remains uncertain.

To leave the matter thus is clearly to be less than fair to what Professor Spurgeon, and her method as developed by others in various directions, in fact achieved. The best parts of her study were valuable and important: how important we are perhaps now prevented from seeing by the fact that not a few of her discoveries have become common currency in later criticism. It helps us to understand *Troilus and Cressida,* for example, to know that there can be found in it a notable concentration upon imagery of taste; it is relevant to the study of *Macbeth* to remember that images of ill-fitting clothes appear repeatedly in the course of the play. These real discoveries called for a development which Professor Spurgeon herself was not always ready to give them: a development that, in one way or another, takes us beyond the card index, beyond the more or less mechanical collation and counting of the images used, into a response to the poetry as a living and dynamic whole, a whole moreover which looks for its completion beyond itself, through incorporation into the ultimate unity of the dramatic action to which it belongs. This is the incorporation at which Professor Wilson Knight has consistently aimed, in what is possibly the most ambitious attempt to interpret Shakespeare that the last half century has produced.

There can be no doubt that Wilson Knight to an eminent degree, and Professor Spurgeon in her own possibly more pedestrian way, have greatly extended our understanding of Shakespeare, and for this we have reason to be accordingly grateful. We shall do well, however, whilst recognizing this, to look a little closely at the "methods," so to call them, upon which these real discoveries are said to be based. In the case of Professor Spurgeon we shall see at once that the "method," in its essence, consists of card-indexing and counting images with a view to establishing their relative frequencies and drawing the corresponding conclusions. The image "X" appears so many times and the image "Y" so many: from the preponderance of either we can draw all kinds of conclusions, which seem to be "scientifically" based, perhaps about the dramatist's own tastes and certainly, it is suggested, about the intentions which underlie a given play. We shall find, I think, on reflection, however, that the poetic image, even if we accept it as a kind of ultimate constituent of poetry, is not readily susceptible to this kind of treatment. Some images belong primarily to literary convention, others impress us as deeply personal in their effect; some, again, belong exclusively to the dramatic personage in whose mouth they are placed and to the situation in which he finds himself, others seem to answer more directly to the expression of the author's own experience. Above all, the poetic image is, more particularly as used by Shakespeare, a living and not a dead thing; and it lives, not dissected and placed in a card index, but in a context, in relation to the intensity with which it is conceived (which varies greatly from one case to another), to the rhythm of the verse that conveys it, and to the total conception of the play in which it is found. Images, in fact, cannot be abstracted from their context, or counted up by a mechanical process as if they were all identical or similar in value. They live, develop, and change by their very nature, and it is precisely the life, the development, and the change which escape classification and call for the critic, or more simply the theatergoer, to make his similarly living response. If the result is, as it must surely be, something less than a scientific certainty, that may be considered by some a pity; but the rest of us may derive some encouragement from the reflection that there are certain areas of life (it may well be the most important) which are, of their very nature, irreducible to the card index and its overgrown and monstrous successor, the computer.

The case of Wilson Knight, which I have associated with that of Professor Spurgeon only on account of the tendency of both to start from a consideration of the poetic image and of its function in the complete dramatic effect, is a good deal more complex. Whether we accept his conclusions or not, there is nothing of the card index or the computer about Professor Wilson Knight's work; and it is just and necessary to say that there has been probably no writer on Shakespeare, in the period which here concerns us, who has opened out more new fields of vision to an understanding of the dramatist in his full life and complexity. Practically everyone who has since written on Shakespeare has had occasion to express his disagreement with many of Wilson Knight's conclusions, in which highly personal applications of ideas derived in varying degree from Nietzsche and from Christian tradition play a large part; but practically all those who have done so have also repeated or developed findings that he was the first to express. And yet, we must add, when all the debts have been fairly acknowledged, the numerous insights recognized for what they are, we often find ourselves asking, as we read or reread these studies, how exactly all this was achieved. The moments of vision are unquestionably there, many and true (and not always recognized as a source by those who have subsequently used them): but there too, surely, are an almost fantastically confused set of religious, "philosophical," and patriotic preoccupations often based, scarcely less than in the case of the card-indexers, upon an extraordinarily naïve conception of what image and metaphor really are. The interrelation of these two aspects—remarkable genuine insights and the tendency to force the text to say what the critic wants it to say—is not difficult to illustrate. An entire book by Wilson Knight—*The Shakespearean Tempest*[6]—sets out to show, for example, the existence through all the dramatist's work of a music-tempest opposition, and traces the presence of this line of imagery in every play that he wrote. The intuition is, beyond doubt, valid and important. The opposition between these two sets of constantly repeated images is *there* and, moreover, *means* something for our understanding of Shakespeare. In the proving of it, however, we are asked to believe that images taken from the early *Henry VI* plays are as valuable, have much the same degree of significance, as others from the unquestioned masterpieces, from *King Lear* and *The Tempest;* and that a burlesque piece spoken by Bottom in his first rehearsal for the Pyramus and Thisbe interlude in *A Midsummer Night's Dream*[7] has to all intents and purposes as much meaning as others drawn, for example, from the undoubtedly Shakespearean part of *Pericles*. This is surely absurd. Similarly in *Antony and Cleopatra*, perhaps the supreme test for a balanced criticism of Shakespeare, the romantic estimate of Antony in terms of "vitality," "transcendence," and "immortality" is stressed by Wilson Knight, if not exclusively, certainly unduly in relation to the merciless realism that accompanies the poetry at each stage in the development of the action. This is, no doubt, for the excellent reason that Wilson Knight himself feels the play in this way; and, so feeling, he has indeed greatly extended our understanding of Shakespeare, but has also on occasion fallen into traps, one-sided and finally confused judgments which are the opposite of our author's dispassionate clarity and balanced strength.

One other tendency in modern Shakespearean studies, related to though not directly deriving from Wilson Knight's work, can appropriately be mentioned at this point. This is the tendency, observable today in many academic quarters, to read into the plays explicit statements of Christian belief and morality. The greater writers of the nineteenth century tended, on the whole, to underestimate the Christian content of Shakespeare's thought, and it is perhaps in reaction to this that many writers in our own time have tended to present him as a moralist of orthodox tendencies and even, on occasions, as something of a theologian. This reaction, if such it is, toward a new orthodoxy has no doubt been carried too far in Shakespearean criticism, and has ended in producing a set of mechanically orthodox readings that are at least as far from what the plays actually offer as the interpretations to which they are opposed. Once again, Shakespearean criticism can only benefit in this situation from the capacity to draw and to maintain necessary distinctions. In view of the admitted lack of external evidence it seems clear that little can usefully be said concerning Shakespeare's personal beliefs, and certain that none of his plays were written to illustrate religious dogmas or to point preconceived moral judgments; on the other hand, it is surely no more than natural that a writer of his time and place should be aware of Christian tradition as an influence molding his thought and that he should even seek, more especially in his later plays, to present in terms of a highly personal reading of that tradition some of his final conclusions about life. The relation of the final romances, in particular, to Christian notions of repentance, atonement, and "grace," is certainly in no sense a matter of simple transcription or direct reflection; but for taking the romances seriously in my final chapter, for reading them as something more than poetic fantasies in dramatic form, I offer no apology. The seriousness and originality of these plays seem to me to be clearly written on practically every page.

In the situation outlined in the preceding paragraphs it seems that the student of Shakespeare will do well to consider his own position with some care. Once again my short introduction of 1938 may serve, even in its one-sided incompleteness, as a starting point. Following a line that was more novel then than it is now—though, of course, I made no claim to be originating anything[8]—I then suggested a possible "approach" through the development of language and verse as seen in the entire course of the dramatist's work, beginning with the individual word and taking it on, in the first instance, into its verse setting. Or, as I put it at the time:

> If a writer's intention is apparent in his choice of subject and general treatment, it has an even closer relation to the words and phrases in which he expresses himself. The word, as we shall see again and again in dealing with Shakespeare, is the product of the most intimate relations of thought and feeling, nervous sensitivity and conscious emotion. Indeed, word and thought, word and feeling, form part of an indivisible process of poetic creation; and, in the greatest poetry, the relation is felt as an identity, so that it becomes impossible to separate the personal development of an experience from its formal expression in words.[9]

And, since the dangers of a mechanical counting of words and images, referred to above, were already apparent, I added:

> It only remains to add that the individual word cannot be considered apart from the verse in which it performs its function. . . . The development of Shakespeare's versification is revealed in a growing flexibility of response to the increasingly complex implications of the individual word. The various stages in the process by which he masters his experience, projects it fully into his plays, are most easily traced by starting from his continual effort to adapt language and verse structure to the growing pressure of his emotions.[10]

In the years that have passed since this point of view was put forward, both the virtues and the limitations of this kind of "approach" have become clearer, to the writer at least, than they were at the time of writing. I should not now be inclined to express the argument in quite the same terms as those I first used thirty years ago. In particular I should be less happy now to talk, a little less than precisely, of Shakespeare's "experience," at least in so far as this might be held to have "biographical" implications, to be related to facts and circumstances in his life about which we can know nothing: nor am I altogether sure that there is a valid distinction between "thought" and "feeling" as elements making up a work of literature, between what I called, rather obscurely as I now find, "nervous sensitivity" and "conscious emotion." I would now say, perhaps more simply, that if it is our aim to define the total impact upon us of a given play, we shall do well to start with the words, the language through which that impact makes itself most immediately felt in any given moment, proceed to the incorporation of the word into the verse structure to which it belongs, see again how this bears fruit in the conveying of such things as character, motive conscious and unconscious, and, finally, draw all these connected and successively expanding aspects of the work with which we are concerned into the complete concept of a *dramatic action*, which is the end and *raison d'être* of the whole.

In other words, we can now see—perhaps more clearly than I originally saw—that the kind of "approach" suggested above is useful only in so far as it leads beyond itself, linking up with the various elements that go to make up the complete dramatic reality. No analysis of the first stage, *the word*, that does not illuminate some part of the last, the complete *dramatic action*, can be valid; but—and to this extent I would stand by my original proposal—we shall understand the *action* itself better if we proceed initially from the smaller unit to the larger, from that in which the individual intention first makes itself felt to the final unity of concept and projection that is the complete work of art. Or, as I put it in 1956, modifying and extending my intentions of 1938:

> The application of this general conception will clearly vary greatly from one play, or one period, to another. When applied to Shakespeare's early work, it is bound to be largely concerned with detecting the birth of tendencies that later found full integration in the unity of his mature masterpieces. Only gradually will it become apparent how these early intuitions, these first motions of personal feeling, are assumed into an adequate dramatic form. If we wish to find traces of true individuality in the plays of Shakespeare's youth, we must look not to the complete work, which is normally still derivative, artificial in conception, but primarily to individual turns of phrase, the occasional striking choice of a word or image to be discerned in otherwise commonplace passages of verse. From these it is

> natural to pass to a study of the way in which the words thus personally used influence the run of the verse itself, expanding into images which are eventually seen to bear significant repetition and to form, with the presentation of character and action correspondingly developed, a more subtle and suggestive unity. It is at this last point that the poetic merges into the dramatic reality. To proceed from the word to the image in its verse setting, and thence to trace the way in which a pattern of interdependent themes is gradually woven into the dramatic action, unifying and illuminating it, is the most fruitful approach—the most accurate and, if properly handled, the least subject to prejudice—to Shakespeare's art.[11]

To turn back to this passage, over the intervening years, is to obtain the sense of a valid, but also a notably one-sided procedure. In the study of Shakespeare's early work, to which reference is made, two simultaneous lines need to be developed. The revealing personal phrase or image is important, both in itself and in relation to the character who utters it or to the situation in which it is spoken; but, side by side with it, an equally valid field of study would show Shakespeare developing and extending his conception of a dramatic action in its entirety, exploring progressively the way in which his dramatic personages throw light upon one another by their comments and reactions being defined as much by what others say of them as through the impact of their own words. Beyond this, again, analysis of the same plays would reveal a dramatist engaged in studying the scope of the dramatic conventions he has accepted, defining the implications of comedy, extending the possibilities of the historical chronicle, even moving from relatively crude beginnings to a more unified and subtle concept of tragedy. All these things, side by side with the attention simultaneously given to the growth of his expressive possibilities in language and verse, show a Shakespeare engaged in realizing the full possibilities, for his own purposes, of an integrated dramatic action.

The stress laid in the preceding argument on the dramatic action implies, as a necessary corollary, awareness that the plays were written for the stage, and for a given type of stage at that. A growing recognition of this reality, indeed, constitutes one of the most fundamental conquests of modern scholarship. Reading in the study can greatly extend our understanding of what Shakespeare wrote, even bringing out points which would normally escape us in the rapid development of a stage action; but in the long run it is to the stage

—and to a particular moment in the development of the theater—that we find ourselves returning, not in a spirit of mere historical reconstruction, but because the conditions of the Elizabethan playhouse need to be present in the minds of those who aim to present the plays in a way that shall be at once modern and—in the deepest sense, one separated from mere historical accident—truly Shakespearean.

Every undergraduate knows that the stage with which Shakespeare was initially familiar, and for which most of his plays were written,[12] descended in a very real sense from the platform used during the Middle Ages to represent thc so-called "miracle" plays. Without entering into details, which are either too familiar to repeat or too intricate to find a place in these introductory remarks, it was like this platform, and unlike most modern stages, in being surrounded on three sides by the public, toward which it was deliberately projected. Furthermore, as it seems hardly necessary to remind the reader, it was divided into various parts, corresponding to different dramatic needs and roughly distinguishable, to modern scholarship, by the names of main, back, and apron stages. These arrangements looked very primitive from a nineteenth-century point of view, but—as has again often been shown—they offered certain important advantages; without some appreciation of these, Shakespeare's conception of a dramatic action must remain largely obscure. It was, in the first place, a stage on which contact between the actors and the public was remarkably direct and intimate: the stock example is the speaking of Hamlet's soliloquies, difficult to deal with on a modern stage without interrupting the flow of the action, but normal and natural in their effect when considered in relation to the stage they were written for.

If *intimacy* was the first important advantage which this stage offered, *flexibility* was certainly the second. The tripartite division of the stage made it easy to maintain a rapid and uninterrupted flow of action. The stock examples, again, are Romeo addressing Juliet on the balcony, Othello strangling Desdemona on the back stage after the main stage has been cleared of the "public" action and the separating curtains have been drawn apart. We might add, in *Henry IV*—Part I, the contrast between the court scenes and their burlesque reflection in Eastcheap, between the aristocratic leaders invoking honor on the field of battle and Falstaff passing his comment on that same "honor" in a spirit at once openly cynical and indicative of life and realism. In each case, dramatic tension and the continuity of the action are maintained to important ends; and the lack of complex scenic effects, apparently an intolerable limitation when considered through nineteenth-century eyes, in fact often supported both. All this is elementary, but it seems important, in considering Shakespeare's work, to remember what a dramatic action is *not*. It is *not*, properly understood, a spectacle to be contemplated externally, still less a photographic imitation of what is sometimes misleadingly called "real life." It is rather, on the contrary, a spoken action, non-realist and conventional by its very nature, requiring the *participation* of the audience as a necessary element; indeed, the concept of scenery and decoration as a kind of subsidiary art added to give more visual attraction is contrary to any serious view of the drama. An outstanding example of the kind of effect at one time lost to the theater, but abundantly open to Shakespeare, was that of the storm in *King Lear*, where the aged king, in the process of creating the external tempest in the only way open to the poet, through his own words, fuses it with the dramatic projection of his own tragic state. Everywhere present, beneath the apparent poverty of the stage conditions available to Shakespeare and his contemporaries, was a wealth of opportunity for the more profound poetic effects which the complication of later ages has often threatened to destroy.

To sum up, then: from a knowledge of the Elizabethan and Jacobean theater it is possible to derive certain consequences which illuminate the Shakespearean conception of poetic drama. In the first place, like his medieval predecessors, Shakespeare based his work on what was still, in its underlying presuppositions, a popular and social conception of the stage and of dramatic art. It is true that by the sixteenth century the participation of the craft guilds, which had been the most obvious sign of this participation, had given way to a more individualistic spirit; but the tradition that considered dramatic representation as a collective act, from which none need be excluded, however illiterate or lacking in social pretensions he might be, was still sufficiently alive to find reflection in Shakespeare's work. We shall not fully understand *Hamlet* if we do not see in the hero's tragedy, besides the intricate analysis of spiritual motives which it certainly conveys, the melodramatic and bloodthirsty story of revenge which so attracted the Elizabethan public. We shall not grasp *all* of the force of *Macbeth* if we only consider the drama of contrary impulses which moves the hero to his choices against a universal background of redemption and damnation, and forget the simple story of crime and punishment, of the destruction which evil brings upon itself, which is an essential part of the complete effect. Shakespeare's greatest plays have, in reality, something of the universal appeal of myth, of the expression of a universal consciousness deeply implanted in the popular mind and accessible, though in varying degrees and ways, to all levels of society. They appeal in different fashions to different levels of understanding, related to one another by the very fact of their common participation, but not identical. There is something in these great plays for the illiterate as for the intellectual, and it is part of their greatness that the immense field of experience which they offer to the latter is still intimately related to the primary emotions which constitute the chief popular appeal of the drama.

Secondly, and possibly even more important: the very structure of the theater in which these works were shown was such as to concentrate attention, not on a spectacle or on the character interpretation of a single actor, however gifted, but on the *action,* in which the artists appeared on the raised and central platform of the stage as intermediaries between the conception of the author and the public, requiring of the latter not only that they watch and listen, but that they participate in the development taking place before them. This sense of *participation,* which had been alive in the Middle Ages as part of a frankly religious manifestation, survived in the sixteenth century in a form akin to that encouraged by myth and legend. In the case of Shakespeare's great tragedies, we are required to participate in the fortunes of the central protagonist—a king, a hero, deliberately exalted above common humanity—either directly or through the comments and reactions of those who surround him: the result is an emotional effect akin to that to which Aristotle, in his basic treatise on dramatic poetry, gave the name of *katharsis* or purification.

Finally (and here we return to our point of departure, justifying our proposal to use sensitivity to living language as a point of departure), this essentially public action is *poetic* in nature, though not—I need hardly say—tied to any particular form of versification. In the best works of the Elizabethan theater, poetry, the vehicle of emotion, and the drama into which it flowers constitute a single and inseparable whole, fused in a unity that goes beyond its separate elements and to which we give the name of *poetic drama.* The personal emotions of the poet extend themselves to the public emotions of the theater, establishing contact with society through the highly conventional and unrealistic medium of the stage. This example has a permanent validity, in so far as the possibilities of the theater, properly considered, lie primarily neither in psychological accuracy of portrayal nor in realistic truth to the surface appearances of life. They lie, rather, elsewhere. Of all artistic forms, the drama is perhaps the most thoroughly conventional, the one that requires from the author the highest degree of identification with the special conditions which its very existence implies. This apparent limitation can, however, if properly understood and accepted, constitute a source of life; because it permits the poetic impulse, with which it is so intimately related, to flower with the greatest intensity, and because it provides the poet with a field of action that, unequaled in emotional depth, transcends the expression of purely personal sentiment. The dramatic poet is as fully poetic, as intense in his expression of emotion, as any other writer in verse; and, in addition, his chosen form obliges him to pass beyond the purely personal, to aim at the creation of a world that, in so far as it is outside himself, is beyond the accidents and prejudices of his own experience. To create is, artistically speaking, to bring into the light an obscure personal emotion, giving it the external appearance of form; the example of Shakespeare shows us how dramatic necessity can be united, continuously and harmoniously, to the ends of personal expression. The theatrical conventions of today have changed in many ways since the sixteenth century, and we should not wish to recreate them in a spirit of mere historical accuracy; but the permanent lessons of the Shakespearean theater are still available, still actual, and still waiting to be reapplied.

PART I

I

The Early Chronicle Plays

HENRY VI–Part I

There is a tendency among modern writers on Shakespeare to find the early series of plays on the reign of Henry VI a good deal more impressive than previous generations would have allowed. Recent stage revivals[1] have brought out a powerful unity in the general conception, suggesting the presence—once strongly denied—of a single author in the treatment of the chronicle material of all three plays; and the discernible variations of style seem more purposeful, more deliberate in their intended effect, than was formerly believed. The author of these plays, whom we may reasonably concede to have been Shakespeare, was possibly the first Elizabethan dramatist to make coherent and meaningful use, on this scale, of chronicle material and, in the process of so doing, to advance an interpretation of historical events which, full as it undoubtedly is of traditional and patriotic echoes, is already notably personal and, moreover, develops remarkably in the process of its unfolding.[2]

In spite of this revaluation, we may agree that the First Part of *Henry VI* is considerably less coherent in its general effect, less marked by the clear presence of a dominating intention, than the later and more individual plays that followed. The series opens with a formal evocation of the death of Henry V, and its treatment of subsequent events turns largely upon two closely related consequences of this loss: on the one hand, what amounts to a prolonged elegiac lament for the dying chivalry of England, and, on the other, the growth in England itself of the savage internal rivalry which ruined the great king's patriotic and warlike achievement. The obsessive presence of these two themes is conveyed through an

121482

episodic, pageant-like conception of drama which is notably less coherent in its effect than the action of the two plays to follow; but, whilst we may admit this inferiority, we may yet find the two aspects of this first play more closely and meaningfully interwoven in the development of the action than may immediately appear.

As a first step, we may note that Lord Talbot, who is undoubtedly on any account the "hero" of this first chronicle, is celebrated indeed in his heroism—the Messenger in the opening scene refers to him as "valiant Talbot," "undaunted spirit," and his whole later history confirms this estimate—but also, and at the same time, that the culminating emotional moments of the action are habitually associated with death, so as to constitute a lament for the older generation of English chivalry in the moment of its passing; in this mood, the play shows us the death of Salisbury—"this woful tragedy" (I. iv)—and that of Bedford—"Undaunted spirit in a dying breast" (III. ii)—both celebrated by Talbot almost in anticipation of his own end. Above all, we are shown Talbot's own death, with which it seems that positive virtue passes finally and irreparably from the life of England:

> How are we *park'd* and *bounded in a pale,*
> A little herd of England's timorous deer,
> Mazed with a yelping kennel of French curs!
> If we be English deer, be then in blood;
> Not rascal-like, to fall down with a pinch,
> But rather, *moody-mad* and *desperate* stags,
> Turn on the bloody hounds with heads of steel
> And make the cowards stand aloof at bay. (IV. ii)

Not all the stress laid here upon defiant heroism can conceal a sense of desperation, of fighting against hopeless odds; and indeed Talbot's last words, when the moment to pronounce them inexorably faces him, balance the craving for immortality against a persistent, almost obsessive sense of vanity and impermanence, which will later receive much finer expression in the final speech of the dying Hotspur:

> Thou *antic death,* which laugh'st us here to scorn,
> Anon from thy *insulting tyranny,*
> Coupled in bonds of *perpetuity,*
> Two Talbots, winged through the lither sky,
> *In thy despite* shall 'scape *mortality.* (IV. vii)[3]

For perhaps the first of many occasions, more particularly when a reaction against "mutability," the prospect of annihilation, is in question, a Shakespearean character seems to be engaged here in asserting emphatically the opposite of what he knows to be reality. The positive affirmation toward which Talbot's declaration ostensibly tends is flawed by its own rhetoric, felt to be poised finally against emptiness; we can hardly avoid feeling in these lines the presence of a persistent note of tragic irony which is surely close to the real, the truly intimate spirit of the general conception.

It is in accordance with this spirit, indeed, that even the emphatic celebration of Talbot's warlike virtues exists side by side throughout with a stressed and unnatural ferocity. This is the note which emerges in his threat to the citizens of Bordeaux:

> if you frown upon this proffer'd peace,
> You tempt the fury of my three attendants,
> Lean famine, quartering steel, and climbing fire— (IV. ii)

where we may feel that he anticipates Henry V before Harfleur,[4] and which, more crudely, finds expression more than once in the savagery of the earlier action:

> Your hearts I'll stamp out with my horse's heels,
> And make a quagmire of your mingled brains; (I. iv)

the same which is again reflected, in another context, in his description of his breaking loose from captivity:

> Then broke I from the officers that led me,
> And with my nails digg'd stones out of the ground,
> To hurl at the beholders of my shame:
> My grisly countenance made others fly:
> None durst come near for fear of sudden death.
> In iron walls they deem'd me not secure;
> So great fear of my name 'mongst them was spread
> That they supposed I could rend bars of steel,
> And spurn in pieces posts of adamant. (I. iv)

No doubt we should be unwise to modernize unduly the spirit of lines such as these. Much in them answers to the typical rant of the "old play," beloved of the Elizabethan groundlings; but, equally surely, we should do wrong to equate Shakespeare's effects here simply with those called forth by those around him, or fail to respond to the presence in this speech of something more, a note of precariousness, a sense of civilized life as balanced on the edge of savagery in a way which the later terms in this series of plays will amply and with full consciousness confirm.

For it is a fact that, Talbot apart, the emphasis throughout this first play is clearly upon a consistent savagery in the living which contrasts with the occasional and precarious chivalry of the dead. It is a savagery, moreover, which stands in the closest relationship to degradation and despair. The squandering by England of her traditional heritage in France is paralleled by bitter quarreling at home, and Talbot himself is successively the victim of betrayal, first at the hands of the ignoble Fastolfe and then, more gravely, at those of York and Somerset, each exclusively dedicated to the pursuit of his selfish ends (IV. iii, iv). As a result of these divisions, victory, won habitually by deceit, falls as though by default to their weak and superstitious foes. Shakespeare's presentation of the French in this play is, indeed, for all its crudity, occasionally more subtle than has sometimes been believed: more subtle even, possibly, than he himself was altogether prepared to recognize. In a play largely devoted to the celebration of Talbot, in whom something of the patriotic virtue of Henry V survives, there could be no place for anything like a modern reading of Joan of Arc. She is accordingly shown in a grotesquely unfavorable light, as devil-inspired, lecherous, and consumed by vanity. Oddly enough, however, we may note even here an occasional moment of greater depth, as though in evasion of the author's plainly declared intention. This is notably apparent in the surprisingly eloquent tone of the lament which she utters over her country's ruin:

> Look on thy country, look on fertile France,
> And see the cities and the towns defaced
> By wasting ruin of the cruel foe.
> As looks the mother on her lowly babe
> When death doth close his tender dying eyes,
> See, see, the pining malady of France. (III. iii)

The horror and the vanity of war is a theme which rarely failed to move Shakespeare to eloquence, and it is not altogether fanciful to find here a first anticipation, dim and distant indeed, of Burgundy's far greater speech, in *Henry V*,[5] upon the waste which follows upon armed conflict. Scarcely less unexpected is the force, relative though it is, with which Joan is allowed at the last to denounce the vices of her English enemies:

> you, that are polluted with your lusts,
> Stain'd with the guiltless blood of innocents,
> Corrupt and tainted with a thousand vices,
> Because you want the grace that others have,
> You judge it straight a thing impossible
> To compass wonders but by help of devils. (V. iv)

We should not, of course, overstress these apparent anomalies in relation to the play's more obvious purposes; but we may feel that they foreshadow, even at this early date and in this, one of the most unsubtle of his plays, something of the characteristic Shakespearean balance and detachment, that they may show a deeper conception in the process of coming to life, however tentatively and even incongruously, in the act of writing.

Perhaps most notable of all, however, in its relation to the later parts of the series, is the tendency, already observable in this First Part, to balance pathos against irony. The Henry VI of this play is a marginal and ineffective figure, not yet endowed to any significant degree with the tragic depth to which he will later, on occasions, arise; but already a few of his utterances point beyond weakness and incapacity to a deeper truth which few of those around him show any sign of grasping:

> O, think upon the conquest of my father,
> My tender years, and let us not forgo
> That for a trifle that was bought with blood. (IV. i)

As a comment on the savage squabbling between the rival "roses," which provides the play with one of its most effective scenes (II. iv), this is not without point. Pathos again, though of a different kind, makes its presence felt in the words of the imprisoned and helpless Mortimer, "Swift-winged with desire to get a grave" (II. v). The death wish, indeed, is strong in many parts of this play, and against it is set, persistently and in disturbing contrast, a notably sardonic quality in the mutual abusings of the lords and churchmen who so shortsightedly and rapaciously indulge their absorbing appetite for power:

> –Gloucester, thou wilt answer this before the pope.
> –Winchester goose, I cry, a rope! a rope!; (I. iii)

attitudes which are contrasted again with the ineffective and despairing common sense which prompts the Mayor of London, in the course of the same scene, to cry: "Good God, these nobles should such stomachs bear!" and to reveal his own pacific nature in his wry comment: "I myself fight not once in forty year" (I. iii). Even La Pucelle contributes, in her own inelegant way, to an effect of the same kind when she says of the body of the Lord Talbot, lying at her feet,

> Him that thou magnifiest with all these titles
> *Stinking* and *fly-blown* lies here at our feet. (IV. vii)

Once more, we should not overstress the significance of this, answering as it does closely enough to an avowedly popular mood: but it may not be altogether fanciful to see at this point something of the spirit of the future Thersites[6] casting a passing shadow over this earlier and immeasurably less subtle play.

HENRY VI–Part II

The above account suggests that *Henry VI*–Part I is, in the main, a crude piece distinguished by occasional moments of insight. Part II is, beyond reasonable dispute, a more closely knit and purposeful performance. Its starting point is the marriage of the unfortunate Henry VI to Margaret of Anjou, engineered in the course of the previous play by the Earl of Suffolk, whose last words as the curtain fell on the action of Part I provide a link with what is to come:

> Margaret shall now be queen, and rule the king;
> But I will rule both her, the king and realm. (*Part I*, V. v)

The results of the mixture of ambition and lasciviousness thus cynically revealed dominate the course of the new play.

The first consequence of this unhappy union is the shameful renunciation by Henry VI of those rights in France which his father had so gloriously maintained and for which Talbot had fought and died. As Gloucester, who now becomes the mouthpiece of the traditional and patriotic order, puts it in his rhetorical question,

> Shall Henry's conquest, Bedford's vigilance,
> Your deeds of war and all our counsel die? (I. i)

The second result, which follows logically from all that has gone before, is the revival of the "ancient bickerings" of the outraged and egoistic lords against the justly hated person of Suffolk; the Cardinal, whom we saw in no favorable light in Part I, gives vent to his intense hatred of Gloucester, whom Buckingham and Somerset in turn distrust, seeing in him an obstacle to their own progress toward the power which they crave for themselves. Beyond these quarrels, which have been carried over from the earlier play, a new and ultimately more sinister force declares itself for the first time through the early soliloquies of the Duke of York, who now announces—though to himself alone—that "A day will come when York shall claim his own" and who is ready to bide his time in the expectation of his opportunity: "Then, York, be still awhile, till time do serve" (I. i). In the declaration of his secret motives through soliloquy, and in his readiness to wait for the action of time to reveal itself on his side, York represents forces that have no precedent in this series of plays. His reflections, with their novel sense of poise and self-awareness, mark the entry into the series, and indeed into Shakespeare's work, of a new political consciousness which, vastly developed, will eventually produce Richard Crookback[7] and, further still beyond him, illuminate certain aspects of characters as different as Iago and Edmund. The conception represented by York is already beyond the reach of *Henry VI*—Part I; and side by side with it, on a lower level of society, we are shown the new craving for self-advancement inspiring John Hume in his insistent desire for wealth: "*Sort how it will,* I shall have gold for all" (I. ii). Here, expressed in plain and simple terms, is the motivation of the new and exclusive driving energy which has everywhere replaced patriotic chivalry as a guide in life.

In this new world, Gloucester stands in growing isolation for loyalty and the rule of law, as Suffolk, Beaufort, and Buckingham join in snarling against him. His essential virtue is revealed on different levels in a series of episodes which amount to a projection of the state of English society. His exercise of justice is portrayed in his resolution of the dispute between Horner and his apprentice Peter (I. iii, II. iii), which is in itself conceived as a commentary upon the aristocratic bickerings which surround the throne, his grasp of truth appears in his exposure of the false "miracle" at St. Albans (II. i), and his personal integrity is shown by his readiness to allow justice to punish his own intriguing wife whom he urges to repent (II. iv). The last of these incidents throws perhaps the clearest light upon his character and his situation. When Eleanor, in the moment of her humiliation, warns him bitterly and truly of the "snares" which his enemies are preparing against him, he replies declaring his readiness to take his stand upon the law:

> I must offend before I be attainted;
> And had I twenty times so many foes,
> And each of them had twenty times their power,
> All these could not procure me any scathe,
> So long as I am loyal, true and crimeless. (II. iv)

Gloucester's attitude, here and throughout the play, is unexceptionable, represents in Shakespearean terms the only possible guarantee for an ordered and humane polity; but in the political world which this play is concerned to present it is also singularly vulnerable.

Gloucester, indeed, for all his virtue and integrity—even, we may say, on account of these—is a man whose attitudes are out of date in the world in which he so disturbingly finds himself. The new queen and his own fellow nobles see him as "insolent," "proud," and "peremptory," presuming upon the virtues which, whilst he maintains his authority, bar their own paths to advancement. They accuse him of their own "rancorous minds," see him as "smoothe Duke Humphrey," assert of him—in terms which later Shakespearean politicians will make their own[8]—that "By flattery hath he won the commons' hearts" (III. i). Against the background provoked by the bitter news of the loss of France, York, seeing that his hour has struck, makes bold to arrest him for treason, and the only reply he can offer is an exposure of the bitter realities of the present:

> Virtue is choked with foul ambition,
> And charity chased hence by rancour's hand . . .
> Beaufort's red sparkling eyes blab his heart's malice,
> And Suffolk's cloudy brow his stormy hate;
> Sharp Buckingham unburthens with his tongue
> The envious load that lies upon his heart;
> And dogged York, that reaches at the moon,
> Whose overweening arm I have pluck'd back,
> By false accuse doth level at my life. (III. i)

In its incisive intensity and truth to character this is writing of a new kind, and answers as such to a fresh vision of public realities in a world from which all sanctions, human and traditional alike, have been debarred; and in the unhappy king's reaction to his faithful servant's plight, a reaction which his wife Margaret dismisses as so much "foolish pity,"[9] Henry himself moves a little nearer to the center of the stage, shows signs of becoming a tragic rather than merely an ineffectual figure. Shakespeare is beginning in this play to consider a problem which will exercise him in later and greater works: the problem represented by the existence of the "good" man in a political order from which pity and humanity have been deliberately excluded. We may agree that Henry remains, as king, ineffectual, whilst sensing also that efficiency, in a world where the appetite for power imposes itself as a uniquely absorbing imperative, seems more and more to imply the sacrifice of common humanity and thereby to forge the circumstances of its own doom.

From the moment of Gloucester's arrest, indeed, the plunge of society into dissolution is most tensely and realistically conveyed. The Cardinal, his chief enemy, ruthlessly brushes aside the law to obtain his death:

> No more of him; for I will deal with him,
> That henceforth he shall trouble us no more; (III. i)

and this resolution is ferociously commended by the queen. The Irish are reported to have risen in rebellion. York, entrusted with the mission of suppressing them, exposes the "policy" of those who are glad to see him away and commends—once more in soliloquy—his own treacherous determination:

> I fear me, you but warm the starved snake,
> Who, cherish'd in your breasts, will sting your hearts, (III. i)

as he stresses his consuming desire to obtain "the *golden* circuit" of which he obsessively dreams. To this end, he proposes to stir up a movement of popular rebellion, making use of Cade as an unconscious tool for ends of his own. A new political force, cunning and thoroughly amoral, exclusively concentrated upon its desire for power, is moving further toward its assertive self-awareness.

Gloucester's tragic end is soon reported (III. ii) as the inevitable culmination of so much savagery. The unhappy king laments his loss, admitting the self-deception which has helped to bring it about, and the queen turns upon him the full ferocity of her disdainful reproach: "Is all thy comfort shut in Gloucester's tomb?" (III. ii). In uttering this question, she speaks more truly than she knows, for we shall soon see that, with Gloucester, hope itself is about to die in Henry's stricken realm. As a first step the people, hitherto passive in their loyalty, are reported to have risen "like an angry hive of bees"; from this turning point, we look forward to the full fury of anarchy unleashed. Meanwhile, the horror of Warwick's description of Gloucester's murdered corpse answers, beyond mere melodrama, to the prevailing spirit of the action:

> But see, his face is black and full of blood,
> His eye-balls further out than when he lived,
> Staring full ghastly like a strangled man;
> His hair uprear'd, his nostrils stretch'd with struggling;
> His hands abroad display'd, as one that grasp'd
> And tugg'd for life and was by strength subdued; (III. ii)

whilst Suffolk, openly accused of murder, answers his accusers with plain and ferocious defiance:

> here's a vengeful sword, rusted with ease,
> That shall be scoured in his rancorous heart
> That slanders me with murder's crimson badge. (III. ii)

By contrast the people, though driven at last to revolt, rise in a mood which is still one of desperation, in "mere instinct of love and loyalty" (III. ii). The queen, on the other hand, is exclusively devoted to the pursuit of her own appetites. She pleads against the banishment of Suffolk, in which she sees the intolerable loss of her lover; and, once she has been deprived of the object of her desire, she is ready in her baffled rage to call upon the forces of "mischance and sorrow" to ruin all alike. Suffolk's answering outburst, in turn, is more than an expression of spleen, proceeds, as he himself confesses, from the intensity of his thwarted passion; as he tells his royal mistress,

> where thou art, there is the world itself,
> With every several pleasure in the world,
> And where thou art not, desolation. (III. ii)

As a final contribution to this accumulation of horrors, and in fitting response to the description of the dead Gloucester, we are given the picture of Beaufort, the most ruthless of his enemies, lying on his own deathbed in what we may reasonably call a dim anticipation of Macbeth's later and far more subtle guilt:

> Died he not in his bed? where should he die?
> Can I make men live, whether they will or no?
> O, torture me no more! I will confess.
> Alive again? then show me where he is:
> I'll give a thousand pound to look upon him.
> He hath no eyes, the dust hath blinded them.
> Comb down his hair; look, look, it stands upright,
> Like lime-twigs set to catch my winged soul. (III. iii)

Death comes habitually, in this play, unnaturally and horribly, the appropriate reflection of unnatural horror in the behavior of evil and shortsighted men.

The rest of the play, which is seen in this way to be centered upon Gloucester's criminal murder, brings an appropriate retribution upon those who have contrived it for ends of their own. The guilty and supremely worthless Suffolk dies at the hands of a mere anonymous captain. Before he is dispatched, his vain appeal in the name of the "noble" blood which his conduct has so consistently belied receives an adequate answer:

> Pool! Sir Pool! lord!
> Ay, kennel, puddle, sink; whose filth and dirt
> Troubles the silver spring where England drinks.
> Now will I dam up this thy yawning mouth,
> For swallowing the treasure of the realm:
> Thy lips that kiss'd the queen shall sweep the ground;
> And thou that smiled'st at good Duke Humphrey's death
> Against the senseless winds shalt grin in vain. (IV. i)

Meanwhile, in Cade's rebellion, the principle theme of the following episodes, the historical panorama is notably broadened as the populace that once listened loyally to Gloucester and applauded his judgments, degenerates into the uncontrolled and predatory mob. The transformation, indeed, is not a pretty one, and Shakespeare does not spare us its brutal significance; but, in considering its full impact, we should not forget that it was York who originally instigated Cade to rise in the pursuit of ends of his own. Clearly enough, the rebellion now afoot is a repudiation of law, learning, society, and natural order. As such it is beyond all possible defense; but it is proper to add that its manifestations, savage and brutal as they are, are yet the response of the people to the brutality and savagery so amply displayed by their supposed "betters." The people, indeed, even in the moment of their rage, still revere the memory of Henry V and recognize that England is "maimed," broken by the conflict in which they participate; though we must add that their own shame is revealed in the ignorance which drives them to the slaying of Lord Say for no better reason than his "speaking Latin" (IV. vii). Adrift in this sea of desperate and meaningless conflict the king is reduced still further to helplessness, whilst his queen is glimpsed, gruesomely but with a dreadful fittingness, avidly and passionately clutching Suffolk's severed head (IV. iv).

Rebellion, indeed, is seen in the concluding scenes of this somber action, engaged in generating its own gathering excess, following to their logical conclusion its perverse laws of negation. Cade orders the records of the realm to be burned and, as he does so, makes his own full assertion of anarchy:

> The proudest peer in the realm shall not wear a head on his shoulders, unless he pay me tribute; there shall not a maid be married, but she shall pay to me her maidenhead ere they have it: men shall hold me *in capite;* and we charge and command that their wives be as free as heart can wish or tongue can tell. (IV. vii)

In the idiom of this play, this represents anarchy bent upon the satisfaction of its baser instincts, exulting in the immediate prospect of destruction. Cade "*in capite*," using the power he proposes to seize for the satisfaction of his baser instincts, is a dreadful parody of true authority. No political realism, however, accompanies the people in their headlong career, and so Clifford, as the emissary of the established "order," finds it easy to separate the rebel leader from his followers by a rhetorical appeal to the patriotic memory of Henry V. The people waver in their response, much as they will do later to the rhetoric of Mark Antony in *Julius Caesar.*[10] They finally abandon the cause of Cade, who is left a man out of his depth indeed, betrayed and brought to an ignominious end, but not altogether a sinister figure in his fall; for with his dying breath he is able to assert that he has been the victim of adverse circumstances, that "famine and no other hath slain me" (IV. x).

At the end of so much bloodshed and ruin, the way is left clear for York, who has been shrewd enough to foresee this moment and to bring it about:

From Ireland thus comes York to claim his right,
And pluck the crown from feeble Henry's head. (V. i)

"Let them obey that know not how to rule" (V. i): this is the voice of a new political spirit, and if it implies a real criticism of Henry's weak and helpless rule, it is nonetheless true that it will, in due course, bring an appropriate doom upon its own head. The content of York's ambition is already implicit in his own words:

This hand was made to handle nought but *gold.*
I cannot give due action to my words,
Except a sword or sceptre balance it:
A sceptre shall it have, have I a *soul.* (V. i)

The equation of the impulses of the "soul" with the craving for a "scepter" and the power that goes with it; the consuming obsession with "gold" which York, echoing that already expressed, in more humble terms, by Hume,[11] now raises to the level of the crown—these things, taken together, represent the strength and the final limitation of the new political spirit. Its immediate manifestation is the clash between York and Somerset and the confrontation of Clifford and Warwick. Clifford refers to his rival scornfully in vivid terms of bearbaiting—

Are these thy bears? we'll bait thy bears to death
And manacle the bear-ward in their chains— (V. i)

even as he calls York's son Richard a "foul undigested lump," in a graphic reference charged with menace for the future. The king is left pathetically in the middle of the disputing factions, bemoaning with bitter truth the death of natural virtue—

O, where is faith? O, where is loyalty?
If it be banished from the frosty head,
Where shall it find a harbour in the earth?— (V. i)

but helpless to impose any semblance of order upon a world empty of valid restraints: a world where the general reaction is summed up in the tone of Richard's final snarl to young Clifford:

—. . . you shall sup with Jesu Christ to-night.
—Foul stigmatic, that's more than thou canst tell.
—If not in heaven, you'll surely sup in hell. (V. i)

On the battlefield at St. Albans, to which all this implacable rivalry naturally leads, and as York kills Clifford, the victim's son reflects the spirit of this entire action by his final dedication, made against a background of universal anarchy, to war and revenge:

> Fear frames disorder, and disorder wounds
> Where it should guard. (V. ii)

Such, concisely and intensely stated, is the state of the world, and the only response to it which the speaker can conceive is expressed in terms of a dedication which can only seek to cover ultimate emptiness. "Let no soldier fly," cries Clifford in his despair, and goes on:

> He that is truly dedicate to war
> Hath no self-love, nor he that loves himself
> Hath not essentially but by circumstance
> The name of valour. (V. ii)

Dedication, accordingly, is to be the order of the day, perhaps because outside the gesture of dedication there lies only the prospect of chaos and meaningless disaster; but, we must surely find ourselves asking, dedication to what? The answer is—to nothing, to a vision of general ruin in a world conceived of as beyond remedy vile and worthless. As Clifford goes on to say, clothing his natural grief in a universal resentment:

> O, let the *vile* world end,
> And the premised flames of the last day
> Knit earth and heaven together!
> Now let the general trumpet blow his blast,
> Particularities and petty sounds
> To cease! (V. ii)

This in turn gives way to the speaker's renewed thought of the death of his father, ruthlessly slaughtered, against all the natural pieties, "in his chair-days": a thought which leads directly to the final statement of appalling and inhuman resolve:

> Even at this sight
> My heart is turn'd to stone: and while 'tis mine,
> It shall be stony. York not our old men spares;
> No more will I their babes: tears virginal
> Shall be to me even as the dew to fire,
> And beauty that the tyrant oft reclaims
> Shall to my flaming wrath be oil and flax.
> Henceforth I will not have to do with pity. (V. ii)

The final statement, with each word brief and tense in its separation, sounds its note of iron in a world of desolation. York's dedication to the ends of power and personal glory have bred at this point their logical and necessary answer. As Clifford declares the turning of his heart, thus unnaturally in the flower of his youth, to the quality of stone, his words look forward to the savage slaughter of Rutland, and of York himself, in the play to follow. Richard, on his side, echoes with his words what has become the pervading spirit of the entire action: "Priests pray for enemies, but princes kill" (V. ii). As the play ends, Clifford affirms once more his determination to continue the struggle, and Warwick, not without a certain irony in view of what is to come, utters his ambiguous prayer for the future: "more such days as these to us befall" (V. iii). Many more, indeed, and even more full of unmitigated horror, there are to be.

HENRY VI–Part III

Enough will have been said by now to suggest that Shakespeare's initial series of plays on English history is more consistent in its design, more purposeful in its presentation of events, than has sometimes been recognized. It foreshadows, indeed, not a few of the points which later plays were to develop. Roughly speaking, it may be said that the *Henry VI* plays turn upon two separate political ideas, each of them amply reflected in the literature of the age. The first of these was the traditional belief, derived from a great body of medieval thought and coloring the familiar medieval view of tragedy, that sin committed by the individual is eventually repaid in the form of retribution upon the sinner; the second, more modern in its implications and supremely reflected for the sixteenth century in the writings of Machiavelli, relates the prevalence of disorder in the state to elements of weakness and indecision in the attitude of its ruler. Both these notions are developed, insistently and side by side, through the various stages of this series. The first finds expression in the ultimate fate of nearly all the principal contenders for power; and the figure of Henry VI in some sense serves to join the two, since it is clear that he is at once a good man against whom sin is almost continuously committed, and a feeble ruler who is disposed at times, moreover, to admit that his own claim to the throne is in some respects uncertain.

However this may be, it is clear, as the curtain rises upon Part III, that the disorder so thoroughly traced in the preceding plays is everywhere rampant and victorious. The bloody victors of St. Albans display their grisly trophy, the head of Somerset, whilst Richard utters his ominous threats against the king himself: "Thus do I hope to shake king Henry's head." York's attitude at the moment of his triumph finds expression in his own words: "By words or blows here let us win our right," and his son urges him to "be resolute" in the pursuit of his ends. On the other side, and scarcely less ominously, Clifford "mourns in steel," whilst in the middle Henry stands helplessly, recognizing, even as Richard calls upon York to "tear the crown from the usurper's head," that his own title is "weak." As the majority of the nobles turn away from a king who thus stands revealed as unready to defend his own rights, Clifford, still dedicated to anarchy and the prospect of revenge, swears to support him "right or wrong"; whilst Henry, in an impossible gesture of weakness which his queen at once sees for what it is, seeks peace for himself and his realm by offering the crown to York, "after my decease" (I. i).

The driving force of the action, however, is by now increasingly concentrated upon the person of Richard, in whom the elements of passion and savagery which everywhere prevail around him appear to have grown to self-conscious and ominous maturity. In this, indeed, he is seen to be his father's son. His desire for power outdoes that of York in emotional intensity—

How sweet a thing it is to wear a crown;
Within whose circuit is Elysium,
And all that poets feign of bliss and joy—

as it rises to the ferocious dedication of his conclusion:

I cannot rest
Until the white rose that I wear be dyed
Even in the lukewarm blood of Henry's heart. (I. ii)

It is perhaps not without meaning that Richard associates the lure of the crown with the "feigning" of poets and so, in a certain sense, with delusion; but it is, at all events, a delusion to which he is passionately and irrevocably committed. Many other personages in this series of plays have *thought* in this way, or something very like it; but none, with the partial exception of York, have declared their motives with this remarkable blend of intense passion and cool clear-sightedness. For this reason alone, if for no other, the immediate future belongs to Richard.

A situation in which motives of this kind so exclusively prevail can only end in slaughter, and this bleak necessity is immediately fulfilled at Wakefield. Clifford at last obtains the revenge to which he has dedicated himself by killing Rutland, "this innocent child," after he has torn him from his tutor's arms. As he declares in the moment of this macabre triumph, revealing once more the obsessive nature of his motivation:

> The sight of any of the house of York
> Is as a fury to torment my soul;
> And till I root out their accursed line
> And leave not one alive, I live in hell. (I. iii)

Not, however, until York has himself fallen into his captor's power is the full extent of the ferocity of his enemies revealed. Even in this series of plays, where savagery pressed to its ultimate limits is the habitual order of the day, the baiting of York on his molehill, adorned with his "paper crown" in what appears to be a sardonic parody of the Passion of Christ, stands out uniquely in the supreme bitterness of Margaret's revengeful taunting:

> Where are your mess of sons to back you now?
> The wanton Edward, and the lusty George?
> And where's that valiant crook-back prodigy,
> Dicky your boy, that with his grumbling voice
> Was wont to cheer his dad in mutinies? . . .
> Why art thou patient, man? thou shouldst be mad;
> And I, to make thee mad, do mock thee thus.
> Stamp, rave, and fret, that I may sing and dance.
> Thou would'st be fee'd, I see, to make me sport:
> York cannot speak, unless he wear a crown.
> A crown for York! and, lords, bow low to him:
> Hold you his hands, whilst I do set it on.
> Ay, marry, sir, now looks he like a king! (I. iv)

In these mockings, conceived with an almost visual intensity worthy, in another artistic order, of Hieronymus Bosch or Breughel, there is brought home to us the Nemesis that has appropriately followed upon York's consuming lust for power. It is the same which, in the not long delayed fullness of time, will also bring retribution upon his killers.

Revenge, indeed, begins to take shape at once in the reflections of Richard, whose purposes, firm in the acceptance of anarchy as the inescapable law of life and self-consciously dedicated to the ends of power, seek to grow now to the full stature they will reach by the end of the play. His thoughts at this point are steeped in a detached, even an ironic estimate, of his situation:

> I cannot weep; for all my body's moisture
> Scarce serves to quench my furnace-burning heart:
> Nor can my tongue unload my heart's great burthen;
> For selfsame wind that I should speak withal
> Is kindling coals that fires all my breast,
> And burns me up with flames that tears would quench.
> To weep is to make less the depth of grief:
> Tears then for babes; blows and revenge for me! (II. i)

This is the definitive birth of a force which York's earlier soliloquies had only foreshadowed, but which now gathers up all the preceding savagery into the power of its concentrated drive.

In contrast to so much dedicated ferocity, the king maintains his precarious foothold, moved by pity to appear a figure at once tragic and politically inept. When Clifford, the latest of his mentors, sweeps aside the motions of compassion—

> To whom do lions cast their gentle looks?
> Not to the beast that would usurp their den— (II. ii)

his answer is a significant inversion of a phrase later to be used by Macbeth: "things ill-got had ever bad success":[12] the expression, indeed, of a true philosophy, as the course of events will eventually show, but of one which is tragically impotent to influence the immediate present. And so from Wakefield we are brought to Towton, where Clifford once again affirms his brutal dedication to revenge—"This is the hand that stabb'd thy father York" (II. iv)—whilst Henry utters in terms of pastoral nostalgia an elegiac lament which we need not dismiss as simply ineffectual:

> Gives not the hawthorn bush a sweeter shade
> To shepherds looking on their silly sheep,
> Than doth a rich embroider'd canopy
> To kings that fear their subjects' treachery? (II. v)

This is no doubt the expression of a hopeless, even finally an irresponsible desire to abdicate, a renunciation from which a king is debarred by the very nature of the office he has assumed. For his refusal to accept responsibility Henry may, as a political figure, fairly be condemned. Machiavelli's "unarmed prophet"[13] can properly be exposed as such, on Machiavelli's terms; but in blaming him we shall also respond to the tragedy implied, in this same scene, by the patterned atrocities unwittingly committed by father against son and son against father, atrocities which lay stress upon a world pitilessly dedicated to self-destruction. Time, however, in these plays, waits for no man. Having uttered his lament, the king is obliged to flee before his victorious enemies, and Clifford, his incongruous support, recognizes that

> The foe is merciless, and will not pity;
> For at their hands I have deserved no pity. (II. vi)

It is now Clifford's turn to die, but whereas—as we may now remember—he was afforded the opportunity to insult, in the person of York, his living enemy, York's sons, Edmund and Richard, joined to Warwick, can only claim the lesser satisfaction of offering outrage upon his lifeless corpse. The note of sardonic frustration which runs through their insults answers very closely to the present spirit of the action.

From the open savagery of battle we pass immediately to that, more disguised but not on that account less vicious in its implications, which rules the political game. The helpless king, found by the hunters who see in him a welcome if unexpected prey, is taken prisoner in "the thick-grown brake" (III. i). Meanwhile Edward, the newly crowned and lascivious king, is engaged in wooing the Lady Grey, a kind of "merry widow" whose eye is firmly fixed upon her own advancement, whilst his brothers ironically look on. Richard, indeed, already desires Edward's ruin in the pursuit of his own ambitions:

> Would he were wasted, marrow, bones and all,
> That from his loins no hopeful branch may spring,
> To cross me from the golden time I look for! (III. ii)

The expression of this desire is followed by a soliloquy in which the speaker contemplates himself, as he examines his motives, in a characteristic mood of ironic detachment:

Why, love forswore me in my mother's womb:
And, for I should not deal in her soft laws,
She did corrupt frail nature with some bribe,
To shrink mine arm up like a wither'd shrub;
To make an envious mountain on my back,
Where sits deformity to mock my body;
To shape my legs of an unequal size;
To disproportion me in every part,
Like to a chaos, or an unlick'd bear-whelp
That carries no impression like the dam.
But am I then a man to be beloved? (III. ii)[14]

The speech, like others which Richard will utter in the later stages of his history, implies an effort to turn deficiency, exclusion from the normal order, into a kind of superiority. It opens with an admission that the speaker feels himself deprived by a trick of invidious fate from the gentle influence of "love" and considers himself accordingly free from the human obligation to correspond to what he dismisses, with an attempted sneer, as "her *soft* laws," as a corrupting force acting upon "frail nature." In asserting his superiority to this "frailty" Richard seeks, indeed, a compensation for his exclusion from a human order which, even as he affects to despise it, he in fact envies; but the stress which his own words lay, almost obsessively, upon "deformity," "disproportion," "chaos," and upon their physical reflection in his own body, shows clearly enough where the true inspiration of so much confidence and self-sufficiency lies. It is enough to make of Richard not merely a "Machiavellian" villain rejoicing in his own capacity to hurt, but the most mature character creation that Shakespeare had at this early stage in his career achieved.

The conclusion to so much keen self-scrutiny is, on the surface at least, the comforting one which the speaker desires. It amounts to a readiness to find congenial the reality which originally moved him to complain against his fate: the reality that the pursuit of power is in effect the only path left open to him:

since this earth affords no joy to me,
But to command, to check, to o'erbear such
As are of better person than myself,
I'll make my heaven to dream upon the crown,
And, whiles I live, to account this world but hell,
Until my mis-shaped trunk that bears this head
Be round impaled with a glorious crown. (III. ii)

We need not deny the force of this "dream," which amounts to an intensifying of York's earlier identification of the crown, the symbol of power, with the richness and the glitter of "gold."[15] It is a "dream" which will bring Richard to the attainment of the ends which his nature craves before finally destroying him. Already, however, the sense that emerges from this, his first fully revealing soliloquy, is that of a monstrous birth, the projection of his own twisted origins into his subsequent career in a world upon which, precisely because it rejects him as "unnatural," he is determined to impose himself. There is meaning in the self-comparison which uses images finally associated with the evocation of a painful, a monstrous labor, to convey the picture of himself as a kind of beast thrusting through the dense tangles of a wood to emerge to his own kind of disillusioned clarity:

> I,—like one lost in a thorny wood,
> That rends the thorns and is rent with the thorns,
> Seeking a way and straying from the way;
> Not knowing how to find the open air,
> But toiling desperately to find it out,—
> Torment myself to catch the English crown:
> And from that torment I will free myself,
> Or hew my way out with a bloody axe. (III. ii)

No simple moral explanation can cover the impression which these words of self-analysis convey. What is suggested here is, indeed, something very like a grotesque parody of the natural processes of birth. Richard feels himself a man "lost," caught in the "thorns" which surround and tear him as he struggles to free himself, "straying from the way" in spite of the intensity of his efforts to find it: a man caught by his own admission in a situation which has elements of claustrophobia about it and seeking, even "toiling desperately," to find the "open air," turning his inescapable disability into the "torment" which his absorbing search for power implies. If the "bloody axe" is the instrument to his hands, which he will wield with ruthless confidence against rivals for the most part as evil as, and far more stupid than, himself, it is one which will never bring him to that "freedom," that liberation from the "torment" of ambition which he recognizes in himself and which constitutes, even beyond his own understanding, the tragic contradiction of his nature. Such is the "explanation," psychologically a good deal more complex than its immediate presentation may suggest, which at this point brings Richard to the surface confidence of his final, consciously "Machiavellian" declaration of political self-sufficiency:

> I can add colours to the chameleon,
> Change shapes with Proteus for advantages,
> And set the murderous Machiavel to school.
> Can I do this, and cannot get a crown?
> Tut, were it further off, I'll pluck it down. (III. ii)

The scene (III. iii) that follows this crucial declaration is, appropriately, an exposure of "realist" diplomacy in its relation to unconfessed personal motives of passion and craving for power. As such, it too may be said to break new ground which Shakespeare will abundantly cultivate in later plays. Lewis of France, with claims of his own discreetly in view, greets Henry's exiled queen and promises her relief; but when Warwick enters, representing the present power of Edward, he turns his attention cautiously to the newcomer:

> Is Edward your true king? for I were loath
> To link with him that were not lawful chosen, (III. iii)

before adding the still more loaded question: "Is he gracious in the people's eye?" This is, in fact, a politician whose thoughts are firmly set upon his own possible advantage. Inspired by these considerations, Lewis agrees to give Bona in marriage to Edward, only to learn as soon as he has done so that the royal lecher who now sits on the English throne has contracted marriage with the widow in whose pursuit he has been engaged at home. In view of this rebuff Margaret is restored to the French king's favor and joined by Warwick in repudiation of the offense to his self-esteem. The movement of the scene, as Warwick and Margaret, who began it as rivals, are joined in friendship, is not without subtlety: "Warwick, these words have turned my hate to love" (III. iii). The new alliance is at once cemented by the betrothing of Warwick's eldest daughter at the shortest notice to Margaret's son;[16] but the best comment on this move in the political game is provided by Warwick himself, when he frankly declares his own motives:

> Not that I pity Henry's misery,
> But seek revenge on Edward's mockery. (III. iii)

Meanwhile, back in England, Richard and his temporary associate

Clarence are equally frank in their ironic comments on Edward's incontinence and on his "well-chosen" bride (IV. i); as Richard puts it:

> God forbid that I should wish them sever'd,
> Whom God hath join'd together. (IV. i)

It is against this presentation of public realities, ironic in its detachment, that the action is ready to move to its conclusion.

As an initial step in this process, Edward, whom Richard has first captured and then released, wins the city of York by a stratagem upon which Richard himself (who more appropriately, indeed?) makes this typical comment:

> when the fox hath once got in his nose,
> He'll soon find means to make the body follow. (IV. vii)

A similar device will be used by John of Lancaster, in *Henry IV—* Part II,[17] to obtain a bloodless victory over the rebel armies at Gaultree Forest. Whilst the civil war thus continues on its somber and ignoble course, Henry VI takes his stand on virtue, but this does not save him from being seized by his enemies in answer to his declarations of good intention. His response is in effect a bitter cry of despair:

> My pity hath been balm to heal their wounds,
> My mildness hath allay'd their swelling griefs,
> My mercy dried their water-flowing tears;
> I have not been desirous of their wealth,
> Nor much oppress'd them with great subsidies,
> Nor forward of revenge, though they much err'd:
> Then why should they love Edward more than me? (IV. viii)

Why, indeed? The answer to this question, whatever it be, is not to be found in this play, which presses forward to its bleak conclusion after the death of Warwick at Barnet (V. ii) and the stabbing of the young prince after the scolding match with Edward, Gloucester, and Clarence. As ever in this series, irony and savagery are joined to the last in destructive and inhuman action.

Finally, as a logical culmination to the whole process, Richard murders the helpless Henry to the accompaniment of a last grim gibe at virtue itself: "Down, down to hell; and say I sent thee thither" (V. vi). This supremely callous act, however, becomes at once the occasion for the most revealing soliloquy that this murderer has yet uttered. Once again Richard contemplates himself, in the light of his deed and those that have gone before, with his characteristic show of detachment—

> I, that have neither pity, love, nor fear—

before he goes on to speak yet again of the "unnatural" and loveless birth which so obsesses him throughout, to justify himself finally in what is surely, beyond his immediate intention, nothing less than a declaration of his limitation as a human being:

> Then, since the heavens have shaped my body so,
> Let hell make crook'd my mind to answer it.
> I have no brother, I am like no brother;
> And this word love, which greybeards call divine,
> Be resident in men like one another,
> And not in me: *I am myself alone.* (V. vi)

"I am myself alone." In these few words, with all that they imply, we may find that Shakespeare has made what is so far his first approach to a profound and finally positive statement about life. Richard has declared his manifesto, his program, which we are called upon to judge in the light of all that we have seen, all that it now illuminates. Evil has become at last not merely an obscure instinct in the hearts of savage men, but fully self-conscious, self-possessed, and self-aware: but, in the very act of so declaring itself, it has announced its isolation, accepted in its own despite its inescapable human—or inhuman—limitation. As the play ends, and against the next threat to peace, humanity, and nature, which is already foreseen by its conscious agent—"Clarence, thy turn is next, and then the rest"—Edward is left to bring the action to a close by saying, with a feebleness that contrasts with the force of what we have just heard: "Here, *I hope,* begins our lasting joy" (V. vii). What will in fact begin, and be brought to its logical conclusion in the next play, is the consummation of Richard Crookback's advance to power.

RICHARD III

In relation to the series of *Henry VI* plays, of which it is the logical conclusion, *Richard III* represents a new, a more elaborate and finished development. The simple construction of the earlier chronicles, which answers, generally speaking, to the sequence of the events described, is replaced by a more deliberately patterned action, in which the principal themes repeat themselves significantly or stand out in deliberate contrast. Phrase responds deliberately to phrase, either ironically or to intensify by choric emphasis a broad tragic effect; incident recalls incident, either in an intentional accumulation of horror or to stress the presence, beneath so much inhumanity, of an obscure and appropriate Nemesis working itself out through the unfolding of events. At the center of this variously contrived structure, focusing upon his own person the elements of self-awareness which we have seen emerging, at first tentatively in York and then more firmly in the stages of his own rise to power, stands the dominating figure of its protagonist. With Richard placed at the center of his play, which he overshadows to a degree that we shall scarcely find repeated in Shakespeare before *Hamlet*, a new type of drama is at once the necessary conclusion of all that has gone before and the expression of a new conception of what the chronicle play implies.

Given this development, and the concept of the dramatic protagonist to which it leads, it is natural that the new play should open with a long and highly individual soliloquy spoken by Richard himself. His definition of his own nature, for which the previous play has prepared us,[18] is principally new in its more controlled and deliberate use of ironic effects. It operates by setting the evident villainy of his intentions against a cool realism which almost, in certain of its pungent phrases and shrewd evaluations, qualifies for definition as comedy:

> I, that am not shaped for sportive tricks,
> Nor made to court an amorous looking-glass;
> I, that am rudely stamp'd, and want love's majesty
> To strut before a wanton ambling nymph;

I, that am curtail'd of this fair proportion,
Cheated of feature by dissembling nature,
Deform'd, unfinish'd, sent before my time
Into this breathing world, scarce half made up,
And that so lamely and unfashionable
That dogs bark at me as I halt by them;
Why I, in this weak piping time of peace,
Have no delight to pass away the time,
Unless to spy my shadow in the sun,
And descant on mine own deformity;
And therefore, since I cannot prove a lover,
To entertain these fair, well-spoken days,
I am determined to prove a villain,
And hate the idle pleasures of these days. (I. i)

The speech, though based on the established attributes of envious villainy, plays down its more obvious rhetorical overtones in the interests of a less grotesque irony and a firmer delineation of character. Although a certain stilted quality survives in the movement of the verse (there is a sense, common to many Elizabethan stage heroes and villains, of the speaker playing up to a dramatically acceptable picture of himself), the general effect is remarkably concise and pointed. Richard's state of mind is conveyed primarily through a series of sharp visual touches—the vision of himself as strutting ludicrously before a "wanton ambling nymph," as being barked at by the dogs as he passes, as spying his misshapen shadow in the sun—and through the sustained contrast, with its implications of contempt and repudiation, between the "sportive tricks" and exigencies of "these fair, well-spoken days" and his own situation as an outsider, "deform'd, unfinish'd," "scarce half made up," "lamely" put together and beyond all remedy "unfashionable." In this way, by making his envy express a criticism which is felt not to be altogether unjustified, the speaker is in some degree humanized, transformed from the abstract incarnation of a traditional vice exploited for melodramatic effect into something like a person: a being whose nature is twisted indeed by his exclusion from "love's majesty" (the phrase stands out forcibly by contrast with the sneer that follows it), but who retains in the cool, pungent run of his comments a definite human plausibility. The contrast between this plausibility and the horror of what Richard actually achieves in the course of the action is a primary factor in the creation of the play's peculiar irony.

It is in accordance with this ironic intention that the first half of the action traces the successive stages of Richard's advance toward his goal. His initial declaration of moral autonomy is almost at once followed by the removal of Clarence, who has been Richard's associate in the preceding play and whose downfall was there foreseen, to the Tower. Richard, having himself instigated it, ascribes the responsibility for this move in characteristically pungent terms to the intrigues of the queen and Mistress Shore:

> The jealous o'erworn widow and herself,
> Since that our brother dubb'd them gentlewomen,
> Are mighty gossips in this monarchy. (I. i)

The critical implication is clear and, once again, not without force; but the speaker, in making it, is moved not by any kind of public spirit—he has just declared his complete separation from society—but by the pleasure which his own superior insight, and the sense of his own capacity to mold the course of events to the ends he has proposed to himself, gives him. It is germane to the situation of the politically aware man, as this play conceives it, that he can only rise further by kicking away the steps that have led him to his present eminence; it is Richard's quality to know and accept this truth, as it is his final tragedy to be inexorably limited by his acceptance of it. With the elimination of Clarence already in his mind, Richard first promises him the disinterested support of a loyal friend and loving brother, and then, left to himself, makes his sardonic comment upon so much capacity for self-deception:

> Simple, plain Clarence! I do love thee so,
> That I will shortly send thy soul to heaven,
> If heaven will take the present at our hands. (I. i)

The ability to *act* the villainies he plans, taking the audience into his confidence with a kind of cheerful *bonhomie* that contrasts with the real monstrosity of his intentions, distinguishes Richard from the other historical personages in this series of plays. Without making him on that account less horrifying as a human being, it adds a fresh dimension to the pattern of crime and retribution with which all the political agents in this ironic melodrama are so obsessively concerned.

Whilst engaged thus in planning death for his brother Richard continues, in his own way, to pursue his concern with life by wooing the Lady Anne. In their meeting, accusation and irony clash as the object of these grotesque advances recalls the saintly figure of the martyred Henry VI to his murderer, who is also, for good measure, the assassin of her own husband, Henry's son:

> – O, he was gentle, mild, and virtuous!
> – The fitter for the King of heaven, that hath him.
> – He is in heaven, where thou shalt never come.
> – Let him thank me, that holp to send him thither. (I. ii)

As she spits "mortal poison" at him in hatred and repulsion, Richard presses his suit, offering his breast for her to stab, declaring his readiness to kill himself at her command. His confidence, of course, is fully justified by the event. Anne surrenders at the end of a protracted verbal struggle and, as she does so, the cool comment of her wooer expresses the satisfaction which his success, and perhaps his sense of having adventured successfully to the very edge of danger, inspires in his keen twisted mind:

> Was ever woman in this humour woo'd?
> Was ever woman in this humour won?
> I'll have her; but I will not keep her long. (I. ii)

Once again, as he seems to stand aside from his projects to take us, his alternately shocked and fascinated audience, into his confidence, Richard adds a new dimension to his villainy, forces us to share after a fashion in the detachment from habitual moral judgments which throughout the first part of the play qualifies the essential savagery of his actions.

A similar impression emerges from his self-presentation to the world around him. Aware of the hostility that his actions will inevitably inspire, Richard cultivates the essentially ironic vision of himself as a "plain" man who laments the refusal of a corrupt and self-seeking world to take him at his own valuation:

> Because I cannot flatter and speak fair,
> Smile in men's faces, smooth, deceive, and cog,
> Duck with French words and apish courtesy,
> I must be held a rancorous enemy.
> Cannot *a plain man* live and think no harm,
> But thus *his simple truth* must be abused
> By silken, sly, insinuating Jacks? (I. iii)

Once more this self-portrayal contains, beneath its essential perversity, a measure of truth. Richard, we may feel, can justly claim a certain superiority to the world of courtly intrigue in which he moves and by which he feels himself rejected: but the exclusion, of course, is also from the natural positives of living, from human sociability as such, and the isolation which he seeks throughout to turn into an asset will bring him in the long run to an appropriate ruin. Meanwhile, however, we can hardly fail to respond to the grimly comic zest which inspires his definition of himself, to those who are already marked down to be the victims of his drive to power, as "too childish-foolish for this world" (I. iii).

The "comedy," nevertheless, if such we can call it, is projected, here and throughout, against an oppressive background of doom. Its principal mouthpiece continues to be Henry VI's widow Margaret, who, having survived the ruin of all her own cherished ambitions, can now denounce all those who surround her as so many

> wrangling pirates, that fall out
> In sharing that which you have pill'd from me. (I. iii)

Margaret, however, is by now no more than a survival from the past, a shadow of former pride. Richard is in a position to answer her by recalling her own ferocities, her part in the murder of York and Rutland so cruelly executed in the moment of her precarious triumph; and to this her only reply can be to urge, as though from the spent ashes of her exhausted passion, yet more death upon those who have replaced her on the summit of glory. To Edward IV's reigning queen she has only this to say:

> If not by war, by surfeit die your king,
> As ours by murder, to make him a king!
> Edward thy son, which now is Prince of Wales,
> For Edward my son, which was Prince of Wales,
> Die in his youth by like untimely violence!
> Thyself a queen, for me that was a queen . . . (I. iii)

The function of Margaret in this play is to give choral emphasis to the pattern of doom that dominates the entire course of the action, and further, in the process of so doing, to expose the essential savagery of Richard's motives:

> Look, when he fawns, he bites; and when he bites,
> His venom tooth will rankle to the death.

The exposure, however, as coming from one whose life is concentrated upon the sterile savagery of the past, falls upon deaf ears in an equally ruthless present. In replying to these denunciations Richard declares, once more in soliloquy and with typical ironic satisfaction, his determination to outdo the world at its own game of hypocrisy, to

> clothe my naked villainy
> With old odd ends, stolen out of holy writ, (I. iii)

and to proceed zestfully with his preparations for the elimination of his brother.

The murder of Clarence introduces a further variation into the general panorama of bestiality and horror. The victim's premonitory dream, in particular, insinuates a new projection of poetry into the realm of subconscious twilight:

> Lord, Lord! methought, what pain it was to drown!
> What dreadful noise of waters in mine ears!
> What ugly sights of death within mine eyes!
> Methought I saw a thousand fearful wrecks;
> Ten thousand men that fishes gnaw'd upon;
> Wedges of gold, great anchors, heaps of pearl,
> Inestimable stones, unvalued jewels,
> All scattered in the bottom of the sea:
> Some lay in dead men's skulls; and in those holes
> Where eyes did once inhabit, there were crept,
> As 'twere in scorn of eyes, reflecting gems,
> Which woo'd the slimy bottom of the deep,
> And mock'd the dead bones that lay scattered by. (I. iv)

This transformation of the reality of "pain," of "the dreadful noise of waters" and "ugly sights of death," into a phantasmagorical vision of treasures beyond value scattered at the bottom of the sea, answers to a kind of poetry which the rest of this play, ferociously concentrated upon brutality and lust for power, can hardly parallel. It is, however, profoundly Shakespearean. For this imaginative transformation of the charnel, this wedding of death to a transfigured, shifting opulence on the ocean bed, it is necessary to look far forward into the dramatist's future poetry: almost as far, we may think even as we establish firmly the essential differences, as the world of Prospero's magic spells and of the "pearls" into which Ariel's song transmutes the supposedly drowned eyes of Ferdinand's "lost" father.[19] The effect, of course, is different, beyond comparison less charged with significance and depth; but, having recognized this, we may also see in the poetic elaboration of this dream a content which, in the act of echoing them and taking up their obsessive rhythms, transforms the repetitive patterns of murder and retribution which principally dominate this play.

A further note of profundity, though of a different kind, is somewhat tentatively struck, again at this point, by one of Clarence's murderers in his reflections upon conscience. "I'll not meddle with it," he concludes;

> it is a dangerous thing: it makes a man a coward . . . it is a blushing shamefast spirit that mutinies in a man's bosom . . . it is turned out of all towns and cities for a dangerous thing; and every man that means to live well endeavours to trust to himself and to live without it. (I. iv)

The results of this "endeavour" on the part of man "to trust to himself," which constitutes precisely Richard's declared program for living,[20] will be made apparent in many of Shakespeare's tragedies, from the present play to at least as far as *Macbeth.* It implies, in the long run, a forcing of reality, a reversal of "nature" which brings its own retribution with it; but the realization, in so far as the murderer's words may be said to imply it, is rejected at this point, fails to exercise any influence upon the course of events. Clarence, left in his extremity to plead for mercy in the name of "the King of kings," is condemned by his own crimes committed in the past, and his murderer's answer is, in terms of this play's retributive pattern, unanswerable:

> How canst thou urge God's dreadful law to us,
> When thou hast broke it in so dear degree? (I. iv)

The saving qualities of compassion can have no place in an action dominated, almost to repetitive obsession, by the prospect of man's inhumanity to man.

Against this background of gathering horror the king, old and mortally sick, flawed by his own moral worthlessness, exacts a momentary show of reconciliation. Buckingham bows to his will, swearing loyalty in terms which his own conduct will shortly turn to irony, and Richard, as usual, passes his own implicit comment on the worth of this fiction by uttering his grotesque parody of repentance immediately before announcing the death of Clarence:

> I do not know that Englishman alive
> With whom my soul is any jot at odds,
> More than the infant that is born to-night;

So speaks the murderer, and caps his gesture with an avowal more fantastic still: "I thank my God for my humility" (II. i). The final comment on this mockery is conveyed, in the scene which at once follows, through the long choric lament of the bereaved and stricken queens:

> – Oh, for my husband, for my dear lord Edward!
> – Oh, for our father, for our dear lord Clarence!
> – Alas for both, both mine, Edward and Clarence!
> – What stay had I but Edward? and he's gone.
> – What stay had we but Clarence? and he's gone.
> – Was never widow had so dear a loss.
> – Were never orphans had so dear a loss.
> – Was never mother had so dear a loss. (II. ii)

The device of patterned lamentation is familiar and, of course, artificial in conception and effect; what is new and striking is the intensity with which it is carried out through the course of the play and, still more, the contrast between these accumulations of grief and the attitude, at once ferocious and ironic, tending to a kind of grim comedy, shown by the murderer. It is, moreover, at the end of these same lamentations that Richard and Buckingham, who have just joined in public expression of loyalty to their king, draw secretly together to plan the death of the young princes and the seizure of the crown.

At this juncture the king dies, whilst the citizens express their expectation of an even grimmer future (II. iii). The queen and her son, set against the background of a state pitilessly dedicated to civil strife—

> blood against blood,
> Self against self— (II. iv)

seek "sanctuary" with the Archbishop of York. Sanctuary, however, is a concept without meaning in the world as this play conceives it, and Buckingham is at hand to give the politician's reason why it should be profaned; as he tells the prelate, not without the man of the world's cynical satisfaction in the contemplation of his supposedly superior realism:

> You are too senseless—obstinate, my lord,
> Too ceremonious and traditional. (III. i)

Inevitably, the attitude which these words represent soon prevails. Richard commits the young princes to the Tower, Rivers, Vaughan, and Grey are brought to their doom (III. iii), thus confirming Margaret's prophecy, and Hastings is executed for his loyalty just after he has expressed, with further unconscious irony, his faith in his murderer's honesty:

> I think there's never a man in Christendom
> Can lesser hide his love, or hate, than he:
> For by his face straight shall you know his heart. (III. iv)

Richard, meanwhile, is busy advancing his cause by appropriate public gestures for the benefit of the unwilling citizens, whose support he requires. These, as reported by Buckingham, are bemused by the course of events, which they find it hard to welcome and cannot aspire to control:

> Now, by the holy mother of our Lord,
> The citizens are mum and speak not a word. (III. vii)

To exercise upon the populace the arts of politic persuasion Richard offers himself to their view, piously flanked by supporting clerics—"See, where he stands between two clergymen!"—as he allows Buckingham to "persuade" him to accept the crown.

Thus far the action of the play, concentrated upon the successive stages of Richard's advance to his goal, have been poised between the horror which his deeds inspire and a kind of detached, ironic comedy which the contemplation of his deeds provokes in him and which, actor-like, he communicates to the audience. As protagonist, he sums up and gathers into his person the savagery which everywhere prevails around him; as self-conscious actor of his own career, he passes on to us, as spectators, a detached and sardonic estimate of his own motives. The crowning, however, represents a turning point after which the spirit of the later action undergoes a notable change. Having obtained the ends he has proposed to himself, Richard is seen increasingly as the victim of his own choices. The horrors he has instigated follow him into his new state and bind him finally and irrevocably to the consequences of his own actions in the past. His first act as king (IV. ii) is to order the murder of the imprisoned princes, who represent an unwitting threat to his new eminence; the next is to plan the death of the Lady Anne—for whom, as he has already foreseen,[21] he has no further use—and to prepare the way for a new marriage by which he hopes to provide for a rule which, as he admits, "stands on brittle glass" (IV. ii). At this point his position shifts from that of the confident outsider, immersed in the contemplation of his control of the world around him, and begins to offer notable anticipations of *Macbeth:* anticipations that occasionally produce remarkable verbal parallels, as when he says, speaking of his own state,

> I am in
> So far in blood that sin will pluck on sin. (IV. ii)[22]

Words such as these, which can hardly be related to anything so concretely expressed in the earlier part of the play, indicate a fundamental shift of emphasis in its later development. Richard, hitherto so keenly aware of himself as the agent of his own destiny, is beginning to feel himself the prisoner of his own actions. The voice of natural pity, so elaborately expressed in Tyrrel's account of the princes' death (IV. iii), is one which he can less than ever afford to recognize, which he needs, even at the cost of forfeiting such humanity as remains to him, rigidly to exclude from his thoughts. There is from now on something increasingly automatic in the royal murderer's grim references to the execution of his plans—"Anne my wife hath bid the world good night"—and even in the attempt to caricature his own behavior as that of "a jolly thriving wooer" (IV. iii). For the first time, we sense a man engaged in whistling in the dark to keep up his own courage, to hide even from himself the sense of intimate emptiness which is beginning to hover obsessively on the edge of his thoughts.

For, in spite of these efforts to maintain the façade of ironic confidence, which are essentially a carry-over from the earlier action, the entire mood of the play is very notably changing. Margaret, backed now by the Duchess of York, continues to sound the familiar note of choric doom; but their lamentations, which Richard had once been able to shrug off, with some justification, as hollow echoes from a withered past, fall now with a fresh urgency, a new sense of tragic issues closing in upon the entire action. Seeing in their unhappy state the fulfillment of Margaret's most bitter prophecies, the royal victims of the murderer's ruthlessness feel themselves reduced to the status of participants in a common vanity to which, no doubt, their own sins, and those of their children, have contributed. As always, Margaret is the most explicit:

> I call'd thee then poor shadow, painted queen;
> The presentation of but what I was;
> The flattering index of a direful pageant:
> One heaved a-high, to be hurl'd down below;
> A mother only mock'd with two sweet babes,
> A dream of what thou wert, a breath, a bubble,
> A sign of dignity, a garish flag
> To be the aim of every dangerous shot;
> A queen in jest, only to fill the scene. (IV. iv)

The old queen's words answer sufficiently, beyond her own grief and ruin, to a change of emphasis in the entire action, which is concentrated now not on the political confidence of the protagonist, but upon the doom which radiates from his actions and drags down his entire world with it. The typical medieval themes of retribution for past sin and of the fall of the presumptuous from their high estate are in process at this point of being gathered into a final tragic resolution.

It is not, however, by these shadows of the past that Richard feels himself immediately threatened. As he returns at the tail end of these laments, and as his victims turn upon him with their bitter accusations, they receive only the ironic blast of his reply:

> A flourish, trumpets! strike alarum, drums!
> Let not the heavens hear these tell-tale women
> Rail on the Lord's anointed! (IV. iv)

The emphasis, however, is now upon concealment, upon the drowning in mere sound of an unpalatable and ominous truth. Against this grotesque background Richard, as though in a final gesture carried over from his former confident self, sets out to woo the Princess Elizabeth and invites to this end the good offices of the queen her mother. The answer he receives, setting irony against irony in an effect of accumulated bitterness, is indeed damning in its effect;

> What were I best to say? her father's brother
> Would be her lord? or shall I say, her uncle?
> Or, he that slew her brothers and her uncles?

Even ironic self-assertion has its limits, and the somber and menacing weight of the queen's final denunciation—

Swear not by time to come; for that thou hast
Misused ere used, by time misus'd o'erpast— (IV. iv)

explicitly reveals them. The fact that, before the long and elaborate exchange is brought to an end, Richard's victim has shown herself to be, in accordance with his own cynical expectations, "Relenting fool, and shallow, changing woman," cannot entirely take the edge from these denunciations or cover the decline in his own original comic energy as the revenges of time begin to take shape against him.

As the scene ends, indeed, confirmation of the changing direction of events reaches the usurper with the news of the Earl of Richmond's return. Richard receives these tidings in a mood which again closely foreshadows that of Macbeth at the end of his tragedy: the mood of a man on edge, veering and changeable, seeking the illusion of relief in what is now rapidly becoming an empty show of decisive action. As his disconnected commands, uttered in haste and stress—"Fly to the Duke"; "Post thou to Salisbury"—mingle with unfinished instructions and impatient gestures—"Why stand'st thou still and go'st not to the Duke?"—his followers are left to grope in ignorance of his intentions, alternately upbraided and confused:

– First, mighty sovereign, let me know your mind,
What from your grace I shall deliver to him.
– O, true, good Catesby; bid him levy straight
The greatest strength and power he can make,
And meet me presently at Salisbury.
– I go.
– What is't your highness' pleasure I shall do
At Salisbury?
– Why, what wouldst thou do there before I go?
– Your highness told me I should post before.
– My mind is changed, sir, my mind is changed. (IV. iv)[23]

This is the voice of a man who feels the control of events slipping from him, who has, perhaps for the first time, no clear vision of where or how far he means to go. The pressure of events only strengthens his disorientation. Lord Stanley is already preparing to desert him, and Richard can only seek to counter this defection by holding his son as hostage; the power which has been obtained by acting against the course of nature now seeks to perpetuate itself through the imposition of unnatural fear. By the time the long scene has drawn to a close, the armies of retribution are gathering against the usurper, as they will later gather against Macbeth, and his own followers—here as at Dunsinane—"on both sides do fight."[24]

Richard's cause, indeed, is already in the process of destroying itself. The treacherous Buckingham, who assisted him in his rise to power, is brought to execution, paying thus for his own sins—

> Wrong hath but wrong, and blame the due of blame—

whilst the armies of Richmond move forward "without impediment," "to reap *the harvest* of perpetual peace" and to restore, with the reign of ordered loyalty, the "*summer fields* and *fruitful vines*" (V. ii) which the usurper's excesses have brought to ruin. It is interesting to see that at this point the ideas of peaceful harmony and natural fertility have already found their characteristic Shakespearean association. Faced by this rising tide of restoration, Richard shows himself still a brave man—like Macbeth after him—and one who, like Macbeth again, seeks the shadow of consolation in intense activity: "For, lords, to-morrow is a busy day" (V. iii).[25] His is an activity, however, which answers to an essentially febrile and incoherent condition. Unlike Richmond, Richard can barely contemplate the foreseen outcome of the action forced upon him. He continues to threaten Stanley, whom he has good reason to mistrust, through the person of his son; but, beyond the steps which immediate necessity imposes upon him, his innermost thoughts are already dominated by the prospect of annihilation, contemplate what his own vivid phrase describes as "the blind cave of eternal night," and are ready to make confession of foreboding:

> I have not that alacrity of spirit,
> Nor cheer of mind, that I was wont to have. (V. iii)

By contrast to this condition we are shown Richmond consecrating himself and his army serenely to "the just God whose captain I account myself," whilst punishment and restoration join hands in his advancing train.

As night falls, and its ghostly shadows reveal to the rival contenders their contrasted images of the past, Richard is left, in a soliloquy perhaps more searching in its implications than anything Shakespeare had yet written, to pronounce his recognition of the egoist's isolated doom:

> What do I fear? myself? there's none else by:
> Richard loves Richard; that is, *I am I*.

NORTHWEST MISSOURI
STATE COLLEGE LIBRARY
MARYVILLE, MISSOURI

The assassin's definition of his state is laconic and direct at the last, as befits a man who has awakened from the dream of action and ironic self-assertion in which he has hitherto sought refuge from an awareness of his real condition. The result of a lifelong dedication to the egoist's desire for power is seen to be the impossibility of self-evasion, of escape from what now emerge, with dreadful clarity, as the limits of the isolated self. As Richard goes on to confess in his last vain effort to come to terms with the situation in which he finds himself:

> Is there a murderer here? no. Yes, I am:
> Then fly. What, from myself? Great reason why:
> Lest I revenge. What, myself, upon myself?
> Alack, I love myself. Wherefore? for any good
> That I myself have done upon myself?
> O, no! alas, I rather hate myself
> For hateful deeds committed by myself!

This is a far cry from the initial confidence of the "Machiavellian" prince, arrogantly dedicated to his own advancement; but it is essential to understand that the end was implied in the beginning, that the whole story answers to an irreversible tragic logic. Before the final bar of a judgment he has never recognized, but which now imposes itself upon him, Richard ends by confessing the isolation which he has chosen for himself and which has now become, by virtue of this very choice, his inescapable limitation:

> I shall despair. There is no creature loves me;
> And if I die, no soul will pity me:
> Nay, wherefore should they, since that I myself
> Find in myself no pity to myself? (V. iii)[26]

To the last Richard is haunted by the thought of exclusion from the world of "love," which he recognizes in his own despite as the natural sign of human solidarity and in the absence of which life presents itself to the egoist as empty, simply void of meaning. This is perhaps the Shakespearean equivalent, more human and less "metaphysical," of the vision of hell which haunted Faustus in Marlowe's great play, where it also produces a last great speech confessing to irreparable loss.[27] It is significant that now, for the first time, Richard confesses that he is *afraid*. "O Ratcliff, I fear, I fear"; and when his servant seeks to restore him to confidence—"Nay, good my lord, be not afraid of shadows"—he can only confess that "shadows to-night" have struck more "terror" into his soul than the "substance of ten thousand soldiers."

Once again, the nature of this confession is full of meaning. In terms of an obliterated distinction between "substance" and "shadow," reality and illusion, the moral duality which everywhere accompanies Shakespearean evil is already presented in the form of a psychological rift, a split in the personality which is the necessary consequence of perverse and unnatural choices. It is worth noting that Richmond has, at this same moment, received the visitation of

> The *sweetest* sleep, and *fairest boding* dreams
> That ever entered in a drowsy head,

and that he is in a position to tell those who follow him;

> I promise you, my soul is very *jocund*
> In the remembrance of so fair a dream. (V. iii)

As so often, and so surprisingly, occurs in this play, we sense anticipations of the vastly enriched world of *Macbeth*.

It is no more than appropriate, accordingly, that in his final oration to his soldiers, Richmond should lay stress upon the return to natural order which his victory will bring with it:

> If you do free your children from the sword,
> Your children's children quit you in your age;

whilst his rival, in contrast, can only seek relief in the illusion, finally self-engendered and self-maintained, that the presages of nature are empty of significance:

> Not shine to-day! Why, what is that to me
> More than to Richmond? (V. iii)

The battle once joined becomes for him a last means of escaping from reality, whilst "conscience" is dismissed, in accordance with the "philosophy" that has consistently ruled his life, as "but a word that cowards use."[28] "Our strong arms be our conscience, swords our law": but the end of this show of confidence is seen, on its own confession, to be at best dubious:

> March on, join bravely, let's to't pell-mell;
> If not to heaven, then hand in hand to hell.[29]

After this last flourish, made less to encourage his followers than to conceal from himself the sense of his own vanity, Richard in a final rousing speech revives for a moment some of his undoubted qualities as a leader of men in his lively dismissal of the enemy before him as

> A sort of vagabonds, rascals, and runaways,

seeing in them no more than

> these bastard Bretons, whom our fathers
> Have in their own land beaten, bobb'd, and thump'd. (V. iii)

To the last he acts bravely in his despair. As his followers report:

> The king enacts more wonders than a man,
> Daring an opposite to every danger:
> His horse is slain, and all on foot he fights,
> Seeking for Richmond in the throat of death. (V. iv)[30]

All this frenzied activity answers finally, as we have already seen reason to suspect, to an attempt at self-evasion, a reaction against recognized vacancy. As we follow Richard to his death, we can hardly avoid establishing a further parallel with Macbeth at the end of his tragedy, equally facing retribution in the person of Macduff. Like Macbeth, he succumbs to the death which the nature of his own choices has finally implied. Richmond is duly crowned (V. v), making his appeal to "smooth-faced peace" and announcing, with the final conquest of evil after its perverse impulse has been at last exhausted, the end of civil strife and the restoration of "smiling plenty" and "fair prosperous days." Shakespeare's first series of chronicle plays has been brought, with the fullness of time, to its logical and impressive conclusion.

II

Titus Andronicus

At approximately the same time as he was engaged on his first series of chronicle plays, Shakespeare embarked, with *Titus Andronicus,* upon his first venture in tragedy. The piece, though hardly attractive on first acquaintance, is more interesting than may immediately appear. Seneca and Ovid share a great part of its literary inspiration between them, not always to its dramatic advantage. Seneca lends his authority to the monotonous pattern of reiterated savageries which dominates the action; and Ovid, to whom Shakespeare was showing his devotion at about this time in the elaborate sensual decoration of *Venus and Adonis* and the more complex moral conflicts of *The Rape of Lucrece,*[1] contributes a scarcely less reiterative thread of images which, largely concentrated upon the story of the rape of Philomel and the revenge of Procne, is alternatively decorative, moralizing, and sensational. Throughout the play, emblematic artifice and ferocious melodrama share between them a tragedy which is crude in its construction and largely monotonous in its striving after effect; but it is fair to add that the monotony answers to a definite unity of style and conception, through which we glimpse at times anticipations of greater plays to come.

For the first time in his dramatic career, Shakespeare makes use of the unique prestige that, for a sixteenth-century mind, surrounded the name of Rome. The opening scene, stiff and immobile with rhetoric, presents the election of the Roman emperor. Whilst Saturninus and Bassianus declare their readiness to accept the verdict of the people, Titus speaks with measured solemnity of his country and with elegiac, almost necrological emphasis, of his own dead:

There greet in silence, as the dead are wont,
And sleep in peace, slain in your country's wars! (I. i)

Against the physical background provided by the massive funeral monument of the Andronici, his son Lucius demands revenge upon "the proudest prisoner" of the defeated Goths, seeking permission to "hew" his limbs and "sacrifice his flesh." The demand is an ominous inversion of the initial contrast between Roman civilization and Gothic barbarity. This is made clear when the captive Queen Tamora pleads eloquently for her son's life:

O, if to fight for king and commonweal
Were piety in thine, it is in these.
Andronicus, stain not thy tomb with blood.
Wilt thou draw near the nature of the gods?
Draw near them then in being merciful. (I. i)

The appeal, addressed to the natural "pieties" which a Roman might be expected to revere, falls upon deaf ears. Lucius mercilessly presses his vengeful demands: "Let's *hew his limbs* till they be clean consum'd." His words show what Tamora is justified in calling "irreligious piety," and cause her son Chiron to ask pertinently: "Was ever Scythia so barbarous?" As his brother Demetrius joins him in invoking the vengeance of the gods, Lucius returns with his freshly blooded sword, announcing with somber satisfaction that "Alarbus' limbs are *lopp'd*," and Titus celebrates a peace which he associates, most typically, with the release which his own slaughtered sons have found in dying for their country's cause:

In peace and honour rest you here, my sons;
Rome's readiest champions, repose you here in rest!
Secure from worldly chances and mishaps!
Here lurks no treason, here no envy swells,
Here grow no damned drugs; here are no storms,
No noise, but silence and eternal sleep:
In peace and honour rest you here, my sons! (I. i)

Whilst Titus, in words which recall those to be spoken, to a very different end, by Duncan's murderer,[2] thus builds upon bloody vengeance his own world-weary, death-directed meditations, the public affairs of Rome slip beyond his control into savagery and ruin.

Life, indeed, continues on its course in spite of these deathward reflections. As Titus' daughter Lavinia enters, she greets her father with a significant inversion of the words he has just spoken: "In peace and honour *live* Lord Titus long!" and is received by him as his "cordial" whilst he weeps "tears of joy"; for a precarious moment the poetry of the play seems to move from death toward a sense of continued life. Death, however, is already firmly enthroned. As the hero rejects the imperial nomination which he might have used for the furthering of peace, Saturninus appeals openly to the sword—

> Andronicus, would thou wert shipp'd to hell,
> Rather than rob me of the people's hearts!—

and Titus makes the fatal error of confirming him with his support. The consequences of his decision are immediately apparent. In the very act of taking Lavinia for his queen, Saturninus reveals his true nature by lusting after Tamora; and Bassianus, when he claims Lavinia for himself, equally sets his own will above the due processes of law. The affirmation of self-will becomes everywhere supreme. When Bassianus announces his determination "to do myself this reason and this right," Titus' brother Marcus supports him by saying "This prince in justice *seizeth* but his own," and Lucius, fresh from the cruel vengeance he has exacted from the Goths, adds emphatically: "And that he *will*, and *shall*, if Lucius live." Titus, for his part, clings obstinately to his own unwise decisions and actually ends by killing the son who stands in his way, to the accompaniment of a typical egoistic brag:

> What, villain boy,
> Barr'st me my way in Rome!

and when Lucius is reasonable enough to point out that he has committed this deed in "wrongful quarrel," his only reply is the unnatural gesture which leads him to disown his own flesh: "Nor thou, nor he, are any sons of mine."

The consequences of Titus' error, and of so much blind self-will, soon emerge. Secure in the possession of arbitrary power, Saturninus renounces Lavinia—"that changing piece"—and takes "lovely Tamora" for his queen. Innocence and lust are visibly personified in these two brides, and the tyrant, following the laws of his own nature, makes the appropriate choice. Titus, faced by this proof of perversity in the man to whose election he has been instrumental, clings to his error, even to the point of refusing burial in the family tomb for the son he has just slain; when his sons finally persuade him against this unnatural decision, his consent is grudgingly and morosely given: "Well, bury him, and bury me the next!" (I. i) Saturninus, meanwhile, pursuing his tyrannical path and seeking to eliminate his rival, accuses Bassianus of "rape" in the person of his discarded bride, but is persuaded by Tamora to "look graciously," in feigned friendship, upon Titus; her real aim is to be avenged upon the Andronici for the sacrifice of her own child. The brutality committed by the Romans upon Alarbus is to be repaid in full measure before the play reaches its desolate conclusion.

The appearance of Aaron, immediately after this long and heavily stylized opening, brings a new sense of life to the play. The part is full of self-conscious overtones, ironies which lend a distinctive quality to its obvious melodrama. Aaron is the theatrical "villain," thoroughly aware of his own evil and dedicated to the pleasure it affords him. Recognizing his own situation as an "outsider," he glories in feeling himself precariously poised over an abyss. His first words place Tamora on the perilous eminence from which they will both eventually fall:

> Now climbeth Tamora Olympus' top,
> Safe out of fortune's shot, and sits aloft. (II. i)

To scale "Olympus' top" is to invite the resentment of the gods; but, meanwhile, Aaron is ready to share his mistress' exaltation and to enjoy the sensation of holding her subject to his will, "fetter'd in amorous chains." For Aaron, precisely because he moves beyond the limits of society, love is an instrument to power, and in this spirit he encourages Chiron and Demetrius to carry out their designs upon Lavinia. Both are fully qualified to be his pupils. They share a common cynicism in their lust, which finds lively expression in Demetrius' attitude to their proposed victim:

> She is a woman, therefore may be woo'd;
> She is a woman, therefore may be won; . . .
> What, man! more water glideth by the mill
> Than wots the miller of: and easy it is
> Of a cut loaf to steal a shive, we know! (II. i)

This is the language, incisive and popular in its effect, which we have been accustomed to hear from the mouth of Richard Crookback;[3] it reflects, basically, the same "outsider's" attitude to life.

With this suitable material to his hands, Aaron proposes the ravishment of "the dainty doe" Lavinia, to be carried out far from the social habitations of man, which are "full of tongues, and eyes, and ears," in the solitude of the woods, "ruthless, dreadful, deaf, and dull." His conclusion, spoken with typical imaginative energy—

> There speak, and strike, brave boys, and take your turns;
> There serve your lust, shadow'd from heaven's eye,
> And revel in Lavinia's treasury— (II. i)

announces the transfer of the action to a new setting and to ferocity of another kind.

The scenes which now follow constitute in some sense the imaginative center of the whole play. In the recesses of the forest, and in the energies of the hunt, the principal characters are taken out of their normal public selves—as they will later be, though to very different ends, in Shakespeare's great comedies, in the Forest of Arden[4] and the sheepfolds of Bohemia[5]—and revealed in the intimacy of their contrasted reactions. For Titus, hunting is still a jocund, essentially a civilized occupation, which contrasts with Aaron's sinister evocations of gloom and obscure horror:

> The hunt is up, the moon is bright and grey,
> The fields are fragrant, and the woods are green:
> Uncouple here, and let us make a bay,
> And wake the emperor and his lovely bride,
> And rouse the prince, and ring a hunter's peal,
> That all the court may echo with the noise. (II. ii)

This might be a first intimation, slight and even crude by comparison, of the spirit in which Theseus and Hippolyta will set forth for the chase in *A Midsummer Night's Dream*.[6] It represents, for the last time in this play, a set of sociable, positive emotions, which are shortly to be plunged into palpable darkness. A hunt of a very different kind, indeed, is already afoot as Aaron, who has already referred to the "wide and spacious" forest walks as "Fitted by kind for rape and villainy" (II. i), lays his stratagem by burying "sweet gold" (II. iii) at the roots of the forest tree.

As he is joined, immediately after this, by Tamora, the woods assume another aspect, become the setting for the triumphant sensuality which she is ready to share with her lover:

My lovely Aaron, wherefore look'st thou sad,
When everything doth make a gleeful boast?
The birds chant melody on every bush;
The snake lies rolled in the cheerful sun;
The green leaves quiver with the cooling wind,
And make a chequer'd shadow on the ground;
Under their sweet shade, Aaron, let us sit,
And, whilst the babbling echo mocks the hounds,
Replying shrilly to the well-tuned horns,
As if a double hunt were heard at once,
Let us sit down and mark their yellowing noise;
And, after conflict such as was supposed
The wandering prince and Dido once enjoy'd,
When with a happy storm they were surpris'd,
And curtain'd with a counsel-keeping cave,
We may, each wreathed in the other's arms,
Our pastimes done, possess *a golden slumber;*
Whiles hounds and horns and sweet melodious birds
Are unto us as is a nurse's song
Of lullaby to bring her babe asleep. (II. iii)

This is surely one of the most impressive speeches of the whole play. Turning to fresh use the Ovidian conventions already familiar in *Venus and Adonis,* it shows us the woods from another point of view, not altogether unlike that already expressed by Titus, but directed to a very different end. Through the evocation of the gay "melody" of the birds, the green leaves "quivering" in the breeze and making their cool "chequer'd shade" whilst the "well-tuned" horns of the hunters contribute their sociable note to the complete picture, we are brought to the hidden embraces of Aeneas and Dido and so to the bliss enjoyed by Aaron and Tamora themselves, "each wreathed in the other's arms," locked in the real if transitory possession of their "golden slumber." The classical conventions, evoked with considerable intensity and skill, provide the background for a sensuality which, like the "snake" coiled deceptively in "the cheerful sun," at the heart of what seems so much idyllic peace, is dangerously and enticingly alive.

Aaron, however, is not concerned with these "venereal signs," for his obsessions lie elsewhere:

Vengeance is in my heart, death in my hand,
Blood and revenge are hammering in my head; (II. iii)

and, apart from this, he "never hopes more heaven than rests in thee." Meeting this dangerous pair as they wander through the wood, Bassianus and Lavinia are imprudent enough to taunt Tamora as Aaron's mistress; and she, as her sons rally around her, introduces yet another variation upon the forest theme, investing it with a new and sinister quality congruent with the dark deed of passion she now urges upon them in pursuit of her revenge:

> A *barren* detested vale, you see it is;
> The trees, though summer, yet forlorn and lean,
> O'ercome with moss and *baleful* mistletoe:
> Here *never shines the sun:* here *nothing breeds,*
> Unless the nightly owl or fatal raven:
> And when they showed me this abhorred pit,
> They told me, here, *at dead time of the night,*
> A thousand fiends, a thousand *hissing snakes,*
> Ten thousand swelling *toads,* as many *urchins,*
> Would make such fearful and confused cries,
> As any mortal body hearing it
> Should straight fall mad, or else die suddenly. (II. iii)

The presence here of all the familiar trappings of melodrama should not obscure the fact that an effect of some subtlety, in relation to the episode as a whole, is being pursued. The serpent of sensuality, basking in the "cheerful" sun, has turned into a sinister image of revenge, dweller in a labyrinth of darkness. The whole nature of the wood has changed to meet this new mood; neither the scene of joyous hunting nor of intense sensual gratification, it has become the home of "barrenness," "where nothing breeds," where deeds of death and destruction are consummated in the dark dead of night.

This transformation of conventional poetry, and all that it implies in terms of moral desolation, is one of the most striking features of the play. It is confirmed in action when Tamora accuses Bassianus of seeking to rape her, and her sons kill him before turning savagely on Lavinia:

> Drag hence her husband to some secret hole,
> And make his dead trunk pillow to our lust. (II. iii)

Lust and death are joined in ironic savagery as the murderers confront the new victim with the full scope of their intentions:

> we will enjoy
> That nice-preserved honesty of yours.

Lavinia's plea for pity, uttered in the name of nature, is answered by Tamora, who recalls the vengeance so brutally exacted on her own child, when she says: "I know not what it means"; as the new victim puts it,

> The milk thou suck'st from her did turn to marble;
> Even at thy teat thou hadst thy tyranny. (II. iii)

The sons of Titus, in turn, find Bassianus' newly slaughtered corpse in the "unhallow'd blood-stained hole," the "swallowing womb" of this "detested, dark, blood-drinking pit." The qualities of the wood have shifted yet again, or at least intensified their horror, to correspond to these new manifestations of human savagery.

Still in accordance with Aaron's plan, the sons of Titus are accused of Bassianus' murder, and Marcus, still following the hunt, comes upon Lavinia ravished, with her tongue cut out, like that of Philomel, and her hands "lopp'd and hew'd" as those of the Gothic prince had been at the opening of the play. The episode finds its culmination in her uncle's long and elaborate lament:

> Speak, gentle niece, what stern ungentle hands
> Have *lopp'd* and *hew'd* and made thy body bare
> Of her two branches, those sweet ornaments,
> Whose circling shadows kings have sought to sleep in,
> And might not gain so great a happiness
> As have thy love? Why dost not speak to me?
> Alas, a crimson river of warm blood,
> Like to a bubbling fountain stirr'd with wind,
> Doth rise and fall between thy rosed lips,
> Coming and going with thy honey breath. (II. iv)

Neither the elaborate expression nor the repugnant quality of the sentiment should conceal from us the continuity of purpose which links this to the rest of the play. Lavinia's torture answers, as the wording of the speech reminds us, to that formerly meted out by her brothers to their defeated foe. The persistent use of images related to trees ("lopp'd and hew'd," "branches"), and the turning to blood of the crystalline streams of pastoral fantasy, both serve to relate these horrors to the woods and natural surroundings which have already been so variously evoked in their relation to human passions and desires; and behind all this, of course, there lies the sustained parallel with the revenge of Tereus which Titus will in due course carry through to its culmination of savagery.

At the end of these crucial scenes the action returns to a simpler pattern of horrors. Titus pleads in vain for his sons, who stand under conviction for murder. The prevailing tone of his plea is, as ever, typically elegiac, the overflow of

> My heart's deep languor and my soul's sad tears. (III. i)

It falls, however, upon totally unresponsive ears. As Lucius puts it, "you recount your sorrows to a stone," and Titus himself is left to conclude that stones have in some sense more feeling than the Romans who reject his prayers. "A stone is soft as wax, tribunes more hard than stones." From now on, the far greater tragedy of Lear is at times faintly foreshadowed in Titus' reflections as he too turns toward madness;

> Why, foolish Lucius, dost thou not perceive
> That Rome is but a wilderness of tigers?[7]
> Tigers must prey, and Rome affords no prey
> But me and mine. (III. i)

As Lavinia, who has already had occasion to compare her enemies to tigers,[8] is brought to her father, tongueless and ravished, Titus is forced to recognize his isolation from humanity in terms which remind us of Timon announcing his last refuge from the ferocity of mankind:

> For now I stand as one upon a rock,
> Environ'd with a wilderness of sea;[9]

we may perhaps find something appropriate in this parallel between two plays each conceived, though with great difference in dramatic and poetic power, as it were at the verge, the extreme limit of possible human attitudes.

As Titus recalls his condemned sons to his ravaged and mutilated daughter, her speechless emotion conveys itself pathetically to his words:

> When I did name her brothers, then fresh tears
> Stood on her cheeks, as doth the honey-dew
> Upon a gather'd lily almost wither'd. (III. i)

Sentiment, however, continues to be poised, in the manner of this play, against a caustic irony. Whilst the father and his remaining children unite in lamenting these cruelties, Aaron enters with news of the emperor's last mockery of justice. Titus is to sever his own hand in the hope of saving his offspring from their fate. Whilst the deceived father expresses his gratitude for this crowning irony—

> O gracious emperor! O gentle Aaron!
> Did ever raven sing so like a lark?—

and disputes with his sons the gruesome privilege of making the sacrifice, Aaron comments with typical sarcasm:

> Nay, come, agree whose hand shall go along,
> For fear they die before their pardon come.

This, in turn, has hardly been uttered, and the sacrifice made, before the messenger returns, bearing two heads and the hand newly sacrificed. As Lavinia kisses her father, Titus, with a last outburst of feeling, says

> that kiss is comfortless
> As frozen water to a starved snake, (III. i)

before bursting out into the frenzied "Ha, ha, ha!" which marks both his final collapse into madness and the confirmation of his dedication to an inhuman revenge. As the scene ends, each brother takes up a severed head, and Lavinia follows with her father's hand grotesquely clenched between her teeth. They go in search of "Revenge's cave," the abode of darkness and unnatural horror, whilst Lucius is sent, in an equally unnatural reversal of patriotic ties, to rouse the Gothic enemy to arms against Rome.

The episodes which follow, presenting Titus as finally mad, are heavy with artifice and sententiousness. His protest against his son's killing of "an innocent fly" is warded off by Marcus when he compares the "victim" to the "empress' Moor"; we are reminded on the surface—but only on the surface—of Lear's greater madness.[10] Finally Lavinia, in an episode toward which one of the play's principal threads of reiterated imagery has been leading, exposes her murderers through the book which tells the story of Philomel, "ravish'd and wrong'd," "Forced in the ruthless, vast and gloomy woods,"[11] in a spot

> By nature made for murders and for rapes. (IV. i)

Nature herself appears to reflect the inhuman aberrations of man, and Titus, though he seems for a moment to turn aside from the vengeance which his sons propose, does so only because his mind is dedicated to a course which will soon reveal itself as still more ferocious and extreme.

At this point a measure of much-needed human relief is afforded, however grotesquely, by the birth (IV. ii) of Tamora's "blackamoor child." With a supreme turn of irony Aaron, defying the general consensus of outraged opinion, begins to celebrate his "first-born son and heir" even as Demetrius threatens, in the play's characteristic idiom, to "broach the tadpole on my rapier's point." The birth in Aaron of a paternal instinct which he declares emphatically against the loathing of the world to which he has attached himself is one of the most effective strokes, poised between irony and grim farce, in the entire play. It leads through his grotesque expressions of endearment—

> Look, how the black slave smiles upon the father,
> As who should say "Old lad, I am thine own"—

to the killing of the Nurse, equally grotesque in the ironic key—

> Weke, weke!
> So cries a pig prepared to the spit—

and to the final paternal caricature which accompanies his departure:

> Come on, you thick-lipp'd slave, I'll bear you hence;
> For it is you that puts us to our shifts. (IV. ii)

This new development in Aaron, not less unexpected for being entirely in accord with the prevailing irony of his presentation, is one of this tragedy's most effective devices.

Titus, meanwhile, dedicated to madness and engaged in shooting arrows bearing messages for the avenging gods (IV. iii), searches for "justice" on land and sea, but finds only its dreadful caricature, revenge; as his nephew Publius puts it in the form of a reputed reply from the other world:

> Pluto sends you word,
> If you will have Revenge from hell, you shall:
> Marry, for Justice, she is so employ'd,
> He thinks, with Jove in heaven, *or somewhere else*,
> So that perforce you needs must stay a time. (IV. iii)

Revenge, indeed, can only come from "hell," from the reversal of all ties of piety and natural feeling, and it is appropriately at this point that news comes (IV. iv) of the return of Lucius, leading the Goths against Saturninus, whilst Tamora prepares to placate Titus in order to stave off the threat to their common rule.

The entry of Lucius with his Gothic allies (V. i) initiates, accordingly, the last stage of the action. Aaron, brought before him, appeals for the only grace that now truly concerns him, the life of his child: "Touch not the boy; he is of royal blood." His appeal is made, in a typically detached way, to the religion of the conqueror, which he does not pretend to share:

> I know thou art religious,
> And hast a thing within thee called conscience,
> With twenty popish tricks and ceremonies. (V. i)

For himself, he admits to the possession of no such "thing," contemplating in equal good spirit the crime against Lavinia—

> she was wash'd and cut and trimm'd, and 'twas
> Trim sport for them that had the doing of it—

and the deception which led to Andronicus' loss of his hand:

> I play'd the cheater for thy father's hand;
> And, when I had it, drew myself apart,
> And almost broke my heart with extreme laughter. (V. i)

Aaron's departure from the play, as consistently unrepentant as when he entered it, is perhaps Shakespeare's most successful achievement in the ironic, "Marlovian" manner. He was to do other things infinitely more worth the doing, but—within the limits he set himself—this is as finished a performance as any.

The approaching conclusion (V. ii) meanwhile brings Tamora, disguised as Revenge, to Titus with her sons. Mad as he is, he recognizes her, and adds Rape and Murder, in the persons of Chiron and Demetrius, to their mother's presence: "Good Lord, how like the empress' sons they are!" This is admirable use of the personifications of the old drama which Shakespeare was even at this moment in the process of outdistancing. Already a deliberately sardonic note prevails over melodrama, as Titus rises to the bitterness of his denunciation:

> Look round about the wicked streets of Rome,
> And when thou findst a man that's like thyself,
> Good Murder, stab him; he's a murderer. (V. ii)

Outmaneuvering Tamora at her own game, he is successful in getting "Rape" and "Murder" to remain with him till he cuts their throats. The way is clear for the final feast, in which the revenge of Philomel—so obsessively present in the preceding action—is finally re-enacted in a spirit of dreadful irony:

> The feast is ready, which the careful Titus
> Hath ordain'd to an honourable end,
> For peace, for love, for league and good to Rome. (V. iii)

The dedication amounts by now to a savage parody of all the public spirit and decorum for which Titus himself stood in the play's opening scenes. With his purpose achieved, and after the general slaughter, it only remains for him to die at the hands of Saturninus, whom Lucius in turn immediately kills.

As the play ends, with its impulse to destruction exhausted in death, Marcus calls the Roman people to restore their unity:

> O, let me teach you how to knit again
> This scatter'd corn into one mutual sheaf,
> These broken limbs again into one body. (V. iii)

With peace and unity thus invoked through the supreme "natural" symbols of concord, which will rarely be far henceforth from Shakespeare's thought, the crimes of the past are exposed and Lucius hailed as lawful emperor. Marcus dedicates to his dead father an appropriate elegy—"Tear for tear and loving kiss for kiss"—and Titus' grandson is called upon, in the name of "kind nature," to add his tears to the general lament:

> Bid him farewell; commit him to the grave;
> Do him that kindness, and take leave of him. (V. iii)

To the last, the pieties of the family stand out, if only by contrast, in this uniquely savage play. Only Aaron, of the survivors, is excluded from them, left "breast-deep in earth" to famish in the sensualist's appropriate torture. To the end, however, he is consistent in his refusal to recognize the existence of good:

> If one good deed in all my life I did,
> I do repent it from my very soul;

only through consistency in ill-doing can the "soul," in which—paradoxically—he has consistently declared that he does not believe, attain the expression of its malevolence. Tamora too remains beyond redemption. "Heinous tiger" to her last breath, she is left without the grace of burial in answer to her own ferocity; for, as Lucius says,

> Her life was beastly and devoid of pity,
> And, being so, shall have like want of pity. (V. iii)

With the fall of the curtain, Lucius declares his intention so to "order well the state" that "like events may ne'er it ruinate."

III

The Early Comedies

THE COMEDY OF ERRORS

Like not a few other great artists, Shakespeare's development at the outset of his dramatic career seems to have been relatively slow. Had he died at the early age of Christopher Marlowe, it is quite possible that we might today have found him the less striking, the less obviously original of the two writers. The judgment, however, would have been rash, even illusory. If we may concede that the impact of Marlowe's genius was at this stage more obviously emphatic, it is at least equally certain that the early plays of Shakespeare show a wider range, a closer adaptation to more varied dramatic ends. We have already traced in the early chronicle plays the growth of a remarkably forceful unifying conception which ended by producing, in *Richard III*, what is in effect a new kind of drama; and we have found even in the apparently unpromising material offered by *Titus Andronicus* anticipations of effects later to be vastly developed. At the same time, in another series of early plays, Shakespeare was engaged in exploring the possibilities of the comic convention, shaping it by a process resembling trial and error into an instrument for expressing the finished statements about life—and more especially about love and marriage as central realities in the pattern of living—that he was already, beneath the obvious desire to entertain, concerned to make. Since Shakespeare embarked upon his career as a comic writer and since he also finished it by writing comedies—albeit of a very different kind—it seems appropriate to give due consideration at each stage to his constantly developing conception of the comic forms.[1]

The first step in this lifelong process may well have been *The*

Comedy of Errors, which seems to have been acted for the first time in 1594 but which was possibly written as much as two years earlier. The play is basically a comedy of "intrigue" conceived on well-established classical lines; the plot is derived from two plays by Plautus[2] and shows a considerable skill in weaving incidents from both these works into a coherent dramatic structure. The result is a formal construction of some intricacy. It is, in fact, through its pleasurable juggling with a plot continually expanding into new situations, repeatedly threatening to escape the demands of dramatic logic and yet always found to be under control, that the piece achieves its effect. On the strictly formal side it is worth noting that Shakespeare accepted the challenge implied in the added intricacy of his plot; the play offers us *two* Dromios against Plautus' one and places *two* women in significant contrast. Since the working out to harmonious conclusions of intricate sets of personal relationships is to be an essential part of Shakespeare's mature comic conception, which none of his greater comedies will fail to use to the full, we should not underestimate the importance of this initial exercise in elaborate plot-making for his developing art.

There is, however, a good deal more than this to *The Comedy of Errors.* That Shakespeare was concerned with an effect more complex than any which mere intrigue plotting could give is suggested by his setting of the comic action in a framework which answers to a different, a notably more serious mood. As the play opens, the Syracusan merchant Aegeon, searching for the wife and child he has lost at sea, finds himself condemned to die in the hostile city of Ephesus. He relates his adventures in verse which, although we may find it relatively crude, conveys a certain sense of solemnity, a suggestion of meanings beyond those immediately apparent. When a Shakespearean character can speak, at this early stage in the dramatist's career, of "the always wind-obeying deep" and of his own ship as "sinking-ripe": when he can answer the Duke's expression of helpless compassion—"For we may pity, though not pardon thee"—by referring to the action of supernatural powers:

> O, had the gods done so, I had not now
> Worthily term'd them merciless to us;

when, finally, he can balance "love" against "loss" as he recalls the son from whom an adverse fate has separated him:

Whom whilst I labour'd of a love to see,
I hazarded the loss of whom I loved: (I. i)

we must feel that we are moving in a world which, for all the obvious difference in depth of feeling and mastery of expression, is not entirely remote from that of the final romances. The antitheses and the solemnity, the balance of loss and gain, suggest a desire to set the main intrigue against a more ample background, less immediately definable in terms of comic incident, than itself.

The opening lines of the principal story (I. ii) serve, indeed, to connect it with what has gone before. Antipholus of Syracuse is shown on his first appearance to be possessed by melancholy, in search of a content which he feels, albeit obscurely, that he needs to find beyond the limitations of the self:

He that commends me to mine own content
Commends me to the thing I cannot get.
I to the world am like a drop of water,
That in the ocean seeks another drop;
Who, falling there to find his fellow forth,
Unseen, inquisitive, confounds himself:
So I, to find a mother and a brother,
In quest of them, unhappy, lose myself. (I. ii)

There is something more here than mere intrigue comedy. Whereas this is habitually and exclusively concentrated upon confusion, upon the entrance mistakenly sought to the wrong house and the blow given and taken in error, Shakespeare's comic incidents normally suggest something beyond themselves, point—on the further side of their surface impact, which we may enjoy for its own sake—to a deeper reflection of the human situation. The speaker of the words we have just quoted is concerned to "find himself"; and the point of the web of errors into which he—and with him those around him—fall in the course of undertaking this search lies in their irrational and finally even sinister inversion of reality. As Antipholus goes on to say of Ephesus:

They say this town is full of cozenage;
As, nimble jugglers that deceive the eye,
Dark-working sorcerers that change the mind,
Soul-killing witches that deform the body,
Disguised cheaters, prating mountebanks,
And many such-like liberties of sin. (I. ii)

The essence of Shakespearean comedy lies in the undermining of the common order of reality, in its temporary substitution by an unfamiliar and more disturbing world from which the principal characters finally return to that same order with their initial preconceptions shattered and their natures correspondingly enriched. At the far end of this exposure to the comic nightmare which is about to engulf him Antipholus, and the rest with him, will see life in something closer to its true nature, will—always within the limits which comedy finally imposes—find himself in his relation to others. The experience will be positively rewarding; but during the course of it, in his in-between state of loss and bewilderment, he will always be on the point of leaving Ephesus and so of placing this happiness behind him, leaving his final reconciliation to the real world and to his own nature unachieved.

The comic nightmare initiated in this way is connected with human relationships and, at their center, with love and its fulfillment in marriage. It is for this reason that Shakespeare, extending the scope of his classical sources, introduces *two* women into his action, contrasting and humanizing them in a way that is entirely his own. Adriana, when she first appears, is moved by jealousy to question the natural dependence of marriage upon a reasonable acceptance of male authority. "Why," she asks, speaking of the men whose freedom she envies, "should their liberty than ours be more?" (II. i). Her companion Luciana bases her reply upon traditional views of the marriage relationship, asserting that "Men more divine, the masters of all these" are, by virtue of their superior endowment with "intellectual sense and souls" "masters to their females," and concludes: "Ere I learn love, I'll practise to obey." The argument is based in the last resort upon an acceptance of natural order. As Luciana forcibly puts it,

> Why, headstrong liberty is lash'd with woe.
> There's nothing situate under heaven's eye
> But hath his bound, in earth, in sea, in sky; (II. i)

but, although this view is clearly intended to prevail, as it will prevail even more emphatically in *The Taming of the Shrew,*[3] there is also some force in Adriana's reply:

> They can be meek that have no other cause.
> A wretched soul, bruised with adversity,
> We bid be quiet when we hear it cry;

But were we burden'd with like weight of pain,
As much or more, we should ourselves complain. (II. i)

There is an element of debate here, a juxtaposition of contrasted points of view, which will be very close to Shakespeare's mature genius; but the possibility of holding the balance should not blind us to the fact that Adriana's jealousy is, as Luciana truly sees, "self-harming" (II. i), and that the comic situations of this play turn repeatedly on people who appear, as we have already seen in the case of Antipholus, to be thrown in upon themselves, humanly isolated in a way which finds its comic reflection in a kind of madness. Adriana echoes Antipholus' original comparison of himself to "a drop of water" seeking its fellow in the ocean[4] when, even in her jealousy, she sets forth a true view of marriage—

For know, my love, as easy mayst thou fall
A drop of water in the breaking gulf,
And take unmingled thence that drop again,
Without addition or diminishing,
As take from me thyself, and not me too—

although she drives it in her obsession to falsely possessive and violent conclusions:

For if we two be one, and thou play false,
I do digest the poison of thy flesh,
Being strumpeted by thy contagion. (II. ii)

These relatively external parallels in word and situation initiate, however imperfectly, comic devices that Shakespeare will later turn to immeasurably greater effect.

The presentation of contrasted attitudes, leading to a truth greater than any single one of them can compass, is extended in the course of the play to other aspects of love. Antipholus of Syracuse expresses his love for Luciana in characteristically romantic terms:

Sing, siren, for thyself, and I will *dote:*
Spread o'er the silver waves thy golden hairs,
And as a bed I'll take them, and there lie;
And in that glorious supposition, think
He gains by death that hath such means to die; (III. ii)

but his use of the word "dote," which responds repeatedly, in Shakespearean comic terms, to the excesses of sentimental passion, is a sure pointer to the true nature of his "glorious supposition," and Luciana has no hesitation in calling him "mad" and in directing him firmly toward sanity through an acceptance of the sober truth of marriage: "Gaze where you should, and that will clear your sight." Only, of course, it is an essential part of the general comic alienation that it is the *wrong* Antipholus whom she is thus soundly advising. Obstinate in the illusion he has chosen to follow, the Syracusan calls her

> mine own self's better part,
> Mine eye's clear eye, my dear heart's dearer heart,
> My food, my fortune, and my sweet hope's aim,
> My sole earth's heaven, and my heaven's claim;

but this, which converts the true language of married love into the excess of love's idolatry, is realistically balanced by his servant's description, in the same scene, of the pursuit to which he has been subjected by the kitchenmaid of Ephesus. For Dromio speaks of love in terms deliberately and exaggeratedly opposite to those used by his master; Luce, he says, makes upon him "such claim as you would lay to your horse": and again: "she would have me as a beast; not that, I being a beast she would have me; but that she, being a very beastly creature, lays claim to me," in order to transform him, as he also says, to "a curtal dog" (III. ii). The point here does not lie in the quality of the humor which is, as is often the case with Shakespeare's early clowns, at once coarse and rather tedious, but in the opposing of an element of realism, stressed even to the point of vulgarity, to the excesses of romantic love. In the end, at all events, Antipholus himself is ready to confess to the existence of a part of "madness" in his love:

> She that doth call me husband, even my soul
> Doth for a wife abhor. But her fair sister,
> Possess'd with such a gentle sovereign grace,
> Of such enchanting presence and discourse,
> Hath almost made me *traitor to myself:*
> But lest myself be *guilty to self-wrong,*
> I'll stop mine ears against the mermaid's song. (III. ii)

By the end of the intrigue he will have been brought from this "madness," this "betrayal" of his own true nature, to "sanity" in another, more positive and inclusive order of things.

Until that conclusion is revealed, however, contradiction prevails everywhere in Ephesus. Adriana's jealousy, and the conflict to which it gives rise, are portrayed with an effort at psychological plausibility that very notably surpasses the hard-boiled, finally pitiless attitudes that Shakespeare might, had he so desired, have taken over from his classical originals. In her resentment she describes her husband as

> deformed, crooked, old and sere,
> Ill-faced, worse bodied, shapeless everywhere;
> Vicious, ungentle, foolish, blunt, unkind;
> Stigmatical in making, worse in mind; (IV. ii)

The concentration upon physical deformity and inadequacy as an instrument of comic ridicule answers fully to the spirit of Shakespeare's Roman models; but it is noteworthy that, in the same breath, Adriana goes on to recognize the difference between what jealousy has made her say and what, in her heart, she knows to be the truth: "I think him better than I say . . . My heart prays for him, though my tongue do curse." In this admission we are shown, if we care to read, the way out of madness and excess, the replacement of irrational possessiveness, and the contrary and self-consuming excesses to which it gives rise, by the natural order of married love.

Meanwhile, and until the moment has come for the truth to be revealed, the world of Ephesian madness prevails as Dromio enters with the news of his supposed master's arrest; as the other Antipholus puts it, only moments later,

> here we wander *in illusions:*
> Some *blessed power* deliver us from hence! (IV. iii)

The Courtezan makes her brief appearance to the Syracusan Antipholus, who sees her as "mistress Satan," whilst his twin of Ephesus is incomprehensibly arrested and subjected to the comic exorcism of Pinch (IV. iv). We can hardly be surprised that Antipholus of Syracuse, finding himself once more at the heart of the nightmare, determines yet again to seek safety in flight: "I will not stay to-night for all the town" (IV. iv).

But his departure, of course, would take him, against all appearances, away from sanity and the true resolution of his problems. It is at this point, accordingly, as master and servant seek refuge in the priory from the lunacy which everywhere surrounds them, that we return to the spirit of the "serious" framework which contains the comic plot. The return, expressed in terms of Shakespearean comedy, is to reality and natural life. Adriana enters, in search of her "poor distracted husband," and the Abbess, in whose hands the final resolution rests, reproves her gravely for the jealousy which has been her own form of insanity:

> And therefore came it that the man was mad.
> The venom clamours of a jealous woman
> Poisons more deadly than a mad dog's tooth. (V. i)

Adriana, in turn, confirms her awakening to reality by taking the rebuke in good part: "She did betray me to my own reproof." The Abbess, in return, agrees to restore her husband "to his wits again," for this is, as she affirms with proper solemnity, "A charitable duty of my order." The pattern, however, is still far from complete. At this point, as Aegeon enters under arrest, we are reminded of the somber framework in which this farce has deliberately been set, invited to contemplate

> the melancholy vale,
> The place of death and sorry execution. (V. i)

As Antipholus of Ephesus makes his entry, demanding "justice" against his wife, the Duke, as though to emphasize the precarious and relative nature of our understanding of life, concludes that all alike have "drunk of Circe's cup" and are accordingly alienated from their right minds. Aegeon, surprised by the failure of the wrong Antipholus to recognize him in the hour of his greatest need, speaks in rueful solemnity of time's betraying action:

> O, grief hath changed me since you saw me last,
> And careful hours with time's deformed hand
> Have written strange defeatures in my face. (V. i)[5]

But even as he exclaims in bitterness against "time's extremity," the entry of the second twin enables the Abbess to bring sanity out of alienation, to clear up the intrigue in what will come to be the constant manner of Shakespearean comedy. The Abbess is recognized to be Aegeon's lost wife and, in the light of this discovery, asserts the restoration of sane harmony, the resolution of past sorrow into present joy:

> Thirty-three years have I but gone in travail
> Of you, my sons: and till this present hour
> My heavy burthen ne'er delivered. (V. i)

The long years of "travail" have at last borne their natural and appropriate fruit. The masters embrace to celebrate their restoration to one another in the sane light of day; and their servants, having renounced all claim to invidious precedence, which their very twinship denies—

> We came into the world like brother and brother;
> And now let's go hand in hand, not one before another— (V. i)

go in to take part in the social consummation represented by what they call "the gossiping."

THE TAMING OF THE SHREW

For what may have been his second exercise in comedy, *The Taming of the Shrew,* Shakespeare took another plot of the "intrigue" type, but developed it in ways which suggest that his experience with *The Comedy of Errors* had made him aware that this type of play would not easily adapt itself to the purposes he already had in mind. *The Comedy of Errors* set its comic action in the "serious" framework provided by its opening and conclusion, thus establishing a contrast which served to point the play's deeper meanings. In *The Taming of the Shrew* the dramatist preferred to incorporate side by side two separate and distinct strands of plot, extracting his comic effects precisely from the constantly shifting interplay between them; but he also provided an Induction, which answers in some sense to the "framework" of the previous play but differs notably from it by the absence of any return to it in the conclusion, the main action being left accordingly open in a way that separates the new play fundamentally from the effect sought and obtained in its predecessor.

The Taming of the Shrew turns, accordingly, upon three different elements of plot, two of which operate at a different level from the third. The first of these is the Induction, which, in the course of the two opening scenes, sets the entire comic action in a framework provided by the transformation of the drunken tinker Christopher Sly into an "aristocratic" spectator of the play which has been arranged for his benefit. Next to this, and answering to the main substance of the comedy, is the popular knockabout story of Katherine the shrew and her marriage to Petruchio, which Shakespeare uses to put forward in comic form certain ideas about marriage and about the natural relationship between the sexes. Finally, the story of Bianca and her suitors, which is derived ultimately from Ariosto's play *I Suppositi*,[6] introduces by way of deliberate contrast a relatively sophisticated element of Italianate comedy. No single one of these diverse threads is perhaps, taken in itself, of outstanding interest or comic value, though we should not underestimate the effect which they are capable of making on the stage; but, taken together, their significance lies, in what is already coming to be Shakespeare's characteristic comic manner, in the way in which they play upon one another to bring out the full intention of the play.

We begin, then, with the Induction, which aims at providing the principal comic story with a framework, a setting which at once isolates it from common reality and conveys, in some measure, an implicit comment upon it. Sly is a man taken out of himself, induced, in the words of the Lord who plans his transformation, to "forget himself"; and then within this illusion, as though to provide an additional element of indirectness, a second deception is set up with the arrival of the players to perform their comedy. The result is an effect of considerable subtlety, which notably exceeds in its complexity anything in the previous play. Having been introduced on the stage to Sly, in his mixture of boorishness and ignorance, we are asked as spectators to stand aside *with him*, to step into the illusion and to watch a further action being carried out on what is, to all intents and purposes, a stage within a stage. The device should save us, among other things, from taking too seriously the story of the shrew and her taming, from reading into it too directly what is apt to strike us as an inhuman and primitive attitude toward women. Compared with Sly, all the characters of the main action appear as what they are, creatures of the stage, instruments of theatrical illusion. In this way, Shakespeare is already foreshadowing his characteristic comic balance between what *is* and what *seems*, between appearance and reality.

Sly, indeed, emerges, when considered in this context, as a figure of some potential subtlety. In the course of his brief occupation of the stage he is imaginatively translated, carried to a new world of the imagination, which he initially resists in the name of common sense but to which he finally succumbs. At first, the luxury to which he awakens from his drunken sleep is contrasted with the prose plainness of his reaction: "Am not I Christopher Sly, old Sly's son of Burton heath, by birth a pedlar, by education a card-maker, by transmutation a bear-herd, and now by present profession a tinker?" (*Induction,* ii); but gradually his unbelief is overcome as he is absorbed into a dream which the reality around him seems to confirm:

> I do not sleep; I see, I hear, I speak;
> I smell sweet savours and I feel soft things:
> Upon my life, I am a lord indeed,
> And not a tinker nor Cristophero Sly. (*Induction,* ii)

Finally it is the reality of his own waking state which becomes for him a "dream," and the present illusion the truth from which he becomes anxious not to awaken; "I would be loath," he says in his new, "transformed" state, "to fall into my dreams again: I will therefore tarry in despite of the flesh and the blood" (*Induction,* ii). Although this device may seem crude in the manner of its development, some of its implications already answer, however dimly, to the nature of drama itself.

Within the framework thus provided, we are given two plots brought together in ways which the dramatist certainly intended to be mutually revealing. The first, and more important, is the "tumbling-trick" or "Christmas gambol"[7] of Katherine's "taming"; the second, more urbane and sophisticated in its effect, is the story of Bianca and her lovers. Taken together, these two stories set a realistic against what purports to be an idealistic attitude toward marriage; but—and it is at this point that we approach the substance of Shakespeare's intention—it is in the end Katherine, the supposedly heartless and rejected shrew, who submits to the balanced, "natural" view of marriage, and the idealized, idolized Bianca who is seen by her final attitude to reject it.

In responding to the impression of barbarism which the "shrew" story may initially make upon us, we shall do well to take into account a number of qualifying factors. Katherine at the outset has good reason to protest against her father's demand that she should marry before her sister. To her reasonable protest against this treatment—

> I pray you, sir, is it your will
> To make a stale of me amongst these mates?— (I. i)

the brief and obstinate assertion of Baptista's bare determination—"Gentlemen, content you: I am resolved"—is less than an adequate answer. If Shakespeare here, as in later plays, is ready to argue in favor of a proper submission as natural, implicit in the order of things, this must emphatically *not* be taken to mean that submission has no limits, that the relationship between father and children, or between man and wife, is conceived by him in one-sided terms of domination and subservience.

Nor, if we care to remember that this is a play, a conventional reflection of life—and one, moreover, which the dramatist has been careful, by setting it within a more "realistic" framework, to remove from immediate reality—shall we find Petruchio as harsh and unreasonable as may appear. The contrast is throughout between his common-sense grasp of real life and the wildly romantic devotion which induces Lucentio to say of the worthless Bianca:

> Tranio, I saw her coral lips to move,
> And with her breath she did perfume the air:
> Sacred and sweet was all I saw in her; (I. i)

to which the servant, in a notably more realistic mood, replies by speaking of his master's infatuation as a "trance" and by advising him to prove the worth of these high-flown assertions by acting in accordance with them:

> if you love the maid,
> Bend thoughts and wits to achieve her.

For all its apparent crudity, Petruchio's attitude has a hardheaded actuality which that of Lucentio lacks. When the latter says,

> Tranio, I burn, I pine, I perish, Tranio,
> If I achieve not this young modest girl, (I. i)

an element of romantic excess, finally self-regarding and self-indulgent, colors his declaration: whereas, when Petruchio declares frankly that his motives are to make his fortune and to see the world:—

> I come to wive it wealthily in Padua;
> If wealthily, then happily in Padua— (I. ii)

we can still leave it to events to show whether the speaker is capable of understanding that there is more than this to marriage, or whether bluntness of this kind is compatible with true feeling.

The entire attitude of Petruchio, indeed, reflects an essential common sense which stands in contrast to the behavior of Bianca's various lovers in this play: to that of Gremio, who, being old, is content to woo her with his wealth,[8] and of Lucentio, whose romanticism turns out, when put to the test, to be compatible with the readiness to deceive which leads him to use a personification of his father to gain his ends.[9] In contrast to so much artifice and deceit, it is revealing to set the terms in which the supposedly insensitive Petruchio describes Katherine to herself mingling burlesque with a forthright, natural strain of poetry:

> 'Twas told me you were rough and coy and sullen,
> And now I find report a very liar;
> For thou art pleasant, gamesome, passing courteous,
> But slow in speech, yet sweet as spring-time flowers:
> Thou canst not frown, thou canst not look askance,
> Nor bite the lip, as angry wenches will,
> Nor hast thou pleasure to be cross in talk,
> But thou with mildness entertain'st thy wooers,
> With gentle conference, soft and affable.
> Why does the world report that Kate doth limp?
> O slanderous world! Kate, like the hazel-twig,
> Is straight and slender, and as brown in hue
> As hazel nuts and sweeter than the kernels. (II. i)

We may feel that Petruchio is in effect revealing the *real* Kate to herself, showing what is—though she does not yet know it and her behavior has so far seemed to belie it—her true nature to a girl who has been systematically belittled by all around her, not excluding her own father. Petruchio is announcing his program, describing Kate less as she is than as she is capable of becoming once he has, by his deliberate use of violence in a stage situation, succeeded in molding her to what the play takes to be the natural, the reasonable attitude to marriage. Petruchio's statement of his positions is habitually extreme, as befits the kind of comedy with which we are here concerned, but the positions themselves are invariably a defense of nature—even when he insists with a brutal directness which such as Lucentio would find intolerably gross upon the childbearing function of woman: "Women were made to bear, and so are you" (II. i)—and stand out by contrast to the facile and disembodied idealism exhibited, in a world finally steeped in self-interest, in an obsessive concern with the dowry, the main chance, by Bianca's devoted servants. When Katherine's father and his own friends are horrified by the "unreverent robes" in which he presents himself for his wedding, Petruchio can retort "To me she's married, not unto my clothes," and go on to say, with striking and characteristic modesty:

> Could I repair what she will wear in me,
> As I can change these poor accoutrements,
> 'Twere well for Kate, and *better for myself.* (III. ii)

In this further contrast between *seeming* and *being,* between the external appearance a man can so easily put on and the reality of his nature, Petruchio shows a moral seriousness which, in our attention to the slapstick action, we can too easily neglect.

Accordingly, as the crude episodes of the "taming" follow upon one another, we are brought to see that Petruchio's treatment of his shrew implies a process of education, that it is aimed, among other things and rather surprisingly, at teaching her to *feel.* This is apparent when he strikes his servants before her and gets her to protest against what seems to be his lack of human consideration. Katherine does in fact develop in the course of the play in the direction of the feeling and humanity which she seemed initially to lack:

> My tongue will tell the anger of my heart,
> Or else my heart concealing it will break. (IV. iii)

If she begins by beating her sister without mercy (II. i), she ends by protesting against her husband's treatment of the Tailor and the Haberdasher (IV. iii); and it is no doubt precisely his intention that she should react in this way. When this advance from the hoydenish invective of the early scenes has been confirmed by her behavior under test, he is ready to respond with a statement of the "natural" relationship between men and women and by an assumption of true marriage. This he does even whilst satirizing the excesses of lovesick romanticism by calling his spaniel Troilus (IV. i) and just at the moment when the third of Bianca's suitors, Hortensio, renounces her in favor of "a wealthy widow" (IV. ii).

The contrast, indeed, to which the play leads us is one between Kate, who, prepared by the rude process of education to which she is subjected, becomes the good wife she has always had it in her to be, and Bianca, the idealized coquette who ends by refusing to obey her husband's command. The play's "philosophy," if so pretentious a word may be allowed, depends upon the assertion of nature which it has all along been Petruchio's function to defend:

> Thus the bowl should run,
> And not unluckily against the bias. (IV. v)

This is the foundation of his whole attitude; and the argument is that when things are so arranged, when the relationships of society run in accordance with and not against "nature," subjection and strife, which are contrasted sides of the same coin, are replaced by free agreement and mutual harmony. Against what may appear to be the spirit of much of its story, the play thus emerges as a civilizing effort on Shakespeare's part, one not essentially out of line with the spirit of his later comedies, which tend always to enhance human relationships, to provide for them a foundation in tenderness and mutual respect.

As the play ends, the husband receives his due—"love, fair looks, and true obedience"—in return for the burden of responsibility he has taken upon himself, and Kate, in the play's most striking utterance, asserts her free conformity with the position he has defended:

> Such duty as the subject owes the prince
> Even such a woman oweth to her husband;
> And when she is froward, peevish, sullen, sour,
> And not obedient to his honest will,
> What is she but a foul contending rebel,
> And graceless traitor to her loving lord? . . .
> My mind hath been as big as one of yours,
> My heart as great, my reason haply more,
> To bandy word for word and frown for frown;
> But now I see our lances are but straws,
> Our strength as weak, our weakness past compare,
> That seeming to be most, which we indeed least are.
> Then vail your stomachs, for it is no boot,
> And place your hands below your husband's foot. (V. ii)

This is emphatically not an argument from subservience or cowed spirit. Kate's "mind," her "heart," and—not least—her "reason" have been as great as those of the two women—Bianca and the Widow—whom the world has so shortsightedly preferred to her and who have just revealed themselves in their essential frivolity. She has had some motive in the course of the action to "bandy word for word"; but it is in the nature of things, which society ignores or distorts at its peril, that the wife is bound to stand to her husband, deferring to his "*honest* will" (the adjective is important in so far as it amounts to the deliberate exclusion of arbitrary domination), as the true subject to his prince. The family requires the one relationship no less than the proper ordering of the state the other. The stress is laid, as it will be so often in Shakespeare's later and more developed plays, on the ordering of things according to "nature," and what Kate has learned in the course of her knockabout tribulations is precisely neither more nor less than to be "natural."

THE TWO GENTLEMEN OF VERONA

The Two Gentlemen of Verona, which may have been written after *The Comedy of Errors* and either before or after *The Taming of the Shrew,* has some claim to be considered Shakespeare's most tedious play. It is more profitable, however, to see it as standing somewhere between these early exercises in comic realism and *A Midsummer Night's Dream.* With *The Taming of the Shrew* Shakespeare seems to have exhausted, at least for the moment, the possibilities of intrigue comedy. Indeed, such a play as *The Comedy of Errors* already combines intrigue a little uneasily with less realistic matter; and now, in *The Two Gentlemen,* he turns away from realism itself to the conventions of courtly love and friendship which he was perhaps already using in the sonnets and which were to be developed in various different forms through his subsequent comedies. The result is a play which foreshadows, although generally in a tentative and imperfect fashion, nearly all the devices he was to use in later and much finer plays.

The central theme of this comedy, which seems to derive from the Spanish author Jorge de Montemayor's *Diana,* written in 1542 and translated by Bartholomew Young, is—for what was to prove the first of many occasions—the difference between appearance and reality, between what *seems* and what *is.* Valentine, who begins by repudiating romantic love in the person of his friend Proteus—

writers say, as the most forward bud
Is eaten by the canker ere it blow,
Even so by love the young and tender wit
Is turn'd to folly— (I. i)

ends by falling a victim to it; Proteus, who declares himself as the play opens "a votary to fond desire," whose heart is "sick with thought," ends by deserting the object of his passion and by betraying his friend. So contrasted, each provides by implication a comment on the other. Thus, when Valentine has so far fallen a victim to the ill he once despised as to invite Proteus to join him in calling Silvia "divine," his friend exclaims "I will not flatter her," and when he falls into the idealistic excess of dignifying Proteus' own mistress Julia with

this high honour—
To bear my lady's train, lest the base earth
Should from her vesture chance to steal a kiss, (II. iv)

his friend repudiates these high-flown words as so much "braggartism." Yet this same realism is in turn exposed when Proteus himself comes to covet Silvia and is ready for her sake to inflict the deepest of "private wounds" upon his lifelong friend.

The point thus made is developed through the entire course of the action, tediously indeed and at times inexpertly, but with some consistency. Valentine, once he has fallen a victim to the passion he formerly despised, expresses his new sentiments with typical excess:

why, man, she is mine own;
And I as rich in having such a jewel
As twenty seas, if all their sand were pearl,
The water nectar, and the rocks pure gold. (II. iv)

This suggests already the characteristic ambivalence which will so often, in the comedies, mark Shakespeare's evocations of romantic love; the "jewel" of the lover's possession is a real one, represents a genuine enrichment of life, but the phrases which reflect this precious possession are often indicative of strain and exaggeration. Proteus, on the other hand, as he finds out that "one nail by strength drives out another," shows the beginnings of psychological analysis. "Love bade me swear, and love bids me forswear"; "Unheedful vows may heedfully be broken"; the speech, as it proceeds, develops into a certain meaningful complexity:

I cannot leave to love, and yet I do;
But there I leave to love where I should love.
Julia I lose, and Valentine I lose:
If I keep them, I needs must lose myself;
If I lose them, thus find I by their loss
For Valentine, myself, for Julia, Silvia.
I to myself am dearer than a friend,
For love is still most precious in itself. (II. vi)

The effort to make Proteus' abrupt transformation credible certainly makes itself felt at this point. Working through the artificiality of the literary conceit, the speech aims at pressing that artifice into the service of a rudimentary analysis. The intention is finally that of the exposure of egoism. Precisely because Proteus can regard it as axiomatic that "I to myself am dearer than a friend"—this reads, indeed, like a transposition into the comic key of Richard III's "Richard loves Richard; that is, I am I!"[10]—he can find in his kind of love an emotion "most precious in itself" and be ready to seek self-gratification through betrayal and abasement. Proteus is disposed to talk easily of "true love," which, he says, "hath better deeds than words to grace it" (II. ii); but, even as he speaks in this way, he is getting ready to betray this truth by his own behavior. Knowing at heart his passion to be "erring" and himself to be "blind," he is nonetheless disposed to go to the depths of degradation to obtain the satisfaction he both abjectly and treacherously craves:

If I can check my erring love, I will;
If not, to compass her I'll use my skill. (II. iv)

In this readiness to set aside all natural ties and obligations in the following of what is finally an irrational and ignoble servitude we find, indicated almost for the first time, one of the constant themes of Shakespearean comedy.

It is significant, in this same connection, that Proteus, who is ready to carry egoism to the point of betrayal, has at his fingertips the most farfetched expressions of romantic idealism. These he uses to advance his cause with Silvia under the guise of advising the aged Thurio to make his own absurd claim:

Say that upon the altar of her beauty
You sacrifice your tears, your sighs, your heart:
Write till your ink be dry, and with your tears
Moist it again; and frame some feeling line

That may discover such integrity;
For Orpheus' lute was strung with poet's sinews;
Whose golden touch could soften steel and stones,
Make tigers tame, and huge leviathans
Forsake unsounded deeps to dance on sands.
After your dire-lamenting elegies,
Visit by night your lady's chamber-window
With some sweet consort; to their instruments
Tune a deploring dump; the night's dead silence
Will well become such sweet-complaining grievance.
This, or else nothing, will inherit her. (III. ii)

It is typical of what will come to be Shakespeare's distinctive comic method that this, which can be read as one of the play's more distinguished expressions of emotion, is at the same time a revelation of the limitations of romantic love. Proteus, in recommending the writing of "some feeling line" to produce an illusion of "integrity," reveals by implication the artifice that underlies his "dire-lamenting elegies," the "deploring dumps" of his self-conscious melancholy. In much the same way, though to much greater poetic effect, Orsino in *Twelfth Night*[11] will at once feel and indulge feeling, combine in his own moody self-awareness the attractions and the shortcomings of romantic love.

Other devices contribute to much the same effect. As in still earlier plays, the comic prose of the servants provides a realistic judgment on the irrational behavior of their masters. Speed asserts the "deformed" vision of Valentine in love:

– You never saw her since she was deformed.
– How long hath she been deformed?
– Ever since you loved her.
– I loved her ever since I saw her; and still I see her beautiful.
– If you love her, you cannot see her.
– Why?
– Because love is blind. (II. i)

As usual we shall not confine the truth to either party to this dialogue; Valentine and Speed each affirm their "truth" and the point of the exchange lies, not in the one-sided assertion of their respective points of view, but in the interplay of contrasted attitudes. A similar effect can be detected, on another level, in the comments of the women who come out of this comedy so much better than the men who respectively idealize or deceive them. When Julia speaks of Proteus' "divine perfection" and of herself as "a true-devoted pilgrim" in the name of love at the very moment when this paragon is engaged in betraying her, the waiting woman Lucetta is perfectly aware that she is speaking "above the bounds of reason" (II. vii); and it is to reaffirm these bounds, to free valid human attachments from excess and "fever," restoring them to their proper place in a sane and balanced conception of life, that Shakespeare's romantic comedy finally aims.

The Two Gentlemen of Verona sets out, in short, to use convention to attain a position from which excess, self-ignorance and self-indulgence have been eliminated. The depths to which these faults can lead are glimpsed, occasionally, in the later scenes. When Proteus sinks into the degradation which his unrequited passion implies, he tells us that Silvia

bids me think how I have been foresworn
In breaking faith with Julia whom I loved . . .
Yet, spaniel-like, the more she spurns my love,
The more it grows, and fawneth on her atill. (IV. ii)

"Spaniel-like"; "fawneth"; Proteus could have used no more characteristic Shakespearean images of abasement and self-disgust to express his predicament.[12]

It is left to Silvia and Julia, who anticipate in this the heroines of later comedies, to oppose to corrupt convention their own firm and clear-eyed view of reality. Silvia denounces Proteus as a "subtle, perjured, false, disloyal man" (IV. ii); and Julia, reading into his devotion to her rival's painted image a reflection of the confused values which have led to her own betrayal, turns her meditation into a repudiation of the "idolatry" which love of this kind implies:

O thou senseless form,
Thou shalt be worshipp'd, kiss'd, lov'd, and adored
And, were there sense in his idolatry,
My substance should be statue in thy stead. (IV. iv)

For this reason the best-known lines in the play, though sung on behalf of the absurd Sir Thurio, in his attempt to seduce Silvia from her true devotion, answer to a truth which in some measure transcends their setting in convention and courtly intrigue:

Who is Silvia? what is she,
That all our swains commend her?
Holy, fair, and wise is she;
The heavens such grace did lend her,
That she might admired be. (IV. ii)

"Holy, fair, and wise" are perhaps terms which surpass anything that this play has to offer. They belong to a kind of idealization which is of its essence literary, and partakes of the limitations of mere literature; but such significance as they have lies in the dramatist's effort to give them a foundation in flesh and blood, to show them as operative in terms of real humanity and normal behavior. The assertion of feminine common sense and good faith represents one of the points in which this pale comedy most closely anticipates the future.

The final restoration of sanity and order is preceded, as it will be in later comedies, by a temporary removal from the court to the simplicities of "natural" life in the forest. The removal is brief, and its effect somewhat ridiculous, but this should not blind us to its connection with later and more impressive devices of a similar kind. In these new surroundings, truth is made apparent, prevails decisively over artifice and error. Valentine, struck to the quick by his friend's betrayal—

I am sorry I must never trust thee more,
But count the world a stranger for thy sake— (V. iv)

is yet capable of rousing Proteus to a confession of "shame and guilt"; having done so, he shows himself magnanimous to the point —realistically absurd, but justified in terms of the comic convention —of making the gesture of renouncing his own love for the benefit of his betrayer:

Who by repentance is not satisfied
Is nor of heaven nor earth, for these are pleased; (V. iv)

to which gesture, Proteus with equal fittingness replies:

O heaven, were man
But constant, he were perfect! That one error
Fills him with faults; makes him run through all the sins. (V. iv)

Ridiculous though it is in terms of real life, the incident can yet be justified in terms of the comic conception. As the play ends, Valentine is declared by the Duke, precisely because he has been constant and has shown himself ready to risk all for Silvia, to be "worthy of an empress' love," and the bandits, to whom the civilized and courtly lovers have been momentarily subjected in order that they may find themselves in new and strange surroundings, are recognized to be "*civil,* full of good," and so fit to return with the rest to the world of civilized and social humanity. Beyond the various absurdities of this conclusion we need to see neither more nor less than a first essay in the more meaningful patterns of later comedies. In these, conventions not altogether dissimilar, though immensely deepened and developed, are to become instruments for the exploration of human relationships, more especially in love, and for the expression of a true attitude to love itself: an attitude in which poetry and realism, romance and comedy, are variously combined. Although it would be dangerous to read too much into this early and imperfect piece, it is worth noting that it ends already with a reconciliation of conflicting opposites, the uniting of its lovers and the return of its outlaws to civilized and social existence: a reconciliation the unreality of which stresses indeed the distance still to be traveled, but which has possibilities of development once the dramatic, poetic, and human contents of the action have been simultaneously expanded.

LOVE'S LABOUR'S LOST

Love's Labour's Lost is at once the most obviously formal and the most immediately impressive of Shakespeare's early comedies. Like much else about the play, its date and the circumstances under which it was written are open to question. The quarto edition is dated as late as 1598, but is described on the title page as "newly corrected and augmented." The strong element of artificiality in the play has been thought to favor the theory of an early dating; but, as we already have occasion to know, an element of artifice is of the stuff of Shakespearean comedy, and the relative polish of a great deal of the writing could very easily point the other way. The use of type names for some of the characters in the quarto text—Braggart for Armado, Pedant for Holofernes, and so on—suggests some connection with the Italian *commedia dell' arte,* and the use of doggerel rhyme and other varied verse forms indicates the presence of an element of deliberate experiment. Possible references to contemporary literary controversies—to the so-called "School of Night," to Nashe, Raleigh, Gabriel Harvey, and others—have been suggested, but are too tenuous to lead to firm conclusions and too complicated to be discussed here.

What is certain is that the play opens with a flourish as Navarre and his companions declare their intention of withdrawing from the claims and distractions of normal society to become "brave conquerors of the world's desires." The artifice of the declaration, with its studied opening gesture to fame, "that all hunt after in their lives," its carefully balanced phrasing—"grace us in the disgrace of death" —and its facile defiance of "cormorant devouring Time" (I. i), leaves us asking ourselves from the first moment whether the course of action upon which this little group is so lightheartedly embarking is either possible or desirable; and much the same impression is left by Navarre's statement that his associates have bound themselves to

> war against your own affections,
> And the huge army of the world's desires. (I. i)

In other words, can the "little Academe" which advances its pretensions with such airy confidence in fact maintain itself "Still and contemplative in living art," or will real life break in, first to disturb its resolution and finally, in its own despite, to enrich its purposes?

Almost from the first moment, indeed, the criticism of artifice makes itself felt within the devoted circle. Its mouthpiece is Biron. Biron is the first of a long series of Shakespearean characters who express themselves with notable detachment on the direction taken by the life around them even as they share in its course; Falstaff is the last and greatest example of this type of comic character, but Biron stands on the early stages of the road which led to that immense achievement. It is Biron who almost at once calls the vows taken by his fellow "academicians" devotion to so many "barren tasks," the pursuit of "things hid and barr'd from common-sense," and who defends his own skepticism by referring explicitly to "nature":

At Christmas I no more desire a rose,
Than wish a snow in May's new-fangled shows;
But like of each thing that in season grows.
So you, to study now it is too late,
Climb o'er the house to unlock the little gate. (I. i)

What is proposed is, in fact, as Biron sees, an "abortive birth"; and his attitude is at once confirmed by the approach of the daughter of the King of France, "A maid of grace and complete majesty," representing in no uncertain terms the entry of the external world and recalling Navarre to those obligations which, most typically, it turns out by his own admission that he has "quite forgot."

As the action expands, the elements of artifice and unreality which have prompted Navarre's project are exposed and criticized from a variety of standpoints. The sum of these, indeed, might be said to be the essence of the play. Nearly all the subsidiary figures who surround the central court situation drop into it from time to time their grain of revealing comment, contribute to an impression in their "betters" of vain and self-absorbed contrivance. Armado, the "refined traveller of Spain," a man in love with his own "fire-new words" (I. i), is obviously himself an object of satire, a parody of certain current literary fashions; but he is nonetheless found to be susceptible to normal human attractions, in the shape of the charms of the country wench Jaquenetta. He may be absurd, himself the object of comic ridicule, but the very fact of his attachment implies an exposure of the pretentious make-believe of his masters. So also Costard, perhaps the most attractive and variously human of Shakespeare's subsidiary comic figures to be created up to this time. It is Costard who asserts with engaging diffidence "the simplicity of man to hearken after the flesh" and who finds it no more than natural that Armado should admit to consorting, in spite of his master's decree, with "a child of our grandmother Eve" (I. i). It is the function of Costard, in short, to call attention to those simple incontrovertible realities which those around him, exclusively concerned with their own notions and the image of themselves which they are concerned to project upon the world, are too busy to take into account. Faced by the incomprehensible fact of the king's life-denying edict, Costard confesses freely that he has paid little attention to it—"I do confess much of the hearing it, but little of the marking of it"—and concludes with typical, if disarmingly confused bluntness: "I suffer for the truth, sir; for true it is, I was taken with Jaquenetta, and Jaquenetta is a true girl; and therefore welcome the sour cup of prosperity! Affliction may one day smile again; and till then, sit thee down, sorrow!" (I. i) Such utterances contain much of the spirit of Shakespeare's later comedy, even look forward in their own slighter way to the tone of Pompey's defense of nature and the flesh in the somber, "realistic" scenes of *Measure for Measure*.[13]

No sooner, in fact, have the two worlds—that of reality and that of self-absorbed intellectual fantasy—been brought together by the entry of the Princess and her companions than the inadequacy of the positions taken up by the "Academe" stands apparent. The newcomers could be described, perhaps a little unkindly, as a band of bluestockings; but their liveliness is apparent in their keen wit, and they bring with them, together with their courtly sophistication, the appeal of life, a kind of fresh air of which this court is badly in need. Subjected to this test, indeed, the proclaimed self-sufficiency of Navarre and his friends very soon collapses. The Princess has hardly made her first entry (II. i) when she refers to Longaville's "short-lived wits" and makes her appeal to what will later become, in *As You Like It*, the spirit of Arden. "The roof of this court," she says to Navarre, speaking of the open air, "is too high to be yours, and welcome to the wide fields too base to be mine." She points too, and in no uncertain terms, to the essential frivolity which has always been implied in Navarre's oath:

> I hear your Grace hath sworn out house-keeping:
> 'Tis deadly sin to keep that oath, my lord,
> And sin to break it. (II. i)

The emphatic terms of this reproof should suffice to tell us that beneath the wit and the artifice serious issues, closely affecting the fabric of human life, are being brought into play.

As we might expect from his attitude at the beginning, it is Biron who reacts most frankly to this exposure of the untenable positions which he and his companions have so lightheartedly assumed. In so doing he sees himself, with characteristic self-dramatization, as "love's whip,"

> A critic, nay a night-watch constable:
> A domineering pedant o'er the boy, (III. i)

one who is, by his own admission, falsely and even absurdly confident of his capacity to impose his own judgment upon life. In this respect, he at once stands with his fellows, whose vow he has after all, however skeptically, taken, and maintains himself at a distance. Ready to confess in the face of reality the inadequacy of the attitudes he has, not without frivolity, assumed, he recalls in the detached frankness of his self-criticism something of the spirit to be displayed, under very different circumstances, by Faulconbridge in *King John.*[14] Like Faulconbridge, Biron is an individualist, with the qualities and shortcomings of the type, a man who can see his own behavior from the outside for what it is but who finds it more difficult to propose to himself with conviction a truly adequate course of action: an anticipation, in short, of those later Shakespearean creations—Falstaff, as we have already said,[15] is the supreme example—who live at once inside and outside their dramatic actions, dominating by the force of their comments upon it the very world to which, when seen from another point of view, they are subject:

> What! I love! I sue! I seek a wife!
> A woman, that is like a German clock,
> Still a-repairing, ever out of frame,
> And never going aright, being a watch,
> But being watch'd that it may still go right!
> Nay, to be perjured, which is worst of all:
> And, among three, to love the worst of all;
> A whitely wanton with a velvet brow,
> With two pitch-balls stuck in her face for eyes;
> Ay, and by heaven, one that will do the deed,
> Though Argus were her eunuch and her guard. (III. i)

Such is the human condition, seen by one who feels the absurdity of his decisions even as, in the interests of a quiet and self-engrossed life, he accepts those which others have made in his name: a state of subjection to the "plague" which Cupid imposes upon those who are rash enough to call into question "his almighty dreadful little might."

Very quickly, indeed, all the "academicians" find themselves forsworn and busily engaged, moreover, in seeking comfort for their wounded self-importance in the assurance that they are not, after all, alone in having deserted their ideals. The revelation of their inconstancy is, like everything else in the play, formal and gradual; each of the victims is placed in a position where, acutely conscious of his own weakness, he can observe that of the others without being himself observed. Biron can still satirize in his discomfiture the excesses of romantic-literary love as he finds them in Longaville:

> This is the liver-vein, which makes flesh a deity,
> A green goose a goddess: pure, pure idolatry— (IV. iii)

even as he goes on to admit, "As true we are as flesh and blood can be." From this position, it is natural for him to argue that the real "academes," "the true Promethean fire," lie, not where he and his master Navarre have perversely sought them, but in the eyes of woman. His argument, still founded upon literary concepts and elaborately artificial in expression, turns nonetheless into the affirmation of a reality that transcends sophistication, that is capable of gathering up "learning" into a more living order, a more valid conception of human relationships. "For where," so the detached and disillusioned courtier finds himself driven to ask,

> is any author in the world
> Teaches such beauty as a woman's eye?
> Learning is but an adjunct to ourself,
> And where we are our learning likewise is,
> Then when ourselves we see in ladies' eyes,
> Do we not likewise see our learning there?

This Platonizing concept leads Biron to an apotheosis of love which is one of the outstanding utterances of the play:

> But love, first learned in a lady's eyes,
> Lives not alone immured in the brain;
> But, with the motion of all elements,
> Courses as swift as thought in every power,
> And gives to every power a double power,
> Above their functions and their offices.
> It adds a precious seeing to the eye;
> A lover's eyes will gaze an eagle blind;
> A lover's ear will hear the lowest sound,
> When the suspicious head of theft is stopp'd;
> Love's feeling is more soft and sensible
> Than are the tender horns of cockled snails;
> Love's tongue proves dainty Bacchus gross in taste:
> For valour, is not love a Hercules,
> Still climbing trees in the Hesperides?

Subtle as Sphinx: as sweet and musical
As bright Apollo's lute, strung with his hair;
And when Love speaks, the voice of all the gods
Makes heaven drowsy with the harmony. (IV. iii)

The splendor of this culmination, and the lines which follow, represent, always within the terms of artifice which the mode of the play imposes, an affirmation of love as a principal source of life, of enhanced vitality; but the artifice acts also, and not less deliberately, to limit the validity of the claim. We know enough of Biron from self-revelation to realize that even this must not be taken too seriously. The deliberate poetic elaboration of his thoughts serves to limit them, placing them as products in some measure of ingenuity and sophistication; and yet the conclusion—

Let us once lose our oaths to find ourselves,
Or else we lose ourselves to keep our oaths—

is serious enough to outlive the spirit of jest implied in the king's summons—"Saint Cupid, then! and, soldiers to the field" (IV. iii)—and to bear what is, in effect, a principal moral of the entire comedy.

The last act of the play is an elaborate drawing together of the separate threads of the action, long and slowly developed, in a manner which will become increasingly typical of Shakespearean comedy, to lead to a conclusion which stresses the relativity of the whole by setting it finally against a background notably greater, more universal in its implications, than itself. The Princess and her companions know well enough that

None are so surely caught, when they are catch'd,
As wit turn'd fool; (V. ii)

and so, precisely with the object of teaching the now crestfallen "academicians" the error of their ways, the situation of the opening is reversed and those who once refused to admit the ladies to their society now approach them in absurd disguise, only to find themselves wittily and heartlessly spurned. It now appears to the discomforted "Muscovites" that Boyet speaks no more than the truth when he asserts that

The tongues of mocking wenches are as keen
As is the razor's edge invisible,
Cutting a smaller hair than may be seen;
Above the sense of sense; (V. ii)

and this they learn to their cost when the Princess briefly and contemptuously dismisses them to the tune of "Twenty adieus, my frozen Muscovites." When, moreover, they have accepted their defeat in the hope of winning clemency, they are still further mocked as so many "Muscovites, in shapeless gear"; and to this they can make no reply which is not in effect a confession of ignominious defeat.

It is, as might be expected, Biron who first sees that he must yield and, abjuring his beloved verbal dexterity—what Moth has ridiculed, not long before, to Costard when he says: "They have been at a great feast of languages, and stolen the scraps" (V. i)—confine himself to the expression of true sentiment in natural and direct speech:

> Taffeta phrases, silken terms precise,
> Three-piled hyperboles, spruce affectation,
> Figures pedantical; these summer flies
> Have blown me full of maggot ostentation:
> I do forswear them; and I here protest,
> By this white glove—how white the hand, God knows!—
> Henceforth my wooing mind shall be express'd
> In russet yeas, and honest kersey noes; (V. ii)

for in such language alone, he concludes, the love which he now proposes can appear as it should, "sound, sans crack, or flaw." The reference to "summer flies" and "maggot ostentation" is enough to communicate to us that the lesson learned by Biron is one that has more than merely verbal or literary reverberations, that it has extended beyond these to cover the field of what is socially and morally appropriate. The learning of this lesson, which begins in the typical manner of this play as a renunciation of literary affectation and ends as an affirmation of natural propriety, is very close to the conception of this and the following comedies.

Side by side with this just, if unceremonious treatment of Navarre and his courtiers, the conclusion sets that of Armado and his followers who are in turn exposed for their more simple pretensions in the burlesque pageant of the Nine Worthies. This serves, on its own level, as a parallel to the "Muscovite" masque which ended in the rout of their "betters." The treatment accorded to the lower orders, however, is notably more gentle than that meted out to Biron and his associates. When the king seeks to discourage them from presenting their show of loyalty, which he expects to find tedious to contemplate, the Princess—rather like Theseus in his attitude toward the "rude mechanicals" and their entertainment in *A Midsummer Night's Dream*[16]—shows that she can combine wit with humanity, as she pleads for the rights of ingenuous simplicity: "That sport best pleaseth that doth least know how" (V. ii). Here again the stress is upon nature, upon good intention and unfeigned spontaneity of gesture; and since it is precisely oversophistication that has been the prevailing fault at the court of Navarre, the plea for its opposite is very much to the point. The pageant itself and the behavior of those who so naïvely take part in it indicate very much the same conclusion. Costard's anxious hope that he was "perfect" in his role as Pompey the Great is set against his readiness to admit to "a little fault"; Sir Nathaniel, entrusted with the part of none less than Alexander, reflects his character, to use Costard's words again, as "a foolish mild man." The emphasis, indeed, is deliberately placed upon mildness, unpretentious simplicity, rather than upon folly; for this is "an *honest* man, look you" and, as such, "soon dashed." The last word is spoken once more, and in inimitable fashion, by Costard: "He is a marvellous good neighbour, faith, and a very good bowler: but, for Alisander—alas, you see how 'tis—a little o'erparted." Even Holofernes the pedant, whom we might reasonably expect to receive shorter shrift, is allowed to utter his protest in terms not devoid of dignity against Biron's too facile ridicule of his efforts—"This is not generous, not gentle, not humble" (V. ii)—and, though we shall recognize him indeed for the absurd figure that he is, we are left with every reason to believe that the Princess at least will be human enough to take his meaning.

With the various threads of the action thus brought together, the last stages of the comedy raise the entire artificial action to a different level by announcing the death of the Princess' father, the King of France. The news is delivered with a blunt directness that makes its own effect in a play so largely devoted to artifice and sophistication:

> the news I bring
> Is heavy in my tongue. The king your father—
> –Dead, for my life!
> –Even so; my tale is told— (V. ii)

and as such it is received. "Worthies, away!" says Biron, responding at once to the change of mood, "the scene begins to cloud"; and, indeed, it is profoundly true to the spirit of Shakespearean comedy that the tragic note should in this way be drawn into its moments of resolution. Under the shadow of this assertion of mortality Biron confesses the nature, as he has now come to see it, of love as a valid and enriching human emotion. The confession is made in such a way as to throw a new light upon the absurdity of his own previous attitudes, and those of his companions:

> And what in us hath seem'd ridiculous,–
> As love is full of unbefitting strains;
> All wanton as a child, skipping and vain;
> Form'd by the eye, and therefore, like the eye,
> Full of strange shapes, of habits and of forms,
> Varying in subjects as the eye doth roll
> To every varied object in his glance:
> Which parti-coated presence of loose love
> Put on by us, if, in your heavenly eyes,
> Have misbecomed our oaths and gravities,
> Those heavenly eyes, that look into these faults,
> Suggested us to make. Therefore, ladies,
> Our love being yours, the error that love makes
> Is likewise yours: we to ourselves prove false,
> By being false for ever to be true
> To those that make us both–fair ladies, you:
> And even that falsehood, in itself a sin,
> Thus purifies itself, and turns to grace. (V. ii)

Once more Biron is left, as his speech ends, balanced between artifice and a deeper content. His speech is, on one level, an elegant dedication of his duties, and those of his friends, to the "fair ladies" that now inspire them; but it is also, beneath its artificial terms, a comic apology for their own defeat. For this is the justification of love in terms of the comic sense of the incongruous, the bringing together of apparent opposites through which Biron now confirms, in his own way, his previous celebration of the lessons to be learned from "a lady's eyes."

The practical consequences of the lesson so learned are not, however, immediately or easily to come into their own. Biron's surrender to his own courtly, sophisticated version of love is a step in the direction of humanity and life; but it is by no means life itself. In the new mood introduced by the news of her father's last surrender to the action of "the sudden hand of death" (V. ii), the Princess refuses to enter too easily into the "world without end" bargain of marriage which is now offered her and her companions by the reformed wits of whom we may say, perhaps, that we are not sure if they yet realize completely that it is for a "bargain" of this nature and this solemnity that they are in fact asking. She prefers for the moment to give its proper due to the obligation of mourning for the dead, and in this her companions follow her. To Navarre she says, with a touch of deliberate and salutary asperity:

> Your oath I will not trust; but go with speed
> To some forlorn and naked hermitage,
> Remote from all the pleasures of the world;
> There stay until the twelve celestial signs
> Have brought about the annual reckoning.
> If this austere insociable life
> Change not your offer made in heat of blood;
> If frosts and fasts, hard lodging and thin weeds
> Nip not the gaudy blossoms of your love;
> But that it bear this trial, and last love;
> Then, at the expiration of the year,
> Come challenge me, challenge me by these deserts,
> And, by this virgin palm now kissing thine,
> I will be thine. (V. ii)

The "forlorn and naked hermitage" to which Navarre is now directed is clearly in some sense the counterpart of the "Academe" into which he formerly planned to take refuge from the world; but the "austere" and "insociable" life which he is to embrace, though only for a time, to expose to "trial" the "gaudy blossoms" of his only too untried love, bear little resemblance to the comfortable and pedantic retreat of his original caprice. Life affirms itself in this way too, imposes some degree of renunciation upon those who would achieve its more lasting gifts. Biron, for his part, receives from Rosaline the same injunction to wait, and added to it the obligation, as penance for his former irresponsibility, to set his vaunted wit in competition with the realities of death and suffering so that only what can stand this severe testing may survive into his changed state:

> You shall this twelvemonth term from day to day
> Visit the speechless sick, and still converse
> With groaning wretches; and your task shall be,
> With all the fierce endeavour of your wit
> To enforce the pained impotent to smile. (V. ii)

"To move wild laughter in the throat of death" is, then, to be Biron's appropriate expiation for past presumption; whilst Armado, on his own more humble level, ends the action by announcing that he has "vowed to Jaquenetta to hold the plough for her sweet love three years." Finally, to his concluding words—"This side is Hiems, Winter, this Ver, the Spring; the one maintained by the owl, the other by the cuckoo"—the songs of Spring and Winter introduce themes older, more close to folk experience, than any touched upon elsewhere in the play. The effect is to set the entire comedy, decoratively indeed but in a spirit that goes beyond mere decoration, in the context of the pattern conferred upon life by the revolving seasons. The cuckoo and the owl, spring and winter, birth and death respectively, give their last words to a comedy which already conveys, beneath its surface polish and elaborate contrivance, no small measure of the Shakespearean intuition of life.

IV

The Sonnets

Certain aspects of the transition between Shakespeare's earliest plays and the more complex modes realized in his later work are usefully approached through the sonnets. Published for the first time as a collection late in the poet's career, in 1609, the sonnets have been variously dated, often to fit in with highly problematic interpretations of unknown facts in his biography. The present tendency seems to favor, on purely scholarly grounds, a relatively early dating; even if we do not follow the theory that certain poems in the series contain references to events connected with the defeat of the Spanish Armada in 1588 and must therefore be ascribed to the very earliest stages in Shakespeare's career,[1] we shall probably find the evidence which points to most of the sonnets as having been written well before the end of the sixteenth century sufficiently convincing. Within the limits of this general conclusion, however, we may equally decide that the poems do not correspond entirely to any single inspiration, or reflect, beneath their variety of theme and treatment, any one stage in Shakespeare's development. It is clear, indeed, that certain common subjects can be detected in the sonnets and are often dealt with in deliberate sequence; but beyond this, it seems possible to conclude that the collection as finally published unites poems originally written at different times and only at a later date brought together in an attempt to give them something like a logical argument and a degree of continuity. The answer to the problem raised by these poems is likely, in other words, to be neither single nor simple; and it may be doubted whether, from this standpoint, anything much more positive can safely be said.

A purely literary approach goes some way to confirm this impression. Although the general level of the poems is remarkably high, and the sense of personal commitment much more marked than in most sonnet series, not all of them are equal in merit. A certain proportion clearly consists of little more than literary exercises, addressed either to a patron of letters or, especially in the case of a few of the later numbers, to a more or less conventional mistress. All, however, conventional or otherwise, show in varying degrees signs of the way in which the sonnet form, by the very strictness of its formal limits, imposed upon language a distinctive economy and intensity; and the best of them develop these qualities to a degree which makes them, within their strictly observed limits, comparable to much in the mature plays. This infinity of variations, indeed, is a most valuable feature of the sonnets, for in it we can trace, perhaps more clearly than elsewhere, some aspects of a process similar to that by which, in the plays we have already considered, conventional plots and versification became molded to the more complex and individual purposes of the later dramas. I say more clearly because the sharply defined limits of the sonnet convention, and the brevity of the poems themselves, make it simpler for us to observe the modifications introduced into them by the author's constantly developing purposes.

The conventions of the sonnet, as already established by such predecessors as Sidney and Spenser, inevitably influenced Shakespeare's own use of the form. Indeed, Shakespeare's achievement might be defined as the playing off of his keen sense of actuality against a conventional basis which gave it both pointedness and enormous possibilities of varying the poetic mood. The relation of personal emotion to an established convention involves a contrast which may be used either to intensify feeling or to indicate the presence of irony by a suggestion of incompatibility with the original mode. This complexity, which is a characteristic feature of many of the best poems in the series, is reflected in distinct linguistic qualities. The sonnet, as Shakespeare found it and as he himself on occasion used it, encouraged great formal ingenuity, which was at times little more than an exercise in poetic sophistication. It affected even punctuation. There is one sonnet in Shakespeare's series (LXXXI) in which every possible pair of lines, if we make exception of the second, the third, and the eleventh, can be read so as to make a complete sentence. The device is, in itself, of little poetic value; but it suggests the degree of formal control behind the sonnets, a control which needed only to be informed by urgency of feeling to produce the subtle intensity of the best of these poems.

The presence in any given sonnet of the characteristic Shakespearean immediacy can, as usual, be gauged by the appearance of a distinctive verbal quality. It makes itself felt in such lines as

> Against my love shall be, as I am now,
> With time's injurious hand crush'd and o'erworn (LXIII)

and the famous

> Lilies that *fester* smell far worse than weeds. (XCIV)

In the first instance, the impression of the passage of time and its action upon the individual is conveyed with a fresh, concrete vividness that produces, moreover, a pairing of words in cumulative effect that is one of the poet's favorite ways of intensifying the emotional content of his poetry;[2] in the second, the striking unexpectedness of "fester" cuts sharply across the conventional associations of "lilies" in a manner that recalls—to go no further—Angelo's tense, clipped utterances at critical moments in *Measure for Measure.*[3] Under the stress of the feeling so reflected, the fashionable weaving of word patterns at which the courtly sonneteers aimed is transformed into a vivid use of the resources of speech to develop a high degree of intensity in a relatively short space. This same keen economy of language, when set in the plays against the prevailing rhetorical structure of the blank verse period, soon produced corresponding modifications in the field of stress. Taken together, these two factors—verbal immediacy developed to an unusual degree and the molding of stress to the movement of living, changing, and developing emotion—account in very great measure for the unique impression produced by Shakespeare's mature poetry. It is probable that the linguistic discipline imposed by the sonnet form upon his natural Elizabethan exuberance was a decisive factor in the formation of the poet's mastery of expression. It made him associate compression with depth of content and variety of emotional response to a degree unparalleled in English (though similar qualities distinguish the best work of Donne and others of his contemporaries) and so give both point and intensity to the development of personal feeling.

These considerations are so important in relation to the emergence of Shakespeare's distinctive modes of expression that it is worth taking a typical sonnet to show how what might have been mere misplaced ingenuity becomes a pregnant poetic device:

When my love swears that she is made of truth,
I do believe her, though I know she lies,
That she might think me some untutor'd youth,
Unlearned in the world's false subtleties.
Thus vainly thinking that she thinks me young,
Although she knows my days are past the best,
Simply I credit her false-speaking tongue:
On both sides thus is simple truth suppress'd.
But wherefore says she not she is unjust?
And wherefore say not I that I am old?
O, love's best habit is in seeming trust,
And age in love loves not to have years told:
　　Therefore I lie with her and she with me,
　　And in our faults by lies we flatter'd be. (CXXXVIII)

The situation announced in the first two lines is, at bottom, the conventional complaint of the lover against the faithlessness of the beloved; yet the development is a good deal more than merely conventional. The transition from convention is marked by fresh linguistic subtlety, seen most obviously in the varied meanings attached to the word "lie." The double sense beneath this word is most clearly conveyed in the final couplet; it implies not only conscious deception but also a lying together as man and mistress. The point, however, lies less in the ambiguity than in its justification, which is not in any way verbal or scholastic, but rather a question of the nature of the experience to be conveyed. The play upon "lie," in fact, enabled Shakespeare to state two emotions contradictory yet simultaneous, both contained in one situation. The lying together, which is from one point of view the natural physical fulfillment of love, is nonetheless based in this case on mutual falsity, for reasons which are made clear in the rest of the sonnet. These reasons are faithlessness, covered by concealment on the part of the mistress, and age and disillusionment on the side of the lover. Shakespeare's use of a deliberate ambiguity in this poem is justified by the precision of his thought, or, more exactly, of his analysis of experience. A line like "I do believe her, though I know she lies" calls for an exactitude of thinking and feeling that a modern reader does not always associate with emotional intensity. It is a type of poetry which justifies ambiguity, because its complexity is balanced by its content, because it is able to gather the divergent possibilities of a single situation into the unifying framework of a realized convention.

These new tendencies in verse and rhythm were closely accompanied, in the most interesting of the sonnets, by the repeated exploration of certain recurring themes. The most important of these look forward, like so much else in the parallel linguistic development, to the plays upon which Shakespeare was engaged between the time when we may suppose him to have written most of these poems and the beginning of what we may conveniently call his tragic period. The linguistic resourcefulness of these poems was occasioned by profoundly personal interests, though these were not necessarily or even probably of the kind favored by the promoters of various biographical theories. The nature of these interests is to some extent indicated by the very choice of the sonnet form. The sonnet, as is well known, based its conventions originally on a highly intellectualized conception of the relations that were held to exist, in a society which we may call aristocratic, between the lover and his mistress, between, respectively, the servant and the source of love. It is true, of course, that in the use of them made by later poets, and very notably by Shakespeare himself, these conventions came to cover a variety of human relationships only very remotely, if at all, connected with this original situation. The majority of Shakespeare's sonnets are not addressed to a woman, but to a man with whom his relations cover varying elements of patronage and friendship, dependence and intimacy; but in spite of this, the spirit of the poems continued to be affected by their origin, and it is true to say that many of Shakespeare's most successful exercises in the sonnet form are more closely related, in spirit and expression, to those of his plays which analyze the nature of human relationship in love than to any other aspect of his work. They represent, in fact, beneath the variety of their subjects and attitudes, a first exploration of themes which were later realized, in either tragic or comic form, in the great series of plays dealing primarily with love which began with *Romeo and Juliet* and *A Midsummer Night's Dream* and ended, many years later, with *Antony and Cleopatra.*

The sonnets, therefore, although they deal with situations that differ very widely from one another, make constant use of imagery connected with the traditional conception of the union between the lover and the object of his desire. This union, when consummated, should find expression in terms of natural increase; the opening sequence, composed of poems addressed to a friend and urging upon him the desirability of marriage, is notably full of references to planting and husbandry:

For where is she so fair whose unear'd womb
Disdains the tillage of thy husbandry? (III)[4]

The necessity for true love to embark upon the adventure of giving, to seek fulfillment in an act of creation, is a theme constantly repeated in Shakespeare's comedies, which turn indeed very largely upon just this kind of situation. The recipient of these early sonnets is constantly being urged to consider the necessity of living, not for himself alone, but in relation to the world beyond himself. The very first poem in the series reproaches him, in effect, for self-centeredness, for refusing to make the creative gesture which ensures the continuity of life and in the absence of which life itself withers in sterile self-contemplation:

But thou, contracted to thine own bright eyes,
Feed'st thy light's flame with *self-substantial* fuel,
Making a famine where abundance lies,
Thyself thy foe, to thy sweet self too cruel. (I)

And again, a little later in the series:

For having traffic with thyself alone,
Thou of thyself thy sweet self dost deceive.
Then how, when nature calls thee to be gone,
What acceptable audit canst thou leave? (IV)

The conclusion to all these early sonnets—that the recipient should fulfill the duty of perpetuating himself through an heir—may be considered conventional in its expression, as is also much of the imagery of usury and law—"audit" and "executors"[5]—used to condemn the "beauteous niggard" and urge him to "bounteous largess";[6] but the intense concentration of the phrases which condemn self-centeredness is remarkable and points to the counterassertion of generosity in giving as a law of life, which the comedies, in particular, will be concerned to develop, equally through convention, as one of their principal themes. When Bassanio, in *The Merchant of Venice,* chooses the casket which urges him to "give and hazard all he hath"[7] and makes himself thereby worthy of Portia's answering self-dedication, he is in effect responding to the same universal law of love by which the whole range of human life is enriched and transformed.

It is interesting, indeed, that so many of the sonnets should lay stress upon this aspect of love; but even more significant, possibly, is the fact that some of the most individual of them are less concerned with this desirable consummation than with the thwarting of this natural and beneficent relationship by shortcomings which seem to be inherent in the very quality of passion. So much is implied even in the relatively conventional numbers of the series, where issues are initially raised which some of the most famous of the later poems will seem to raise to the status of a universal and somber law of life. Human love and friendship, according to the mood expressed in some of the most striking of the sonnets, are inevitably vitiated by inconstancy: not, however, merely by the conventional inconstancy of the courtly sonneteers, the theme of endless doleful and ultimately self-regarding complaints (Shakespeare dealt faithfully with these in many of his comedies),[8] but by a flaw, or vice, felt to be inseparable from the nature of passion itself. The subject of a considerable proportion of the sonnets that have a genuine claim to individuality is, in one form or another, this inescapable thwarting of the natural human desire for union and increase:

> Let me confess that we two must be twain,
> Although our undivided loves are one; (XXXVI)

the "loves" which should be "one," "undivided," because it is in the nature of love to seek unity in the creative gift of self to its object, are in fact inexorably separate, rendered "twain" by what amounts to a contrary and tragic fatality. This frustration, as we have said, is felt as a *necessary* flaw at the heart of passion; and this flaw tends to be identified, in the sonnets with which we are concerned, with the action of impersonal and destructive time.

The sense of the hostility of time, indeed, is fundamental not only to the sonnets but to many of the plays of this period in Shakespeare's career. The theme was a commonplace of the age, associated with the Platonizing philosophy of the court poets, which contrasted the ideal perfection of eternity with the corruptible realities of earthly existence, and with the religious "pessimism" of medieval tradition. Both these elements are variously present in Shakespeare's work, but in the sonnets it is the newer, the more "modern" attitude which on the whole prevails:

Time doth transfix the flourish set on youth
And delves the parallels in beauty's brow. (LX)

Ruin hath taught me thus to ruminate,
That Time will come and take my love away. (LXIV)

O fearful meditation! where, alack,
Shall Time's best jewel from Time's chest lie hid? (LXV)

Time is conceived in many of the most striking of these poems as a conditioning element in human experience, which it first brings into being and then, following inexorable laws of its own, proceeds to destroy. The apparent solidity and permanence of natural objects and human creations—"brass," "stone," and "gates of steel"; "earth," "boundless sea," and "rocks impregnable"[9]—are equally destined to decay by a process against which human endeavor can only set its fragile and finally impermanent aspirations. Natural fear of the action of time, conceived now as an eternal process of attrition, neither beginning in a definite act of creation nor directed toward a meaningful and redemptive conclusion, is not balanced in these poems by any consistent residue of traditional morality, still less by any sense of the possible significance as well as of the inevitability of death. Renaissance feeling regarded time as the enemy and solvent of personal experience, which it wears remorselessly into insensibility. Shakespeare gave this feeling magnificent expression when he transformed the classical commonplace *Tempus edax rerum*[10] into the somber intensity of the opening of Sonnet XIX:

Devouring time, blunt thou the lion's paws,

where the epithet "devouring," which belongs naturally to the lion, is transferred to "time," thus creating a very intricate balance of emotions. The lion naturally raises associations of splendid life and activity as well as of a menacing terror; but the transfer of "devouring" indicates that the end of all this activity is a fatal consuming, a wearing down of life into pure annihilation. The verb "blunt" shows the typical sensing of the intangible in terms of the immediate life of the fingertips; it simply makes more intense by contrast the energy which is so wastefully subdued to the consuming action of mutability.

The attitude expressed by the sonnets toward the relationship of time to individual experience, and especially to the personal ties of love and friendship, is accordingly various and even contradictory. At times the poet expresses his conviction, in harmony with the poetic conventions, of the permanence and unique validity of emotion in its different forms; and then his attitude is that stated in one of the most famous and eloquent of all the sonnets:

> Love's not time's fool, though rosy lips and cheeks
> Within his bending sickle's compass come;
> Love alters not with his brief hours and weeks,
> But bears it out even to the edge of doom. (CXVI)

Splendidly as this conviction is expressed, however, there is about the sonnet, and more especially about its closing lines, a suggestion of the rhetorical, of an effort to carry conviction by mere weight of affirmation:

> If this be error, and upon me proved,
> I never writ, nor no man ever loved.

The conclusion surely conveys an odd sense of weakness and insecurity after the powerful development which has preceded it. The "bending sickle's compass" is, in terms of language and rhythmic vigor, superbly real in comparison with the lame, unsupported weight of assertion in which the poem is supposed to culminate.[11] The poet is saying, in effect, that the experience with which he is dealing *must* have a timeless validity, because to accept the contrary would be to convert the experience itself into something tragically meaningless. It is precisely this situation, this sense of emotional conviction balanced by rational doubt, that makes its contribution, with other elements, to the tragedy of *Romeo and Juliet*[12] and that was eventually more comprehensively dramatized in *Troilus and Cressida.*[13]

Under such circumstances it is not surprising that, in other moods, a contrary attitude prevails. Such is the case in the opening lines of the almost equally famous Sonnet CXXIX:

> The expense of spirit in a waste of shame
> Is lust in action.

The force of this opening answers to something more than a moralizing reflection on the nature and impermanence of passion. The familiar condemnation of "lust" is extended, by the very force of its expression, to something like a judgment on the nature of love itself. Under the pressure of mutability our spiritual instincts appear, at times, baseless illusions which no logical reading of the facts appears to justify. "Love," thus considered, becomes identified with "lust," changes from the most intense and valuable of human experiences in time into an expenditure, of "spirit" indeed, because some of our deepest aspirations are involved, but destined to sterility, to lose itself in a "waste"—a desert which is at the same time a useless giving out of life—"of shame." This sonnet and the one quoted above represent, in fact, the two contrasted sides of a single picture. Both are reactions to the facts implied in human subjection to the temporal process which governs our lives. Love and friendship, which is a reflection of love, are seen in these poems as a reaction against the process of temporal decay, an attempt to grasp through accepted experience an intuition of permanent spiritual value; but precisely because they are born in time, they are destined to destruction. What is rooted in time, and owes its nature to time, time itself destroys. If man, as a temporal unity of body and spirit, can only perceive spiritual values under the guise of time, it is equally true that his perceptions are, in time, fatally transient. Shakespeare's reaction as poet to this necessity underlies the bitterness which is to be found in many of his sonnets and which inspires much in the plays most closely related to them.[14] Since love and friendship, though so desirable, appear to be dedicated to vanity, the poet's vision of them becomes at times vicious and repellent; the very value which is presumed to be in them only makes them, by a strange paradox, more potent to corrupt. "Lilies that fester smell far worse than weeds." The action of time becomes associated with the corrupt inconstancy of the flesh, as though one necessarily implied the other. A great part of Shakespeare's tragic experience can be described, from this point of view (there are, of course, many others), in terms of a reaction against his consciousness of the somber implications of the temporal nature of man; of the quality of that reaction the most individual of the sonnets, written as they presumably were still relatively near the outset of his career, provide an illuminating illustration.

We are now in a position to see that Shakespeare's use in many of the sonnets of imagery compounded of contradiction is directly related to the nature of the experience he wished to convey. The final ambiguity with which these poems are concerned lies in the simultaneous fulfillment and destruction of the values of human life by time; it depends not upon a verbal interest, but upon an emotional situation of tragic depth and content. This situation will be carried on, absorbed into vaster constructions covering a far wider range of human experiences, in the dramatic works of Shakespeare's maturity. The great tragedies, though they are of course far from being confined to this single aspect, can be seen as forming a continuous process in the exploration and extension of it; and each stage in this exploration, this extension, involves a further organization of verse and language. The comedies too are engaged, from their own point of view, in illuminating other areas, not finally unrelated, of the same field. From *Romeo and Juliet* and *A Midsummer Night's Dream,* through *Troilus and Cressida* and *Twelfth Night* to *Antony and Cleopatra,* there is a continual development from original ambiguity, which expresses a clash within experience, to a fully organized verse which in turn implies a harmonious ordering of the elements of experience and with it the complete realization of the dramatist's art.

V

From *Romeo and Juliet* to *Richard II*

The impression left by a survey of Shakespeare's earliest work is, perhaps, of a variety even greater than the not inconsiderable achievement. The young dramatist whose first series of plays on English history shows such considerable intellectual grasp in conceiving and following through a complex pattern of political behavior was at the same time engaged in evolving, through successive experiments in dramatic structure, a type of comedy which might answer to the variety and balance of what he had to say. If none of these first plays, considered in its own right, gives at first sight quite that impression of dominating personal genius which we may derive from Marlowe's work at its best, it is at least equally certain that Shakespeare's production during these years, taken as a whole, already points to a scope and breadth of interest quite beyond the reach of his most brilliant contemporary.

At some time immediately after the writing of these first plays, and well before the turn of the century, Shakespeare built, upon the foundations thus securely laid, the first unquestioned masterpieces of his career. Within what was certainly a very brief period of time—not, we may assume, much more than two years,—he produced successively his first great tragedy, *Romeo and Juliet,* a comedy of startling brilliance, *A Midsummer Night's Dream,* which views the same central theme of love in a completely different light; and—as if this were not enough—a historical play, *Richard II,* which gives the chronicle type of drama an entirely new dimension and lays the foundations for a whole series of still greater plays to follow. The ability to achieve so high a standard of excellence in so many different undertakings within so short a period of time, and at so early a stage in his development as a dramatist, is in itself a testimony to the unique nature of Shakespeare's genius.

ROMEO AND JULIET

Romeo and Juliet, Shakespeare's first youthful tragedy—if we exclude for the present purpose *Titus Andronicus*—has a number of clear points of contact with the sonnets. These are most obviously apparent in the style of the play, which here and there incorporates actual sonnets into the dramatic structure and makes at all times a considerable use of sonnet imagery; but the theme too turns, as in some of the sonnets we have just considered,[1] upon the relation of love to the action of time and adverse circumstance. At least one of the questions that the tragedy poses is, indeed, familiar from the sonnets. To what degree can youthful love be regarded as its own justification—"bears it out even to the edge of doom,"[2] as the sonnet has it—or, alternatively, to what extent do the lovers share the conviction that this is simply an empty, rhetorical affirmation? The answer the play gives lies not in any simple assertion, whether affirmative or otherwise, but rather in a balance of contrasted realities. The Prologue strikes a sinister note from the outset by telling us that we are about to witness "the *fearful* passage of a *death-marked* love"; but it is necessary to add that the disaster to which this love will be brought is in great part a result of the hatred of the older generations, in which the young participate, if at all, as victims involved in a situation not of their choosing. Though the young lovers are indeed "star-crossed," destined to die, their response to experience, and the contrast with those around them who only *believe* that they are reasonable and mature, gives the relationship to which they have pledged their generosity a proper measure of validity. Their love must indeed accept the reality of death, which its very origin and nature demand; but once this has been accepted, it remains true that a sense of incommensurate worth, of *true* value, survives to color their tragedy.

The Prologue has no sooner been spoken when the circumstances that will lead fatally to the destruction of love are introduced in the shape of the irrational vanity of the Capulet-Montague feud. The servingmen who so touchily eye one another in the streets of Verona are at once lecherous and self-important, uneasily conscious of breaking what they know to be the law even as they insult their opposites. The masters, on this first showing, are little or no better than their men, combining touchiness and senility in a particularly distasteful way. Their wives know them better than themselves; when Capulet testily calls for his sword to join in the melee, his wife says ironically: "A crutch, a crutch! why call you for a sword?" (I. i), and Lady Montague is equally at pains to hold back her husband from "seeking a foe." On the more active side, reason is habitually overruled by brute instinct, Benvolio's sensible attitude—"I do but keep the peace"—balanced by Tybalt's irrational spoiling for a fight: "I hate hell, all Montagues, and thee!" (I. i). The fair comment on so much obstinate and "canker'd hate" is left, here as it will be throughout the play, to Prince Escalus, who shows himself conscious, as an impartial ruler, of the ruin to which these senseless attitudes will lead, and who does what he can to hold them in check. We may conclude by the end of this opening that, if this is a fair picture of "experience," there is likely to be something to be said in favor of the romantic idealism of youth.

Romeo himself, however, is by no means romantically presented on his first appearance: not, at any rate, if "romanticism" means an acceptance of him at his own estimate. Benvolio tells us of having seen him stealing furtively, almost as a man ashamed, "into the covert of the wood," and Montague speaks of him locking out "fair daylight," making "himself an artificial night" (I. i). Even in the conventional idiom of *The Two Gentlemen of Verona,* we should recognize these as unfavorable signs. They prepare us for a Romeo who is at this stage in love with himself as Rosaline's unrequited lover, a Romeo

> to himself so *secret* and so *close,* . . .
> As is the bud bit with *an envious worm;* (I. i)

a creature, in other words, "doting" rather than loving, perversely enamored of his own self-centered and melancholy reflections. The distance he will cover in his progress through the play needs to be measured against the deliberate conventionality of this beginning.

All this is amply confirmed when Romeo himself appears and utters his first elaborate "complaints":

O brawling love! O loving hate!
O anything, of nothing first create!
O heavy lightness! serious vanity!—

to which, shortly after, he adds further considerations on a more sententious level:

Love is a smoke raised with the fume of sighs;
Being purged, a fire sparkling in lovers' eyes;
Being vex'd, a sea nourish'd with lovers' tears:
What is it else? a madness most discreet,
A choking gall and a preserving sweet. (I. i)

This is a Romeo who can indeed say of himself, a good deal more truly than he yet knows, "This is not Romeo: he's some other where," even as he complains from a point of view still naïvely limited to the self that his mistress has no share in love's generosity, that she will not *give* herself in fulfillment of its essential law. To Benvolio's question, "Then she hath sworn that she will still live chaste?" Romeo replies:

She hath, and in that sparing makes huge waste;
For beauty, starved with her severity,
Cuts beauty off from all posterity. (I. i)

This is, of course, an argument familiar from the sonnets,[3] and one which this play will in due course turn to serious ends. Romeo is still speaking within the limits of convention, urging upon the object of his desire that generosity which he has not yet had occasion to show in himself. He is soon to find a love that is ready to give for what is, in the eyes of the world, folly; but, until this is so, his character cannot begin to develop to its true tragic stature.

At this point, and after some talk of Capulet's forthcoming feast, we turn from Romeo to Juliet, who is urged by her mother to think of marriage and who replies, in her still unawakened simplicity: "It is an honor that I dream not of" (I. iii). Juliet, indeed, is surrounded here, as she will be almost to the end of the play, by the "experienced," by those who are always ready to give their advice on the proper conduct of her life. Such is the Nurse, with her combination of easy sentiment and deep-rooted cynicism, her belief, at once normal and senile in its discursive presentation, that love is a prompting of the flesh which is destined to find its social fulfillment in a suitably contrived marriage; such too is her own mother, who looks back complacently on the destiny which at some remote moment in the past gave her to Capulet and which she is ready to elevate, for her daughter's benefit, into a universal pattern:

> By my count,
> I was your mother much upon these years
> That you are now a maid. (I. iii)

As Lady Capulet goes on to refer to Paris' suit in language deliberately and appropriately contrived—

> This precious book of love, this unbound lover,
> To beautify him, only lacks a cover— (I. iii)

Juliet, the moment of whose awakening is still to come, can only reply in the simple terms of filial obedience.

As Romeo moves toward the fatal meeting with Juliet, his attitude is set in contrast to that of Mercutio, who offers him advice in terms of an essentially worldly common sense, which is not on that account less relevant to his state of sentiment. Mercutio is convinced that the supposed tribulations of love have an easy remedy which he and his friends propose to apply:

> we'll draw thee from the mire
> Of this sir-reverence love, wherein thou stick'st
> Up to the ears. (I. iv)

The famous "Queen Mab" speech, to which these exchanges lead, is a brilliant exercise in poetic bravura, of the type to which Shakespeare, in the first flush of his creative powers, was especially attracted. It is, however, also more than that, insomuch as it emphasizes, against Romeo's superficially settled attitudes, the inconstancy of human impulses in the state of love, the lively unpredictability of love itself:

> This is that very Mab
> That plats the manes of horses in the night,
> And bakes the elf-locks in foul, sluttish hairs,
> Which once untangled much misfortune bodes:
> This is the hag, when maids lie on their backs,
> That presses them and learns them first to bear. (I. iv)

The similarity between this and the habitual language of Puck, in *A Midsummer Night's Dream*, is surely not accidental; there is the same sense of the mischievous and the incongruous, even the same faintly sinister delight in the upsetting of fixed sentimental attitudes and unalterable moral categories. This is essentially a *comic* attitude to love, as different from Romeo's self-absorbed devotion to Rosaline as it will prove to be from his dedication to Juliet. Romeo moves at this point, as he will continue to do, in a sphere entirely remote from Mercutio's comic exhortations; but it is notable that he answers his friend's exuberance with a first obscure intimation of fear. When Mercutio has confessed that his talk has been of "nothing but vain fantasy," "thin of substance as the air," and "more inconstant than the wind," Romeo recognizes his foreboding in the face of the still unknown future:

> my mind misgives
> Some consequence, yet hanging in the stars,
> Shall bitterly begin his fearful date
> With this night's revels, and expire the term
> Of a despised life closed in my breast,
> By some vile forfeit of untimely death. (I. iv)

Romeo's concern for his "despised life" still answers to his early sentimental state, which finds in pessimism an intimate, finally self-indulging necessity; but it remains true that it is at this point that the play's persistent association of love and death enters the hero's mind for the first time.

In this way we are brought to the fatal ball in the house of the Capulets. Old Capulet, most typically, plays his part as host to the accompaniment of jests about "corns" and memories of his lost youth:

> I have seen the day
> That I have worn a visor, and could tell
> A whispering tale in a fair lady's ear, (I. v)

and so forth for as long as his relations and friends will bear with him; but, as he goes on to confess to his cousin, "you and I are past our dancing days," and the present lies with Romeo as he forms his fatal question:

> What lady's that, which doth *enrich* the hand
> Of yonder knight?

It is typical of Romeo that his first reference to Juliet should speak of her in terms of "enrichment," the enhancing effect proper to beauty; significant too that his first reaction to the sight of her should give him the force to break through all former artifice, to rise to what, though still romantic in inspiration, is in effect a new intensity:

> O, she doth teach the torches to burn bright!
> It seems she hangs upon the cheek of night
> Like a rich jewel in an Ethiop's ear; (I. v)

a beauty capable, indeed, of transforming life, but which he can also, with what is already a sense of foreboding, hail immediately afterward as "Beauty too rich for use, for earth too dear." Already, moreover, the world is ominously present at the birth of this new vision, and answers to the lover's rapt confession of his transformed state—"I ne'er saw true beauty till this night"—with Tybalt's harsh recognition—"This, by his voice, should be a Montague"—even as he calls for his sword. The sinister note has been struck once and for all, briefly but not on that account less powerfully, in spite of Capulet's determination that his feast shall not be interrupted, and in spite of the confrontation of Romeo's unruly enemy with the old man's stubborn "will." Yet again, as will occur so often in this play, age and youth, authority and passion meet, as Capulet's angry assertion of his right to command—"Am I the master here? or you? go to"—meets the younger man's grudging aside:

> Patience perforce with wilful choler meeting,
> Makes my flesh tremble in their different greeting, (I. v)

and as this in turn leads to the threatening conclusion:

> this intrusion shall,
> Now seeming sweet, convert to bitterest gall.

The spare, tense economy of these exchanges is the sign of a dramatist working at the height of his newly discovered and continually expanding powers.

The first exchange between Romeo and Juliet, which follows immediately on this clash of contrary and headstrong wills, is carried on, by a most effective contrast, in artificial sonnet form, which makes it a matter of "saints" and "pilgrims," the expression of a still strained and tense devotion. As the lovers exchange their first kiss, however, it is already to a play upon "sin" which carries threatening overtones:

– Thus from my lips by thine my sin is purg'd.
– Then have my lips the sin that they have took.
– Sin from my lips? O trespass sweetly urged!
Give me my sin again. (I. v)

At this point, if ever, we may feel familiar poetic conventions in the process of being brought to what is finally a dangerous, a precarious life. Indeed, when Juliet, after Romeo has left her, says:

If he be married,
My grave is like to be my wedding-bed, (I. v)

the play's characteristic note of ominous splendor is being firmly struck; we may already sense, however obscurely, that this love is destined to end in death, but that death itself may be ennobled by the dedication which love can bring to its acceptance. For the immediate moment, moreover, we should note that the new situation is conveyed through a corresponding development in character; for Juliet, who has hitherto shown herself submissive to parental authority, being now newly born to love learns at once to disguise her true feelings. Already she has shown enough presence of mind to preface her question about Romeo's identity by enquiries about two other guests, whose identity in no way concerns her; and when she has been betrayed by the intensity of her own feeling into crying, incautiously,

Prodigious birth of love it is to me,
That I must love a loathed enemy, (I. v)

and is challenged by the Nurse to explain her outburst, she turns aside the threatened revelation with a beautifully offhand reference to

A rhyme I learn'd even now
Of one I danced withal.

By the end of this admirably contrived scene, a situation as tensely actual, as ominously poised over contradiction, as any briefly conveyed in the sonnets is being endowed with dramatic life.

In the episode which follows, after the Chorus has further underlined the elements of foreboding which accompany the birth of this love, Mercutio proceeds with his taunting of Romeo for his infatuated devotion to Rosaline. "Speak but one rhyme, and I am satisfied," he urges, continuing his comic attack upon the romantic excess to which he still believes his friend is subject; but he fails, of course, to obtain the response of his victim, whose heart and mind are fully engaged elsewhere. Romeo's true answer, indeed, is uttered before Juliet:

> But soft! what light through yonder window breaks?
> It is the east, and Juliet is the sun! (II. ii)

In the invocation which follows, the expression is, of course, still conventional in form, still a reflection of some of the most familiar motives of the poetry of courtly love:

> her eyes in heaven
> Would through the airy region stream so bright
> That birds would sing and think it were not night.

Beyond this deliberate play with words and conceits, however, we can respond also to a process by which true sentiment, not necessarily of a mature or admirable kind, is engaged upon the task of filling out convention, endowing it with life. The young lover, as he contemplates the object of his desire, projects his sensuous imagination into the celebration of her person:

> See, how she leans her cheek upon her hand!
> O, that I were a glove upon that hand,
> That I might touch that cheek! (II. ii)

The urgency of the expression, in fact, though still extreme and precarious in its quality, is being made to answer to the reality of intense emotion: "Call me but love, and I'll be new baptized"; "dear saint." We are not being invited here to any easy identification with the lover's new states of feeling. The language which prevails in this speech, and through the greater part of the entire episode, is at once plainly excessive, even an indulgence of sentiment, and, in terms of romantic love, expressive of a true devotion, entirely different from the superficial, self-centered attitudes which have prevailed, almost up to this moment, in Romeo's declarations of his love for Rosaline. The new situation is far more complex, a far more intricate compound of conflicting realities. Because this new love bears within itself an element of excess, a neglect of all realities except those which its own consummation involves, it will end in death; but because it is also a true emotion (and true not least in relation to the aged experience that sets itself up so consistently to thwart it, to deny its truth), because its intensity answers, when all has been said, to love's *value*, it will be felt to achieve, even in its inevitable frustration, a certain measure of triumph over circumstance.

The element of contradiction makes its presence felt throughout this famous scene. Juliet, here as nearly always a good deal more realistic than Romeo, knows from the first that their love is surrounded by a sinister reality which its material circumstances confirm:

> The orchard walls are high and hard to climb,
> And the place death, considering who thou art;

to which his passionate reply is at once, when viewed in terms of worldly common sense, a further expression of excess, and, in relation to the new vision which has taken possession of him, a sign of the nature of true love:

> With love's light wings did I o'erperch these walls,
> For stony limits cannot hold love out:
> And what love can do, that dares love attempt.

The Romeo who speaks after this fashion, and who goes on to say:

> wert thou as far
> As that vast shore wash'd with the farthest sea,
> I would adventure for such merchandise,

is clearly a new person in relation to the conventional lover whom Mercutio and his friends could justly ridicule in the opening scenes. His eyes have been opened to the reality of love as an "adventure," involving the total commitment of self, the willingness to risk all to obtain the rich "merchandise," the prize of great value which love—if in fact it is a central reality in human experience—implies. This gesture of the gift of self, however, is at once necessary and dangerous, balanced over a void. This is recognized again, and in a new way, by Juliet when she answers Romeo's entranced declarations with a direct simplicity of her own and calls for an answering directness and simplicity from her lover:

> O gentle Romeo,
> If thou dost love, pronounce it faithfully.

Romeo's far-flung declarations of the value and intensity of love call, as their natural counterpart, for plainer, more naturally human decisions, and it is these which Juliet is here emphasizing. By so doing, she does not, of course, call in question the truth and validity of the emotions which have transported Romeo to what is in effect a new life; but she is saying that these transports call for translation into a more intimate key, demand incorporation into a more common, but not on that account a less precious or valid reality.

The following duet, as we may properly call it, carries on this balance of intensity and artifice, idealism and reality:

> – Lady, by yonder blessed moon I swear,
> That tips with silver all these fruit-tree tops,–
> – O, swear not by the moon, th' inconstant moon,
> That monthly changes in her circled orb,
> Lest that thy love prove likewise variable.
> – What shall I swear by?
> – Do not swear at all;
> Or, if thou wilt, swear by thy gracious self,
> Which is the god of my idolatry,
> And I'll believe thee. (II. ii)

Juliet prefers plain statement to Romeo's elaborate declarations of faith; declarations, moreover, made in the name of the "inconstant" moon, and so ominously suggesting impermanence. "Do not swear at all," she pleads, or swear, if at all, by the plain object of her love, his "gracious self"; but she too strikes the note of impermanence in her confession of "idolatry," which at once answers to a true intensity and places it in the expression whilst leading to her final confession of misgiving:

> I have no joy of this contract to-night:
> It is too rash, too unadvised, too sudden,
> Too like the lightning, which doth cease to be
> Ere one can say, "it lightens." (II. ii)[4]

Throughout this exchange, the imagery of night which provides the appropriate conditions for the romanticism that unites these lovers is also the background, finally embracing a sinister element, against which love shines out in real but precarious and transitory splendor. Having thus expressed the misgivings which already shadow her love, and which she is more ready at this stage to grasp than Romeo, Juliet counters them with her affirmation, equally splendid and more positive in its implications, of love's inherent generosity:

My bounty is as boundless as the sea,
My love as deep; the more I give to thee,
The more I have, for both are infinite. (II. ii)

This is the central Shakespearean affirmation that love asserts itself through giving, and that its gift is of the kind which enriches and is an indication of value, of "infinity." In the light of this, her repeated returns to the casement to salute Romeo yet again are, dramatically speaking, profoundly true to life. They serve to rouse Romeo from the misgivings to which he has been subjected, and which in his case are associated with night and the illusion of dreams—

I am *afeard*,
Being in night, all this is but a dream,
Too flattering-sweet to be substantial—

until his doubts are finally dispelled in the positive affirmation of his outburst: "It is my soul that calls upon my name," and in the final blended dedication:

– I have forgot why I did call thee back.
– Let me stand here till thou remember it.
– I shall forget, to have thee still stand there,
Remembering how I love thy company.
– And I'll still stay, to have thee still forget,
Forgetting any other home but this. (II. ii)

Poised against a background of night and impermanence love asserts briefly, for the duration of this scene, its anticipation of life and permanence to come.

As this statement of dedication draws to a close, we are brought back once more in contrast to the world of experience, which returns this time in the shape of Friar Lawrence, who—unlike the other old men in this play—is aware that the young have feelings of their own, but who, being himself old, is debarred from sharing the reality of their feelings. It is within the limits of his understanding of life that he should see birth and death as related processes of nature:

The earth that's nature's mother is her tomb;
What is her burying grave, that is her womb;

it is also within his capacity to make allowances, theoretically and as an observer, for the contradictory principles that he sees, not without a certain subtlety of vision, as exercising their dominating and opposite action upon human nature:

> Two such opposed kings encamp them still
> In man as well as herbs, grace and rude will. (II. iii)

Yet, whilst recognizing in the Friar this true moralizing vision, we must also feel that the entry at this point of Romeo, "wounded" and seeking the remedy for ills which are beyond all abstract cure, represents in most vivid form the impact of real life upon theory and remote moralizing. The Friar contemplates the lover's predicament from his own point of view, which Romeo must find irrelevant; for him Juliet is one more "young woman" among many, with whom a young man has fallen in love. The Friar, moreover, is interested in this love, not in itself but as an instrument for ending, as he hopes, the family feud by which Verona is so intolerably divided; to this worthy end he will set his own typically old man's contrivances into action, only to discover for himself the truth that so many others will experience, mainly to their own undoing, in this play, that life will always tend to move, beyond the attempted control of those who seek to direct it in accordance with ends of their own, to its own conclusions.

It is in this spirit that the Friar agrees, although with foreboding, to perform the marriage that Romeo demands of him. He accedes, in fact, whilst Romeo, again prophetically, brings together love and death as he asserts the *value* of his devotion:

> come what sorrow can,
> It cannot countervail the exchange of joy
> That one short minute gives me in her sight:
> Do thou but close our hands with holy words,
> Then *love-devouring death* do what he dare,
> It is enough I may but call her mine. (II. vi)

This, with its desire to crowd the unique intensity of love into "one short minute," and to set the achievement of this union against the devouring action of time, is close in spirit to the great sonnets on mutability. It amounts to a renewed and intensified bringing together of the contrary sensations which make up what we can properly call the "metaphysical" heart of this play. The Friar, speaking as ever in terms of experience, utters his contrasted warning against the perils which these one-sided ecstasies imply: "These violent delights have violent ends," he says, and, going on to speak, in terms which again touch upon a central contradiction of the tragedy, of "immoderate appetite," he urges the pair to "love moderately." This, of course, he is able to do precisely because he is a spectator, separated by age and outlook from the imperious claims of passion. His attempts to understand the situation of the lovers are, indeed, rather conscientiously painstaking than successful. "O, so light a foot," he says feelingly of Juliet,

> Will ne'er wear out the everlasting flint;

and this, if it is true, as seen from one point of view, is from another —that of the lovers themselves—besides the point. It is a view spoken from the standpoint of "experience," knowledge of the ways of the world, which ignores, however, the reality of that engagement in their emotion which is, in this same scene, the substance of Juliet's reply to Romeo:

> They are but beggars that can count their worth;
> But my true love is grown to such excess,
> I cannot sum up sum of half my wealth. (II. vi)

Here we have a familiar cluster of ideas associated with love and indicating its essential value. The refusal to consider emotion in terms of mere accountancy, to "count their wealth," saves lovers, in the moment of their mutual engagement, from being "beggars," gives to their "true" emotion such "excess"—and here the elements of truth and exaggeration are deliberately balanced one against the other—that it escapes all temporal estimates of value and asserts, however dangerously and precariously, its own valuation. In phrases such as these, which the estimate of "reason" represented by such as Friar Lawrence finds finally incomprehensible, but in which love's generosity imposes, whilst the mutual commitment lasts, its own conviction, the conventional poetic idea of "love's wealth" points beyond any limit of mere convention to the heart of the tragedy which here concerns us.

The outside world, however, though the lovers can succeed at certain moments in ignoring it, is still there, ready to strike; as Benvolio says, immediately after Juliet has spoken in this way, "The day is hot, the Capulets abroad" (III. i). Mercutio, reasonable after his own fashion to the last, exposes in no uncertain terms to his friend the essential vanity of all the family quarrels by which Verona is divided. "Thou wilt quarrel," he points out, "with a man that hath a hair more, or a hair less, in his beard than thou hast"; but as soon as Tybalt appears, dangerously on the warpath, he is as obstinate in refusing to give way as any of the others:

> –By my head, here comes the Capulets.
> –By my heel, I care not; (III. i)

and again, still more stubbornly, "I will not budge for no man's pleasure, I." The double stress on "I" is proof that, in despite of his qualities of human and reasonable detachment, Mercutio is as subject as any other man to the irrational folly which prevails in both parties, and therefore as incapable as any of the rest of escaping the doom that awaits them all. It is striking to note that, in the midst of so much unreason, it is only Romeo, in his new situation, who expresses himself with realism to the man who insists in regarding himself as his mortal enemy:

> I do protest, I never injured thee,
> But love thee better than thou canst devise; (III. i)

in view of these words there is supreme irony in the fact that when Romeo, immediately after, intervenes to separate Mercutio and Tybalt, the only result is that his enemy is able to stab his friend under his arm. Once again, death makes his entry, but this time not in words alone, but in its irreparable reality, to be saluted by the dying Mercutio in phrases which contrast to magnificent effect, by their very sobriety, with all the alternately exuberant and fevered poetry which has decorated its impact to such varying effect in the preceding course of the play. "The hurt cannot be much" says Romeo, at once expressing a friend's irrational hope and, we may feel, seeking to hide from himself the appalling consequences of his well-meant gesture. Mercutio's reply transposes the whole incident to a new level of tragedy. "No," he says, with a rueful gravity to which the survival of his old humorous tone lends a further dimension, "'tis not so deep as a well, nor so wide as a church-door; but 'tis enough, 'twill serve"; and again: "ask for me to-morrow, and you shall find me a grave man" (III. i). In this way, and to the accompaniment of Mercutio's last pun, the whole emotional quality of the play undergoes, in effect, a transformation. Nothing even in romantic and youthful love will be the same after Mercutio's departure as it was before it. The dying man's last judgment upon the events which have led to his death is indeed clear and final. "A plague o' both your houses"; in the light of the unanswerable truth which this represents, Romeo's hesitant plea—"I thought all for the best"—may strike us as a pathetic illusion, finally something less than adequate. Romeo, indeed, is driven to feel his own responsibility for what has happened, and to fall in reaction, when Tybalt returns, into something very like the revenger's base rant. "Fire-eyed fury be my conduct now," are the words he utters, just after he has said of himself, dwelling upon his love:

> O sweet Juliet,
> Thy beauty hath made me effeminate. (III. i)

We need not necessarily feel that the new mood of "fury" is more manly—though Romeo may wish, as he speaks, to believe it so—than the "effeminacy" which inspired him to behave reasonably toward the man he is now about to kill. At all events, it is the facts, rather than his attempt to react to them, that seriously count at this stage. As Romeo, in his new desperate mood, dispatches Tybalt and accepts Benvolio's advice to flee, the action has passed beyond human control to fall under the influence of the "stars" as the Prince pronounces, in stern justice and for the public peace, the sentence of banishment upon the latest murderer.

It is significant that it is precisely at this moment, when the course of events can clearly be seen passing beyond the lovers' possible control, that Juliet shows more clearly than ever before that she has become a good deal more than the unawakened adolescent of the opening scenes. If she now calls upon "love-performing night," it is in no mere prolongation of the earlier romantic exchanges—and, indeed, in this sense it has always been Romeo, rather than herself, who has felt so intensely the attractions of the extinction of light—but in search of the full physical consummation of her love. Her words are in this sense precise and firm:

> O, I have bought the mansion of a love,
> But not possess'd it, and, though I am sold,
> Not yet enjoy'd; so tedious is this day
> As is the night before some festival
> To an impatient child that hath new robes
> And may not wear them. (III. ii)

Her new intensity, however, is not unrelated to a note of hysteria, and there is indeed something surprising in the presence, in the passage just quoted, of imagery that actually carries a hint of the brothel ("possess'd . . . sold . . . enjoy'd"); we should not suggest that Juliet's love is affected, in its quality, by these undertones, but that they answer to a new complexity, a shift toward darkness in the moral tone, that is making itself felt elsewhere. Similarly, when the Nurse enters, bringing, as she fears, news of Romeo's death, it is indeed hysteria that plays a major part in the conceptual impression of her contrary emotions:

> Hath Romeo slain himself? say thou but "I,"
> And that bare vowel "I" shall poison more
> Than the death-darting eye of cockatrice:
> I am not I, if there be such an I,
> Or those eyes shut, that make thee answer "I."
> If he be slain, say "I" . . . (III. ii)

The expressions of contradiction are prolonged through this speech to remarkable effect:

> O serpent heart, hid with a flowering face! . . .
> O nature, what hadst thou to do in hell,
> When thou didst bower the spirit of a fiend
> In mortal paradise of such sweet flesh?
> Was ever book containing such vile matter
> So fairly bound? O, that deceit should dwell
> In such a gorgeous palace! (III. ii)

The last phrase is, in its intensity of contradiction, almost worthy of *Othello*. There is about all this a new sense of tragic complexity, and with it a new depth of psychological penetration, which is the result of balancing against one another the splendors and the impossibilities of romantic love. Juliet, awakened from adolescence into maturity, is discovering that "deceit" can dwell in the "gorgeous palace" of her dedication, seeing beneath the "mortal paradise," at once sublimated and subject to decay, of the "sweet flesh" in which the perfections of her lover are dangerously "bowered," a "spirit" indeed but—disconcertingly, opposed to the original simplicity of her youthful idealism—one which reveals itself under the external manifestations of a "fiend." The contradictions which the knot of human passion bears within itself are affirming themselves to this young but rapidly maturing imagination with almost intolerable intensity.

Meanwhile, and at her side in the moment of stress, the voice of "experience" continues to assert itself in the observations of the Nurse. Hers, wrapped in kindly forms, is the voice of a universal cynicism about the possibilities of love itself:

> There's no trust,
> No faith, no honesty in men: all perjured,
> All forsworn, all naught, all dissemblers. (III. ii)

It is finally, beneath its appearance of wisdom and detachment, a self-centered, an impotent voice—"These griefs, these woes, these sorrows, make me old"—one concerned only with its own situation. To Juliet it can bring no comfort, and she surrenders to the unique, impossible reality of her love as she affirms, at once naturally and against all reason, that

> My husband lives, that Tybalt would have slain;
> And Tybalt's dead, that would have slain my husband:
> All this is comfort. (III. ii)

The stressing of the fact that Romeo is now not merely her lover, the object of her romantic devotion, but her married "husband" is designed to give to this assertion of "comfort" in disaster an element of the natural; but Juliet herself must know, even as she speaks, that her situation, and that of Romeo, are not so simple, and indeed she follows this expression of an impossible hope with a recognition of the opposite reality:

> "Romeo is banished": to speak that word,
> Is father, mother, Tybalt, Romeo, Juliet,
> All slain, all dead. (III. ii)

The premonition of death, once uttered, inevitably affirms itself in her thought. The end of all this tragic excess lies, most typically, in her own prayer: "death, not Romeo, take my maidenhead." It is left to the Nurse to maintain, in her own way and against the direction of her young mistress' mood, the ends of life as she declares her readiness to seek out Romeo for Juliet's "comfort"; and to this proposal Juliet—who has, in the last analysis, no alternative—at the end accedes.

It is appropriately left to the Friar to keep up the note of foreboding. Romeo, he says, is "wedded to calamity," as he brings him the news that he has been banished. Romeo's reply, affirming the love-centeredness of all his thought—

There is no world without Verona walls,
But purgatory, torture, hell itself— (III. iii)

is from his point of view, outside both the excesses and the transforming effect of love, nothing less than a blasphemy; for Romeo's reactions are based upon the exclusive element of obsession in his passion—

heaven is here,
Where Juliet lives—

and find issue in the fevered contradictions of his high-flown, conceited utterance: "This may flies do, but I from this must fly" (III. iii). Once more, the element of artifice in these words is deliberate, answers to a distraught and finally—as far as it goes—a corrupting emotional state; but though the Friar can reasonably urge "philosophy" upon his penitent, his words remain those of an observer, outside both the splendor and the peril of the lover's state, and Romeo can tell him with natural indignation:

Hang up philosophy!
Unless philosophy can make a Juliet,

and point out, with bitter truth, that his mentor is in no position to feel the valid, the essential truth of his situation: "Thou canst not speak of that thou dost not feel." As though to support the pressure of experience upon him, the Nurse also enters, to report that Juliet is in like case; but her reproach to Romeo for what she sees as his excessive despair—"stand, an you be a man"—is, like the Friar's, at once objectively true and, from the victim's point of view, an irrelevance.

The truth is that Friar Lawrence, representing a common sense which is second nature to him, speaks at this moment of what he does not understand. An onlooker from the outside, he sees in Romeo's transports of frustration and grief only "the unreasonable fury of a beast," and finds it natural to reprove the young man for his betrayal of true manliness:

Thy noble shape is but a form of wax,
Digressing from the valour of a man, . . .
And thou dismember'd with thine own defence. (III. iii)

It is important, at this point, to see that this judgment, which is the type of many others made in the course of the play, is at once true, needing to be said, and—as seen from the standpoint of the victim —besides the point, uttered by one who cannot, by his very nature, understand what is really at stake. In the same way, the Friar's attempts to console Romeo, combining encouragement with reproach—

> thy Juliet is alive,
> For whose dear sake thou wast but lately dead . . .
> Happiness courts thee in her best array;
> But, like a misbehaved and sullen wench,
> Thou pout'st upon thy fortune and thy love:
> Take heed, take heed, for such die miserable— (III. iii)

constitute at once a valid warning, which the final tragedy will terribly confirm, and amount—seen from the standpoint of Romeo's absorbing and consuming passion—to so much irrelevant and facile moralizing. Before the play ends the Friar's faith in "experience" as a guide in life will lead him to conclude that everything has its remedy, is susceptible to a little rational manipulation; and it is in this spirit, well-meaning but shortsighted, finally complacent, that he plans the stratagem that will only serve to hasten the concluding disaster. For he and the Nurse who so admires him—"O, what learning is!"—are, in the last analysis, essentially of the same kind.

"Experience," meanwhile, in the grosser and more insensitive form represented by old Capulet, is busy about its own shortsighted plans. "Well, we were born to die" is his characteristic comment on Tybalt's death, and it is decided that Juliet, in order to shake her from her supposed grief for the dead man, will be bundled as quickly as possible into marriage with Paris. Once again, facile good intentions serve only to hasten disaster. It is against this ominous background that Romeo and Juliet achieve (III. v) the brief consummation of their mutual love. It is a consummation, as we now have reason to expect, which is at once intense, contradictory, and finally poised over fear: fear, above all, for the future, whilst life is being plucked, in intense and breathless haste, from the insubstantial present. The nightingale sings in "the *fearful* hollow" of her lover's ear, and Romeo, exultant as he is in the moment of achievement—

> Night's candles are burnt out, and *jocund* day
> Stands tip-toe on the misty mountain tops—[5]

can only precariously maintain his happiness. "I must be gone and live, or stay and die." Life is, for him, with Juliet, and absence from her means death; so that, when Juliet—as ever more realistic at heart—clings desperately to what she knows to be an illusion—"thou needst not to be gone"—he is ready to deny truth in the name of his love: "I'll say yon grey is not the morning's eye." Once again, however, the end of love is foreseen to lie in death: "Come, death, and welcome! Juliet wills it so." Even, however, as Romeo accepts the illusion upon which his life now rests, it is Juliet who returns to daily reality—"It is the lark that sings so out of tune"—and who foresees that they must separate. Truth, in other words, stands most delicately balanced against illusion; to decide which is which, and to what end they are interwoven, could be described as precisely the crux of this tragedy. As Juliet admits that "more light and light it grows," it is left to Romeo to make his comment of tragic foreboding: "More light and light: more dark and dark our woes."

At this point reality intervenes in yet another form, as the Nurse interrupts the lovers to bring news, with daybreak, of the approach of Lady Capulet. There is once again an ominous note in Juliet's last question, "thinkst thou we shall ever meet again?" and though Romeo's reply seems to suggest confidence—

> I doubt it not; and all these woes shall serve
> For sweet discourses in our time to come—

the sinister death note reaffirms itself in the last words which, in the event, Juliet will speak to her lover alive:

> O God! I have an ill-divining soul.
> Methinks I see thee, now thou art below,
> As one dead in the bottom of a tomb. (III. v)

At the last she is left to rely upon fortune—that deity "fickle" in the eyes of the world, tending at all times to impose separation—to send Romeo back to her arms.

The world beyond the lovers proceeds, meanwhile, on its own paths of misunderstanding. Lady Capulet believes that her daughter weeps for Tybalt and offers, in typically "experienced" terms, her moralizing consolation:

> some grief shows much of love,
> But much of grief shows still some want of wit.

As always, "experience" seeks the solution to all problems in "moderation": seeks it precisely where love, of its very nature, is unable to find it. It is noteworthy, however, as a sign of the way in which the complexities of maturity are imposing themselves, that when Romeo is mentioned, Juliet shows herself old enough to dissemble to her mother. "Indeed," she says,

> I never shall be satisfied
> With Romeo, till I behold him—dead;

what she does not know, and what constitutes, of course, the irony of this situation, is that this "satisfaction" is very shortly to be granted her. Her mother, meanwhile, has come to bring her news of the "wedding" which has been arranged by the elderly and the "experienced" for what they have decided is her own good; and her more formidable father now enters to confirm his "decree." At this point, we are clearly shown the fundamental insensibility of those who claim to be versed in the ways of the world: shown it nowhere more obviously than in Capulet's unreasoning rage at Juliet's timid attempts to cross him—"My fingers itch!"—and scarcely less evidently in her own mother's callous remark: "I would the fool were married to her grave." And so, indeed, she shall be, sooner than Lady Capulet knows; but meanwhile the Nurse is allowed to utter her protest in the name of a certain human feeling—"You are to blame, my lord, to rate her so"—only to evoke the father's egoistic stressing of what he believes to be his own unrewarded care and toil:

> Day, night, hour, tide, time, work, play,
> Alone, in company, still my care hath been
> To have her match'd. (III. v)

It is, in fact, his own self-esteem which feels itself affronted by his daughter's obstinacy, and which prompts him to turn her away unless she is docile to his will. Juliet, indeed, faced by a situation slipping beyond all possible control, feels herself caught in a trap:

> Alack, alack, that heaven should practise stratagems
> Upon so soft a subject as myself;

but when she seeks advice from the Nurse, who has so recently shown her some measure of understanding, it is only to be told that Romeo is a "dishclout" in comparison with Paris; there is point indeed in her own final disenchanted comment: "Well, thou hast comforted me marvellous much."

Thus abandoned by those from whom she might have expected help, Juliet decides to turn to the Friar, only—by yet another ironic mischance—to find Paris, her discreet and honorable suitor, in advance of her at his cell. Even as she asks for counsel, she already sees her ultimate "solution" in the death which is pressing itself upon her intimate reflections. Rather than be forced to marry Paris, she says,

> shut me nightly in a charnel-house,
> O'ercovered quite with dead men's rattling bones,
> With reeking shanks and yellow chapless skulls;
> Or bid me go into a new-made grave,
> And hide me with a dead man in his shroud;
> Things that to hear them told, have made me tremble. (IV. i)

Her thoughts are full of the charnel-house, the obsessive presence which will from now on live in her mind side by side with love. Precisely these things, which she now regards with horror, she is fated to do; but we should recognize too that these forebodings, excessive as they are, are spoken in the name of loving faith:

> I will do it without fear or doubt,
> To live an unstain'd wife to my sweet love.

Strong in the love which this determination reflects, Juliet is able at this crisis to dissemble beyond her years. Her deception of her father, in the very act of professing filial obedience (IV. ii), is no doubt a sin, but a sin conceived in the name of natural love and in the face of an egoistic and unimaginative opposition; once more, we find ourselves faced with the play's central tragic contradiction. To affirm the rights of love, Juliet finds herself driven to dissemble; her situation is one which can, of its nature, have no happy solution, but we cannot—unless we are ready to share the egoism and incomprehension of her parents—simply leave her condemned of deception.

Alone with her resolution, Juliet is not surprisingly given over to fear. She confesses to feeling "a faint cold fear" which "thrills through her veins" (IV. iii) as she, who has found her elders so lacking in understanding, contemplates the possibility that even the Friar may be ready to betray her. The thought drives her back upon her increasing obsession with mortal decay, as she contemplates in her imagination the tomb

Where bloody Tybalt, yet but green in earth,
Lies festering in his shroud,

and thinks of the dreadful possibility of her awakening by his side:

Alack, alack, is it not like that I
So early waking, what with loathsome smells
And shrieks like mandrakes torn out of the earth,
That living mortals hearing them run mad:
Or, if I wake, shall I not be distraught,
Environed with all these hideous fears? (IV. iii)

Meanwhile, in the scene which at once follows these somber premonitions (IV. iv), the preparations for life and festivity are afoot, and the Nurse, foreseeing an imminent marriage, is in her element; just before she discovers Juliet's "death," and in the presence of her "body," she jests broadly over the coming consummation of her wedding:

Sleep for a week; for the next night, I warrant,
The County Paris will set up his rest
That you shall rest but little. (IV. v)

Gross and insensitive as they no doubt are, these are after all words of life; and it answers to the play's intention that they are the prelude to the Nurse's own discovery of what she thinks to be, not life, but, its opposite, the image of death. Capulet too, in his lament, equally joins love and death as he reveals the "truth" to Paris:

O son, the night before thy wedding-day,
Hath death lain with thy wife; see, where she lies,
Flower as she was, deflowered by him. (IV. v)

The Friar, for his part, adds his appropriate note to the whole by stressing another kind of life:

confusion's cure lives not
In these confusions. Heaven and yourself
Had part in this fair maid; now heaven hath all . . .
Your part in her you could not keep from death,
But heaven keeps his part in eternal life. (IV. v)

We need neither reject this simply as so much abstract moralizing, nor accept it as the last word on the tragedy which is now approaching its final stages. It represents the voice of "experience," which belongs to but does not exhaust the total impact of life. "She's best married that dies married young"; "Nature's tears are reason's merriment"; it is hard not to feel, as we hear these hard things so easily said, that from this sententious "wisdom" something—which is, perhaps, finally life itself—has been excluded.

The illusion of life, indeed,—if illusion it be—is precisely what Romeo expresses in the very next scene:

> My bosom's lord sits lightly in his throne,
> And all this day an unaccustom'd spirit
> Lifts me above the ground with cheerful thoughts.

It affirms itself even against the contrary sensations which have taken possession of his sleep:

> I dreamt my lady came and found me dead—
> Strange dream, that gives a dead man leave to think!—
> And breathed such life with kisses in my lips,
> That I revived and was an emperor.
> Ah me! how sweet is love itself possess'd,
> When but love's shadows are so rich in joy! (V. i)

Here the central contrast which we have followed through the whole course of the play presents itself from yet another standpoint. The force of love affirms itself, momentarily, in and through an illusion that yet partakes of life; but Romeo has no sooner spoken than Baltasar enters with news of Juliet's "death," and her lover's answer corresponds to yet another change of mood: "Is it e'en so? then I defy you, stars!" (V. i) Where Juliet visited the Friar in search of advice and consolation, Romeo in the madness of his desperate resolve now seeks out the sinister apothecary—sinister by his own account (V. i)—to obtain poison for the ending of his life. Meanwhile, to emphasize the operations of a malignant fortune beyond human control, Friar John's mission has gone astray, undoing all Lawrence's previsions, and Juliet is left, in his own words, as "Poor living corse, closed in a dead man's tomb!" (V. ii)

The last scene of the tragedy opens with Paris at the monument, uttering over Juliet's "tomb" his own decent lament in sonneteering terms. He is interrupted by Romeo in his new mood of desperate, essentially death-directed resolution:

> I will tear thee joint by joint
> And strew this hungry churchyard with thy limbs:

The time and my intents are savage-wild,
More fierce and inexorable by far
Than empty tigers or the roaring sea. (V. iii)

The lover's thoughts revolve characteristically in his mad excess of grief—a fitting pendant to the almost equally mad excess which formerly marked one extreme of his love—round the obsession of the charnel—"Thou detestable maw, thou womb of death"—but it is worth noting that, even as he declares himself to Paris as "a desperate man," he can still address his rival as "Good gentle youth." As he goes on to say, still to Paris, and with profound truth: "By heaven, I love thee better than myself"; the mood is one which, as has often been pointed out, reminds us of Hamlet, whom he also now resembles in being driven unwillingly to kill. Awakening almost at once to the desperate reality of his deed, he sees his victim as joined obscurely to himself in a common adverse fate—"one writ with me in sour misfortune's book"—in an attitude which combines a measure of true nobility with a touch of self-compassion.

These events lead to their culmination in the moment at which Romeo looks on Juliet as she lies on her "tomb" as on a marriage bed, and sees in his grim surroundings, which the radiance of her presence in his imagination transforms, "a feasting presence full of light." We may legitimately ask ourselves whether this represents reality, of an imaginative kind, or illusion in the eyes of common sense; and the answer is surely both. There follows Romeo's noble hymn to death, or rather to beauty as transfigured by love and thereby rendered triumphant over circumstance and the grave:

Thou art not conquer'd; beauty's ensign yet
Is crimson in thy lips and in thy cheeks,
And death's pale flag is not advanced there; (V. iii)

but, of course, in reacting to and accepting the beauty of this, we shall not forget that the point lies, though Romeo is unaware of it, in the fact that Juliet is *alive*. Meanwhile, love and the desire to die are romantically (or shall we say, pathetically? or even self-indulgently? or, possibly, both?) fused in Romeo's words:

shall I believe
That unsubstantial death is amorous,
And that the lean abhorred monster keeps
Thee here in dark to be his paramour? (V. iii)

The truth is that "the palace of dim night" exercises upon Romeo here, as it has done to less extreme effect earlier in the play, a profound attraction, which persuades him to seek his repose, "here, here," "with worms that are thy chamber-maids"; the slightly sententious tone is surely part, though we may agree that it is not all, of the complete effect. Romeo's final nostalgia is, at all events, for "everlasting rest," for the opportunity to

> shake the yoke of inauspicious stars
> From this world-wearied flesh; (V. iii)

and we should perhaps be chary of either accepting this mood at its declared value or of exclusively condemning it. Whilst giving its full worth to the romantic power which inspires Romeo's words, we need not take him at this moment entirely at his own self-estimate; for the speaker is moved, on his own confession, by a "desperate pilot," the end of whose guidance will be to lead him to run on "the dashing rocks" his "sea-sick weary bark." Never in Shakespeare, surely, is suicide accepted quite simply at its own essentially self-dramatizing estimate; though we must add, to do justice to the complete effect, that here it is given its full value, in terms of the poetry, as an element in romantic love. Romeo's final words before he kills himself sum up precisely this vital contrast, as they join life and death in a reflection of the play's complex mood: "Thy drugs are *quick*" (*quick* in the double sense of *rapid* and *alive*), "Thus with a *kiss* I die." There could be no more fitting conclusion than this "metaphysical" balance of contrasted emotions for a play which has turned from the first upon the twin realities, at once separate and identical, of love and death.

Immediately after this last gesture the world returns, in the shape of a Friar Lawrence now moved, most significantly, by fear. The limitations of "experienced" detachment, even when joined to recognized virtue and good intention, have by now been thoroughly exposed. As Juliet, too late, awakens, he can only call her from

> that nest
> Of death, contagion, and unnatural sleep;

only confess at the last his own human limitations:

> A greater power than we can contradict
> Hath thwarted our intents.

In a last effort to remedy what is in fact beyond mending, the Friar proposes to direct Juliet to a monastery, but here once more his measure of understanding and his desire to contrive for the best are powerless before the unanswerable vehemence of her retort: "Go, get thee hence, for *I will not away*" (V. iii). For her imagination, centered on love as the source of life to the exclusion of all other realities, the "poison" on Romeo's lips may yet be a "restorative." None other, indeed, is logically available to her; for she is ready to die where she has been awakened to life, to seek in death the only remedy for her tragic situation.

To the aged survivors, now belatedly chastened by the tragedy that they have helped to bring about, the spectacle before them of the youthful dead comes as a reminder of their own approaching end; as Lady Capulet puts it,

> this sight of death is as a bell
> That warns my old age to a sepulchre.

The Prince, as representative of law and civilization in a city where both have been set aside to tragic effect, is left to denounce a feud that has been the cause of so much death and loss, where life and unity might have resulted from the consummation of love in marriage:

> See, what a scourge is laid upon your hate,
> That heaven finds means to kill your joys with love.

Or, as he puts it in the act of winding up this tragic action, "A glooming peace this morning with it brings."

A MIDSUMMER NIGHT'S DREAM

Good reasons exist for supposing that *A Midsummer Night's Dream* must have been written at a date not very distant from that of *Romeo and Juliet.* There are moments, indeed, when the play may strike us as a comic counterpoise to the "romantic" tragedy, exploring through the comic conventions other aspects of that irrational but vital impulse, in the name of which the young lovers of Verona chose death as an alternative to the extinction of their mutual relationship. Through convention, in fact, Shakespeare works out in this play a pattern of contrasted attitudes to the love which seems to elude reason and, at times, to convert human beings into its slaves; a pattern, moreover, which is set finally in the framework of a rational and social attitude to marriage.

This attitude is given its expression, also in poetic terms, through the relationship of Theseus and Hippolyta, whose "nuptial hour," we are told as the action opens, "draws on apace." Theirs is presented as a love compatible with experience, conscious of its true nature and of the dangers inherent in passion, but confident also of the ability of civilized human beings to turn passion to positive and beneficent ends. Theseus speaks of his past "desires" as lingering on into the present, and makes a frank confession to his future bride of the part once played by violence in the beginnings of their own relationship:

> Hippolyta, I woo'd thee with my sword,
> And won thy love, doing thee injuries. (I. i)

This amounts to a recognition that love is compatible with the cruel and the irrational, as indeed much in the coming action will confirm. Side by side with this, however, and representing not the past but the present and the anticipated fulfillments of the future, Theseus asserts the ability of rational maturity to incorporate this vital impulse into the social and essentially civilizing dance of life, which this play will aim at reflecting in dramatic form; as he at once goes on to say, still to Hippolyta,

> I will wed thee in another key,
> With pomp, with triumph, and with revelling. (I. i)

The "wooing" of the past, based on the immediate and even dangerous impulses of individual passion, is now to find its consummation in the social celebration of marriage; but before it does so, before the conclusion here anticipated is turned into the final reality, we shall have occasion to observe the operations of passion to less social ends, in a variety of contrasted situations and in surroundings which imply a deliberate withdrawal from the world of human and social living.

Scarcely, indeed, has Theseus stated these intentions with regard to his marriage than he is interrupted by the entry of Egeus, "full of vexation," inspired by bitter resentment against his own child.

Once again, as in *Romeo and Juliet*, although to different ends, we are made aware of the shortsighted confidence of "experience" in its ability to assert its own designs at the expense of others. The father, in his determination to *impose* his own view upon his daughter, dismisses Hermia's declared preference for Lysander as a mere question of deceitful "feigning" and unnatural "love-tokens," finally as a manifestation of her perverse and unnatural "cunning"; against this, he clings obstinately to the father's right to filial "obedience," only to rouse against himself the irrational reality of a love which he can neither understand nor allow for, in "stubborn harshness."

Theseus, required to assert his authority in this dispute, does so in the name of an acceptance of natural dependence as the indispensable foundation of truly ordered and social living. The choice he places before Hermia is one between submission and death: death or, alternatively, an unnatural, lifelong renunciation of love itself. In so doing, he acts as a ruler, as the voice of reason and natural law whose concern it is to direct the impulses of passion into their established and indispensable social channels. Hermia, however, protests against his decision, claiming the privilege, upon which true love must rest and which is equally a part of life, of seeing with her own eyes. "I would," she says, "my father look'd but with *my* eyes," rather than with those of the experienced "judgement" to which he lays claim and which Theseus, as the voice of authority, is properly concerned to defend. Her plea is one uttered in exclusive attention to the satisfaction of her own impulses, and as such we shall not be tempted to accept it as it stands; but neither, on the other hand, shall we follow Egeus in his shortsighted and obstinate refusal to allow it any consideration at all. In point of fact, the action of the play will turn out to depend, to no small extent, precisely upon what different "eyes" see in love, and it will be the harmonizing of these visions, rather than any arbitrary choice between them, that will finally constitute its substance. Already, Theseus' own position shows itself more understanding than a mere affirmation of authority would require. As Hermia clings to her decision with an obstinacy equal to that of her father, Theseus warns her that the consequences of her refusal to listen to reason will be the denial of natural life, a sterile obligation

> To live a *barren* sister all your life,
> Chanting *faint* hymns to the *cold fruitless* moon.

He shows himself in this aware of the difference which separates such as Hermia, whose natural end is fulfillment in marriage, from those whose renunciation of the world is firmly founded, who in full knowledge *choose* the spiritual life. "Thrice-blessed," indeed, he warns her, are those

> that master so their blood
> To undergo such maiden pilgrimage;

but, for the rest, for those who are called to live naturally in the world, the position is otherwise:

> *earthlier* happy is the rose distill'd,
> Than that which, *withering* on the *virgin thorn*,
> Grows, lives, and dies in single blessedness.

It is a feature of Theseus' maturity, of the grasp of reality that makes him fit to rule, that he is capable of balancing these two attitudes, the spiritually dedicated and the naturally human, giving to each its appropriate value and demanding the one-sided rejection of neither.[6]

This truth, however, can only be finally affirmed at the end of an action that, until its conclusion, will mainly be concerned with the interplay between various partial attitudes to love. Hermia and Lysander, as lovers, live in their own world, which has its own laws, but which is not in any event that of mature and reasonable experience. Their confidence is placed fully in that world and the vision which it imposes. As Lysander, appealing to reason from *his* own standpoint, says to his rival:

> You have her father's love, Demetrius;
> Let me have Hermia's: do you marry him:

an argument based on exclusive concern with his own compulsions, which Egeus is able to take up by asserting in turn his essentially *proprietary* view of his paternal rights:

> true, he hath my love,
> And what is *mine* my love shall render him. (I. i)

Lysander's reply to this is a claim to social equality with his rival and, more important, an assertion of the rights which, in his view, and Hermia's, the fact of love reciprocated in itself confers; but it is important to note that, whilst speaking thus in the defense of his own interest, he is ready to dismiss the love of others, as in the case of Helena, as so much irrational excess:

she, sweet lady, *dotes,*
Devoutly dotes, dotes in *idolatry;* (I. i)[7]

from which we are left to conclude that love, blind to its own partiality, is characteristically clear-sighted in relation to that of others.

Left alone after Theseus has declared his judgment, Lysander and Hermia consider the nature of love more closely. It is, they are aware, essentially ill-starred—"The course of true love never did run smooth"—but equally they know by personal experience that it is "hell to choose love by another's eyes." Its willfulness is, in fact, at once its strength and its weakness, and its background is impermanence, an inescapable subjection to time and circumstance. As Lysander says:

if there were a sympathy in choice,
War, death, or sickness did lay siege to it,
Making it momentary as a sound,
Swift as a shadow, short as any dream;
Brief as the lightning in the collied night,
That, in a spleen, unfolds both heaven and earth,
And ere a man hath power to say "Behold!"
The jaws of darkness do devour it up:
So quick bright things come to confusion. (I. i)[8]

Here, clearly, we have an echo of the characteristic mood of Romeo, not less poignant or charged with feeling for being translated from a tragic to a comic action. Hermia is ready to accept the truth of her lover's comment, which she regards as the description of "a customary cross"; but it is worth noting that she does so in the name of "fancy," and therefore, up to a point, of illusion. In this spirit, which amounts to a decision to evade reality by attempted flight, Lysander persuades her to leave Athens with him; and she, as she accepts his proposal, swears to keep faith by Cupid, who is, however, notoriously fickle, by "the simplicity of Venus' doves," who represent in fact anything but simplicity, and—most significantly of all—"By all the vows that ever men have broke." The essentially dual nature of passion, compounded of simplicity and deception, could hardly be more strongly affirmed.

The "simplicity" of love, indeed, is immediately shown in a new light by the entry of Helena, in whom the same exclusive devotion evokes no response from its declared object. In the exchange between herself and Hermia the cross-complexities of love are given their full value. Hermia, resting upon her own recent experience, stresses its transforming and essentially irrational power:

> Before the time I did Lysander see,
> Seem'd Athens as a paradise to me:
> O, then, what graces in my love do dwell,
> That he hath turn'd a heaven into a hell;

whilst Lysander, equally concentrated on the satisfaction which his own position seems to afford him, touches somewhat patronizingly on the same theme in his final good wishes for Helena: "As you on him, Demetrius *dote* on you." To this Helena, in turn, can only answer that it is precisely Demetrius, whom she vainly loves, who "dotes," not on her, but on her rival. Both love's strength and its weakness, accordingly, are seen to lie in its compelling power to act transformingly upon the real; as Helena goes on to say:

> Things base and vile, holding no quantity,
> Love can transpose to form and dignity;
> Love looks not with the eyes, but with the mind;
> And therefore is wing'd Cupid painted blind:
> Nor hath love's mind of any judgement taste;
> Wings, and no eyes, figure unheedy haste:
> And therefore is love said to be a child,
> Because in choice he is so oft beguiled. (I. i)

This is the sentence that sums up the meaning of what we have seen and are to see. The lovers themselves confirm it by their uncertain and unreasoning choices, as well as by the obstinacy with which they maintain them against all contrary considerations; and now Helena herself, having just admitted all this, is immediately inspired to betray the confidence of her friend in the hope of obtaining love's reward at her expense.

The entry of Bottom and his friends (I. ii) introduces a further contrast, another plane of the complete action. The play they are preparing to perform before Theseus is in effect something very like a parody of Romeo's tragedy; it is "the most lamentable comedy, and most cruel death of Pyramus and Thisby." The time, however, has hardly come for this part of the action to be developed, and so the actors are soon replaced by the fairies (II. i), as life in its social and civilized forms gives way to the mysteriousness of the woods, where the irrational but potent impulses it normally covers will be released and where its capacity to master these by gathering them into a more comprehensive humanity will be in some sense tested. As we are introduced to this new facet of the action, it is clear that even in the fairy realm passion has introduced its all too human disorder. Oberon, according to Puck's report, is "passing fell and wroth," consumed with jealousy for his queen and with desire for the boy attendant whom she has enticed from his service; and Titania, on her side, clings to her conquest, "perforce withholds the loved boy,"

> Crowns him with flowers, and makes him all her joy: (II. i)

treats the page, in short, exactly as she is shortly to treat the grotesquely transformed person of Bottom the weaver. As a result of this tense situation, the entire fairy realm is plunged into disorder. As Puck again reports:

> all their elves for fear
> Creep into acorn cups and hide them there;

and it is precisely this disorder that Puck in turn, as the very spirit of irresponsibility, makes particularly his own.[9]

Oberon and Titania, when they finally meet from opposite sides, accuse one another mutually and with considerable heat. Oberon is said to be "amorous," in all the human sense of that word, and Titania is reminded of her former passion for Theseus in words which, spoken as they are in the woods, the home of the dark and irrational forces in life, are not devoid of a sense of menace:

> Didst thou not lead him through the glimmering night
> From Perigenia, whom he ravished? (II. i)

There is indeed a sinister element in this fairy realm, one associated with the action of "blood" and the darker side of the passions, not in any way less real than that of lyrical fancy and poetic decoration to which we can all respond. Titania speaks with feeling of "the forgeries of jealousy," and nature itself is seen as subject to profound disturbance; the winds, "as in revenge," have sucked up "contagious fogs" from the sea, and "the seasons alter," are subjected to an unnatural process of change:

> the spring, the summer,
> The childing autumn, angry winter change
> Their wonted liveries; and the mazed world,
> By their increase, now knows not which is which:
> And this same progeny of evil comes
> From our debate, from our dissension. (II. i)

In the face of this situation, Oberon sticks obstinately to the demand that his caprice be satisfied, denying all responsibility—"Do you amend it, then; it lies in you"—whilst Titania defies him in the name of her infatuation: "The fairy land buys not the child of me." Their final parting is, inevitably, on terms of mutual defiance, with Oberon declaring that he will use the services of Puck to subject his queen to "torment"; and it is in this mood that he at once sends the spirit to seek the flower called, not without meaning, "love-in-idleness," the properties of which are such that they will make

> man or woman *madly dote*
> Upon the next live creature that it sees. (II. i)

By the action of this plant, Titania will be induced to confound her sense of reality, to pursue "with the soul of love," which is thereby reduced to the absurd and the sinister, "lion, bear, or wolf, or bull," and, perhaps even more ignominiously than these, "meddling monkey" or "busy ape." The only reason which Oberon has for exposing her to this treatment is the hope that she may thereby be induced to "render up her page to me."

It is precisely at this point, when all the irrational and potentially destructive qualities of love seem to have been confirmed in the fairy order, that Helena enters "doting," in vain pursuit of the same Demetrius who declares himself ready to "slay" his rival Lysander even in the act of confessing that Hermia, the object of his passion, in turn "slays" him by her failure to respond to his love. What better example could we find than this of love's excess, of the reflection of fairy perversity in human dedication to madness? In this spirit, Demetrius goes on to berate Helena soundly, whilst she in turn confesses to her abject state with a comparison of supreme indignity:

> I am your spaniel; and, Demetrius,
> The more you beat me, I will fawn on you, (II. i)[10]

only to receive his heartless reply: "I am sick when I do look on thee," and to be threatened, at least by implication, with the loss, in addition to all else, of "the rich worth of your virginity." Helena, thoroughly caught in the trap of her unrequited love, can only answer with the abject recognition of her abasement: "you in my respect are all the world." Love, translated from its original courtly setting to the woods, has become a force that operates by reversing the normal order of things, that can hint at a sinister note when Helena says "Apollo flies, and Daphne holds the chase," and find it amply confirmed when Demetrius, in the obsession of his own passion, utters his final threat to her: "I shall do thee mischief in the wood." Even after this, however, her irrational subjection to passion is such that she can say:

> I'll follow thee, and make a heaven of hell,
> To die upon the hand I love so well; (II. i)

whilst Oberon, on his return, declares that he is ready to make Titania full of just those "hateful fantasies" that we have heard uttered in the human order.

In the scene which follows (II. ii), Oberon's purpose is at last fulfilled as Titania sleeps to the insistent evocation of beasts and insects shadowing her slumber, and as Oberon himself utters his culminating malevolence: "Wake when some *vile* thing is near." No sooner has this been accomplished than the connection with the human action is drawn still closer, as Lysander and Hermia enter, devoted to one another but exhausted by their prolonged wanderings in the woods. Lysander is still able to speak, poetically, of their being united as "one heart," whilst Hermia shows herself more realistically aware of the dangers that encompass human relationships in the forest when she urges him to "lie further off." No sooner have they succumbed to sleep, and after Puck, following his fairy master's instructions, has thrown his charm in the wrong man's eyes, than Helena enters, still "doting" upon the uncourteous Demetrius. As Lysander awakes, the web of unreason is drawn even tighter as he succumbs to his new love for Helena and makes his appeal—not, precisely at this moment, without irony—to what he is pleased to think of as reason:

> The will of man is by his reason sway'd,
> And reason says you are the worthier maid. (II. ii)

There could hardly be a more inauspicious moment for asserting the supremacy of "reason" in the affairs of passion. The entire action in the woods, on the fairy and human levels alike, indicates that the will of man is moved in these matters by irrational factors, and indeed to Helena the sudden change in Lysander appears as one "mockery" more, even as Lysander himself renounces, in most unreasonable terms, the love he formerly professed for Hermia:

> For as a surfeit of the sweetest things
> The deepest loathing to the stomach brings,
> Or as the heresies that men do leave
> Are hated most of those they did deceive,
> So thou, *my surfeit and my heresy,*
> Of all be hated, but the most of me! (II. ii)

Where, we may well ask after this, does "doting" end and true love begin? The scene is brought to its appropriate conclusion when the abandoned Hermia awakes, dreaming of a "crawling serpent" at her breast, only to find Lysander gone and herself alone and subjected to terror in the woods.

This is the appropriate moment to extend the comic pattern further by bringing Bottom and his group to the heart of the action. Bottom and Titania are now to provide the supreme example, central to the whole play, of love's incongruity; and on the verge of this revelation the weaver's mixture of simplicity and basic common sense is appropriately stressed. Puck intervenes to place the ass's head on Bottom, whilst his friends flee from him in fear, but whilst he himself retains his self-confidence and fundamental aplomb: "this is to make an ass of me; to fright me if they could. But I will not stir from this place." This is the same confidence which will enable Bottom to fall easily into his new role as Titania's consort, treating the attendant fairies with deference and even a certain dignity: the same which, more importantly, renders him immune to the fantasies that surround him in the forest, although insensible at the same time to its magic. Therein lies the essence of his attitude to love, and of his situation at this moment. Titania, on the other hand, is fully subjected to the follies and excesses that accompany unreasonable love. She, as she awakes, "dotes" on her grotesque companion, whom her imagination entirely transforms from his reality. "Mine ear," she says,

> is much enamour'd of thy note;
> So is mine eye enthralled to thy shape; (III. i)

NORTHWEST MISSOURI
STATE COLLEGE LIBRARY
MARYVILLE, MISSOURI

for "doting" enters through the senses, and true love, as distinct from enslavement to passion, calls for the confirmation of the mind.[11] Bottom's realistic comment upon this—"you should have little reason for that; and yet, to say the truth, reason and love keep little company together now-a-days" (III. i)—has serious meaning, uttered though it is in an absurd situation, appropriate to the spirit of comedy; and as much can be said of his retort to Titania's further excess, "Thou art as wise as thou art beautiful": "Not so, neither; but if I had wit enough to get out of this wood, I have enough to serve mine own turn" (III. i).[12] The wood, indeed, is in no sense a substitute for daily living in the workaday world. The appropriate home of a fairy, it can provide no permanent habitat for the human beings who will in due course return, with their minds and hearts suitably chastened and enriched, to normal social living; and, in so far as Bottom holds on to this truth in the midst of his grotesque translation, he is affirming a reality central to the entire conception.

The full meaning of this episode is, indeed, considerably more various and complex than any mere response to the obvious comic situation can suggest. Titania, duped as she is by Oberon's plot, is still "a spirit of no common rate." As such, she is able to respond, even in a situation calculated to make her words palpably absurd, to the vision of love as a purifying and essentially ennobling force. She can tell Bottom, in words which convey more than the obvious absurdity which her situation imposes:

> I will purge thy mortal grossness so,
> That thou shalt like an airy spirit go; (III. i)

and before the web of confusions in which they are both involved is ended, Bottom will have assimilated at least something of this point of view. The marriage of incongruities, indeed, as reflected in love and now supremely embodied in the inversion of normal human qualities and attitudes in the woods, is the essence of Shakespeare's comedy in this play.

In the episodes which follow this grotesque confrontation of "spirit" and "flesh," the fairy and the mortal worlds, irrationality and subjection to the forces in nature which evade reasonable control everywhere prevail. Oberon, in his confirmed malice, is ready to see Titania "dote," and Puck finds pleasure in being able to bring him the news that she is so far alienated from her true self as to be in love with a "monster." Nature, indeed, is in the process of becoming more than a little sinister as the instrument of Puck's malicious devices:

> Their sense thus weak, lost with their fears thus strong,
> Made senseless things begin to do them wrong . . .
> I led them on in this distracted fear,
> And left sweet Pyramus translated there:
> When in that moment, so it came to pass,
> Titania waked, and straightway loved an ass. (III. ii)

Against this background, with all the normal attributes of reason suspended as each character pursues his exclusive, irrational desire, Demetrius enters, rebuked by Hermia for having, as she believes, killed Lysander; and of the supposed victim, Demetrius can only say, with significant brutality, "I had rather give his carcass to my hounds." For Puck, such excesses are no more than a pleasurable confirmation of his own conviction of human folly. As he says, contemplating the results of his own handiwork and with visible satisfaction, "Lord, what fools these mortals be!" For it is, as he himself declares, his nature to be "best pleased" by those things that "fall preposterously." The situation is next still further complicated by the appearance of Lysander, who swears to his love for Helena, who in turn is determined to reject him. Once more the elements of reason and illusion are subject to significant inversion. Lysander, justifying his change of devotion, argues that he now has the "judgement" which he formerly lacked; Helena replies by asserting that he is essentially unchanged, that he is without "judgement" now, as in the past.

Further to complicate the intrigue, Demetrius, at this point awakened, addresses himself to Helena in terms which are, always within the prevailing convention, frankly and undisguisedly sensual:

> O, let me kiss
> This princess of pure white, this seal of bliss; (III. ii)

but the object of this address sees in it, in her own state of puzzled resentment, only "spite," "hell," and mockery, and is led by this to make her own counterappeal for a properly civilized behavior:

> If you were *civil* and knew *courtesy*,
> You would not do me thus much injury.

These are values, however, which do not belong to the woods, which will have in due course to be sought by a suitably chastened and enlightened return to social reality. Meanwhile, and until this can take place, all are alike involved in the bonds of confusion to which their own one-sided attitudes have brought them. Hermia, conscious of being plunged in "dark night," trusts to her hearing, not to the plain evidence of her eyes, which has deserted her; but Lysander has been vouchsafed the visible manifestation of his new love—

> Fair Helena, who more engilds the night
> Than all yon fiery oes and eyes of light— (III. ii)

even as he declares that his former love for Hermia has turned to "hate." Helena, however, far from accepting this shift in the direction of her own former desire, can only see in all this a "confederacy" against herself on the part of all the rest: this is what has resulted from seeking to follow the love of the eyes in the wood, where its operations are subject to irrational fairy powers. Under the pressure of these powers, the friendship which formerly united the two girls in the civilized, human world and which Helena now recalls—

> So we grew together,
> Like to a double cherry, seeming parted,
> But yet an union in partition— (III. ii)

is also on the point of breaking. As she asks,

> will you rent our ancient love asunder,
> To join with men in scorning your poor friend? (III. ii)

The plea, however, is made against a background of gathering confusion. Lysander turns on Hermia in abuse—"Hang off, thou cat, thou burr! vile thing"—even as she pleads: "Since night you loved me; yet since night you left me"; and when Helena in turn asks to be forgiven for having betrayed her to Demetrius and to be allowed to "bear her folly," forgiven, back to Athens, all the reply she gets is: "Why, get you gone; who is't that hinders you?" All this "jangling," meanwhile, in which human beings are seen to be caught inextricably in the consequences of following exclusively their own passions, is esteemed by Puck a "sport," even as Lysander, vainly chasing Demetrius through the forest in search of vengeance, confesses himself fallen "in dark uneven way." By the time this web of intensified cross-purposes has been completely woven all the lovers, having followed their fanciful and unreal purposes to this sorry end, are ready to express themselves as thoroughly chastened. Helena is concerned only to seek relief "from those that my poor company detest," and Hermia confesses that her legs "can keep no pace with my desires."[13] As both pairs, overcome by exhaustion, at last address themselves to rest, all await the break of day and the moment to seek rescue from this maze of madness in a return to normal life in Athens.

Until, however, Titania has been released from her spell, there can be no question of the lovers—and ourselves with them—finding themselves out of the wood. Pending her deliverance, and plunged in her own parody of a falsely romantic vision of love, she still sees in the grotesque person of the translated Bottom her "gentle joy," whom she addresses in terms which we have by now learned to find typical: "O, how I love thee! how I *dote* on thee" (IV. i). In these terms Antipholus of Syracuse, also subjected to "madness" in *The Comedy of Errors,* expressed his impossible love for Luciana;[14] so too, the pale lovers of *The Two Gentlemen of Verona* addressed themselves to the objects of their sentimental "idolatry."[15] Oberon, exercising the privilege of an observer, confirms this "dotage" in his queen, whom, however, he is now ready to release from what he calls "This hateful imperfection of her eyes" (IV. i). He declares that everything that has happened in the woods as the result of his own devices shall be remembered only as the shadow of deformed passion, as "the fierce vexation of a dream," once the dreamers have been recalled to their true selves, awakened from the following of desire in the night of error to the light of day and the truth of reason.

On the heels of these declarations, Titania accordingly at last awakes. She confesses that she has indeed seen "visions," but of herself as "enamoured of an ass"; as Oberon puts it, not without a certain stressed cruelty: "There lies your love." With the return of reason thus confirmed on the fairy level, it is time for Theseus and Hippolyta to enter in "the vaward of the day," as the sound of hunting horns greets the morning to awaken the human sleepers at Theseus' command. The stress is laid now upon harmony, the bringing together of "discord" into music, the uniting of the sounds of nature to those of human sociability in "one mutual cry." Lysander, restored to normal life, acknowledges his disobedience and Demetrius confesses that his recent behavior has reflected an unreasonable fury; now, however, "in health," he finds himself in a position to recognize his "natural taste" for Helena and its power to replace his former unreasoning desire for Hermia. Theseus, with the ground thus prepared, "overbears" Egeus' continued demand for punishment, and calls for reason and concord to be cemented in the social and civilizing bonds of marriage, to which religion will lend its appropriate sanction:

> in the temple, by and by, with us
> These couples shall eternally be knit. (IV. i)

The lovers on their side, thus prompted, awaken to a dialogue which carries its own answering note of solemnity as they balance the insignificance of the past against the noble and mutually enriching prospects of the present:

> – These things seem small and undistinguishable,
> Like far-off mountains turned into clouds.
> – Methinks I see these things with parted eye,
> When every thing seems double.
> – So methinks;
> And I have found Demetrius *like a jewel*,
> Mine own, and not mine own. (IV. i)

The awakening is one that, in characteristic terms of Shakespearean comedy, hovers on the intuition of a new life.[16] To complete it with the inclusion of the comic incongruous, Bottom, in the very act of standing finally confirmed as an object of ridicule, asserts in terms which seem to go beyond the obvious reality of his situation the vision by which he too is possessed:

> I have had a most rare vision. I have had a dream, past the wit of man to say what dream it was.

The substance of his dream, indeed, turns out to be nothing less than an echo, comically confused, but nonetheless compacted of reality, of St. Paul's vision of love as a transforming and unique power:[17]

> The eye of man hath not heard, the ear of man hath not seen, man's hand is not able to taste, his tongue to conceive, nor his heart to report, what my dream was. (IV. i)

From these words, we may gather that Bottom has his own contribu tion to make, from the standpoint of comedy, to the play's variations upon its central theme. For love, as this comedy conceives it, is seen to be at once a folly and to carry within itself, obscured indeed and even subject to absurdity, but nonetheless real, a glimpse of the divine element in human life; and at this point the ridiculous and the sublime meet in what is perhaps the play's deepest, most profound moment.

Vision and illusion are, indeed, explicitly blended in the opening of the final scene (V. i), where the various elements of the action are drawn together, mutually reinforcing one another in Shakepeare's characteristic comic manner. Theseus, speaking with the voice of reason, finds an element of excess in the respective visions of "the lunatic, the lover, and the poet," but even in his words the divine faculty of "imagination" is granted its transforming power side by side with the delusions born of mere "frenzy." In the light of the action we have just witnessed, the contrary judgments which the contemplation of human behavior invites when inspired by passion are held in a delicate balance. The imagination, romantically conceived, truly sees "visions," of the kind which inspired Romeo and Juliet in their mutual affirmations of love's truth and validity, but equally from the realistic point of view, as we have had ample occasion to see in the forest, the possibilities for misunderstanding and deception are great indeed:

> in the night, imagining some fear,
> How easy is a bush supposed a bear! (V. i)

But, even as Theseus thus judiciously holds the balance, Hippolyta in her reply lays the stress finally on something more than mere deluded fancy. In her eyes at least,

> all the story of the night told over,
> And all their minds transfigured so together,
> More witnesseth than fancy's images,
> And grows to something of *great constancy;*
> But, howsoever, strange and admirable. (V. i)

In the long run the imaginative vision imposes itself upon the images of mere "fancy," confirming the realities we have glimpsed beneath the distracted behavior of the human lovers in the wood and asserting itself even beneath the obvious comedy of Bottom's "translation."

As the lovers enter against the background which this opening exchange provides, the social and civilizing vision of love begins to impose itself. They are "full of joy and mirth" in contrast to their past trials, and Theseus greets them as "gentle friends," with the wish that "joy and fresh days of love" may reign in their hearts. Lysander, in turn, speaks for them all as he makes the appropriate reply. "More" joy and love than that which has been desired for themselves, he desires to Theseus and Hippolyta,

> Wait in your royal walks, your board, your bed! (V. i)

This is the vision of the marriage union as life-giving in its effects, joining body and soul, reason and feeling, imagination and fancy in its essential "truth." Against it, however, Theseus, as he looks forward to the entry of Bottom and his companions with the Pyramus play, can still speak of "the anguish of a torturing hour." In easement of this "anguish" the lovers, whom we have watched in the woods during their action of passion, are now themselves to witness another action in which romantic love is exposed to ridicule: and their reaction to what they see enacted—their charity, or lack of it, in the light of their own recent experiences—will throw light upon what kind of men and women they are. As Theseus says in his conclusion, defending in advance the good faith which will render acceptable even the absurdities of these self-appointed actors,

> never anything can be amiss,
> When simpleness and duty tender it. (V. i)

The lesson is once again that prompted by the masque of the Nine Worthies at the end of *Love's Labour's Lost:*[18] the lesson which Theseus again sums up when he says:

> Love, therefore, and tongue-tied simplicity,
> In least speak most, to my capacity: (V. i)

the lesson which the loyalty of the simplehearted in itself conveys and which the arrogant and the sophisticated ignore at their own peril.

The Prologue to the play confirms precisely this lesson with its initial words: "If we offend, it is with our good will." As Lysander comments, going rather beyond the surface mockery in search of the deeper meaning to which Theseus has just pointed: "A good moral, my lord; it is not enough to speak, but to speak true." The play itself, after this beginning, goes on to a sufficiently close parody of the Romeo attitudes to love and death; "the cranny, right and sinister" through which Pyramus and Thisbe speak, "the grim-look'd night," the "night with hue so black" that envelops their meeting—all are familiar elements, transposed into another key, from the tragedy. Hippolyta, rather rashly, is inclined to dismiss all this as "the silliest stuff that ever I heard," but Theseus in his reply penetrates more deeply to the spirit of this comedy when he says: "The best in this kind are but shadows; and the worst are no worse, if imagination amend them" (V. i); and Bottom, in a kind of parody of deeper intuitions of reconciliation and life, says of the lovers with his habitual touch of unconscious poetry: "the wall is down that parted their fathers."

The last word of the play, however, is not allowed to rest here. It is left principally, and in the first place, to Oberon as he delivers his celebration of married fruitfulness:

> Now, until the break of day,
> Through this house each fairy stray.
> To the best bride-bed will we,
> Which by us shall blessed be;
> And the issue there create
> Ever shall be fortunate. (V. i)

There is good reason to suppose that these lines, and indeed the play as a whole, were written with a definite marriage celebration in view; but Shakespeare was always capable of wedding such particular ends to his own more universal purposes, and these words in fact amount to an appropriate rounding off of the entire action.[19] In spite of this, however, they are not quite the end. To Puck, left alone on the stage, words are given which convey, if only in passing, a note somewhat more sinister in its effect. He speaks as "The *iron tongue* of midnight hath told twelve," under the influence of "the *heavy* gait of night," when the world of spirits emerges to come into its own, and his conclusion has a distinctive quality which has been present as an element in the play from the first and which now seems to come forward to affirm itself alone:

> Now the wasted brands do glow.
> Whilst the screech-owl, screeching loud,
> Puts the wretch that lies in woe
> In remembrance of a shroud.

Now it is the time of night,
That the graves, all gaping wide,
Every one lets forth his sprite,
In the church-way paths to glide:
And we fairies that do run
By the triple Hecate's team,
From the presence of the sun,
Following darkness like a dream,
Now are frolic . . . (V. i)

In these final references to Hecate and the graveyard, to dreams and night, we may perhaps see something rather more than mere surface decoration, find a reminder of the life of which we have recently caught disturbing glimpses in the woods: a life now set indeed in the civilized Athenian framework which opens and closes the action, but felt nonetheless to be disturbingly endowed with a reality of its own. Love, though the bringer of light and life, has also its places of darkness, as we have had occasion to see from time to time in the recent alienations from reason, and though we must believe that the civilizing and rational order of marriage finally prevails in *A Midsummer Night's Dream*, it is not against a vacuum or in the absence of contrary realities that its triumph in this great comedy must be set.

RICHARD II

It is a remarkable sign of Shakespeare's creative energy at this early stage in his career that, at much the same time as he conceived the two great plays we have just considered, he must have embarked, with *Richard II*, on a venture of a very different kind. The play is one which, on a superficial view, it may be easy to underestimate. The style in which it is written is highly formal and elaborate: so much so that it may seem at first sight to be lacking in the vigor of real life. The formality and the elaboration, however, correspond to an acute and already highly personal reading of historical events. In Shakespeare's very selective treatment of this royal tragedy, careful study can detect a consistent concern to distinguish between fiction and truth, or—to put the matter in another way—to show the downfall of a traditional conception of royalty and its replacement by a political force at once more competent, more truly self-aware, and more precariously built on the foundations of its own desire for power. The problems, moral and political alike, posed by this development will provide the starting point, a few years later, for a series of plays that represent one of the highest points in the dramatist's earlier career.[20]

In accordance with this general purpose the action of *Richard II* opens on a note of high formality, as the feudal lords Bolingbroke and Mowbray are uneasily confronted under the eyes of their king. Both these courtly rivals, presented in the initial act of replacing unity by strife, allegiance by passionate self-assertion, are still grouped in a pattern of loyalties dependent upon the crown; but, although they are at first careful to maintain the appearances of loyal respect, their formal statements of allegiance are soon replaced by blunt expressions of mutual defiance.

> *Now,* Thomas Mowbray, do I turn to thee,
> And mark my greeting well; (I. i)

and as Bolingbroke goes on to deliver his bitter challenge, and receives the tense, strained rhetoric of his rival's reply, we are made aware that the formality of the original exchanges is being replaced by something else, by a mood which includes, among other things, a notable sense of artifice and strain.

The change of tone is explained at least in part by the nature of the grievances which separate these rival lords; for these, and their final relation to the king himself, are something less than transparent. The main charges in Bolingbroke's indictment are solid enough. They include the embezzlement of royal revenues for "lewd employments," persistent intrigue, and, above all, a part in the plotting of the Duke of Gloucester's death; the last accusation, most ominously of all, involves the king himself, the center of the feudal structure of loyalty to which lip service is still being paid, in ambiguity and a suggestion of guilt. Mowbray's reply, though rhetorically impressive, is notably evasive in the realm of fact. *Part* of the money received from the royal treasury was, he admits, held back, but—so it seems—to repay a debt contracted on another occasion; and whilst denying that Gloucester's death lies to his charge, he admits to neglect of his "sworn duty" in that case and confesses, though with affirmations of subsequent repentance and reconciliation, to a plot against the life of Richard's uncle, John of Gaunt. Whatever the precise facts may be—and they are left deliberately vague—this is clearly a world more complex than that of rhetorical defiance and knightly conflict: and in it the king himself, though maintaining an attitude of royal impartiality, is more deeply involved than he cares to admit.

Richard's increasing evasiveness, indeed, is a notable feature of these early scenes. His first interventions in the quarrel are proper statements of detachment:

> Mowbray, impartial are our eyes and ears . . .
> He is our subject, Mowbray; so art thou:
> Free speech and fearless I to thee allow. (I. i)

So indeed should a king speak and act in the following of his vocation; but as the accusations implicitly approach his person, there is an increasing sense that this fracas is touching dangerous ground. Almost imperceptibly, this possibility affects the firmness of the royal stand. As Mowbray persists in answering defiance with defiance, Richard's initial gesture of peacemaking takes on a cynical, almost a bored expression:

> Let's purge this choler without letting blood . . .
> Forget, forgive: conclude and be agreed;
> Our doctors say this is no month to bleed. (I. i)

Is this to be ascribed to intelligence or to indifference, to superior understanding or to a tendency in the speaker to evade the decisions and responsibilities to which his office calls him? Perhaps the answer lies finally in the spirit which seems to prevail throughout these early episodes of feudal rivalry. Perhaps the very elaboration of the conflicting expressions of defiance points to an underlying void which is filled, on the plane of action, by less respectable motives; and perhaps it is significant that Richard's own regality, which he knows so well how to present in impressive gestures and declarations, can easily turn into a kind of bored indifference which reflects his sense of insecurity. Possibly, indeed, neither the honor which these contending lords so glibly affirm that they value above life nor Richard's own poses of royal impartiality are altogether what they seem to be. In the world of lyrical rhetoric which surrounds the initial court action they are no doubt appropriate, but in the sphere of personal and political responsibility the reality is more obscure, less graciously defined. Richard himself seems to recognize this when, at the end of this first scene, he follows his final assertion of authority—"We were not born to sue, but to command"—with a rueful admission of helplessness: "Which since we cannot do," and only partially covers the lapse by the concluding statement of his purposes: "to make you friends" (I. i).

It is not until after this scene, and the following interrupted tournament, that we see Richard in the company of his favorites, and the presentation of the man begins to prevail over that of the feudal monarch. With Bolingbroke banished and out of mind—as Green puts it: "Well, he is gone; and with him go these thoughts" (I. iv)—a new tone of thriftless cynicism makes itself apparent in the royal comments. The most damaging expression of this is the tone in which he greets the news of John of Gaunt's sickness:

> Now put it, God, in the physician's mind
> To help him to his grave immediately. (I. iv)

The wish is particularly meaningful because Gaunt, besides being Richard's uncle, represents on his deathbed the traditional spirit of an England associated, for this play, with Edward III and his blood: when Richard desires his death so as to be able to plunder "the lining of his coffers" to provide him with soldiers for the Irish wars, it is in effect his own vocation that he is setting aside. This becomes clear when Richard and Gaunt are directly confronted. Gaunt's famous speech on England (II. i), so easily reduced to a set piece of poetic virtuosity, has a place of its own in the main development. Stylistically, its heightened lyricism is linked to the early court scenes, belongs—like them—to a past which is already succumbing to the inner hollowness that undermines it:

> The setting sun, and music at the close,
> As the last taste of sweets, is sweetest last; (II. i)

the elegiac note so powerful in Gaunt's words anticipates, beyond his own death, the passing of an order which Richard's authority can no longer effectively maintain.

Gaunt's poignant references to the past indicate, indeed, death and loss in the present. His speech is marked further by a Christian tone which both contrasts with his nephew's present cynicism and anticipates the religious note which Richard's later utterances will associate with the spectacle of royalty overthrown. As Gaunt's words rise to their highest intensity in the contemplation of sacred majesty, England becomes

> this teeming womb of royal kings,
> Fear'd by their breed and famous by their birth,
> Renowned by their deeds as far from home,
> For Christian service and true chivalry,
> As is the sepulchre in stubborn Jewry
> Of the world's ransom, blessed Mary's son. (II. i)

England, in its state of ideal unity, is an anticipation of perfection—"This precious stone set in the silver sea"; "This other Eden, demi-paradise"—and the substance of this blessed state is conveyed through a sublimation of the chivalry which survives, as a shadow blemished with strife and egoism, in Richard's own court. The presence of a Christian aspiration will be balanced, in the king's own later tragic utterances, by a sense of betrayal, the shadow of the gesture of Judas which will accompany him through his decline. Meanwhile, we have "This land of such *dear souls,* this *dear, dear* land" (II. i): beneath this poignant assertion of patriotism there lies the expression of a tragedy, reflected in Gaunt's own death, which seeks in the religious reference a universal expression.

Seen against this background, Gaunt's denunciation of Richard acquires a deeper meaning. The exchange between them is nicely balanced between feeling and artifice:

> – I mock my name, great king, to flatter thee:
> – Should dying men flatter with those that live?
> – No, no, men living flatter those that die.
> – Thou, now a-dying, say'st thou flatterest me.
> – O no! thou diest, though I the sicker be. (II. i)

The ideas of flattery and truth, health and sickness, life and death, are interwoven in a way which has relation to the complete conception. Gaunt is dying indeed, and his world with him: but Richard too is set on the path to decline, and his sickness, moreover, is that of his country. Against these realities, the final denunciation put into Gaunt's mouth—"Landlord of England art thou now, not king" (II. i) —is seen in its full meaning. England is described, by contrast with the preceding lyricism, as in a state of sickness; for it has been Richard's crowning irresponsibility to commit his "anointed body," the health of which so closely figures that of his realm, to "those physicians that first wounded thee." The consequences of this betrayal still lie hidden in the future. Meanwhile, Richard's reaction to his uncle's rebuke confirms the moody, contradictory facets of his nature:

> let them die that age and sullens have;
> For both hast thou, and both become the grave. (II. i)

Immediately afterward, however, this bitterness is seen to imply an awareness of his own state and of the baseless fictions of loyalty which surround him. When York tries to turn his anger by affirming that Gaunt speaks out of love for him, and compares that love, with unconscious irony, to that which Bolingbroke still professes, Richard's reply penetrates for a moment to the reality of events to come:

> Right, you say true: as Hereford's love, so his;
> As theirs, so mine; and all be as it is. (II. i)

This mood of disillusioned fatalism, mingling insight with a touch of self-indulgence, is very close to Richard's nature. To set this incipient tone of tragic bitterness side by side with the childish callousness which prompts him, in the very shadow of his uncle's death, to seize his revenues, is to respond to a character and a situation which are growing in close relationship toward the revelation of their full reality.

These intimations of growing instability in Richard are followed by a notable change in the attitude of those who have so far professed allegiance to him. In York's defense of Bolingbroke's rights, traditional feudal ideas merge into the defense of selfish interests. On the one hand, the claim of lineage, the rights of normal inheritance, are being properly defended by "the last of noble Edward's sons"; on the other, a world of covetousness and mutual distrust is already feeling its way toward the overthrow of legitimate authority. What is in York indecision, a clash of loyalties, is soon seen to involve in others a more direct awareness of threatened interests. After Richard has left, Northumberland adopts a tone which will be associated with his name in the following plays; the king is "not himself," and the envious counsels of his flatterers will translate themselves into acts "'Gainst us, our lives, our children, and our heirs" (II. i). The true implications of the rivalries with which the play opened are now emerging in their double nature. If the disintegration of loyalty proceeds from the unworthiness of its royal fountainhead, it is nonetheless in the form of unwarrantable resentment, the maintenance of selfish positions, that it extends itself.

Disintegration, indeed, is the final impression left by this scene with which the first stage of the play draws to a close. In the mounting indignation of the nobility, balanced between patriotic concern and self-interest, we see reflected the breaking unity of the English state. The episode ends, significantly, after Northumberland's remarkable phrase,

> even through the hollow eyes of death
> I spy life peering, (II. i)

with the announcement of Bolingbroke's return. The action is now embarked upon the course which it will follow to the end of the play. The return of Lancaster, as he will from now on call himself, is simultaneously a necessity, if the foundations of order are to be restored upon the firm, conscious exercise of authority, and an expression of rebellious selfishness, defeating its own purposes by the perverse nature of its claim. The contradiction thus indicated between means and ends, between Lancaster's desires and the manner in which he usurps the crown, will dominate the following history.

From this moment up to the encounter between Richard and his rival the scope of the action narrows to present a clash of personalities. The tragic impotence of the king is balanced by his rival's purposeful advance toward the ends he has proposed to himself. From the moment of his setting foot again in England, Bolingbroke's advance is as cautious as it is sure. Potentially useful allies, like the young Harry Percy, he greets with effusive thanks and a tactful indication of recompense to come:

> And as my fortune ripens with thy love,
> It shall be still thy true love's recompense; (II. iii)

but to those of his enemies who, like the royal favorites Bushy and Green, fall into his hands, justice is inflexibly administered. In his separation, at such moments, of spiritual and political responsibilities—

> Bushy and Green, I will not vex your souls,
> Since presently your souls must part your bodies— (III. i)

Bolingbroke shows himself already the father of the future Henry V;[21] solicitude in the spiritual order can exist side by side with the firm execution of justice, but the one must not interfere with the practical necessities of the other. It is always expedient, moreover, that the sentence should be publicly justified before it is carried out, and so—

> to wash your blood
> From off my hands, here *in the view of men*
> I will unfold some causes of your deaths. (III. i)

That in this particular case Henry is an instrument of justice is not to be doubted; but the anxiety to seek public justification for his necessary ruthlessness will be passed on by him to his son and may, on future occasions, find less impeccable causes on which to exercise itself. For the moment, the firm command—"My lord Northumberland, see them dispatch'd"—is significantly followed by an expedient gesture of courtesy to Richard's queen ("Take special care my greetings be deliver'd") and by the practical aphorism which brings this episode to a close: "Awhile to work, and after holiday" (III. i).

It is no accident that the presentation of this firm dedication to the job in hand should be followed by Richard's return to the scene. He too has been away, spending in Ireland the resources plundered from Gaunt, and his return is the occasion for a typical display of sentiment, marks the reunion of "a long-parted mother" with the child who "plays fondly with her tears and smiles in meeting." Richard as he returns to face his formidable rival at once expresses tragic sentiments and plays with his emotions, "weeping, smiling," as he greets the earth which both inspires him to genuine love and is used by him as the occasion for a self-conscious display of emotion. As he goes on, in the course of the same speech, to compare his enemies to "spiders" and "heavy-gaited toads," to "stinging nettles" and "lurking adders," Richard in effect reduces tragedy to melodrama. Beneath the artifice and the pathos which are so closely interwoven in what he says, we may feel the presence of that distraught and essentially morbid, febrile imagination which is as much part of his nature as the capacity to respond with an impressive show of tragic dignity to his situation as a king betrayed. His emotions, indeed, have throughout an unconscious as well as a conscious content; and this gives the character, beyond its conventionality and its public significance, a depth and complexity possibly greater than any so far attained by Shakespeare in his dramatic development.

These qualities soon reveal themselves in terms of his incapacity to face practical necessity. Confronted by immediate danger, Richard is ready enough to take up the conception of the divine vocation which justifies his kingship, to assert that

> Not all the water in the rough rude sea
> Can wash the balm from an anointed king; (III. ii)

but it is not long before we are brought to see that this rhetorical confidence is balanced in him only by personal weakness and an intimate disposition to give way to despair. Within five minutes of having thus placed his confidence in God, he is considering, not without a kind of complacency, a certain self-regarding pleasure in the contemplation of disaster, the possible loss of his realm:

> Say, is my kingdom lost? why, 'twas my care;
> And what loss is it to be rid of care? . . .
> Cry woe, destruction, ruin and decay;
> The worst is death, and death will have his day. (III. ii)

The fact is that, personally and politically, Richard is not equipped to cope with his enemies. His best, his most nearly profound utterances, reveal incapacity to act consistently, even a marked tendency to hysterical evasion of the truth. A tragic sentimentalist by nature, though one capable from time to time of rousing himself moodily and dangerously to resentful action, he uses his moments of misfortune to elaborate his woes poetically, even to take a kind of perverse pleasure—actor-like—in expressing his unhappy state.

These outbursts lead finally, in the culminating speech of the scene, to a full expression of despair. As always, a certain conventionality persists in the tone of Richard's lament, but can be felt in the process of giving way to a stronger current of emotion:

> For God's sake, let us sit upon the ground
> And tell sad stories of the death of kings—
> How some have been deposed, some slain in war,
> Some haunted by the ghosts they have deposed,
> Some murder'd by their wives; some sleeping kill'd,
> All murder'd. (III. ii)

Basically, of course, this famous speech rests on a series of medieval commonplaces, presents a traditional catalogue of the misfortunes that, by the compensating action of Fortune's wheel, accompany the dangerous exaltation of the king. The examples are familiar; but in the flow of the expression, the rise of the voice to the longer period in "Some haunted by the ghosts they have deposed," and the fall to

"All murder'd," we find conveyed, side by side with a true tragic sense, a notion of the insignificance which haunts the pomp of royalty, this particular speaker's capacity for dwelling on his own tragedy, exacting from his plight a sad refinement of sensation. Richard, true to character, at once expresses his tragedy in terms which genuinely move us—for it is a true tragedy, and it is an anointed king whom his subjects, sworn to loyalty, are about to betray—and finds a certain self-regarding pleasure in the consideration of his unhappy condition; so that it is not surprising that the speech, after the grave beauty to which it has risen in the contemplation of the vicissitudes of royalty, falls away into hysteria and self-pity:

> Cover your heads and mock not flesh and blood
> With solemn reverence. Throw away respect,
> Tradition, form, and ceremonious duty,
> For you have but mistook me all this while.
> I live with bread like you, feel want,
> Taste grief, need friends. Subjected thus,
> How can you say to me I am a king? (III. ii)

There is still an appeal here to the traditional sanctions that accompany the royal office, to the "reverence," "form," and "ceremony" that surround a legitimate king; but it is at the same time an appeal theatrically conceived, a turning of tragedy to self-exhibition which at once attains, in the broken rhythm of the final lines, a real pathos and covers a weak man's resentment against what he prefers to regard as the incomprehensible turns of fate.

Such a man can be no rival for the clear-sighted and ruthless politician who is determined to replace him on the throne. The "brazen trumpet" of Bolingbroke's messenger conveys "the breath of parley" into the "ruined ears" of Richard, pitifully sheltered behind the "rude ribs" of his ancient castle. The forms of loyal service, which the newcomer is at first careful to maintain, conceal the realities of domination, the "tender show" of "stooping duty" is stressed almost subserviently to cover the bare grasping of power that underlies it. Northumberland, bringing what is in effect his new master's ultimatum, and disposed to respond to the new situation with a courtier's eye firmly fixed upon the main chance, covers it with a wealth of stylistic affectation. Richard, on his side, is perfectly aware of his situation. It has never been intelligence he has lacked, but something else, less easily definable but not, for a man placed as he is, less important. We may, if we will, call this something consistency of character; and its lack expresses itself, even as he replies with an assumption of weakness, in the awareness that a stern reality is undermining the content of his words:

> We do debase ourselves, cousin, do we not,
> To look so poorly, and to speak so fair. (III. iii)

Already, indeed, Richard looks forward to the march of events which, derived in great part from his own weakness, is leading inexorably to a tragic conclusion:

> Oh God, oh God, that e'er this tongue of mine,
> That laid the sentence of dread banishment
> On yon proud man, should take it off again
> With words of sooth! O, that I were as great
> As is my grief, or lesser than my name!
> Or that I could forget what I have been,
> Or not remember what I must be now! (III. iii)

Here, at least, the utterance is simple, direct enough to pass beyond artifice and pretense to penetrate to the true extent of a royal tragedy.

More often, however, Richard's sense that the reversal of his original judgment will undo him expresses itself in what he knows to be, even as he speaks, "idle talk." This is apparent in the elaborate self-exhibition of "What must the King do now? must he submit?" and the lines which follow:

> I'll give my jewels for a set of beads,
> My gorgeous palace for a hermitage,
> My gay apparel for an almsman's gown,
> My figured goblets for a dish of wood,
> My sceptre for a palmer's walking staff,
> My subjects for a pair of carved saints,
> And my large kingdom for a little grave,
> A little, little grave, an obscure grave;
> Or I'll be buried in the king's highway,
> Some way of common trade, where subject's feet
> May hourly trample on their sovereign's head;
> For on my heart they tread now whilst I live;
> And buried once, why not upon my head? (III. iii)

In these words, and in the rest of the speech, artifice, weakness, and pathos are variously interwoven. It is interesting to compare this utterance to that, partially similar, which expressed Henry VI's nostalgia for the simple life when faced with the horrors of civil war.[22] The artificial construction is parallel, but is put to ends substantially different; for in Richard, far more than in Henry, it is a kind of pathetic self-pity, as much the exhibition of sorrow as grief itself, that prevails. Sensing that he is doomed, Richard exploits his condition self-consciously; but his artifice, besides being moving as related to a royal tragedy, is sufficiently realized in terms of character to evoke that compassion which only the emotions of a person can give. For Richard, even as he "plays the wanton" with his woes, is aware that just this is what he is doing:

> Would not this ill do well? Well, well, I see
> I talk but idly, and you laugh at me. (III. iii)

The speaker's feeling, precisely by being aware of its artificial expression, becomes more real than that of Henry VI, less confined to the literary order and more capable of arousing pity.

The end of this confrontation confirms the situation of its central figures by giving them external projection. Brought back to reality by Northumberland's blunt request, "may it please you to come down," Richard takes up once more the image of the sun of royalty which his rival has applied to him: "Down, down I come, like glistering Phaeton." The image, besides answering to the speaker's characteristically aesthetic self-awareness, leads directly to the meeting with Bolingbroke, in which power, still cloaked in the forms of loyalty, is brought face to face with helplessness, with what Northumberland, typically cruel to the fallen, brushes aside as "the fondness of a frantic man." Henry, kneeling in the external show of deference, calls upon his followers to "show fair duty to his majesty"; but Richard, not content to respond to these empty shows, penetrates more directly to the bare facts of his situation when he says, calling upon his rival to rise:

> Up, cousin, up; your heart is up, I know,
> Thus high at least, although your knee be low. (III. iii)

To the newcomer's sober statement, "I come but for mine own," he replies, with a still more penetrating realism, "Your own is yours, and I am yours, and all," and follows this, most realistically of all, with his rejoinder to Bolingbroke's empty offer of service:

Well you deserve; they well deserve to have,
That know the strong'st and surest way to get. (III. iii)

The distance traveled by Richard since the early scenes of courtly pageantry is never more apparent than at this moment, in which his personal tragedy is seen as the foundation for a long political development to follow after his death.

From the moment of his spectacular descent "into the base court," Richard's fate is to all intents and purposes sealed. The latter part of the play confirms his fall and consummates the process of his rival's rise to power. The proclamation of Bolingbroke as king is followed by the demand, pitilessly pressed, that his predecessor should publicly renounce his office: "Are you contented to resign the crown?" (IV. i). In Richard's reply, complex and contradictory by comparison with this ruthless challenge, the germ of many later Shakespearean developments can be discerned. His thoughts turn, not merely on natural grief, but on a sense of vanity—*nothingness*—which the very artificiality of the expression paradoxically deepens:

Ay, no; no, ay; for I must nothing be; . . .
Make me, that *nothing* have, with *nothing* grieved,
And thou with all pleased, that hast all achieved!
Long mayst thou live in Richard's seat to sit,
And soon lie Richard in an earthy pit! (IV. i)

We must feel at this moment that the word nearest to the speaker's heart is, after all his elaborations, *nothing,* and that his mood issues in an intense craving for the release from effort and choice which only death can bring. But the *nothingness,* it must be added, is also reflected in Bolingbroke's absorbing pursuit of power. Richard's attitude to his political responsibilities is of course extreme, one more example of his essential self-indulgence; but his comment at this decisive moment in his fortunes is also relevant for the usurper who is now, with little but devices of policy in his mind, preparing to replace him on the throne. *Nothing, nothing:* in the long run any relevant conception of political power will have to come to terms with the challenge which that word implies and which so much of the public behavior shown in this play amply confirms.

Meanwhile, however, the case against Richard is bitterly pressed home. To his final, exhausted question, "What more remains?" there corresponds, not any expression of human compassion on the part of his enemies, but the prosecution of the accusations prepared against him:

> No more, but that you read
> These accusations and these grievous crimes, (IV. i)

followed by an admission that the real purpose of this proceeding is to justify the usurper in the eyes of the world. Surrounded by so much ruthless calculation, Richard's very real weaknesses become increasingly subsidiary to the pathos of his tragedy as king deposed. His reply to Northumberland raises to a fresh level of poignancy the Christian parallel which runs as a principal thread of feeling through the tragedy:

> Nay, all of you that stand and look upon,
> Whilst that my wretchedness doth bait myself,
> Though some of you with Pilate wash your hands
> Showing an outward pity; yet you Pilates
> Have here deliver'd me to my sour cross,
> And water cannot wash away your sin. (IV. i)

Our reaction to this is necessarily double. Richard is engaged to the last in exhibiting his emotions, playing with feelings the seriousness of which we cannot, in the light of his known failings and consequent responsibility for his state, fully accept; and yet the betrayal, based on the calculation that everywhere surrounds him, implies a setting aside of every normal human obligation, and its effect is deepened by the fact that it is a king whom his subjects, sworn to loyalty, are engaged in deserting. It is the tragedy of betrayal, as well as that of fallen royalty, that is being enacted round Richard's isolated and unhappy person; and the treachery, moreover, is doubly personal, insomuch as Richard has, by his own past behavior and dubious choices, betrayed himself before he was in turn betrayed:

> Nay, if I turn mine eyes upon myself,
> I find myself a traitor with the rest. (IV. i)

Richard has betrayed the office which he has held unworthily, and the betrayal has bred a corresponding treachery which leads to his destruction. Bolingbroke, in a way not finally dissimilar, will prove in due course to be divided between the political virtues that are undoubtedly his and a desire for power which is ominously reflected in the court of timeserving and ambitious lords who seek their own convenience by accompanying his rise to authority.

Beneath the conventionality of Richard's expression lies, indeed, an effort to define his relation to the tragic course of events. This culminates in his request for a mirror, in which once more artificiality, conscious self-exhibition, and a measure of true self-exploration are variously blended. Henry, now secure master of the situation, contemptuously accedes to the latest emotional trick of his victim, whilst Northumberland, ruthless as ever, presses the charges against him—

> Read o'er this paper while the glass doth come—

and stresses yet again the political motive beneath his disapproval of his master's careless concession:

> The commons will not then be satisfied. (IV. i)

When the mirror is at last brought, Richard contemplates his features in it with a kind of tragic self-analysis. This opens, as he breaks the glass, with a typically artificial statement: "How soon my sorrow hath destroy'd my face"; but the comment offered by Bolingbroke points to a deeper contrast between shadow and reality, which is not without tragic content:

> The shadow of your sorrow hath destroy'd
> The shadow of your face.

Bolingbroke perhaps speaks here more deeply than he knows; but the observation produces from Richard, as he takes up the related concepts of "shadow," "sun," and "substance," an indication of the deeper roots of his tragedy:

> Say that again.
> The shadow of my sorrow! ha! let's see!
> 'Tis very true, my grief lies all within;
> And these external manners of laments
> Are merely shadows to the unseen grief
> That swells with silence in the tortured soul;
> There lies the substance. (IV. i)

One can trace in Shakespeare's work the various stages of a process by which literary artifice, expanding in complexity and psychological correspondence, becomes an instrument of self-analysis. We have already found ample traces of this development in *Romeo and*

Juliet;[23] and now the person of Richard, as revealed here, represents a further important stage in the same process. For Richard, as will later be the case for Hamlet, the outer forms of grief are mere "shadows" of the "substance" within;[24] between the tragic content of the two characters there is, of course, no comparison, but a process could be traced by which the artifice of the one is transformed into the greater complexity of the other. Once more, the later plays in the series will throw light on the nature of this transformation.[25] For the moment, Richard's sense of his tragedy leads to the final breakdown, which accompanies his request for "leave to go"

> Whither you will, so I were from your sights,

in which the measureless bitterness of his situation is amply expressed.

By the last scenes of the play, Richard has been awakened in no uncertain terms from his former "dream" of worldly felicity to "the truth of what we are":

> A king of beasts indeed; if aught but beasts,
> I had been still a happy king of men; (V. i)

though we may doubt even now whether, beneath the pathos and the horror, the speaker has understood how far he is himself connected with the world which he has found such good reason to despise. Everything in the action at this stage—Richard's increasingly severe imprisonment, the fear which prompts York servilely to accuse his own son of treason to his new master (V. ii, iii)—confirms this bitter estimate. Richard's last speech, the immediate prelude to his murder, opens against this somber background of fear and treachery, with what seems at first sight an academic exercise in poetic pessimism:

> I have been studying how I may compare
> This prison where I live unto the world. (V. v)

An oddly remote occupation, we may be tempted to conclude, for a king plunged into darkness and solitude, and moreover about to die; but, apart from the fact that a certain measure of artifice is in character, still answers to this particular king's nature as revealed throughout, the development of his thoughts moves beyond mere artifice to achieve a more valid tragic effect. As his meditations move to their climax a deeper effect is attained, a more felt reference to the human situation touched upon, when Richard returns to the idea of *nothing* which has been so persistently present as a background, expressed and implied, to his thoughts:

> whate'er I be,
> Nor I nor any man that but man is
> With *nothing* shall be pleased, till he be eased
> With being *nothing*. (V. v)

Here, at least, beneath the carefully balanced expression, is a serious attempt to make words respond to feeling, in something like a tragic statement about life. Richard feels that what he is about to say is valid not only for himself, but "for any man that but man is," who shares the essential limitations of the human state. It is worth noting, moreover, that this increase in depth is at once followed, most improbably in terms of realism, by the playing of "music," in what we may consider a first dim foreshadowing of one of the mature Shakespearean symbols. The harmony, suitably contradictory in its effects to match the speaker's thoughts—

> how sour sweet music is,
> When time is broke and no proportion kept!—

resolves itself into an attempt at more subtle analysis:

> here have I the daintiness of ear
> To check time broke in a disorder'd string;
> But for the concord of my state and time
> Had not an ear to hear my true time broke. (V. v)

Beneath the artificial balance of the phrasing, the speaker is attempting a valid statement on his condition and the errors which have brought him to it, and in the observation which follows—"I wasted time, and now doth time waste me"—he almost succeeds. Even the elaborate expression has a certain justification in terms of character, as the utterance of one who has habitually *acted* on his royal stage, observed, as it were, his attitudes with an eye to public effect and personal gratification:

> Thus play I in one person many people,
> And none contented. (V. v)

The devices of this speech, to convince fully, would need to be filled out with a sense of personal commitment to a degree here never quite attained: but, imperfect though it may be, the meditation does foreshadow later developments in the presentation of the tragic hero. Certainly the murder which follows is, by comparison, a pedestrian piece of melodrama. Perhaps Richard's last individual word is spoken in his bitter comment to the Groom on the value of human titles and honors: "The cheapest of us is ten groats too dear" (V. v). This is at once legitimate comment and the confirmation of a character, the evaluation of an inhuman situation and the expression of a king who has always tended to find in an effective show of cynicism a refuge from the collapse of his self-indulgent sentiments.

After the murder, the play ends with a brief and sinister indication of the triumph of the new order. Already, it is becoming clear that Bolingbroke's crime, tacitly admitted as such, will bring neither personal nor political peace. The "latest news" is that the "rebels"—not now his own supporters, but those who have in turn risen against his usurped power—have "consumed with fire" the town of Cicester. On all sides, executions respond to a renewal of civil strife; the heads of numerous "traitors"—so called by he who has just ceased to be such—are on their way to London, and the spiritual power, henceforth to be increasingly involved in political intrigues, is curtailed by the death of the Abbot of Westminster and the banishment of the loyal and plain-spoken Carlisle. Upon this catalogue of mischance and cross-purposes, the murderers of Richard enter with his body, not to be commended for their "deed of slander," but yet to pin firmly on the real assassin the guilt to which he himself admits. To Exton's unanswerable "From your own mouth, my lord, did I this deed," Henry can only correspond with a statement of moral contradiction, the first of those that will be almost habitual in his mouth:

> They love not poison that do poison need,
> Nor do I thee: though I did wish him dead,
> I hate the murderer, love him murdered. (V. vi)

Here is the politician, typically engaged in shuffling off the responsibility for his decisions upon others; but beneath the careful balance of the phrasing, the "guilt of conscience" is firmly placed where it belongs, and the new king's last words announce the intention, which will accompany him to his death as an unfulfilled aspiration, to redeem his "guilt" by a spiritual enterprise in the Holy Land. This aspiration, the failure to fulfill it, and its transformation into a more limited national purpose under his son are the themes of the later, greater plays to follow.[20]

VI

King John and *The Merchant of Venice*

KING JOHN

After the achievement represented by the three great plays considered in the last chapter, Shakespeare seems to have produced two pieces comparatively tentative, even in some respects unsatisfactory in quality. The first of these, *King John,* must have been written between his two series of plays on English history and occupies something like an intermediate position between them. It is, indeed, one of his most curious and uneven efforts. Much of the writing is strikingly disjointed, either over-rhetorical or simply excessively contrived in relation to the meanings conveyed; but these factors, which go together with a dramatic structure that seems in some ways oddly primitive, a survival from cruder conceptions of what constitutes a chronicle play, now and then give way to a more profound effect, answer to an unmistakably personal reading of history. These more successful moments are almost invariably associated with the figure of Philip Faulconbridge, the Bastard.

The play opens with a set-piece disputation over rival claims to the English throne between King John and an ambassador from France. John is clearly the subject of approval in so far as he affirms his rights against the foreign claimant; but the justice of his position in relation to his nephew Prince Arthur soon becomes the subject of doubt in the comment made, for his ears alone, by Elinor, the queen mother; strength rather than right—"Your strong possession much more than your right" (I. i)—must be, she says, the foundation of her son's confidence in his cause. No sooner has this been said, and after John has announced his intention of pursuing the war with funds to be derived from the properties of the Church, than a "strange controversy" between Robert Faulconbridge and his bastard brother, Philip, comes before him for judgment. In a world where the principles of legitimacy and order are evidently in peril, the Bastard, as the illegitimate son of Richard Coeur de Lion, is ready to rely upon his own wits and strength and to give up whatever claim he may have to the Faulconbridge inheritance to pursue an adventure which, though less certain in its results, may bring him far greater rewards:

> Brother, take you my land, I'll take my chance.
> Your face hath got five hundred pound a year,
> Yet sell your face for fivepence and 'tis dear. (I. i)

The expression of his decision, made before his royal origins are finally confirmed, is typical in its easy confidence and contemptuous dismissal of safe, respectable motives as a guide in life. When Queen Elinor finally discloses that he is indeed her grandson, his reception of this support is as characteristic in its easy aphoristic style as it is frankly amoral in essential content:

> Madam, by chance but not by truth? what though?
> Something about, a little from the right,
>   In at the window, or else o'er the hatch;
> Who dares not stir by day must walk by night,
>   And have is have, however men do catch:
> Near or far off, well won is still well shot,
>   And *I am I*, howe'er I was begot. (I. i)

The phrase "I am I" is, of course, an echo from Richard Crookback,[1] and much in the Bastard's attitude to life at once reminds us of that previous incarnation of political energy and carries us, in certain respects, as far forward as the Edmund of *King Lear*, whose attitude toward "legitimacy"[2] Faulconbridge would certainly have understood. For the moment, perhaps, it is enough to say that when the Bastard thus defines himself in his relation to the world, he is at once pointing to the virtues that will distinguish him, always *within this world*, from the alternately corrupt and pusillanimous dignitaries who surround him, and suggesting what will prove to be on a longer view, his essential limitations as a human being.

For the moment, it is the virtues that most clearly stand out. The Bastard goes on to declare himself careless of hereditary distinctions, which he is inclined to think of as having little or no substance —"For new-made honour doth forget men's names"—and to parody the artifices of court life to considerable effect:

> And when my knightly stomach is sufficed,
> Why then I suck my teeth and catechize
> My picked man of countries: "My dear sir,"
> Thus, leaning on my elbow, I begin,
> "I shall beseech you"—that is question now;
> And then comes answer like an Absey book:
> "O sir," says answer, "at your best command;
> At your employment: at your service, sir":
> "No sir," says question, "I, sweet sir, at yours," (I. i)

until at the last he is able to gratify himself with the detached irony of his conclusion:

> this is worshipful society,
> And fits the mounting spirit like myself;
> For he is but a bastard to the time
> That doth not smack of observation. (I. i)

"Observation," indeed, the dispassionate weighing of men and situations as they are in a world in which neither hereditary pretensions nor excess of moral scruples appear conducive to advancement, or indeed, even to survival, is the peculiar and appropriate gift of the "mounting spirit." It is a gift which this particular student of life exercises with a frankly confessed eye to his own advantage: an eye which falls short of deliberate dishonesty—for, as he himself goes on to say, "I will not practise to deceive"—but which remains confident of its owner's ability to outdo the deceiver, if need be, at his own game: "Yet, to avoid deceit, I mean to learn."[3] This, indeed, is very much the spirit in which Faulconbridge considers his own origins. When his mother confesses, at the end of this first scene, that he was born in sin, his reply is a notably cheerful, "Madam, I would not wish a better father," which he follows up with a still more cheerful defiance:

> Who lives and dares but say thou didst not well
> When I was got, I'll send his soul to hell. (I. i)

The combination of easy confidence and rhetorical bravado, firm self-reliance and a careless attitude toward most merely external forms and prejudices, answers very exactly to the tone of many of the most interesting parts of the play.

It is not long before Faulconbridge is able to apply this outlook to the necessities of foreign war. The episode which presents the rival armies of England and France before the uncommitted walls of Angiers (II. i) is no doubt long and clumsily developed; but it serves to show the prevailing political attitudes and to present the Bastard in action against a typically "politic" background. Lewis the Dauphin declares himself for Arthur, whilst his follower Austria adds a typically sanctimonious comment, upon which the action to follow will cast an odd light:

> The peace of heaven is theirs that lift their swords
> In such a just and charitable war:

to all of which the French king at once adds his more realistic observation for the benefit of all concerned:

> We'll lay before this town our royal bones,
> Wade to the market-place in Frenchmen's blood. (II. i)

He goes on to accuse John of being a usurper, after which, to the accompaniment of mutual scolding from the womenfolk, the two kings compete ruthlessly for the support of Arthur, who is in the unhappy position of wishing to choose neither: "I am not worth this coil that's made for me."[4]

After these preliminaries have been disposed of, both monarchs in turn state their claims formally to the beleaguered citizens, who cautiously prefer to await the issue of battle before giving access to either. Faulconbridge, assuming the typical role of an impartial bystander, belittles both claimants by referring caustically to the presence of "bastards" on either side; though he is himself dedicated to the English cause, and will in due course show himself capable of patriotism, his service is offered in a spirit of detachment from rhetorical excess and pretension of all kinds. When the battle is finally joined, he rejoices, but still after his own fashion, without illusion or excessive commitment, at the prospect of action:

> Ha, majesty! how high thy glory towers,
> When the rich blood of kings is set on fire!
> O, now doth Death line his dead chaps with steel;
> The swords of soldiers are his teeth, his fangs;

And now he feasts, mousing the flesh of men,
In undetermined differences of kings.
Why stand these royal fronts amazed thus?
Cry "havoc!" kings; back to the stained field,
You equal potents, fiery kindled spirits!
Then let confusion of one part confirm
The other's peace: till then, blows, blood, and death! (II. i)

This is rhetoric of a peculiar kind, drawn to the prospect of chaos and death even whilst it reacts against both by asserting the attraction of action as an end in itself: rhetoric ultimately poised, like so many of Faulconbridge's utterances beneath their patriotic surface, on the border line of satire. In a logical extension of his essential common sense, and in a situation which offers little incitement to look beyond it, he goes on to propose that John and Philip should sink their differences in common action against the defiant citizens, taking up their quarrel again only after this obstacle has been overcome. The terms of his advice amount to a mockery of both parties for their common inadequacy:

these scroyles of Angiers flout you, kings,
And stand securely on their battlements,
As in a theatre, whence they gape and point
At your industrious scenes and acts of death. (II. i)[5]

After they have got themselves by concerted action out of this ridiculous position, in which their self-esteem inevitably suffers, he suggests that they leave the arbitration of their quarrel to the fickle resolution of Fortune. This is "counsel," "policy," of a finally disillusioned kind in which the Bastard delights, seeing in it the only acceptable proof of man's capacity to dominate the course of events in what is, he suspects, in the last resort a meaningless world; though it should be noted that, for all his talk of "Fortune" as the ultimate arbiter, he is careful to weight his advice cannily in favor of his own side by ensuring that, in the battle to come,

From north to south,
Austria and France shoot in each other's mouth, (II. i)

thus advancing their mutual destruction.

The consequences of this strange argument are not far removed from the farcical. Seeing the danger which threatens from the acceptance by the rival monarchs of Faulconbridge's proposal, the citizens hastily seek safety in proposing a political marriage, of the kind which Shakespeare uses more than once in his historical plays.[6] Let Lewis the Dauphin, they suggest, seek the hand of John's niece, Blanch of Spain. The politicians take up this idea with alacrity, and though Blanch is something less than enthusiastic about her future husband—

> Further I will not flatter you, my lord,
> That all I see in you is worthy love— (II. i)

Lewis' interested acceptance carries the day. Once again the Bastard is left to make his sardonic comment, this time in the sonnet form appropriate to a parody of love. "This is pity now," he says of the prospective bridegroom,

> That, hang'd and drawn and quarter'd, there should be
> In such a love so vile a lout as he. (II. i)

We are not to forget, of course, as we follow these proceedings, that agreement between these recently embattled rivals is being reached at the expense of Constance and Arthur, whom the French have pledged themselves, with repeated invocations of morality, both religious and political, to support in a just cause. The last word remains yet again with Faulconbridge as he utters, in words marked by even more than usual of his typical linguistic vigor and by the comparative complexity of life which distinguishes it from most of the play, his disenchanted comment upon the operations of "commodity" as the ultimate, if unconfessed arbiter of public conduct:

> John, to stop Arthur's title in the whole,
> Hath willingly departed with a part:
> And France, whose armour conscience buckled on,
> Whom zeal and charity brought to the field
> As God's own soldier, rounded in the ear
> With that same purpose-changer, that sly devil,
> That broker, that still breaks the pate of faith,
> That daily break-vow, he that wins of all,
> Of kings, of beggars, old men, young men, maids,
> Who, having no external thing to lose
> But the word "maid," cheats the poor maid of that,
> That smooth-faced gentleman, tickling Commodity. (II. i)

In a speech of this kind we can sense something of the process by which the natural exuberance of Elizabethan speech was molded into Shakespeare's own charged and sensitive expression. The hurried, almost chaotic unfolding of the Bastard's thought is typical of much contemporary writing, but more personal to Shakespeare is the vivacity of illustration and the ready recourse to familiar, even popular personifications. The speed with which the abstraction "Commodity" is visualized as a plausible, "smooth-faced gentleman" by a series of graphic illustrations—"purpose-changer," "sly devil," "broker" that "breaks the pate of faith"—the very confusion which causes us to hesitate between ascribing the relative in the last lines to the "maids" or to "Commodity" itself: all these show, if we will, a certain incoherence, but are redeemed by the powerful vigor which indicates the impact of a personal utterance.

This impact is, of course, a reflection of the Bastard's own personality, of the extent to which he is not subdued, like those around him, to the quality of the action in which he moves. He stands out in a world in which the rival factions, though always ready to ascribe to "conscience," to the highest motives, the buckling on of their armor, are moved in fact by self-interest and political design. His attitude toward surrounding events is one which we are invited at once to share and to feel as a problem. He appears, on the one hand, to stand out as honest judge and bluff commentator in a play which he dominates by his levelheaded impartiality; on the other, although this is not entirely clear in *King John,* the very amorality which his attitudes imply will turn, in the long run, into the problem of the man of drive and intelligence whose motives are entirely limited to immediate political ends.[7] Although Faulconbridge succeeds in imposing his dispassionate and detached view of the world around him, we should note that at the last he recognizes that he too belongs to the world of "commodity," even though—unlike the rest—he makes no attempt to disguise its true nature either from himself or from those who associate with him. As he asks himself, assessing his motives with his usual honesty:

> why rail I on this Commodity?
> But for because he hath not woo'd me yet:
> Not that I have the power to clutch my hand,
> When his fair angels would salute my palm;
> But for my hand, as unattempted yet,
> Like a poor beggar, raileth on the rich.

Well, whiles I am a beggar I will rail
And say there is no sin but to be rich;
And being rich, my virtue then shall be,
To say there is no vice but beggary. (II. i)

The Bastard justifies himself finally in relation to the standards upheld by those around him. Not a few of his attitudes will be found again, considerably developed and transformed, in later plays, notably in some parts of *Henry IV* and, as we have already suggested, in certain aspects of the character of Edmund in *King Lear*. It is only in these later works that the virtues which he represents are seen to be founded, paradoxically, upon his limitations, and so to raise the problem of the relation of what we may call, in the widest sense, "politic" behavior to a moral conception of life.

In the scene (III. i) which follows this central speech, the unhappy Constance is left to rail against Fortune, whilst the politicians on either side, having completed their betrayal of her cause by mutual consent, go through the motions of comforting her. Once again, as she turns indignantly on Austria, the last word is left with the Bastard in exposure of his enemy's mixture of sanctimonious "virtue" and cunning; and, as the victim of these taunts utters his braggart assertions of outraged vanity—"O, that a man should speak these words to me!"—and calls upon his rival to make his mockery good, the latter echoes Constance's denunciation in his own ironic refrain: "And hang a calf-skin on those recreant limbs." At this point the scope of the action is further extended by the intervention of Pandulph, "of fair Milan cardinal," a typical political cleric who denounces John in the interest of Holy Church and is denounced by him in terms which seem to echo the original Protestant "morality" which preceded Shakespeare's play.[8] Philip, also challenged by the churchman for deserting the cause he has sworn to uphold, utters his plea for peace and honest dealing with a certain eloquence. "Shall these hands," he asks,

so lately purg'd of blood,
So newly join'd in love, so strong in both,
Unyoke this seizure and this kind regreet?
Play fast and loose with faith? so jest with heaven,
Make such unconstant children of ourselves,
As now again to snatch our palm from palm,
Unswear faith sworn, and on the marriage-bed

Of smiling peace to march a bloody host,
And make a riot on the gentle brow
Of true sincerity? (III. i)

The question falls on deaf ears. For the Cardinal only hatred of England, which has threatened the material interests of the Church, counts, and, instigated by him, both sides return to arms. In the battle which follows the Bastard soon has the satisfaction of killing Austria (III. ii), whilst John, with typical duplicity, urges Hubert to dispose in secret of the life of Arthur. In much of this part of the play, as in Constance's melodramatic speech craving death—

O amiable lovely death!
Thou odoriferous stench! sound rottenness!— (III. iv)

we may feel the expression balanced between irony and horror, realism and rhetoric, and moving toward new complexities of feeling. Philip comments significantly on these excesses when he tells Constance that she is "as fond of grief as of your child" (III. iv), and Pandulph insinuates that, with the murder of Arthur, which he foresees and approves, Lewis' chance to seize the English crown will come, and with it the opportunity to advance the interests of the Church:

How green you are and fresh in this old world!
John lays you plots; the times conspire with you! (III. iv)

This is the voice of the ecclesiastical politician, secure—or so he believes—in his understanding of an aging world and of public motives for what they are.

In contrast with so much ruthless calculation Hubert refrains, in a scene which plays deliberately and with some elaboration upon sentiment (IV. i), from carrying out John's command to blind the helpless Arthur. The assembled English lords have by now reason to suspect their king's intentions and, when Hubert falsely announces the Prince's death, accuse him bitterly of foul play. From now to the play's desolate conclusion they are left torn between treason and righteous indignation, whilst retribution is announced in the extreme form of a foreign invasion of England and the ear of the unhappy queen mother is reported to be "stopp'd with dust" (IV. ii). Finally, after Peter of Pomfret has uttered his prophecies of foreboding against the king, Hubert announces that "Young Arthur is alive," thus making unnecessary John's hysterical efforts, which later Shakespearean murderers will echo, to shift the blame for his intended crime from his own shoulders.

Here, however, the tragic irony which is so heavily labored throughout assumes control of the course of events. Arthur kills himself in despair (IV. iii), thereby carrying out his uncle's unnatural purpose, but at a time when John for reasons of cowardice and policy has decided to desist from it. The king fails, accordingly, to get any undeserved credit for his change of plan, and the incensed nobles press for revenge. They turn first upon Hubert, but are put off in characteristic terms by Faulconbridge, who treats Salisbury with a display of his usual aplomb:

> Put up thy sword betime;
> Or I'll so mark you and your toasting-iron,
> That you shall think the devil is come from hell; (IV. iii)

he fails, however, to prevent the English nobility from seeking help traitorously in the French camp. As a result of this failure the Bastard is left, in a typically sudden shift of mood, to utter what are possibly the most profound words of the whole play. He, who has always presented himself to the world with a show of self-confidence, now declares himself, in this moment of abandoned loyalties, as a man lost, bewildered by the situation in which he finds himself:

> I am amazed, methinks, and lose my way
> Among the thorns and dangers of this world. (IV. iii)

The confession strikes a fresh note in the strange compound of incongruities that makes up his character; and, basing himself upon it, he goes on, in the mood which the contemplation of so much cowardice and unworthy motivation imposes, to utter more clearly than elsewhere his personal vision, disillusioned and somber in its clear-sightedness, of the state of the nation which he has sincerely, on his own terms, desired to serve:

> From forth this morsel of dead royalty,
> The life, the right and truth of all this realm
> Is fled to heaven; and England now is left
> To tug and scramble and to part by the teeth
> The unowed interests of proud-swelling state.

All that remains, according to this same vision, is a bare prospect of anarchy and civil ruin:

> Now for *the bare-picked bone of majesty*
> Doth dogged war bristle his angry crest
> And snarleth in *the gentle eyes of peace:*

or again, perhaps even more forcibly, more vivid in its presentation of a seemingly irreversible process of social decay:

> Now powers from home and discontents at home
> Meet in one line; and *vast confusion* waits,
> As doth a raven on a sick-fallen beast,
> The imminent *decay* of wrested pomp. (IV. iii)

Against this denuded vision of disaster, Faulconbridge can only continue to assert, as he has consistently done, his own virtues of disillusioned self-reliance, affirming a kind of tough loyalty to himself—and to the England with which, in spite of all, he has chosen to identify his fortunes—in the face of a hostile, broken, and ignoble world:

> Now happy he whose cloak and cincture can
> Hold out this tempest. (IV. iii)

To survive without committing an act of essential self-betrayal, without surrendering to a degradation which can only end in anarchy and ruin, is as much as the self-reliant man, drawing about himself such defenses as he can muster in his own bleakly isolated person, can hope at this inauspicious moment to achieve.

The Bastard, however, is alone in England in showing this reaction to the blows of an adverse fate. John is revealed by contrast as a man terrified, ready to cling to any hope, however ignoble, which may save for him the crown, and with it his skin. All around him is shifting and baseless. The Cardinal, once he has achieved his political ends, is ready to invoke peace in terms which join arrogance to calculation. "It was my breath," he tells the cowering English king, "that blew this tempest up" to punish John for his "stubborn usage" of the Pope; but now that the erstwhile rebel is showing himself "a gentle convertite"—the phrase, addressed to whom it is, covers a wealth of irony—he is ready to act as peacemaker: "My tongue shall hush again this storm of war" (V. i).

Scarcely have these arrogant and shameless words been spoken than Faulconbridge returns to confirm the death of Arthur—responsibility for which John seeks to pin on Hubert—and to announce that the French are in London. He makes a characteristic effort to rouse the king to put a brave face upon adversity, as he is himself ready to do:

> Grow great by your example and put on
> The dauntless spirit of resolution; (V. i)

but John, deliberately turning his back upon this appeal, prefers to rest his illusions upon the "happy peace" which he hopes the papal legate will secure for him. Amid so much base calculation and intimate betrayal, the Bastard's call to arms leaves him, in replacement of his cowardly and shameless king, the immediate arbiter of events.

The mastery of Faulconbridge remains limited, however, as he at heart knows, by the nature of the corrupt cause to which he stands committed. A sense of unworthiness and divided loyalty dominates the last stages of the action as Salisbury, bound in spite of himself to the support of a foreign invader, laments the part which circumstances force him to play in civil war and his own country's ruin:

> is't not pity, O my grieved friends,
> That we, the sons and children of this isle,
> Were born to see so sad an hour as this;
> Wherein we step after a stranger, march
> Upon her gentle bosom, and fill up
> Her enemy's ranks,—I must withdraw and weep
> Upon the spot of this enforced cause,—
> To grace the gentry of a land remote,
> And follow unacquainted colours here? (V. ii)

The spirit of this lament, which the contrast with the Bastard's loyalty suggests is too easily uttered, will be echoed, in more poignant terms, by Henry Bolingbroke from his throne at the opening of *Henry IV*—Part I.[9] Lewis, as an interested party, seeks to persuade Salisbury that this unnatural action will end in benefits for all concerned; but, even as he brings his argument to a close by saying "even there, methinks, an angel spoke" (and there is a pun here upon the "angel" coin, the price of treachery) the "holy legate" enters—he, of all men, most committed to political maneuvering—to urge the reconciliation which the interest of his Church now demands. The course of events, however, has moved beyond the control of clerical intrigue, and Lewis can have no further use for offers of reconciliation. In the terms of his own blunt retort: "What is that peace to me?" (V. ii). The Bastard, who sees his self-reliance thus justified is left to welcome the refusal of the enemy to treat, and to utter, in typically heightened, rhetorical terms, as befits the finally dubious cause he has been obliged to espouse, the English defiance.

The final battle is accordingly joined (V. iii), with John already stricken by mortal sickness. The wounded French noble Melun, brings news to the English of the ruthless design which now inspires their unnatural ally: "Fly, noble English, you are bought and sold!" (V. iv) The adjective is, perhaps, excessively kind to these unwilling traitors, but the news comes, at all events, as a comment upon John's illusion that peace can be bought for his own advantage. The English, indeed, are at last in the process of learning their bitter lesson. They declare their return to their natural allegiance:

> We will untread the steps of damned flight,
> And like a bated and retired flood,
> Leaving our rankness and irregular course,
> Stoop low within these bounds we have o'erlook'd,
> And calmly run on in obedience
> Even to our ocean, to our great King John; (V. iv)

once again we seem to anticipate Henry IV, this time in his final exhortation to the rebels on the eve of Shrewsbury.[10] For John's tainted cause, however, this reversal comes too late. Hubert brings news of his poisoning (V. vi)—at the hands, appropriately, of a treacherous monk—and Faulconbridge confesses that his own power has been scattered in The Wash. John makes his last entry, feeling the poison within him as the "hell" he has amply deserved (V. vii), whilst the Dauphin, answering to the legate's persuasions, makes his offer of peace after the English king has died. The Bastard, facing a still uncertain future, continues to pin his faith to self-reliance. The blessings of peace, he says, will the more readily be consolidated if based upon preparedness for continued war; and, to further this end, he offers his "faithful services" to the new occupant of the throne. His last exhortation to England—

> Nothing shall make us rue,
> If England to itself do rest but true— (V. vii)

may be said to wring a practical and patriotic moral out of the sorry series of events we have been called upon to contemplate.

THE MERCHANT OF VENICE

By comparison with Shakespeare's earlier exercises in the comic form, *The Merchant of Venice*, which may have been written in 1596, seems—together with *A Midsummer Night's Dream*—to announce the transition to a more elaborate conception of comedy. The play is in certain respects a little tentative, not altogether assimilated to a single dominating conception. The contrast between Belmont and the Rialto, romantic love and the pursuit of wealth through merchant endeavor, is perhaps incompletely worked out, and the allegory of the caskets can scarcely bear the burden of moral significance which seems to be thrust a little halfheartedly upon it. Above all, the disturbing presence of Shylock threatens to load the comedy with a somber sense of reality that leaves it by contrast, and in his absence, strangely deprived of solidity and meaning. Originally conceived as an object of repudiation, even of ridicule, Shylock almost ends by shattering the framework of comic artifice by introducing a dark and twisted strain from real life; but, although we may think that his presence in a certain sense unbalances the play, *The Merchant of Venice* excels Shakespeare's earliest comedies in the skillful blending of its various elements and indicates, in its greater complexity and more varied reflection of reality, an approach to some of the more permanent features of his mature comic creations.

The action opens, as will often be the case in later comedies, and notably in *Twelfth Night*,[11] upon characters whose reflections are tinged with melancholy, an indefinable discontent with their present state of life. The wealthy merchant Antonio, who appears to lack nothing that riches can provide, is nonetheless possessed, as his first words indicate, by a kind of boredom, dissatisfied, beneath all the opulent references to the world of merchant adventure which surrounds him, with the kind of existence to which he feels himself obscurely condemned:

In sooth, I know not why I am so sad:
It wearies me; you say it wearies you;
But how I caught it, found it, or came by it,
What stuff 'tis made of, whereof it is born,
I am to learn. (I. i)

Much the same is true, though in a different way, of Portia. Committed as a rich heiress in the golden seclusion of Belmont to her father's choice, which she respects as in natural duty bound but cannot fail to find constraining, she confesses that "my little body is aweary of this great world" (I. ii). Each feels confined to an existence which seems to exclude the decisive act of self-surrender, of free dedication to the claims and opportunities which life offers and which finally justify it. Before the play ends Antonio will have found, and taken, his chance to escape this limitation in the opportunity, which is also the risk, of dedicating his wealth, and with it his life, to the happiness of his friend Bassanio; and Portia, in turn, already senses in the gift of herself in marriage a means of release from the golden cage in which she must otherwise decoratively and uselessly dwell.

Seen from this point of view, the long-drawn-out symbolism of the casket episodes acquires a new significance. Portia's first two suitors are found, each in his own appropriate way, to be wanting. Morocco chooses gold, "which many men desire" (II. vii), only to find that his choice brings him, not life, but its opposite: in the words of the inscription in his casket, "Gilded tombs do worms infold." Arragon, in turn, chooses silver in the name of self-esteem and receives, not the award he has rashly assumed to be his due, but the "fool's head" that this self-regarding choice brings with it:

Some there be that shadows kiss,
Such have but a shadow's bliss. (II. ix)

Each of these weighty personages in effect chooses self and is subjected to the mockery his choice invites. The attitude of Bassanio, for whom Portia has been instinctively waiting, is different. His first words on the subject of his love reveal him as the typical romantic lover in his most positive aspect:

her sunny locks
Hang on her temples like a golden fleece;
Which makes her seat of Belmont Colchos' strand,
And many Jasons come in quest of her. (I. i)

That Bassanio may strike us in realistic terms as a thin character, even as one suspiciously ready to rest his hopes upon the sacrifice of his friend, is not important. He is to be judged in terms of the romantic comedy to which he belongs; and it is as such, as a "Jason" dedicated to love's adventure and disposed—unlike his rivals—to risk for it, that he shows himself ready in the moment of his trial to give in order to receive, to choose inner reality rather than the deception of outward show. Taking the risk which the injunction on his casket conveys, and which is in these comedies a law of life—"who chooseth me must give and hazard all he hath" (II. vii)—he receives his appropriate reward in the graceful simplicity of Portia's answering self-surrender:

> You see me, Lord Bassanio, where I stand,
> Such as I am; though for myself alone
> I would not be ambitious in my wish,
> To wish myself much better; yet for you
> I would be trebled twenty times myself;
> A thousand times more fair, ten thousand times
> More rich;
> That only to stand high in your account,
> I might in virtue, beauties, livings, friends,
> Exceed account: but the full sum of me
> Is sum of something which, to term in gross,
> Is an unlesson'd girl, unschool'd, unpractised;
> Happy in this, she is not yet so old
> But she may learn; happier than this,
> She is not bred so dull but she can learn;
> Happiest of all in that her gentle spirit
> Commits itself to yours to be directed,
> As from her lord, her governor, her king.
> Myself and what is mine to you and yours
> Is now converted: but now I was the lord
> Of this fair mansion, master of my servants,
> Queen o'er myself; and even now, but now,
> This house, these servants, and this same myself
> Are yours, my lord: I give them with this ring. (III. ii)

Once again, as in the case of Bassanio, it is easy to misinterpret this, to find Portia's self-presentation as an "unlesson'd girl" disingenuous, even artful, in view of her own later mastery of the complexities of the trial scene. This, however, is once more to ignore the comic terms on the basis of which she was created. What is in question here is not psychological realism but the familiar accountancy of love, which rests on giving rather than on seeking to take, and which finds its fulfillment in generous and free self-dedication as opposed to the vanity of self-assertion. In Portia's lines we may properly feel that the content of Katherine's final speech on the marriage relationship in *The Taming of the Shrew*[12] has been taken up and given a new depth of personal tenderness and a greater humanity of content.

The ideals and satisfactions of romantic love, however, are not allowed to stand alone in this play. In choosing to help Bassanio, Antonio has accepted the risk which the leaden casket enjoined. By so doing, he has taken upon himself the rule of friendship and opened to himself the possibility of obtaining its true wealth, which is not to be assessed in terms of temporal merchandise; but his choice exposes him to the hazards of the world and through them to the real possibility of tragedy. The real world, which shadows the colorful and self-absorbed society of the Rialto, is represented not merely by the brightly colored talk of argosies and swelling sails, of merchandise and far-flung affairs—topics in which this society delights—but by the somber reality of Shylock.

The interpretation of Shylock's part in the play calls in any event for considerable firmness in discrimination. It may even be that Shakespeare, when he embarked upon his comedy, was not in every respect fully conscious of what he was in fact bringing into being. It is essential, of course, to avoid the modern temptation to sentimentalize Shylock, or to read his character in terms of our own preoccupation with racial realities. The melodramatic villain, the heartless usurer, and the enemy of Christianity all belong to the conception, and an Elizabethan audience would certainly have found nothing unusual or unseemly in the final downfall of all three. This downfall is amply accomplished before the end of the play and is certainly essential to its intended effect; but even before Shakespeare Marlowe had gone a considerable way, in the early scenes of his *Jew of Malta*,[13] to apportion blame between the races, and what Shakespeare has done in *The Merchant* is to follow his instinct for powerful dramatic effect to the extent of conferring upon his Jew, at the moments when that effect requires them, a consistency and human solidity which, reflecting disquieting aspects of the real world, threatens at times to break through the elaborate poetic fabric of his Venetian romance.

An unprejudiced reading of the play, indeed, can leave us in no doubt concerning the scope of this achievement. The contemptuous treatment afforded to Shylock by the Christians, not excluding Antonio, is, of course, to be seen primarily through Elizabethan eyes. It is justified, in these terms, by the generally accepted need to repudiate the position of one who sins by taking "A breed for barren metal of his friend" (I. iii), who seeks, in other words, to make inanimate gold "breed" and so assume a function properly confined to living creatures. The rejection and final punishment which this aberration brings upon the sinner is both in itself appropriate and necessary, by contrast, to bring out the truth implied in both Antonio's generosity and Portia's essential plea for "the quality of mercy" (IV. i). Shylock, in fact, is brought to ruin because these positive virtues are beyond his comprehension; but Shakespeare's instinct for a dramatic situation was not thereby prevented from giving due force, when the situation called for it, to his response to the contempt of his enemies and even to the appeal to racial tradition implied in his quoting of the Old Testament story of Laban (I. iii) and elsewhere. Similarly, the betrayal of the Jew by his own daughter is clearly to be regarded as justified both as an act of religious conversion and as an escape from what are finally inhuman attitudes; but though Shylock is evidently at once comic and ignoble when presented, in Salanio's description (II. viii), as confounding the loss of Jessica with that of his "ducats," there are moments when his deprivation of both is invested with a degree of passion that, while it cannot justify him, does add to the initial effect a note at least akin to tragedy. When Tubal reports that one of Antonio's creditors has been seen abroad with "a ring that he had of your daughter for a monkey," Shylock's reaction–

> Thou torturest me, Tubal: it was my turquoise; I had it of Leah when I was a bachelor: I would not have given it for a wilderness of monkeys– (III. i)

is sufficiently steeped in emotion, personal and, as it were, racial, to produce an effect that finally evades the merely comic. Incidents of this kind are common in Shakespeare's presentation of Shylock; they are used, beyond the evident intention of condemning the usurious unbeliever, beyond even that of showing an incompletely human being entrapped in the insufficiency of his own attitudes, to lend depth and dramatic verisimilitude to the Jew's passion, to what is seen at certain culminating moments to be his intense desire to *survive* by clinging to his own separate standards. This is the desire which makes him, on his first appearance, declare himself ready to "buy with you, sell with you, talk with you, walk with you," but not, on the other hand, "to eat with you, drink with you, nor pray with you" (I. iii); to cling, in other words, by every means in his power—including, notably, his command over money—to his separate identity in a world implacably, if reasonably, hostile to everything for which he stands.

It is his understanding of these deeper issues behind Shylock's admitted "villainy," even his rejection of the human law of compassion, that enables Shakespeare to present the Jew's reactions to Christian society with a force that makes it impossible for us simply to pass them by. It is not in any sense that Shylock is to be regarded as being in the right. On the contrary, his attitudes are based on what all the comedies agree in regarding as basic human limitations, blind spots which, when persisted in, make a balanced and fully human life unattainable. Shylock is finally condemned by his persistence in his own perverse choices, by the warped attitudes which prompt him to reject life when it is offered him upon the only terms on which, according to these comedies, it is available; but the rejection itself is rendered dramatically understandable, takes possession of our minds as a dark and twisted strain that threatens at times to affect our attitude to the play as a whole. His retort to Antonio's initial request for a loan, so spare and tense with passion against the brilliant but relatively trivial decoration that surrounds it, is charged, on any interpretation, with the unmistakable accents of reality

> Go to, then: you come to me, and you say
> "Shylock, we would have moneys": you say so;
> You, that did void your rheum upon my beard,
> And foot me as you spurn a stranger cur
> Over your threshold: moneys is your suit.
> What should I say to you? Should I not say
> "Hath a dog money? is it possible
> A cur can lend three thousand ducats?" or
> Shall I bend low and in a bondman's key,
> With bated breath and whispering humbleness,
> Say this,—
> "Fair sir, you spit on me on Wednesday last;

> You spurn'd me such a day; another time
> You call'd me dog; and for these courtesies
> I'll lend you thus much moneys"? (I. iii)

Here, if anywhere, the compulsive dramatic instinct is at work conferring life upon a character beyond all possible abstract limits or over-all necessities. The development of the rhythm, with its repetition of key words ("moneys," "dog," "cur"), the calculated pauses, the breaks in the flow of the argument after the accumulation of indignant irony (the short "Say this" following the broad sweep of the preceding line): all this shows verse no longer dominated by the rigid pattern of sound but reaching out in the movement of thought and emotion to convey the true springs of the speaker's emotion.

All this does not mean, as we have said, that we need be tempted to simplify the reading of the character so presented. The conventional Elizabethan view of the Jew and the usurer continues to be, at this point as always, the foundation of Shakespeare's conception of Shylock, as, indeed, the entire comic conception requires it; but, whilst he has taken this view as his starting point, and is on the way to accepting it for his conclusion, his sense of dramatic contrast is clearly at work humanizing it, balancing it—even at some risk to the effect made by his play as a whole—against other factors that, if they do not contradict, at least profoundly modify it. The modification sometimes even threatens to color our view of Shylock's Christian opponents, those whom the general line of the comedy would have us see as uniformly benign and superior. It produces, in reply to the explosion of resentment just quoted, Antonio's ruthlessly complacent expression of superiority:

> I am as like to call thee so again,
> To spit on thee again, to spurn thee too;

so that we may even feel that, when he explicitly tells Shylock:

> If thou wilt lend this money, lend it not
> As to thy friends; . . .
> But lend it rather to thine enemy;
> Who, if he break, thou mayest with better face
> Exact the penalty, (I. iii)

he is in effect inviting the fate which will in due course threaten to undo him. The appropriate reversal of this episode comes, indeed, when Antonio is driven to throw himself upon the Jew's mercy, only to receive what is, always within its own terms, the unanswerable logic of his reply:

> I am a Jew. Hath not a Jew eyes? hath not a Jew hands, organs, dimensions, senses, affections, passions? . . . If a Jew wrong a Christian, what is his humility? Revenge. If a Christian wrong a Jew, what should his sufference be by Christian example? Why, revenge. The villainy you teach me, I will execute; and it shall go hard but I will better the instruction. (III. i)

We have already stressed that the temptation to whitewash Shylock in the light of our own notions in these matters must be avoided. To "better instruction" in this way is by no means to escape the charge of "villainy" which remains firmly fixed; but recognition of this evident reality need not lead us to ignore the plain evidence of the text, which gives this same "villainy" a real, if perverse, motivation, or to discount the full balance that his sense of a dramatic situation imposed at this and other points on Shakespeare's conception.

It is in the light of these considerations that we may best approach the famous trial scene (IV. i) where the two worlds of romance and reality which divide the play so uneasily between them are finally brought together. The presence of elements of artifice and make-believe derived from traditional storytelling, and not on that account less effective on the stage, should not blind us to the serious nature of the conflict here presented. Shylock, whose attitude to Antonio we have seen to be more complex, even in its admitted perversity, than a simple Gentile view would be ready to recognize, has recourse to a justice which he feels to be, for once, on his side. Antonio himself recognizes the strength of the Jew's position in terms of law:

> The Duke cannot deny the course of law:
> For the commodity that strangers have
> With us in Venice, if it be denied,
> Will much impeach the justice of his state;
> Since that the trade and profit of the city
> Consisteth of all nations; (III. iii)

for reasons characteristically mercantile, and in themselves entirely respectable, the powers that rule Venice are obliged to reject humanity in the name of the law upon which their credit is founded. This obligation gives Shylock the opportunity which turns eventually into the occasion of his downfall. By the opening of this scene we shall certainly have learned not to underestimate Shylock, or to give his outbursts of dark and twisted emotion less than their share of human value; but we must add that his own appeal to justice is seen at the crucial moment to be limited by this same resentment, to remain bound up in self and blind to the higher human reality of compassion. It is for this reason, now seen in its relation to the preceding symbolism of the casket scenes, that Portia, transformed from the object of Bassanio's romantic love into the mouthpiece of a more universal law, intervenes in the proceedings. She does so to a double end. In the first place, and throughout the earlier part of the long scene, she grants the Jew, in the name of justice, all that in justice is his right. By so doing, she underlines the reality of Antonio's "hazard," by which he is finally to be redeemed; but, having done this, she goes on to raise her plea beyond "justice" to invoke a "mercy" which is beyond all covenant of law, and which is the gratuitous gift of "heaven": a "mercy" of which all men, just and unjust, Christian and Jew alike, stand in need. Unless we grasp its place in the complete conception we shall not respond fully to Portia's most famous utterance:

> The quality of mercy is not strain'd,
> It droppeth as the gentle rain from heaven
> Upon the place beneath: it is twice blest;
> *It blesseth him that gives, and him that takes:* . . .
> It is an attribute to God himself,
> And earthly power doth then show likest God's
> When mercy seasons justice. *Therefore, Jew,*
> *Though justice be thy plea, consider this,*
> *That, in the course of justice, none of us*
> *Should see salvation: we do pray for mercy;*
> *And that same prayer doth teach us all to render*
> *The deeds of mercy.* (IV. i)

It would be wrong indeed to read as a mere set piece a speech the leading ideas of which will be echoed in later plays, from *Henry V* to *Hamlet* and *Measure for Measure,*[14] which threatens indeed to burst the bonds of comedy and to anticipate a more profound and complex vision of life. Meanwhile the last lines, more especially, constitute the deepest, the most permanent "meaning" of Shakespeare's play, and provide—among other things—the foundation of an outlook from which Shylock, who has himself so passionately invoked "justice," may fittingly be judged. For Shylock, in the very moment of seeming to obtain the judgment which is recognized to be his due, is condemned by his failure to temper "justice" with "mercy," recognizing thereby his share in the universal human situation. He too needs "mercy," and is called upon to "give" as well as to exact; and because this lesson of the caskets, translated from allegory to a situation tense with human drama, fails to move him, the very "justice" he has invoked finally breaks in his hands and he is judged in the light of the narrow and implacable standards upon which he has chosen to take his stand.

With the departure of Shylock we return, a little uneasily, to the world of poetry and artifice which has generally prevailed whenever he has been absent from the stage. As the various pairs of lovers finally come together, in the appropriate comic manner, romance and music are united in a poetic effect which is sometimes principally decorative (as in the famous duet "In such a night" (V. i) between Lorenzo and Jessica, where the beauty of the verse cannot quite lead us to forget the element of deception and heartlessness by which their love has been shadowed), but which occasionally rises, as in Lorenzo's most eloquent utterance, to a more profound "Platonic" statement of spiritual harmonies:

> How sweet the moonlight sleeps upon this bank!
> Here will we sit, and let the sounds of music
> Creep in our ears; soft stillness and the night
> Become the touches of sweet harmony.
> Sit, Jessica. Look how the floor of heaven
> Is thick inlaid with patines of bright gold;
> There's not the smallest orb which thou behold'st
> But in his motion like an angel sings,
> Still quiring to the young-eyed cherubins;
> Such harmony is in immortal souls;
> But whilst this muddy vesture of decay
> Doth grossly close it in, we cannot hear it. (V. i)

The enchanted harmonies of music become here the reflection of something more profound, a deeper intuition, glimpsed if not retained, of universal fitness. The absorbing beauty of life which everywhere surrounds man and his inability to maintain other than fugitively his hold upon it becomes at such moments the pervasive background of Shakespeare's comic devices.

It only remains to mention in conclusion the episode of the lovers' gift to Portia and her maid of their rings and of their final return to their respective owners. Drawn in all probability from a story by Boccaccio, the incident parallels in a broadly comic key the central moral of love as consisting of accepted risk, of the spontaneous and irrevocable gift of self. The rings were originally conferred as pledges of mutual fidelity. Portia now confiscates them in the name of "justice"—to remind us that, in "justice," "all men are frail"—and returns them, on the plea precisely of Antonio, who has already shown under sterner circumstances his readiness to make the life-giving gift of self for his friend. As he now says:

> I did once lend my body for his wealth;
> Which, but for him that had your husband's ring
> Had quite miscarried: I dare be bound again,
> *My soul upon the forfeit,* that your lord
> Will never more break faith advisedly; (V. i)

and Portia makes the return, in answer to Antonio's renewed, but this time spiritual, guarantee, in a comic reflection of "mercy," of that capacity for tolerant and compassionate understanding upon which alone any durable human relationship can be founded. Thus expressed, it may seem that the device can hardly bear the burden of meaning placed upon it, and this is indeed an impression which a good deal of this play is likely to give us. The entire action is dominated, possibly even beyond the author's initial intention, by the human and dramatic stature of Shylock; but, for all the imperfect co-ordination—as we may feel it—of the various elements which compose it, *The Merchant of Venice* not only lives as the dramatic retelling of more than one ancient and familiar story, but suggests themes which elsewhere—in the relation of reality and make-believe which Shakespeare used so triumphantly in his later, greater comedies—were to be more profoundly and coherently developed.[15]

VII

Henry IV—Parts I and II, and *Henry V*

The series of plays initiated with *Richard II* and developed, some three years later, through the two parts of *Henry IV* and *Henry V*,[1] represents without doubt one of the peaks of Shakespeare's achievement during the earlier period of his dramatic career. Its starting point is, in accordance with the inherited conception, an adaptation to the exigencies of Tudor political thought of traditional conceptions of monarchy.[2] The royal office is assumed to be divinely instituted, the indispensable guarantee of order in a state nationally and patriotically conceived; the political thought expressed in these plays combines the fervent nationalism of the day with sacramental notions of monarchy more venerable than itself. In the period covered by this series, however, the emphasis rests on the interruption of the relationship which should naturally exist, according to the traditional view, between king and subject, on the disastrous consequences of that interruption, and on the restoration of ordered rule, after the uneasy interim of Henry IV's reign, on a more secure, if more limited, basis under the authority of his son.

Shakespeare, however, who shared with Machiavelli—the real Machiavelli, not the conventional "Machiavel" of the Elizabethan imagination, whose relevance to the dramatist's thought has been greatly exaggerated—a keen awareness of the political realities of his age, used this story to develop insights of his own into the questions raised by the attainment and exercise of power. The story he inherited presented an appropriate motive in the portrayal of Prince Hal, whose progress from dissolute heir apparent to responsible monarch gives a main thread of continuity to the series. Hal's career, of course, can properly be seen in traditional terms as a manifestation of Christian kingship. This, indeed, is the foundation upon which Shakespeare's design unequivocally rests; but, although this reading of his hero's character is never irrelevant, or less than properly impressive, it comes increasingly to be seen in relation to unanswered, and perhaps unanswerable, questions which are implicit in the very attainment of his necessary and patriotic ends. What, to put the matter in slightly different terms, are the personal as distinct from the political qualities that go to the making of a king? The answer emerges in several stages, each of which is at once based on inherited notions of the political character and vastly extends the implications of these notions, passing from an affirmation of the necessity of kingship to a searching consideration of the qualities and limitations of the public personality.[3]

HENRY IV–PART I

The expository scene which opens the First Part of *Henry IV* shows Bolingbroke weighed down, as the concluding scenes of *Richard II* have anticipated,[4] by thoughts of anarchy and civil war. Its background is the bitter memory of "civil butchery," of strife between rivals "All of one nature, of one substance bred," clashes within the body politic that can only serve to wound and destroy it. To counter the threatened renewal of this condition, the new king calls upon his barons to unite, under the sign of the cross, for the liberation of the Holy Sepulchre:

> Therefore, friends,
> As far as to the sepulchre of Christ,
> Whose soldier now, under whose blessed cross
> We are impressed and engaged to fight,
> Forthwith a power of English shall we levy;
> Whose arms were moulded in their mothers' womb
> To chase these pagans in those holy fields
> Over whose acres walk'd those blessed feet
> Which fourteen hundred years ago were nail'd
> For our advantage on the bitter cross. (I. i)

The tone of this appeal, at once eloquent and nostalgic, is one of emotional compensation, of the casting off of a personal burden of sin. Henry already knows at heart that his desire to play properly his royal role is flawed past mending by the way in which he has so recently come to the throne. His murder of Richard fatally engendered the strife which he now aims at ending. No sooner has he affirmed his purpose than "heavy news" comes "all athwart" from Wales to force a postponement of the crusading project. The reign which opens with the summons to a holy enterprise will end, after years of weary disillusionment, in a room "called Jerusalem,"[5] which will be his nearest approach to the Holy Land; and in between it will have seen little but plot and counterplot, battles in which victory serves only to sow the seeds of further civil strife.

Already, indeed, Henry feels himself obscurely punished for his sins not only as king in the weariness which his opening words betray, but in his son's notorious dedication to the "riot and dishonour" visibly incarnate in the person of Falstaff.[6] To the tavern, accordingly, and to Falstaff in it, the action logically turns. Falstaff's opening question to Hal—"What time of day is it, lad?"—is at once a challenge to the basic assumptions of the serious action and an indication of his own limitation. Falstaff, as the Prince brings out in his elaborate reply, lives by repudiating time. Time is at this stage no concern of his, as it is of the politicians who will become—as we shall see[7]—in ever increasing measure its victims, but the very fact that he ignores its call to the exercise of responsible choice implies that he will himself have to be repudiated before the Prince can take up a vocation in which he will be at once conscious of time and, in some measure, its victim. The process of repudiation is foreshadowed from the very outset of their relationship. As Falstaff's imaginative energy asserts itself through the flaunting of his irresponsibility, his refusal to be bound by common human limitations, so does the Prince withdraw into detachment, into a refusal to be committed, that is equally typical of his own nature. Falstaff's spacious references to thieves as "squires of the night's body," "Diana's foresters . . . governed, as the sea is, by our noble and chaste mistress the moon" are balanced by Hal's more realistic estimate of the ultimate prospects of robbery:

> . . . the fortune of us that are the moon's men doth ebb and flow like the sea, being governed, as the sea is, by the moon. As for

> proof, now: a purse of gold most resolutely snatched on Monday night and most dissolutely spent on Tuesday morning; got with swearing "Lay by" and spent with crying "Bring in"; now in as low an ebb as the foot of the ladder, and by and by in as high a flow as the ridge of the gallows. (I. ii)

From the imaginative fancy of the devotees of thievery as "the moon's men," governed by the varying tides of fortune, to the stark reality of the gallows a single logically defined sequence imposes itself. The bringing back of Falstaff's irresponsible exuberance to dispassionate reality and implied condemnation is typical of the Prince. From the first he is presented in ultimate detachment from Falstaff. There is in his future development no real conversion, because the moral estimate of his temporary companion is from the beginning firmly present in his mind. The divergence of spirit thus indicated belongs to the central conception of the play.

For it is necessary, in considering the effect of the scenes of low life which so abound in this play, and which constitute so splendid a manifestation of its comic inspiration, to arrive at a balanced estimate of the part played in them by both the leading actors. In the case of Falstaff, we shall no doubt need to take not a few traditional elements into account.[8] He bears about him elements of the buffoon, the Vice of the medieval stage, and incarnates the temptations against morality and duty which the young king-in-the-making will be required to abjure. He is not, however, entirely bound by limitations of this kind. The Falstaff of *Henry IV*—Part I, besides representing the vices which Hal must put aside in the following of his vocation, increasingly stands out from the political action in which he moves, serves as a connecting link between two contrasted worlds, the tavern world of comic incident in which he is at home and the world of court rhetoric and political decision to which he also has access. So situated in two worlds and confined entirely to neither, his is a voice that lies outside the prevailing political spirit of the play, that draws its cogency—though of a limited kind, condemned even as it is expressed for being partial, for the sin of mistaking the part for the whole—from the author's own insight expressing itself in a flow of comic energy. From this standpoint, and without ignoring the other, the very real darker side of the picture, we may say that Falstaff represents certain valid aspects of the humanity which it seems that the public man must necessarily exclude.

That humanity is full of gross imperfections, which must end by destroying the life they seem to affirm; but the Falstaff of this play, whilst he shares these imperfections and is indeed their supreme incarnation, is not altogether limited to his role of scapegoat and instigator of corruption. The comic spirit which went to his creation has other facets, less morally austere but not on that account less relevant to a balanced view of life. His keen intelligence, his real understanding, his refusal to be fobbed off by empty or hypocritical phrases—these are characteristics that enable him, in his most successful moments, to transcend his world and to become the expression of a great and completely serious conception. Nothing Shakespeare had so far done in the comic spirit—or even, perhaps, was subsequently to do—can overshadow this achievement.

Against it, equally a necessary part of the complete effect, we need to set the detachment and self-awareness of Falstaff's princely associate. Both are shown, at the end of this first "comic" scene, in Hal's soliloquy. This touches on a theme always close to his father's heart[9] and stressed throughout as a constant feature of the family character: the tendency to live for public effect, to grade behavior to the reaction that it is desired to produce in the world. The impression made by the soliloquy is explained in part by the nature of the material inherited by the dramatist. The Prince, as he appeared in the popular account, was an outstanding example of the dissolute young man who, when faced by grave responsibilities, underwent a kind of moral conversion and finally made good in the sphere to which he was called. The story, thus conceived, was too familiar, too powerful in its evident appeal, to be ignored; on the other hand, its conception of character and motive was too naïve to appeal to a Shakespeare already moving toward the mood in which he was shortly to produce *Hamlet*. Faced with this dilemma, the dramatist chose to accept the very improbability of the story and turn it to account. The Prince, from his first appearance, has substantially made his choice; he looks forward to a reformation which, precisely because it has never really been in question, is partly moved by a political calculation which reflects his father's character. In this way what no doubt began as a simple self-revelation, an explanation uttered with an eye to the future, ended as something rather different. If it is Hal's destiny, as the story demands, to change, or rather to *be seen* to change, it is at least in part because he is aware that a transformation of this kind will attract popularity; for it is a fact of public life that "nothing pleaseth but rare accidents" (I. ii) and these the political realist will be careful to supply. The whole process of "reformation," as Hal describes it in these initial reflections, has a surface quality, glitters with a kind of metallic speciousness over previous faults "like bright metal on a sullen ground"; and its purpose is to "*show* more goodly" and "attract more eyes." The "conversion," thus partially transformed from an edifying example to a deliberate instrument of policy, enters into the permanent characteristics of the House of Lancaster. The future Henry V, destined to become an incarnation of the political virtues (which are in no sense to be despised), begins by conditioning intimate conviction to the public display of moral qualities; for behind Shakespeare's acceptance of a traditional story lies the sense, which grows as the action develops, that success in politics implies some measure of moral loss, the sacrifice of more immediately attractive qualities in the distinctively personal order.

The scene which follows (I. iii) returns, following the play's characteristic construction, to the "serious" action to show the split between the king and the rebels in the process of coming into being. If Henry's kingship is in danger of being rendered sterile in its higher aspirations by the circumstances which led to his seizure of the crown, a similar frustration accompanies those who, having helped him to the throne to further selfish ends of their own, now wish to curb his power. Worcester refers meaningfully to

> that same greatness too which our own hands
> Have holp to make so portly, (I. iii)

and Hotspur, a little later, puts the relationship in less flattering terms when he describes his associates as the "base second means," "the cords, the ladder, or the hangman" involved in the late king's murder. Desire for power prompted the rebel leaders to give their assent to the crime of regicide, and now fear prompted by a mutual awareness of guilt makes inevitable the clash between the usurper and those who formerly served his ends. The result is an endless distrust, the consequences of which finally conclude, in this play, at Shrewsbury.

Against this background and after the demonstration, just witnessed, of Hal's political detachment, yet another contrast—that between himself and Hotspur—begins to take shape. Hotspur's first speech, describing the courtier who brought the king's request for his prisoners after Holmedon, is finely conceived in the comic spirit; this is the man of action at his best, still sure of the validity of his values, direct, incisive, impatient of artifice and intrigue. What takes place after the king's angry departure, however, shows the subjection of this impulsive warrior to the labyrinth of politic behavior. His first response to Henry's final demand is stated with an emphasis that betrays the tendency, always innate in him, to develop his emotions in excess of their cause:

> An if the devil come and roar for them,
> I will not send them: I will after straight
> And tell him so;

but Northumberland's immediate interruption counsels "pause" and heralds, with the entry of Worcester, the change from emotional conflict to statecraft and the devices of "policy." Worcester is subtle enough to play upon this same impulsiveness by stressing the "matter deep and dangerous" "full of peril and adventurous spirit" (I. iii) of the plot he is about to unfold. Hotspur's reaction to the prospect of hazard introduces for the first time the abstract "honour" which represents at once the weakness and the strength of his position:

> Send danger from the east unto the west,
> So honour cross it from the north to south,
> And let them grapple. (I. iii)

"Honour," thus followed, is in the process of converting itself for Hotspur into an emotional stimulus which, as it is mentioned, rouses an infallible response in high-sounding rhetoric. It is not difficult to see, in these outbursts, a comic anticipation of qualities which will find later expression in the subtle blend of "nobility" and failure which characterizes so many of Shakespeare's tragic heroes. Othello, Antony, and Coriolanus, each in his own distinct way, reflect in their rhetoric a tendency to justify themselves, or to conform to an idealized presentation of their own behavior in the very moment of failure; and if Hotspur is less subtly and, for the most part, less tragically conceived, the balance of true emotion and emptiness, the reliance on a noble conception barely developed beyond its verbal value reflects the moral adolescence which, to some degree and maintaining all the necessary differences, he shares with them. It would be hard to imagine a better foil to the dedicated and self-reliant competence which we have already seen taking shape beneath Hal's apparent dissolution.

Before the scene has ended Worcester, with all the politician's contempt for the simple values of the man of war, has involved his nephew in a web of intrigue. He persuades him first of all to give up his prisoners, retaining only the son of Douglas; and having done this, he turns from Hotspur to plot the more devious intricacies of "policy" with Northumberland:

> Your son in Scotland being thus employ'd,
> Shall *secretly into the bosom creep*
> Of that same noble prelate, well beloved,
> The archbishop. (I. iii)

The ambiguity which balances the idea of a serpent creeping into a prelate's bosom against the implications of "noble" and "well beloved" is typical of Worcester's world. Hotspur, out of his depth, salutes his uncle's contrivance as "a *noble* plot," whilst Worcester more accurately reveals its foundations in guilt and expediency:

> 'Tis no little reason bids us speed,
> To save our heads by raising of a head;
> For, bear ourselves as even as we can,
> The king will always think him in our debt,
> And think we think ourselves unsatisfied,
> Till he hath found a time to pay us home. (I. iii)

Fear, in this world, breeds fear, and produces the very rebellion which fear itself, working through a conscience of guilt, would desire to avoid. The end of the scene shows us Worcester about to "*steal* to Glendower and Lord Mortimer," seeking in dubious unity the remedy to "much uncertainty." Northumberland it leaves, not less typically, unsure of himself and of the future ("we shall thrive, I trust"), and Hotspur, a stranger in this world of intrigue with which he is nonetheless ready to compromise his "nobility," clings to the supposed certainties of action with a rhetorical gesture which is really an evasion of the choices in which he finds himself involved:

> Uncle, adieu: O, let the hours be short
> Till fields and blows and groans applaud our sport. (I. iii)

These are, indeed, Hotspur's only constants to guide him through a world of shifting uncertainties; how inadequate they are, how opposed in their simplicity to the controlled self-awareness of the Prince, time will show.

After these opening scenes, which have mainly presented the contrasted facets of the political action, the interest shifts to embrace a comic parallel to the central theme. This change of vision has a double purpose; it extends the social range covered by the play, presenting a popular reflection of the prevailing crisis of authority, and further develops Hal's relation to Falstaff. The robbery itself is an active manifestation of disorder; it is no accident that the object of a theft in which the heir to the throne plays an ambiguous part is money on its way to the royal exchequer. The essence of the adventure (II. ii) lies in the contrast between Falstaff's participation, shameless, corrupt, and ridiculous by turn, and the Prince's blend of diversion and detachment. Falstaff appears more than ever the incarnation of "misrule," distinguished—always within his dedication to dissolution—by the capacity to confer upon his own monstrosity an unexpected, paradoxical normality. His triumphs, such as they are, depend on the evasion of facts, whereas the superiority of the Prince rests on the dispassionate observation of them. The ability to detach himself from his surroundings is at once Hal's virtue and in some sense his human limitation. After the trick played upon Falstaff, he says of his companion that he "*lards* the lean earth as he walks upon." The image is, of course, appropriate to the incarnation of "riot," open debauchery, and exorbitant "misrule." The Prince, with his habitual clear-sightedness, imposes his vision of things; but this peculiar type of physical imagery, the product of a certain calculated and superior vulgarity, will be echoed at various stages of the later action. Its relation to Falstaff's "fleshly" inversions of the spirit of Puritan morality is very close to the central conception.

The scene at Eastcheap (II. iv) which follows the robbery is, besides being the longest, one of the most important in the play. During its course, the various aspects of the complete action, thus far separately presented, are drawn together in their mutual relationship. The Gadshill adventure, recently worked out in reality to Falstaff's discomfiture, is gone over in retrospect and modified, in the process, by the comic imagination of the victim. The Prince carries on his jest at the expense of his companion, who simultaneously admits his defeat and evades it, transforms it into something different; and finally, in the incident to which the whole scene leads, both combine to enact in comic anticipation the crucial meeting between father and son, at which the latter will accept the responsibilities imposed upon him by birth and the former find some compensation for the disappointment which his own past actions have inflicted upon him.

Falstaff's account of the robbery, and his subsequent exposure, bring into play what are in effect two worlds, two contrasted attitudes to life. His comic imagination plays upon the incident, transforming it at will and making of it a satire of the exaggerations of heroic warfare. "Eight times thrust through the doublet, four through the hose . . . I never dealt better since I was a man": so might one of the warriors in the serious action glorify his own prowess. The same expansive comic energy, using the properties of the popular stage to superb effect, has just produced a picture of the fat knight, in his own words, as beating the future king out of his kingdom "with a dagger of lath" (II. iv) and driving his subjects before him "like a flock of wild geese." Here, as always, until he is curbed by the imposition of fact, Falstaff represents life, the refusal to be bound by moral categories which, necessary in themselves, are so often limited, even selfish, in their particular application. His imagination habitually transcends his situation, escapes its immediate cause to rise to a generality of statement that is, in his mouth, at once grotesque and variously true. So is it with his denunciation of the "cowardice" of his fellows. To discuss whether Falstaff is or is not a coward is finally irrelevant, because the character is not, at these moments, conceived in terms of realistic motive at all; it is rather that the categories of cowardice and valor have become, while he speaks, momentarily irrelevant. So much is this so that social necessity, which demands the acceptance of responsibility, the subjection of individual impulse to the general good, leads finally to his elimination, but will run the risk in eliminating him of killing the vitality it also needs. To put the matter in another way, we may feel at these moments an affinity with Falstaff as he rejects the common categories of virtue; but—we must add—by these categories, in spite of him, life must finally be lived, and only in the light of their necessity is the protest against them comprehensible.

For this reason, the Prince is there to correct the balance. As Falstaff's imagination moves away from the original sordidness of the Gadshill incident, so does Hal's dry precision take pleasure in exposing the facts of the case; and the exposure, again most typically, leads to that insistence upon sweat and grossness—"thou clay-brained guts, . . . thou whoreson, obscene, greasy tallow-catch"—which is at once the true reverse of Falstaff's exuberant fleshliness and a sign of the compensating vulgarity which, in these comic scenes, so persistently shadows the speaker's cold-blooded, efficient habits of thought. The clash of personalities ends, as usual, in a deliberate exaggeration on either side of the contrasted physical qualities which incarnate their respective natures. On the side of Falstaff, as seen by the Prince, we have "this sanguine coward," "this huge hill of flesh," images which expand, affirm themselves, as they convey the speaker's disapproval; on the side of Hal, as pictured by his disreputable associate, we have "you starveling, you elf-skin, you dried neat's tongue, you bull's pizzle, you stock-fish," and the rest. Both are exaggerations, exaggerations respectively of warm corruption and cold efficiency, each revealed through its physical qualities; but it is certain that, on this level, Falstaff will have the best of the argument, and so the Prince, to reassert himself, returns to his own realm of sober fact and reason: "when thou hast tired thyself in base comparisons, hear me speak but this." Hal's dominion is, in the long run, that of the "plain tale," the unvarnished fact; Falstaff's is that of the comic fantasy playing upon reality, transforming it to ends in which truth and falsehood, life and illusion, are blended. Both act in accordance with their own natures. The Prince, devoted to the concrete, the practical, will eventually become the representative of a morality dedicated primarily to necessary political ends; Falstaff, in whose phrases life thrusts insistently through all barriers and confinements, will be at once intensely alive and impatient of necessary order. The one will achieve his just purposes at the expense of some aspects of humanity; the other, whilst remaining human to the last, will end by distorting humanity to his own monstrous image, making it necessary for the moral judgment to disown him to escape the threat of complete anarchy.

Not, however, until the parody of the interview between Henry IV and his son is the connection between the "serious" action and its "comic" reflection made finally clear. The episode, of course, anticipates the real confrontation to follow; it is moreover an anticipation critical in kind, bringing out certain flaws in the situation which it exposes to comic scrutiny:

> *Falstaff:* . . . this chair shall be my state, this dagger my sceptre, and this cushion my crown.

> *Prince:* Thy state is taken for a joined-stool, thy golden sceptre for a leaden dagger, and thy precious rich crown for a pitiful bald crown! (II. iv)

The juxtaposition of the two speeches is not without meaning. Falstaff starts from the humble objects around him and subjects them in parody to a certain imaginative transformation. The chair becomes "my state," the false dagger a "sceptre," and the cushion a "crown"; whilst for the Prince, who follows the inverse process in his concentration upon the real, the same state is restored to its true nature as a "joined-stool," the "golden sceptre" becomes once more a dagger of "lead," and the "rich crown" the pitiful "bald crown" of advancing years. The process on either side is not without relation to the main conception.

As much can be said of Falstaff's behavior after ascending his mock throne. This is, as we have said, a parody of the scene to follow between father and son; it is also a mock enthronement of "misrule" in the spirit of carnival which leads finally to its necessary exposure. His description of the Prince, using the supposed words of his father, contains an element of sardonic caricature: "That thou art my son, I have partly thy mother's word, partly my own opinion, but chiefly a villainous trick of thine eye, and a foolish hanging of thy nether lip, that doth warrant me" (II. iv). It is not thus, of course, that Henry will actually speak to his son; but the disillusioned clarity, even the coarseness of the description, corresponds to something really present in the family nature, which makes itself felt repeatedly in the Prince's attitude toward his tavern life—especially in his moments of association with Poins—and is related to the detachment which is one ingredient of his political sense. For, in the light of what we have just seen, there is more than a little relevance in the question put by Falstaff into Henry's mouth: "Shall the son of England prove a thief and take purses?" (II. iv)

If this were Falstaff's last word he would be something less than the great comic creation he is. When he goes on to point to himself as the "virtuous man" whom the Prince should keep by him, he is clearly saying the opposite of what Henry *must* say; and yet the following description carries enough life with it for us to realize that the circumstances which demand Falstaff's banishment also involve a loss which no necessity, political or moral, can make altogether irrelevant. For Falstaff, as he presents himself for this particular purpose (and his imagination can compass many presentations for many, even contradictory, ends) is

> A goodly portly man, i' faith, and a corpulent; of a cheerful look, a pleasing eye, and a most noble carriage. (II. iv)

For all its admitted comic quality, there is no mistaking the positive, life-reflecting tone of that description. The speaker is imaginatively identified with his words even as he laughs at himself through them. When he makes the king say he sees "virtue" in his eye, he is clearly mocking himself, and the image of the tree which is known by its fruit reaffirms the specific religious undertone, which is at once an object of ridicule in its Puritan implications, and a measure or standard; and yet when he stresses age in himself, "inclining to three-score," it is a real pathos that he is reducing to absurdity, and humor of this kind can only proceed from a certain honest candor of approach. "Goodly" and "cheerful" in his portliness, we can neither accept Falstaff as representing a sufficient view of life nor follow the Prince in his dismissal of him. He is there at the heart of the play, and his comments, though never all the truth and often indeed a deliberate reversal of it, are always relevant to its complete definition.

This emerges clearly enough when it becomes the Prince's turn to parody his father. Falstaff becomes the butt of a grossness that is surely relevant to the character; in this parody of the relationship between father and son, the Prince heaps upon him such epithets as "bolting-hutch of beastliness," "swollen parcel of dropsies," "huge bombard of sack," and "stuffed cloak-bag of guts." It is noteworthy, in an episode so variously related to popular traditions, that the king's supposed denunciation should turn largely on familiar conventions. If the "roasted Manningtree ox with the pudding in his belly" derives explicitly from a popular feast, the further evocations of the "reverend vice," "grey iniquity," and "vanity in years" clearly require for their appreciation a backward glance to the "morality" tradition. This variety in his traditional and popular derivations largely accounts for the unique fascination exercised by Falstaff; it is as though many anonymous figures, consecrated by established custom and related to living popular traditions, were brought together, at once united and transformed, in this figure of swelling, if unregulated, vitality and comic vigor.

From participation in this wealth of disordered life the Prince is by the very responsibilities of his position largely excluded. We have only to compare the spirit of his denunciation with Falstaff's equally material, but more human, exuberance to see that a deliberate contrast is being pointed. The tone adopted by the Prince is no doubt a necessary corrective; it certainly brings out a true aspect of Falstaff's "three score years of aging villainy," and the repudiation is undoubtedly necessary if Hal is to fulfill his vocation. The truth, however, is so stated as to bring out certain less attractive qualities in the speaker, which may assist him in gaining his political ends but which are not thereby made more humanly acceptable. It is as though Hal, whose every action tends to calculation, felt for his companion the repulsion inspired in the practical intellect by something which it can neither understand, ignore, nor, in the last resort, use. The Prince, in echoing Falstaff's idiom, brings to it a cold, efficient intensity that points to an underlying aversion. The flesh, with which the finished politician needs to reckon, is nevertheless an object of repulsion to him. Beneath the burlesque and the rowdiness we may already look forward to the final rejection.

Falstaff, indeed, in a plea not less pathetic for being a parody based on monstrous presumption, finally justifies himself in terms of human normality:

> If sack and sugar be a fault, God help the wicked! if to be old and merry be a sin, then many an old host that I know is damned: if to be fat be to be hated, then Pharaoh's lean kine are to be loved. (II. iv)

The plea is steeped in sentiment, even in the exploitation of feeling, and to that extent it cannot be admitted; but, as an expression of human qualities that Hal may be the poorer for having to exclude, it is supported by a religious reference that attains, through and in despite of parody, a force of its own. This morality justifies, at least as part of the complete effect, Falstaff's final appeal against dismissal: "banish plump Jack, and banish all the world." Banish Falstaff, in other words, and banish everything that cannot be reduced to an instrument of policy in the quest for a success that is, in its absence, haunted by a sense of emptiness. It is true to the Prince's nature, and to the exigencies of his vocation, that he can already reply without hesitation, speaking in anticipation of his own future action as much as in parody of his father's present attitude: "I do, I will" (II. iv). The long scene ends with Hal's statement that "we must all to the wars," pointing to the change of spirit that will from now on overtake the action. Henceforth neither he nor Falstaff will be devoted entirely to the life of comic freedom, and their actions, like those of everyone else in the play, will look forward to the resolution at Shrewsbury.

By the end of the great tavern scene, the two main threads of the early action—the serious and the comic, the aristocratic and the popular—have been brought together, presented as mutually and variously illuminating. Thus united, they lead to a scene (III. ii) of central importance to the whole design, in which the king and his son are at last confronted and the choice between public vocation and private dissolution, ordered royalty and the chaos of "misrule," finally made. Upon this choice depends the health of the English polity, already presented in its various elements as subjected to the disorder which emanates from the suspect origins of Henry's kingship. This decisive meeting is placed between two episodes which indicate between them the point of balance reached by the action as a whole. The first (III. i) stresses the growth of mutual recrimination in the rebel camp, and in the second (III. iii), the Prince and Falstaff meet in their tavern surroundings for the last time (in this play) and the subjection of the comic action to warlike events is finally confirmed.

The first scene turns initially on a clash between Hotspur and Glendower, in which neither is seen to advantage. If Glendower is a mixture of superstition, vanity, and incompetence whose self-regard prompts him to see insults at every turn, Hotspur, the admired soul of "honour," is not only ready to carve his own country into the spoils of war but to quarrel over the division; and when at last he has forced Glendower to agree to his proposal, he admits in effect that his obstinacy has been the product of ill-tempered spleen:

> I do not care; I'll give thrice so much land
> To any well-deserving friend;
> But in the way of bargain, mark ye me,
> I'll cavil on the ninth part of a hair. (III. i)

Here, at least, the reverse side of Hotspur's "generosity" is apparent. Having risked the unity of the enterprise to which he is committed, he is able, having got his way, to thrust aside his anger with an offhand "I do not care" and a specious show of magnanimity; but the stubborn obstinacy of his final words, and the pursuit of his feud with Glendower to a point at which it places the common interest in jeopardy, are revelations of an unstable and immature outlook.

It is left, as usual, to Worcester to provide a "politic" comment on these developments. Hotspur is rebuked for

> Defect of manners, want of government,
> Pride, haughtiness, opinion and disdain;

and, at the end of the scene, the comic contrast between Mortimer's "romantic" interlude with his wife, in which Glendower's "magic" devices seek to bridge the gap of language between them, and the ironic comments of Hotspur and Lady Percy continues to indicate flaws in character with economy and relevance. Hotspur's concealment of tenderness, of which he is made ashamed by the excessively facile emotions before him, once more suggests an incomplete attitude to personal relationships:

> Swear me, Kate, like a lady as thou art,
> A good mouth-filling oath, and leave "in sooth,"
> And such protest of pepper-gingerbread,
> To velvet-guards and Sunday-citizens. (III. i)

The comment contains both a true criticism of the false conventions which surround Mortimer's "romance" and an implied exposure of the speaker's own limitation to a set of prejudices imposed upon him by character and class alike. The traditional aristocrat's pride in his own plain speaking and his contempt for the pretensions to breeding so absurdly assumed by the lower orders are here combined in an admirable portrait from which neither detachment nor a certain affection are absent. In its modest way, this piece of "popular" comedy already reflects the mature Shakespearean capacity for extracting a variety of meanings form the dramatic presentation of human relationships.

With the movement of the scene to the king's private counsels (III. ii) the relation of the play's "personal" to its "political" theme is at last directly explored. The confronting of Henry with his son has, of course, a "public," rhetorical value which the traditional story imposed. Henry's opening words, however, modify this conception to include a more intimate concern. Prince Hal, destined to become the incarnation of political virtue, is in his unregenerate state a "scourge" in the hands of God, a reminder to his father of the "displeasing service" performed by him in the past:

I know not whether God will have it so,
For some displeasing service I have done,
That, in his secret doom, out of my blood
He'll breed revengement and a scourge for me;
But thou dost in thy passages of life
Make me believe that thou art only marked
For the hot vengeance and the rod of heaven
To punish my mistreadings. (III. ii)

The stressing of the theme of retribution corresponds already to an intimate sense of tragic fatality.[10] The "doom" is "secret," the "revengement" obscurely bred out of the sinner's own blood to chastise him; and yet the sense of guilt which burdens the speech is presented in relation to an overmastering sense of expediency. What Henry condemns in his son is finally a public, a political blemish. His preoccupation is with the "low" and "inordinate" nature of desires that do not correspond to the princely standing of his heir; Hal's "attempts" are "poor," "bare," "lewd," and "mean," his pleasures "barren," and the essence of his faults a surrender to "rude society" which prejudices his "greatness" and is incompatible with the obligations of his "princely heart." From the very first the tragic quality of Henry's intimate meditations is associated with the public, visible nature of the vocation he has dubiously assumed and which is turning into the consuming burden of his life.

As Henry's long reflections develop we suspect, indeed, not for the first time, that the only true *moral* criterion of this king has been, from the beginning, *political* effectiveness. His thoughts, as he contemplates his past career, turn with preference on an estimate of the public effect of a show of "virtuous" discretion:

By being seldom seen. I could not stir
But like a comet I was wonder'd at;
That men would tell their children "This is he";
Others would say "Where, which is Bolingbroke?" (III. ii)

The use of modesty to arrive at a position of pride, of concealment to attract universal attention, is deeply implanted in this essentially, exclusively public personality. Bolingbroke, in his own words, "*stole* all courtesy from heaven," "dress'd" himself in a humility which is clearly less a moral virtue than a device of policy. For Henry the criterion of morality has always tended to be success; and, that being so, it is not surprising that his son should have learned, when necessary, to separate feeling from the necessities of political behavior and that filial tenderness, real as it is in him in his moments of deeper sincerity, should exist side by side with a readiness to subject personal considerations to public achievement. In the realization, born of bitter experience, that the quest for this achievement can also be an illusion lies the secret of the tragic note which dominates the king's later years.

His father's reproaches lead at length to the Prince's reaction, in which, for the first of many occasions, denigration of his character exacts the response of a fixed, firm intensity of purpose. "I will redeem all this on Percy's head," he replies, and goes on to paint a picture of himself as a ruthless warrior which will be repeated in due course, and in terms not altogether dissimilar, by Henry V at the gates of Harfleur:[11]

> I will wear a garment all of blood,
> And stain my favours in a bloody mask,
> Which, wash'd away, shall scour my shame with it . . .
> Percy is but my factor, good my lord,
> To engross up glorious deeds on my behalf;
> And I will call him to so strict account,
> That he shall render every glory up,
> Yea, even the slightest worship of his time,
> Or I will tear the reckoning from his heart,
> This, in the name of God, I promise here. (III. ii)

The total effect of this speech is not easily to be described. The reformation of the private dissolute into the public figure is, without doubt, essential to it; the Prince is vowing himself to duty, and his behavior will never again be what it was in the irresponsible early scenes. Yet there are other aspects of this dedication which need equally to be considered. Among them is the emphasis on "I,"[12] a cold determination which the speech also shows and which is, at least in part, a reaction against the galling superiority attributed to his rival; for behind the phrase "your unthought-of Harry" bitter resentment exists side by side with filial concern. It is the birth of a rigid war machine as well as a prince finding his true nature that is being evoked here, and the culminating dedication to "God" needs to be seen simultaneously under both aspects if the full value of the scene is to be realized. "I will tear the reckoning from his heart": from this moment, an iron fatality has been set in motion which will assert itself on the field at Shrewsbury and—finally—at Harfleur and at Agincourt.

The following scene (III. iii), carrying on the device by which the "serious" action and its comic reflection are alternately developed, shows a parallel shift in spirit. Falstaff's first words take us back to the "action" on Gadshill, but in a changed and chastened mood: "Bardolph, am I not fallen away vilely since this last action? do I not bate? do I not dwindle?" Falstaff can still look upon himself with comic detachment, as when he says that "my skin hangs about me like an old lady's loose gown," or compares his "withered" state to that of an "old apple-john"; but the emphasis on age and exhaustion is new, and the elements of the following comedy equally indicate a change of attitude. Immediately after these first indications, the comic phrases turn upon conceptions of repentance and amendment, already used by Falstaff when, in the first tavern scene (I. ii), he had spoken of "giving over this life"; but whereas repentance had there been made light of, the new utterance is perceptibly more somber in tone:

> Well, I'll repent, and that suddenly, while I am in some liking; I shall be out of heart shortly, and then I shall have no strength to repent. (III. iii)

No doubt the element of religious parody is still present here, but Shakespeare has a way of combining various purposes in a single phrase, and the change of spirit at this point, confirmed as it is by what follows, is a clear sign that the discomfiture of "misrule" is acting as a limiting factor on the free expansion of the comic spirit.

The dialogue which follows relates this shift of feeling to other facets of the character. When Bardolph comically falls in with this feigned spirit of repentance by saying "you cannot live long," Falstaff replies by taking up the other, the "fleshly" and disorderly side of his nature: "Come, sing me a bawdy song; make me merry." This continual capacity to move from one aspect of his presentation to another is of the essence of the complete conception. At this point it turns into a satire upon gentility. "I was as virtuously given as a gentleman need to be," Falstaff begins, weighing comedy with a certain mock nostalgia implied in his backward glance to a lost past. As a "gentleman" Falstaff was "virtuous," but mildly so, "virtuous *enough*"; and the following phrases balance virtue with its opposite in humorous antithesis:

> swore *little;* diced not above *seven times a week;* went to a bawdy-house *not above once in a quarter—of an hour;* paid money that I borrowed, *three or four times.* (III. iii)

The whole is a satire on the life lived "in good compass." At the end of it, Falstaff falls back on yet another of his traditional aspects, that which he derives from the Vice, the incarnation of disorder and the refusal to accept "rule"; for, in his own words, which characteristically combine his moral with his physical qualities, "now I live out of all order, out of all compass." Bardolph, in taking up this last phrase, stresses the purely physical aspect of thus living "out of compass"; but the physical is, of course, a reflection of the moral reality, and Falstaff, in asserting his freedom, is in fact limiting it, relating it to a spiritual tradition which the play in its moments of greatest depth at once accepts and balances against a profound if anarchic vitality.

This last consideration is important. Falstaff's utterances are habitually steeped in tradition, religious and theatrical, and upon the variety of his reaction to tradition depends a good deal of the force of his presentation. He shares with his audience a whole world of imagery, a common inheritance which gives him reality more especially by contrast with the orators and politicians of the "serious" action. The ease with which the theatrical passes into the religious reference is clearly seen in his comment on Bardolph's nose, to which he refers as "a death's head or a memento mori"—"I never see thy face but I think upon hell fire and Dives that lived in purple" (III. iii). In such phrases we feel what the strength of a still living popular tradition could offer to the dramatist. Assimilated into Falstaff's utterances as their natural background, it enables him to bring to his criticism of his political "betters" a realism that is, in its profounder moments, neither self-regarding nor altogether cynical, but derived from a balanced view, still accessible to the author for dramatic purposes, of man's nature and destiny.

The reverse side of the picture is stressed, almost at once, with the entry of the hostess. This brings out the predatory Falstaff, ready to exploit human weakness, to borrow mercilessly, and to accuse his companions of having stolen his possessions. His attitude to the hostess is marked by a persistent emphasis upon the flesh: an emphasis unredeemed by the spirit of comedy and intended to stress the sordid manifestations of appetite in an aging cynic:

> There's no more faith in thee than in a stewed prune; nor no more truth in thee than in a drawn fox; and for womanhood, Maid Marian may be the deputy's wife of the ward to thee.

Even at this point, however, the more serious aspects of the conception impose themselves. Faced by the unanswerable truth of the Prince's denunciation—"there's no room for faith, truth, nor honesty in this bosom of thine"—and the relation of it to his physical enormity—"it is all filled up with guts and midriff"—Falstaff can still balance this evocation of the life lived "out of all compass" with a deeper, more tragic intuition which makes itself felt not less on account of the comic use to which it is put. At his most serious moments—for in him comedy repeatedly touches the serious—Falstaff gives his comic utterances a taste of universality by relating them to the familiar drama of mankind worked out in the individual between birth and death, and in the race between the Creation and the Last Judgment: "Thou knowest in the state of innocency Adam fell; and what should poor Jack Falstaff do in the days of villainy? Thou seest I have more flesh than another man, and therefore more frailty" (III. iii). To take this too seriously would be as misleading as to deny it all seriousness. Falstaff's tone is in part comic, mocking religious phraseology for ends of his own; but the reference to the flesh includes the meaning sanctioned by Christian tradition, and it is in his sense of the relationship between the two realities that Falstaff acquires his full stature. We need not, should not, say that he simply accepts the Christian tradition. A great part of him clearly does not, and he will be finally repudiated in consequence by a Prince whose indispensable vocation rests precisely upon that tradition; but the tradition is present, alive even in the utterances that express his refusal to submit to it, and giving him, even in this refusal, a complexity that enables him at his best to dominate an action whose internal logic drives it increasingly away from him. This, however, is an anticipation of things to come. For the moment, the spirit of comic independence reasserts itself in Falstaff's remark on rebellion: "Well, God be thanked for these rebels, they offend none but the virtuous," which at once confirms disorder and repudiates, in the act of inverting its own phraseology, the "virtue" which will increasingly wear a political garb in the development of the series.

In the last stages of *Henry IV*—Part I, the various threads of the action are drawn together to meet at Shrewsbury. As the moment of decision approaches, Northumberland's "politic" infirmity shows the remaining rebel leaders seeking to evade the bitter truths which at heart they recognize. Hotspur and Douglas, as men of action, meet the news with a specious show of confidence, based on the readiness to see things as they are not:

Douglas: A comfort of retirement lives in this.
Hotspur: A rendezvous, a home to fly unto,
If that the devil and mischance look big
Upon the maidenhead of our affairs. (IV. i)

Worcester, as the "politician" of the conspiracy, knows better. Persuasiveness and "reason," born of cunning and experience, are his gods; but for all this he is a rebel, and as such driven to exclude the operations of true reason as fatal to his own projects. He admits this flaw when he tells his associates:

For well you know we of the offering side
Must keep aloof from strict arbitrement,
And stop all sight-holes, every loop from whence
The eye of reason may pry in upon us. (IV. i)

The fruits of rebellion are, like its origins, disunity and chaos; this truth illustrates a fatality of which Worcester is dimly aware, which he strives to exclude, but which is seen at this moment in the process of overtaking the enterprise to which greed and the desire for power originally committed him.

The end of the scene, with the intervention of Vernon, introduces in contrast a conception of chivalry which is, by any standard, superior in strength and consistency:

I saw young Harry, with his beaver on,
His cuisses on his thighs, gallantly arm'd,
Rise from the ground like feather'd Mercury,
And vaulted with such ease into his seat,
As if an angel dropp'd down from the clouds,
To turn and wind a fiery Pegasus,
And witch the world with noble horsemanship. (IV. i)

A reader used to the complexities of Shakespeare's mature judgments—and this play already reveals a considerable degree of maturity—will not give to this description either more or less value than can properly be attached to it. Already we have been presented with enough material to form a realistic and in some respects a limiting judgment of the type of humanity which Hal has inherited and which he will shortly elevate to a supreme political virtue. These limitations, however, belong to the human rather than to the political order, and are compatible with supreme value in action. This value is here caught in its first public revelation. Henry is here embarked on the process of development which will finally lead him to the triumph of Agincourt, a triumph which his very shortcomings will enable him to attain more securely by excluding all the complexities which might have undermined the self-confidence necessary to his patriotic function.

Certainly by the side of this resplendent martial confidence Hotspur's rhetoric strikes us as hollow, in a relevant sense as *dated:*

> No more, no more: worse than the sun in March,
> This praise doth nourish agues. Let them come;
> They come like sacrifices in their trim,
> And to the fire-eyed god of smoky war
> All hot and bleeding will we offer them:
> The mailed Mars shall on his altar sit
> Up to the ears in blood. (IV. i)

The emphasis on "blood," the adolescent insensibility turned into verbal ruthlessness point, by contrast with the preceding picture of Hal's martial regeneration, to an essential emptiness. The Hotspur here revealed is connected with the object of the Prince's previous satire on his rival's domestic behavior.[13] He appears as a man who has failed to mature, whose "honour"—overtaken by the changing times—is in the last analysis an empty rhetorical device, and who will shortly be eliminated from a world in which he has resolved to play a part without understanding the true nature of the issues in which his fate and the maneuvers of the politicians around him have involved him.

These maneuvers are seen in operation in the episodes which lead, through a varied compound of deception and misunderstanding, to the final resolution. The king makes Worcester and Vernon a generous offer of peace in which he sees the hope of a restoration of natural order based on the free recognition of just authority. His action in so doing is proper to a king; but the origins of his power, which he would now prefer to forget, make their endless consequences felt to frustrate his intentions. Worcester, on his side, is driven first to shut out reason and then to conceal the fact that peace has been offered. His reasons amount to a denial of the rebel's ability to choose responsibly:

> It is not possible, it cannot be,
> The king should keep his word in loving us;
> He will suspect us still and find a time
> To punish this offence in other faults. (V. ii)

Worcester's distrust, like Henry's tragedy, has its origins in the past. It owes its existence to the initial crime by which the seeds of disorder and suspicion were sown to work themselves out on either side in conflict. Both parties in this action are as much victims of "fortune" as conscious agents of their respective purposes. Both evoke "honour" and other lofty sanctions to confer dignity upon their cause; but, though their culpability can never be equal, it remains true that crime born on either side of self-interest is bearing fruit in unnecessary bloodshed.

Against this background the rivalry between Hal and Hotspur is marked by the chivalrous modesty of the challenger. Vernon's emphasis on the Prince's transformation needs to be set against the play's various attitudes to Hotspur, in whom we should not, like the cynical Worcester, see simply what is implied by the caustic phrase: "A *hare-brain'd* Hotspur, governed by a spleen" (V. ii). This is certainly part of the truth about Hal's rival; but another view would discover in him a manifestation, inadequate but sincere, of honorable chivalry. This type of chivalry can achieve the romantic quality of

> I will embrace him with a soldier's arm,
> That he shall shrink under my courtesy, (V. ii)

lines which might have been uttered, later in Shakespeare's career, by Coriolanus or his rival Aufidius.[14] As in the case of the Roman heroes, it combines an attractiveness of its own with an insufficiency which will be finally demonstrated in the warrior's own field of action. Most significant, perhaps, in this respect is Hotspur's assertion, as the scene ends, of the helplessness of human values against the action of time:

> O gentlemen, the time of life is short!
> To spend that shortness basely were too long,
> If life did ride upon a dial's point,
> Still ending at the arrival of an hour.
> An if we live, we live to tread on kings;
> If die, brave death, when princes die with us! (V. ii)

In this speech, Hotspur touches on something relevant not only to an understanding of his own nature but to the history as a whole. The rhetorical flourish of his conclusion cannot conceal the fact that, as in so many of the sonnets, which deal with similar themes, it is a sense of the precarious, the transitory quality of the emotional impulses that appear to constitute life that dominates the speech. It makes Hotspur's affirmations of "honour," if not empty, pathetic and ultimately invalid; and the sense of their inadequacy is shortly confirmed by his death at the hands of a more controlled and mature conception of duty associated with the growth of the ideal king.

The battle episodes to which these preliminaries lead turn upon a nice opposition between traditional concepts of "honour" and a critical presentation of the heroism of war. Sir Walter Blunt, who dies for his King (V. iii), is seen as something less than a master of his fate. For Hotspur, to whom the simple idea of "honour" has always been a sufficient guide, he was a "gallant knight"; but his slayer Douglas, a character less committed to the heroic idea and indeed drawn on lines altogether more barbarous, utters his epitaph in savage terms in which frustrated impatience and a certain rough contempt both play their part:

> A fool go with thy soul, whither it goes!
> A borrowed title hast thou bought too dear. (V. iii)

As usual, something like the last word is left with Falstaff, whose part in the battle is not circumscribed to the mixture of self-interest and heroic values by which the main political actors are at once moved and limited. "Sir Walter Blunt: here's honour for you! here's no vanity!" To appreciate the comment we need to sense the touch of mortality which underlies it. "Vanity," of course, offers a double sense, that of pride (which ends in the traditional fall) and that of nothingness, futility, itself related to death and to the sense of empty "honour" that has brought it upon the victim.

Falstaff's exchange with the Prince, which concludes this scene, answers to a similar intention. Hal, as befits his regenerated state, is concerned with the death of the "noblemen" who lie

> stark and stiff
> Under the hoofs of vaunting enemies; (V. iii)

we need not call the phrase insincere, but there is something limiting about its rhetorical quality which Falstaff is perfectly fitted to take up. He does so, first in his own parody of warlike boasting—"Turk Gregory never did such deeds in arms as I have done this day"—and then by giving Hal his "pistol," which turns out to be a bottle of sack. What is at stake here is not cowardice or its opposite, but rather the assertion of an independence that refuses to accept verbal values at their own estimate, but which plays upon them by converting humor and farce into a distinctive irony. Such is the spirit of his famous comment on Blunt's sacrifice: "I like not such grinning honour as Sir Walter hath: *give me life:* which if I can save, so; if not, honour comes unlooked for, and there's an end" (V. iii). In the phrase "give me life" may be found the key to this judgment in which we may detect, if we will, a foundation of fear, but in which this "cowardice," if it exists, is transformed by self-awareness into something very different; for this is a comment on the waste implied (among other things: the judgment is relevant, not final) in a battle so many of whose causes have been shown to be suspect. Falstaff is, let us say, a coward who can contemplate his own cowardice with detachment; and, by so doing, he offers an estimate of the heroic values, which are themselves related to a positive interpretation of life, but which need the operation of this objective check to prevent them from degenerating into a verbose pose.

The Prince, meanwhile, follows his own path, which leads him, through the rescue of his father from death at the hands of Douglas (V. iv), to the final confrontation with Hotspur. With this, the central duel between rival conceptions of "honour" and their relation to the "destiny" which overshadows them is at last brought to a head. These conceptions are, indeed, mutually exclusive; this is implied in the Prince's words "Two stars keep not their motion in one sphere," and the type of "glory" with which both are here concerned is not of the kind that can be shared in life. The clash between them follows, and ends in Hotspur's death. His last speech is important in its suggestion of a relationship between the speaker's conception of "honour" and certain themes growing to mature expression in Shakespeare's work at this time. Hotspur, dying, affirms the value of the "proud titles" of glory above those of "brittle life"; but in the adjective there is a sense of hollowness which contrasts with the content of the vaguely conceived "titles" themselves and suggests that sense of tragic emptiness which Shakespeare comes increasingly to set in pathetic contrast to the heroic ideal. The whole of Hotspur's response to his rival's final words is wrapped in a characteristic pessimism:

> They wound my thoughts worse than thy sword my flesh:
> But thought's the slave of life, and life time's fool;
> And time, that takes survey of all the world,
> Must have a stop. (V. iv)

To interpret this adequately is to be aware of a conflict more subtle than may immediately appear. It is at once an attempted excuse for inner emptiness, for chivalrous values seen at the decisive moment to be void of true significance, and a pathetic affirmation of the tragedy which the recognition of this reality implies. The sense of the passage of time, unredeemed by a corresponding conception of "value," is typical of many of the sonnets[15] and of much of Shakespeare's work at this period. Originally relatively abstract in expression, we see it now gaining a personal and pathetic quality which will eventually affect the dramatist's attitude to his tragic heroes.

At this point, indeed, Hotspur is at once expressing disillusionment and, in expressing it, seeking a last emotional compensation. At Shrewsbury he has fallen before a conception of honor deeper and, as the future will confirm, more effective than his own; but he has fallen also on behalf of the policies incarnated in Worcester, policies which his emotion has too readily accepted but which are less creditable than those which his own nature should have been able to assimilate. His death leaves us with an impression poised between the tragic and the ironic, adequately summed up in the self-conscious pathos of his reference to the "earthy and cold hand of death" and in the contrast of attitudes contained in his conqueror's brief completion of his final "food for—": "For *worms, brave* Percy." This is simply one aspect of the fatality that overshadows a battle in which the rebels fail to attain their end and in which it is foreseen that the king will equally be prevented from achieving the unity for which he is *now*, but too late, genuinely striving.

The Prince's oration over his dead rival is, as far as it goes, fitting and impressive, one more sign of his growing stature; but it belongs, like so much in his nature, to the *public* rather than to the truly personal order. In calling Hotspur "great heart" and "so stout a gentleman" he affirms the values of courtesy which are to be a part of his own royal virtues; but, even in so doing, in the lending of his "favours" to cover his enemy's "mangled face" with "rites of tenderness," we may feel a weight correspondingly laid on vanity:

> When that this body did contain a spirit,
> A kingdom for it was too small a bound;
> But now two paces of the vilest earth
> Is room enough. (V. iv)

Beneath the formal quality of this epitaph lies a preoccupation with the "vanity" upon which Falstaff has already touched in irony; the modification of the chivalrous note by a qualifying sense of tragedy is full of meaning for the interpretation of later plays.

It is no accident that Falstaff has been a spectator of this duel of contrasted incarnations of "honour." Before the battle, his contact with the popular sphere implied a parallel, at once cynical and humorous, to the serious action, and now his mock death carries this parallel to a logical culmination; whilst the Prince, having delivered his chivalrous epitaph over Hotspur, turns to a comic shadow of it in his reflections over Falstaff's body:

> O, I should have a heavy miss of thee,
> If I were much in love with vanity!
> Death hath not struck so fat a deer to-day,
> Though many dearer, in this bloody fray. (V. iv)

The easy flow of rhyme offers a clear contrast to the preceding heroic seriousness, and even the reference to "vanity" rouses echoes from the past action. The Prince's humor, with its somewhat self-conscious disclaimer, "If I were much in love with vanity," is indeed in character, as is the pun on "deer" and "dearer," which is of a kind that can be paralleled elsewhere in his utterances. Comic as the speech is in intention, its spirit is that of a commentary offered in character, a placing of what has gone before; nor is this mock death, and the Prince's equally mock farewell, at this moment in which he has decisively confirmed himself in his "serious" political function, entirely without significance for their future relationship.

Falstaff's comment after his "resurrection" contains as usual an assertion of simple vitality against the claims of verbal obligation: "To die, is to be a counterfeit; for he is but the counterfeit of a man who hath not the life of a man: but to counterfeit dying, when a man thereby liveth, is to be no counterfeit, but the true and perfect image of life indeed" (V. iv). The stress laid upon "life," in its "true and perfect image," illuminates the function of Falstaff in this play without, however, exhausting it. In the light of this assertion, the speaker's "cowardice" is seen to include a positive comic value, and even the final stabbing of Hotspur's dead body and the taking of the grotesque burden on his back, though no doubt it is the final manifestation of the braggart soldier of theatrical convention, contains also an ironic reference to the serious, "chivalrous" combat we have just witnessed. At this point, the last word of the play has really been spoken. The final scene (V. v) simply winds up the political action, justifies Henry against the treachery of Worcester, and allows the Prince to express himself with proper generosity toward Douglas. The king's concluding reference to the future campaigns against his remaining enemies places us on the threshold of the play to follow.

HENRY IV–PART II

Henry IV—Part II, although carrying on the design initiated in the preceding play,[16] differs in certain respects from its predecessor. Henry IV, whose struggle to assert his kingship had provided a principal thread of action in Part I, has ceased in the sequel to exercise any positive influence over the course of events. As a result, the state of England—more extensively and realistically portrayed than before—is shown as given over to anarchy and corruption. Aged and cynical rebels share a sense of adverse fatality with the king whom they originally backed in his crime of usurpation; whilst in the popular sphere, a predatory and decaying Falstaff exercises his wits in drawing from misery, corruption, and impotence an uneasy and parasitic sustenance. The consequences of the crisis in authority initiated by Bolingbroke's murder of Richard cover the entire realm and threaten its vital unity with extinction. It would hardly be possible to stress more forcibly the urgency, the indispensable need, of Henry V's approaching affirmation of authority.

The earlier political action is concentrated, as though to emphasize the prevalence of disorder, upon the counsels of the rebel leaders. These are developed with an elaboration which is perhaps best studied in the words spoken by Northumberland when the news of defeat at Shrewsbury is finally brought home to him:

> In poison there is physic; and these news,
> Having been well, that would have made me sick,
> Being sick, have in some measure made me well:
> And as the wretch, whose fever-weaken'd joints,
> Like strengthless hinges, buckle under life,
> Impatient of his fit, breaks like a fire
> Out of his keeper's arms, even so my limbs,
> Weaken'd with grief, being now enraged with grief,
> Are thrice themselves. (I. i)

The verse is, in ancestry, clearly that of the early Shakespeare. The machinery is prominent to a degree that would never be tolerated in the greater plays; but there is a feeling, too, that the poet is reaching out through these devices to new elaborations of experience. The speech aims, however obscurely, at a new effect, an attempt to carry the shifts and tensions of consciousness in the strain of self-definition. In Northumberland's mind health and sickness, action and renunciation, are chaotically intertwined. "Poison" comes to him, or so he would like to think, in the form of "physic"; the bad news that, in a state of health, would have reduced him to sickness, has now, precisely because he is "sick," created in him an illusion of health. The intention, moreover, is not simply to contrast age and weakness with the need for decisive action. It is to convey in the motion of the verse the tragic disharmony that exists in the old man and unites him to a history not less tragically conceived. The words "well" and "sick," as he uses them, shift in their context, refer at different moments to his own condition and to the news he has received. It is the effect of perversity in rebellion to produce a state of moral "sickness" which the external action confirms and which, in the last analysis, Northumberland shares with the king he is striving to overthrow.

Northumberland, to put the matter in another way, is not simply a figure to be observed and analyzed in terms of motivation. From the beginning, his helplessness is related to an overriding sense of tragic circumstance. His first words, spoken to Lord Bardolph,

> The times are wild; contention, like a horse,
> Full of high feeding, madly hath broke loose
> And bears all down before him, (I. i)

have already conveyed a sense of impending disaster which, superbly embodied in the blind sensual energy of the horse, looms over the petty drama of senile indecision enacted, as it were, beneath its menacing shadow. Now, as defeat is confirmed, the threat extends itself, is concentrated upon a vision of universal chaos:

> Let heaven kiss earth; now let not Nature's hand
> Keep the wild flood confined! *let order die!*
> And let this world no longer be a stage
> To feed contention in a lingering act;
> But let one spirit of the first-born Cain
> Reign in all bosoms, that, each heart being set
> On bloody courses, the rude scene may end
> And darkness be the burier of the dead! (I. i)

Here, if anywhere, rhetoric touches, through the broken and hysterical reaction of a defeated old man, upon the universal implications of sedition. The rebels of this play are no longer primarily crafty politicians, realistically presented. The emphasis now is hardly upon responsibility at all. The dim figures who have survived the disaster at Shrewsbury are no longer, like Hotspur and Douglas, active and impetuous leaders; nor are they even particularly crafty, as Worcester had been, or, like Glendower, opinionated and obstinately vain. Their personal qualities, such as they are, have been relegated to the background; like Northumberland himself, though in varying degrees, they have become old and disillusioned shadows, no longer in control of the events which they have set in motion and which now push them on to conclusions only foreseen as disastrous.

The lengthy ratiocinations of Lord Bardolph and his fellow conspirators in the next political episode (I. iii) show them wrapped in the foreboding,

> Conjecture, expectation, and surmise
> Of aids uncertain,

which their arguments strive to conjure. They are built on an elaboration of concepts which finally, somewhat like that of the Greek leaders in *Troilus and Cressida,* excludes true purpose.[17] The initial emphasis on the need for decision—the answer of "*instant* action" to the challenge offered by "the *present* quality of war"—fades into a contrary stagnation. This development answers to a natural process; for, as Bardolph recognizes,

a cause on foot
Lives so in hope, as in an early spring
We see the appearing buds; which to prove fruit,
Hope gives not so much warrant as despair
That frosts will bite them. (I. iii)[18]

The imagery, like so much in the sonnets and plays of this period, rests upon convention, but the contrast between "spring" growth and the lack of final fulfillment, between deceptive "hope" and harsh reality, is very close to the sense of frustration which dogs the rebel leaders in these scenes. This is already, in an elementary form, the problem with which Agamemnon and the Greek leaders will so long and vainly wrestle under the walls of Troy.[19]

The last of these early political scenes (II. iii) confirms the death of virtue and its replacement by senile indecision in an age of self-seeking policy. Northumberland is striving to maintain against his wife and Percy's widow the outward appearance of self-respect. It is his "honour," he argues, which is "at pawn," imposing upon him a course of action which he tacitly admits to be irrational. The word, so closely associated with her husband's memory, prompts Lady Percy to affirm the passing, in his person, of an order that died finally, as at once inadequate and incompatible with the spirit of the successful politicians of these plays, at Shrewsbury. Her answer to Northumberland's wavering appeal to "honour" is clear and decisive; for when "honour" was alive, incarnate in Hotspur, he deserted it, leaving "two honours lost, yours and your son's" (II. iii). Her outburst culminates in the celebration of a chivalrous ideal at once compelling, endowed with a magnetism of its own, and irretrievably lost. Hotspur is remembered as the norm of aristocratic conduct, the inspiration by whose light

Did all the chivalry of England move
To do brave acts.

The inspiration, however, led only to public disaster and personal loss. Hotspur is dead, "food for worms."[20] Those who have survived him—and not on the rebel side alone—share between them a world of calculation, to which Northumberland has already accommodated himself. The adjustment, dishonorable as it is, will not bring with it the safety for which he craves. He admits that, if he is to fight, it will be as a victim caught in a web of circumstances from which there is no final escape:

> I must go and meet with danger there,
> Or it will seek me in another place
> And find me worse provided. (II. iii)

In the end, however, the instinct to temporize prevails, and the aged politician's last words confirm the uncertainty which derives from subjection to a temporal process which he knows to be beyond his control:

> 'Tis with my mind
> As with the tide swell'd up unto his height,
> That makes a still-stand, running neither way. (II. iii)

"Time and vantage" are in charge of events, and no decision grasped at by Northumberland's tortuous and infirm mind can turn aside the approaching execution of his fate.

The presentation of a Falstaff in some respects notably changed from his previous image provides a parallel to the "serious" episodes we have just considered. His words and actions still contain a commentary on public events, but the spirit of that commentary has undergone a certain transformation. No longer felt to stand in some measure apart from the events in which he participates, he has become subdued to the tone of the life around him. If he feels his years as a burden, so do the politicians who have accompanied, with approval or dissent, Henry's rise to power; and, if he is diseased, we have seen that disease is both the counterpart of rebellion and a sign of the disorder which it will be Hal's stern duty to extirpate from the imperiled body of his realm.

In the light of this general statement, it is worth noting that Falstaff's first words in this play refer to his need to consult a physician. His "water," according to the doctor, is "a good healthy water," but "for the party that owed it, he might have more diseases than he knew for" (I. ii). The statement links the aging Falstaff to the infirm plottings of the rebel leaders and, beyond these, to the state of the English kingdom infected—as the action will progressively show—by the dubious origins of its king's authority. It is true that Falstaff can still turn his circumstances to laughter, be "the cause that wit is in other men"; but his jokes under the new circumstances deviate significantly from the best of those in Part I, are attuned to the changed world in which he finds himself. In his grotesque picture of himself as "a sow that hath overwhelmed all her litter but one" the self-consuming consequences of anarchy are emphasized in the act of reducing them to laughter; and this gives way, in his following reference to the Prince—"He may keep his own grace, but he's almost out of mine, I can assure him" (I. ii)—to a first comic inversion of what will eventually be his own rejection. The physical embodiment of "riot" announces himself, in his growing presumption, as able to reject the master who will finally reject him.

These opening manifestations are preliminary to the main purpose of the scene: the clash between Falstaff, in whom the spirit of anarchic self-assertion is embodied in the flesh, and the claims of control incarnated in the figure of the Lord Chief Justice. The exchange between them culminates in due course in a statement of irreconcilable positions:

– Well, the truth is, Sir John, you live in great infamy.
– He that buckles him in my belt cannot live in less.
– Your means are very slender, and your waste is great.
– I would it were otherwise; I would my means were greater, and my waist slenderer.
– You have misled the youthful prince.
– The young prince hath misled me; I am the fellow with the great belly, and he my dog. (I. ii)

Beneath the play of verbal opposites lies a contrast close to the central conception. To the Chief Justice's moral accusation Falstaff replies with an assertion of physical expansiveness, but, in accordance with the mood that increasingly prevails, physical freedom corresponds to profligacy, expansion becomes "waste," and finally Falstaff turns his physical bulk to an evocation of penury and the Prince whom he is accused of leading astray into the "dog" who leads the beggar in his helplessness. Falstaff's wit still imposes itself but its end is now, not the expression of a criticism of life, but an evasion of the claims of restraint, which will nonetheless prove inescapable for serious and comic, virtuous and profligate alike.

The final exchanges answer to the same spirit. The Lord Chief Justice counters Falstaff's insolent reference to "the capacities of us that are young" with a bitterly realistic catalogue of decay:

> Have you not a moist eye? a dry hand? a yellow cheek? a white beard? a decreasing leg? an increasing belly? is not your voice broken? your wind short? your chin double? your wit single? and every part about you blasted with antiquity? (I. ii)

The Falstaff of Part I would never have been subjected to so merciless an exposure and would never have accepted it if he had;[21] but now his fictitious affirmation of perennial youth—"I was born about three of the clock with a white head and something a round belly"—and his satire on Puritan piety—"For my voice, I have lost it with halloing and singing of anthems"—affect us chiefly as echoes of earlier, more carefree felicities. These are indeed "costermonger times," corresponding to an aging world in which "virtue" is neglected and the figure of "valour" has become that of the soldier returning broken from the wars and reduced, as Falstaff also puts it, to the miserable occupation of "bear-herd." In Falstaff himself, impecuniousness has similarly become "consumption of the purse," an "incurable malady," whilst "age" and "covetousness" are no less intimately connected than "young limbs" and "lechery"; but—as he goes on to say—"the gout galls the one, and the pox pinches the other" (I. ii), so that the final effect is one in which comedy seems well on the way to the sardonic cynicism affected by Thersites in *Troilus and Cressida.* Falstaff, with the "gout" or the "pox" and affected by the "incurable" disease of poverty which borrowing "only lingers out," ends by seeing in the circumstances of war no more than a means of putting off his inevitable exposure: "A good wit will make use of anything: I will turn diseases to commodity" (I. ii). That the Prince will be amply justified in rejecting a Falstaff so conceived is not open to question; but the fact that the companion of his former tavern exploits so expresses himself is a sign not only of his own decline in years and comic energy, but of that of the world in which he and the Prince both move.

Lest we should fail to relate this change in Falstaff to the surrounding action, the scenes which follow introduce a Prince almost equally subdued to the general disenchantment. Hal's attempt to convey to Poins, in whom—as he well knows—the world's reactions are reflected, the sorrow which his father's illness inspires in him is met with complete incredulity. Poins' skepticism, which confirms his own intimate mood, is met by an appeal to the future development already foreseen: "let the end try the man." The end will bring triumph, self-mastery, and self-affirmation; but even these desirable ends have their price, as is implied in the melancholy which peers through self-exculpation in the following phrase:

> I tell thee, my heart bleeds inwardly that my father is so sick: and keeping such vile company as thou art hath in reason taken from me all ostentation of sorrow. (II. ii)

The "vile company" which, in his first soliloquy,[22] Hal accepted as a means to his political education, confident that he could discard it at will, has become a constraining factor in his life. Poins, no longer merely the companion of his leisure hours, now appears as an epitome of what the world thinks about him—"never a man's thought in the world keeps the road-way better than thine"—and if the element of condescension, the belief that company can be assumed and discarded like an old coat, is still present, there is also a new sense of confinement, of being caught in circumstances formerly accepted in levity which oblige the speaker to keep his deepest emotions to himself, making them lie as an undivulged burden at his heart. For one brief moment, we see Hal as the victim of his own past choice, oppressed with emotions which he cannot, having chosen his own peculiar path to public success, allow himself freely to express.

The great tavern scene (II. iv) in which this part of the action culminates is designed to recall the Prince's former adventures at Eastcheap.[23] Once more Hal, subjected to Falstaff's ironic comments, discovers his identity; and once again Falstaff, asserting himself in the spirit of "riot," parodies the serious claims to valor of his aristocratic betters. The difference in mood, however, is more significant than these parallels. Falstaff, whose influence over the Prince is to all intents and purposes dead, continues to be presented in decline. His victory over Pistol is a poor shadow of the exuberance which had once triumphed, in imaginative retrospect, over the "men in buckram"[24] and which is now reduced to mere evasion, to an effort to escape the imposition of fact. The spirit of comedy, modified to meet the approaching vindication of moral order, is blended with pathos, burdened with a sense of the corruption of human values by time and ill-living.

Behind these intimations of decay the scene stresses, through the relationship between Falstaff and Doll Tearsheet, the presence of a compensating humanity. This is accomplished with no undue concession to sentiment, no disguise of the corrupting effects of senile appetite: "If the cook help to make the gluttony, you help to make the diseases, Doll; we catch of you, Doll, we catch of you; grant that, my poor virtue, grant that." The combination of realism and decayed sentiment, ironic resignation and an echo of compassion ("my poor virtue") reflect a situation already charged with human complexity; and to it Doll, destined by the weakness of her sex to bear the "huge full hogshead," the monstrous weight of Falstaff's carnality, responds by clinging to his faded physical exuberance as to the shadow of life:

> Come, I'll be friends with thee, Jack: thou art going to the wars; and whether I shall ever see thee again or no, there is nobody cares. (II. iv)

To her flushed imagination, his "victory" over Pistol presents itself as a heroic episode, to be celebrated in a grotesque parody of the bombastic rhetoric so prominent in the Ancient's own utterances:

> Ah, rogue! i' faith, I love thee: thou art as valorous as Hector of Troy, worth five of Agamemnon, and ten times better than the Nine Worthies. (II. iv)

The effect here is purely comic; and in Falstaff's complacent appreciation of his own worth it is a similar absurdity, the contrast between his claim and its miserable object, that counts. This incongruity, however, bears with it an intimation of decline that ends by attaching itself to Doll's fuddled emotions. Thus moved, she takes up the image of the "martlemas," the boar destined for slaughter at the outset of winter, and invests it, beneath the obvious comedy, with a characteristic pathos:

> Thou whoreson little tidy Bartholomew boar-pig, when wilt thou leave fighting o' days and foining o' nights, and begin to patch up thine old body for heaven? (II. iv)

At this point, the grotesque endearments of the prostitute, presented without abuse of sentiment, touch upon the scene's distinctive undertone of moral tragedy. If a sense of age and impotence now surrounds Falstaff, and if his behavior, no longer fresh and freely personal, is concentrated on the sordid realities of brawling by day and lechery by night, the change carries with it an awareness of impending dissolution. A note of moral reflection colors, albeit unwillingly, the twilight of his relationship with Doll, and makes it the occasion for some of the deepest sentiments of the play.

Doll's expressions of affection, indeed, finally inspire the most unequivocal of all Falstaff's intimations of decline: "Peace, good Doll!

do not speak like a death's-head: do not bid me remember mine end." The phrase, in cutting right across the simplified effects of realistic comedy, connects Falstaff with the dark feeling of the political action, a connection made still more explicit, a moment later, in Poins' ironic comment on his relations with Doll: "Is it not strange that desire should so many years outlive performance?"[25] Once more, as in Part I—though toward ends notably transformed—the "low" episodes echo their aristocratic counterpart and Falstaff's burden of disease and concupiscence is presented as a reflection of the malady and disharmony shared by the senile rivals who, prior to the Prince's affirmation of his royal vocation, divide between them the public life of England.

It is on a return to this blend of sentiment and tragedy that the exchange with Doll ends. "I am old, I am old," Falstaff repeats, receiving in return another of those answers in which calculation and gross sentiment shade into an intimation of deeper feeling: "I love thee better than I love e'er a scurvy young boy of them all." This declaration in turn inspires the reply, "Thou'lt forget me when I am gone," in which the recognition by age of its own impotence is touched, at least for a moment, by the shadow of true emotion. The effect of these somber reflections is greatly enhanced by their setting in the surrounding comedy, which leads finally to the renewed exposure of Falstaff. When the Prince and Poins reveal their identity, he still has presence of mind to recover, to return to an echo of his former attacking mood; for the exclamation "Ha! a bastard son of the king's? And art thou not Poins his brother?" shows him stressing the community between Hal and his associate to which these scenes more than once revert. His gift for evasion, however, is now exercised under unfavorable conditions. The presence of moral reality which colors, however unwillingly, his thought makes itself felt when he crowns Doll's question to the Prince, "What says your grace?" with the embittered pun: "His grace says that which his flesh rebels against." The echoes which derive from this wry evocation of the conflict between body and spirit are manifold. To link it with the reference, which immediately precedes it, to Lenten abstinence and the illegal eating of flesh, is to approach very closely the intimate spirit of this scene; and to see its further relation to the contrast between law and its evasion, moral rigor and unregulated appetite, setting the choice thus postulated against the background of burning in hell-fire, is to respond to some of the somber undercurrents which, associated with age, decay, and approaching retribution, amount to a profound transformation of the entire comic effect.

By the end of the second act the internal strife and decay which threaten Henry IV's England with dissolution have been extensively portrayed. Both in the rebel counsels and in the tavern world from which Hal is detaching himself, the shadow of age and impotence lies heavily over the action. The presentation of the king, from whose false position—false at least in its origins—this disorder springs, now marks a turning point in the entire history. Henry's old age is dominated by disappointment and by an obsessive preoccupation with infirmity:

> Then you perceive the body of our kingdom
> How foul it is; what rank diseases grow,
> And with what danger, near the heart of it. (III. i)

The enterprises planned in the earlier part of the reign have all remained without fulfillment. Accepting this frustration as part of the nature of things, Henry's strongest emotion has become a nostalgia for peace and sleep. This nostalgia is born less of immediate experience than of a sense of the meaningless procession of events beyond human control:

> O God! that one might read the book of fate,
> And see the revolution of the times
> Make mountains level, and the continent,
> Weary of solid firmness, melt itself
> Into the sea!

This stressed subjection to mutability derives ultimately from the king's contemplation of his past career, in which he now sees nothing but division proceeding (in great part by his own act) out of original concord:

> 'Tis not ten years gone
> Since Richard and Northumberland, great friends,
> Did feast together, and in two years after
> Were they at wars: it is but eight years since
> This Percy was the man nearest my soul,
> Who like a brother toil'd in my affairs,
> And laid his love and life under my foot. (III. i)

The lesson of the past comes home to him at the end of his career with the force of a universal law. Recalling Richard's original prophecy—

> The time will come that foul sin, gathering head,
> Shall break into corruption— (III. i)[26]

the king has come to read into the subsequent history of his reign a confirmation of the operations of fate; but it is his tragedy that, having accepted the reality of his condition, he is no longer in a position to derive benefit from any practical lesson to be drawn from it:

> O, if this were seen,
> The happiest youth, viewing his progress through,
> What perils past, what crosses to ensue,
> Would shut the book, and sit him down and die. (III. i)

A sense of the weight of necessity, of an obscure fatality born of human error and bearing down upon individual helplessness, is the only lesson derived by Henry from the long chain of events which has brought him to exhaustion and his kingdom to the verge of dissolution.

The transfer of the action to Falstaff's exploits in Gloucester (III. ii) further underlines this impression of "necessity." In his relations with Shallow and Silence, he is brought into touch with the very embodiments of powerless senility. "Mad Shallow," "lusty Shallow," shifting from the contemplation of mortality—"death, as the Psalmist saith, is certain to all; all shall die"—and the memory of his youth at the Inns of Court to matters of hard calculation—"How a good yoke of bullocks at Stamford fair?"—is thoroughly in keeping with the spirit of the play. The switch from tragic impotence to the shrewd bargaining of the market place is various in its implications. It stresses the speaker's lack of sensibility, his senile tendency to turn, without any sense of incongruity, from universal tragedy to the petty routine of avarice; but equally the emphasis on the market place points in its own way to the continued processes of life which individual decline cannot altogether obscure. Life goes on even under the shadow of death; its manifestations, grasping, absurd, and inadequate though they may be, are variously interwoven with the sense of mortality which the action at this stage so strongly conveys.

Falstaff himself has no illusions about the world around him, or about his own place in it. He sees to the "bottom" of Shallow—"Lord,

Lord, how subject we old men are to this vice of lying"—in his mixture of present helplessness and remembered, or coveted, lechery; he can do so because he knows that the cynical observer and his victim are alike in being "time's subjects." "We have heard the chimes at midnight, Master Shallow" (III. ii), and the echoes which these chimes evoke touch life at many points. Falstaff's own vision is, like so much else in this play, the product of experience colored by age. His previous repudiation of "honour" bears fruit in his changed attitude to the human victims of civil strife. The "food for powder"[27] which he had led to battle at Shrewsbury now speaks to him through Feeble, who has also been pressed into a cause which has no meaning for him and who resigns himself to his probable fate in words which recall those once spoken by the Prince to Falstaff himself at Shrewsbury, "a man can die but once: we owe God a death."[28] The words are similar, but the attitude of Falstaff, confronted with all that they imply, has changed. Whereas his reply to the Prince had been tinged, beneath its evident disrepute, with irony and wit, had implied an affirmation of the rights of life beyond the selfish calculations of politicians, the Falstaff of Part II, after allowing Mouldy and Bullcalf to buy their freedom, is content to accept his victim's submission to his fate; for such, and no other, is the nature of things, and in Gloucestershire, as in the counsels of kings and courtiers, *necessity* justifies all: "if the young dace be a bait for the old pike, I see no reason, *in the law of nature,* but I may snap at him. *Let time shape,* and there an end" (III. ii).

The scenes which follow lead to the final resolution of the political crisis. To rebels aware of participating in a state of organic failing and sickness which embraces the entire state—as York puts it, echoing his king,

> we are all diseased,
> And with our surfeiting and wanton hours
> Have brought ourselves into a burning fever,
> And we must bleed for it— (IV. i)[29]

the action of time opposes, on the loyalist side, the representatives of a new generation. The responsibilities abdicated, to all intents and purposes, by Henry are now momentarily concentrated upon John of Lancaster. What has been in Henry IV a tragic sense of adverse fatality becomes in his sons a practical grasp of human limitation. Having played no part in the crime which brought their father to the throne, the Prince and his brother are free to attain all that he can no longer hope to achieve. Yet—since the past after all lives on in their present circumstances—the achievement itself, positive and necessary as it is, loses some of its savor. The cool competence of Lancaster's handling of the rebels, his impeccable appeal to all the correct doctrines lead up to the hollow victory at Gaultree, adequately summed up in his parsimonious ascription of it to divine collaboration: "God, and not we, hath *safely* fought to-day" (IV. ii). The voice that speaks throughout this scene is the voice of political sufficiency, condemning its enemies—justly—for their shallowness, in perfect mastery of the course of events. It is a voice that we shall hear again in Henry V, deepened indeed by reference to other, less merely political values, but present as a factor determining the new king's decisions and contributing to his success.

As usual, the final comment is left to Falstaff, who, though in some ways the shadow of his former self, can still assert himself on occasions against the prevailing tone of the action. The taking of Colevile after the rebel surrender reflects upon the spirit of the political exchange we have just witnessed. Colevile speaks bitterly of the "betters" who have led him to his fate; and both he and Falstaff are in turn commented upon, flatly and coldly, by the presiding genius of this unsavory action. For Falstaff, Lancaster has a level-toned rebuke, the theme of which has often been anticipated by Hal in the tavern:

> These tardy tricks of yours will, on my life,
> One time or other break some gallows' back; (IV. iii)

and for Colevile, "famous rebel," he decrees "present execution." In the political sphere the triumph of loyal efficiency is as complete as it is salutary; yet even here we are allowed, before the scene ends, a glimpse of Falstaff's judgment on Lancaster and, through him, on so much in this play. He describes Prince John as "a young, sober-blooded boy," one of those who "when they marry, get wenches" (IV. iii). The rich flexibility of the prose, as it flows on in a succession of phrases like "apprehensive, quick, forgetive, full of nimble, fiery and delectable shapes," emphasizes by contrast the coldness which has inspired the successful princes and leaders in their vindication of the principle of authority. The phrasing, indeed, is a product of "inflammation," and Falstaff has no illusions about his own pretensions to heroism. "Some of us," he comments, would also be "fools and cowards," were it not for the artificial heightening of the emotions; but emotion of any kind comes as a natural relief after the action we have just witnessed.

The two scenes (IV. iv, v) which follow take us back to the infirm king, now about to die with the weight of his past acts lying heavily upon his conscience. His comment on his son, whom Warwick attempts to defend, is one in which skepticism and bitterness prevail:

> 'Tis seldom when the bee doth leave her comb
> In the dead carrion; (IV. iv)

and, a little later, he receives the news of the defeat of the rebels in a mood that recalls the contradictions of the aged Northumberland:

> And wherefore should these good news make me sick?
> Will Fortune never come with both hands full,
> And write her fair words still in foulest letters?
> She either gives a stomach and no food;
> Such are the poor, in health; or else a feast
> And takes away the stomach; such are the rich,
> That have abundance and enjoy it not. (IV. iv)[30]

It is—as we have seen—no accident that the king and his former accomplice, now his defeated enemy, are thus bound together by subjection to age and the sense of a lack of solid achievement. Both belong to a world in which sickness and decline prevail, and are mirrors of inner tragedy. Both are victims rather than agents, once their respective selfish choices have been made; and both stand, without the prospect of entering it, upon the threshold of a world in which the criterion of effective success will be married to a simple and positive set of moral judgments.

The birth of this world is confirmed in the next scene (IV. v), as the Prince is reconciled to his father on his deathbed and assumes, in all its glory and burden, the vocation his birth has imposed upon him. The fatal decision, to which the whole action has been tending, is now expressed in two speeches. In the first, the king, conscious of the approach of death, gathers up his sense of vanity in one complete evocation of the rule of "riot" which, as he foresees, will fall upon England when his son is crowned. Beyond the vanity of death, he sees another, still more bitter vanity, the dissolution of everything for which he has striven into the chaos of "misrule":

For the fifth Harry from curb'd license plucks
The muzzle of restraint, and the wild dog
Shall flesh his tooth on every innocent.
O my poor kingdom, sick with civil blows!
When that my care could not withhold thy riots,
What wilt thou do when riot is thy care?
O, thou wilt be a wilderness again,
Peopled with wolves, thy old inhabitants! (IV. v)

In this speech Henry is affected personally, tragically if we will, by the foreseen ruin of the structure to which he has so painfully devoted his life; for his son's assumption of the crown will, he anticipates, lead to the destitution of his officers and the abandonment of his decrees. In the culminating part of the speech, the whole "public" significance of the Falstaff scenes is summed up in a bitter apprehension of chaos. "Form," by which alone the fragile political structure can be maintained through allegiance to its royal keystone, will be mocked and "vanity" rule to the dissolution of civilized customs. The gold which is, in the crown, the emblem of kingship will "gild" the shame of misrule, and the result will be an endless disorder in which "riot," deprived of its mask of conviviality, will assume its true visage of predatory ruthlessness, to the dissolution of the national community and of all civilized life.

To this bitter reproach the Prince replies with an expression of filial reverence which at last reconciles him to his father. His kneeling is an exterior expression of obedience, the sign of a "most inward true and duteous spirit"; and it leads to an affirmation of the conversion which has been from the first anticipated and is now at last a reality:

If I do feign,
O, let me in my present wildness die,
And never live to show the incredulous world
The noble change that I have purposed! (IV. v)

It is noteworthy, however, that this "conversion" is still essentially a *public* matter, a question of showing the "incredulous world" to what extent it has misjudged the future king. We need not, should not, affirm that this makes the Prince insincere; for he is a public figure and his emotions are necessarily publicly, politically conceived. If this play contains deep personal feeling, this lies precisely in the gap which is felt at certain moments to separate public from private emotion; where the one is triumphant in the necessary assertion of authority, the other sees in the exercise of the royal power a burden of responsibility almost intolerable to be borne, a constricting framework enclosing life and making the king's office barely human in its implications. This latter sense the Prince expresses as he sums up the content of his meditations on the crown:

thou, most fine, most honour'd, most renown'd,
Hast eat thy bearer up. (IV. v)

The incidence here of intense private sentiment is communicated in words which point to the presence of inherited, traditional feeling. For this play shows emotion of a tragic kind making itself felt, in its attitude to the royal office, partly through traditional conceptions and partly in contrast to them; and in the shifting relationship between these two strains lies the explanation of some of the deepest effects which it is capable of producing.

At the end of his speech, the Prince asserts his own attitude to the crown in a spirit which combines sober resolution with a touch of pessimism:

Thus, my most royal liege,
Accusing it, I put it on my head,
To try with it, as with an enemy
That had before my face murder'd my father,
The quarrel of a true inheritor.
But if it did infect my blood with joy,
Or swell my thoughts to any strain of pride;
If any rebel or vain spirit of mine
Did with the least affection of a welcome
Give entertainment to the might of it,
Let God for ever keep it from my head,
And make me as the poorest vassal is,
That doth with awe and terror kneel to it! (IV. v)

The sense of the crown as an "enemy" is close to the deeper feeling of much of the play, and cuts across the confidence required by the "public" action in a way that we can only call tragic. As a public figure, Hal has justly asserted his determination to maintain the power which God has conferred upon him; but here, in the face of his father's disillusionment, he speaks of the crown as a "murderer" and abjures the very "strain of pride" which other words of his, not so very long before, seem to have reflected. His vocation is a severe and somber one, and to rejoice in it at this moment, in the presence of a father who has, indeed, been "murdered" by the weight of it, would be to show a "rebel spirit," an "infection" of the blood. On the threshold of his assumption of the power he is vowing to maintain, the Prince shows himself aware of the need to keep in check the temptations which accompany the exercise of authority; in this sense of a tension between control and the assertion of self-will lies, as we shall see,[31] the key to certain elements in the nature of Henry V.

The father's reply is poised to the last between contradictory emotions. He is happy to hear this rehabilitation of his son's "public" character and filial devotion; but in his "latest counsel" his thoughts turn back to the "by-paths and indirect crook'd ways" by which he achieved the crown. As he looks back upon his reign, he sees it as showing the response of anarchy to the anarchy which his own actions first set loose:

> For all my reign hath been but as a scene
> Acting that argument;

and even though his death "changes the mode," so that what in him was vile "purchase" is translated "in a more fairer sort," it is worth noting that his last advice is still pessimistically conceived:

> all my friends, which thou must make thy friends,
> Have but their stings and teeth newly ta'en out. (IV. v)

Surely in this use of the word "friends" we may detect the presence of a deep tragic irony. It confers upon the dying king, as he takes his leave of life, a sense of ironic fatality against which even his son's determined practical affirmation seems strangely limited:

> My gracious liege,
> You won it, wore it, kept it, gave it me;
> Then plain and right must my possession be:
> Which I with more than with a common pain
> 'Gainst all the world will rightfully maintain. (IV. v)

The words "right" and "rightfully," "plain" as their sense is to the speaker, show already the virtues and the limitations of the future Henry V. It is no part of the Prince's nature to look too closely into the origins of his power, with which his father has been so closely concerned. By refraining from so doing, by regarding his inheritance of the crown as a sufficient reason for affirming the justice of his holding of it, he lays the foundations for his future success and for the precious unity of his kingdom; but, amply justified though he is in the political order, and though confidence in his own right is a proper attribute of kingship, we cannot but sense that "public" necessity has triumphed over the personal theme, and that from now on individual feeling will have no primary part to play in what is becoming, more than ever before, an essentially political action. Its exclusion, together with that of anarchy, "riot," and indulgence, will be confirmed in the last meeting with Falstaff.

First, however, the new king has to be reconciled to the personal embodiment of the justice upon which his power will rest. The Lord Chief Justice stresses his position as the "image" of the royal power, and insists upon the dependence of rule itself on a proper respect for the sanctions embodied in his office:

> Behold yourself so by a son disdain'd;
> And then imagine me taking your part,
> And in your power soft silencing your son:
> After this cold consideration, sentence me. (V. ii)

Henry, in his reply, assumes the impersonal function required of him. Publicly, he announces his determination to "stoop and humble" his intents to "your well-practised wise directions," to what is, in effect, less a moral conception than one of policy and practical wisdom; though in saying this one does not assert the presence of deceit, but rather of a necessary Machiavellism, an understanding of what political effectiveness *really* implies, as essential to his conception. The gesture of acceptance having been made, as befits a king who is renouncing not only his unruly past, but in some sense the free impulses of his own youth, the speech rises to a firm affirmation of self-control, as impressive as it is curiously strained, emptied of normal feeling:

> The tide of blood in me
> Hath proudly flow'd in vanity till now:
> Now doth it turn and ebb back to the sea,
> Where it shall mingle with the state of floods
> And flow henceforth in formal majesty. (V. ii)

This is an assertion of moral power rather than of human understanding. Behind the image of the tide so impressively evoked, there is a sense of the various resources of man turned, harnessed to an end, which is that gravely subsumed under the title of "formal majesty." The tone of this powerful declaration of intent prepares us, once Falstaff has been finally rejected, for the spirit in which Henry V will exercise his authority.

Falstaff, meanwhile, receives the news of the old king's death by vowing himself, and his companions in Gloucestershire, to the last and most presumptuous adventure of "appetite";

> Away, Bardolph! saddle my horse. Master Robert Shallow, choose what office thou wilt in the land, 'tis thine . . . I know the young king is sick for me. Let us take any man's horses; the laws of England are at my commandment. Blessed are they that have been my friends; and woe to my lord chief justice. (V. iii)

In the light of vain assertion on this scale, any sentimental approbation of Falstaff is placed firmly out of court. This is the voice of "appetite" approaching its prey in the prospect of anarchy: rapacious, cruel—as in Pistol's echoing comment on the Chief Justice: "Let vultures vile seize on his lungs also!"—and blown out, no longer merely with good living, but with the arrogant self-confidence that anticipates in reality nothing but its own ruin. The "pleasant days" of Pistol's dream will be confronted with reality in the icy wind of righteous authority that blows from Westminster; but, inhuman as the wind may seem and to some extent be, the reality of the corruption it blows away will amply justify it.

These preliminaries, and the somber little episode of Doll Tearsheet's arrest which follows them,[32] throw light upon the famous crux which rounds off the play—the rejection of Falstaff by Henry as he assumes his responsibilities. Falstaff comes to Westminster full of his new and sinister confidence. He will "leer" upon the king to attract his favor, he will assume "earnestness of affection," "devotion," associating feelings which may once have possessed a certain sincerity with his new spirit of conscious calculation. The crowning moment is reached when Pistol, having recalled Doll's imprisonment, prompts the pretentious confidence of his reply—"I will deliver her" —and utters the final phrase, "There roar'd the sea, and trumpet-clangour sounds" (V. v), in which poetry and base rhetoric are so richly combined. The moment for settling accounts has at last come and it will show, among other things, that Doll is far beyond Falstaff's power to save.

The encounter, indeed, balances the contrasted themes of the play to remarkable effect. The breaking of the wave of Falstaff's enthusiasm against the fixity of the royal purpose is admirably conveyed in dramatic terms. "God save thy grace, king Hal! my royal Hal!" Falstaff cries, transported by the prospect of his coming prosperity; and after Pistol has echoed him—"the heavens thee guard and keep, most royal imp of fame!"—he further adds "God save thee, my sweet boy!" only to find these transports checked by the cold austerity of Henry's indirect rejoinder: "My lord chief justice, speak to that vain man." This in turn leads Falstaff to express—this time in terms which reflect, exploiting it if we will, genuine personal pathos—his inability to believe what he has heard: "I speak to thee, my heart," deliberately ignoring the Lord Chief Justice's reproof: "Have you your wits? know you what 'tis you speak?" before he receives finally, from the king's own mouth, the decisive, unanswerable rejoinder: "I know thee not, old man." The whole exchange is, in its brevity, marvelously varied, charged with the contrasted emotions that go to make up the play. From this moment, the full content of the scene is, to a discerning attention, apparent.

Shakespeare, indeed, not only accepted the artistic difficulty involved in the rejection, which the nature of his material and his own earlier presentation of Falstaff imposed upon him, but wove it into his own conception. There is no doubt that the change noted in the presentation of Falstaff in this play aims, among other things, at making the rejection both feasible and necessary. The Falstaff of Part I would never have allowed himself to be turned off without visible reaction, an aged, broken shadow, beneath his cynicism, of his former self. It is not accidental that he has been given a new burden of age, lechery, and disease, which fits the changed spirit of the play even as it justifies, and not only in political terms, his treatment at the hands of his former friend. When Henry denounces Falstaff as

> So surfeit-swell'd, so old, and so profane,

he is responding to the traditional content of his theme, which called for the young king to reject "riot" on the threshold of his new responsibilities. He makes, in other words, a true criticism, which an Elizabethan audience would not have found excessive; and the criticism is backed up with the austerity of a great religious tradition when he adds:

NORTHWEST MISSOURI
STATE COLLEGE LIBRARY
MARYVILLE, MISSOURI

Make less thy body hence, and more thy grace.

From the *public* standpoint, which also carries with it in this case a moral and religious implication, this judgment represents a culminating point in the entire history. Henry, as king, cannot but make it, and by making it he lays the foundations of political and moral salvation for his kingdom.

Yet there is, equally, another side to the picture. Though the king's words must be given their proper value, the same applies to Falstaff's repeated criticisms of the royal family, which have run as an accompaniment through the preceding action and are no less part of the truth. This balancing of the issues, which should not be confused with indifference and unwillingness to assert judgment, is profoundly Shakespearean in its effect. The contrasted personalities of Falstaff and Prince Hal are seen as occupying no more than a part of the whole field of reality which conditions their dramatic being; they are complementary aspects of a creation whose principle of unity lies not solely in the vision of either but in the integration of the various standpoints which constitute the dramatic material as a whole. Henry's judgments, valid and inevitable as they are, suffer—like those of other Shakespearean characters—from being too easily made. Never is this more so than at this moment, in which he assumes the dignity and impersonality of his vocation. The denial of past friendship involved in "I know thee not, old man," the tight-lipped implication of disgust in his advice to "leave gormandizing," the studied gesture to the gallery, so appropriate in one whose life is to be lived from now on as a public function: "Presume not that I am the thing I was"—all these are as revealing as the afterthought by which Falstaff, banished scarcely five minutes before, is arrested and thrown into prison. This final stroke has been variously interpreted by those who wish it to fit in with their conception of the new king's character; but surely, however we may choose to connect it with Henry's transformed nature, its final meaning is related also to the blow it strikes at Falstaff's halfhearted attempt to revive his confidence—"I shall be sent for soon at night"—and to the dissipation of the hopes, themselves connected with the exploitation of Shallow to which he clings. We can feel for Falstaff at this moment without accepting his point of view, just as we can applaud the new king for his resolve without ceasing to count the human cost, not least for himself, of his decisions. This interplay of intimate motives, all relevant and none final, we should by now have learned to see as a characteristic manifestation of Shakespeare's genius.

The final condemnation is accompanied, typically, by Lancaster's flat and unpleasing comment:

> I like this fair proceeding of the king's:
> He hath intent his wonted followers
> Shall all be very well provided for.

The concluding provision for Falstaff, though it clearly corresponds to an effort to justify the royal action in public terms, is only on the public plane satisfactory:

> For competence of life I will allow you,
> That lack of means enforce you not to evil:
> And, as we hear you do reform yourselves,
> We will, according to your strengths and qualities,
> Give you advancement. (V. v)

Though perhaps a sufficient justification of the king, it does not help us to form a kinder estimate of the man. The comment surely needs to be read in the light of Falstaff's death as announced in *Henry V*. Far from being an afterthought, or—as some have held—a practical device to dispose of a character whom Shakespeare himself, having created him, could neither repeat indefinitely nor allow to dominate his historical conception, Falstaff's death is surely the logical conclusion of this action. Death and mortality are woven into the fabric of this great series of plays, and if the political development is dominated by these realities, so that only the frigid imposition of the will to govern, exercised in the common good, can obtain some measure of triumph over it, it is logical that the humanity which that will cannot compass, having undergone a corruption of its own, should finally die. Fair provision by the grace of the new order is no destiny for the creature that Falstaff has been. Even in his old age, his spirit is nearer to the related decay and tenderness of the exchanges with Doll Tearsheet:[33] and since neither tenderness nor decay have henceforth any real part in the new king's character, his death, and not merely his exposure as a symbol of "riot," is inevitable.

There is no need, in the last analysis, to be sentimental on behalf of either the Prince or Falstaff. The "unpleasantness" in their relationship is a necessary part of the play. It springs from all that is most personal in its conception; it translates yet again into dramatic terms the "disease" which we have found hanging over the English state, and it relates all the divisions between age and youth, action and inaction, anarchic folly and cold calculation which embody that disease to a developing split in the dramatist's conception of the world as his plays reveal it. The precise meaning of this bitter contrast between aged dissolution and the controlled frigidity so unnaturally ascribed to youth needs to be defined in relation to certain of the sonnets,[34] to *Troilus and Cressida,* and to *Measure for Measure.*[35] *Henry IV*—Part II provides, in a word, through the presentation of a society in which the normal attributes of life are subjected to a peculiar and disquieting inversion, a fruitful approach to the issues more completely handled by Shakespeare in the first plays of his full maturity.

HENRY V

The political success aimed at by Henry IV is finally achieved, in the last play of the series, by his son. The general theme of *Henry V* is the establishment in England of an order based on consecrated authority and crowned by action against France. The conditions of this order are, again in accordance with the main conception, moral as well as political. The crime of regicide which had stood between Bolingbroke and the attainment of peace no longer hangs over Henry V—unless as a disturbing memory—and the crusading purpose which had run as an unfulfilled aspiration through the father's life is replaced by the reality, at once brilliant and ruthless, of the son's victorious campaign.

This, as critics have not always realized, is less a conclusion than a point of departure for the understanding of *Henry V.* It was the conditions of kingship, at least as much as its results, that interested Shakespeare in these plays: and these conditions are viewed, by the time the last of them came to be conceived, in a light definitely akin to the tragic. The problem of political unity and that of personal order have been brought in the course of these historical studies into the closest relationship. The former has been achieved, in the preceding plays, by the development of a political capacity that recalls, in various of its aspects, the Machiavellian conception of the Prince; but success of this kind increasingly poses for Shakespeare, whose thought was at once more traditional and less limited to the political than that of the great Florentine, wider problems more definitely moral, even religious, in kind. Just as the state, already in *Henry IV*—Part II, is regarded in its divisions as a diseased body ravaged by a consuming fever, so is the individual seen increasingly as torn between the violence of his passions and the direction of reason; and just as the remedy to political anarchy lies in unquestioned allegiance to an authority divinely constituted, so does personal coherence depend upon the submission to reason of our uncontrolled desires. The link between the two states, political and personal, is provided in these plays by concentration upon the figure of the king. The problem of the state becomes that of the individual at its head. The king, who properly demands unquestioning allegiance from his subjects, is first called upon to show, through the perfection of his dedication, a complete and selfless devotion to his office. The personal implications, as well as the patriotic triumphs, which that devotion brings with it are considered in *Henry V*.

It demands, in the first place, an absolute measure of self-domination. Called upon to exercise justice and shape policies for the common good, the king can allow no trace of selfishness or frailty to affect his decisions. He must continually examine his motives, confirm them in the light of reason; and this means that he is engaged in a continual struggle against his share of human weakness. As the play proceeds, we become increasingly aware that there is in Henry an uneasy balance between violent passion, in certain of its forms, and firm self-control. The control is, indeed, an essential part of his political capacity and of his personal stature. Without it, Henry would not be a true king at all; but, precisely because he is a man and not a crowned puppet, there are times when an unmistakable sense of constraint makes itself felt, as for instance in his greeting to the French ambassador:

> We are no tyrant, but a Christian king;
> Unto whose grace our passion is as subject
> As are our wretches fettered in our prisons. (I. ii)

The harshness of the comparison is, to say the least, remarkable. Such control, though admirable, and doubly so in a king, is necessarily precarious. The passions, "fettered," treated with a disdain similar to that which, as Prince Hal, he has already displayed to the considerations of normal feeling when the fulfillment of his vocation imposed the renunciation of his past, may be expected to break out in forms not immediately attractive.

Almost at once, in fact, they do so. The French envoys, in fulfilling their mission by presenting him with the Dauphin's tennis balls, touch upon a raw spot in Henry's sensibility; they expose him to ridicule and, worst of all, they refer—by the observation that "You cannot revel into dukedoms here"—to the abjured but not forgotten past. Henry's reaction, in spite of the opening affirmation of self-control, takes the form of one of those outbursts which are habitual with him whenever his will is crossed. As when France was to be "bent" or "broken,"[36] his rhetoric, measured and even cold on the surface, is full of accumulated passion:

> When we have match'd our rackets to these balls,
> We will, in France, by God's grace, play a set
> Shall strike his father's crown into the hazard. (I. ii)

The reference to "God's grace," rarely omitted from Henry's official utterances, clearly befits a Christian king, and we need not deny its propriety; but from the personal point of view, which the play is also concerned to stress, the note of resentment which rises through the speech is equally significant. It rankles at this point until the real motive, or an important part of it, becomes at last explicit:

> we understand him well,
> How he comes o'er us with our wilder days,
> Not measuring what use we made of them. (I. ii)

The personal offense once mentioned, the considerations of conscience are swept aside, at least for so long as the new emotion is in command. The horrors of war, the slaughter and misery attendant upon it, are once again mentioned, but only that he may disclaim responsibility for them. The tone of his words, following the swell of emotion, rises to one of ruthless and triumphant egoism:

> But *I* will rise there with so full a glory
> That *I* will dazzle all the eyes of France,
> Yea, strike the Dauphin blind to look on us.
> And tell the pleasant prince this mock of his

> Hath turn'd his balls to gun-stones; and his soul
> Shall stand sore charged for the wasteful vengeance
> That shall fly with them: for many a thousand widows
> Shall this his mock mock out of their dear husbands;
> Mock mothers from their sons, mock castles down;
> And some are yet ungotten and unborn
> That shall have cause to curse the Dauphin's scorn. (I. ii)

"*I* will rise there"; "*I* will dazzle all the eyes of France." The Dauphin's gibe has set free Henry's "fettered" passions and these express themselves in a cumulative vision of destruction. The tone of the utterance—the impact of "strike," the harsh reference to the balls which have been turned to "gun-*stones*," the sense of irresistible, ruinous force behind "mock castles down"—reflects the new feeling and anticipates the later, more masterly picture of Coriolanus in action.[37] This is not to say that we are to regard Henry as a monster at this point, or to deny that a proper sense of royal responsibility underlies his words. He is uttering a warning, condemning the real irresponsibility of others; but the speech has, beyond this, an intimate content which is also part of the complete effect. The sense of power, inhuman and destructive beneath the surface of righteous anger, has been unleashed in the king. The responsibility for coming events, already assumed by the Archbishop of Canterbury earlier in the same scene, has now been further fastened upon the Dauphin, and Henry is in a position to announce his coming descent upon France with a phrase that incorporates into his new vehemence the convenient certainty of righteousness:

> But all this lies within the will of God,
> To whom I do appeal.

No doubt the conviction is sincere; but the fact remains that the will of God and the will of Henry, now fused in the passion released by the Dauphin's jest, have become identical.

It is not until the opening of the French campaign that Henry's utterances are translated into action. The poetry of war in this play deserves careful attention. Much of it, corresponding to the spirit of the patriotic chronicle, is full of life and vigor; such is the elaborate description in the Prologue to this same act of the "fleet majestical" which bears the English forces to Harfleur. The king "embarks his royalty" on a "brave fleet," adorned and lighted by the dawn:

behold the threaden sails,
Borne with the invisible and creeping wind,
Draw the huge bottoms through the furrow'd sea,
Breasting the lofty surge: O, do but think
You stand upon the rivage and behold
A city on the inconstant billows dancing;
For so appears this fleet majestical. (III. Prologue)

Such imagery, splendidly and consciously laden for its effect, is a contribution to the spirit of the play. It may be that some of its deeper notes are not included in it, but the effect of a pageant, of the confident display of might in beauty, is undoubtedly part of Shakespeare's debt to his theme which, whilst balancing it against other elements, it was no part of his intention to forgo. If, in much of this play, he qualifies the note of majesty with more somber and reflective tones, the effect of these tones is in part gained by the contrast with the appeal of majesty itself.

Yet when, immediately after, Henry himself appears, much of his first utterance, as he incites his followers to battle, has about it a strong flavor of artificiality and strain:

Then imitate the action of the tiger;
Stiffen the sinews, summon up the blood,
Disguise fair nature with hard-favour'd rage;
Then lend the eye a terrible aspect;
Let it pry through the portage of the head
Like the brass cannon; let the brow o'erwhelm it
As fearfully as doth a galled rock
O'erhang and jutty his confounded base,
Swill'd with the wild and wasteful ocean.
Now set the teeth and stretch the nostril wide,
Hold hard the breath and bend up every spirit
To his full height. (III. i)

There is about this incitation something forced, incongruous, even (if we may risk taking the point a little too far) slightly absurd. The action of the warrior is an imitation, and an imitation of a wild beast at that, carried out by a deliberate exclusion of "fair nature." The blood is to be summoned up, the sinews stiffened to the necessary degree of artificial savagery, while the involved rhetorical comparisons which follow the references to the "brass cannon" and the "galled rock" strengthen the impression of something very like unreality. In stressing this note of inhumanity, the speech does not intend to deny the poetry of war, which, as we have just seen, Shakespeare expresses most fully in certain passages from the various prologues of this play; but, as later in *Coriolanus,* he balances the conception of the warrior in his triumphant energy as "a greyhound straining at the leash" against that, not less forcible, of a ruthless and inhuman engine of destruction. Both ruthlessness and splendor are inseparable aspects of the complete picture.

Henry's treatment of the governor and citizens of Harfleur relates this conception of the warrior to tensions already apparent in his own character. Not for the first time, two scenes are placed together to point a contrast. The way in which he presents his ultimatum is full of that sense of conflict between control and passion that was so prominent in his early utterances. The grotesque inhumanity implicit in his words is balanced by a suggestion of tragic destiny. Beneath his callousness is a sense that the horrors of war, once unleashed, freed from the sternest control, are irresistible. His soldiers, he warns the governor, are still held uneasily in check. "The cool and temperate wind of grace," whose control over passion is the mark of a Christian soldier, still exercises its authority; but "licentious wickedness" and "the filthy and contagious clouds" of "*heady* murder" threaten to break out at any moment. In his catalogue of the horrors of war stress is laid upon rape and the crimes of "blood." The "fresh-fair" virgins of Harfleur will become the victims of the soldiery, whose destructive atrocities are significantly referred to in terms of "liberty":

> What rein can hold licentious wickedness
> When down the hill he holds his fierce career? (III. iii)

The process of evil, once unleashed, follows courses fatally determined; but Henry, having described them in words which emphasize his awareness of their horror, ends by disclaiming all responsibility for them, just as he had once disclaimed all responsibility for the outbreak of the war. The whole matter, thus taken out of his hands, becomes indifferent to him:

> What is't to me, *when you yourselves are cause,*
> If your pure maidens fall into the hand
> Of hot and forcing violation? (III. iii)

Yet this very assertion of indifference carries with it, at bottom, a sense of the tragedy of the royal position. Only this denial of responsibility, it would seem, only the exclusion of humanity and the acceptance of a complete dualism between controlling "grace" and the promptings of irresponsible passion, make possible that success in war which is, for the purposes of this play, the crown of kingship.

For it would certainly be wrong to suppose that Shakespeare, in portraying Henry, intends to stress a note of hypocrisy. Rather, his purpose is to bring out the burden of royalty, to point to certain contradictions, human and moral, which seem to be inherent in the notion of a successful king. As the play proceeds, Henry seems at times to be, at least in a moral sense, almost the victim of his position. The treasonable activities of Cambridge, Grey, and Scroop are indications of the duplicity with which monarchs are fated by their position to deal. Somewhere at the heart of this court there is a fundamental flaw which must constantly be allowed for by a successful ruler. It appears to Henry, in his dealings with the conspirators, as something deep-rooted enough to be associated with the original fall of man:

seem they religious?
Why, so didst thou: or are they spare in diet,
Free from gross passion or of mirth or anger,
Constant in spirit, not swerving with the blood,
Garnish'd and deck'd in modest complement,
Not working with the eye without the ear,
And but in purged judgement trusting neither?
Such and so finely bolted didst thou seem:
And thus thy fall hath left a kind of blot,
To mark the full-fraught man and best indued
With some suspicion. I will weep for thee;
For this revolt of thine, methinks, is like
Another fall of man. (II. ii)

It is remarkable that Henry, in meditating upon this betrayal, should return once more to that theme of control, of freedom from passion, which is so prominent in his own nature. By concentrating on the functioning of the body, and on the sense of mutual divergence between eye, ear, and judgment in the difficult balance of the personality, the speech sets spiritual control in contrast with a sense of anarchy that proceeds, most typically, from the contemplation of physical processes. "*Gross* passion"—the adjective is significant—is associated with the irrational "swerving of the blood," and the judgment which controls it needs to be "purged" by fasting ("spare in diet") before it can attain a scarcely human freedom from "mirth or anger." By thus emphasizing the difficult and even unnatural nature of such control, the speech casts a shadow, at least by implication, over that of Henry himself; but it is also seen to be necessary, inseparable from his office. The administration of justice, upon which depends order within the kingdom and success in its foreign wars, demands in the monarch a detachment which borders on the inhuman. The state must be purged of "treason lurking in its way" before it can be led, with that single-mindedness of purpose which is both Henry's strength and, perhaps, in the long run, his limitation, to the victorious enterprise in France.

It is clear, indeed, that *Henry V* represents, however tentatively, a step in the realization of themes fully developed in the tragedies. Inheriting from his sources the conception of a victorious king, perfectly aware of his responsibilities and religiously devoted to the idea of duty, Shakespeare seems, in the most individual scenes of his play, to emphasize the difficulties of the conception, the obstacles, both personal and political, which lie between it and fulfillment. These difficulties, however, never amount to a questioning of the royal judgment. Even in the disguised Henry's debate with Williams and Bates on the morning of Agincourt (IV. i), where the implications of his power are most searchingly discussed, the king's right to command obedience is never in question. For Bates the duty of a subject lies in loyal execution of the royal will, and the responsibility for wrong action rests beyond the simple soldier with the king: "we know enough, if we know we are the king's subjects." Nor does Williams, though more skeptical in his attitude, question the postulate that the subject is bound to obey; for to disobey, as he puts it, "were against all property of subjection," and the emphasis is still upon the "proportion" to be observed between king and subject, directing head and executing body, and upon the proper submission which the successful prosecution of the military effort requires.

Henry, of course, accepts this view of his position; but although the questionings of his followers do not—and cannot—lead him to doubt his own authority, they do force him to reflect deeply upon the weaknesses which even kings cannot overcome. "The king is but a man as I am; the violet smells to him as it doth to me; . . . all his senses have but human conditions; his ceremonies laid by, in his nakedness he appears but a man; and though his affections are higher mounted than ours, yet when they stoop they stoop with the like wing." There is about the argument a universality which transcends the royal situation. Men, differentiated by vain "ceremony," are united in their common "nakedness," and the most notable feature of human behavior seems to the speaker to be its domination by impulse, its helplessness before the stooping of the affections.[38] In this respect the king is one with his men; and just because he is so like them, because his senses too "have but human conditions" and are constantly liable to break through the guard of rigid self-control imposed upon him by his vocation, there is something precarious, potentially disproportionate in his absolute claim upon the allegiance of his followers.

The royal isolation is further underlined by Williams when he points out the spiritual consequences of a conflict for which the king has accepted full responsibility: "For how can they [Henry's soldiers] charitably dispose of anything when blood is their argument? Now, if these men do not die well, it will be a black matter for the king that led them to it" (IV. i). These words repeat once more, but with a greater urgency, a preoccupation with the horrors of war which Henry has already expressed, even if he succeeded in shaking off responsibility for them, to the French envoys and the governor of Harfleur. They imply, beyond the sense of responsibility which derives from the traditional conception of monarchy, a contrast—already familiar—between the Christian law of "charity" and the impulse to destruction that threatens it in the necessary acts of war with the consequences of unlimited brutality. The connection between this conflict of flesh and spirit and the tendency of human societies, states and families alike, to dissolve by the questioning of "degree" into anarchy is not established in this play as it is in the tragedies which followed. But Hamlet himself might have reflected like Henry on the precarious basis of human pretensions, and Angelo defined in similar terms the catastrophic realization of it brought about by his encounter with Isabella. Had Henry once followed his line of speculation far enough to doubt the validity of his motives for action, or—on the other hand—had he given free play to the sinister impulses dimly recognized in himself, he would of course have been the protagonist of another and quite different play; but the possibilities are there as a premonition, a first indication of issues brought fully to light in later actions.

For the moment, Henry counters the implications of this argument by pointing out that soldiers "purpose not their death, when they purpose their services." Williams' somber reflections, however, impose themselves upon him, attach themselves to his own meditations, and are profoundly echoed in his own words. Connecting war with sin, he repeats the tone of earlier statements: "Besides, there is no king, be his cause never so spotless, if it come to the arbitrement of swords, can try it out with all unspotted soldiers: some peradventure have on them the guilt of premeditated and contrived murder; some, of beguiling virgins with the broken seal of perjury" (IV. i). The result is, in part, a fresh emphasis on meticulous self-examination as a means of conserving spiritual health—"Therefore should every soldier in the wars do as every sick man in his bed, wash every mote out of his conscience"—and, in the verse soliloquy which closes the scene, one of those outbursts of nostalgic craving for release which have appeared already, in his father's mouth, in *Henry IV*—Part II, and which will be reflected with a new, more *physical* apprehension of existence in Hamlet's soliloquies and in the Duke's incitations to Claudio in *Measure for Measure:*

> what infinite heart's ease
> Must kings neglect, that private men enjoy! (IV. i)

The craving for "heart's ease" in this long speech is still, generally speaking, what it is in *Henry IV:* a desire to be freed from the burden of an office in which human purposes seem fatally divorced from human achievement. The development of the verse is still painstaking, leisurely in the expansion of its long periods, and a little rhetorical; but there are moments which foreshadow the association in *Hamlet* of this nostalgia with a desire to be free from the encumbrances, the "fardels,"[39] the "things rank and gross in nature"[40] by which the flesh persistently seems to obstruct the workings of the spirit. "Greatness" is a "fiery fever" which consumes its royal victim like a bodily disease, and the contrasted peace of the humble subject is described with a curious ambiguity of tone:

> Not all these, laid in bed majestical,
> Can sleep so soundly as the wretched slave,
> Who with a body fill'd and vacant mind
> Gets him to rest, cramm'd with distressful bread. (IV. i)

In the association of peace with bodily fullness and vacancy of mind, in the impression, harshly and directly physical, behind "fill'd" and "cramm'd," there is a distinct suggestion of certain descriptions of satiated, idle contentment in plays as far apart as *Troilus and Cressida* and *Coriolanus*. Here already such imagery represents a kind of residue, intractable and irreducible, in direct contrast to the king's increasing emphasis on the need for spiritual discipline. It is no more than a suggestion, unabsorbed as yet into the main imaginative design of a play conceived on different, simpler lines; but, tentative as it is, it stands in a certain relationship to the clash of flesh and spirit—"passion" and "grace"—which exacts continual vigilance from Henry and which is slowly moving through these developments of imagery to more open realization.

A similar potential cleavage can be detected in the treatment of the two sides drawn up for battle at Agincourt. Shakespeare differentiates between the French and English forces in a way which sometimes seems to foreshadow the balance held in *Troilus and Cressida* between Greeks and Trojans, though it is true that the unfavorable estimate of the English, which is scarcely compatible with the spirit of the play, is expressed only in the words of their enemies. The English are morally worthy of their victory, but the French account does go a little way to anticipate the possibility of criticism. The French, combining a touch of the unsubstantial chivalry of Troilus with a more than Trojan emptiness, are, like the Trojans, and more justly, defeated; the English, whom they represent as gross and dull-witted, are as undeniably successful as the Greeks. Shakespeare's handling of the battle carries on this conception. The French, trusting in a thin and rhetorical belief in their own aristocracy, rush hastily and incompetently to their deaths; the English, deriving their spirit from their king, win the day by their perseverance and self-control. Self-control, however, which is—as in Henry himself—not without some suggestion of harshness and inhumanity. Henry's righteousness does not prevent him from inflicting merciless reprisals on his prisoners, and, though these matters need to be looked at in the spirit of the times, and the play is careful to emphasize the base act of treachery which rouses Henry to righteous anger, there is something finally sardonic about Gower's comment that "the king, *most worthily,* hath caused every soldier to cut his prisoner's throat. O, 'tis *a gallant king*" (IV. vii). By such excellence, Shakespeare would seem to say, must even the most just and patriotic of wars be won.

There is, indeed, a good deal of throat-cutting in this play. The king's ruthlessness, a logical consequence of his efficiency, needs to be seen against the human background which Shakespeare provided for it, most noticeably in the comic scenes which turn on the behavior of the common soldiery. There is little room in *Henry V* for the more expansive notes of comedy. Shakespeare's delineation of character is, indeed, as clear-cut as ever, and his dialogue abundantly if discreetly flavored with the sense of humanity; but there is about the humor of these scenes a certain desiccated flatness that contrasts sharply with the exuberance of earlier plays. Bardolph, Pistol, and the others, no longer enlivened by contact with Falstaff, quarrel like curs and—where occasion presents itself—steal like the creatures of rapine that they are; and their jokes turn largely upon the bawdyhouses which will swallow them up on their return to England, and upon the cutting of throats. "Men may sleep and they may have their throats about them at that time; and some say knives have edges" (II. i). Nym's remark, itself dark and enigmatic, is prefaced by a somber, fatalistic "things must be as they may," which modifies the comic sententiousness of the speaker and implies a certain resigned acceptance of the ordering of life.

The humorous conception of the characters, in short, is toned down to fit in with a spirit no longer essentially humorous; and this applies not only to Nym but to his companions in arms. Fluellen and Gower, Williams and Bates are distinguished, not by comic vitality or by the penetration of their comments on men and events, but by their qualities of common sense and by an attitude of tough loyalty and dedication to the work in hand; and it is by their devotion to the strictly practical virtues and by their definition of their various national idiosyncrasies that they live. The best of these comic episodes is contained in Fluellen's expression of devotion to his king after the great victory has been won: "I will confess it to all the 'orld; I need not to be ashamed of your majesty, praised be God, *so long as your majesty is an honest man*" (IV. vii). Should we need a word to describe the best positive values of this play, those which distinguish it from mere patriotic rhetoric on the one side and sardonic pessimism on the other (and both moods are constituent parts of it), it would be the word "honest" as here used; honesty which can offer loyalty whilst maintaining independence of judgment, and which is brought out, as much as the cruelty which balances it, by the somber circumstances of war which no merely patriotic show of rhetoric or romantic comradeship in death can conceal. These soldiers, revering the necessary form of monarchy, can yet see in it the reflection of their common humanity. It is this reflection, by which they are ennobled, which has brought them to victory over enemies for whom "common" humanity is no object of reverence or understanding. If this understanding points eventually to an intuition increasingly tragic in its implications, it is also related to the patriotic purposes which equally prevail in this play.

It is by his possession to an eminent degree of precisely this kind of virtue that Henry finally affirms himself as a king. His essentially "political" wooing of Katherine of France at the end of the play most nearly approaches true emotion when, in his characteristic, direct prose, he contrasts the passing nature of man's decorative virtues with the constancy of a "good heart":

> a speaker is but a prater; a rhyme is but a ballad. A good leg will fall; a straight back will stoop; a black beard will turn white; a curled pate will grow bald; a fair face will wither; a full eye will wax hollow; but a good heart, Kate, is the sun and the moon; or rather the sun and not the moon; for it shines bright and never changes, but keeps his course truly. (V. ii)

This, at least, belongs rather to Henry's virtues than to the political arrangements being proposed. The same virtues enabled him, on the morning of Agincourt, to unite his followers in the true fellowship of "a band of brothers." They are, indeed, no mean virtues, but they are necessarily dedicated in this play to the public, the political sphere, and in a world which is no longer—for better or worse—that of *Henry IV*—Part I. Falstaff himself, out of place in this world, is remembered in his death, serving as a kind of measure by contrast with which Shakespeare emphasizes what seems to be a changing vision of humanity. This death—it is worth noting—is ascribed directly to the king, who has "killed his heart"; and Nym, repeating that phrase of resignation which conveys so much more than he realizes of the spirit of this new world, relates Henry's treatment of him to an obscure, inherent fatality: "The king is a good king; but *it must be as it may;* he passes some humours and careers" (II. i). His companions who remain must now accommodate themselves to the times. They do so by abandoning domestic crime to follow their king to France. War and its prospects of plunder are for them no more and no less than a means of livelihood and an alternative to preying upon one another. As Bardolph puts it: "We must to France together; why the devil should we keep knives to cut one another's throats?" (II. i). The end of their adventure—after the stern episode of Bardolph's hanging for sacrilege—is contained in Pistol's final speech, revealing the death of Nell, "of malady of France" (V. i), and his own anticipation of his future:

> Old do I wax; and from my weary limbs
> Honour is cudgelled. Well, bawd I'll turn,
> And something lean to cutpurse of quick hand.
> To England will I steal, and there I'll steal:
> And patches will I get unto these cudgell'd scars,
> And swear I got them in the Gallia wars. (V. i)

For Pistol is the last and least worthy survivor of another world, and his anticipated future and the king's plain and dispassionate honesty each looks forward, in its own way, to a very different one to come.

It is indeed significant, in making a final estimate of this play, that the account in it of the death of Falstaff is, by common consent, the most human and deeply felt thing in the entire story. In an action where the touchstone of conduct is success, and in which humanity has to accommodate itself to the claims of expediency, there is no place for Falstaff. Shakespeare had already recognized this, and prepared us for the necessary changes, when he accepted the logic of the "rejection" scene and of the events leading up to it; and now his end affects us tragically as the last glimpse of another and, in part, a less somber world. No doubt there is a patriotic purpose, not irrelevant to the play, and no doubt Shakespeare conceived his successful monarch with that purpose in mind. One aim does not, in Shakespeare, necessarily exclude another; and the fact remains that as we consider the uncompromising study of achieved and just success which rounds off this trilogy, a certain coldness takes possession of us as it took possession, step by step, of the limbs of the dying Falstaff. We too, in reaching the end of this sober, balanced presentation of public virtue, find ourselves in our own way "babbling of green fields."[41]

THE MERRY WIVES OF WINDSOR

It will hardly be necessary to deal at any length with *The Merry Wives of Windsor.* To say this is not to deny the piece its characteristic virtues. The comic intrigue, leading to the exposure of a jealous husband and frustrating the shortsighted matchmaking of a pair of parents, is skillfully handled and conveys a lively sense of the middle-class scene; the action works out effectively enough on the stage and there is no reason why we should belittle or deny the achievement which this represents. The previous series of historical plays, however, having introduced us to Falstaff, makes it inevitable that we should look first to him in any play in which he appears; and the fact is, quite simply, that the Falstaff of *The Merry Wives* strikes us as making what we can only call a posthumous appearance, seems to represent no more than the halfhearted revival of a character originally conceived in a very different spirit.

It might seem sufficient to leave the matter thus, were it not that certain incidents—and more particularly the conclusion of the play—are there to leave an impression which is, in the last analysis, rather different. Falstaff bundled into the basket of dirty clothes and thrown into the Thames, or Falstaff dressed up to evade discovery as Mrs. Ford's "maid's aunt, the fat woman of Brentford" (IV. i) and soundly beaten in his disguise, we can accept as a creation which, although it has little or nothing to do with the Sir John we have known, exists farcically in its own right; but Falstaff in the guise of a "woodman," making his appeal to the "hot-blooded gods" of antiquity and excusing himself in the name of the frailties committed by these same gods—"When gods have hot backs, what shall poor men do?"—is, to some extent at least, another matter. The scene under the oak in Windsor Park seems to answer, beneath its obvious farcical content, to an exorcizing process, represents the final projection of "riot" and "misrule" into a form of monstrous and presumptuous fleshliness which is to be cast out, expelled through the words of incantation uttered over his supine form by the "fairies" in disguise:

Fie on sinful fantasy!
Fie on lust and luxury!
Lust is but a bloody fire,
Kindled with unchaste desire,
Fed in heart, whose flames aspire
As thoughts do blow them, higher and higher. (V. v)

The song is uttered over a Falstaff stripped of all his attributes of comic energy, left with only the monstrosity of his fleshly appetites, and, as such, ready for expulsion from the life of society; and it concludes, significantly, in what are, still beneath their obvious farcical connotation, in effect ritual words of expulsion:

Pinch him, fairies, mutually:
Pinch him for his villainy:
Pinch him, and burn him, and turn him about,
Till candles and starlight and moonshine be out. (V. v)

The words, in their mixture of nonsense and incantation, read very like the confused memories of a rite of purification. As such they link Falstaff, even in his new fallen state and in the exclusion which is decreed over him "mutually," in the name of society, to a kind of life deeper, more profoundly related to immemorial instincts and ancestral memories, than any to which the main comic action would seem to lead us: a life which may make the play itself more adequate, as the last appearance of this great comic creation, than the general tone of the rest of the action would in itself justify.

VIII

The Great Comedies

Relatively little that really illuminates has been written upon Shakespeare's comedies. This is perhaps due in part to the presence in them of an important element of convention, which has to be mastered before the human content of the plays, their relation to normal experience, can begin to make itself felt. A similar element no doubt exists also in the tragedies and the historical plays, but in these the universal significance of the dramatic action asserts itself more obviously and directly. Othello and Lear,—and, we might add, Henry V—are recognizable human beings, facing predicaments and challenges which may be on a different scale from those familiar in ordinary life, but to which, nonetheless, we can readily respond. In Shakespeare's comedies, however, a content not finally dissimilar in kind is canalized into conventional forms. Artificial situations, contrived marriages, elaborate happy endings, all set in countries of the imagination, frequently act, even while they exercise their magic upon us, as impediments to full and direct participation in the dramatist's intention: impediments which, without doubt, it is well worth overcoming, but which call for a special effort, a particular kind of attention, before the necessary fullness of response can be achieved.

That the effort *is* worth making is not seriously open to question. At approximately the same time as he embarked, in his second great series of plays on English history, on an extended exploration of the implications, personal and public alike, of political behavior, Shakespeare chose to develop his own concept of comedy, already approached in earlier plays, to reflect other aspects, not finally less serious or compelling, of human behavior. In *Much Ado About Nothing* he allowed his mind and imagination to play, with unique wit and brilliance, upon the validity and the limitations of love in a brittle and scintillating society. In *As You Like It,* he followed this remarkable success by a greater, involving the creation of an entire comic world which reflected, beneath the deliberate conventionality and artifice of its forms, some of his deepest and most personal intuitions concerning the nature of human life; and finally, in *Twelfth Night,* these same intuitions found projection in one of the most consistent, as well as the most intangibly elusive, of all his creations. Nothing that he was later to write—not even *Hamlet, King Lear,* or *Antony and Cleopatra*—can diminish the value of these successive triumphs, or prevent us from seeing them as what they are, the most individual—in some sense the most harmoniously finished—of all his earlier achievements.

MUCH ADO ABOUT NOTHING

Much Ado About Nothing is not, perhaps, one of the most immediately attractive or satisfying of Shakespeare's comedies. None, indeed, contains more moments of striking verbal brilliance, or carries on with greater assurance the game of polished and slightly heartless repartee which often seems to constitute the main business of life in Messina. To pass, however, from an appreciation of these epigrammatic felicities to more direct consideration of the persons who utter them and the situations which inspire them may be to risk a certain disenchantment. It is easy enough to respond to the vivacity of some of the characters and situations and one can be tempted to concentrate on the exchanges of wit between Beatrice and Benedick to the exclusion of practically everything else in the play, finding Hero by comparison the most colorless of heroines and Claudio positively unattractive. To lay emphasis in this way upon the obvious brilliance of certain parts is, however, to do less than justice to a play which its author undoubtedly conceived as a coherent and indivisible whole. *Much Ado* is, above all, a highly formal comedy working through strict conventions and a progressive interplay of situations which are revealed in their true nature through mutual contrast and which, in the process of this revelation, illuminate various facets of truth and illusion in the central reality of love.

The starting point of the action is the return of a group of courtiers from the wars. In these, "a young Florentine called Claudio" has—we are told—borne himself "beyond the promise of his age" to "better expectation" (I. i). The play, however, sets out to show Claudio under a different aspect as he declares his love for Hero, the daughter of the governor of Messina, a girl whom he confesses that he has scarcely had occasion to see but whose outward appearance strikes him—to use his own words—as a "jewel" of great price to force the idea of marriage upon him. The nature of this love, however, is expressed rather by omission than through any sign of positive emotion. Hero must be the least articulate of all Shakespeare's heroines; and Claudio, when he is left alone with Don Pedro, declares himself in a way which suggests that his newly discovered feeling for her rests on a very slender foundation of knowledge. "I looked upon her," he says, referring back to his recent past,

> with a soldier's eye,
> That liked, but had a rougher task in hand
> Than to drive liking to the name of love:
> But now I am return'd and that war-thoughts
> Have left their places vacant, in their rooms
> Come thronging soft and delicate desires,
> All prompting me how fair young Hero is,
> Saying, I liked her ere I went to wars. (I. i)

The tone of this is lukewarm enough to suggest that Claudio's newly found "soft and delicate desires," the conclusion that he formerly "liked" Hero but has only now had time to give the matter serious thought, are signs of his unpreparedness to offer the object of these "desires" anything like the deliberate and conscious gift of self in which true love consists. That he himself feels a lack of confidence in his own capacity to love is indicated, indeed, by the fact that he has just begged Don Pedro, in an oddly tentative manner—"My liege, your highness now may do me good"—to take up his cause with Hero; and his diffidence is matched in turn by the older and more experienced man's perhaps overconfident readiness to serve his turn.

Side by side with this gauche and diffident pair, she almost entirely tongue-tied, he alternately diffident and inclined to set too high a worth upon his own feelings, the opening of the play offers us two other characters—Beatrice and Benedick—who seem to be only agreed in believing that they are indifferent to one another and have seen through love itself as an illusion. It is in this conviction that Benedick comments, with partial truth, on Claudio's new feelings toward Hero. When Claudio, seeking support for his own precarious decision, asks him, "Can the world buy such a jewel?" Benedick replies: "Yea, and a case to put it into"; and when he goes on to say: "In mine eye she is the sweetest lady that ever I looked on," Benedick's retort is a confident assertion of his own realism: "I can see yet without spectacles, and I see no such matter" (I. i). This deliberate deflation of the excesses of romantic love is, of course, amply familiar to us from earlier plays, and there is no reason why we should not allow it a due measure of validity in this case. We should, however, also by now know enough of the spirit of Shakespearean comedy to refrain from taking Benedick's confident attitude simply at its face value. Once more we are being offered different views of the same reality as seen through the deceptive medium of individual eyes; views which we might call respectively romantic and realistic, in whose clash and interrelation lies a great part of the substance of the play. Even without foreseeing the eventual outcome, we may be certain that the truth will lie neither with Claudio's halting assertion of his attraction for Hero nor with the bold and self-confident denial of its validity which his critic rashly sets up in opposition to it.

It should be noted, as a first step in penetrating the true complexity of the offered pattern, that Benedick's assertiveness is from the first itself subjected to the criticism of Beatrice, who, before he has spoken to Claudio or even appeared on the stage, has already referred slightingly to the quality of Benedick's wit. "In our last conflict four of his five wits went halting off, and now is the whole man governed with one: so that if he have wit enough to keep himself warm, let him bear it for a difference between himself and his horse; for it is all the wealth that he hath left, to be known a reasonable creature" (I. i). The intention of placing the pretensions of merely verbal wit in its relation to truly rational and human attitudes is clear enough and answers to an important aspect of the play. Nor is this, in turn, the last word about this relationship of seeming contraries; for it is to be noted that Beatrice, even as she expresses her contempt for Benedick, is presented as anxious to have news of him, whilst Benedick, in the very act of responding to general expectation by making his own depreciating remarks about Beatrice, pays a kind of left-handed tribute to her beauty; "there's her cousin," he says, "an she were not possessed with a fury, exceeds her"—that is, Hero—"as much in beauty as the first of May doth the last of December" (I. i). Each in effect expresses with the scintillating verbal brilliance which is available to them in such abundant measure, and which constitutes at once their attraction and their final limitation, an attitude to the other which ministers to their respective self-conceits but which is in reality founded on something less than a true understanding of their real needs and motives.

In this way, the pattern of contrasted opinions which is to dominate the coming action is already set forth in the opening scene. We are to see whether Claudio's romantically superficial view of his new love can stand the test of exposure to reality, and at the same time whether those who so articulately and confidently defend themselves from love by asserting loudly and insistently their superiority to its compulsions can in fact maintain their declared confidence. A brief exchange between Claudio, Don Pedro, and Benedick states the future pattern in its plainest terms as they declare their respective attitudes to Hero:

> *Claudio:* That I love her, *I feel.*
> *Don Pedro:* That she is worthy, *I know.*
> *Benedick:* That I neither *feel* how she should be loved, nor *know* how she should be worthy, is the *opinion* that fire cannot melt out of me. (I. i)

Each speaker's choice of words is designed to bring out the foundations of his own position and, with it, its partiality. Claudio "feels" that Hero is worthy of his love, resting his newly acquired belief upon mere unsupported sentiment which events will prove to be powerless in the face of apparent, if perverse, reason. Don Pedro, in whom the voice of experience speaks with appropriate assurance, "knows" upon good grounds that she is worthy of the devotion offered her, and acts perhaps with a slightly too easy confidence as a result of this rational conviction; but Benedick, strong only in the appearance of reason to support what is in fact nothing better than his own "opinion," based on the plain incapacity, where matters of love are concerned, either to sympathize or to understand (to "feel" or to "know"), *thinks* that he knows that both are wrong. There, in a few words, is the design of contrasted attitudes and prejudices which reflect, in the last instance, self-centered and self-justifying needs and which this comedy will be concerned to bring to a formal and harmonious conclusion.

The impulse required to set the entire intrigue in motion is provided, from outside, by the malevolence of Don John. To take this personage realistically, or to seek to provide him with adequate motivation for his behavior, is to misunderstand the spirit which prevails in this comedy. Don John represents, in relation to the rest, the dash of bitterness required to bring out the elements of contradiction and fictitiousness which prevail in those around him. As the play opens, he has been forcibly reconciled, after undergoing a defeat which he continues to resent, to his legitimate brother Don Pedro; but the sting of bastardy remains strongly implanted in him and, after having initially declared himself as a man "not of many words," a taciturn exception in a supremely articulate society, he soon goes on to declare his true motives in terms which closely echo the terminology of certain of the sonnets:

> I had rather be a *canker* in a hedge than a *rose* in his grace; and it better fits my *blood* to be disdained of all than to fashion a carriage to rob love from any: in this, though I cannot be said to be a flattering honest man, it must not be denied but I am a plain-dealing villain . . . If I had my mouth I would bite; if I had my liberty, I would do my liking: in the meantime let me be that I am, and seek not to alter me. (I. iii)

The presence in this self-revelation of a number of elements common to other and more developed Shakespearean villains need not induce us to go beyond seeing in Don John the essentially flat, finally impersonal creation that he is. His attitudes are those of self-sufficiency and consciously willed isolation that constantly accompany evil in the plays; but it is not in this case required that they should reveal themselves through individual or realistic motivation. It is enough that Don John, in a spirit of envious self-sufficiency which covers his own conviction of essential inferiority, should declare through this initial self-revelation his purpose of twisting love to his own ends of defeated and embittered resentment. He is to be the "canker," passionately inspired by his sense of social exclusion to destroy the "rose" of natural love and normal sociability;[1] but, since this is a comedy and accordingly dedicated by definition to a harmonizing conclusion, the end of his intrigues can only be to bring out more deeply the true nature of love and to obtain, as the contrary of everything that he has desired, its consummation in personal union and social harmony. Meanwhile, and until the time comes for his designs to be unmasked, it is enough to see that the news of an intended marriage presents itself to him as an occasion "to build mischief on," and that the decision of the brother whom he hates to woo Hero on behalf of Claudio becomes—for his perverted vision—possible "food" to nourish his resentment.

The various relationships thus presented in the opening scenes of the action tend, according to the purpose which prevails in this comedy, to be brought together in a formal dance of balanced relationships. The true nature of this dance will not be apparent until the end of the play, when the chief actors in its development will at last be brought into a true and fruitful relationship with one another; meanwhile, the intervening state of intrigue and confusion is fittingly symbolized (II. i) in the form of a masked gathering and through the ill-assorted partnerships to which it gives rise. Before the beginning of the dance in which it is to culminate Beatrice sums up the "tart" character of Don John—"I never can see him but I am heart-burned an hour after"—even as she confirms, to her own subsequent discomfiture, her obstinate determination to avoid marriage "till God make man of some other metal than earth" (II. i). The proviso is, of course, an unrealistic one in so far as it is precisely to the "earthiness" of their natures that men and women owe their impulse to submit themselves to one another, and to reality, in marriage. In so far as she is declaring her superiority to this universal human condition Beatrice is taking her stand upon pride and imperfect knowledge of herself and of life; but there is eloquence and a true sense of reality in her pressing of her own argument: "Would it not grieve a woman to be overmastered with a piece of valiant dust? to make an account of her life to a clod of wayward marl?" (II. i). We may feel at this point that the speaker is responding to the realities of the human situation more seriously than she can yet know: more seriously certainly than when she goes on to impose upon the diffident Hero her own arrogant view of marriage:

> wooing, wedding, and repenting, is as a Scotch jig, a measure, and a cinque pace: the first suit is hot and hasty, like a Scotch jig, and full as fantastical; the wedding, mannerly-modest, as a measure full of state and ancientry: and then comes repentance, and, with his bad legs, falls into the cinque pace faster and faster, till he sinks into his grave. (II. i)

As a principal vehicle of the comic spirit, Beatrice at this point stresses the incongruity which forms part of the spirit of love. By so doing, she contributes an essential element to the complete effect; but she is also indulging, through her unmatched gift of verbal brilliance, her own precarious sense of superiority to the universal condition of that "piece of valiant dust," that "clod of wayward marl" which is, even more truly than she knows, man, and the immediate reflection, in terms of action, of what she has said is the series of misunderstandings and mistaken identities which constitute the first of the two formal dances between which the main action is situated.

The pattern of confused identities which it will be the concern of the play to unravel is, indeed, brought to a head as the various partners address themselves to one another beneath the protection which their respective masks afford. Don Pedro approaches Hero with the intention of wooing her, not for himself, but on behalf of Claudio. Baltasar presents himself to Margaret, who rejects him, and Hero's gentlewoman Ursula truly recognizes Don Antonio, who strenuously denies his identity; and, finally, Beatrice herself recognizes Benedick beneath his mask, but pretends to fail to do so in order to make jest the more freely at his expense. Last of all, as a fitting pendant to these various cross-purposes, real and contrived, Don John recognizes the disguised Claudio, but pretends to believe that he is addressing himself to Benedick in order to poison the mind of his victim by insinuating that Don Pedro, whom Claudio has entrusted with the furthering of his cause with Hero, is in fact engaged in wooing her for himself. The fact that these insinuations and misapprehensions, advanced in each case under the cover of mistaken identities, are taken up to disproportionate and sometimes potentially tragic conclusions lends its characteristic tone of polished and enticing bitterness to the shifting fabric of hearsay and prejudice —"Much ado about nothing"—which constitutes the material of this comedy.

With Don John's insinuation, of course, these masked cross-purposes impinge upon the main action. Claudio, confirming his inexperience and his lack of faith in the depth and reality of his own love, shows himself at once ready to take them at their declared value. His failure to believe either in himself or in the declared object of his devotion is made evident in the compound of naïvety and cynicism which his own words reflect:

Friendship is constant in all other things
Save in the office and affairs of love:
Therefore all hearts in love use their own tongues;
Let every eye negotiate for itself,
And trust no agent; for beauty is a witch,
Against whose charms faith melteth into blood.
This is an accident of hourly proof,
Which I mistrusted not. (II. i)

Claudio is here engaged in persuading himself of the truth of Don John's perverse axioms, which have become for him a matter of "hourly proof"; the cynicism of inexperience, unsure of itself and seeking assurance at the cost of its own disillusionment, is fittingly molded to the "canker" of Don John's craving to belittle and destroy the realities from which it feels itself excluded. To add a further complication to this pattern of perverse "seeming," moreover, Benedick at once confirms Claudio in his unnatural belief when, speaking out of his own allegedly greater experience of these matters, he assures his puzzled friend that "the prince hath got your Hero," even as, reflecting on the undignified manner of his own recent treatment at the hands of Beatrice, he expresses his resentment at "her base though bitter disposition." Having thus uncovered the real weakness behind Claudio's too facile assumptions, we are now further shown that Benedick, for all his stressed pride in his own shrewdness, is himself incapable of declaring the true nature of love.

Benedick's own position, and that of Beatrice in relation to him, is indeed revealed by a number of seemingly inconsequential touches to be less firmly founded than either would like to believe. As much is implied in the statement of his desire to avoid at all costs "three words' conference with this harpy" (II. i), and, equally, in Beatrice's finally rueful comment to Claudio on her own position with regard to marriage: "Thus goes everyone to the world but I, and I am sun-burnt; I may sit in a corner, and cry heigh-ho for a husband" (II. i). Even before the plot to bring them together, and to make each recognize in the other a suitable match has been set afoot, the ground is carefully prepared for us to recognize that she would be "an excellent wife for Benedick" and he in turn, in Don Pedro's phrase, "not the unhopefullest husband that I know" (II. i). The central part of the action, which follows naturally from the several misunderstandings of the masked dance, will turn appropriately on two contrasted intrigues: one of them a positive, matchmaking device designed to bring together a pair who only need to know themselves and one another better to recognize that they are in fact destined one for another, the second corresponding to the darker side of the comedy and concentrating on Don John's machinations against Claudio and Hero, projects recognized to be "athwart" and to proceed from a mind that confesses itself to be "sick" in its own "displeasure" (II. ii).

The first plot, concerning Beatrice and Benedick, achieves its ends without much difficulty. We know that the mind of each runs upon the other, although this reality has so far expressed itself characteristically in verbal repudiation. Just before he falls, Benedick invites retribution upon himself by passing an easy judgment upon Claudio for his simplicity: "I do much wonder that one man, seeing how much another man is a fool when he dedicates his behaviours to love, will, after he has laughed at such shallow follies in others, become the argument of his own scorn" (II. iii). This, in effect, is exactly what he himself proceeds to do. Already he insinuates that marriage might, under certain circumstances, become a possibility for himself: "till all graces be in one woman, one woman shall not come in my grace" (II. iii). By saying as much as this, Benedick is in effect raising the question of the nature of love, which consists largely in the ability to create the perfection of its object; for it is precisely the image of such perfection that the lover, by the very fact of being in love, creates to his own satisfaction in the recipient of his devotion. It is not surprising, in view of this, that once the comedy that is to ensnare him has been acted out for his benefit, his first words are an acceptance of the deception that, in the last analysis, answers to his intimate desires. Benedick, like Beatrice when her turn comes shortly after, is intelligent enough to know that there is truth in the judgments that he has overheard concerning his own presumption and self-love; and so he is led, like her again and in spite of his usual brilliant, if limited, range of perception, to overlook the element of deception and enticement that is also there. "This can be no trick"; the "wise" bachelor is caught in his own appropriate trap as he confesses that it is his destiny to be "horribly in love." His surrender amounts to an acceptance of his own part in the universal human condition, a recognition of the falsity both of his publicly flaunted judgments of Beatrice and of the supposedly superior insight on which he has prided himself; as he goes on to say, in rueful self-defense:

> doth not the appetite alter? a man loves the meat in his youth that he cannot endure in his age. Shall quips and sentences and these paper bullets of the brain awe a man from the career of his humour? No, the world must be peopled. (II. iii)

And so, he first reacts with an excessive and finally comic modesty against his former self-confidence—"I must not seem proud; happy are they that hear their detractions and can put them to mending"—and then, when the still unconverted Beatrice comes to invite him to dine with the rest of the company, is ready, lover-like, to read the most absurd and improbable meanings into her plain words.

Beatrice, however, is by now equally ready to fall into the trap which Hero, Margaret, and Ursula have set for her. The accusation which they prepare against her, and which she overhears, is the appropriate one of self-absorption:

> her wit
> Values itself so highly, that to her
> All matter else seems weak: *she cannot love,*
> Nor take no shape nor project of affection,
> She is so *self-endeared.* (III. i)

This is an apt definition of the barrier which Beatrice—once more like Benedick—has hitherto been so busy erecting against nature, and which is now shown to be—as we might have expected—powerless to stand out against reality. In answer to this accusation, Beatrice—like Katherine the shrew, with whom she has some points of contact[2]—makes her appropriate and natural submission to the reality of love, when she says:

> Benedick, love on; I will requite thee,
> Taming my wild heart to thy loving hand; (III. i)

for it is clear by now that Beatrice, again like Benedick, knows the truth of love at the bottom of her heart and is ready to recognize it:

> For others say thou dost deserve, and I
> Believe it better than reportingly. (III. i)

Once more, answering to the spirit of this most deliberately formal of comedies, disguise and the appearance of deception become instruments to lead to the recognition of "nature" and the manifestation of truth.

On his next appearance, indeed, Benedick shows all the traditional signs of a man in love. Whilst this thread in the intrigue is being drawn to its appropriate and positive conclusion, however, the other, darker side of the comedy cuts across the newborn harmony with Don John's false substantiation of his accusation against Hero. He too makes his appeal, after his own fashion, to the "plain" evidence of the eyes; as he says to his brother and to Claudio:

> If you dare not trust that you see, confess not that you know: if you will follow me, I will show you enough; and when you have seen more, and heard more, proceed accordingly. (III. ii)

His appeal is in effect to false sight and false certainty, and the strength of his position lies in the fact that his victim, Claudio, is ready in his inexperience to take falsity for truth and to base his actions upon his illusory conviction. Claudio's reply to Don John's insinuations against Hero is, in effect, a statement of false determination: "If I see anything to-night why I should not marry her to-morrow, in the congregation, where I should wed, there will I shame her" (III. ii). The attitude is one which, on its very different level of intensity, recalls Othello's perverse demands for "ocular proof" and the complacency with which he contemplates the appalling and unnecessary decision to which Iago has brought him: "Good, the justice of it pleases."[3] Claudio's determination reflects, of course, a different situation, proceeds from one who is, by comparison with Othello, hardly a "character" at all; but the point is that his appearance of decision, which ministers finally to a certain naïve self-esteem in himself, rests in fact upon the false evidence of the eyes, upon an inadequate conception of love, and, in the last analysis, upon his own inexperienced weakness.

It is at this point, however, even as Don John arranges for Borachio to impersonate a lover in incriminating posture at Hero's window, that a further turn is given to the comic screw, as the villains are overheard describing their device and attributing it to their master. By this development, the false and the cunning, whose vision of reality is perverted to answer to their own malevolence, place themselves unwittingly in the hands of those who show, beneath their confused use of words and concepts, a certain basic loyalty and soundness of response. The attitude which we are invited to adopt toward Dogberry and his watch is not, of course, a simple one. Their verbal errors can be regarded as a deliberate comic inversion of the dexterity so abundantly displayed by most of the principal actors in this comedy; if Dogberry is far from attaining the polished brilliance which comes so readily to such as Benedick, his misuse of words is equally prompted by self-conceit, by a foolish and ignorant determination to display in the hearing of others his own imagined superiority. Some of the errors, however, and more often those of his followers than of Dogberry himself, convey meanings more profound than the speakers themselves can know. The first words exchanged by the watch are in this respect not without significance:

> *Dogberry:* Are you good men and true?
> *Verges:* Yes, or else it were pity but they should suffer salvation, body and soul. (III. iii)

The emphasis, beneath the comic confusion, is already upon essential goodness and truth, upon the capacity for "salvation, body and soul"; and in a situation where the perversion of keen sight in the name of ends falsely reasonable is engaged in furthering division and hatred, these are the qualities which need to be invoked from beyond the limits of sophistication to enable the truth to be declared. We shall not forget that, in *Love's Labour's Lost,* it was Costard, himself not above confusing meanings, who pointed to some of the firmer realities of his play,[4] and that, in *A Midsummer Night's Dream,* Bottom was vouchsafed his moment of "vision"[5] even as he assumed the ass's head which his relatively simple presumptions invited.

The revelation of truth through the mouths of the ignorant is not arrived at, indeed, without overcoming a fair share of comic obstacles. The time needed for the truth to be overheard is only obtained through Dogberry's absurd instructions to the watch to refrain from doing their obvious duty by immediately arresting the delinquents;[6] and Dogberry himself, indeed, is so taken up with what he regards as his superior command of language, so full of a kind of self-esteem which naïvely reflects that shown, sometimes to more vicious effect, by his "betters," that the final exposure of Don John's intrigue comes about almost too late and runs the risk of being impatiently brushed aside, in his haste to be elsewhere, by Leonato. Here, however, it is Leonato who is displaying shortsightedness, unwillingness to wait upon the truth which is always liable to emerge from the least likely quarters; for, if Dogberry's confusions are a part of the general effect of comic incongruity, it is not less so that it is in such hands and mouths as these that the truth is finally deposited. "Asses" though they may appear in the eyes of the sophisticated, Dogberry and his fellows yet cling to reality as they understand it, and by so doing they finally become instrumental to saving all. In spite of the self-importance which could easily make of him an officious busybody or petty tyrant—"I am a wise fellow; and, which is more, as pretty a piece of flesh as any is in Messina" (IV. ii)—Dogberry and his fellows are seen to be instruments of truth; the contrasted facets of appearance and fact, pretension and reality, which answer to the comic method of this play are nowhere more tellingly exemplified.

Before this revelation can take place, however, the action shifts back to its more somber plane as Claudio and Hero meet in church for the expected celebration of their marriage. Hero has approached this moment in a typical state of apprehension. "My heart is exceedingly heavy" (III. iv), she confesses; and Beatrice in turn has given this mood a comic reflection in her own transformed state by confessing herself as in "the sick tune" for her new love, and as being "exceedingly ill" for a husband. In her case, however, it is the laws of life, of normal humanity, that are asserting themselves, as we may gather from the tone and content of Margaret's jesting observation:

> I cannot think . . . that you are in love, . . . or that you can be in love. But Benedick was such another, and now is he become a man; he swore he would never marry; and yet now, in despite of his heart, he eats his meat without grudging: and how you may be converted I know not; but methinks you look with your eyes as other women do. (III. iv)

Against the perverse declaration of their respective inclinations, Beatrice and Benedick have in fact accepted their true natures as "woman" and "man" respectively; there could be no better foil to the confused tale of willfulness, misunderstanding, and malevolence that we are now to witness.

The marriage ceremony, to which all this has been leading, is in many respects the center of the entire pattern of the play's various "seemings." Offered Hero, "this rich and precious gift," in marriage, Claudio rejects her as "this rotten orange," making perverse appeal to what he holds to be the difference between reality and appearance:

> O, what authority and show of truth
> Can cunning sin cover itself withal!
> Comes not that blood as modest evidence
> To witness simple virtue? Would you not swear,
> All you that see her, that she were a maid,
> By these exterior shows? But she is none:
> She knows the heat of a luxurious bed;
> Her blush is guiltiness, not modesty. (IV. i)

The language at this point, and in much of what follows, notably outstrips comic convention in a way that may reasonably remind us of Shakespeare's "problem" comedies. "Cunning sin" covers itself, to the confusion of the simple, with the "authority and *show* of truth," and the blush on the cheeks of the accused comes as evidence falsely "modest" to counterfeit "*simple* virtue." Obsessive concentration upon his own imaginings—"the heat of a luxurious bed"—impels Claudio to reply to Hero's bewildered defense of her virtue —"*seem'd* I ever otherwise to you"—with an agonized repudiation of all appearances:

> Out on thee! *Seeming!* I will write against it:
> You *seem* to me as Dian in her orb,
> As chaste as is the bud ere it be blown;

for, as he adds, though the former object of his love "seems" thus, though her external aspect is consonant with the impression of remote and undeveloped chastity, the reality is brutally otherwise:

> But you are more intemperate in your blood
> Than Venus, or those pamper'd animals
> That rage in savage sensuality. (IV. i)

The exaggeration behind Claudio's new attitudes reflects itself in his hysterical concentration upon "blood," the savage forces of animal desire which contrast so strangely with the previous remoteness of his too facile idealism. This is, in effect, the other side of the essential inexperience we have already observed in Claudio; and we may even feel that Don Pedro's readiness to accept the testimony of false appearance at this point throws a light of its own upon his earlier confidence in taking up the young man's errand. Claudio is now obsessed, precisely because his previous attitudes failed to take reality into account, with a new and distorted sense of the difference that appears to separate "outward graces" from "the thoughts and counsels of the heart." Having begun by placing reliance too easily upon the external appearance of things, he now reacts equally unilaterally in the direction of disillusionment as to the true nature of the reality which underlies them. The sudden change in his outlook shows a considerable insight into the vagaries of the romantic imagination.

Something of the same kind can be said of the other characters who participate in this surprising and unnatural inversion of former attitudes. Hero's father, Leonato, for example, falls into a hysterical excess not altogether unrelated to Claudio's own:

> But *mine*, and *mine* I loved, and *mine* I praised,
> And *mine* that I was proud on, *mine* so much,
> That I *myself* was to *myself* not *mine,*
> Valuing of her,—why, she, O, she is fallen
> Into a pit of ink, that the wide sea
> Hath drops too few to wash her clean again,
> And salt too little which may season give
> To her foul-tainted flesh! (IV. i)

So much emphasis upon "mine," upon "myself," can hardly fail to bring home to us the element of self-centered obsession which colors this hysteria, which expresses itself in the contrast between the conventional content of certain images—"a pit of ink," "the wide sea"—and the bitter emphasis on the "foul-tainted" flesh which stands out against them. We are reminded, in anticipation, of the way in which Leontes, in the earlier part of *The Winter's Tale,* meditates with equal frenzy and equal lack of a sense of reality upon his wife's imaginary betrayal; reminded, too, of the obsession with "nothing,"[7] vanity, intimate disaster, which this reversal of his cherished and self-gratifying attitudes produces in his mind.

In the face of so much accumulated unreason and hysteria, the Friar speaks to restore the voice of sanity in the light of his own greater and more balanced experience. "Call me a fool," he says,

> Trust not my reading nor my observations,
> Which with experimental seal doth warrant
> The tenour of my book; trust not my age.
> My reverence, calling, nor divinity,
> If this sweet lady lie not guiltless here
> Under some biting error. (IV. i)

Benedick, too, has enough grasp of reality to ascribe the deception to its true source in Don John. To remedy matters in accordance with the general comic design, the Friar proposes a new "seeming" in the form of a public announcement of Hero's "death." This, he argues, will serve to bring back the natural emotion of pity, in accordance with that very inconstancy which he affirms to be a normal law of human behavior; for

> what we have we prize not to the worth
> Whiles we enjoy it; but being lack'd and lost,
> Why, then we reck the value, then we find
> The virtue that possession would not show us
> Whiles it was ours. (IV. i)

This we may take to be, in a sense, the "philosophic" foundation of the entire action. Claudio, whose original attraction to Hero rested on no firmly founded conception of her "value," lost her to the accompaniment of a general depreciation of her real worth. Only through the experience of her "loss" will the true quality of the "jewel" thus so lightly surrendered come to be appreciated, by him and the world, for what it really is.

The news of Hero's "death" will—to put the matter more concretely—serve, in the Friar's plan, to lead Claudio from his superficial fancies to the true "imagination" of love as "value" and source of life. "So will it fare with Claudio," he says:

> When he shall hear she died upon his words,
> The idea of her life shall sweetly creep
> Into his study of imagination;
> And every lovely organ of her life
> Shall come apparell'd in more precious habit,
> More moving-delicate and full of life,
> Into the eye and prospect of his soul,
> Than when she lived indeed; then shall he mourn,
> If ever love had interest in his liver,
> And wish he had not so accused her,
> No, though he thought his accusation true. (IV. i)

The intensity of the expression here—the emphasis on "life" at the moment when death is supposed to triumph, the stressed pairs of words ("eye and prospect," "moving-delicate," and so forth), the emphasis laid on "soul" and on the capacity of the imagination to render "true" even what might appear false to the eye of reason—all confirm that we are at a crucial stage in the play's development.

It is through this device, belonging to the order of comic convention, that life will finally assert itself in this play in a more mature and adequate conception of the married relationship and its implications.

Beatrice, too, as Hero's cousin, is affected by the new emotional stresses that have entered the action. Under their influence, she recognizes her love for Benedick and receives his answering surrender. As a sign of the reality of his love, Benedick declares his readiness to do for her anything she may require; and in her reply she is led by the new tragic situation not to romantic declarations or to further jest, but to the passionate if natural excess implied in the intensity of her command to her newly found lover: "Kill Claudio!" At this point, the continuing demands of comedy stand delicately poised against a fundamentally uncomic situation. That Beatrice, who has hitherto shown her easy mastery of the polished and pointed phrase, should thus find herself reduced to uttering a bare and savage request for vengeance, shows an incongruity that carries comic implications of a kind; and that the reasonable Benedick, of all men, should find himself placed as a result of his new love in a situation so foreign to everything he has stood for in the past, is frankly—if disconcertingly—absurd. Newly reconciled to love, Benedick finds himself confronted with a demand that takes him far beyond the common sense and detachment on which he has been accustomed to pride himself. To refuse his mistress' command would seem to imply turning his back on his new love, whilst to accept it means going beyond the dictates of reason and humanity; for, when Beatrice goes on to say: "O God, that I were a man! I would eat his heart in the market-place" (IV. i), the intensity of her feelings is clearly leading her—and threatens to lead Benedick—into a false situation. Benedick's first reaction to this command to become the instrument of vengeance upon Claudio is the reasonable one we might expect from him: "not for the wide world"; but his new and unforeseen love has placed him too in a new situation and he finally accepts the charge laid upon him: "By this hand, Claudio shall render me a dear account" (IV. i). By the end of this crucial scene, all the principal actors find themselves committed far beyond their original expectations; and it is from their commitment, even from their errors and excesses—because these too are, after all, a reflection of real life—that the final resolution will emerge.

As the action approaches its concluding stages, indeed, something of the same kind is suggested when Leonato's otherwise self-engrossed lamentations point to a similar repudiation of abstract, "philosophic" consolation:

> 'Tis all men's office to speak patience
> To those that wring under the load of sorrow,
> But no man's virtue nor sufficiency,
> To be so moral when he shall endure
> The like himself. (V. i)

"I will be flesh and blood" he determines, basing his resolve on the knowledge that

> there was never yet philosopher
> That could endure the toothache patiently. (V. i)

In this mood, his own passion, and that of Antonio with him, leads them both to draw their swords in search of vengeance upon Claudio for Hero's despised honor; and even Don Pedro, though he speaks in terms which are reasonable by contrast with most of what surrounds him, is mistaken in persisting in his belief that Hero was properly accused. When Benedick, newly dedicated to courses which his former self would certainly have condemned as signs of unreason, makes his appearance, Claudio, looking for relief in his friend's famous "wit," receives instead his unexpected challenge to a duel; for Benedick, who is by now thoroughly out of his habitual role as a "humourist," challenges him in the name of the honor with which his new love has confronted him. "You are a villain; *I jest not,*" he says, as though anticipating that the world will find it hard to accept him in his new guise, and continues, with the solemnity that befits his new convictions: "You have killed a sweet lady, and her death shall fall heavy on you" (V. i). Claudio on his side, by now thoroughly estranged from his original role of devoted lover, directs himself in jest to love's latest victim and is joined in this by the "reasonable" Don Pedro, who asks: "when shall we set the savage bull's horns on the sensible Benedick's head?" The "moral" of this transformation, however, and of its opposite, as undergone by the victim of these jests, is that the merely "sensible" also has its limitations; for both Claudio and Benedick are being driven, each from his own very different starting point, to acknowledge the force of reality.

Behind these confusions the moment of clarification is already approaching. Benedick has brought news of Don John's escape, and the watch now intervene with Borachio's confession. The terms of this touch closely upon the play's central theme, the contradiction between true and deceptive vision, reality and "seeming"; for, as the repentant instrument of villainy says, "I have deceived your very eyes," and, more appositely still, "what your wisdoms could not discover, these shallow fools have brought to light" (V. i). As we have already had occasion to observe, it is in accordance with the intention of this comedy that truth should be discovered in unexpected ways and in unusual places. To those who find their own folly, their subjection to appearance, thus exposed, this revelation comes as "iron" and "poison"; and by it Claudio is led—though, as he thinks, too late—to return to the "truth" of Hero as he once "felt" it and as he now, on more firm and rational grounds, knows it to be:

> Sweet Hero! now thy image doth appear
> In the rare semblance that I loved it first.

In this conviction, and sobered by the loss which he believes he has brought upon himself, he accepts "penance" and is urged by Leonato, in return for the forgiveness offered him, to take his niece in marriage. We shall clearly not interpret this in any merely realistic sense. It belongs to the framework of the comic convention, represents a situation no more "real," though far less moving in its effect upon us, than the "resurrection" of Hermione at the end of *The Winter's Tale*.[8] Overwhelmed by this gesture of what he calls "overkindness," Claudio accepts the offer in his new and chastened mood; for he has, of course, sinned by believing too readily the accusations which envy and the desire to slander have brought against his love and which his own moral levity has induced him to accept as true.

The affair of Beatrice and Benedick, meanwhile, remains to be rounded off in a suitably lighter key. Benedick, uneasy in his new state as lover, calls upon Margaret to help him in preparing nothing less than a sonnet for his mistress; there could be no better comic proof of his "conversion" from the man he has been. His wit has been "blunted," subjected to that of his new mistress, which he now recognizes ruefully to be "quick" and alive; and it is only left for him to cast an equally rueful eye upon his new state by reference to the accepted models:

> in loving, Leander the good swimmer, Troilus the first employer of panders, and a whole bookful of these quondam carpetmongers,

> whose names yet run smoothly in the even road of a blank verse, why, they were never so truly turned over and over as my poor self in love. (V. ii)

Recognizing his own failure as a rhymer, Benedick goes on to confess that he loves, in some measure, "against his will." The confession is significant; in their new relation to one another, Beatrice and Benedick both find that their former selves survive to plague them with the distance that separates past presumption from present reality. As Beatrice sums it all up: "Thou and I are too wise to woo peaceably."

In this way we move to the conclusion (V. iv), which is developed in terms appropriate to the prevailing comic convention. Claudio marries the veiled woman presented to him as Hero's substitute, and finds, of course, that it is Hero herself restored to life; whilst Beatrice and Benedick, albeit with some show of unwillingness to defend their wounded self-respect, declare in the eyes of the world the love which so unexpectedly unites them. Nothing less than sonnets by both of them have been discovered, and Benedick—capable to the last of playing to the gallery—agrees to take Beatrice "for pity," and she to "yield" to him "upon great persuasion." The final word upon their union is given to Benedick when he says: "man is a giddy thing, and this is my conclusion" (V. iv). It is also, perhaps, something like the last word on an action which is brought to a conclusion with a formal dance of partners, this time unmasked and truly united: a dance in relation to which even the "brave punishments" promised by Benedick—the humorist, be it noted—for the villainous Don John must take second place.

AS YOU LIKE IT

At the time, approximately, of his investigation, in the second great series of English historical plays, of the implications of the exercise of authority, Shakespeare's comic genius reached, in *As You Like It*, perhaps for the first time the measure of its full possibilities. Through and by means of convention, a statement about life is conveyed, without sententiousness or undue solemnity, in the appropriate forms of comedy: a statement centered upon the nature of love and friendship, considered—as they had already been considered in earlier comedies and in some of the most interesting of the sonnets—as basic human experiences in themselves of value, but which extends from these to cover a concept of *sociability*, of true *civilization*.

The opening scenes of *As You Like It*, indeed, introduce us to the issues of human life in society under a variety of conventional forms which are seen to concern both the *family* and *society* as a whole. In case we should be under any temptation to think that the artificiality of these forms, their obvious dependence upon devices of literary origin, provide justification for interpreting the play as an evasion, an escape into a world of mere poetic fancy, we should note that the initial emphasis is strongly upon *disorder*, upon the sinister reversal of the most natural human relationships. The disorder thus introduced into the action at once assumes a double form. In the first place, we learn that Orlando, as the younger of the two brothers, has been subjected by his senior, Oliver, to whose care his father entrusted him on his deathbed, to a tyranny or "servitude" which has reduced him to a status approaching that of a beast and prevented him from growing through the necessary process of education—what Shakespeare will elsewhere call *nurture*, or *art*, seeing in it the appropriate and indispensable complement of *nature*[9]—into true gentility. "My father," he accuses his brother, "charged you in his will to give me good education; you have trained me *like a peasant*, obscuring and hiding from me *all gentlemanlike qualities*" (I. i). It is precisely because his remains, in spite of this treatment, a noble nature—"the spirit of my father grows strong in me"—that Orlando announces his determination, as the play opens, no longer to "endure" this subjection.

The tyrannical treatment of Orlando by his brother, moreover, takes place in relation to another equally unnatural situation. Parallel to it, and in a wider sphere, the prevalence of an essential disorder in society is confirmed in the supplanting of the legitimate and beneficent rule of "the old Duke" by the arbitrary authority of "the new Duke" who has usurped his position. For those who may be tempted to see, here and elsewhere in Shakespeare's comedies, no more than an elaborate game of make-believe, it is worth reflecting that these, though treated in a different and more indirect way, are the themes which will reappear in many of his greatest tragedies, not excluding *King Lear*. Though here subject to convention, transcribed as it were into a comic key, they are not on that account to be taken less seriously as dramatic reflections of real life.

The consequences of these reversals of nature and of civilized order make themselves apparent in the early stages of the action. Oliver makes use of a wrestler, a dispassionate and largely tongue-tied incarnation of brute force, to execute his plot against Orlando. In order to persuade him to this he pretends to detect an unnatural evil in his brother in very much the same terms as Edmund will later use for the discrediting of Edgar in the eyes of his overcredulous father.[10] "It is the stubbornest young fellow of France," he says, and goes on to ascribe to him what are in effect his own unnatural faults: "full of ambition, *an envious emulator* of every man's good parts, *a secret and villainous contriver* against me *his natural brother,*" and to urge him to mingle brutality with dissimulation: "therefore use thy discretion; I had as lief thou didst break his neck as his finger." Before he has finished, Oliver's persuasiveness rises to even more unnatural levels of falsity: "And thou wert best look to't; for if thou dost him any slight disgrace, or if he do not mightily grace himself on thee, he will practise against thee by *poison, entrap thee* by some *treacherous device,* and never leave thee till he hath ta'en thy life by some *indirect* means or other; for, I assure thee, and almost with tears I speak it, there is not one so young and so villainous this day living" (I. i). It should be noted, however, as a most significant conclusion to this long list of what are essentially his own blemishes, that Oliver, when left to himself, is obliged to recognize the true virtue of his brother, which in fact he envies for the attraction it exercises over the rest of men: "Yet he's *gentle;* never schooled, and yet learned; full of *noble device;* of all sorts *enchantingly beloved;* and indeed so much *in the heart of the world* . . . that I am altogether *misprised*" (I. i).

These attitudes of envy and unreasonable resentment are soon seen to reflect themselves in the wider ranges of the society with which the play is concerned. In much the same way as Oliver, and on his more ample stage, the new Duke is, by comparison with his gentle and humane predecessor, thoroughly suspicious and tyrannical. He exiles Rosalind from his court in a completely arbitrary fashion—"Let it suffice thee that I trust thee not" (I. iii)—and even, once she and his own daughter Celia have sought their liberty in flight, threatens his creature Oliver with the confiscation of his property if he fails to ensure the rapid return of the fugitives into his power

(III. i). The tone of all these early court episodes, with their sense of a world increasingly subject to degeneration as it ages, is summed up by the courtier Le Beau when, in the act of bidding farewell to Orlando as he sets out upon his exile, he makes his own comment on what have become the sorry ways of society:

Sir, fare you well:
Hereafter, *in a better world than this,*
I shall desire more love and knowledge of you. (I. ii)

The aspiration for "a better world," and the awareness of living in a worse, are placed in the mouth of one who is old enough to remember the times when such a world actually existed. Though it may seem at this stage to be little more than a pathetic nostalgia for the impossible, it will in due course be satisfied, not by translation to an imaginary Arcadian perfection—though such a translation answers to a necessary and revealing stage in the complete conception —but by the restoration of order and humanity to the real society —"real," naturally, in terms of the conventions which the play uses— from which they have been unnaturally banished.

Even in a world of the kind so bitterly rejected by Le Beau, however, certain positives survive. Among them is the firm friendship which unites Rosalind and Celia, who might easily have been, given the situation of their respective parents, rivals, but who are in fact no such thing; for Celia declares herself ready from the first to acknowledge the wrong which has been done to her friend's father and even to offer such restitution as may be in her power in the future. "You know," she says, "my father hath no child but I, nor none is like to have: and truly, when he dies, thou shalt be his heir; for what he hath taken away from thy father perforce, I will render thee again in affection" (I. ii); for to do otherwise would be, as she at once goes on to say, to make of herself a "monster." In a similar way Orlando, in the very moment of his trial, has fallen in love with Rosalind and received from her the token of true faith which he will carry with him into exile. Throughout the various stages of this opening, we may say that convention is being consistently used to reflect the complexity of real life.

It is the aim of this comedy, still working through the conventions it has chosen, to bring these tensions to a harmonious resolution which will itself answer to the genuine positives, both personal and social, of real living. This resolution is to be sought through the displacement of the action in a direction which appears at first sight (but at first sight only) to be away from common reality; by moving it, in other words, to the Forest of Arden, where love and other human relations are to be taken temporarily into the state of nature, and where the simplicities of the primitive world (itself presented in terms thoroughly and deliberately conventional) will be set in contrast to the corrupt state of sophistication which we have already seen in action. This removal, it need hardly be repeated, is not a mere "escape" from reality, does not in any sense constitute the final answer toward which the comedy may be said to move. The "state of nature," as the play presents it, is as artificial, as remote from the true reality of the condition it purports to represent, as the "sophistication" which it replaces. Both, indeed, are instruments for asserting, within the limits of comedy, permanent truths about life which they do not directly or "realistically" reflect. Rosalind, Celia, and Orlando leave the court in search of "liberty," freedom from restraint and corruption. They will find this in the forest, and with it what is even more important, a degree of self-knowledge, a fresh understanding, itself expressed within the limits that their author has chosen to accept, of what life really is; but at the end of the action they, and with them all the others concerned, will have to return, bringing with them the insights they have acquired in the course of their adventures, to the social and civilized world, the distinctively human order of life with which the play is finally concerned.

So much, indeed, is implied in the opening presentation of the Forest of Arden (II. i), which is considerably more complex than may at once appear. Our first information about life in the forest comes from the wrestler Charles, who touches upon some of the main themes in its presentation when he tells Oliver that, according to report, the old Duke has already sought refuge there,

> and a many merry men with him; and there they live like the old Robin Hood of England; they say many young gentlemen flock to him every day, and fleet the time carelessly, as they did in the golden world. (I. i)

The "golden world" is, accordingly, set in an ideal past, presented as a compound of legendary antiquity, of the reign of the gods and goddesses in Arcadia, and of the original timeless innocence which existed in the Garden of Eden before the Fall. The ability to neglect the action of time, indeed, is essential to the conception, the key at once to its attraction and to its final insufficiency. At some period in the past, during the generation of Orlando's virtuous father, who was not accidentally named Sir Rowland de Bois, a creature by implication of the woods, the forest world of ordered harmony and simple, unchanging human happiness corresponded to an ideally natural ordering of society, which is then supposed actually to have existed in court and state; but since the passing of that mythically fortunate generation, forest and court, ideal and reality have become grievously separated, and the consequent loss for mankind, tantamount to a kind of Fall from original grace, may be said to be symbolized in the figure of the faithful Adam, whose name is again not without significance and who is obliged, after his banishment from a corrupted society, to pass his old age wandering through Arden in painful search for the ideal order to which he once belonged and to the reality of which his continued loyalty to Orlando testifies. To put the matter in this way is, of course, to risk loading with abstract and theoretical meanings what is, in fact, in the play admirably light and effortlessly poetic; but the point is one which needs to be made, even with this danger in view, if the final, *unsolemn* seriousness of Shakespeare's conception is to receive its due.

The contrast between an ideal order, which those who desire it can only seek in the forest but which they will not ultimately find there, and the remembered experience of the real world to which, as human beings, they belong is one which dominates the entire presentation of the action in Arden. The forest is like the "golden world" in partaking of a kind of timelessness, which seems indeed, to those who have recently escaped from the anxieties and mutual distrusts of their corrupted social world, to be a necessary condition of the ideal. "There's no clock in the forest," as Orlando points out to Rosalind.[11] He goes on, however, to speak himself of that time which "travels in divers paces with divers persons" and which necessarily accompanies the lover's awareness of his condition (III. ii); and Touchstone, an unwilling refugee on his own lower level, is expressly observed by Jacques in the act of consulting his "dial" in the forest, and overheard by him relating the moment of time to the sense of inevitable decay which so persistently accompanies life in the real world and which no amount of dedication to pastoral make-believe can finally ignore:

And so, from hour to hour, we ripe and ripe,
And then, from hour to hour, we rot and rot;
And thereby hangs a tale. (II. vii)

The reality of this "tale" is germane to the entire conception of this comedy, and indeed to all Shakespeare's exercises in the comic form from now on.[12]

All the attitudes of those who have entered Arden imply, in fact, each after its appropriately diverse fashion, not only the attraction of an ideal aspiration, but, side by side with and consistently coloring it, the awareness of an actual Fall from original innocence. The woods are said by the old Duke, who has sought refuge in them from the trials to which he was subjected by the unnatural action of his brother, to be "More free from peril than the envious court." This is true and important; but the very statement implies that the memory of "peril" and "envy" are still very much alive in his mind as he speaks. If he is able, in his new state, to say, somewhat sententiously, that he can find

tongues in trees, books in the running brooks,
Sermons in stones and good in everything,

and to declare that he feels no desire to change his condition, there is at least equal meaning in his recognition that

Sweet are the uses of adversity;
Which, like the toad, ugly and venomous,
Wears yet a precious jewel in his head. (II. i)

The reality of the "jewel," though we are asked by the very rules of the comic game to accept it, need not lead us to neglect the ugliness and poison of the toad which bears it; and the Duke's courtly companion Amiens remains fully aware during his enforced sojourn in the realm of "nature" of what he calls the "stubbornness of fortune"[13] which has brought him there. More than once, indeed, there are hints of real contradictions beneath the apparent simplicity of the pastoral ideal; for those who have found refuge in the forest from the pressures of a hostile world are still under the manifest necessity of living at nature's expense, of killing the deer—"poor dappled fools,"[14] as they are decoratively called—upon whom their sustenance depends. Theirs is a situation into which the melancholy observer Jacques reads, not without a characteristic sense of pleasure, a moral which has a certain relation to real life, as he professes to see in his companions

> usurpers, tyrants, and what's worse,
> To fright the animals and to kill them up
> In their assign'd and native dwelling place. (II. i)

It is indeed upon the animals, the real representatives of "nature" in the forest, that the human intruders are obliged in their extremity to prey simply to keep themselves alive. Whatever else it may be, the forest is *not* conceived as a place where the laws of common life are permanently suspended in the interests of an effortless and simple existence.

It would perhaps be nearer the truth to say that it is a place where each human actor finds what his own nature prompts him to discover. To Amiens' song, with its touching expression of the desire to believe that those who are fortunate enough to live "Under the greenwood tree" in daily contact with nature are rendered free thereby of the less attractive aspects of life in society, finding there

> No enemy
> But winter and rough weather,

Jacques at once responds with the disillusioned spirit of his parody:

> Here shall he see
> Gross fools as he,
> An if he will come to me. (II. v)

Both Amiens and Jacques are partially right, respond in their contrasted reactions to elements genuinely present in the human situation; but the central issue at stake in Arden, which is not finally to be resolved there, concerns not these separated fragments of vision, but, in the last resort, the complex and mutually enriching links between "nature" and civilization.

To the world of nature thus conceived the main actors of the play accordingly come, to seek what is in essence a measure of self-clarification. The first to decide to join the former Duke by taking refuge in the forest is Orlando, who is accompanied in his journey there by his faithful servant Adam, in whose aged person the traditional ideals of fidelity and service, which have been so harshly exiled from Duke Frederick's corrupt and sophisticated court, are still alive. Adam, strong in the firm and unshakable possession of essential human values, which his subjection to the harsh realities of old age and exile cannot obscure, knows in the act of leaving it that "this house"—the court—has become "but a butchery," an abode of deception and treachery upon which he comments without illusion:

> Know you not, master, to some kind of men
> Their graces serve them but as enemies?
> No more do yours: your virtues, *gentle* master,
> Are *sanctified and holy traitors* to you.
> O, what a world is this, where what is comely
> *Envenoms* him that bears it. (II. iii)

It is in reaction against a world of this kind that Rosalind and Celia, as we have learned already, have abandoned the court to go

> in *content*
> To *liberty* and not to banishment. (I. iii)

What all four find in the forest, however, is a reality in some respects very notably distinct from any conception that they, or we, may harbor of merely idyllic peace. The aged Adam is driven to the verge of utter exhaustion in what Orlando, taking pity upon him, calls "this *uncouth* forest" (II. vi),[15] before he finds himself forced to threaten Duke Senior to obtain the food of which both are by now desperately in need: forced, in other words, to sin against his own civilized and sociable values and to make himself, in the eyes of his former sovereign, "a rude despiser of good manners," a man "empty" of essential "civility" (II. vii). In a way finally similar Rosalind and Celia go through much the same kind of experience; for they too are reduced to confess their weariness after long hours of wandering through the forest, and the clown Touchstone, whom they have so strangely chosen for their incongruous companion in their adventure of "liberty" and who clearly has no illusions about the real meaning of the state of nature, has no better than this to say of his enforced surroundings: "Ay, now am I in Arden; the more fool I; when I was at home, I was in a better place," and concludes, in a typical mood of detached fatalism, that "travellers must be content" (II. iv). We may think that the best comment on Arcadian illusion is conveyed through the shepherd Colin, when he says of his master, from whom Rosalind and Celia are hoping to get relief in their extremity:

My master is of churlish disposition
And little recks to find the way to heaven
By doing deeds of hospitality. (II. iv)

The exercise of "hospitality" is clearly under any circumstances a virtue, a distinctively human and humanizing quality; but we are not to assume that it is necessarily more prevalent in the order of pastoral simplicity than in the world of normal social intercourse. We must surely conclude, at the best, that the original dwellers in this pastoral "paradise" are scarcely the idealized and gentle "swains" that a more superficial use of the convention would have made of them.

It is worth noting, moreover, that those who find themselves driven by adverse circumstance to enter Arcadia bring their true, their civilized natures with them. When the Duke reproves Orlando for having so rudely interrupted his rustic feast, the latter replies that he is, in spite of the circumstances in which he now finds himself and which have driven him to this excess, a man who has "some *nurture*," a true measure of civility, in his nature. His final appeal for understanding is made to those who have known civilized behavior in the real world of human society:

If ever you have look'd on better days,
If ever been where bells have toll'd to church,
If ever sat at any good man's feast,
If ever from your eyelids wiped a tear
And know what 'tis to pity and be pitied,
Let *gentleness* my strong enforcement be; (II. vii)

for, as he goes on to imply, to "lose and neglect the creeping hours of time" in the forest may be a temporary necessity which exile imposes, but can never be a permanent answer to the challenge, essentially sociable and human in its nature, of real life. The Duke's table, set out among the trees for the feast which Orlando has so rudely interrupted, in itself represents a *social* act, and as such a positive good, in contrast, precisely, to the evil which has driven those who are now joined around it to seek refuge, in temporary renunciation of their full human stature, in the freedom of the forest. The final resolution of the issues raised in the course of the action must lie, in the last resort, not in Arden, which is essentially and of its nature a place of transition, even in a very real sense of illusion, but elsewhere.

The forest, accordingly, is to be seen above all as a place where basic human attitudes are put variously to the test; these concern more particularly love and its reflection in friendship. First and outstanding among the various pairs who meet in these new surroundings are Orlando and Rosalind, who find in Arden the love which they sought at the court, but which they were debarred from bringing to its natural consummation there. Their relations in the forest become the occasion, in the first instance, for the criticism which Rosalind, taking advantage of her disguise as the page "Ganymede," passes upon what she calls the "quotidian," the feverish excesses, of romantic love. It is not from this kind of love, upon which so many preceding Shakespearean comedies have passed judgment, that the protagonists of this play will derive the strength to overcome the trials to which they are respectively subjected. When Orlando, speaking of the qualities of love, asks her "What are his marks?" she replies by cataloguing the conventional signs of the lovesick devotee which she is happy not to find in him:

> A lean cheek, which you have not; a blue eye and sunken, which you have not; an unquestionable spirit, which you have not; a beard neglected, which you have not . . . then your hose should be ungartered, your bonnet unbanded, your sleeve unbuttoned, your shoe untied, and everything about you demonstrating a careless desolation. (III. ii)

By the absence of all these signs, Rosalind concludes that Orlando is —to her relief and his credit—"no such man"; and, having thus established the essential sanity which makes him attractive in her eyes, she goes on, still in the light of the comic spirit, which is marked by its readiness to accept the incongruous and the irrational as aspects of life, to consider the nature of love itself, which she finds to be a madness indeed—it could not otherwise be the proper substance of comedy—but a madness both universal and necessary to life; for, if it may be admitted, in terms of realistic common sense, that love is "merely a madness" which "deserves as well a dark house and a whip as madmen do," the fact remains, and is not less incontestable, that "the reason why they"—the generality of lovers—"are not so punished and cured, is that the lunacy is so ordinary that the whippers are in love too" (III. ii).

Rosalind's own attitude to love, to which these exchanges lead, and which is more directly developed in the second scene in which, still speaking as "Ganymede," she discusses the matter with Orlando (IV. i), is a characteristic compound of humorous detachment and frank acceptance. Unwilling to take romantic love at its own incurably pretentious estimate, she remarks that "The poor world is almost six thousand years old, and in all this time there was not any man died in his own person, videlicet in a love cause," and goes on to comment sharply enough upon some of the most illustrious literary examples of this excessive passion:

> Troilus had his brains dashed out with a Grecian club; yet he did what he could to die before, and he is one of the patterns of love. Leander, he would have lived many a fair year, though Hero had turned nun, if it had not been for a hot midsummer night; for, good youth, he went but forth to wash him in the Hellespont and being taken with the cramp was drowned; and the foolish chronicles of that age found it was "Hero of Sestos." (IV. i)

The last word, however, is not allowed to rest here. The conclusion which confirms these critical estimates goes on to lend them a deeper, even a more tragic content which is an essential part of the complete effect: "But these are all lies: men have died from time to time and worms have eaten them, but not for love" (IV. i). Real men have not, and indeed, it would seem, should not *die* romantically in pursuit of their irrational passions; but whether, and to what extent, it may be said that they should *live* for and by them is a question that still remains to be asked.

It is a question which Rosalind herself goes on to answer, at least by implication. Her attitude to Orlando is forthright, impatient of all forms of romantic excess; when he says, with a certain touch of the pretentious, that her frown might be sufficient to "kill" him, her retort is "By this hand, it will not kill a fly," and she goes on from this to assert against the more absurd excesses of romantic devotion her own more realistic view of the volubility of men and women alike in love. "Men," she says, "are April when they woo, December when they wed: maids are May when they are maids, but the sky changes when they are wives"; and yet again, when, in his devotion, Orlando ventures to call her "wise," her answer is conceived in the essence of the comic spirit of incongruity:

> the wiser, the waywarder: make the doors upon a woman's wit and it will out at the casement; shut that, and 'twill out at the key-hole; stop that, 'twill fly with the smoke out at the chimney. (IV. i)

It is necessary to the comic effect, however, that these sallies should not remain the last word. Orlando believes throughout that he is speaking to "Ganymede," and Rosalind's awareness of this invariably conditions her replies. At the last she is ready, even as she continues to speak in this way, to recognize in more intimate terms to Celia her own servitude to "that same wicked bastard of Venus that was begot of thought, conceived of spleen, and born of madness": let him, she concludes, in apparent but profoundly natural contrast to so much that she has said in her moments of purely comic inspiration, "be judge how deep I am in love" (IV. i).

Side by side with the central romantic situation, carried on by Rosalind in her disguise, other aspects of love are presented, and fall under her comment, in the story of the shepherd Silvius and the Phebe who is the object of his unreasoning and servile devotion. Silvius is the romantic lover personified in all his excess, who is content to see his disdainful mistress as his "executioner" (III. v) and who, by the very fact of so doing, ensures that this—an "executioner" —is precisely what she shall continue to be for him. When Phebe, however, in her disdain for this abject follower, aspires beyond him to none other than "Ganymede," Rosalind exposes the tyranny she exercises over him in no uncertain terms, stressing both the human content of love (and the equally human limitations which go with it) and the need for self and mutual respect in its conduct. To Silvius she urges the claims of a proper self-respect, based upon a genuine and necessary realism, against the excesses of sentimental self-abasement in all its forms:

'Tis not her glass, but you, that flatters her;
And out of you she sees herself more proper
Than any of her lineaments can show her; (III. v)

whilst to Phebe, on her side, she lays stress upon the positive human good of marriage, and upon the need to found this central relationship upon a true knowledge of the self and of its accompanying limitations. "Mistress, know yourself," she says, and goes on to add what amounts to a command to sanity and a proper sense of proportion:

down on your knees,
And thank heaven, fasting, for a good man's love:

to end, more sharply still, with a call to realism in self-assessment and in the estimate of what life may really offer her:

> Sell when you can: you are not for all markets:
> Cry the man mercy: love him: take his offer. (III. v)

The mercantile form of this advice is deliberate, represents an emphatic call to realism and a proper sense of truth; but it is significant that it falls, as far as the recipient is concerned, upon deaf ears. Entrapped, little though she is prepared to recognize it, in the illusion of her supposed "love" for "Ganymede," Phebe ignores this advice to content herself with the considerable good which is hers for the having, and even seeks to use her victim, Silvius, to convey her impossible message to Rosalind. Silvius, by his acceptance of this ignoble mission, in reality confirms his own state of servitude, his inability to respect himself properly as a human being; the awakening of this pair to sanity, to the appropriate recognition of things as they really are, and so to the need for building their own lives upon a natural and realistic foundation, will only come with the final resolution.

Yet another aspect of love, in some sense marginal to the main action but not on that account less relevant to it, is provided by Touchstone, who is brought, albeit with more than a touch of unwillingness, to recognize the place of marriage in any truly "natural" scheme of life:

> As the ox hath his bow, sir, the horse his curb, and the falcon her bells, so man hath his desires; and as pigeons bill, so wedlock would be nibbling. (III. iii)

For Touchstone this uneasy compulsion presents itself in the forest in the ill-favored form of the country wench Audrey. Unwilling as he is to accept even the possibility of a permanent commitment to this grotesque partner—who, however, responds adequately to his own nature—Touchstone at first sets his mind upon an uneasy and evasive compromise. He will "marry" her through the offices of the hedge-priest Oliver Martext, and so leave open to himself the avenue for a possible escape from servitude; but when Jacques points out that this attitude cannot lead to any true or valid marriage—"this fellow," he says, "will but join you together as they join wainscot" (III. iii)—he ends by agreeing, with some unwillingness, to seek a "true priest" to carry out the appropriate offices to unite them. In this way, he accepts the necessity of marriage, which has been brought home to him in the forest but which cannot receive its final consummation there—again to follow Jacques' phrase—"under a bush like a beggar."[16] For Touchstone, too, marriage presents itself with a social, a distinctively human form of challenge, and by the end of the play he will be ready to take his Audrey as she is, recognizing in her "an ill-favoured thing," indeed, "but mine own," and living in the hope that he too may yet find, when he returns to the real world in the company of his incongruous bride, the "pearl" concealed in his "foul oyster."[17] An element of relativity, of the irreducible tendency of human nature to remain on the margin of the beautiful and harmonizing visions which the imagination proposes to it, is essential to Shakespeare's comic vision in its profounder moments, and here, in Touchstone's wry inconclusiveness, it is finely incorporated into the vision of Arden.

Finally—and at this point we are brought directly back to the wider purposes by which the action is governed, and which will eventually preside over its resolution—love plays its part in the forest by healing the original breach between Orlando and the brother who initially drove him into exile. Seeking out his banished brother in the forest, and thereby exposing himself to the kind of danger to which he had once been ready to leave Orlando, Oliver falls asleep under a tree and is rescued—and rescued precisely by a deed of courage which involves the shedding of this same brother's blood—from the dangers represented, in terms which unite the pastoral order to a kind of symbolic meaning, by a serpent and a lioness. In other words, when Oliver, suitably repentant, carries to Rosalind a bloody napkin as a sign of his rescue, he shows himself, according to his own admission, "converted" by the "kindness, nobler than revenge" (IV. iii),[18] which he has encountered in the very person whom he once so grievously wronged. Thus finding reconciliation in the forest, the brothers make their peace and Oliver, restored to true civility as distinct from its false and sophisticated reflection, given "fresh array"[19] and "entertainment" by the Duke, falls in love with Celia and declares himself content to renounce the "estate" which he now recognizes that he has wrongfully administered, and, furthermore, to "live and die a shepherd" (V. ii). In this way, and in accordance with the conventional pattern of the play, the natural relationship between the brothers is at last re-established for the general good of society. Orlando, bringing with him the natural virtues that have always been his, returns to the world of "nurture" to which he truly belongs, whilst Oliver, who has previously shown himself so unnatural in his state of worldly sophistication, retires in a mood of chastened contemplation to seek true understanding of the world and of himself in the natural simplicities.

What we have witnessed through the central part of the play has been, in essence, a set of variations on the theme of love and on that of the true sociability which accompanies it and confers meaning upon personal relationships. By the time these variations have been fully worked out in the Forest of Arden, we are ready for the final resolution which will be contrived by Rosalind in her understanding, now deepened by the effect upon her of her recent experiences, of the true nature of love as a cementing and positive influence, at once central and salutary, upon human life. On the verge of this resolution, the complaints of the still unsatisfied lovers strike her comically as "the howling of Irish wolves against the moon" (V. ii), residues of an excess of romantic self-centeredness which can achieve only its own madness. To each of those thus situated she offers her help, in appropriate but still enigmatic form, with the end of enabling them to take up their proper places in the final dance of civilized harmonies to which the whole action is now tending. "To-morrow," she tells them, "meet me all together," and then goes on to distribute to each, in riddling form, her assurance that they shall find what is proper for them and what, indeed, in so far as they know themselves they truly desire:

> (*to Phebe*) I will marry you, if ever I marry woman, and I'll be married to-morrow: (*to Orlando*) I will satisfy you, if ever I satisfied man, and you shall be married to-morrow: (*to Silvius*) I will content you, if what pleases you contents you, and you shall be married to-morrow. (V. ii)

Then, after having thus announced in enigmatic form the approaching consummation, Rosalind ends by calling each of those who hear her to the appointed place of meeting:

> (*to Orlando*) As you love Rosalind, meet: (*to Silvius*) as you love Phebe, meet: and as I love no woman, I'll meet. (V. ii)

The artifice of the final resolution, founded in this way upon the recognition of natural instinct and the need to incorporate it into a wider context of human realities, is set in turn against the spirit of the Page's song, with its emphasis upon the order of the seasons as the appropriate setting for love:

It was a lover and his lass,
With a hey, and a ho, and hey nonino,
That o'er the green corn-field did pass,
In the spring time, the only pretty ring time,
When birds do sing, hey ding a ding ding,
Sweet lovers love the spring— (V. iii)

and on the need to take "the present time," the offered moment of living experience, against the background of a mutability which originally conditions it and against which its absorbing human reality is now affirmed. The progress from winter bareness to the promise of spring—from "Blow, blow thou winter wind" to the spring time of love reborn—answers to the general structure of the play, which is now in the process of being rounded off to its natural conclusion: for love, in the concluding words of the song, "is crowned with the prime" and the moment of its consummation is at hand.

And so, as the play is drawn to its harmonizing close, still in the forest, but with an eye now clearly directed to the reality, human and social, which lies beyond these Arcadian limits, Rosalind and Celia make their solemn entry, appropriately accompanied by Hymen, the god of marriage, who declares his intent to "bar confusion" in the name of a conception of married union that can now reflect, in its mingling of joy and gravity, the order of nature itself: for, as the song which announces their entry puts it,

There is mirth in heaven,
When earthly things made even
Atone together:

and again, when the various couplings are at last complete in the "atonement," the restoration of unity which has made them possible:

Wedding is great Juno's crown:
O blessed bond of board and bed!
'Tis Hymen peoples every town;
High wedlock then be honoured:
Honour, high honour and renown,
To Hymen, god of every town! (V. iv)

No sooner have these celebrations of marriage been sanctioned by this note of due solemnity, than the time comes for all those concerned to leave Arden for the last time: to leave it in order to make their necessary return to the world of social and civilized realities to which they are at last ready to be incorporated. Duke Frederick, having declared himself "converted" to a new and more responsible outlook upon life, restores his crown to its rightful owner and renounces the "world" which, by his previous perverse acts, he has helped to plunge into confusion; and Duke Senior, taking up his former role, which has always been his by right, calls upon all those present to join him in the dance of married harmonies which reflects, in its grave and entranced unity, the universal harmony of nature:

> Play, music! And you, brides and bridegrooms all,
> With *measure heap'd in joy*, to the measures fall.

The last word is left, however, not to him, but to Jacques, the detached and melancholy observer, who is now allowed to call each to the place in the dance, the harmonious "measure," which corresponds to him. To the restored Duke he says:

> You to your former honour I bequeath;
> Your patience and your virtue well deserves it;

to Orlando, who has won his Rosalind,

> You to a love that your true faith doth merit;

to Oliver:

> You to your land, and love, and great allies;

to Silvius:

> You to a long and well-deserved bed;

and, finally, to Touchstone, who has declared his readiness to take his new-found Audrey to himself in marriage:

> And you to wrangling; for thy loving voyage
> Is but for two months victuall'd. (V. iv)

In thus taking upon himself the words which distribute to each his appropriate part in the measure, it may seem at first sight that the detached and self-centered Jacques is going beyond his limitations; but further reflection may suggest to us that the last word rests thereby, as the spirit of comedy will have it, with a certain note of relativity which serves to balance and qualify the preceding statement of universal harmonies.

Some such note of relativity is, indeed, appropriate to the play's complete comic effect. To allow it a place in his conception Shakespeare has introduced into his play two characters—Touchstone and Jacques—who stand, each in his own very different way, somewhat apart from the main unifying conception. The unwilling submission of Touchstone to the married state we have already considered; it represents, in the typical Shakespearean way, the voice of reality qualifying the truths and harmonies glimpsed by the imagination through the forms of sophisticated comedy as developed in the main action. Jacques himself, who has commented with sharp detachment on Touchstone's weaknesses, lies—contented as he is with his self-centered and self-chosen melancholy—in a rather more fundamental way apart from the general pattern. His comments—including those which go to make up his famous speech on the seven ages of man (II. vii), which it is too easy to quote out of its context as a detached expression of the author's "philosophic" wisdom—provide at all times a qualifying background to the more positive assertions which prevail elsewhere. As such, they fulfill a necessary role in the complete and balanced conception with which the play is concerned; but to impose upon them a seriousness which is certainly not intended is to falsify the author's intention and the part assigned to the speaker in the action as a whole.

The force of Jacques' successive vignettes of representative states of life answers, indeed, rather to a distinctively comic vision than to any profound insight into the nature of reality. The "whining schoolboy" creeping, "like snail," unwillingly to school already reflects a humorous conception, and so, even more definitely, do the essentially satirical comments which follow on the conventional lover,

> Sighing like furnace, with a woeful ballad
> Made to his mistress' eyebrow,

and on the soldier,

> Jealous in honour, sudden and quick in quarrel,
> Seeking the bubble reputation
> Even in the cannon's mouth. (II. vii)

We have met both these personages elsewhere in the plays, and shall have occasion to meet them at times in other, more serious contexts;[20] but the spirit in which both they and the "justice,"

> In fair round belly with good capon lined,

are conceived is one in which the comic intention, alternately tolerant and sharply reflective of human frailties and idiosyncrasies, prevails. Slightly sententious and finally self-gratifying in tone, like nearly everything said by Jacques in the course of the play, these observations are certainly not to be taken simply at the speaker's own valuation. The context in which they are uttered is carefully designed to make this clear. Just as Jacques, at the end of his speech, has allowed himself the pleasure, in a final artificial flourish, of reducing the state of man in his old age to one of impotence and vanity—

> second childishness and mere oblivion,
> Sans teeth, sans eyes, sans taste, sans everything— (II. vii)

the entry of Adam, who represents visibly those positives of loyalty and faith which the melancholy "philosopher" cannot understand or relate to his own reading of life, serves to remind us that there are other possible views of old age and, indeed, by implication at least, of human existence as a whole. It is precisely these views, based upon positive acceptance and participation, that the main comedy is concerned to advance.

For the fact is that Jacques' "wisdom" is founded at each turn upon his limitations. He is fitted by his nature to expose the elements of vice and disorder which undeniably occupy so large a place in human existence—it is, of course, his self-declared vocation, perhaps a little too readily accepted, to "Cleanse the foul body of the infected world" (II. vii)—but the sufficiency which his every utterance implies is not in turn without its own Achilles' heel. It is worth remarking that the old Duke, as he rebukes him for his overfacile moralizing, stresses in no uncertain terms the roots of his "philosophic" misanthropy, his complacent declaration of his own superiority to the motives of lesser men in a very real subjection to the elements of selfishness and lust which he so readily condemns in others:

> thou thyself hast been a libertine,
> As sensual as the brutish sting itself;
> And all the embossed sores and headed evils
> That thou with license of free foot has caught
> Wouldst thou disgorge into the general world. (II. vii)

"Brutish sting"; "embossed sores"; "headed evils"; "disgorge"; the connection with the maladies of the "infected world," and the clear statement that Jacques himself shares fully in the evils he is so apt to denounce from the standpoint of his self-asserted superiority, are too powerful for them to fail in making their point. It is noteworthy that Jacques' only defense against this accusation lies in the claim that the vices which it gives him such pleasure to expose are in fact universal attributes of human society:

> Why, who cries out on pride,
> That can therein tax any private party?
> Doth it not flow as hugely as the sea,
> Till that the weary very means do ebb?
> What woman in the city do I name,
> When that I say the city-woman bears
> The cost of princes on unworthy shoulders?
> Who can come in and say that I mean her,
> When such a one as she such is her neighbour?
> Or what is he of basest function,
> That says his bravery is not on my cost,
> Thinking that I mean him, but therein suits
> His folly to the mettle of my speech?
> There then; how then? what then? Let me see wherein
> My tongue hath wrong'd him; for if it do him right,
> Then he hath wrong'd himself; if he be free,
> Why then my taxing like a wild-goose flies,
> Unclaim'd of any man. (II. vii)

This is possibly Jacques' most truly eloquent utterance, and we need not give less than their true value to its central themes, of which echoes may be found as far away as *King Lear;* but this does not mean that we are invited, either at this point or ever, to accept this moralizing entirely at its own estimate. Jacques is laying claim here to the status of a satirist, a self-appointed cleanser of the social Augean stables; and his vision is of the kind which, though it is keen enough to penetrate to certain truths, is also limited by the element of self-satisfaction which has inspired it. We are told elsewhere of Jacques that he is one who sucks his melancholy "as a weasel sucks eggs"; and it is there, precisely, that his final limitation as a human being lies. For his function as critic, though it enables him to mirror truly certain aspects of human nature, is nonetheless self-appointed, self-regarding, and incomplete, even destructive of true order. It is significant that Orlando, when the occasion arises, shows clearly that he has little use for him or for the kind of vision which he represents. When Jacques is moved to criticize Rosalind's name adversely for no more solid reason than his own unsupported prejudice, Orlando's retort is quite simple and conclusive: "There was no thought of pleasing you when she was christened" (III. ii); and when Jacques invites Orlando to join him in his favorite pastime of "railing against our mistress the world, and all our misery," the reply amounts again to a reaffirmation of perspective, an exposure of the limitations of all "philosophy" of this kind: "I will chide no breather in the world but myself, against whom I know most faults" (III. ii).

It is, accordingly, Jacques' limitation, as critic and as human being, to fail to understand the necessary truth which this observation contains. True criticism and true moralizing can only rest on the foundation of an adequate self-knowledge, which will tend in turn to make the criticism and the moralizing themselves less absolute and less self-satisfied. The "observer" who claims the privilege of passing superior comments upon the life around him without accepting the responsibility of sharing it finally rules himself by his own attitudes out of court. The spirit of "philosophic" melancholy as represented in Jacques has, indeed, its moments of insight, its partial truths, to offer to the rounded and balanced vision of life at which this comedy aims; but it is *partial*, no more than a single ingredient, and by no means the most important one at that, in a more ample and positive complete effect. It is for this reason that Jacques, after having become, as we have seen, for a brief moment the spokesman of the conclusion, leaves the harmonious and "social" order whose formation he has just confirmed to contemplate in isolation the repentance of the "converted" Frederick:

> To him will I: out of these convertites
> There is much matter to be heard and learn'd. (V. iv)

"Much matter," in other words, to be "sucked out," after the fashion of the weasel with the egg. As ever, Jacques' motive is, in the last analysis, "observation," the gratifying of a self-regarding curiosity based on a kind of personal impotence, an inability to participate fully and naturally in the processes of life; and, since his attitude is one which implies throughout an incapacity for genuine *giving*, for the positive acceptance of an order, at once natural and distinctively human, beyond the isolated self—the acceptance by which, in love or otherwise, the self is at last justified—he remains a mere marginal presence in the process by which that order is finally, within the scope of the distinctive comic vision, consummated.

TWELFTH NIGHT

Shakespeare's comedy of *Twelfth Night* seems to have been written for presentation, possibly in 1602, to a polite audience on the occasion of the religious festivity which the title recalls and which coincides with the end of the Christmas celebrations. If this is so, a good deal of light is thrown upon the different elements which combine to make up one of the most varied and subtly unified of Shakespeare's comedies. *Twelfth Night* adds to many of the qualities of a masque, an aristocratic entertainment, those of a kind of children's merrymaking, an occasion for dressing up in order to mock the absurdities committed in all seriousness by their elders. Very roughly speaking, for the comedy is even less adapted than most to this kind of dissection, one could say that the element of masque prevails in the "poetic," romantic part of the action, and that the sentiments and situations developed in this are given a comic reflection in the prose underplot which at each turn accompanies and is interwoven with it. The result is a construction notably different in kind from that of *As You Like It,* and one perhaps even more satisfying, more closely knit and diversely subtle in its interplay of contrasted levels of meaning.

The "serious" part of *Twelfth Night* deals principally with conceptions of romantic love derived from the literary taste, aristocratic and sophisticated, of the day. Shakespeare, as usual, transforms his material in the process of developing it, makes it the vehicle for purposes which are unmistakably his own. The play's concern with love is represented, on this level and as the action opens, by Duke Orsino and Olivia. Orsino's famous first speech—

> If music be the food of love, play on;
> Give me *excess* of it— (I. i)

together with what follows in the brief opening scene, reveals his attitude in love as a blend of sentiment and artifice, true dedication and elaborate self-centeredness; it is at once an eloquent statement and, by implication, a criticism of the play's courtly romantic theme. Orsino is a fine creature, a superior being who is capable, and knows himself to be capable, of responding to the most exquisite and valuable human emotions. We shall not fail, here or later, to respond to the real beauty of the poetry in which these emotions are expressed; but this does not mean that the speaker of it is beyond criticism, or that his attitudes do not require, like those of lesser beings, to be taken out of themselves, extended beyond the sphere of self-contemplation in which they can easily lose themselves. The "spirit of love" which dominates Orsino's heart and mind is, in other words, both a true passion and a subtle form of emotional indulgence; apprehended by him as "quick and fresh," possessed of a capacity that "receiveth as the sea" and transforms all that it touches into imaginative wealth, it is at the same time an "appetite" that craves its own "excess," that tends inevitably, as it approaches the satisfaction it so intensely craves, to "sicken" and "die": so that everything which it receives falls, by an appropriate law of compensation,

> into *abatement* and *low price*
> Even in a minute. (I. i)

There is clearly a contrast here with the true love which, in the familiar terms of Shakespearean comedy, essentially enriches and adds to the content and value of life. In this strangely contradictory emotion, in which Orsino's "desires," as he confesses, pursue him "like *fell* and *cruel* hounds," he seeks in the last analysis a concession to sentiment, a "surfeit" of feeling which expresses itself most clearly in his longing for "sweet beds of flowers" and in the surrender to love thoughts which "lie *rich* when canopied with bowers" (I. i).[21] In the implications of this "richness," half rare value and half cloying surfeit, lies the key to an understanding of Orsino's state as the comedy opens.

Something of the same kind can be said, in a rather different way, of Olivia, the unresponsive object of this devotion. She, too, in Valentine's account of her, combines true sorrow for her dead brother with a dwelling upon what have come to be for her, paradoxically, the elaborate sweets of melancholy:

> like a *cloistress* she will *veiled* walk,
> And water once a day her chamber round
> With eye-offending brine: all this to season
> A brother's dead love, which she would *keep fresh*
> And *lasting*, in her sad remembrance. (I. i)

Once again, as in the case of Orsino, we shall not be tempted to simplify this situation to produce a one-sided reading of the play's intention. Olivia, as we shall see her in the course of the action, is—like Orsino—a creature of rare worth and strong humanity of sentiments; she shows herself perfectly capable of living up to her position as mistress of a great house, and there is nothing in itself unworthy about the persistence of her genuine grief for the brother she has lost. There is, however, in terms of the comic intention, another side to the story. To live thus, for reasons however laudable in themselves, in the past, to keep the memory of death alive in what is finally a self-absorbed and self-regarding dedication to grief, is to sin against life, to close the doors willfully upon its necessary renovation. Orsino, like other comic characters we have had occasion to meet, is, in a relevant if not exclusive sense, in love with love, Olivia enamored essentially of her own sorrow. Precisely because their potential human value, as revealed in the intense poetic quality of their sentiments, is so great, so exceeding the common measure, they will have to learn to go in each case beyond these initial attitudes, to accept the experience which life offers them on terms finally not of their own making. Throughout this opening, Shakespeare is engaged in the characteristic task of giving courtly and romantic feeling—and, with it, the genuine and natural human emotions which it threatens to carry to exclusive excess—its due, at the same time as he is limiting it, indicating the degree of selfishness which accompanies its expression and which will have to be transformed, in the course of the action, by exposure to more normal and ultimately positive forms of living. These too will be expressed within the conventional limits which the comic form imposes.

The primary instrument of this transformation is, of course, Viola, whose readiness to rely upon her own resources—like that shown by Rosalind in a similar situation in *As You Like It*—contrasts from the first with the attitudes that prevail at Orsino's court. This is made clear as soon as she appears, immediately after we have seen Orsino and been told of Olivia's grief, as a shipwrecked fugitive on the Illyrian coast. Her first thought for her brother is an expression of positive hope: "Perchance he is not drown'd": a hope founded upon the Captain's report of his last glimpse of him as one "most *provident* in peril," whom he saw

> bind himself,
> *Courage* and *hope* both teaching him the practice
> To a *strong* mast that *lived* upon the sea; (I. ii)

a hope which rests finally upon the quality which she detects in the Captain himself and to which she can respond because it answers to her own essentially realistic and positive intuition:

> There is a fair behaviour in thee, Captain;
> And though that *nature with a beauteous wall*
> *Doth oft close in pollution,* yet of thee
> I will believe thou hast a mind that suits
> With this thy fair and outward character. (I. ii)

It is because she is aware of the existence of "pollution" as a possibility shadowing life that Viola can become the mouthpiece for life's positive affirmation. These same qualities accompany her as Orsino's messenger to Olivia. Her attitude to the romantic terms of the message with which she has been charged is characteristically detached. "I took great pains to study it, and 'tis poetical" (I. v), and indeed Olivia herself is prepared to believe that Orsino's declarations are "feigned." When, in the course of the same scene, Olivia asks her how she would behave if she were to find herself in the position of an unrequited lover, Viola's reply is an affirmation, blunt and pointed for all the indirectness which her situation imposes, of the real compulsions of passionate devotion. Unlike the romantic sentiment which luxuriates in its own frustrations, true love cannot accept rejection:

> If I did love you in my master's flame,
> With such a suffering, *such a deadly life,*
> In your denial I would find no sense;
> I would not understand it. (I. v)

Romantic love is here being subjected to criticism on what are, in effect, its own terms. The implication is that passion such as Orsino's, in so far as it is self-centered and self-consuming, is finally unreal, fails to project itself in the forms which itself assumes to be appropriate. If Viola, speaking as "Cesario," were to feel for Olivia as her master declares himself to feel, she would

> Hollo your name to the reverberate hills,
> And make the babbling gossip of the air
> Cry out Olivia. O you should not rest
> Between the elements of air and earth,
> But you should pity me. (I. v)

The presence, at this point and elsewhere, of obvious elements of poetic convention in Viola's statements of love's sincerity should not obscure the relevance of this passage to the play's main theme, which is the exploration, even within and through convention, of real life. Viola has already expressed to Olivia, in terms familiar to us from the sonnets, her conviction that the very nature of love implies the responsibility of *giving,* in the absence of which its creative possibilities languish, turn in upon themselves to wither and die:

> Lady, you are the *cruellest* she alive,
> If you will lead these graces to the grave
> And leave the world no copy; (I. v)[22]

she now further suggests, by implication at least, that Orsino's real, though unconfessed, tendency to accept the situation in which he finds himself, extracting from the contemplation of Olivia's rejection of himself a refinement of melancholy, is a sign of the unreality of his passion. It is a large part of her function in the play to act as the instrument by which this unreality is broken down and love restored to its true possibilities through a positive and life-giving contact with things as they are.

The same function emerges, perhaps even more clearly, in the course of the scene (II. iv) in which Orsino presses Viola to carry his message yet again to the irresponsive object of his desire. To his declaration, still essentially complacent, of a love "more *noble* than the world," based upon an attraction of "soul" which he likes to think should be irresistible, she opposes a sense of the limitations which real life, the very fact that another person, with feelings and desires of her own, is involved, may impose upon this kind of passion; she asks him quite simply: "But if she cannot love you, sir?" Orsino, most typically, cannot conceive that this is even a possibility. "I cannot be so answered," he replies, precisely because his thought is fixed upon himself, in contemplation of his own situation; and when Viola, drawing now upon sentiments which she is not in a position to express openly, indicates a possible parallel with the sufferings of "some lady, as perhaps there is," whose passion for him may be as great and as hopeless as that from which he believes himself—perhaps even a little in excess of the facts—to suffer, his reply is a refusal to believe that anyone but himself—and, in particular, any mere *woman*—can harbor so intense, so absolute a dedication. "There is," he says,

> no woman's sides
> Can bide the beating of so strong a passion
> As love doth give my heart.

For Orsino, in his essential complacency, it is obvious that "women lack retention," the capacity, upon which he so prides himself and to which Olivia's disdain allows him to give such deliciously elaborate expression, to persevere in feeling. The love of these lesser creatures is of a kind essentially different from his own superior sentiments. It may, in the conventional terms of his own poetry, "be called *appetite*,"

> No motion of the liver, but the palate,
> That suffer *surfeit, cloyment, and revolt;*

whereas his own feeling is, as he concludes with at least a touch of implied self-congratulation,

> all as *hungry* as the sea,
> And can digest as much. (II. iv)

The recourse to images of hunger and surfeit, rooted as they are in poetic convention, is nonetheless deeply significant. It is of the essence of the play's attitude to its "romantic" theme that Orsino's own love is, in part at least, an "appetite," cloying in its initial conception and deliberately mannered in its expression, an imposition of sophisticated and artificial attitudes upon genuine human emotion. Its final perversity is reflected in the fact that it insists in coveting the wrong object and will accordingly need to be rededicated before the action can be rounded off in the grouping of appropriately united couples with which the play concludes.

This transformation is brought about through the familiar comic device of an assumed disguise which involves a young woman in the temporary concealment of her sex and after exposure to the various misunderstandings to which this leads. The complications, artificial as they may appear, are an essential part of the play's complete development. Viola, as she receives the ring which conveys the awakening of Olivia to her infatuation for "Cesario,"[23] finds herself caught up in the unforeseen consequences of her own devices; as she says, in language which conveys a meaning beyond mere convention and romantic fancy:

> Disguise, I see thou art a *wickedness,*
> Wherein *the pregnant enemy* does much.
> How easy is it for the *proper-false*
> In women's *waxen hearts* to set their forms!
> Alas, our *frailty* is the cause, not we!
> For such as we are made of, such we be. (II. ii)

Something of the complexity of real life is here reflected, in and beneath the forms of convention. "Disguise" is a reflection of Shakespeare's lifelong preoccupation with "seeming," with the falsity beneath which men and women seek to hide, from others and perhaps most intimately of all from themselves, the intricacies of their own natures. In tragic terms this could amount to a "wickedness," a reflection of ultimate falsity, and the fact that Viola can use this very word here is an indication that the tragic emotion is not entirely absent; but it is the end of comedy, as this play conceives it, to trace out these and similar complexities, beyond all possible human intention, to the ends of life, so that there is meaning, a significant acceptance of the way in which these ends impose themselves, in Viola's final, half-humorous renunciation of her own capacity to mold the course of events to her immediate purpose:

> O time! thou must untangle this, not I;
> It is too hard a knot for me to untie! (II. ii)

It is, perhaps, the human determination to bend life, prematurely and unilaterally, to its own partial ends that produces tragedy, and the wiser readiness to wait for the unfolding of the natural pattern after its own fashion that allows the comic resolution of harmonies to grow to its completion in the fullness of time.

Viola, however, though she shows herself wise enough to admit that neither she nor any other human being can, in the long run, control the course of life, shows a very considerable capacity for understanding the nature of its operations; and that too is a part of the comic vision as this play conceives it. She can, as a sign of this realization, take up and give full value, a genuine human meaning, to Orsino's more self-centered and circumscribed melancholy. When, in urging upon her the necessity of love, he affirms, with the characteristic dying cadence of his romantic musings, that

> women are as roses, whose fair flower
> Being once display'd, *doth fall that very hour,*

she can take up the truth contained in his observation, less in the spirit of self-immersed gloom in which it is uttered than as the reflection of a universal flaw felt to exist at the heart of life:

> And so they are: alas, that they are so;
> To die, even when they to perfection grow! (II. iv)

Immediately afterward, she goes on to set this same melancholy in relation to her own situation by referring, since the nature of her disguise makes it impossible for her to speak directly of her own state, to the "history" of her supposed sister:

> She never told her love,
> But let *concealment,* like a worm i' the bud,
> *Feed* on her damask cheek: she *pined* in thought;
> And with *a green and yellow melancholy*
> She sat like patience on a monument
> Smiling at grief. (II. iv)

This, though it may appear at first sight to be a mere echo of Orsino's mood, is in effect different. Viola is lamenting the unnatural and apparently insoluble plight in which she finds herself, not giving it poetic decoration or luxuriating in the "dark" thoughts which it inspires in her. Though she speaks, as always, within the limits of her appropriate poetic convention, she also speaks to ends that are distinctively her own. It is the necessity for "concealment" that leads in her case to a melancholy conceived of as "green and yellow," out of season and inevitably self-consuming in its effect upon the sufferer; and the way out of this unhappy state will lie, not in the romantic lover's surrender to delicious sadness, but in the advancing of love beyond this introverted stage in relation to the rest of life.

The impact of reality, indeed, makes itself felt from the moment in which Olivia is driven, in her own despite, to make open declaration of her love for "Cesario." In this way life affirms itself, in the characteristic fashion of Shakespearean comedy, by breaking through the barriers which artifice and pretense have been engaged in setting up against it; and, as it does so, Olivia recognizes the implications of her surrender in a speech which is itself full of disturbing and, at first sight, unexpected echoes:

> I did send,
> After *the last enchantment* you did here,
> A ring in chase of you: so did I *abuse*
> *Myself*, my servant, and, I fear me, you:
> Under your hard construction must I sit,
> To *force* that on you, in *a shameful cunning*,
> Which you know none of yours: what might you think?
> Have you not set mine honour at the stake
> And baited it with all *the unmuzzled thoughts*
> That *tyrannous heart* can think? To one of your receiving
> Enough is shown: a cypress, not a bosom,
> Hides my heart. (III. i)

To respond adequately to this confession is to sense, beneath the conventional forms, a soul caught in the contradictions which its own appetites, developed in a situation of long and perverse self-concealment, have imposed; those references to self-abuse, those "unmuzzled" notions of a "tyrannous" desire, can only be exorcised by being brought out into the open, related in a natural way to the daylight realities of life. Meanwhile, and until this can take place, the ambivalences of desire are expressed, after the fashion of this play, in which disguise habitually answers to the unavowed complexity of human impulses and appearances, through a typical interplay of double situations. Olivia, in a first tentative groping toward self-clarification, asks "Cesario": "I prithee, tell me what thou thinkst of me?" and the exchange is continued in these terms:

> –That you do think *you are not what you are.*
> –If I think so, I think the same of you.
> –Then think you right: I am not what I am.
> –I would you were as I would have you be!
> –Would it be better, madam, than I am?
> I wish it might, *for now I am your fool.* (III. i)

The results of a situation compounded of misunderstandings and concealment, implying a refusal on the part of so many of those most directly concerned to recognize the claims of life for what they are, become apparent when the supposed "Cesario," herself caught, though in this case through no fault of her own, in the consequences of her own disguise, is driven by the declaration of Olivia's passion for her to renounce the impossible mission with which she has been entrusted by Orsino:

> never more
> Will I my master's tears to you deplore. (III. i)

Not till the end of the play, when the time comes for the shedding of disguises and for the assumption by each character of the part which properly corresponds to him or herself in the whole, will the imperious and life-conferring compulsions of love find their appropriate consummation in a comic reflection of real, as distinct from artificial, humanity.

The way out of this complex of misunderstandings lies through the revelation that Viola's twin brother, Sebastian, has survived the perils of shipwreck to which he was exposed at the beginning of the play. Once more the new situation is introduced through an appropriate inversion of common reality. Sebastian, meeting Olivia, who believes him to be "Cesario" and consequently the object of her own newly awakened devotion, appears to himself to be living in a world of fantasy in which the laws which govern daily reality are strangely suspended: "Or I am *mad*, or else this is a dream." So might Antipholus of Syracuse have spoken in Shakespeare's early exercise in comic form;[24] but here, since the content of the "dream" answers to his true and natural desires, he declares himself disposed to allow it to continue: "If it be thus to dream, still let me sleep" (IV. i). The "dream" that thus answers to the intimate compulsion of real life tends, in terms of Shakespearean comedy, to merge into the reality of daylight. When we next meet Sebastian, he has received the gift of the "pearl" which confirms Olivia's dedication to him of herself and is able to distinguish the genuine and life-giving magic of his new bewitchment from the aberrations of mere lunacy:

> though 'tis *wonder* that enwraps me thus,
> *Yet 'tis not madness.* (IV. iii)

This answers to the general trend of the comic conception, which is consistent in moving away from "madness" and the various forms of self-deception, with which the earlier part of the action has been so closely concerned, in the direction of sanity and normal fulfillment.

To look upon life with "wonder," a proper sense of reverence, is to be, in Shakespearean comic terms, the opposite of mad. Olivia herself is at last brought out of her self-imposed isolation, as she in turn begs Sebastian to confer upon her "the *full assurance* of your *faith*" to the end that

> *my most jealous and too doubtful soul*
> May live at *peace*. (IV. iii)

She has come by the end of the play to understand that she is a creature whose destiny lies in marriage, that real peace will lie for her not in surrender to the self-deceiving mirror she has set up before herself under the pretext of dedication to the dead, but in the full acceptance of life as offered in the present; as Sebastian has just said at the opening of the scene, opposing the firm grasp of reality which he shares with his sister to so much indulgence of cloistered feeling: "This is the air: that is the glorious sun" (IV. iii). Things, to put the matter in its simplest terms, are first and foremost what they are; and in a joyful acceptance of their present reality, positive, freely given, and "glorious," triumphant over the shades of night and over all forms of self-imposed delusion, lies the key to true living.

By the time the action has been brought to a close the ends conceived in this way have been triumphantly achieved. Neither the initial devotion of Orsino nor Olivia's reiterated sorrow emerges at their original self-estimate. When, in the final scene (V. i), Orsino marries, not Olivia, but the Viola who has conquered his true affection with her combination of self-reliance and feminine grace; when Olivia has awakened from the dream constituted by her dedication to a sterile melancholy; when, through these developments, the clear "air" and the "glorious sun" of life have asserted themselves to ends of harmony and fulfillment, the true purpose of the make-believe with which the play seems, on this level, to have been so long concerned is at last apparent. The romantic visions of devotion which originally inspired these courtly sentimentalists contain within themselves positive elements, emotions natural and necessary to a full and truly civilized life. They are visions, however, which now call in a new spirit for more adequate objects of dedication, and these have been provided in the course of the action. Both Orsino and Olivia have learned that the compulsive force of the passions to which they have been respectively dedicated is such as to draw them finally beyond themselves, demanding from each the acceptance of a fuller, a more natural and spontaneous way of living.

The "lessons" which emerge in this way from the main action of *Twelfth Night* are reinforced and diversified by an underplot which gives a new and profoundly Shakespearean content to the comedy of character which Ben Jonson had only recently exhibited in his play *Every Man in his Humour.*[25] Jonson's comedy of "humours" is, in its essence, an attempt at psychological realism: based upon principles which purported to be "scientific" (within the limitations of the age), it replaced poetry by prose, fancy by the realistic delineation of personality. Shakespeare, in so far as he chose to make use of this conception of comedy, modified this "realistic" bias in the direction of the very different imaginative ends he had in view. Though the comedy of his underplot carries social implications which make their presence felt from time to time, these implications are generally subsidiary to the unifying, harmonizing purpose which dominates the play as a whole. *Twelfth Night* is more indivisible in its effect, less easily separable into elements significantly contrasted, than any preceding Shakespearean comedy; but within this imaginative unity, this uniquely pervasive "Illyrian" quality, the comic scenes in prose make their effect by asserting a firm reality, itself suitably transformed to correspond to the general mode, against the deliberately poetic elaboration which prevails in the more aristocratic, courtly sphere of the action. No more suitable foil, indeed, could be imagined to the conventionality, the poetic artifice, which Shakespeare was in this play at once concerned to use and, as he made use of it for ends essentially his own, to criticize.

The general aim of the prose scenes is, accordingly, to balance the elaboration which so largely prevails in the courtly action with a more direct reflection of real life, comically conceived. In Sir Toby Belch, Maria, and Sir Andrew Aguecheek, as they carry on their intrigues in the backstairs region of Olivia's mansion, we may discern, in distinctively social terms, a reflection of the underside of that aristocratic life which has found elsewhere in the play its more elegant expression. Like Falstaff, with whom he has occasional points of contact, Sir Toby is no paragon of virtue. The product of a decayed feudal order, he lives by his wits and is ready to exploit the pretensions of Sir Andrew for the sake of his "three thousand ducats a year": the means of life offer themselves as they come, and it does not behoove such as Sir Toby—or Falstaff—to be overdelicate in his acceptance of them. Neither he nor Maria, however, are, like their "betters," self-deceivers in the name of a supposed refinement; and it is here, above all, that the parallel with Falstaff, translated though it is into the very different terms of this play, holds good. In Sir Toby's presentation of him, Sir Andrew emerges as a caricature of his courtly superiors: as one who claims to play the "viol de gamboys," to speak three or four languages, and to possess, in Sir Toby's not disinterested estimate of his social virtues, "all the good gifts of nature," but who is also seen (by Maria, who is not easily deceived) to be a "fool" and "a great quarreller," saved from disaster only by his possession of "the gift of a coward to allay the gust he hath in quarrelling" (I. iii). For his intrigues and his basic cynicism, Sir Toby will be sufficiently punished when his misplaced ingenuity leads him to have his head broken for his rashness in crossing swords with Sebastian (V. i); but for the measure of genuine attachment to life which enables him to comment by implication upon his niece's self-centered and self-consuming melancholy—"What a plague means my niece to take the death of her brother thus? I'm sure care's an enemy to life" (I. iii)—he is rewarded at the last (if reward it be) by marriage to his kindred spirit in humor, Maria.

Over both these personages, indeed, and over the prose episodes of the play as a whole, the comic spirit projects a light of its own, as distinct from Jonson's more explicitly moralizing genius as can readily be imagined. It produces a compound of Illyrian fancy and truth to nature which refuses either to belittle or, alternatively, to inflate into false seriousness: the spirit which finds expression in Maria's retort to Sir Andrew—"thought is free" (I. iii)—and in the consistent repudiation of vain self-righteousness and officious self-approval in all their forms. These comic episodes represent—to put the matter in another way—the spirit of "Twelfth Night," the setting free of natural instincts normally under restraint: instincts which are often absurd in the way in which they manifest themselves, but which possess—at least when set against the aristocratic pretensions which prevail elsewhere—a genuine life of their own. When Malvolio utters his protest against "riot" in the name of the decorum and self-importance which he associates so complacently with his own person —"My masters, are you mad? or what are you? Have you no wit, manners, nor honesty, but to gabble like tinkers at this time of night? . . . Is there no respect of place, persons, nor time in you?" —Sir Toby can retort, "We did keep time, sir, in our catches," and go on to deliver the most powerful of his repudiations of pretentious and self-admiring virtue: "Dost thou think because thou art virtuous, there shall be no more cakes and ale?" (II. iii).

The protest against pretentiousness in all its forms is maintained indeed, through the underplot in a variety of ways. Olivia's supposed letter to Malvolio (II. iv) and the form of Sir Andrew's challenge to "Cesario" (III. iv) both carry satires of courtly conventions, of love and "honour" respectively; and both, moreover, in so far as they involve personages from the "serious" action, bringing them out of their usual sphere and exposing them to situations which reveal them in a certain absurdity, tend to join the play's two levels in a revealing unity. No one in the action is finally altogether exempt from the operations of this kind of comic inversion. Even Viola, who has chosen—albeit for excellent motives—to practice a kind of deception, is entrapped for a moment in the unforeseen consequences of her own assumption of disguise when she reacts in natural fear to the challenge which Sir Toby has prepared for Aguecheek; although, of course, her own attitude to the business of the duel is, most typically, one of engaging common sense and candor: "I am one that had rather go with sir priest than sir knight. I care not who knows so much of my mettle" (III. iv). The rich and varied fusion of realism and convention in a series of comic effects which answers perfectly to the prevailing Illyrian mood is perhaps the play's supreme achievement.

The central figure of the underplot, however, upon whose person the various intrigues finally turn, is of course Malvolio. As Olivia's steward he represents her dignity, which he associates ridiculously with his obsessive sense of his own, and bears her messages to those who live in her domain; in so doing, he brings together the two worlds of aristocratic sophistication and realistic "humour" which, by their continual interplay, make the theme of the comedy. Malvolio is admirably chosen to play this part. The comedy which surrounds his person turns upon the familiar Shakespearean contrast between reality and self-estimation; the contrast which also, under other forms, dominates the presentation of his mistress and Orsino. Whereas they deceive themselves as to the real nature of their emotions, and choose to live in a world of their own imagining, Malvolio, not less self-consciously attached to "virtue" and to his own conception of his dignity, is caught by Maria "practising behaviour to his own shadow" (II. v) and imagining, in the same scene, his own advancement and the putting in his place of Sir Toby. "You are idle shallow things," he says in his infatuation to those who are engineering his downfall, "I am not of your element" (III. iv). The self-love which leads him to respond to the challenge which his enemies place before him in the form of an illusory prospect of exaltation—"some are born great, some achieve greatness, and some have greatness thrust upon 'em" (II. v)—is not devoid on occasion of a certain crazed dignity; but it leads him at the last to a series of misfortunes from which he is never truly delivered.

In this last respect, Malvolio is unique in the play. The presence of a disturbing quality beneath the obvious comedy of his presentation is most apparent when he finds himself, through the devices of Maria and those who accompany her, imprisoned in darkness and visited by Feste the clown in his disguise as Sir Topas (IV. ii). The essence of the comic effect at this point lies in the fact that Malvolio, though impenetrably deceived as to his own nature, clings to solid and tangible reality against the illusions to which he is so mercilessly subjected. When Feste transforms the "prison" verbally into an abode of nobility and light—"it hath bay windows *transparent* as barricadoes, and the clearstories towards the south—north are as *lustruous as ebony*" (IV. ii)—he insists that the place of his confinement is, as in reality it is, "dark as hell"; and if the comedy strikes us, at this point, as unusually sardonic in its implications, this is related to Feste's stressing of the fact that the "darkness" in which he finds himself thus enveloped has a moral significance for the victim's own nature. "I say there is no darkness but ignorance" is Feste's retort to Malvolio's insistence that he is in truth plunged into a real physical obscurity; and the point of the comment is that this darkness is a reflection of the lack of proper self-understanding which has led Malvolio to live in accordance with a fictitious conception of his own dignity not altogether unlike that shown by his "betters," but from which, in contrast to them, he shows to the last no sign of awakening:

> I say, this house is as dark as ignorance, though ignorance were dark as hell; and I say, there was never man thus abused. I am no more mad than you are. (IV. ii)

In so far as it is a matter of distinguishing truly between external realities, Malvolio's protest corresponds to an undeniable truth. The comedy of his situation—if comedy we can call it—turns upon the fact that, lucid as he is in his attitude to his physical surroundings, he is yet—like many of those who surround him, but to a far less curable degree—the prisoner of his own self-estimate.

There is, accordingly, in Malvolio's vicissitudes a note which transcends the obvious comedy of his situation and which ends by affecting with a certain uneasiness the celebration by the humorists of their triumph over him. At the end of the play Malvolio alone fails to join the final procession of characters awakened, each on his or her appropriate level, to the claims of reality. His last protest to Olivia contains a note of accusation which seems to evade the comic spirit, or at least to live unquietly in relation to it:

> Why have you suffer'd me to be imprisoned,
> Kept in a dark house, visited by the priest,
> And made the most notorious geck and gull
> That e'er invention play'd on. *Tell me why.* (V. i)

The answer is, of course, that he has made his own prison, that the darkness to which he has been confined reflects his own attitude to life; but the insistence with which the question is posed and Malvolio's invincible inability to see the answer stand out with an odd effect of incongruity from the general orientation of the final scene. His last letter of protest to his mistress is couched in terms of a certain dignity, and Orsino himself is ready to concede that "This savours not much of distraction": as neither, indeed, did his previous comment, addressed to "Sir Topas" in the hour of darkness, concerning "the opinion of Pythagoras" upon the soul's immortality: "I think nobly of the soul, and in no way approve his opinion" (IV. ii). It is Malvolio's defect to be inextricably rooted in a fixed idea of things, in which he himself occupies the center, as he shows at the last when he responds to Orsino's efforts "to entreat him to a peace" in the interests of the general harmony that has just been established with the bitter and uncomprehending cry: "I'll be revenged on the whole pack of you" (V. i). This defect makes him a legitimate object for the comic derision which so abundantly overtakes him in the course of the play, and for which we need not pity him; but, for all the absurdity of his yellow stockings and cross-garters, in spite of the obvious parody of a vain self-righteousness held to be "Puritan"—though we should note in passing that Maria expressly denies (II. iii) that he is any such thing—Malvolio's demand for a satisfaction that his need for self-justification craves, but which he cannot in the very nature of things hope to obtain, places him in a certain sense outside the play's comic spirit, relates him finally to other and perhaps more disturbing orders of reality.

By this time, we have reached the end of the play in one of those scenes of reconciliation and married fulfillment toward which Shakespearean comedy so insistently tends. Sebastian has been united to Olivia, who has been thereby restored from her melancholy self-contemplation to the claims of real life. Antonio, the sea captain, has affirmed his place in the world of Illyrian fantasy in the name of true friendship and honest constancy, values for which he has already declared himself ready to risk his life in a hostile environment for the sake of Sebastian:

> my desire,
> More sharp than filed steel, did spur me forth . . .
> . . . my willing love,
> The rather by these arguments of fear,
> Set forth in your pursuit; (III. iii)

generous sentiments nobly confirmed in action, which now find their appropriate setting in a world where acceptance and mutual forgiveness prevail. Having been involved, with danger of his life, in the "Cesario"-Viola-Sebastian confusion, Antonio emerges at the last into the light of day, to the dawning of which his loyalty and steadfast faith have contributed. Only the remnants of Orsino's jealous resentment at Olivia's marriage to another than himself now remains to shadow, though only for a moment and in passing, the final resolution. In a first and typically impulsive reaction to the frustration of his long-cherished designs, he seeks satisfaction in the thought of revenge:

> my thoughts are *ripe in mischief;*
> I'll *sacrifice the lamb that I do love,*
> To *spite* a raven's heart within a dove. (V. i)

To this "savage" jealousy, which prompts Orsino, even at this late stage, to contemplate the killing of the object of his love in a last appropriate gesture of self-torture, Viola replies by the offer of her readiness to give her own life:

> I, *most jocund, apt, and willingly,*
> To do you rest, a thousand times would die,

even as she declares the true object of her love:

–Where goes Cesario?
– After him I love
More than I love these eyes, *more than my life,*
More, by all mores, than e'er I shall love wife.
If I do feign, you witnesses above,
Punish my life for tainting of my love. (V. i)

"More than I love these eyes, more than my life": here we have, concentrated into a few intensely spoken words, the real turning point of the whole episode. Love has at last been declared in its full truth and boundless generosity; and now the priest's revelation of Olivia's marriage to Sebastian begins to shift the clouds, whilst the return of a suitably chastened Sir Toby, with his head broken for his past presumption, finally reveals the truth in a suitably comic manner. Sebastian, restored to the sister whom he feared that "the blind waves" had devoured, finds that the action of the waves has been less "blind" than he had thought, and goes on to ask questions which are, in terms of the Shakespearean comic vision, a prelude to reconciliation—"What countryman? what name? what parentage"[26]—and is greeted as a "spirit" restored:

A spirit I am indeed;
But am in that dimension grossly clad
Which from the womb I did participate. (V. i)

As a "spirit" of this kind, immortal but compact with life and corporal "dimension," he greets "drowned Viola" as his restored sister. In the light of this revelation, Olivia recognizes her "mistake" and accepts Sebastian for himself; whilst, last of all, Orsino responds to the declaration of Viola's faith, waking from his own fantasies to take her for his bride:

When that is known, and *golden time* convents,
A solemn combination shall be made
Of our dear souls.[27]

The world of child-like fantasy and theatrical illusion which belongs to the spirit of this play merges here, with a delicate and ethereal intensity, into something deeper, more profound in its human reverberations, than itself. There can be few points in Shakespeare's earlier writing at which we can feel ourselves so close to the world of symbolic transformations which will prevail, at the end of his career, in *The Winter's Tale* and *The Tempest.*

From this final restoration of harmony Malvolio, as we have already seen, is excluded. It only remains to say that Feste, too, stands —as he has stood throughout the play—rather outside the prevailing mood. The spirit of his own distinctive comedy, which is on occasions by no means devoid of malice, responds to constantly shifting attitudes, moods more complex and varied in their implication than may at first appear. These are related at each turn to the state of the developing action. His first song (II. iii) affirms love as natural and real. "Every wise man's son" knows that "Journeys end in lover's meeting," and this may perhaps imply a criticism of the love which feeds upon itself in self-contemplation; but, equally, the background of all human sentiment is impermanence, so that "In delay there lies no plenty" and "Youth's a stuff will not endure." In a spirit not finally dissimilar he has already made his appropriate comment on Olivia's dedication to grief when, after asking her the reasons for her mourning, he induces her to declare her belief that her brother is in "heaven" and concludes: "The more fool, madam, to mourn for your brother's soul being in heaven" (I. v). Feste's moods are, indeed, as varied as the constantly shifting emotional texture of this most finely woven of plays. He can respond to Orsino's melancholy—"Come away, come away, death" (II. iv)—as readily as to any other emotion which is at once true, humanly valid, and open to criticism for the excess or self-centeredness with which it is sometimes pursued; equally, he can apply himself to burlesquing the pretensions of Malvolio. An element of mastery, indeed, of drawing the sources of his life from outside the main action of the play, is an essential feature of this Fool. In his position as a licensed jester, Feste is able to move freely among his superiors, and shows himself no respecter of persons when he replies to Orsino's query, "how dost thou, my good fellow?" with the sharp and detached realism of his reply: "the better for my foes and the worse for my friends" (V. i). In this way he answers, perhaps even better than most, to the constant tendency of Shakespearean comedy to qualify its own imaginative harmonies with a profound sense of the element of relativity, of a final uniqueness and autonomy, which underlies all human experience. When the time comes for him to utter the song which rounds off the play, he conveys a mood enigmatically compounded of realism and fancy, truth and illusion, which is perhaps the last and deepest impression we retain from Illyria. The song passes from a wistful evocation of the innocence of childhood—"When that I was and a little tiny boy"—to wry and disillusioned comment upon mature reality:

> But when I came to man's estate . . .
> . . . 'Gainst thieves and knaves men shut their gate, (V. i)

and goes on to envelop the whole in the pervasive and intangible melancholy of the refrain: "For the rain it raineth every day." For Illyria, too, in spite of all the beauty of imaginative fancy which has gone to its poetic creation, is a dream; and it is of the essence of Shakespeare's mature comedy—and in this, as in other respects, *Twelfth Night* will remain unsurpassed till *The Winter's Tale* and *The Tempest*—to touch the poignant, and to extract from its sense of the passing and the insubstantial some of the deepest and most individual of his dramatic effects.

PART II

IX

The Problem Plays

The period that followed immediately on the completion of the English historical trilogy consisting of the two parts of *Henry IV* and *Henry V*[1] is one of peculiar importance for an understanding of the development of Shakespeare's art. His dramatic production at this time is marked by an intensifying of the tragic feeling already discernible in parts of *Henry V* and of the plays that preceded it. This tragic feeling, however, did not immediately attain clear, direct expression. The plays that followed *Henry V* are, on the contrary, remarkably obscure in intention and sometimes even in expression: so much so that Shakespeare criticism has generally agreed to give them the significant name of "problem" plays. Comedies, in the formal sense, but conceived in a spirit almost entirely opposed to that of Shakespeare's earlier comedies and indeed of comedy in general; tragedies in which the heroes are actuated by no clear motives, but rather grope in a kind of spiritual darkness, seeking to clarify their own impulses—such are the typical productions, at once intensely interesting and deeply disquieting, of this moment in the dramatist's development. Though not the period in which he produced his greatest masterpieces, almost all the themes of the great tragedies made their first appearance in the obscure and difficult plays of these years.

From the point of view of Shakespeare's developing dramatic art, these plays show a notable concentration on two related problems—the consistent presentation of character and the projection into a coherent dramatic pattern of complex states of experience. The two problems are naturally related, and advance in dealing with the one is therefore accompanied by growing success in mastering the other. As we read the problem plays in the order they were presumably written in we shall see how the issues with which they deal are first sorted out, divided into clear-cut conflicts capable of dramatic representation, and then, by a further refinement, revealed as conflicting aspects within a single mind. In *Troilus and Cressida*, the prevailing impression is one of a separation into two opposed and mutually exclusive camps, each corresponding to one isolated reading of experience; the tragedy of the central pair of lovers lies in the incapacity of their pale emotion to bridge this gap, and such unity as the play achieves is obtained less through dramatic means than through the interplay of related images in a common poetic mood. In *Hamlet*, on the other hand, the spiritual conflict, though still imperfectly defined, radiates from a complex central character, who simultaneously interprets the world around him and, in interpreting it, reveals the extent of his own infirmity; the hero is not perfectly fitted to his dramatic setting, but his awareness of the discrepancy constitutes the root of a genuine personal tragedy. In *Measure for Measure*, finally, contradictions related to those of the previous plays are set against an objective conception of law to see whether, or to what extent, they can be resolved by accepting it; and though the final result is rather a deepening of self-knowledge in the protagonists than the achievement of spiritual coherence, the dramatic presentation of conflicting values is, at its culminating moments, clearer than ever before. All these plays are concerned, each after its fashion, with the effort to arrive at some kind of personal order in a world dominated by contradiction and obscurity. Though none of them can be said to attain more than a very partial measure of it, each represents in its own way an important step in Shakespeare's advance toward maturity of vision and in the mastery of his dramatic craft.

TROILUS AND CRESSIDA

The close relationship between the values of love and war—one of the most marked features of *Troilus and Cressida*—corresponds to a conception of dramatic unity which, although its antecedents can be traced respectively to the sonnets and the historical plays, was, at the time of writing, new in his work. The novelty consists in uniting, in a manner mutually illuminating, a personal theme and its public, "social" extension. Instead of a political conflict objectively observed and commented on by a character (such as Falstaff) who stands, in a sense, outside it, we are presented with a personal issue—the story of two lovers of opposed parties—set in the context of the Trojan War. The situation of the lovers is variously connected with the cleavage between the warring parties to which they respectively belong; and the connection thus dramatically established is further strengthened by the pervasive presence of imagery that suggests disruptive tendencies barely contained within a common way of feeling. The result, in terms of poetic drama, is less a finished and coherent creation than a statement of emotional ambiguity, the reflection of an experience deprived of order and seeking clarification through its own expression.

This ambiguity, in so far as it affects the personal action, is connected with themes that found expression, perhaps in some cases almost simultaneously, in the sonnets.[2] Taking as his point of departure the conventional subject of so many Renaissance sonneteers—the union with his mistress desired by the poet—many of Shakespeare's most individual sonnets convert this theme, which is applied to a variety of human relationships, into an apprehension of the parallel fulfillment and destruction of human values by time. Time, which brings passion to its consummation, implies equally its decline; for the union of love, the very desire for which is inconceivable apart from its temporal setting, demands as a necessary condition an unattainable eternity. The desire for unity is inevitably preceded by a state of separation, and to this tragic separateness it equally inevitably, in the flesh, returns:

> Let me confess that we two must be twain,
> Although our undivided loves are one. (Sonnet XXXVI)

The action of time, which is at the same time creative and destructive, which both makes love possible and destroys it, is the unavoidable flaw at the heart of passion. The dramatic presentation of this contradiction, in the setting of a "political" situation which in some sense reflects it, is the theme of *Troilus and Cressida.*

The flaw thus introduced by time into human experience is represented dramatically in the separation which overtakes the two lovers, a separation foreseen from the beginning and implicit in the logic of events. Of the spirit of this separation, Troilus' leave-taking is possibly the clearest expression:

Cressida: And is it true that I must go from Troy? . . .
Is it possible?
Troilus: And suddenly; where injury of chance
Puts back leave-taking, justles roughly by
All time of pause, rudely beguiles our lips
Of all rejoindure, forcibly prevents
Our lock'd embrasures, strangles our dear vows
Even in the birth of our own labouring breath;
We two, that with so many thousand sighs
Did buy each other, must poorly sell ourselves
With the rude brevity and discharge of one.
Injurious time now with a robber's haste
Crams his rich thievery up, he knows not how;
As many farewells as be stars in heaven,
With distinct breath and consign'd kisses to them,
He fumbles up into a loose adieu,
And scants us with a single famish'd kiss,
Distasted with the salt of broken tears. (IV. iv)

The verbal intricacy of this speech is highly characteristic of the play and helps to throw light upon the peculiar nature of its inspiration. The experience reflected in it is, verbally at least, tremendously rich, endlessly elaborate, but the ordering of it is not equal to the complexity. The adverse action of time upon the parting lovers is represented by an astonishing number of verbs—"puts back," "justles roughly by," "rudely beguiles," "forcibly prevents," "strangles"—but the emotion does not *develop*, does not acquire added coherence in the course of its expression. It remains a long and acutely sensed effort to express a state of conflicting feeling. It belongs, in short, to a period in Shakespeare's development in which the keenness of his apprehension of certain elements of experience was not accompanied by a corresponding sense of order and significance; for the attainment of that order and significance in his love poetry we have to wait until *Antony and Cleopatra*.

Nonetheless, though unsatisfactory, the experience behind these lines is highly individual. In each of the verbs of parting there is an element, sharply and vividly realized, of harsh and hostile physical contact. This labored feeling is balanced by the poignant thinness of the positive love imagery which so inadequately accompanies it.

Troilus, whose awareness of separation is so acute, so tangibly conceived, can only express his passion in images as intense as they are airy and essentially bodiless. Love is indeed "rich" in his estimation, fit to be mentioned with the "stars in heaven"; but it can only be expressed in "sighs" and "labouring *breath*," in the hurried breathlessness of "distinct *breath* and consign'd kisses," and in the intensely palated but transitory delicacy of "Distasted with the salt of broken tears." Opposed to this "airy," pathetic passion, the full brunt of the senses is felt in every phrase that stresses parting. "Rudely," "roughly," "forcibly," time and hostile circumstance undermine the tragic brevity of love, so that the "lock'd embrasures" which should normally convey the intensity of physical union are felt to be only an effort to snatch a moment's identity in the face of events which are forcibly drawing the lovers apart. The parting imposed by external circumstances, indeed, is subsidiary to a certain weakness inherent in passion itself. The ideal, which is perfect union, is desired intensely, but is light as "breath" or "air"; and the bodies through whose coming together alone this intensity can be enjoyed are always, while they are united, "labouring" against a tendency to separate. Their "labour," irrevocably frustrated, issues in nothing tangible or permanent. Throughout *Troilus* the elements in love that make for separation are too strong for those that desire union, and "injurious time" is the process by which separation is born out of desired consummation.

Troilus and Cressida, then, in so far as it deals with the central pair of lovers, projects a metaphysical situation into the evocation of a personal relationship. The play is, in this as in other respects, the product of a profound uncertainty about the value of experience. The consequence of this uncertainty, as it affects more particularly the love poetry of Troilus, is the corruption of romantic sentiment. Once again, we are taken back to the sonnets. The sensation conveyed by some of the most individual of these poems turns upon a combination of conventional Petrarchan devices with an intense and normally disturbing sensual quality; the familiar image of the lily, to take an obvious example, with its associations of beauty and purity, is transformed by a magnificent juxtaposition of convention and immediacy into the potent corruption of "Lilies that *fester* smell far worse than weeds."[3] A somewhat similar effect, dramatically presented, is apparent in Troilus' first account of Cressida:

I tell thee I am mad
In Cressid's love; thou answer'st "she is fair";
Pour'st in the open ulcer of my heart
Her eyes, her hair, her cheek, her gait, her voice,
Handlest in thy discourse, O that her hand,
In whose comparison all whites are ink
Writing their own reproach, to whose soft seizure
The cygnet's down is harsh, and spirit of sense
Hard as the palm of ploughman. (I. i)

The underlying convention here is clearly Petrarchan, romantically abstracted from common reality. It makes itself felt in the assertion that Troilus is "mad" for love, in the strained use of "pour'st" and "handlest" to describe Pandarus' speech, in the comparison of Cressida's hand to the "cygnet's down," and in the introduction of "ink" to bring out by contrast its superlative whiteness. But the conventional imagery is transformed, as it were, from within in a manner so closely bound up with the convention that it acts as a corrupting agent, intimately related to the surface sentiment. By giving deep sensuous value to the Petrarchan images, it conveys simultaneously an impression of intense feeling and an underlying lack of content. "Handlest in thy discourse" is a farfetched literary image; but it brings with it a notable keenness of touch which is developed in the contrast between harshness and the "soft seizure" of the cygnet's down, between the hardness of the ploughman's hand and the almost unnatural immediacy of "spirit of sense." Yet the conventional note remains, and with it the feeling that Troilus' passion, for all its surface intensity, has an inadequate foundation, is vitiated by the strained self-pity which allows him to refer to "the open ulcer of my heart," and by the weakness to which he confesses in the course of the same scene: "I am weaker than a woman's tear."

It is important to realize why this weakness, which Cressida after her own fashion shares with her lover, does not produce a tragedy of character, but of situation. The tragedy indeed consists less in the personal suffering of the lovers than in the overriding influence exercised by time upon all human relationships and feelings. In *Antony and Cleopatra*, at least while the lovers are united by their feeling for one another, personal emotion has become strong enough to overcome mutability; in *Troilus*, the supremacy of time is never really questioned, and so a consistent status as persons inevitably eludes the lovers. Their weakness reflects the uncertainty of mood in which the play was conceived and to which they owe the peculiar poignancy, more than sentimental and less than tragic, with which they meet their personal fortunes. Antony and Cleopatra, as lovers, are fully drawn human beings because their love, while it lasts and within its own clearly defined limitations, is valid and confers upon their emotions a full personal value. Conversely, the complete realization in evil of Regan and Goneril in *King Lear,* with the sensual ferocity that characterizes their behavior, proves that when he wrote that play, Shakespeare felt himself able to distinguish between the various elements in his moral experience without falling into ambiguity and confusion. Antony and Cleopatra, Regan and Goneril have full reality as characters precisely because they proceed from a clear understanding in their creator of the value of human emotion as distinct from the evil possibilities implied in it. *Troilus and Cressida,* however, with its intuition of passion as vain and transitory, is compatible with no such individuality of presentation; for time, as it is understood in this play, destroys personal values and makes them invalid.

This limiting observation can be applied with equal force to the behavior of both lovers, and through the entire action. Cressida's falseness does not spring from a deep-seated perversity or even from a strong positive attraction for Diomed, but from the mere process of events, from a flaw inherent in the human situation. Her tragedy, such as it is, derives from awareness of her helplessness. We feel it in her pathetic appeal when Troilus prepares to leave her after the night they have spent together:

Prithee, tarry;
You men will never tarry, (IV. ii)

and in the moment of self-knowledge in which she tells him:

I have a kind of self resides with you,
But an unkind self that itself will leave
To be another's fool. (III. ii)

There is something in the expression of this uncertainty, half punning and conventional, that makes it difficult to conceive of Cressida as a fully realized being. At most, she lives for us only in the mood of the moment, with barely a sign of that responsibility and consistency which is involved in the very conception of character. Any attempt to subject her inconsistency to a moral judgment, of the kind that the medieval elaborators of this legend had in mind when they denounced her "faithlessness," is out of place because the spirit in which Shakespeare created her made it impossible for her to be shown as really responsible for her actions; and without responsibility there can be no moral evaluation. When she comments in the early part of the play on her refusal to reveal her feelings for Troilus:

> Yet hold I off. Women are angels, wooing;
> Things won are done; joy's soul lies in the doing, (I. ii)

her aphoristic lines are not a revelation of wantonness, but simply an impression of the sense, which constitutes the only true tragedy of this play, of the impossibility, the meaninglessness of constancy in a world where time dominates human relationships and where attraction and separation seem necessary and connected aspects of a single situation.

This impossibility also dominates the poetry of Troilus himself and is there further developed from its original basis in romantic sentiment. Troilus' passion, even before it is faced with the necessity for separation, is strong only in anticipation. The intensity of its sensations is conveyed in a refinement of physical feeling, in an attempt to embody in terms of the senses an insubstantial and incorporeal emotion:

> I am giddy; expectation whirls me round.
> The imaginary relish is so sweet
> That it enchants my sense; what will it be,
> When that the watery palates taste indeed
> Love's thrice-repured nectar? death, I fear me,
> Swounding destruction, or some joy too fine,
> Too subtle-potent, tuned too sharp in sweetness,
> For the capacity of my ruder powers:
> I fear it much, and I do fear besides
> That I shall lose distinction in my joys . . . (III. ii)

The sensations of this passage are intense enough, but only through the palate and the senses; like the corresponding emotions of Cressida, they scarcely involve any full personality in the speaker. Troilus' emotions are concentrated on "expectation," on the "*imaginary* relish," and he feels that the "watery palates" will be too weak to sustain the actual consummation. The whole speech turns upon this contrast between the refined intensity of feeling which he seeks, self-consciously and with a touch of indulgence, in "Love's *thrice-repured* nectar," and the giddiness, the "swounding destruction," which would follow its impossible consummation. The experience of love, it is suggested, is so fine, so "subtle-potent," that it surpasses the "ruder powers" of the body and remains an incorporeal aspiration which the senses strive vainly to attain.

Yet, by a strange contradiction, it is precisely because fulfillment in love is sought by Troilus exclusively on the sensual level that it proves unattainable. We can see now why the poetry of this play makes such extensive use of the imagery of taste, why Cressida, for example, says, before she leaves Troy for the Greek camp:

> The grief is fine, full, perfect, that I taste. (IV. iv)

Taste is a sense at once luxurious, delicate, and transitory; also it can be connected, in gross opposition to Troilus' bodiless idealism, with digestion and the functioning of the body. For the weakness of Troilus' passion, as we have already suggested, implies that it is patent of corruption: and that corruption—it can now be added—is the logical consequence of an effort to extract from the refinement of the sensual a substitute for spiritual experience. Immediately before the speech just quoted there is a striking turn of phrase in his appeal to Pandarus:

> O, be thou my Charon,
> And give me swift transportance to those fields
> Where I may *wallow* in the lily-beds
> Proposed for the deserver. (III. ii)

The ideal aspirations of Troilus remain abstract, intangible; such intensity as they achieve derives from their subjection to time, from his awareness of their own transitory nature. But this impermanence makes them bodiless, so that the sensual instincts, unable to associate themselves fully with the insubstantial ideal of union in a mutual passion, express themselves both weakly and basely, "wallowing" like a pig in clover, in what would be, if it were more forceful, a corrupt satisfaction.

This special use of the contrasted implications of sensual experience is extended in the course of the play from the personal to the public action, and contributes thus to the unity of its conception. The refined imagery of taste given to the Trojans, and especially to Troilus, reflects a bodiless ideal which becomes, in the mouths of the scurrilous Thersites and the Greek cynics, a series of clogged, heavy references to the digestive processes. Thersites has "mastic jaws," and Achilles calls him "my cheese, my digestion," whilst Agamemnon tells Patroclus that Achilles' virtues

> like fair fruit in an unwholesome dish
> Are like to rot untasted. (II. iii)

In fact, the very sense that expresses the related intensity and lightness of Trojan passion becomes, in the Greeks, a symbol of inaction and distemper out of which issue the boils, "the botchy core" (II. i), of Thersites' disgust.

In this way we pass from the individual to the public action, from the love of Troilus and Cressida to the war between the Greeks and Troy. This connection between the private and the public theme is indeed the most original feature of the play. The two parties, like the two lovers, are divergent within a common type of feeling. The Trojans share the fragile intensity of Troilus. They are deeply concerned with the value of "honour" and with a view of love that aspires to be idealistic, while Hector shows the virtues of war which are so noticeably absent from the bulky Ajax and the graceless Achilles. Typical of them is the speech in which Troilus explains the case for continuing the war:

> But, worthy Hector,
> She is a theme of honour and renown;
> A spur to valiant and magnanimous deeds,
> Whose present courage may beat down our foes,
> And fame in time to come canonize us. (II. ii)

Yet the lightness and grace of this idealism covers a certain artificiality. The verse itself is unsubstantial and the expression vague and high-flown. It reads, at this stage in Shakespeare's development, like a survival from earlier plays set against the contortions and involutions of so much of *Troilus.* The impression is neither accidental nor isolated. Hector's reasoning in the same scene shows clearly that the arguments advanced by Troilus are as flimsy in content as their expression is tenuous. For all this "honour," for which Troilus is ready to fight and, if need be, to die, is directed to the defense of Helen, whose worth has been destroyed by the manner in which she has been stolen from Menelaus. Even Paris can only argue that the original dishonor of her rape should now be redeemed by the heroism shown in her defense. The tone of the Trojan references to Helen contrasts strangely with the idealism of their declared intentions. Paris pleads that he

> would have the *soil* of her *fair* rape
> Wiped off in honourable keeping her,

and Troilus, conveying a slight but unmistakable twist to conventional imagery, declares that Paris

> bought a Grecian queen, whose youth and freshness
> Wrinkles Apollo's and *makes stale* the morning. (II. ii)

The juxtaposition of "fair" and "soil," "freshness" and "stale," touches the basic weakness of Trojan idealism, and points to the way in which that idealism is organically connected in its expression with the sluggish inertia that prevails in the Greek camp.

The true nature of this Trojan weakness is perhaps most explicitly stated by Troilus when he sets forth, in an attempt at reasoned expression, his argument for the continuation of the war:

> I take to-day a wife, and my election
> Is led on in the conduct of my will;
> My will enkindled by mine eyes and ears,
> Two traded pilots 'twixt the dangerous shores
> Of will and judgement: how may I avoid,
> Although my will distaste what it elected,
> The wife I chose? There can be no evasion
> To blench from this, and to stand firm by honour. (II. ii)

Troilus' terminology is indefinite and the expression of his argument, like so much of what passes for discussion in this play, far more complicated than its content. There seems at one point to be an opposition of "will," which we may associate here with sensual impulse, and "judgement," by which this impulse should normally be restrained and directed; the opposition, in short, of sensuality and moral control, which becomes a little later the central theme of *Measure for Measure.*[4] In that play, however, the moral conflict is explicitly stated, and—what is more important—takes shape in a dramatic clash of clearly defined personalities; in *Troilus and Cressida* there is only an uncertainty, a sense of uneasiness, which the notable incoherence of the expression reflects. The conclusion reached by "judgement" is that affirmed by Hector—that purposeful action must follow from a dispassionate weighing of alternatives in the light of the principles of reason—but the whole trend of Troilus' reply is to annihilate, or at least willfully to confuse, the distinction between "will" and "judgement" themselves, to show that "judgement" is powerless and irrelevant once the sensual will has impelled man toward action. In other words, the basis of Troilus' "honour" is simply sensual impulse, and its weakness lies largely in his unwillingness to recognize this fact, and in the abstraction and lack of content that follow in the train of this evasion.

In a way very typical of this play, the discussion turns into a debate, conducted on lines that recall the traditional procedure of the schools, on the relative merits of reason and honor as guides in life. Its central crux is a conflict between opposed interpretations of *value*. Troilus, the romantic, if we may so agree to call him, needs to feel himself supported by a belief that man can create his own values, that he can confer worth upon the object of his strivings by the unsupported strength of his own subjective engagement. "What's aught but as 'tis valued?" he asks; but Hector, older and more experienced, better able to contemplate his own motives and to distinguish in them between what is genuinely valid and what proceeds from the need to justify illusion, replies by arguing the need for an external confirmation of value, the support of subjective estimation by a genuinely objective consensus. In his own words, spoken in answer to his brother:

> value dwells not in particular will;
> It holds his estimate and dignity
> As well wherein 'tis precious of itself
> As in the prizer. (II. ii)

Acting upon this conviction, Hector is sufficiently outspoken on the subject of Troilus' infatuation:

> Is your blood
> So madly hot that no discourse of reason,
> Nor fear of bad success in a bad cause
> Can qualify the same? (II. ii)

The argument—though Troilus rejects it and Hector himself fails to follow it to its conclusion—once more binds the personal love theme to that of the justification of public action. Troilus—and in this he is typical of the Trojans—refuses to admit the weakness of his conception of honor, which is, however, implied in the very situation which brought the war into being: for the reality of Helen, as Hector points out, does not correspond to Troilus' embroidered and Marlovian conception of her:

> Brother, she is not worth what she does cost
> The holding. (II. ii)

But this same lack of solid foundation is apparent, as we have seen, in the undertones of Troilus' own poetry, where the unacknowledged sensual basis of his idealism refuses to be entirely suppressed. Underlying the "poetical" quality of Troilus' emotional flights, there is a distinct strain of coarseness and inertia. It appears in the references, so typical of this play, to the "soiled silks" and the "remainder viands" which are thrown away "because we now are full." Most typical of all, in the determination to hide its own weakness which it implies, is the Trojan reaction to reason:

> Nay, if we talk of reason,
> Let's shut our gates, and sleep: manhood and honour
> Should have hare hearts, would they but *fat* their thoughts
> With this *crammed* reason: reason and respect
> Make *livers pale* and lustihood deject. (II. ii)

This insistence upon mental inertia and the obstruction of physical processes, as applied to reason, stands in significant contrast to the lightness and artificiality of Troilus' idealistic outbursts, but they are organically related to them. The Trojan devotion to honor, Shakespeare would seem to infer, is devotion to an abstraction that has no sufficient basis in reason, that is, in fact, no more than an empty justification of impulse: but—it is equally important to realize—to abandon honor for its lack of rational foundation is to expose oneself to the danger of lethargy, to a rooted disinclination to act at all.[5] Once more we are faced with the split between motive and impulse, moral *value* and sensual substitutes, which dominates this play without a real glimpse of resolution.

The analysis of this important scene suggests how the contrast between the Greek and Trojan parties, which most critics of the play have noted, is modified by significant points of contact. The Trojans, for all their concern to defend "honour," as they conceive it, against the Greeks, are strangely related to their enemies. This relationship, of course, is openly "symbolized" in the combat between Hector and Ajax (IV. v), when Hector refuses to carry on the duel with his "cousin-german" and Ajax agrees to call a truce. But the contacts established through a common type of imagery are still more important for an understanding of the play. In the Greek camp, we find fully explicit the staleness which Trojan "honour" has tried to ignore. Where the Trojans reject reason in favor of ill-considered action, the Greeks accept it and are reduced to inaction. Agamemnon's very first speech, as the head and cornerstone of Greek unity, shows how inconclusive are the intellectual processes so painfully followed by the leaders who accompany him and how closely related they are to the views expressed by Troilus on "crammed reason":

Princes,
What grief hath set the jaundice on your cheeks?
The ample proposition that hope makes
In all designs begun on earth below
Fails in the promised largeness; checks and disasters
Grow in the veins of actions highest reared,
As knots, by the conflux of meeting sap,
Infect, the sound pine and divert his grain
Tortive and errant from his course of growth.
Nor, princes, is it matter new to us
That we come short of our suppose so far
That after seven years' siege yet Troy walls stand;
Sith every action that hath gone before,
Whereof we have record, trial did draw
Bias and thwart, not answering the aim
And that unbodied figure of the thought
That gave it surmised shape. (I. iii)

Agamemnon's thought proceeds not from point to point according to a definite rational sequence, but by a series of indeterminate digressions which reveal his incapacity to come to a conclusion. His labored illustrations and the theoretical observations which accompany them destroy the coherence of an argument which they do nothing to further; as so often in this play, there is no recognizable development of thought to justify the complexity. The repeated doublings of words—"tortive and errant," "bias and thwart"—all lay emphasis upon obstruction, upon the speaker's struggle against obscure impediments which hinder the Greeks from successful action; and the use of unusual and unassimilated Latinized words, such as "conflux" and "tortive," produces a similar sense of resistance and difficulty. More significantly still, these obstructions are associated with disturbances and interruptions in organic growth. The prospect of hope "fails in the promised largeness," does not grow to its anticipated stature. "Checks and disasters" are intertwined with natural growth, and the very rising of the sap in the "sound pine," which is so eminently a natural process, produces infection and distortion in the growth of the tree. Most important of all, because corresponding to the spirit expressed by Troilus, thought is "unbodied" and its processes, separated from the actual course of events, are equally cut off from the sensual immediacy which finds irresponsible expression in the comments of Thersites. The keen nervous quality so noticeably lacking in the theoretical observations of the Greek leaders breaks out significantly in Thersites' sweeping affirmation of anarchy and disorder; in a similar manner, Troilus' disembodied idealism covers a sensual impulse which he refuses to recognize.

It is only natural that this discrepancy in the Greeks between thought and action should be expressed in terms of physical disorder; and here the link with the Trojans becomes even more explicit. Thersites' boils and plague-spots are related to Agamemnon's laborious thoughts on authority just as Troilus' contempt for "crammed" reason and his insistent sense of soilure and physical obstruction are connected with his abstract idealism. The vital point in Shakespeare's presentation of the Greeks is this association of continual ratiocination with a complete overthrow of "degree" in their ranks; they are entirely unable to turn council into united action. The position in the Greek camp is briefly summed up by Thersites, whose clear-sightedness can produce nothing but stagnation: "Agamemnon is a fool to offer to command Achilles; Achilles is a fool to be commanded of Agamemnon; Thersites is a fool to serve such a fool; and Patroclus is a fool positive" (II. iii). While Agamemnon, Nestor, and Ulysses scheme and discuss, Ajax and Achilles "fust" out of action; the hand that executes is out of touch with the "*still and mental* parts" that contrive the conduct of the war. Perhaps the point is most clearly made by Ulysses in his account of the pride which keeps Achilles in his tent:

> imagined worth
> Holds in his blood such swoln and hot discourse
> That *'twixt his mental and his active parts*
> Kingdom'd Achilles in commotion rages
> And *batters down himself*. (II. iii)

The conflict in Achilles between personal pride and duty to the Greek cause is stated here in terms of "blood," of sensual passion; the implications of "swoln and hot," suggesting feverish disorder due to extreme intemperance, are unmistakable. The adjective "kingdom'd," like so many of the words which characterize the poetry of this play, is not fully explicit, but it clearly refers the personal issue back to the general theme of "degree." The individual warrior, like the Greek polity at war, should be a unity founded upon "degree"; and "degree" in the individual is an ideal correspondence between thought and action, impulse and control, "blood" and "judgement."[6] It is Achilles' tragedy, like that of all the Greeks, whose hope of final victory depends upon his return, to find himself involved in strife between his "mental" and his "active" parts to an extreme which leads him, in self-consuming conflict, to destroy his own manhood, to "batter down himself."

On both sides in this presentation of the Trojan War, indeed, it would seem that the balance between emotion and reason is profoundly disturbed. The "cunning" of the Greek leaders is manifestly out of touch with practical considerations and expends itself in an activity completely disproportionate to the desired end: "it will not in circumvention deliver a fly from a spider, without drawing their massy irons and cutting the web" (II. iii). Himself like a boil on a disordered body, Thersites dismisses the warrior Ajax—the incarnation, after Achilles, of Greek prowess in the field—as a mindless brute—"thou hast no more brain than I have in mine elbows"; "thou art but here to thrash Trojans" (II. i)—and sees in the war itself nothing but lechery and unreason. On the Trojan side the infidelity of Cressida finally undermines Troilus' faith in "honour" as a basis for action and leaves him dimly aware of the incompatible and contrary elements which underlie what he had assumed to be the indivisible simplicity of passion. Confronted by Ulysses with the direct proof of betrayal, he says:

> Within my soul there doth conduce a fight
> Of this strange nature, that a thing inseparate
> Divides more wider than the sky and earth;
> And yet the spacious breadth of this division
> Admits no orifex for a point as subtle
> As Ariadne's broken woof to enter.
> Instance, O instance! strong as Pluto's gates;
> Cressid is mine, tied with the bonds of heaven:

Instance, O instance! strong as heaven itself,
The bonds of heaven are slipp'd, dissolved and loosed:
And with another knot, five-finger-tied,
The fractions of her faith, orts of her love,
The fragments, scraps, the bits and greasy relics
Of her o'er-eaten faith, are bound to Diomed. (V. ii)

All the characteristics of the love poetry of Troilus can be recognized here—its tenuous and unnaturally refined expression, its subtlety in dealing with distinctions within an apparent unity, its sensuous thinness balanced by the imagery of disgust and repletion which connects it with the verse given to the Greeks and indicates the unifying factor in this play. For the ambiguous attitude toward experience which so deeply exercised Shakespeare in many of his sonnets is the determining factor in his presentation of both parties. Proceeding from his sense of the disharmony introduced by their subjection to the temporal process into the love of Troilus and Cressida, it extends to embrace the two parties in their fantastic and unreasonable conflict. The Trojans follow a false idealism, which deceives itself with talk of "honour," but is really based on "blood" and ends in a pathetic and helpless realization of its own insufficiency; the Greeks elaborate endlessly a "judgement" that is out of touch with the instinctive sources of action, until Agamemnon's chaotic reasoning finds its proper counterpart in the distorted bitterness of Thersites' diseased sensibility.

Read in this way, *Troilus and Cressida* emerges as an attempt to give expression to a fundamental flaw felt to exist at the heart of human experience, and not readily to be described. The final difficulty is the lack of that *degree,* proper and natural order in distinction, which Ulysses abstractly perceives in the longest and most famous of his speeches:

Take but degree away, untune that string,
And, hark, what discord follows! each thing meets
In mere oppugnancy: the bounded waters
Should lift their bosoms higher than the shores,
And make a sop of all this solid globe:
Strength should be lord of imbecility,
And the rude son should strike his father dead. (I. iii)

From this general proposition he goes on to paint, in words of universal resonance, his culminating picture of a world in anarchy:

NORTHWEST MISSOURI
STATE COLLEGE LIBRARY
MARYVILLE, MISSOURI

Force should be right; or rather, right and wrong,
Between whose endless jar justice resides,
Should lose their names, and so should justice too.
Then everything includes itself in power,
Power into will, will into appetite;
And appetite, an universal wolf,
So doubly seconded with will and power,
Must make perforce an universal prey,
And last eat up himself. Great Agamemnon,
This chaos, when degree is suffocate,
Follows the choking. (I. iii)

In this speech, which represents so much more than a mere reflection of political orthodoxy, we find supremely expressed, in terms of the disorder introduced by passion or "appetite" into the human organism, the nightmare of mere "chaos" which, present on both sides in the conflict between Greeks and Trojans, is the real theme of this fascinating and disturbing play. The Trojans seek to ignore the limitations of passion in a bodiless idealism; the Greeks, quite incapable of idealism, are weighed down by all that the Trojans try to forget. Both sides are bound together by the occasion of their quarrel; as Thersites says: "All the argument is a cuckold and a whore" (II. iii). Troilus, in one magnificent phrase, sums up the crux from which the varied contradictions of the play draw their interest:

> This is the monstruosity in love, lady, that the will is infinite and the execution confined, that the desire is boundless and the act a slave to limit. (III. ii)

The infinity sought by the will is the idealistic love of Troilus, which neglects the wearing action of time and the related inability of passion to live up to ideals of love and honor which can only be redeemed from abstraction by integration into an adequate conception of value; and the very boundlessness of the desire, when it encounters the limits imposed by time and the body to which, in the absence of such an integration, it feels enslaved, turns to the clogged inertia of Achilles and the endless self-scrutiny of the Greek camp.

HAMLET

In their various ways the critics of *Hamlet* agree that the subject of the play is a frustration. The hero's speculations on action proceed from his creator's consciousness of a flaw felt to exist at the heart of human experience, the nature of which we can only hope to understand in so far as it has been projected into a dramatic sequence adequately corresponding to it. This, stated in general terms, is the key to the problems which the tragedy so notoriously raises. A frustration of the kind reflected in *Troilus and Cressida* or in *Hamlet* can never convey an initial effect of clarity, because it implies that the experience with which it is concerned has not been previously mastered, that the action which reflects it on the stage —though not necessarily confused or contradictory in its dramatic effect—is itself conceived as in some sense an act of definition. *Hamlet* is a problem play precisely because Shakespeare, when he wrote it, was engaged, for reasons which it cannot be the task of criticism to establish, in reducing to order a whole world of disturbing ideas and emotions by giving them significance in a balanced and dramatically effective creation.

Some part of the difficulty of interpreting the play is no doubt due to the fact that the commonplace Elizabethan story of revenge, already popularized in all probability by Thomas Kyd some ten years before Shakespeare may have written his play, does not lend itself naturally to the type of experience which Shakespeare wished to make it express. Revenge implies swift action based on clear-cut and primitive convictions leading, as its principal theatrical attraction, to the remorseless shedding of blood. It thrives, dramatically speaking, on an undeveloped passion for melodrama; the one thing not readily squared with it is the subtle exploration of states of conscience and feeling issuing in profound inaction. In making this point it is not suggested that the difficulties of *Hamlet* are purely or principally of an external order, to be ascribed in any important sense to an imperfectly judicious choice of plot. As a dramatic structure the play is admirably conceived, supremely effective in the theater, clear and concrete in its development and final resolution. The difficulties proceed rather from the nature of the experience which the play so uniquely reflects. *Hamlet* dramatizes a story, chosen in part out of external considerations, in which intense personal engagement makes its presence felt; but the emotion which this engagement generates is of its nature such that it can only attain a due measure of objectivity in the process of working itself out. *Hamlet* is—to put the matter briefly—a masterpiece of exploration, and the initial effect of obscurity which it is apt to make upon us is a necessary part of the price we pay for participating in the process of relentless probing by which this exploration is conducted.

Hamlet, however, though it recalls many motives of *Troilus and Cressida,* is a great deal more than a repetition of that play. The thwarting of action by self-scrutiny which is connected with the development of disease in the human organism is indeed common to Hamlet and the Greek leaders. Fortinbras' attack on Poland becomes

> the imposthume of much wealth and peace,
> That inward breaks, and shows no cause without
> Why the man dies. (IV. iv)

The feeling of this, and of a good deal else in the play, could be paralleled from Ulysses' speeches. But the advance in *Hamlet* is apparent in its more dramatic quality and in its more profound penetration of the instinctive foundations of character. Hamlet's soliloquies are far less "rationalized," less theoretical and exterior in their effect, than Ulysses' reflections upon time, order, and human motivation. The laborious machinery of ratiocination is replaced by subtle and truly dramatic shifts of feeling. In the "To be or not to be" speech—to limit ourselves to the most familiar example of all—Hamlet's contrasted moods are *felt* in the movement of the verse, in language that reflects through the varied and precise operation of the senses the constantly fluctuating relation of thought to emotion. More ample resources of language are being brought into play; we feel the sharp immediacy of the vernacular ("To *grunt* and *sweat* under a weary life") contrasted with the remote Latinity of "quietus" and "consummation." The conflicts in Hamlet's mind are no longer arguments but *states* of experience in which sense and thought are fused in the study not of an idea, but of a character.

The mention of character suggests a further new development in *Hamlet.* The divisions upon which the story of *Troilus* turns belong, as we have seen, to the metaphysical rather than to the human order. The central clash of feeling is between living emotion and impersonal, destructive time, and the love of Troilus for Cressida, hopelessly involved in a situation not of its own making, is felt as a light, almost a disembodied aspiration. In *Hamlet,* on the other hand, contradictions too complex and, so to speak, too *human,* to be thus neatly separated are brought together into one person whose relation to the action, though not completely clarified (for he is himself engaged in an inconclusive effort to achieve self-definition), is varied and continuous. Instead of a division of opposites, conceived in relative abstraction, we are presented with a central figure whose motives penetrate the action at every point, seeking clarification through contact with it and illuminating it, in turn, by the centrality of its presence. In pursuing the duty laid upon him by his father's ghost, Hamlet brings to light a state of disease which affects the entire field presented to his consciousness; and, in the various stages through which this infection, this "imposthume," is exposed, he explores progressively the depths of his own infirmity.

In accordance with this conception, the first part of the play gradually concentrates its latent discords upon the revelation of the Ghost. This is not, as we may assume it to have been in the original melodrama, a simple call to action, an unambiguous appeal to filial piety; nor, on the other hand, can Hamlet's attitude toward it be accounted for, as some writers have argued,[7] principally by his uncertainty as to the nature, good or evil, "heavenly" or "hellish" in its origins, of its inspiration. The matter is more complex than either of these attitudes would suggest, more closely related to the intimate contradictions of the play. *Both* aspects are in some degree relevant to a proper understanding of the Ghost, and the link that unites them is to be sought ultimately in Hamlet's own mind. The Ghost, in fact, acts upon Hamlet as a disturbing influence, imposing upon him a clear-cut filial obligation, to which all that is positive in his being responds, at the same time that it confirms the presence around him of sinister realities which he feels, even as he repudiates them, to be obscurely related to stresses in his own nature. In this way, far from leading to resolution through the action proposed by the original story, its message plunges the hero and his surroundings into obscurity and doubt.

Obscurity and doubt, indeed, accompany the first appearances of the Ghost. Horatio says that at the cockcrow "it started like a *guilty* thing" (I. i), and that its coming "bodes some strange eruption" (I. i) to the state. This "eruption" is present as an ill-defined foreboding in the minds of those who await its coming on the battlements of Elsinore. Francisco, the common soldier, is "sick at heart" (I. i), and his "sickness," after finding an external projection in the feverish preparations for war reported by Marcellus, is more intimately related to the latent tensions of the play in Horatio's account of the threat from Norway which has inspired them:

> young Fortinbras,
> Of unimproved metal *hot* and *full,*
> Hath in the skirts of Norway, here and there,
> *Shark't up* a list of *lawless* resolutes,
> For *food* and *diet,* to some enterprise
> That hath a stomach in't. (I. i)

This type of imagery, describing social maladies in terms of the unbalance which "blood"-inspired "appetite" provokes in normal physical processes, links *Hamlet* in spirit to the other problem plays. Its dramatic counterpart is the revolt, repeatedly revealed in the course of the action, of youth against age, impulse against experience, restless self-will against the complacency of established authority. Fortinbras is expressly described as a young man defying his "impotent and bed-rid" uncle in pursuit of his own predatory ends. His behavior, which provokes from Denmark the correspondingly tense and strained reaction implied in Marcellus' talk of "sweaty haste" and "nightly" toil (I. i), will be paralleled by that of Laertes and, in a certain sense (in so far as Claudius claims "parental" tutelage over his nephew), of Hamlet himself; they point to a widespread dislocation of natural functioning, centered ultimately upon the inversion of normal relationships which accompanies the usurped royalty of the Danish king.

At this point it is well to bear firmly in mind, as we follow the deliberately slow and intricate development of the action, with its sense of plot and counterplot, its references to the "old mole" (I. v) working below the surface of the earth and to the "enginer" "hoist with his own petard" (III. iv), that *Hamlet* is something more than the inwardly directed tragedy of an exceptionally complex and self-aware individual. Not all criticism of the play has recognized sufficiently the importance of its *political* aspect, the fact that its hero is, whatever else he may also be, a public figure, a prince and an heir apparent, whose relation to Claudius is colored from the outset by the ambiguous relationship in which they stand with respect to one another. When Hamlet, on his initial appearance, stands pointedly aside in the presence of his uncle's assembled court, listening to the flow of bland, respectable commonplace which comes so readily and, it seems, so impressively from the throne, and inserts from time to time the obscure comments which reflect what is to us his still unexplained bitterness—"I am too much i' the sun"; "A little more than kin and less than kind" (I. ii)—it is not the barbaric drama of some remote Danish principality that stirs our interest but something nearer both to Shakespeare and ourselves: the intrigue and the treachery that accompanied the maneuvering for power in a Renaissance court. Beneath Claudius' impressive ability to assume, on the surface and in the public eye, the appropriately judicious and authoritative mask, which has even led some students of the play to minimize the full extent of his malignity,[8] lie the obsessive realities of insecurity, ruthlessness, and hunger for power which it is Hamlet's tragedy that he can only meet on their own level, by answering spying with counterespionage, cruelty with the deliberate suppression of pity, and usurpation with murder. By so doing, by experiencing to the full the claustrophobic quality of this corrupt and unnatural court, he finally exposes the "imposthume" implicit in Claudius' rule and rids Denmark of the poison at its heart; but this is not accomplished before he has himself been destroyed by his recognition of the link which binds him, in his own despite, to the reality he is called upon to destroy.

The revelation of this state is, in accordance with the essentially exploratory spirit of this play, gradual and indirect. The reversal of the natural foundations of authority in Claudius' rule is first reflected in a strictly subsidiary fashion, through the relation of Polonius to his children. In Polonius, with his mixture of "policy" and self-satisfied "experience," impotence, and complacency, the claim of paternity to proper respect appears as a mockery. His senile distrust of youth, which fails to assert itself against Laertes when the latter presses his determination to return to Paris, imposes upon Ophelia his own interpretation of love, at once cynical and life-denying:

I do know
When the blood burns, how prodigal the soul
Lends the tongue vows . . .
Do not believe his vows, for they are brokers,

Not of that dye which their investments show,
But mere implorators of unholy suits,
Breathing like sanctified and pious bawds,
The better to beguile. (I. iii)

The sense of resentful distrust, of natural emotion belittled and entangled in ambiguous complexities of expression, will be linked in due course to Hamlet's own repudiation of love to contribute to the final definition of his tragedy. Polonius the moralist, as he denounces passion, involves his own counsel in equivocation. Envy inspires, at least in part, his repudiation of "blood," of an experience which age no longer permits him to feel; and the reference to "brokers" and "investments" ("broker" with a subsidiary sense of "pander" and "investments" in the double sense of financial interests and transforming garments), the intricate relationship between the surface of "pious" propriety and the compound of cynicism and resentment that underlies it, corresponds to the spirit of courtly dissembling which the speaker, in his position of trusted, experienced authority, so weightily upholds. Polonius' treatment of his children, and their contrasted reactions to him, rebellious and unnaturally submissive respectively, indicate in the personal order the profound dislocation of normal relationships which prevails beneath the bland surface of Claudius' rule and extends like a stain over the entire field of his authority.

Only gradually, as his own misgivings find expression, is this dislocation related to the sense of intimate betrayal which Hamlet, still obscurely, associates with his father's loss and the "appetite" so unnaturally revealed in his mother. The disgust revealed in his first soliloquy (I. ii) still precedes rather than derives from his external situation. It is a revulsion against the "too too solid flesh"—"solid" and, if a relevant subsidiary meaning be accepted, "sullied," stained by its unescapable materiality[9]—that oppresses him, producing the desire—essentially unstable, immature, self-centered—that it should "melt," "dissolve into a dew"; and this in turn is extended to find expression in his vision of the world as an "unweeded garden," possessed by "things *rank* and *gross* in nature," "weary, stale, flat, and unprofitable." The tone at this point reveals rather an internal disaffection, not devoid of emotional self-indulgence, than a mature judgment, and the "incest" attributed to Gertrude, referred to in such a context, is at least as much a projection as a source of inner conflict. Not for the first time in Shakespeare's writing of this period, the type of physical reference which pervades the speech indicates the presence of unassimilated feeling. Already the world has been spoken of in terms which convey, in many of the sonnets and in *Troilus and Cressida,* a repudiation of "appetite"; the effect produced by "rank and gross," the sense of dregs and disenchantment implied in "stale," point to the disillusionment which overtakes time-conditioned love. The attempt to provide this type of emotion with an objective equivalent, to project it into a dramatic conception, is fundamental to the play.

A certain projection, indeed, is achieved during the same speech in Hamlet's comparison of the two kings, his father and his uncle, to Hyperion and a satyr respectively;[10] but the terms of the comparison, far from reflecting the moral clarity at which he aims, confirms the persistence of the infirmity which inspired it. A figure noble, remotely classical, and *dead* has been replaced by another, a gross, repellent threat to purity, but alive; and in this substitution is reflected not so much the particular tragedy of a son, or even the degradation of a mother's affections, as the inevitable corruption of human feeling. *Both* kings, the living as well as the dead, bear relation to Hamlet's own state; bound to him by ties of blood, *both* affect aspects of his being from which he cannot, in the last analysis, free himself. The sources of his disgust, though never fully explicit, can be derived, still in the course of this speech, from his account of the relations between Gertrude and her dead, her idealized husband. His father's love for his mother had, as their son now recalls it, a precarious artificial quality, as though its object needed to be protected from physical contact, even to the extent of not permitting the wind to "visit" her face "too roughly"; but her response to it is associated, still in his memory, with a passionate intensity of craving that again reminds us of certain passages from *Troilus:*

> she would hang on him,
> As if *increase of appetite* had grown
> By what it *fed* on. (I. ii)

Such a passage will show why some critics[11] have found the emotion expressed in *Hamlet* excessive, imperfectly related to its causes as dramatically presented. It is—be it noted—Gertrude's relation to her first, not her "incestuous," husband that is being recalled; and the impression conveyed is not that of a particular, unlawful relationship, nor even simply of the sensual weakness which has borne fruit in his mother's infatuation for Claudius, but of a corruption present at the heart of passion and affecting all human relationships. That corruption, both in love and in the experience which finds in love one particularly intense expression, seeks in this tragedy an adequate dramatic projection.

Because Hamlet's infirmity, by its very nature, resists full definition, the final revelation of the Ghost (I. iv, v), while it relates his disgust at last to an external motive, deepens the sense of conflict which envelops his being. It shows Claudius to be not only the supplanter of his father's love but his murderer; it adds a public cause of resentment—that of having been deprived of the royal succession—to Hamlet's intimate grief. Yet, rather than illuminating, the Ghost's story extends the area of obscurity which surrounds Hamlet's malady. As a result of it, his mind and the condition of the world are united as aspects of a single infirmity. That "something is rotten in the state of Denmark" (I. iv) he has known from the start, though his sense of Gertrude's "incest" has never seemed a sufficient cause of his reaction; but now, when it appears that such a cause has been revealed, the infamy he is called upon to destroy is linked to the unease that already weighs upon his heart:

> The time is out of joint; O, cursed spite,
> That ever I was born to set it right. (I. v)

External disease and inner disaffection, far from finding resolution in the prospect of the action imposed upon them, exasperate one another in mutual aggravation. The rest of the play will mainly confirm that in the world which the author's experience at this stage postulates as uniquely and obsessively real they are incapable of resolution.

After the revelation of the Ghost, the main action is concentrated on the efforts of the protagonists to clarify their position with regard to one another. Here, perhaps, more obviously than at any other stage in its development, a claustrophobic sense of Renaissance court intrigue permeates the action. Both Claudius and Hamlet, while suspecting that their own situation is not in certain important respects what it appears to be, have suspicions to confirm. Claudius increasingly relates to Hamlet's person the insecurity which he senses beneath the surface tranquillity of his rule, and Hamlet has learned from the Ghost that his own disaffection is connected with his uncle's criminality and, more obscurely, with the unnatural relationship that binds the latter to his mother. Each, therefore, sets himself to observe the behavior of the other, with a view, ultimately, to clarifying his own situation; but each, by a twist deeply characteristic of this play, does so by dissembling, by reflecting in a deliberate tortuousness of approach the obscurity of his moral state. Claudius, seeking to involve Hamlet in a double intrigue, makes use of elements which derive from the ambiguous character of his royal authority. Besides setting Rosencrantz and Guildenstern to spy upon him, thus bringing him into contact with the corrupt servility that has replaced true loyalty at Elsinore, he involves his relations to Ophelia in the servile maneuverings of the "politic" Polonius. To these devices, each calculated both to confirm his sense of the "rottenness" that surrounds his uncle's authority and to magnify his intimate disgust, Hamlet responds with a counterintrigue, which equally corresponds to his own abnormal condition, for the madness he feigns is at once a disguise deliberately assumed and the manifestation of a true moral infirmity. The threads of the action, thus involved in plot and counterplot, are finally drawn together in the play scene (III. ii), which serves as a point of focus, concentrating upon itself the preceding intrigue and making possible the progressive revelation of disease which follows. Itself a fiction, but a fiction reproducing life, it exposes the false foundations of Claudius' rule and, at the same time, makes it possible for Hamlet, who alone is in a position to grasp the full significance of his uncle's involuntary self-betrayal, to begin his exposure of the relationship which binds the remaining protagonists (grouped as they are round the dramatic representation of their king's actual crime) to the central corruption.

At this stage, then, the area of Hamlet's infirmity is extended by contact with the external world. The verbal duel with Rosencrantz and Guildenstern concentrates his mind, already possessed by an inner incompatibility, upon the courtly fiction which surrounds him. They are, by their own admission, parasites, reflections of the falsity which emanates from Claudius and disguises itself under the outward appearances of duty; "indifferent children of the earth," dwellers "in the secret parts of Fortune" (II. ii), their phrases seem expressly fashioned to touch the hidden roots of his loathing, to confirm his estimate of a society to which, even as he repudiates it, he feels himself obscurely connected. As always, his distaste expresses itself in the extension to his surroundings of his own unease. His thought, embracing the universe in the process of turning in upon itself, offers him the prospect of feeling himself, in abstraction from the outer world which he cannot accept in its common reality, "king" of a space at once "infinite" and finally empty; but, in so doing, it leaves him the victim of the "bad dreams" to which he is led by the contrast between the vague "infinity" of his aspirations and the reality of the "prison"—Denmark, the world, his own mind—in which an inner incompatibility compels him to live. The exposure of this situation culminates in the great prose speech (II. ii) in which the spiritual dignity of man ("*noble* in reason," "*infinite* in faculty," angelical, divine) is set against the vanity implied in "quintessence of dust"; while its setting, the "goodly frame" of the firmament, becomes, as he contemplates it in the light of his rooted distaste, "a most *sterile* promontory." Here, as elsewhere, Hamlet's thought at once embraces and rejects a thin, abstract "infinity." In the name of this "infinity," for which it craves without being able to embody it, it spurns the concrete, the limited, which it persistently associates with corruption but to which its expression is obstinately tied.

The second intrigue to which Hamlet is exposed touches even more closely the roots of his malady. His love for Ophelia, in which his desire for purity—purity, nobility, and infinity represent the persistent but abstract aspirations of his thought throughout the play—might have found expression in an emotion which, while partaking of the flesh, could have been raised to the spiritual, becomes the occasion for the cynical devices by which Polonius offers to discover the truth for his master. Polonius, indeed, has from the first involved Ophelia's purity in his own impotent resentment against the flesh. Her love, tender, abstract, and inexperienced, like most of the shades of positive emotion which so ineffectually cross the stage in this tragedy, has been subjected to a process of denigration against which it can offer no positive assertion of its own validity. It is this denigration which finally penetrates Hamlet's own mind, finds its ally there in the obscure resentments which are so prominent in his nature, and provokes—more especially when he realizes that Ophelia's love is being turned into a trap against himself—the bitter, self-centered cruelty of his repudiation. For Hamlet's anger is only in part caused by his discovery of the intrigue to which he has been so shamefully exposed. Its sources are ultimately more personal, more closely related to his own moral dilemma. Love, trapped in the "prison" of the flesh and unable to conceive other than an abstract, bodiless "infinity," is exposed to decay; and so, reacting against it with an asceticism based finally on resentment, Hamlet incorporates his intimate disgust into the madness which is at once a disguise, a refuge, and a manifestation of despair. Divorced by an obstacle which remains beyond definition from its natural roots in the flesh, and moved by a passionate loathing of physical processes, his reason turns upon his former love in a mood akin to hatred: "I say we will have no more marriages . . . To a nunnery, go!" (III. i) To grasp the full range of feeling here, we should be aware that "nunnery," in Elizabethan low speech, could bear the sense of "brothel"; so that among other things the bitter references to "painting" in which Hamlet, with a self-righteousness that is also part of the character, expresses his disgust fall naturally into place. The ideal of chastity, remote but intensely desired, and the reality—as the speaker conceives it—of universal and inevitable promiscuity are united in one complex reaction. "Go thy ways to a nunnery!" he repeats, because otherwise physical union with Ophelia may produce more creatures "indifferent honest," condemned to experience the decay of "nobility" which has become for Hamlet a universal attribute of life. Thus inspired to revulsion, he first shatters Ophelia's spirit and is finally responsible for her death.

To this exposure of Hamlet's infirmity through its relation to the world around him corresponds, in these same scenes, the gradual undermining of Claudius' apparent confidence and royal control. Although the self-betrayal induced by the play scene is the first clear revelation of his divided state, the discrepancy between inner reality and surface appearance has already been indicated in his comment, delivered as an aside, on Polonius' plans to entrap Hamlet through Ophelia:

Polonius: We are oft to blame in this—
'Tis too much proved—that with devotion's visage
And pious action we do sugar o'er
The devil himself.
Claudius: O, 'tis too true;
How smart a lash that speech doth give my conscience!
The harlot's cheek, beautied with plastering art,
Is not more ugly to the thing that helps it
Than is my deed to my most painted word. (III. i)

The action of *Hamlet* is, in its inner logic, the progressive revelation of a state of disease. The king's reference to "painting" belongs to the same range of feeling as that of Hamlet's own denunciation of woman. It reduces the show of regality in Claudius to a mask, sugared over with a false surface, plastered to conform to a fictitious pose; and by so doing, it both prepares the way for Hamlet's exposure of the corrupt reality beneath it and indicates the presence of contradictions not unrelated to those in the hero's own mind. The effect is the highly disturbing exposure of what, before being an external reality, is an intimate state of disharmony.

It is at this turning point in his relationship to the world around him that Hamlet, left to digest these shattering revelations of intrigue and treachery, utters the most famous and most intimate of his soliloquies. It would be wrong to see in his reflections the unfolding of a consistent, "philosophic" line of thought; what is in fact conveyed is the fluctuation of feeling in response to the contradictory and frustrating impulses of emotion. Ostensibly, indeed, the soliloquy presents an incitement to action. "To be or not to be": in other words, to act or not to act, for action is the necessary confirmation of being, even—so Hamlet initially appears to propose to himself—when it has become the act of self-destruction. If all action in life has been made to appear senseless, there may even be an attraction, a kind of *nobility* ("whether 'tis *nobler* . . ."), in the act of killing oneself to escape this necessary senselessness:

> To die: to sleep;
> No more; and by a sleep to say we end
> The heart-ache, and the thousand natural shocks
> That flesh is heir to, 'tis a consummation
> Devoutly to be wish'd. (III. i)

Here, if anywhere, we have the play's nearest approach to a "romantic" Hamlet, a Hamlet who considers, nostalgically and with a certain complaisance, the prospect of annihilation as release, restful abdication from the need to make senseless decisions and to undertake useless and equivocal duties.

The best comment on the "nobility" of this resolve is that it does not maintain itself. In what follows, Hamlet's reflections, though he still attempts to present them to himself as rationally persuasive, turn into the expression of a flawed and disaffected consciousness:

> To die, to sleep,
> To sleep, perchance to dream; ay, there's the rub. (III. i)

Brusquely interrupted by this sharp recall to reality, as it cuts across the accumulated nostalgia of the preceding lines, Hamlet's meditations turn once again to dwell upon the all too human and tangible causes of his disaffection. The long and laboriously built-up list of indignities to which he now gives free rein—

> the whips and scorns of time,
> The oppressor's wrong, the proud man's contumely,
> The pangs of despised love, the law's delay,
> The insolence of office, and the spurns
> That patient merit of the unworthy takes— (III. i)

are still intended, by the gathering force of their massed emphasis, to carry him to his self-annihilating decision; but they lead only to a sharp confrontation with the nakedly sensed reality of the instrument of suicide—the "bare bodkin"—and stand revealed by the end of the speech as expressions not of determination, but of his innate desire to regard *all* action as inescapably flawed.

Under the impulse of these somber reflections Hamlet's thought turns back upon itself in the direction of the obscure stagnation which is finally congenial to his nature. After recognizing the existence of a "dread" of "something" beyond definition, some dark and indefinitely menacing reality concealed in the aftermath of annihilation, the pressure of emotion gathers momentum, emotional commitment, in the carry-over of the period which evokes

> The undiscovered country from whose bourn
> No traveller returns, (III. i)

only to be pulled up yet again in the brief and vivid phrase "*puzzles* the will," where the emphasis is set plainly and tensely upon personal disorientation. In this way, a response to the rhythmic development of the soliloquy allows us to feel the successive stages by which real uncertainty overcomes the initial show of resolve, by which "conscience"—or self-awareness—supports intimate disorientation, and by which a "cast of thought" recognized to be "pale" and ineffectual ends by tainting—the implication of infirmity in "sicklied o'er" is full of meaning in its relation to the imagery of disease which so abounds throughout the play—what Hamlet, as a rational human being capable of "nobility," needs to consider "the native hue of resolution." In the absence of inner consistency "enterprises" potentially of supreme value as acts of decisive self-affirmation ("of great pith and moment") fade from their illusory attraction,

turn away
And lose the name of action. (III. i)

In this speech, significantly placed at the very heart of Hamlet's tragedy, the possibilities of verse as an immediate reflection of inner tensions are exploited as never before in Shakespeare's work. The conflicts in his mind, far from being merely arguments or even statements of a clear-cut moral dilemma, are revealed as states of conscience in the very act of seeking self-definition, subjected to the ebb and flow of a constantly shifting and developing emotion.

The various strands of intrigue which have been used to explore Hamlet's malady and its relation to "the state of Denmark" are finally brought together in the play scene (III. ii). This, by re-enacting the past, recalls the occasion of the corruption which now covers the entire action with its ramifications. Above all, it shatters the appearance of royal self-control which Claudius has so far presented to the world—like a painted mask covering the reality beneath—and brings to the surface the split which his guilty act first introduced into his conscience. Immediately after the end of the play episode, we see him striving impossibly to pray, caught in an awareness of his state, but unable—like Macbeth after him—to retreat from the position in which he has placed himself:

O limed soul, that struggling to be free,
Art more engaged! (III. iii)

The contamination produced by association with Claudius' rule affects to some degree all those who surround him, so that none—from the moment of his self-betrayal—can live at ease with himself or his surroundings. All of them, indeed, are involved through Hamlet's bitter asides in the falsity, the inner hollowness, of the central situation. The appearance of ordered peace hitherto offered by his uncle's rule having been finally destroyed, his nephew is ready to probe ever deeper into the corruption which surrounds him and which, as we have seen, ultimately covers the central action as a reflection of his own state.

If the scenes which lead up to the play episode are concentrated upon it, as upon a central point of focus, those which follow expand from it as consequences of the situation which it has revealed. The next decisive moment is represented by Hamlet's interview with his mother (III. iv). This penetrates more deeply than ever before into the roots of the disease which, emanating from Hamlet himself, expands from his wounded nature to cover the entire action. The sense of his mother's guilt in relation to his uncle has been from the first a pervasive though imperfectly defined presence in Hamlet's mind. Only now, however, after the situation revealed by the Ghost has been confirmed, is he ready for a direct attack upon it. The attack opens, after the elimination of Polonius—dismissed as "a wretched, rash, intruding fool," an irrelevant intruder who has so far merely obscured the central clash of "mighty opposites"[12]—with a contrast that can be linked significantly to Hamlet's first soliloquy. "Look here," he tells Gertrude, "upon this picture, and on this":

> The counterfeit presentment of two brothers.
> See what a grace was seated on this brow;
> Hyperion's curls, the front of Jove himself,
> An eye like Mars, to threaten and command;
> A station like the herald Mercury
> New-lighted on a heaven-kissing hill;
> A combination and a form indeed,
> Where every god did seem to set his seal
> To give the world assurance of a man:
> This was your husband. Look you now, what follows;
> Here is your husband; like a mildew'd ear
> Blasting his wholesome brother. Have you eyes?
> Could you on this fair mountain leave to feed,
> And batten on this moor? (III. iv)

The point of this contrast can only be understood after due appreciation of its linguistic qualities; for, as so often occurs in this play, what is stated is not in perfect accord with the manner of its expression. Ostensibly the passage contrasts two realities, one uniformly perfect, the other equally uniformly corrupt; but a careful reading will show that, while the corruption is indeed beyond question, its presence is not entirely without relation to the perfection set against it. That the representation of the two brothers should be described as a "counterfeit" already indicates that Hamlet, even as he elaborates his comparison, is following his familiar course of loading it with an ambiguous content that reflects his own instability. The son presents his father's memory in terms of literary comparisons of classical origin—Hyperion, Jove, Mars, Mercury[13]—and the result is a perfection abstractly, decoratively conceived. Memory, indeed, is thin, transient, so that if his father lives still in Hamlet's mind, it is in the main nostalgically, because his "wholesomeness" —the word has also been used before[14]—represents at best a distant aspiration to set against the presence, active and sensibly conceived, of corruption. It is only when we pass from the dead father to the living uncle that the force of direct expression is felt in the image of the "mildew'd ear," in the positive power of "blasting," and in the implications, so often paralleled in *Troilus and Cressida,* of "feed" and "batten." The speaker's mind is clearly involved in distinguishing between abstract perfection and concrete deficiency, between a spiritual concept precariously projected into literary imagery and a sense of corruption, ultimately physical in its expression, as pervasive as it is disturbing.

This sense of frustration, of an inability to impose his idealism upon reality, is no doubt connected with the cruel, destructive tone of Hamlet's moralizing. This cruelty, the product of a kind of inverted self-indulgence, indicates once more the presence of a rooted spiritual infirmity; and in giving rein to it, his emotions induce in those around him the disintegration of their seeming integrity by exposure to the stresses present in their own natures. As he arraigns Gertrude, Hamlet at once leaves her hopelessly divided—that is implied in her exclamation, "O Hamlet, thou hast cleft my heart in twain!"—and, under the guise of performing a salutary act of moral surgery, finds a certain savage satisfaction in exposing further the roots of the division in his own soul. The presence of the "flesh" as an object of loathing which weighs upon his consciousness inspires, at least as much as it proceeds from, his revulsion against his mother's "incest":

Rebellious hell,
If thou canst mutine in a matron's bones,
To flaming youth let virtue be as wax
And melt in her own fire; proclaim no shame
When the compulsive ardour gives the charge,
Since frost itself as actively doth burn,
And reason panders will. (III. iv)

The sources of Hamlet's disgust, here as always, are intimate rather than external, moved by the tension within himself which divides flesh from spirit, leaving the latter, as in *Troilus,* thin, abstract, and disembodied, but expressing the former with a force and consistency of repudiation unequaled in the more abstractly conceived play. When he proceeds to accuse Gertrude of living in "the rank sweat of an enseamed bed," of being

> Stew'd in corruption, honeying and making love
> Over the nasty sty,

we must feel at once that there is something excessive about the emotion conveyed, that its roots lie not in the external facts of Hamlet's situation, but in an intense distortion, imperfectly understood by the speaker himself (and perhaps by his creator) within his own experience.

Once again we have touched upon that discrepancy, so to call it, between the inner emotion and its dramatic manifestation which is so persistently to be felt in *Hamlet*. The "nasty sty" is not primarily the reality that underlies the marriage of Claudius and Gertrude, but the conviction, produced by the stress of imperfectly balanced feelings, that the unsavory quality of this particular relationship covers a universal human weakness. Dramatically speaking, no doubt the emotion is not fully dominated, projected into the external action; and yet, as we compare this utterance with its parallels in *Troilus and Cressida*, we must feel the advance in *weight*, in concrete reference, to be as notable as it is disturbing. In *Troilus*, the flesh is felt only in separation, in the frustration of a disembodied desire. In *Hamlet* this subsidiary presence of the flesh is in process of becoming an essential element in experience; its immediate relevance is felt in new linguistic power, in a subjection to ends which, if still in some respects incoherent, are truly representative of the sonnet artifice the other play never entirely loses. Reason, which one side of Hamlet's nature wishes to see allied to the natural human functions in action, takes the form of a loathing of all bodily contacts, leaves the field open, by its withdrawal into a disembodied "spirituality," for a repudiation, itself pervertedly sensuous, of the life of the senses. The feeling thus expressed brings to a head reactions spread through the play in the form of a bitter preoccupation with physical decay: "The sun *breeds maggots* in a dead dog, being *a god kissing carrion*" (II. ii). The mention of "god" is to be associated with the same "god-like" reason which, as the force of "breed" indicates, serves in Hamlet's mind only to pander to the lust-inflamed will.

Thus far, the course of this tragedy can be conceived as corresponding less to a consecutive series of events moving logically toward an appointed end (in the manner of Shakespeare's mature plays) than as a succession of attempts at self-clarification on the part of the hero, each of which culminates in an analytic soliloquy and reaches out, as it were, to seek illumination through relation to the surrounding world. Self-clarification, however, is conceived as a necessary prelude to action: in this case the filial duty exacted from Hamlet by his father's Ghost. Hamlet's concern with action, upon which his dilemma is finally concentrated, is most fully developed, immediately after his confrontation with his mother, in the course of his meditations upon the martial enterprise of Fortinbras (IV. iv). It is essential to realize that Hamlet, following one of the principal convictions of traditional thought, regards action as natural to the rational and undivided personality. The ability to act is the mark of "god-like" reason in man, the chief sign of his superiority over the "beast," whose only concern is "to sleep and feed." There is, in other words, no question of the rightness or otherwise of revenge. Hamlet's task chiefly interests Shakespeare as an act which requires the unity of purpose and sentiment in a harmonious personality. But, as the entire action shows, it is precisely the lack of this union which constitutes Hamlet's problem. In his own inaction he is moved to envy Fortinbras ("a most delicate and tender prince": we can feel the lightness, the spontaneity of the verse in contrast to the speaker's own clogged doubts), but with an envy which turns to criticism almost imperceptibly in the course of the expression. If the soldiers before him are moved by what Hamlet recognizes to be "*divine* ambition" ("*divine* ambition": "god-like reason"; the parallel is not without significance), it is nonetheless to be noted that they are "puffed" by its presence in them—the word carries a suggestion of vanity and inflation—so that we are prepared, in Hamlet's following meditations, to coincide with him in seeing them as absurdly "making mouths at the invisible event," grotesquely agitating themselves, with a vain conviction, for a mere "egg-shell."

Thus far the criticism, expressed in verse which reflects the shifting consciousness of the speaker, has followed the lines of Falstaff's attitude toward "honour."[15] The next sentence, however, while it continues the train of thought, turns upon an ambiguity which involves a further complication of feeling:

> Rightly to be great
> Is not to stir without great argument,
> But greatly to find quarrel in a straw
> When honour's at the stake. (IV. iv)

The two statements thus combined have the appearance of a noble and consistent attitude based on "honour," but they are actually in virtual contradiction. Reason, it is suggested, does not allow a man to act except upon a sufficient cause, upon the foundation of "great argument"; but "honour," based on natural feeling, insists that it is right and noble to act "greatly," with magnanimity, even when "reason" has concluded that the ground for action is an inadequate "straw." Falstaff's realistic skepticism has, in short, been taken up into a mood at once deeper and less conclusive, based no longer on the detached observation of reality but upon an intimate sense of conflict. "Honour," satirically conceived in the earlier comic spirit, has now become a necessary good, an incentive to action of a kind with which Falstaff had never been concerned; but, in the mood in which Hamlet considers it, it is also less than acceptable to reason. The two contrary attitudes, thus assumed into a single character, constitute the basis of the tragic discord.

The expression of this dilemma gives a fuller meaning to the general definition attempted in the opening lines:

> What is a man,
> If his chief good and market of his time
> Be but to sleep and feed? a beast, no more.
> Sure, he that made us with such large discourse,
> Looking before and after, gave us not
> That capability and god-like reason
> To fust in us unused. (IV. iv)

The argument seems simple enough, but once more the expression of it suggests rather a conflict of feeling than the triumphant demonstration of a truth rationally established. The sense of man's nobility, his "large discourse" and "god-like" reason, is balanced by the sluggishness of "sleep" and "feed" (we are reminded of the food imagery so prominent in *Troilus and Cressida*) and still more by the contrary implications of "beast" and the musty vanity of "fust." The intensity with which these words underline the note of stagnation forbids us to pass them by; they are the key to the emotional undercurrents which dominate the speech. It is Hamlet's desire to see action and its rational sanction fused in "god-like" action. The exercise of reason, however, produces an exactly contrary effect to that which is declared to be its proper end. Instead of justifying, it convinces the speaker of the uselessness of the action proposed to him; he has to choose between action, which is natural and in itself desirable, but—to the eye of reason—"*gross* as earth,"[16] and rational thought, which is "divine," but leads, in the speaker's disaffected state, merely to immobility.

By this stage in the play the divisions in Hamlet's own nature are amply reflected in the surrounding action. The last scenes, indeed, are less the logical working out of a dramatic process than the revelation of a complete disintegration. With the apparent self-control of Claudius visibly broken, Polonius eliminated, and Gertrude divided against herself, infection is spreading through the Danish court like a stain; its next advance involves Ophelia. Gertrude and Ophelia, indeed, occupy in *Hamlet* an intermediate position which turns finally into their peculiar tragedy. Bound simultaneously to the corrupt royalty of Claudius, Gertrude by marriage and Ophelia as the daughter of his instrument Polonius, and to Hamlet as mother and lover respectively, the growth of palpable division within the state is reflected in their intimate disunion. Gertrude, like Claudius himself, though in a subsidiary sense, is subjected to an inner conflict beyond all possible resolution; Ophelia is driven to a madness which is the true counterpart of that feigned by Hamlet, and which has for its elements sorrow at her father's death and a sense of personal betrayal. Her innocence, the product of a calculated sheltering from the world, is finally brought into touch with death and with its visible manifestation—corruption in the "cold ground" (Hamlet's irony, too, has dwelt insistently on "the convocation of politic worms" at work on the body of Polonius)—at the same time that her shattered integrity reveals itself in the form of equivocal songs. The final account, by Gertrude, of her suicide mingles innocent beauty with artifice, the sad virginity implied in "cold maids" with the "*grosser* name" given to the flowers of nature by "*liberal* shepherds." The whole description, moreover, is involved, as befits the victim, in a sense of elegiac helplessness:

long it could not be
Till that her garments, heavy with their drink,
Pull'd the poor wretch from her melodious lay
To muddy death. (IV. vii)

That even innocence should find its pathos expressed through artifice is indeed typical of the spirit, ambiguous and, to use one of its own characteristic expressions, "muddied," impure, which has now taken possession of the play.

During these later scenes, the corruption in which the whole of Denmark is involved is exposed in all its ramifications. Claudius, acutely aware of himself as surrounded by the suspicions of the people,

> *muddied,*
> *Thick*, and *unwholesome,* in their thoughts and whispers
> For good Polonius' death, (IV. v)

also sees in the "secret" return of Laertes another stirring of violent, youthful "blood" in the infected body of his state. The idea of infection is now obsessively present in his utterances. Of his supposed "indulgence" to Hamlet, he says:

> so much was our love,
> We would not understand what was most fit,
> But, like the owner of *a foul disease,*
> *To keep it from divulging, let it feed*
> *Even on the pith of life.* (IV. i)

This intimation of infirmity can be supported by his further comment on his own state:

> diseases desperate grown,
> By desperate appliances are relieved,
> Or not at all, (IV. iii)

and, most significantly of all, by his own definition of his relation to Hamlet:

> like the hectic in my blood he rages,
> And thou must cure me. (IV. iii)

The bond which unites these "mighty opposites" so closely in their common tragedy, and which is now approaching its final resolution in death, is nowhere more exactly stated. Claudius' final intrigues, indeed,—the dispatch of Hamlet to England, the use of Polonius' death and Ophelia's tragic end to involve Laertes in a web of intrigue—are no more than attempts to conceal what the remorseless development of events is already revealing, to cover the "imposthume" of his own state, from which that of Denmark derives, by extending the area of the disease. His devices, however, like the state of mind which produced them, hopelessly divided against itself, are finally deprived of all true conviction.

Something not very different can be said, at this stage, of Hamlet himself. When he returns for the final reckoning, he does so in a state that is, in one sense, a reflection of clarity achieved—for the subsidiary issues of the action, personified in Rosencrantz and Guildenstern, in Polonius, even in Ophelia, all instruments of the central corruption which emanates from his uncle's power, have been cleared away—but with a lack of belief in the efficacy of his personal intervention which proceeds finally from his sense that the disease he aims at curing is intimately related to his own state. The king will die, because death is the end to which his nature tends, and Gertrude too will be carried away by the intrigue in which her own weakness has involved her; but restoration cannot be personified in Hamlet, who is himself mortally affected. His return is from the first involved in death—he reappears in a cemetery and struggles vainly with Laertes in Ophelia's grave (V. i)—and the final resolution which fate puts into his hands is surrounded by obscurity and misunderstanding. Claudius, intending to poison him, in fact poisons Gertrude; Laertes, hoping to avenge his father's death, is caught in the trap he has agreed to lay for his enemy; and Hamlet himself only carries out the Ghost's command after he has realized that he is himself finally, inescapably involved in the pattern of death which has woven itself round his person. The whole of the last scene represents rather the final working out of a mortal process of disease than the triumphant execution of a natural duty. It is as though the poison originally poured by Claudius into his brother's ear, like

> a most instant tetter, barkt about,
> Most lazar-like, with vile and loathsome crust, (I. v)

has extended its action from the "smooth body" of Hamlet's father to cover the entire court of Denmark grouped for death round the infected person of its usurping king.

In this way the last scene reflects the spirit which, in greater or less degree, has prevailed throughout the play. Hamlet's efforts to follow the course of duty have been throughout obstructed by an inner conflict, a settled disgust, the true extent of which is only gradually revealed in the course of the action. This conflict, or disgust, is spread through the entire tragedy, into which it instills a pervasive, violent poison, associated in some degree with the disorder of the "blood" in and through which it works. The poison is present in all the protagonists and in the state which is their common environment; but it works always *from within* outward, revealing its full power to destroy in the course of its development. It is supremely present beneath the suave surface of Claudius, whose usurped authority is undermined in the course of the play by guilt and fear; but it is also present in Gertrude, whose weakness has led to the marriage which her son, finding in it an exterior projection of his inner disgust, regards as "incestuous." It can be found in the senile self-regard of Polonius, more especially in his attitude toward youth and passion, and eventually breaks through to the surface in the madness of the shattered Ophelia; Laertes, the representative of hot, idle youth, shares it, and so does even the active, confident Fortinbras in his irresponsible military adventures. Above all, it is present in Hamlet himself, whose actions throughout are peculiarly calculated to bring about its exposure in those around him. By the end of the play Hamlet has revealed all the evils which surround him and has shown them to be variously, if obscurely, related to the stresses, which constitute the real center of the tragedy, in his own soul. By bringing them to the light, and by finally carrying out as a passive instrument the mission imposed upon him, he leads those who surround him, with himself, to the death that is their common end. The spirit of this tragedy is still involved in contradiction, still imperfect in its clarity of conception; but never so far in Shakespeare's work has an emotional situation been so variously reflected in an elaborate dramatic action. The fact is of decisive importance for an understanding of the dramatist's complete development.[17]

MEASURE FOR MEASURE

Few of Shakespeare's plays have given rise to more contrasted interpretations than *Measure for Measure*. Most of the difficulties derive ultimately from the discrepancy which is generally felt to exist between the play's formal assumptions and a prevailing spirit which is, for the greater part of its development, notably incompatible with them. Formally speaking, *Measure for Measure* is a comedy, and as such dedicated to a reconciling and harmonizing conclusion, which is indeed worked out with considerable ingenuity in the long and intricate final scene. The most individual episodes, on the other hand, are notably uncomic, dedicated not to reconciliation but to the exploration of insoluble conflicts and somber moral realities. The preoccupation with the flesh, already present as one element among many in *Hamlet*, acquires greater weight and consistency in *Measure for Measure*, and to it corresponds a "law" which is "reason" made more personal, more immediately realized in answer to a more concrete sense of moral realities.

The need for constant moral standards, and for their enforcement by the civil power, is the starting point of the action. It is to strengthen this enforcement that the Duke, at the beginning of the play, calls upon Angelo to replace him; and even Claudio, who is most interested in the loosening of bonds that condemn him to immediate death, agrees that the sentence passed upon him is just. His plight, he tells Lucio, proceeds

> From too much liberty, my Lucio, liberty;
> As surfeit is the father of much fast,
> So every scope by the immoderate use
> Turns to restraint. Our natures do pursue,
> Like rats that ravin down their proper bane,
> A thirsty evil; and when we drink we die. (I. ii)

Claudio's words, however, do more than confirm the necessary severity of the law. Their apparent directness is capable of sustaining the weight of the moral contradiction upon which the whole play turns. The linguistic power of *Measure for Measure,* far from expanding easily into lyricism or rhetoric, is subordinated to a supple bareness and concentrated most often upon an intense underlining of the value of single words. This does not mean that the effect is necessarily simple. No word in Claudio's speech is logically superfluous, but more than one is, in its context, surprising. The verb "ravin," for instance, suggests bestial, immoderate feeding, and so "appetite," but the next line proceeds, through a "thirsty evil," to transfer the metaphor to drinking; the shift of the image and the sharp focusing of impressions by which it is accompanied are characteristic of Shakespeare's mature art. The effect is to transfer attention almost imperceptibly from the idea of Claudio's condemnation to another which, without directly questioning the first, yet profoundly modifies it. The repellent impression summoned up by "ravin" and maintained by the reference, at once contemptuous and loathing, to "rats" is unobtrusively transformed into an evocation of natural thirst; the evil remains, and is uncondoned, but its relation to the normal human situation has gone through a decisive change. The whole passage, indeed, is designed to stress the deep-seated contradiction involved in the very nature of passion. Human nature, Claudio says, is driven to pursue the object of its desire like a rat whose natural, or "proper," thirst impels it to swallow the "bane" which must inevitably, once swallowed, kill it. Passion, indeed, coveted and pursued in full "liberty" beyond the limits of the moral law, leads fatally to destruction; but—and here Shakespeare restores the balance necessary to his conception—it is a bane *proper* to humanity, which craves free satisfaction as the thirsty animal craves for water and which man cannot therefore, even if he should so desire, hope to suppress.

The reservations implied in Claudio's confession of guilt gain fresh power, a little further on, from one of the few speeches in *Measure for Measure* in which strong and simple emotion triumphs over the discipline habitually imposed upon it. When Lucio brings news of Claudio's arrest to Isabella, he describes her brother's sin in lines where intensity of feeling breaks with tremendous effect through the deliberate, restrained tonelessness of so much of this play:

> Your brother and his lover have embraced:
> As those that feed grow full: as blossoming time,
> That from the seedness the bare fallow brings
> To teeming foison; even so her plenteous womb
> Expresseth his full tilth and husbandry. (I. iv)

The writing of such a speech implies new possibilities in Shakespeare's art. Not only are various of its images vastly developed in *King Lear* and later plays, but the very movement of the verse is more rich and complex in the command of words behind "seed*ness*" and "*plenteous* womb," in the concentration that can use both "feed" and "husbandry" to express the fertility of passion. The effect is to give to the natural instinct behind Claudio's sin a full and triumphant expression. The bane is, after all, inescapably "proper" to humanity. His love for Juliet, expressly related to the fullness of the harvest and to the physical satisfaction that follows eating, is as inevitable as the return of the fertile "blossoming time" to the dead, bare fallow; and, like that return, it is life-giving, "plenteous," "teeming." In the light of the undeniable vitality so expressed, the problem of "liberty" in its relation to the moral order acquires a new urgency. It represents an intuition which must not indeed overstep the restraining limits of the law but which must somehow, in the interests of harmony, be freely incorporated in them.

The balance thus held in the individual utterance is consistently maintained in Shakespeare's presentation of life in Vienna. The life of the city is based upon the natural order uncurbed by any reference to the moral law; the Duke himself, we are told, has withdrawn into the cultivation of his personal interests, allowing common life to develop in accordance with its own instincts. The result has been an unchecked spread of what the moral law condemns as vice and this spread is associated, in the realistic scenes presenting the street life of the city, with corruption and death. Vienna is undermined by decay, and the imagery of venereal disease dominates Shakespeare's presentation of its life. The jesting conversation of the courtiers and men of the world in this play turns insistently, even monotonously, upon the threat of sexual disease; but beneath the levity which springs from long familiarity there appears a deeper note of fear. The courtiers of Vienna and the parasites who prey upon them are aware of the frightening moral emptiness which their maladies imply. When one of his friends observes to Lucio, "Thou art always figuring diseases in me; but thou art full of error—I am sound," he replies, with at least a hint of the profound religious seriousness which animates this play: "Nay, not as one would say, healthy; but so sound as things that are hollow: thy bones are hollow; impiety has made a feast of thee" (I. ii). Beneath this hollowness, which is more than physical, lies that fear of death which is in *Measure for Measure* the beginning of wisdom.

Here too, however, there is another side to the picture. The "bane" that has poisoned Viennese society is still, to return to Claudio's key phrase, "proper" to it. It is still a consequence, however tainted by human perversity, of natural human failings. This is a fact with which the law itself must eventually come to terms. The examination of the bawd, Pompey, by Escalus, the representative of the Duke's justice, sets before us in concrete form some of the intricacies which human nature imposes upon the necessary administration of justice. Pompey, when challenged, makes no attempt to deny his trade. He simply denies the utility of trying to suppress it. "Truly, sir," he says, "I am a poor fellow that would live." The discussion that follows proceeds in the most direct and telling simplicity:

> *Escalus:* How would you live, Pompey? by being a bawd? What do you think of the trade, Pompey? is it a lawful trade?
> *Pompey:* If the law would allow it, sir.
> *Escalus:* But the law will not allow it, Pompey; nor it shall not be allowed in Vienna.
> *Pompey:* Does your lordship mean to geld and splay all the youth of the city? (II. i)

The point is crudely, even cruelly made, but its implications are tremendously serious. To re-establish the law in Vienna is, as we have seen, vitally necessary. Failure to deal with the diseases of which Pompey is a symptom involves the collapse of society under the double burden of physical disease and moral dissolution. Yet upon what human instinct, if Pompey is right, can the law be based? For Pompey, and for the great unconscious mass of humanity, the law is no more than a matter of verbal caprice. The trade of bawd is "unlawful" in Pompey's eyes, not because it degrades man's true dignity, but simply because the law in its mysteriousness "will not allow it." To find for the law a necessary sanction in experience without depriving it of the firmness and impartiality upon which its maintenance depends is the task which ultimately faces the Duke in *Measure for Measure*.

Before he has gained the experience necessary to carry it out, however, the Duke has to learn from two simplified solutions of the moral problem. His own error has been an excessive faith in "liberty," in permitting human instincts to grow uncurbed until they threatened to undermine the fabric of society. His abdication, besides clearing the way for Angelo's rigid enforcement of the letter of the law, brings him into contact, through Isabella, with a virtue whose perfection implies a complete withdrawal from human affairs. Both Angelo and Isabella have their own way of imposing "law" upon the flesh: ways which are found to be inadequate and, indeed, by a strange irony, mutually destructive, but through the contemplation of which the Duke gains at least some of the understanding upon which true justice rests.

The attempt to enforce the law by delegating authority to Angelo fails. It fails ultimately because of the deputy's lack of self-knowledge. Angelo believes that he has, by the force of his own virtue, dominated passion, whereas in reality he has simply passed it by. Lucio, whose remarks are so often revealing, describes him as a man whose blood is "very snow-broth," who "rebates and blunts" his "*natural* edge"—the adjective is important—by opposing to it an abstract discipline conceived in "the mind," in "study and fast," and ultimately powerless before what Escalus calls "the resolute acting of the blood" (II. i); his inexperience is enough to disqualify him as a lawgiver. That is what is implied in the offhand and unsubstantiated claim with which he backs his rejection of Escalus' plea for Claudio:

> You may not so extenuate his offence,
> For I have had such faults. (II. i)

Angelo condemns Claudio in reality because he finds his crime inconceivable, and for the same reason he eventually falls. Self-deception, however, is only the first stage in his progress. The ignorance upon which his virtue is so precariously based can turn, with catastrophic suddenness, into the complications of vice.

Measure for Measure is not the only play in which Shakespeare suggests the possibility of a development of this kind. In the preoccupation which other plays reveal with the conflict between passion and controlling reason, his heroes are often moved to admire the man who seems to have dominated his lower instincts. "Give me"—says Hamlet to Horatio—"that man that is not passion's slave" (III. ii); and his desire is simply an extension into the personal sphere of Ulysses' abstract insistence upon "degree." Yet here too there is another side of the picture. Reason that is not fully harmonized with a rich and free emotional life may easily become an imposition concealing every kind of dangerous thwarted instinct; and *Measure for Measure* is only one of several plays written at this time in which Shakespeare concerns himself with situations where that balance is difficult to maintain. The man born free of passion is evidently to be admired and envied; but his freedom may imply a coldness, an indifference to feeling that only partially covers latent impulses of cruelty and domination. The position is perhaps most clearly stated in a famous sonnet:

They that have power to hurt and will do none,
That do not do the thing they most do show,
Who moving others, are themselves as stone,
Unmoving, cold, and to temptation slow;
They rightly do inherit heaven's graces . . . (Sonnet XCIV)

The application to Angelo is obvious. In him too there is a stony virtue which depends upon the innate sluggishness of the blood, upon the fact that he has been from birth "cold" and "to temptation slow." More important still, he has "power to hurt" and exercises it implacably against Claudio; and, most significantly of all, the blamelessness upon which his claim to judge rests is a deception, a concealment of deeper and more unrealized instincts. Angelo, like the man in the sonnet, does not do the thing he most does show. The deception is not less dangerous for being, at the outset, unconscious. Indeed, it is more dangerous, for the ignorance that covers it makes it peculiarly liable to perversion. Angelo's control is of the kind that can turn, almost without warning, into a desire for domination which aims in complete ruthlessness at the goal appointed by his lower instincts.

This is precisely what happens when he meets Isabella. When he finally becomes aware of his feelings toward her he expresses himself in terms which are pregnant with sexuality and self-will:

I have begun;
And now I give my sensual race the rein;
Fit thy consent to my sharp appetite;
Lay by all nicety and prolixious blushes,
That banish what they sue for; redeem thy brother
By yielding up thy body to my will. (II. iv)

The most remarkable thing about this speech of Angelo's is the completeness with which it accepts, and makes its own, the impulse to recognized evil. For it is not sufficient to say that Angelo is weak-willed or that his normal self-control has been undermined by irrational forces. It is rather that the passion to which he has denied all natural expression has now taken complete control of his will, which reveals itself as forcibly in the direction of carnal desire as it had previously been affirmed in moral rigor and "firm abstinence." Thus impelled, it proceeds, by a remorseless internal logic which will become more and more characteristic of Shakespeare's tragic figures, along the road that leads to destruction.

Isabella's virtue, though standing at the other extreme from Angelo's, is related to it by a common foundation in inexperience. When the play opens, she is about to take her vows of profession as a nun. The fact is in itself significant. Virtue in *Measure for Measure* is habitually on its guard, defending itself by withdrawal against the temptations that so insistently beset it. Isabella's opening exchange with the nun who accompanies her stresses the note of retreat and mortification. Considering the rules to which she is shortly to submit herself, she desires an even stricter seclusion from the world:

Isabella: And have you nuns no farther privileges?
Francisca: Are not these large enough?
Isabella: Yes, truly. I speak not as desiring more;
But rather wishing a more strict restraint
Upon the sisterhood, the votarists of Saint Clare. (I. iv)

It is significant too, in view of all that is to follow, that Francisca goes on to emphasize one particular feature of the enclosure:

When you have vow'd, you must not speak with men,
But in the presence of the prioress;
Then, if you speak, you must not show your face. (I. iv)

To grasp the spirit in which this retirement is conceived, we must see it in relation to the necessity for enforcing the law at any cost. Virtue and chastity need to be restored in a world where every unrestrained instinct threatens to violate them; and just as the lawgiver must defend them by imposing "The needful bits and curbs to headstrong weeds,"[18] so must the individual preserve them in himself even at the cost of renouncing a society which seems to incline almost universally to corruption. Isabella, by entering the convent, is simply carrying to its logical extreme the fulfillment of a moral duty.

Mere restraint, however, is not in her case enough. Before she can take her vows, human claims of a kind which no exclusion can solve call her away from the cloister. Lucio brings the news that her brother, at the point of death, places his last hope in her intervention. The terms in which this hope is expressed by Claudio himself are an indication of the hazards, so far unsuspected by Isabella, which beset virtue in this play:

> bid herself assay him:
> I have great hope in that; for in her youth
> There is a prone and speechless dialect,
> Such as move men; besides, she hath prosperous art
> When she will play with reason and discourse,
> And well she can persuade. (I. ii)

The qualities upon which Claudio relies are not, typically enough, those of simple virtue. In his view, at least, his sister can "play with reason" and mold the wills of men subtly—even if innocently, in complete unconsciousness of artifice—to her purpose. Most significantly of all, her main power lies in the "prone and speechless" attractions—there is even a faint suggestion of invitation and artful passivity in the adjectives—of her youthful person. It is not of course that she is dishonest or that she sets out to appeal deliberately to Angelo's baser instincts. It is simply that she is a woman and that therefore her power over men, which she has yet to begin to understand, is bound to become a temptation. If Isabella's virtue does not fully satisfy, that is not primarily through any obvious moral deficiency in her own nature (though attempts have been made to find one) but simply because the state of simple virtue does not exist in *Measure for Measure.* Chastity there is surrounded by reservations not of its own making, flaws related to the flesh and inherent in the human situation. If Isabella has any fault, it is that she is unaware of these flaws and reservations. Her retirement is too simple, her virtue too little grounded in experience to correspond to the spirit in which this play is conceived. In the very readiness with which she accepts the mission that Lucio urges upon her—

> Commend me to my brother: soon at night
> I'll send him certain word of my success— (I. iv)[19]

there is, besides proper feeling for her brother, a touch of inexperience that will eventually lead her into a situation with which she is in some respects unqualified to deal. It is certain that the path to Claudio's salvation will be longer and harder than she yet realizes.

The two scenes which portray the encounter between Angelo and Isabella (II. ii, iv) owe much of their effect to the fact that each is peculiarly fitted to bring out the weakness of the other. The first is devoted substantially to the downfall of Angelo. His utterances, short and ambiguous in her presence, become after her departure charged with the imagery of desire:

> she speaks, and 'tis
> Such sense, that my sense breeds with it.
>
> The tempter or the tempted, who sins most?
> Not she, nor doth she tempt, but it is I
> That, lying by the violet in the sun,
> Do as the carrion does, not as the flower,
> Corrupt with virtuous season. Can it be
> That modesty may more betray our sense
> Than woman's lightness? Having waste ground enough,
> Shall we desire to raze the sanctuary,
> And pitch our evils there? (II. ii)

The peculiar verbal texture of these speeches is already familiar in works of this period. The play, in the first tentative aside, on the double meaning of "sense"—"sense" as "meaning" or "understanding" and "sense" as "sensuality"—conveys perfectly the half-conscious process by which Angelo's self-control has been undermined; the type of ambiguity so prominent in the more analytic sonnets is being effectively projected into a personal and dramatic situation. The opening lines of the later speech, in turn, clearly recall the "god kissing carrion" of *Hamlet* and, perhaps even more clearly, the "lilies that fester" of the sonnet. Compression in the syntax is once more a sign of emotional pressure, though still scarcely understood by the speaker. Angelo does not pause to develop the comparison between "I" and the "carrion"; he gives them simultaneous existence in a single image which brings out, in the first dim moment of realization, the significance of his new state. His will, clarifying its sinister purpose in the very process of expression, reveals itself as a destructive instinct perversely incited by the mere presence of virtue to the satisfaction of its corrupt desires. The "carrion" element of passion, always present beneath his modesty, is breaking out in a form even more dangerous than the evils he had so confidently undertaken to suppress.

The connection between Angelo's "foulness" and its opposite in Isabella is the key to all that follows. Having abandoned himself to his instincts, he proceeds at their next meeting to work upon her with consummate dialectic skill. Desire, far from undermining his intelligence, sharpens it, gives it fresh power to penetrate and destroy. When he repeats his sentence, she takes her stand on the contrast between the absolute claim of the law and the pitiful incapacity of its human instruments. "'Tis set so down in heaven, but not in earth" (II. iv). The argument is dangerous because, though just, it can be turned logically against herself. If Claudio's sin is not, at least on earth, beyond forgiveness, if frailty can indeed be an adequate reason for relaxing the severity of the law, then

> Might there not be a charity in sin
> To save this brother's life? (II. iv)

Isabella, still ignorant of the sinister purpose behind all this, falls into the trap. She declares her readiness to take upon herself responsibility for the decision to which she is pressing Angelo:

> Please you to do't,
> I'll take it as a peril to my soul,
> It is no sin at all, but charity. (II. iv)

The exclamation, generous as it is, proves fatal. Isabella's plea, taken up with evil intention, recoils against her own position. If pity is a sufficient reason for relaxing the statutes, she herself can plausibly be summoned to relax them too. The conscience of the lawgiver, if—as Isabella has still every reason to suppose—his intentions are pure, is not necessarily less inviolate than that of the virgin; indeed, if the present state of Vienna is any indication, his responsibility may be greater and the call for firmness more urgent. As Angelo, taking up her very words, at once retorts:

> Pleased *you* to do't at peril of *your* soul,
> Were equal poise of sin and charity. (II. iv)

Angelo does not go so far as to deny that the act which he is about to urge upon Isabella is a sin. He merely shows that the charity upon which she so passionately calls can be invoked against her; events will show how far she can maintain the rigidity of her virtue without sacrificing some of her own humanity.

Isabella, of course, when she has understood the drift of Angelo's proposal, refuses to consider it. She refuses in terms that, besides reflecting the impulsiveness of her character, point to the presence of tense and unrecognized elements, finally not devoid of erotic implications, beneath the emphasis of her repudiation:

> were I under the terms of death,
> The impression of keen whips I'ld wear as rubies,
> And strip myself to death, as to a bed
> That longing have been sick for, ere I'ld yield
> My body up to shame. (II. iv)

It is not necessary to go so far as to find this actually repellent; but it does show a remarkable insight into the psychological pressures that sometimes find issue in the craving for martyrdom and which foreshadow, in the case of Isabella herself, a comprehensible but nonetheless self-centered breakdown into hysteria. When she has finished, Angelo can quietly, logically return to his point:

> You seem'd of late to make the law a tyrant;
> And rather prov'd the sliding of your brother
> A merriment than a vice. (II. iv)

At this point Isabella begins to realize the weakness of her position. She admits as much in her reply—"To have what we would have, we speak not what we mean." This is not the kind of answer likely to dissuade Angelo. "We are all frail," he insists, and once more Isabella falls into the trap laid for her. "Else let my brother die," she exclaims, and Angelo uses her appeal to press home the implications of his original argument. "Nay, women are frail too," he insinuates, and goes on to make his logical deduction:

> Since, I suppose, we are made to be no stronger
> Than faults may shake our frames—let me be bold—
> I do arrest your words. Be that you are,
> That is a woman; if you be more, you're none. (II. iv)

The argument, though perverse, brings out complexities which Isabella is unfitted to recognize. She originally brought forward the admission of man's natural weakness as a reason for relaxing the rigor of the law; Angelo, not less logically, though moved by the selfishness of his own desire, bases upon the very same recognition his demand that she should surrender herself to his will.

What are we to conclude from this? Not certainly that Angelo is right and Isabella wrong. Her main point—the essential distinction between "ignominy in ransom" and the graciousness of "free pardon" —stands, and Angelo's lust is clearly the enemy of virtue. Yet we do wrong, beyond this, to simplify Shakespeare's conception by looking for "solutions" to clear-cut moral problems. The dilemma set before Isabella—to surrender her virginity to buy her brother's life— the play is not primarily concerned to solve; it merely gives her two opposed attachments, both right and both involved in contradiction by an evil quite beyond her control. But, once this has been granted, it is hard not to feel in her virtue at least a touch of willful egoism:

More than our brother is our chastity . . . (II. iv)

Take my defiance!
Die, perish! Might but my bending down
Reprieve thee from thy fate, it should proceed.
I'll pray a thousand prayers for thy death,
No word to save thee. (III. i)

It is not the sentiment that surprises, but the manner of its expression. That Isabella should, in such a case, refuse indignantly is natural; that she should turn upon her brother, accuse him of cowardice and even—as she condemns him to death—cast upon him the shadow of bastardy is less so.[20] The egoism which prompted Angelo to will the evil conceived in his "appetite" is not totally absent from Isabella's defense of her chastity. "Virtue," as each of them conceives it, is still a partial and abstract thing, still an imposition of the reason planted a little aridly upon a whole world of sentiments and reactions which remain outside it and take refuge in the humanity, corrupt and hollow though it be, of Pompey and Lucio. Both lack the self-knowledge that true moral maturity requires. Both are themselves in need of judgment and both, before they can be adequately judged, must be considered in the light of an experience more mature and impartial than their own.

That experience, to the degree in which this play offers it, is provided by the Duke. The figure of the Duke, as Shakespeare conceives him, hesitates between two aspects. He is both inside the action, as the indispensable instrument of a remarkably involved and tortuous plot, and outside it, judging with compassionate detachment the events to which his own abdication has given rise. As a character within the action, the Duke's self-confessed weakness, born though it is of tolerance and the readiness to understand, has contributed to the intolerable state of Viennese society. As a detached "symbol" of truth in judgment, on the other hand, his understanding is presented in a way that tends to affirm it as absolute and perfect. Angelo himself, when finally exposed, ascribes to Vincentio certain attributes of divinity:

O my dread lord,
I should be guiltier than my guiltiness,
To think I can be undiscernible,
When I perceive your grace, *like power divine*,
Hath look'd upon my passes. (V. i)

The transition between these two positions takes place during the course of the action. A retired and even ambiguous figure in the early scenes, the Duke comes forward increasingly as the plot advances. In the later episodes he holds the threads in his hands, directs them, and provides by his observations upon them the most impartial comment. No other Shakespearean character, at this stage in the poet's career, had been conceived with an intention so clearly, if intermittently "symbolic"; it is even possible to think of the Duke, in this light, as a first approximation to Prospero.[21]

The emphasis upon superior detachment must not lead us to think of the Duke's function in terms of providing solutions, more or less clearly defined, to the problems raised in the course of the play. Shakespeare was elaborating a state of experience, not answering an abstract question; and this state was essentially a strife, a disharmony still far from resolution. "Solutions" in Shakespeare are not intellectual statements; they are only apprehensible in a gradual harmonizing of themes, to which the functions of plot and character become increasingly knitted. The contradictory elements of experience are reconciled, if at all, in the process of living them out. The reconciliation toward which they are moved is not imposed in abstraction, but slowly and patiently attained through a steady incorporation of the most diverse elements. In *Measure for Measure,* at any rate, in spite of its "comic" presuppositions, it is still premature to speak of this kind of resolution. The Duke does not, in any primary sense, offer solutions; rather he is steeped in the mystery and obscurity so typical of the play. To Lucio he is "the old fantastical duke *of dark corners*" (IV. iii), and Escalus tells us that he has always been "one that, *above all other strifes,* contended especially *to know himself*" (III. ii). This description is significant. Both Angelo and Isabella have failed in self-knowledge, in awareness of the complex knot of good and evil which centers on human passion. A lawgiver must be aware of this complexity, must seek to harmonize the natural sources of experience with the moral "law." The Duke's own self-knowledge, however, still hangs in the balance. It is still a "strife," a "contention," a matter of working out obscure and even contradictory impulses that refuse, so far, to submit to a common unity. The fact that he exists at all, that Shakespeare was able to conceive a judgment based upon true impartiality, points to the direction in which his interests were moving; but between the conception and such fulfillment of it as was attained in the plays of his later maturity lies the prolonged experience of the tragedies.

The Duke's distinctive contribution to *Measure for Measure* really begins when, having assumed the Friar's role, he confesses Claudio (III. i). He introduces in his great opening speech a fresh fact in relation to which the problems raised by the desires of the flesh need to be reconsidered. This fact is the universal relevance of death:

> Be absolute for death; either death or life
> Shall thereby be the sweeter. (III. i)

To Claudio's confession of hope—"I've hope to live, and am prepared to die"—the Duke replies with a reasoned pessimism whose acceptance of death places it beyond the uncertainty which inevitably accompanies and often flaws all human desire. Death is the common destiny of man and simply to rebel against it is the act of a child; but to consider in the light of it the passions and appetites which have brought Claudio—and Vienna—to such tragic consequences is the beginning of wisdom.

The beginning but not the end. Men do well to accept the idea of death as an element inextricably interwoven, through the action of time, into every moment of our living experience. Without that acceptance there is no true maturity, but without a corresponding sense of life there is no vitality at all. The reaction against death, like that against the letter of the law, affects *Measure for Measure* at every level. The problem of Pompey, as it faces Angelo and Escalus, is balanced for the Duke by that of Barnardine. Like Pompey, like so many other characters in the background of this play, Barnardine has no conception of the moral law. He is, in the words of the Provost, "a man that apprehends death no more dreadfully but as a drunken sleep; careless, reckless, and fearless of what's past, present, or to come: *insensible of mortality, and desperately mortal*" (IV. ii). The Duke, whose sense of the moral law is so closely bound up with his awareness of mortality, cannot consent to his execution in such a state. He finds Barnardine

> A creature unprepared, unmeet for death;
> And to transport him in the mind he is
> Were damnable. (IV. iii)

Damnable: the sense of moral issues implicit in our acts and prolonging themselves to eternity is throughout distinctive of the Duke's outlook. The acceptance of the moral law is bound up with a deeper, profounder respect for human life. This does not, of course, invalidate the law itself, or diminish the need for its enforcement; but it does underline the almost infinite patience and understanding which that enforcement involves. Barnardine, though only a minor presence in *Measure for Measure,* has a distinctive part to play in it; and Shakespeare, in allowing him to play it, enriches notably the moral pattern of his conception.

The reservations represented by Barnardine are taken up on a higher level—as they were with Pompey in the matter of judgment—by Claudio and Isabella. As the dialogue between these two proceeds after the Duke's departure, the emphasis slowly but decisively shifts from death to its opposite—that is, to Claudio's keen desire for life. Even in the Duke's speech, where the feeling for death is most intense, we feel the horror of the

soft and tender fork
Of a poor worm. (III. i)

This horror can be paralleled in *Hamlet.* So much can hardly be said of the way in which Isabella's attempt to minimize the pangs of death turns into an acute realization of the actual nervous "pang" of dying:

Darest thou die?
The sense of death is most in apprehension;
And the poor beetle that we tread upon,
In corporal sufferance finds a pang as great
As when a giant dies. (III. i)

Clearly this is no sort of argument for death. The emphasis is no longer where the Duke had left it, upon the peace of death, but rather upon the pain involved in the passage to extinction. The body reacts with vivid sensual immediacy against the consolation offered to it. The reaction, proceeding as it does from the nervous sensibility, is completely spontaneous; and gradually it communicates itself to Claudio. At first he is resolved to die that his sister's honor may be saved; but the resolution that expresses itself in the phrase "I will encounter darkness as a bride" (III. i) is really a rhetorical effort to force himself to accept a fate which he regards as inevitable. It does not live long. As Claudio slowly comes to realize that he *might* live, his resolution palpably wavers. The first resolve had been clear-cut, decisive: "Thou shalt not do it"; but when his sister, with that strain of moral ruthlessness which is part of her nature, and—as we now know—of her weakness, forces him to face his position with the unambiguous order: "Be ready, Claudio, for your death to-morrow," he hesitates. "Yes," he answers, but with deliberation and as though his thoughts were fixed elsewhere; and indeed they pass, in the phrase that immediately follows, to considerations that affect him more nearly:

> Sure, it is no sin;
> Or of the deadly seven it is the least. (III. i)

The phrase amounts to a plea to Isabella to change her mind. To meet death boldly when no hope of life remains is a thing a man owes to his self-respect, but to choose it when it might be avoided, even with shame, is far harder. It calls for a degree of detachment and determination which few young men—or, indeed, few of any age—can claim to possess. Claudio tries to show he has acquired them, but fails.

In the remark just quoted, if anywhere, lies the moral issue beneath the whole incident. The conception of *Measure for Measure* rests upon a balance between two aspects of human passion: the natural and proper instinct upon which it rests and the dissolution and disease to which its unchecked indulgence leads. Claudio's phrase holds the balance perfectly. The idea that it would be "no sin" for Isabella to lie with Angelo is no part of Shakespeare's conception. It *is* a sin, and *deadly,* barely redeemable. Claudio has committed this same "deadly sin"—and the phrase has behind it the force of a Christian tradition to which Shakespeare in this play firmly adheres—but he has also committed the most natural, the most spontaneous of the seven; for his sin, though he recognizes it to be grievous in social terms, has involved that offering of self which is, in Shakespearean terms, the law of love, and so of life. Isabella, when she turns on him in her anger, fails to take this into account. It is not her decision which is wrong, but her expression of it which is—from the level of compassionate understanding at which the Duke aims—inadequate; and Claudio's profoundly human observation compels us to recognize this. Having made it, he falters and then visibly breaks down. His instincts, refusing to accept the extinction decreed for them, react against the abstract resolution previously imposed upon them:

> Ay, but to die, and go we know not where . . .
>
> The weariest and most loathed worldly life
> That age, ache, penury, and imprisonment
> Can lay on nature, is a paradise
> To what we fear of death. (III. i)

This is the fear of *Hamlet* once again, the dread of uncertainty following extinction; but it is that fear expressed with a physical immediacy rarely known in the earlier play. The emphasis in Claudio's tremendous outburst of horror is all upon the sensitive apprehension of life, upon the immediate opposition between the "sensible warm motion" of the living body and the "cold," rotted "obstruction" which reduces it to a "kneaded clod"; even the life of the "delighted spirit" in the cosmic obscurity of the afterstate is sensually conceived. The impending presence of death has brought out in Claudio a fear whose very weakness is natural, human: a fear which Isabella's virtue has not sufficiently allowed for, but which the Duke in his compassionate understanding will accept.

It is from this point, indeed, that his activities of reconciliation begin to take shape. Having overheard the dialogue of Isabella and Claudio he begins to take steps to ward off the consequences of Angelo's wickedness. These steps are plunged for a time into obscurity during which the issues are delicately balanced, poised between life and death. He works, it is worth noting, at night. This part of the play, in which the mysterious intrigues of the Duke and Angelo strive for supremacy, is full of references to "the heavy middle of the night" (IV. i), to "dead midnight" (IV. ii), and—perhaps most significantly of all in its sense of deception and disappointment —to "lights that do *mislead* the morn" (IV. ii). The intricate mechanism of the plot at this point, which is often brought forward as evidence of Shakespeare's lack of interest in his theme, but which is better seen as corresponding, however obscurely, to the harmonizing conventions of comedy, may be more significant than it looks. The Duke, for all his detachment, is not fully in charge of events. He is learning, not less than the others, from experience, and only differs from them in the wider range of his sympathy. The control of evil is *not* in his hands; its machinations often find him unprepared, leave him groping hastily in the darkness for an improvised remedy. That is why the resolution of this play, directed toward a clarification which has no place in the outlook of the characters themselves, cannot completely satisfy. The external and the inner situation simply do not correspond. When Angelo, by a crowning perfidy, sends word that Claudio's execution is to be put forward so as to take place before the meeting in which Isabella is to buy his life, the Duke is almost forestalled. Only by a rather unconvincing trick of substitution does he avert tragedy. This is clearly no way for an allegedly semi-"divine" figure to behave, and Vincentio, no less than Prospero after him, is strangely capable of very human contradictions and irritability; but perhaps we should be wrong to stress excessively the "divine" attributes in either figure. Both, after all, are involved in events which they themselves have helped to bring about, and are in the process of understanding their own situation in relation to these events. In the confusion which life offers to the seeker after moral clarity the opportunity to do good presents itself in strangely haphazard ways; and the Duke, with no more than an unusually awakened moral sense to see him through the surrounding darkness, grasps them and turns them to his own ends. In so doing, he increases the area of his understanding and shows his humanity.

Measure for Measure, then, offers no real "solution" to the problems it raises. The problems, indeed, interested Shakespeare at this moment more closely than the possible solutions. The contradictions so essential to the play were to be worked out later, with far greater resources and in other styles. Here the resolution is no more than hinted at. The clearing-up in the last scene is little more than a piece of able manipulation. In spite of its undoubted technical skill, the full body of experience never really informs it, as it has informed the episodes of anguish and division, to give it a corresponding life. But suggestions of greater clarity can be found. They express themselves, in that very fourth act which seems so given over to tortuous obscurities, in a rising series of dawn images, which become more powerful as the Duke begins to feel his mastery of the situation. These culminate in his great prose speech to the Provost:

> Look, the unfolding star calls up the shepherd. Put not yourself into amazement how these things should be: *all difficulties are but easy when they are known* . . . Yet you are amazed; but this shall absolutely resolve you. Come away; *it is almost clear dawn.* (IV. ii)

But the "symbolism," if such we may call it, remains elementary. All the forces of life and fertility suggested in Lucio's great speech on

Claudio's love[22] are not yet behind it to give it life and adequate content. This strengthening has yet to grow out of the whole body of the tragedies. The theme of *Measure for Measure* is still the interdependence of good and evil within human experience as centered in the act of passion. The mature tragedies which follow are to separate the elements within this complexity; this separation will result in a more complete projection of the individual experience into a more plastic and sensitive dramatic form.

ALL'S WELL THAT ENDS WELL

All's Well That Ends Well, which shows in the matter of plot contrivance superficial points of contact with *Measure for Measure,* is by any account a curiously indecisive piece. Two distinct themes are clearly intended to illuminate one another, but can scarcely be said to come together with complete harmony. The first aims at exploring, through the relationship of Helena and Bertram, the connection between personal *virtue* and inherited *honor;* the second relates this theme to the story of a sick and aging king, his "miraculous" cure through Helena's faith in her dead father's remedy, and the winning by her, through her own personal merits and faith, proved in adversity, of a Bertram who strikes us throughout as remarkably unworthy of her. It is, indeed, in the actions of Helena and in her relation to the courtly world around her that the play most consistently comes to life.

The virtues of Helena display themselves in a world notably dominated by an awareness of the adverse action of time. The king, as it opens, is said to have "abandoned his physicians"; having "persecuted time with hope," he has found at the last "no other advantage . . . but only the losing of hope by time" (I. i). His physician, whose skill and integrity were such that he was *almost* able to "make nature immortal," is dead, and has confirmed by his death his share in what are evidently the limitations of all human effort: "he was skilful enough to have lived still, if knowledge could be set up against mortality" (I. i). The elaborate balance of the prose in these early scenes answers once more to Shakespeare's efforts to turn the conventions of comedy to distinctive use as the reflection of real life.

This situation produces in the king a deep nostalgia for the past. Like other Shakespearean comic characters, notably in *As You Like It*,[23] he habitually sees virtue in relation to the *dead*, and more especially in Bertram's father, in whom "wit," divorced from its degeneration into modern levity, was still compatible with true "honour," who was conscious of his appropriate place in society and was yet scrupulously deferential toward those of lower station; whom memory, in short, presents as an example, the incarnation of courtly virtue, to a decadent present:

> Such a man
> Might be a copy to these younger times;
> Which, follow'd well, would demonstrate them now
> But goers backward. (I. ii)

We shall not, if we wish to be true to the play's intention, equate this nostalgic attitude with the author's complete thought; but it remains true that these memories produce in the king a typical old man's pessimism, which he expresses feelingly in the remembered words of his departed friend:

> "Let me not live," quoth he,
> "After my flame lacks oil, to be the snuff
> Of younger spirits, whose apprehensive senses
> All but new things disdain; whose judgements are
> Mere fathers of their garments; whose constancies
> Expire before their fashions." (I. ii)

Although this is not what the play finally aims at saying, though its final affirmation will not be placed in the mouth of tired old age, there is strength enough in the expression—and more particularly in the equation of the rash judgment of youth with the outer "garment" of reality—to lead us to give it due weight in the complete picture.

Inspired by these thoughts to a sense of his own irrelevance, the king goes on to express his desire to follow his generation into oblivion. The conflict in his exhausted frame between "nature," the instinct for life and its acceptance, and "sickness" is one that he is now conscious of lacking the strength or the living motivation to resolve. He, and his state with him, are aware of being dominated by the force of decline and death, await—but not yet with the hope of receiving it—the continual, the daily re-created "miracle" of life renewed.

Against this background, the comedy shows us two young people asserting their own natures in strongly contrasted ways. In the court a certain feverish craving for activity in the young answers to the impotent skepticism of old age: the "gentry," we are told, are

> *sick*
> For breathing and exploit, (I. ii)

in much the way that Fortinbras, in the opening scene of *Hamlet,* was said to be defying his "impotent and bed-rid uncle" in the pursuit of his predatory ends.[24] Bertram, the son, as we have seen, of a worthy but *dead* father, reflects a similar situation. He is the external copy of the parent whom the king in his nostalgic memory exalts:

> thou bear'st thy father's face;
> Frank nature, rather curious than in haste,
> Hath well composed thee; (I. ii)

there remains the question whether the inner, personal reality of so noble a father—his "moral parts"—have also descended to his son. For, as his mother clearly sees, Bertram, though resplendent in the superficial courtly virtues, enjoys these by inheritance rather than by merit of personal affirmation; he is, moreover, recognized by her to be, as a courtier, "unseason'd," imperfectly prepared to cope with a dangerous and declining world, so that her advice to him as he leaves to seek his fortunes is defensively conceived. "Love all," she urges him, but *"trust a few"*; and again:

> be able for thine *enemy*
> Rather in power than use;
> . . . be check'd for *silence,*
> But never taxed for speech. (I. i)[25]

Once these precautions have been taken for the defense of virtue in a treacherous environment, the rest must lie in the will of "heaven," and his mother, beyond praying for him, can do little to save her son from the perils that must infallibly await him.

Already, however, Bertram is contrasted—still in the Countess' mind—with Helena, who backs the "hopes" that her "education" promises with a virtue that is not merely inherited but consciously and personally affirmed: "she derives her honesty and achieves her goodness" (I. i). Unlike so many of the older generation, Helena is not overawed by the recognition of mortality; she grieves naturally, as in filial duty bound, for her dead father, but refrains from that "excess" of grief which she truly defines as "the enemy of the living." As the play opens, her life is concentrated upon the reality of the love which she feels for Bertram and upon which she—after the fashion of other Shakespearean heroines[26]—is ready to stake her being:

> there is no living, none,
> If Bertram be away. (I. i)

It is typical, however, of the quality of Helena's devotion that it should be compatible with a firmly realistic estimate of practical possibilities. She is aware that the object of her love is, in terms of the worldly values of the court, impossibly beyond her reach; "twere all one," she confesses, with a characteristic combination of realism and commitment,

> That I should love a bright particular star
> And think to wed it, he is so above me. (I. i)

Similarly the picture she draws of the object of her desire is one in which idealization and realism are significantly blended:

> 'Twas pretty, though a plague,
> To see him every hour; to sit and draw
> His arched brows, his hawking eye, his curls,
> In our heart's table; heart too capable
> Of every line and trick of his sweet favour:
> But now he's gone, and my idolatrous fancy
> Must sanctify his reliques. (I. i)

"Idolatrous"; "sanctify"; the implications of these words, so often used of love with a finally limiting implication in Shakespearean comedy,[27] show Helena engaged in placing the image of courtly perfection which she has herself a little artificially evoked. Bertram's "arched brows," his "hawking eye," his "curls": these things, though answering to true emotion as written in her "heart's table," are yet the reflections of a reality in some sense strained and artificial. The heart, indeed, is only "*too* capable" of responding to these superficial graces, of registering "every line and trick" of these surface splendors; but the full reality of her love, which is to be affirmed, through the comic convention, in the experience of loss and repudiation, will be shown in the course of the play to rest upon a deeper and more genuine human content.

It is through Helena's exchange, in this same opening scene, with the incongruous Parolles that love begins to emerge, beyond these initial limits of convention, in something of its true strength and weakness. Parolles, indeed, is a kind of touchstone, not altogether unrelated in function to the character so named in *As You Like It*.[28] The product of the disillusioned skepticism of the society upon which he lives as a parasite, he touches the action at many points, alternately deflating pretension by the assertion of his own distillation of cynicism and prompting those around him to reaction. Parolles, indeed, is a kind of desiccated Falstaff, deprived of the greater character's distinctive comic energy but perhaps rendered by this deprivation even more indestructible, more obstinately and clingingly attached to the surface of existence; and as such Helena, with her ability to penetrate to fundamental reality, responds to him. Helena is fully aware of Parolles' human limitations. She knows that he is "a notorious liar," "a great way fool," and "solely a coward." As such, she is ready to repudiate him and all that he stands for; but beyond these indignities she can also appreciate in him a certain consistency of outlook which is to be recognized, in contrast to so many courtly attributes that pretentiously claim more, as belonging to the indestructible fabric of life. As she strikingly puts it:

> these fix'd evils sit so fit in him,
> That they take place, when virtue's steely bones
> Look bleak i' the cold wind. (I. i)

For it is also true to this play's intention that "cold wisdom" should be seen, in its self-satisfied superiority, as waiting ignobly on the "superfluous folly" which everywhere surrounds it.

It is accordingly in contact with the reality represented by Parolles that love begins to appear in something of its true nature; for, if it is to be more than the matter of abstract idealization and verbal conceit to which the courtly outlook habitually limits it, it will have to be seen to come to terms with a more disillusioned and realistic estimate. When Parolles urges, against facile idealization, that "there was never yet virgin got till virginity was first lost," when he dismisses virginity itself as "against the use of nature," he is at once echoing Falstaff and, in his own cynically limited way, asserting certain claims of life: though, yet again, his references to sale and "commodity" as the ultimate criterion—"off with't, while 'tis *vendible*"—point to his own anti-romantic bias and worldly limitation. Again, when he comments "your old virginity is like one of our

French withered pears, it looks ill, it eats drily, . . . it was formerly better" (I. i), it is his own pessimism that echoes Falstaff's phrases and attitudes[29] without sharing in Falstaff's distinctive zest. It will be no part of Helena's reaction to endorse positions so belittling of love, and therefore so far removed from her own frank positives; but it is in reaction to Parolles and all that he stands for that the central truths which it is her part to affirm will begin to take shape in the course of the play.

By her readiness to meet Parolles on his own ground Helena shows, indeed, that there is more behind her own attitudes than mere romantic yearning for an unattainable love. Her virtue is proved from the first to be compatible with a due measure of realism and plain speaking. She stresses, in terms familiar from the sonnets, her awareness of the infinite contradictions which love implies—"His jarring concord, and his discord dulcet," "His faith, his sweet disaster" (I. i)—but her estimate of Bertram and his ambitions is, at the end of it all, realistic and true. "The court's a learning place, and he is one," she reflects, leaving the phrase deliberately and ominously unfinished: "one," in short, to whom she feels herself attracted even as she recognizes that mere attraction is no guarantee of permanence or objective worth, that the "pity" is that "wishing well" has "not a body in't." She is equally clear concerning her own prospects in love, as one of "the poorer born"

> Whose baser stars do shut us up in wishes;

but against this, it is her own freedom and responsibility that she emphasizes, underlining in the deliberately stressed and sententious rhyme with which the positive statements of this play are habitually put forward her confidence in the capacity of human beings to shape their fate to their desires:

> Our remedies oft in ourselves do lie,
> Which we ascribe to heaven: the fated sky
> Gives us free scope; only doth backward pull
> Our slow designs when we ourselves are dull. (I. i)

In this conviction she brushes aside the "impossible" and places her trust in the conscious possession of a "merit" that has nothing to do with inherited position:

> Who ever strove
> To show her merit, that did miss her love? (I. i)

This is realism, though of a kind very different from that shown by Parolles: a kind which will prove effective precisely because it is not shortsightedly limited to the material appearance of things. The "king's disease" will provide the opportunity, which her proper faith in herself and her love enables her to grasp, to work what will appear to the realists and the "experienced" to be nothing less than a "miracle." It is perhaps the central paradox of this comedy that Helena's belief in "miracle," or its possibility, is based in the last analysis upon a firmly realistic trust in her own resourcefulness, upon what her own faith, and her readiness to accept the risk implied in it, may be expected to achieve.

In this spirit Helena confesses to the Countess, Bertram's mother, the love which she bears her son. To the Countess' declaration of faith in her virtue and modesty, and in the naturalness of love itself —"Our blood to this, this to our blood is born" (I. iii)—she responds by declaring, in terms of romantic convention, her readiness to live as Bertram's "servant" and to die, if need be, as his "vassal." Beyond this, however, she stresses equally her determination to *merit* the love she is seeking:

> I follow him not
> By any token of presumptuous suit;
> *Nor would I have him till I do deserve him.* (I. iii)

Given the values which prevail around her, Helena is bound to confess that she does not "know how that desert should be"; but, though she is aware that, by the standards of the world, she "strives against hope" and "loves in vain," it is of the nature of her love to persevere in the disinterested gift of self and to expect to generate further love in the process of giving:

> in this captious and intenible sieve,
> I still pour in the waters of my love,
> And look not to lose still. (I. iii)

Her confidence in her love is related to her faith in her father's remedy, through which she expects to achieve the "miracle" of the king's cure. To restore the king to health, and thereby to obtain her "impossible" love, she is ready to stake everything, even her "well-lost life"; by this declaration she unites the two central themes of the play in a common gesture of generosity and confidence in the positive laws of life, a readiness to give all in order to obtain the all-embracing fulfillment she so confidently and spontaneously seeks.

In Helena's program of action we have been brought to see the reality of "honour." Bertram, meanwhile, is preparing to "woo" the same deity under a more superficial aspect. His is the young man's enthusiasm for appearance, for the heady challenge of the "brave wars" to which he is ready, neglecting the more prudent counsel of his elders, to "steal away" (II. i). Once more his attitudes receive their implicit evaluation in Parolles' echo of the soldier's bombastic talk of "Mars' novices" and of Captain Spurio, "with his cicatrice, an emblem of war," and in his own bravado claim to have inflicted that wound: above all, in his avowedly cynical advice to Bertram to cultivate those who "wear themselves in the cap of the time" and "move under the influence of the most received star" (II. i). Such, concludes Parolles, with a clear reflection of courtly values and the military pretensions which go with them, are to be followed, "though the devil lead the measure" (II. i).

In the central confrontation, to which all this leads, youth and age, faith and skepticism, meet face to face. The king, confirmed in his knowledge of the world, refuses to be "credulous" where the possibility of his own cure is concerned; Helena in her reply stresses the *value* of her father's "receipt," which she declares to be stored up,

> as a triple eye,
> Safer than mine own two, more dear. (II. i)

This, indeed, is the turning point of the entire action. Helena, having declared her readiness to face the supreme risk to obtain the prize of love, is brought to the decisive test. Her exchange with the king is once again given solemnity through the high sententiousness of rhyme. The emphasis rests, quite deliberately, on a supernatural intervention. In her plea, Helena stresses the discontinuity of what she offers with all merely human intervention, asserts the force of "*inspired* merit" against "worldly breath," and goes on to state:

> most it is *presumption* in us when
> *The help of heaven* we count the act of men, (II. i)

before concluding: "Of heaven, *not me,* make an experiment." Following logically from this, she goes on to take up the king's challenge by laying her own existence in the balance. If she fails in her healing mission, her own life shall be forfeit: "With vilest torture let my life be ended" (II. i). Confronted by this gesture of faith, the king in turn accepts the offered "hazard" against all the claims of "common sense," the consensus of worldly wisdom and recognized experience. As he lays stress on the mortal consequences of failure Helena confirms, for the last time and unequivocally, her readiness to take up the challenge before her:

King: Sweet practiser, thy physic I will try,
That ministers thine own death if I die.
Helena: If I break time, or flinch in property
Of what I spoke, unpitied let me die. (II. i)

This gesture of faith, however, has its reverse side. In the event of success, Helena is ready to put forward her claim to the reward for which she has chosen to risk her life. She affirms her right, once the cure has been effected, to marry the lover of her choice; and this the king, following what we know to be the normal law of comedy, is ready to grant her.

A variety of standpoints, all in varying degrees worldly and sophisticated, surround this central confrontation. Lafeu, in particular, is inclined, as an old courtier, to hold that "miracles are past" and belief in their possibility invalidated by the findings of "philosophical persons" who have made "modern and familiar, things supernatural and causeless" (II. iii): though he tends finally to reject these skeptical attitudes in the light of his own conviction, scarcely less detached in its final implications, of the relativity of all human knowledge:

> Hence it is that we make trifles of terrors, ensconcing ourselves into *seeming knowledge,* when we should submit ourselves to *an unknown fear.* (II. iii)

Against this background, nonetheless, it emerges as a fact, true if incomprehensible in the eyes of the world, that the "miracle," "the rarest argument of wonder that hath shot out in our latter times" (II. iii), has taken place. The king has indeed been restored to health, against his own expectations and those of the world; and it is left, most unexpectedly but with a kind of wry propriety, to Parolles to salute the cure as an effect of "great *transcendence*" and to prompt Lafeu to declare in turn the "showing of a heavenly effect in an earthly actor" (II. iii). For the space of this incident, with its persistent overtones of spiritual meaning, we feel ourselves in a world not unlike that of certain prose scenes in *The Winter's Tale.*[30]

Having won her crucial victory of faith, Helena is asked to choose her reward from among those of "noble father" set before her. In her own words, at once confident and profoundly humble, "*Heaven hath through me* restored the king to health" (II. iii); and now, in the light of this achievement, she does not so much offer to "take" Bertram as to "give" herself to him, much as Portia in *The Merchant of Venice*[31] gave herself to Bassanio in response to his choice of the casket:

I give
Me and my service, ever whilst I live,
Into your guiding power. (II. iii)

Here, however, Bertram reveals himself inadequate. Unlike Bassanio, he has chosen no casket, made no demonstration of his readiness to accept the risk which love of its very nature implies. He refuses the "gift," preferring false "honour" to true "value," for reasons typically self-centered and frivolous:

She had her breeding at my father's charge.
A poor physician's daughter my wife! (II. iii)

In vain the king calls upon him to reflect that "Good alone is good without a name," whilst "great additions," where they swell in the absence of virtue, can only produce "a dropsied honour" (II. iii). The matter has in fact passed beyond his control; for, when the young man boorishly insists in his attitude—"I cannot love her, nor will strive to do't" (II. iii)—Helena answers his ungenerous repulse by declaring her refusal to take an unwilling lover and by assuming, in the moment of adversity, the guise of a penitent pilgrim.

From this moment until the end of the play, interest passes from Helena to Bertram, who, following his superficial values in the quest of "fortune" through "hazard," leaves for the wars with Parolles as his appropriate attendant. Parolles, as usual, stands in a double relationship to his master, whom he at once echoes and, by implication, exposes. His rhetoric is the hollow counterpart to Bertram's "honour," though his observations are also those of one who knows, after his fashion, "what is man" and who, in so far as his knowledge contains elements of truth, surpasses in some measure the confessed ignobility of his role. In accepting Parolles as experienced guide and mentor in the ways of the world, Bertram reveals the insufficiency of his own insight into life. Lafeu judges him more accurately when he penetrates to his essential hollowness: "the soul of this man is in his clothes" (II. v). Parolles lives parasitically upon a society which affirms indeed the values of war and "honour," but which finds its appropriate symbol in the *drum*, hollow and high-sounding, for which he is verbally—but only verbally—ready to risk himself. His reality, as the Countess truly sees it, is that of "a very tainted fellow" (III. ii), corrupting and himself the product of corruption; although it is true that in his very ignobility he reflects life under certain of its aspects, more real after their own fashion than the empty verbiage of self-flattering honor by which so much of the world around him is inspired.

The "drum" episode ends with the exposure of Parolles as an insubstantial "bubble": an exposure which in turn implies that of the values followed by Bertram, who placed his trust in Parolles' supposed "knowledge" and "valiance" precisely because these, in their lack of solid content, mirrored his own defects. By comparison with Bertram, indeed, Parolles shows himself, in the moment of his downfall, at once more patently corrupt and, after his fashion, more honest. His reply to the Second Lord's contemptuous question, "Is it possible he should know what he is, and be that he is?" is a plain affirmation of his obstinate will to survive. "Let me live" (IV. i): the very simplicity of this aspiration marks its separation from Bertram's more pretentious ignobilities, gives the speaker, within the limits which his nature imposes, a certain counterbalancing actuality and truth.[32]

Bertram, meanwhile, follows his own shabby path to personal degradation. His attempt to seduce Diana is marked by a typical combination of facile sentiment and shallow sensuality. "Love is holy," he pleads, only too easily, as he asks his intended victim to surrender to what he calls, revealingly enough, his "*sick* desires" (IV. ii). We have here the familiar ingredients of Shakespearean "doting,"[33] the selfish and one-sided parody of true love: "doting," moreover, turned to something more corrupt than itself, passing beyond mere folly to what remarkably resembles viciousness. Diana, the object of this mean assault, shows herself by contrast ready, with her feminine realism and refusal to be taken in by empty and high-sounding phrases, to expose Bertram's craving as an ignoble caricature of love. His behavior she sees, as a woman, to answer to permanent aspects of weakness and egoism in the male sex:

> Ay, so you serve us
> Till we serve you; but when you have our roses,
> You barely leave our thorns to prick ourselves,
> And mock us with our bareness. (IV. ii)

As Bertram confirms his willingness to surrender the ring handed down to him by his forebears—with all its associations of faith and "honour"—in order to obtain the satisfaction which his "will," his sensual desire, so ignobly craves, her attitude touches the heart of the matter. To Bertram's emphasis on the "honour" that derives solely from inheritance, and which he is now in effect revealing in its true shallowness, she opposes a more personal and human conception—

> Mine honour's such a ring:
> My chastity's the jewel of our house,
> Bequeathed down from many ancestors;
> Which were the greatest obloquy in the world
> In me to lose— (IV. ii)

until he is driven to lay down the very nobility and honor to which he pretends—

> Here, take my ring:
> My house, mine honour, yea, my life be thine— (IV. ii)

in a self-centered and selfish impulse which seeks in reality nothing beyond the satisfaction of its own craving.

It should be noted that the course of this singularly unattractive episode is marked by a further string of accompanying comment, put into the mouths of anonymous attendants and expressed in the play's typically disenchanted and somber prose. The two Lords who observe Bertram's adventures are fully convinced both of the need to resist the baser promptings of the flesh and of the universal force of these promptings in relation to the human situation. "Now, God delay our rebellion! as we are ourselves, what things we are!" as one of them puts it, only to arrive at a characteristically pessimistic conclusion: "Merely our own traitors" (IV. iii). These generalizations are shown in what follows to be compatible with a full measure of realism. The end of Bertram's line of conduct is clearly seen to be an ignoble self-destruction—"he that in this action contrives against his own nobility, in his proper stream o'erflows himself" (IV. iii)—and against this perversity is set, as a redeeming feature, the reality of Helena's "holy undertaking" and her supposed entry, after a sanctified death, into "heaven." The general reflection on human life by which these comments are rounded off—

> The web of our life is of a mingled yarn, good and ill together: our virtues would be proud, if our faults whipped them not; and our crimes would despair, if they were not cherished by our virtues— (IV. iii)

is typical, in its grave and balanced detachment, of the mood which prevails in the most individual passages of this least spontaneous of comedies.

Whilst Bertram is thus engaged in the pursuit of his ignoble ends—again in the words of the attendant Lord, "this night he fleshes his will in the spoil of his honour" (IV. iii)—the time of resolution is at hand. Its first stage is represented by the final exposure of Parolles, who maintains in the face of it his claim to represent a permanent and indestructible aspect of life. "Simply the thing I am," he affirms, "shall make me live" (IV. iii); in this obstinate relation to reality, exercised in the face of rejection and contempt, we are once again close to the prevailing spirit of this enigmatic and dryly conceived action. Helena, too, as she returns from her "pilgrimage" to contemplate the disenchanting reality of her lover, echoes Diana in striking the note of man's frailty and irresponsibility. "O strange men!" she exclaims,

> That can such sweet use make of what they hate,
> When saucy trusting of the cozen'd thoughts
> Defiles the pitchy night: so lust doth play
> With what it loathes for that which is away. (IV. iv)

In reality, however, though she is still dead in the eyes of the world, the moment of final clarification is already foreshadowed—"the time will bring on summer"; "All's well that ends well" (IV. iv)—and Helena herself, celebrated by the Clown as "the herb of grace" (IV. v), will be instrumental in bringing it into being.

The closing scene, intricate and drawn out in a manner familiar from earlier comedies, provides perhaps the closest parallel with *Measure for Measure;* it also displays fugitive points of contact with the "symbolic" romances of Shakespeare's last years. As it opens, the king and the Countess are at one in condemning Bertram for his indulgence of self-will to the point of rebellion and at the expense of his true "honour"; though the Countess is ready to allow his conduct the excuse of "*Natural* rebellion, done i' the blaze of youth" (V. iii). By following his impulses to this unworthy end, Bertram is seen to have renounced the high good offered to him beyond his deserts:

> He lost a wife
> Whose beauty did astonish the survey
> Of *richest eyes*, whose words all ears took captive,
> Whose *dear perfection* hearts that scorn'd to serve
> Humbly call'd mistress. (V. iii)

In this way, it is made clear that Bertram, by rejecting Helena, has done *to himself* "the greatest wrong of all"; but the king, in whom the sense of age and nostalgia for the vanished past remain strong, remarks that

> Praising what is lost
> Makes the remembrance dear,

and declares his readiness to forgive a fault which is in any event beyond human remedy:

> The nature of his great offence is dead,
> And deeper than oblivion do we bury
> The incensing relics of it. (V. iii)

At this point, we may feel the presence of the "symbolic" overtones which will announce the prospect of reconciliation in the final romances, and which is clearly intended to set the tone, poised between resignation and understanding, for what is to come.

When Bertram finally makes his appearance the king confirms his readiness to forget the past. "All is whole," he declares; for

> we are old, and on our quickest decrees
> The inaudible and noiseless foot of time
> Steals ere we can effect them. (V. iii)

Bertram, on his side, seems to have learned wisdom at least in relation to Helena,

> she whom all men praised and whom myself,
> Since I have lost, have loved. (V. iii)

The sense of a pervading regret for "love that comes *too late*," the pessimism of an old age that sees life and perfection fading irreparably into the past ("That's good, that's gone"), continues to color the king's reflections and answers to the spirit of an action concentrated now upon the contemplation of human values seemingly lost and awaiting, in a spirit that once again anticipates certain effects of the last comedies, the "miracle" of resurrection.

The path to the final resolution, however, is still beset by obstacles. As the king recognizes as Helena's the ring now offered by Bertram to Lafeu, and as Bertram holds to his denial that it was ever hers, the direction of the action seems to change yet again. Bertram is still less than honest in his story of how he came by the ring. As though in response to his evasions the mood of the scene notably darkens; the king confesses himself moved by "conjectural fears" of foul play at Helena's expense and orders the young man's arrest, whilst Diana comes forward to confront him with his past behavior toward herself and to claim redress for the wrong supposedly done to her. Bertram, ungenerous and frivolous almost to the last, thrusts her aside as "a fond and desperate creature" and makes a last appeal to his decidedly soiled "honour":

let your highness
Lay a more noble thought upon mine honour
Than for to think that I would sink it here. (V. iii)

The king, reverting to a principal theme of the play, retorts that this honor can only be bound to the reality of his "deeds," which stand at present visibly compromised. As Diana challenges him on oath to recognize the reality of his treatment of her, Bertram plunges deeper into ignominy, dismissing her as "a common gamester to the camp"; but the truth is by now ready to emerge, and he receives the eloquence of his intended victim's retort:

O, behold this ring,
Whose *high respect* and *rich validity*
Did lack a parallel; yet for all that
He gave it to a commoner of the camp,
If I be one. (V. iii)

Out of his own vain words, Bertram stands most effectively condemned. His former associate Parolles, the shadow of his earlier pretensions, now emerges most appropriately to confirm the truth of Diana's assertion in the face of her would-be seducer. The "burr"[34] indeed sticks, though Bertram is capable of a last desperate effort to shake him off as "one with all the spots o' the world tax'd and debosh'd" and to present himself as a victim deceived, "subdued to her rate" by Diana's "infinite cunning," before bringing his self-defense to a typically ignoble close:

> I had that which any inferior might
> At market-price have bought. (V. iii)

A modern view of Bertram might tend to find some excuse for him as the victim of a deceitful stratagem, tricked into a marriage which he has been from the first unwilling to contemplate. Such an interpretation, however, though it may help to account for the notable lack of conviction with which Bertram's final acceptance of Helena is portrayed, would be contrary to the artificial laws of comedy, which regard substitution of the kind practiced by Helena and Diana as justified by the nature of the good which is to be gained by their use. In terms of the action to which he belongs, and outside which we are not called upon to consider him, Bertram stands condemned by his own attitudes and behavior, and his only prospect of redemption will lie at the last in the positive good of marriage, which, having finally set aside his perverse and negative attitudes, he will be brought by Helena's faith and resourcefulness to accept.

Bertram's efforts at self-exculpation are indeed by now as vain as they are unattractive. As Diana continues to press him for the return of the ring the falsity of his account of how he came by it is exposed and he can only "confess" the truth. Once more, and for the last time, Parolles has a relevant comment to offer. Bertram, he says, has indeed loved Diana "as a gentleman loves a woman": in other words, and more explicitly: "He loved her, and loved her not" (V. iii). The king, in his reply, stresses with equal truth the equivocal standing of Parolles himself—"As thou art a knave, and no knave" (V. iii)—even as Lafeu recalls the episode of the drum to his confusion.

Finally, as the comedy draws to its appointed close, the true history of the ring given unwittingly by Bertram to Helena is revealed in riddling form, and Helena herself, now pregnant with the fruit of her stratagem in the form of Bertram's child, "resurrected." "One that's dead is quick" (V. iii): once again, in spite of Bertram's obstinate shabbiness and the notably perfunctory manner in which he asks for pardon and declares his readiness to be reconciled to Helena, we are in a world which foreshadows that of the final romances. "The bitter past, more welcome is the sweet" (V. iii): an apt phrase, indeed, to sum up the complex of mingled emotions which this play, so oddly balanced between faith and skepticism, innocence and cynicism, leaves us.

X

The Mature Tragedies

In the series of great tragedies which followed *Measure for Measure*, Shakespeare's art attained a more varied and controlled expression. We are no longer dealing with "problem" plays, in which the presence of unresolved dilemmas, uncertainties incapable of clear artistic statement, makes itself felt. The conceptions elaborated in the new plays are, indeed, more complex than ever before, the interrelation of themes even further extended; but there is no longer any sense of that gap, which we must feel even in *Hamlet*, between purpose and achievement, between emotion and the dramatic conception through which it expresses itself. Above all, the tragic conflicts which predominate in these plays correspond to states of feeling more firmly defined, more clearly conceived in terms of a possible resolution. If the range of experience is far more ample than any we have so far considered, certain possibilities of harmony have grown, tentatively at first and then more clearly, to keep pace with them. By the end of the series a definite clarity has imposed itself, always within the prevailing tragic conception, upon the dramatic presentation of these plays. Having passed through *Othello*, *Macbeth*, and *King Lear*, in which the heart of the tragic experience is revealed in its full intensity, we are ready for *Coriolanus* and *Antony and Cleopatra*, which are as clear, lucid, and controlled in their conception as *Hamlet*, at the other end of the series, was dark, contradictory, and intractable. But it is essential to realize, if we are to understand the nature of the Shakespearean experience, that the later plays in the series could never have been conceived without the earlier.

As usual, the advance in artistic maturity first makes itself felt in greater linguistic range and power and then expands to cover the other elements of dramatic expression. As the contradictions of the problem plays are progressively mastered, the poetry which formerly expressed them becomes not only vastly extended in range but correspondingly harmonized, subject to a greater degree of emotional unity; and this unity is in turn reflected in a clearer conception of character and in a more truly dramatic presentation of conflict. There is not, at this stage, any suggestion of a change in the prevailing tragic mood. The subject of all these great plays can be described, in general terms, as the working out to its inevitable conclusion of the disruptive effect of the entry of passion into normal human experience. By this entry the balance, essential to right living, between the passionate and rational elements in the personality is overthrown, and what should have been orderly, vital, and purposeful is plunged into disorder, death, and anarchy. The novelty of Shakespeare's work at this period lies not in the mood expressed, but in the scope and growing clarity of the expression. As the tragedies follow one another, the conflict between passion and reason ceases to be shown in the form of an internal cleavage, such as that observed in *Hamlet.* It becomes something more truly dramatic, a clash between contrasted and opposed personalities and orders, which reflects in turn an effort to separate the factors within experience which, by accepting the place ascribed to them in a balanced set of values, move toward unity and development, from those which, by pressing their claim to absolute independence, make all harmonious integration impossible. In other words, the opposition between reason and passion, first isolated—through Othello and Iago—in a dramatic conflict of personalities and then projected, in *Macbeth* and *Lear,* beyond the individual hero to the state and universe which surround him, is merged increasingly into another, of greater significance and profundity, between highly personal conceptions of "good" and "evil."

OTHELLO

Othello is, by common consent, one of Shakespeare's most completely "objective" plays. The internal conflict of *Hamlet,* the identification of the hero's tragedy with the effort to achieve self-definition, is now polarized into a more obviously dramatic opposition between the Moor and his envious lieutenant Iago. The substitution as vehicles of the tragic emotion of one complex and incoherent character by two sharply defined personalities in conflict implies a different kind of play and brings with it a new and in some ways a clearer conception of the tragic protagonist. Othello is the first of a series of Shakespearean heroes whose sufferings are explicitly related to failings in themselves, but who manage in spite of this to attain tragic dignity. Like Antony and Coriolanus after him, he dramatizes as "nobility" what emerges, in certain important respects, as his own incapacity to cope with life; and, as in their case, the very weakness by which Iago engineers his downfall is turned into true tragedy.

The dramatic construction of the play turns, accordingly, upon the close, intricate dovetailing of the two contrasted characters of the Moor and his Ancient. At the center of the action, a tragic compound of nobility and weakness, stands Othello. That the Othello of the early scenes is truly and worthily a hero, who dominates his surroundings by the consistent simplicity of his attitudes and behavior, is not seriously open to question. Leader in war of the armies of the republic to which, as an alien stranger, he has sworn allegiance, savior of Venice from her traditional Turkish enemy, his merits are universally recognized, his authority in the moment of peril beyond discussion. Shakespeare, however, has been equally careful from the first to suggest the presence of certain weaknesses, potential if not yet actual, beneath the impression of strength and consistency which his hero initially presents to the world. One can detect in Othello from the first a revealing tendency to self-dramatization. His first utterance is a round assertion—full, splendid, rhetorical—of his royal lineage and of his services to Venice:

> My services, which I have done the signiory,
> Shall out-tongue his complaints. 'Tis yet to know,—
> Which, when I know that boasting is an honour,
> I shall promulgate,—I fetch my life and being
> From men of royal siege; and my demerits
> May speak, unbonneted, to as proud a fortune
> As this that I have reacht: for know, Iago,
> But that I love the gentle Desdemona,
> I would not my unhoused free condition
> Put into circumscription and confine
> For the sea's worth. (I. ii)

One need not deny the compulsive power of this rhetoric, whilst recognizing a certain theatrical quality in the gesture with which he underlines the nobility of his origins and which makes him say, not without a certain unconscious irony, "When I know that boasting is an honour." These rapt declarations do not constitute boasting, if only because boasting implies a self-consciousness in conceit which is far from the essential simplicity of the character; but they show a certain complacency, equally barbaric, which has already allowed Iago to dismiss his speeches maliciously as "bombast circumstance" (I. i), and which will shortly induce him to caricature his description of his love-making as so much "bragging" and "fantastical lies" (II. i). The complement of this self-centeredness—the defect, Iago again tells us, of "a free and open nature"—is the simplicity that leads Othello to think "men honest that but seem to be so" (I. iii), to misread the motives of those around him in the light of his own naïve self-esteem.

These limitations are scarcely important for as long as Othello is confined to the field of action. In war, indeed, where confidence and self-affirmation are the order of the day, they may be positively advantageous; but in personal relations, more particularly in an alien society and in the unfamiliar complexities of love, the situation is very different. Othello, in spite of himself, submits with a touch of unwillingness to love, finding it somehow incongruous with the "unhoused free condition" in which the active simplicity of his nature has so far found expression; and even the encounter with Desdemona, whose love can so easily become for him a cause of "circumscription and confine," merely underlines the possibility of tragedy. For Othello, as the entire action will show, is rarely able to get sufficiently far from himself to offer Desdemona the disinterested dedication in which true love consists. His happiness in the opening scenes is genuine and moving; but it is also, like everything else in his character, self-centered, naïve, even egoistic in its expression, and his account before the Venetian senate of his manner of wooing makes this clear. He begins, not without a certain theatricality, by asserting his ignorance of life as lived beyond the narrow circle of soldiery:

> little of this great world can I speak,
> More than pertains to feats of broil and battle, (I. iii)

before going on to evoke, with his usual splendid vigor, the way in [illegible], but also of an age in which adventures and discoveries had married fantasy to daily life, should not prevent us from seeing in his words the exposure of a decidedly one-sided conception of love. It was, in fact, by his passionate, simple-minded delight in his own magnificent career that Othello won Desdemona, taking her from her aristocratic surroundings and introducing her to a world at once elemental, strange, and full of possible misunderstandings; and—we could fairly add—it was in part because the conquest ministered to his self-esteem that he valued her:

> She loved me for the dangers I had pass'd
> And I lov'd her *that she did pity them.* (I. iii)

There is nothing accidental about this declaration, before a foreign and potentially hostile audience. If Desdemona's love for Othello was founded on her spontaneous admiration for the person whose adventurous story had captivated her youthful imagination, his for her was, by his own account, less a return of personal feeling than an extension of his self-esteem. "I loved her that she did pity them": Othello's estimate of his situation is nothing if not simple; but events will show that this simplicity is terribly, tragically vulnerable.

For we can never forget that Othello is, after all, a foreigner in Venice. For the cultured and skeptical Venetians around Desdemona, her relations with the "lascivious Moor" are mysterious, unnatural, and deeply disturbing. In the eyes of her own father, who holds to the last that his child has deceived him, Desdemona's action proceeds from a perversion of the judgment and passion is a poison which acts through the erring senses to enslave the will:

> A maiden never bold;
> Of spirit so still and quiet that her motion
> Blush'd at herself; and she—in spite of nature,
> Of years, of country, credit, everything—

To fall in love with what she fear'd to look on! . . .
I therefore vouch again,
That with some mixtures powerful o'er the blood,
Or with some dram conjured to this effect,
He wrought upon her. (I. iii)

In his perplexity Brabantio lays exaggerated emphasis upon his daughter's submissiveness until simplicity itself becomes, in this world of sophistication and skepticism, faintly equivocal. The adjectives "still" and "quiet" and the suggestion, barely indicated, of shame in "blush'd at herself" stand in a peculiar relationship to the mixtures "powerful o'er the blood" which are said to have overcome her judgment. To say this is not, of course, to accept Iago's account of Desdemona as "a super-subtle Venetian" who has molded the "erring barbarian" (I. iii) to her purposes; though it is true that Brabantio's parting words—spoken, we may feel, in the resentful impotence of old age—do something to endorse this view:

Look to her, Moor, if thou hast eyes to see:
She has deceived her father, and may thee. (I. iii)

Iago—as we shall see—invariably pushes his own interpretations of human motive to the extreme which his peculiar logic demands and in so doing falsifies it. He represents only one possible attitude—the least flattering—to love, but Brabantio's reaction is there to underline its relevance to what we may call the Venetian atmosphere of the play and even to our estimate of Desdemona's part in it. Like Isabella and even Ophelia before her, Desdemona has the power to exercise upon men an influence of whose nature and strength she remains until the last moment very largely unaware; and this power, given a perversely logical interpretation in Iago's "philosophy," becomes an occasion of dissolution and destruction.

In the light of all this, there is something ominous in the terms in which Othello begs the Duke and his counselors to allow his wife to accompany him to Cyprus:

Vouch with me, heaven, I therefore beg it not
To please the palate of my appetite;
Nor to comply with heat—the young affects
In me defunct—and proper satisfaction;
But to be free and bounteous to her mind. (I. iii)

The sentiment is unexceptionable, but the resolution is a little too easily made. Not for the first time, Othello dismisses confidently the

very failings with which in the event he is to stand condemned
references to "heat" and to "the palate of my appetite," which
trast so oddly with the vague, confident opulence of his plea, ta
forward to his own behavior as the tragedy unfolds itself. In vi
the fact that the despised elements of sensuality are shortly to
their way into Othello's mind till his utterances are saturated
them we are justified in allowing them even at this early stage
importance than he is ready to concede to them. Equally, in
second part of the same speech we may read an unconscious irony into the contemptuous dismissal of the possibility that the mere "disports" of love may undermine his devotion to the serious business of war:

> when light-winged toys
> Of feathered Cupid seal with wanton dullness
> My speculative and offic'd instruments,
> That my disports corrupt and taint my business,
> Let housewives make a skillet of my helm,
> And all indign and base adversities
> Make head against my estimation. (I. iii)

Once more the facility of the contrast indicates danger for the speaker. Othello, who here ostensibly dismisses love in the name of his "speculative and offic'd instruments" spurns it in effect as a "circumscription" of his simple, barbaric selfhood, of a conception of his own dignity which is essentially instinctive, unreasonable; by so doing he reveals his peculiar vulnerability to the irrational forces of animal feeling. Indeed the whole of his subsequent history is a tragic comment upon this facile opposition between the "serious and great business" of generalship, in which he finds a satisfaction not less passionate for being ostensibly divorced from love, and the fatal promptings of an "appetite" whose real power and importance he never admits or understands and which therefore ruins him.

If Othello's "nobility" provides one of the main conceptions upon which the closely knit structure of the play rests, the "critical" skepticism of Iago is certainly the other. Through his plotting, the mysterious poison which had worked, according to her father, on Desdemona's "still and quiet" nature becomes an active and sinister reality. For Iago *is* that poison, no longer hinted at or obscurely present in minds never fully conscious of it, but turned to destructive activity. His acts present themselves as the consequences of a "philosophy"—if we may call it so—which regards Othello's downfall as being as inevitable, as rooted in the nature of things, as his love. Since time dominates human experience, and since spiritual *value*—which Hamlet had so passionately and so vainly sought—dwells only "in particular will,"[1] love becomes for Iago merely an appetite, "a lust of the blood and a permission of the will" (I. iii). One object, therefore, may satisfy desire as readily as another. The "permission of the will" is indeed required, suffices to distinguish man from the beast; but, since, according to Iago, the object of this will can be nothing other than physical satisfaction, the attainment of this becomes the only imperative which the will can recognize.

This line of thought leads Iago, logically enough, to a pessimistic interpretation of love; for satisfaction, in experiences purely physical, leads necessarily to satiation, and this in turn to a craving for change. According to his "philosophy," there is nothing in the world of "nature" to prevent desire from passing easily—and meaninglessly—from one object to another. In the particular case of Desdemona he contends that it *must* so pass:

> Mark me with what violence she first loved the Moor, but for bragging and telling fantastical lies; and will she love him still for prating? Let not thy discreet heart think it. Her eye must be fed; and what delight shall she have to look on the devil? When the blood is made dull with the act of sport, there should be, again to inflame it and to give satiety a fresh appetite, loveliness in favour, sympathy in years, manners and beauties; all of which the Moor is defective in; now, for want of these required conveniences, her delicate tenderness will find itself abused, begin to heave the gorge, disrelish and abhor the Moor; very nature will instruct her in it and compel her to some second choice. (II. i)

Satiety; second choice: on these words, Iago will build something like a destructive "philosophy" of love. The transient nature of all physical passion will do more than incline Desdemona to be unfaithful; it will *compel* her, with a determinism of its own, and once the original impulse toward Othello has been exhausted, to choose again. Love, being merely a prompting of the senses to which the will gives assent, needs to be continually "inflamed" if the "blood" is not to be "made dull with the act of sport." For love, as in *Troilus,* is simply an "appetite," intense but impermanent, like all sensual experience, and in particular like the impressions of taste. That which was—to use another of Iago's characteristic phrases—as "luscious as locusts" will soon become "as bitter as coloquintida" (I. iii); full, in the moment of fulfillment, of "relish," of "delicate tenderness," it must continually be "fed," lest it turn to "abhorrence," "disrelish," and "heave the gorge" in nausea at the object of its former choice. The original impulse, once satisfied, fatally demands renewal; without this, it turns to indifference and even to loathing.

We shall not understand fully the implications of Iago's reading of love unless we appreciate not only the extent to which they echo prejudices actually present in what we may call the "Venetian" atmosphere of the play, but also the nature of the bond that, beneath every surface appearance, unites him to the object of his envy and hatred. At first sight, the Ancient is everything that his general is not, cynical, "intellectual," and detached where Othello is passionate and trusting to the point of folly. These qualities, however, are in certain important respects less opposed than complementary. If Othello's passion tends to express itself, as we have seen, with a certain remoteness from the realities of sexual attraction, Iago's cynicism and belittlement of natural emotion, though uttered from his mask of worldly common sense and "honest" plain speaking, are saturated with the feeling of "blood." "Blood," or sexual emotion, is the driving force of his intelligence, although it is a force always controlled and criticized by that intelligence. He tells Desdemona on her arrival at Cyprus that he is "nothing if not critical" (II. i) and he shows Roderigo a passionate (that is the only word for it) contempt for the operations of "appetite"; but it is "appetite," though belittled and despised by one whom a deep personal impotence seems to debar from the experience of it, that is at the root of the man, criticism and all. This is apparent in the temper of his remarks to Roderigo advancing the claims of reason and control:

> If the balance of our lives had not one scale of reason to poise another of sensuality, the blood and baseness of our natures would conduct us to most preposterous conclusions; but we have reason to cool our raging motions, our carnal stings, our unbitted lusts. (I. iii)

How intensely we feel "blood" at work here in the very criticism of passion! "Reason" balances—"poises," as Iago so precisely puts it—the scale of sensuality, foreseeing in the unchecked operation of our fleshly instincts the "most preposterous conclusions"; but the vigor of the references to "raging motions," "carnal stings," and "unbitted lusts" demonstrates beyond all possible error the source of Iago's peculiar vitality in action. His intellect dwells from the first pungently, insistently, upon the elements of bestiality which underlie human passion and which he is driven by a compelling need to expose; but the presence in his own thwarted and resentful mind of the despised emotions is implied in the very intensity with which they are contemplated. It is impossible not to feel the obsessive sexuality which inspires his feverish activity in the dark at the opening of the play. Revealing itself in the persistent animality with which he incites Roderigo to disturb the "fertile climate" in which Othello dwells and so to "poison his delight" ("poison," indeed, is one of the images most characteristically present in his mind, a key to his mode of operation throughout the play), it dominates both the man and the scene:

> Even now, now, very now, an old black ram
> Is tupping your white ewe. Arise, arise;
> Awake the snorting citizens with the bell,
> Or else the devil will make a grandsire of you. (I. i)

The grotesque tone of the last lines in itself reflects the intimate source of the intensity behind Iago's every action. The "passionate" Othello never, until his enemy has injected his peculiar poison into his mind, expresses himself in love with such physical intensity as the "skeptical," ostensibly controlled Iago; in this apparent paradox lies a principal key to the interpretation of the whole play.

In the light of this situation, much of the dramatic action of *Othello* acquires a deeper meaning. Above all, Iago's "philosophy" gives a clear logical expression to the doubts and reservations which from the first accompany the hero's love in the minds of those who surround him. Brabantio had believed that his daughter's choice was against the rules of nature; Iago, on the contrary, believes not only that the choice was natural, but that "nature," which had brought her to it, would drive her inevitably to change. The facts appear to bear him out, in so far as he succeeds in undermining Othello's love for Desdemona; but before the beginning of the destructive process that he foresees and makes it his business to bring about, we are given one brief glimpse of Othello's happiness. Separated by stormy seas during their voyage to Cyprus, he meets Desdemona once more and enjoys a brief moment of fulfillment which, it seems, nothing in life can equal. His one desire is to hold this moment, to make it eternal:

> If it were now to die,
> 'Twere now to be most happy; for I fear,
> My soul hath her content so absolute
> That not another comfort like to this
> Succeeds in unknown fate. (II. i)

Yet, even here, at the moment of his "absolute" content, Othello *fears*. This precarious moment, he senses, will never find its fellow, for the temporal process is one of dissolution and decay. Only death can come between this communion and its eclipse; but death, of course, implies the annihilation of the personality and the end of love. Like a harmony which has reached the culmination of its development, this love must either cease or turn to the discord which Iago, in a prophetic aside, foresees:

> O, you are well tuned now:
> But I'll set down the pegs that make this music. (II. i)

In the extended use, against a background of tempest at sea, of the musical metaphor of harmony as a symbol of spiritual concord, the play anticipates some of the techniques which will be developed, to very different ends, in *Pericles* and *The Winter's Tale;*[2] but the device remains inevitably unsustained in a play in which the elements of destruction and discord clearly prevail. Already Iago has been present to observe this reunion and to color Desdemona's forthright declarations of devotion with the insertion of his own worldly and persistently disparaging comment; and, as soon as she and Othello have left the scene, his destructive cynicism returns—in the tone of his prose dialogue with Roderigo—to become the driving force of the action. From this moment until the final disaster it never really loses the initiative.

The transition from concord and the anticipation of married fulfillment is indicated with considerable care. In the scene which follows the reunion of the lovers (II. iii), the motives of felicity and disillusionment are simultaneously developed. It is night, the night in which Othello has announced "the celebration of his nuptial," but also the night in which Iago's activity will turn rejoicing into savagery and drunkenness. His instrument to this end is Cassio, in whom all his unflattering conclusions with regard to love appear to him to find their confirmation. We shall only understand Iago's part in this tragedy if we realize that he plays throughout upon the real weaknesses of his victims. These weaknesses he elevates, following his "philosophy," into consistent principles, reading into what is largely infirmity, susceptibility, or indecision a positive tendency to evil; but his observations, though they do not account fully for the behavior of his victims, and indeed consistently pervert their underlying motives, invariably pick on something really vulnerable in them. That something is normally connected with desire or "appetite." Cassio is by inclination a courtier, proud of his ability to respond easily to beauty and to insinuate the pleasing compliment; he is also, as his regretted susceptibility to drink suggests, something of a sensualist. His imagination, stirred by Iago, lingers upon Desdemona with intense but passing approbation. She is "exquisite," "a fresh and delicate creature," with an "inviting" though—he hastens to add—"a right modest eye." There is nothing particularly vicious about all this, but it is enough to enable Iago—considering Cassio in the light of his own jealousy and of his disparaging convictions about life—to see him as one who puts on "the mere form of civil and humane seeming for the better compassing of his salt and most hidden loose affection" (II. i). The description is highly typical. Iago cannot conceive of human weakness as other than fully conscious. Believing in the controlling powers of "corrigible authority" (I. iii), because he senses in them his own instrument for the exercise of power over others, he is led to rationalize Cassio's failing, turning susceptibility into positive cunning; but the short encounter with Bianca (III. iv) is there, with its glimpse of callous and superficial worldliness, to show that his judgment is not altogether unrelated to reality. Having observed in Cassio just sufficient "loose affection" to make his accusations plausible, he uses him to bring out Othello's unconsidered sensuality, to ruin his judgment and destroy his peace.

By inflaming the fuddled Cassio to riot Iago releases the forces of passion on the island. As the drunken revelry, prevailing, takes the mind prisoner, jealousy creeps into Othello's mind through Iago's action upon the instability which makes his will, unknown to himself, the slave of passion. Once his happiness has been disturbed, the tone of his anger contrasts significantly with his earlier assertions of self-control:

Now, by heaven,
My blood begins my safer guides to rule,
And passion, having my best judgement collied,
Assays to lead the way. (II. iii)

For the first time, Othello admits that his anger may be powerful enough to poison his judgment, his "*safer* guides" as he ominously calls them, and to carry him into ill-considered courses. Iago has already begun to work upon his weakness. He has known from the first that this is a victim who will allow himself to be led "tenderly" by the nose, "as asses are" (I. iii). His confidence rests on his reading—one-sided and cynical indeed, but not on that account less effective for the end he proposes to himself—of the Moor's simplicity. Othello, as we have seen, tends to neglect the part played by physical desire in a love in the conduct of which he needs to feel himself "free and bounteous," at once truly generous and flattered in his vulnerable self-esteem; Iago, for whom *all* love is simply the gratification of this desire, gives a very different interpretation of his victim's character:

His soul is so *enfetter'd* to her love,
That she may make, unmake, do what she list,
Even as her appetite shall play the god
With his weak function. (II. iii)

It was precisely this idea of being "enfettered" by his love that Othello had so confidently rejected in bringing Desdemona to Cyprus; it had offended his belief in himself both as a warrior and, more intimately, as a man. But Iago's action, based as always on the rationalization of affection as "appetite," aims at the dissolution of this heroic simplicity, seeks to subdue Othello by rousing the bestial instincts which slumber beneath the surface of his personality.

In this he succeeds with surprising ease: surprising, that is, unless we remember how the way has been prepared by the stress laid upon the Moor's disastrous ingenuousness. The long and intimate scene (III. iii) placed at the very heart of the play, in which Othello is progressively "infected" with Iago's malignant attitudes, is also a revelation of the extent to which these two central characters are connected within their opposition, related to one another as light to darkness, as contrasted but finally complementary aspects of a single reality. Iago knows at the outset that his victim, once confused, is lost, and so his primary aim is to involve him in uncertainty. For

Othello, once placed in doubt, is quite incapable of suspending judgment. Suspense affects his self-confidence, contrasts with the capacity for quick and firm decision upon which he prides himself. He demands an immediate resolution, which can in practice be nothing but an acceptance of Iago's insinuations:

> to be once in doubt
> Is once to be resolved; exchange me for a goat,
> When I shall turn the business of my soul
> To such exsufflicate and blown surmises,
> Matching thy inference. (III. iii)

Few things in Othello are more revealing than this habitual tendency to protest rhetorically against the presence of the very weaknesses that are undoing him. He refers contemptuously to the "goat," the most notorious symbol of sensuality, just as Iago is engaged in poisoning his mind through his "blood"-inspired imagination; and the reference, strengthened by the sense, in "exsufflicate," of the beast breathing heavily in the external signs of passion, is at once grotesque and significant.

Flattering the "free and open" nature in which his victim so naïvely prides himself, Iago proceeds to clip the wings of his freedom and to convert his frankness into suspicion. He recalls the persistent misgivings that have from the first surrounded this marriage—"She did deceive her father, marrying you" (III. iii)—and stresses the inequality of "clime, complexion, and degree" in a way at once calculated to hurt Othello's pride and to emphasize his ignorance, as a foreigner and a man of alien race, of Desdemona's true motives. Above all, he insinuates that her apparent purity of purpose may conceal a sensual corruption of the will:

> Foh, one may smell in such a will most rank,
> Foul disproportion, thoughts unnatural. (III. iii)

The last assertion is really the important one. The others do little more than prepare the ground for it. Iago's purpose is, in his own words, to "act upon the blood" (III. iii), to make the sensual basis of Othello's passion come to the surface, not to give body and content to the reality of love, but in the form of passionate and destructive jealousy. The victim's mind must be infected. Iago's conception of love as so much corrupt "appetite" is to take possession of him, exploiting unsuspected facets of his nature, demoralizing him and destroying his integrity. He must be brought to see Desdemona as Iago, in his "philosophy," insists that she really is. She is natural, "the wine she drinks is made of grapes" (II. iii); therefore her "blest condition" must be fatally, inevitably subject to inconstancy.

It is worth noting that Iago has begun to act upon Othello by throwing doubt upon the purity of his own thoughts. The Moor believes that men "should be what they seem" (III. iii); his whole life has been founded on the assumption that our motives are few and our spiritual needs simple, our actions completely and unequivocally under our control. Iago implies that the assumption is dubious, that not only the motives of others, but even our own are open to obscure and scarcely apprehended reservations:

> Utter my thoughts? Why, say they are vile and false;
> As where's that palace whereinto foul thoughts
> Sometimes intrude not? (III. iii)

This is a typically sophisticated "Venetian" conclusion, and one which perfectly fits Iago's purposes. It is because his "philosophy" enables him to establish contact with the lower, unconsidered elements of his victim's emotional being that he is able to destroy Othello's simplicity and to reduce him to a mass of contradictions and uncontrolled impulses. Having once deprived him of the certainty which his nature craves, he plays upon his sensual fancy, recreating Cassio's "dream" with obsessive insistence—the product, perhaps, of a certain thwarted "appetite" in himself—upon the grossness of physical contacts, makes him *visualize* the sin by which Desdemona is offending his self-esteem. Othello has already offered a glimpse of how completely his being is anchored upon his faith in his love; as Desdemona leaves him he has said, in a first obscure glimpse of the horrors which await him:

> Perdition catch my soul,
> But I do love thee! and when I love thee not,
> *Chaos is come again.* (III. iii)

Now, dimly aware of the prospect of this "chaos" opening before him, he makes his impossible, absurd demand for instant proof. The completeness of his fall is reflected in the grotesque irony which his demand implies. "Villain, be sure thou prove my love a whore" (III. iii); from which point Iago leads him on with a sneer that works like poison on his fantasy:

how satisfied, my lord?
Would you, the supervisor, grossly gape on?
Behold her topp'd? (III. iii)

Here, besides rousing still further the sensual elements in his imagination, Iago touches Othello at a most vulnerable point; he offends him intimately in his personal respect. The reaction is a characteristic mixture of pathetic bewilderment and defiant self-esteem. Conscious of the racial difference which separates him from the Venetians around him and vaguely aware of a mortifying social inferiority—

Haply, for I am black,
And have not those soft parts of conversation,
That chamberers have— (III. iii)

he thrusts aside the doubt that assails him in the man of action's superior reference to "chamberers," only to fall at once into further uncertainty of a more concrete and, perhaps, for him of an even more mortifying kind:

or, for I am declined
Into the vale of years. (III. iii)

The instinctive reaction—"yet that's not much"—is not sufficient to undo the final impression of failure, openly recognized in the conclusion—

I am abused, and my relief
Must be to loathe her— (III. iii)

in which misery and offended self-respect compete for precedence. Iago's very boldness has won his point. He must have been very sure of the Moor's blindness to work upon him with so gross a caricature, but his confidence has been justified by the event. For the caricature, for all its grossness, has roused not Othello's indignation, but his outraged self-esteem and has brought to the surface the destructive forces of his neglected animal instincts.

A few ambiguous phrases from Iago have been enough—with Cassio's invented intrigue and a handkerchief fallen and found by chance—to reduce Othello to an absolute slavery to passion. The slender basis of the intrigue, far from being a sign of weakness in the play,[3] is a deliberate and necessary part of its intention. Iago himself, in a solitary moment, describes perfectly his own method and achievement:

> The Moor already changes with my poison:
> Dangerous conceits are in their nature poisons:
> Which at the first are scarce found to distaste,
> But with a little act upon the blood,
> Burn like the mines of sulphur. (III. iii)

The relation of poison to taste, and of both to the action of the "blood," is by now familiar. It has marked the process which has reduced Othello's barbaric egoism to incoherence, his heroic rhetoric to a grotesque echo of his enemy's cynicism. Above all, he has been induced to see himself as betrayed, and it is typically the knowledge, rather than the betrayal, which affects him:

> I had been happy, if the general camp,
> Pioners and all, had tasted her sweet body,
> *So I had nothing known.* (III. iii)

The form of this confession is highly revealing. The problem of Othello is revealed here as a problem of consciousness, of the relationship of instinctive life to critical detachment. The intense and pathetic sense of isolation, of the irrevocable loss of what might have been, as it makes itself felt in the evocation of Desdemona's "sweet," "tasted" body, is balanced in Othello by an infantile readiness to be deceived, to accept as true less than what his reason—however unreasonably, even pervertedly—has told him to be the truth.

By the end of this scene, Othello's new "knowledge" has had two consequences. It has destroyed his heroic simplicity of judgment, upon which his real nobility has been based, and it has roused his own sensual impulses to destructive fury. From now on, sensual passion and prowess in action are, in Othello, mutually exclusive; the entry of the one implies the dissolution of the coherence and self-confidence necessary to the other. It is significant that, when he becomes aware that his peace is undermined beyond hope, he refers to his loss, not first of Desdemona, but of his integrity as a warrior:

> Farewell, the tranquil mind, farewell, content!
> Farewell, the plumed troop, and the big wars
> That make ambition virtue. (III. iii)

For the last time, Othello looks back in this speech to his former greatness. From now on, he is a man submitted to two main influences, both equally destructive: on the one hand the loss, so intimately felt, of his military glory; on the other, that sense of Desdemona's supposed promiscuity which grows upon his imagination until Iago can make the ironic comment: "I see, sir, you are eaten up with passion!" (III. iii)

The scene in which these developments take place forms a kind of pivot upon which the whole subsequent action turns. The end of it is marked by an exchange which, in another context, would strike us as a piece of grotesque parody, but which here, confirming Othello's consecration to self-deception, conveys an appalling irony which is all its own. Prompted by Iago's deliberate sneer—"your mind perhaps may change"—the barbaric warrior vows himself, finally, once and for all, in the name of the very consistency he has always prized, to destruction:

Like to the Pontic sea,
Whose icy current and compulsive course
Ne'er feels retiring ebb, but keeps due on
To the Propontic and the Hellespont;
Even so my bloody thoughts, with violent pace,
Shall ne'er look back, ne'er ebb to humble love,
Till that a capable and wide revenge
Swallow them up. Now, by yond marble heaven,
In the due reverence of a sacred vow
I here engage my words. (III. iii)

The vow, made in the name of a "compulsive," an irreversible passion, to which the speaker is now enslaved, is offered to a "marble" heaven, reflects the motion of an "icy" current, answers to a will petrified or frozen, caught in the savage and unreasoning thrust of its own egoistic and "blood"-inspired purposes. Thwarted in a love which he has never really understood in its true nature of mutual dedication, Othello's egoism announces itself as consistent in revenge, decisive, irresistible; all the intensity of personal feeling which was never fully gratified in his relations with Desdemona are to be exercised in exacting retribution for the ruin of his integrity.

To the rhetoric of this inhuman resolve, Iago's voice, shriller and more highly pitched, answers as he too kneels in a grim parody of the unnatural dedication which he has himself brought into being:

Witness, you ever-burning lights above,
You elements that clip us round about,
Witness that here Iago doth give up
The execution of his wit, hands, heart,
To wrong'd Othello's service! Let him command,
And to obey shall be in me remorse,
What bloody business ever. (III. iii)

To the ample, barbaric gesture, at once irresistibly powerful and "stony," deprived of life and flexibility, of the hero who has just renounced his heroism with his humanity, answers the clipped, almost falsetto tones of the betrayer who, by engineering the "currents" of Othello's passion into the channels he has prepared for them, is engaged in completing the destruction of love, the ruin of "nobility," in accordance with his consistent and all-absorbing aim.

The increasing insolence of Iago's attitude as he comes to realize that his success is assured is brought out with increasing force in the scenes that follow. Perhaps the irony reaches its climax when the plotter makes his victim stand aside and assist in silence at what he imagines to be Cassio's account of Desdemona's infidelity (IV. i). Every word is a mortal wound for Othello's pride. Iago sneers, and disclaims the sneer with a phrase that is itself an affirmation of contempt:

Othello: Dost thou mock me?
Iago: I mock you! no, by heaven,
Would you would bear your fortune *like a man!* (IV. i)

He roundly taxes the heroic Othello with lack of manliness:

Whilst you were here o'erwhelmed with your grief—
A *passion most unsuiting such a man*—
Cassio came hither . . .

Marry, patience;
Or I shall say you are all in all in spleen,
And *nothing of a man.* (IV. i)

Nothing could do more than this savage element of caricature in Iago's treatment of Othello to convey the degradation of the victim; no better foil to the Moor's earlier rhetoric—rhetoric which stands in the closest relationship to the subsequent tragedy—could be conceived.

As the plot advances, and as Iago's control over his intrigue grows, the sensual element becomes increasingly intense and disturbing in the victim's utterances. We see and feel its effects when he falls into a fit, drags himself along the ground, and mutters frenziedly, in the presence of his exultant enemy, about "noses, ears, and lips" (IV. i). We feel them in those bestial phrases in which his outraged egoism, deprived of expression in the natural simplicities of action, gropes blindly toward its revenge: "I'll tear her all to pieces!" "I see that nose of yours, but not that dog I shall throw it to" (IV. i); and still more in the combination of affronted self-respect and rising savagery which prompts the exclamation, "I'll chop her into messes; cuckold me" (IV. i). But they appear most clearly of all, and in closer relation to the love they are corroding, in that terrible scene (IV. ii) in which the crazed Othello turns, with a mixture of intensely frustrated physical attraction and open repulsion, upon Desdemona. The feeling is, at certain moments, curiously reminiscent of the sonnets. Desdemona is addressed as a "*rose*-lipp'd cherubin" —such imagery, a compound of poetic convention and deep emotion, is very characteristic—and his loathing for her finds expression in typical sense imagery:

Desdemona: I hope my noble lord esteems me honest.
Othello: O, ay; as summer flies are in the shambles,
That quicken even with blowing. O thou weed,
Who art so lovely fair and smell'st so sweet
That the sense aches at thee, would thou had'st ne'er
been born. (IV. ii)

The mention of "weed," the reminiscence of convention behind "lovely fair," and the keen evocation—almost unnaturally sensitive—of the faculty of smell are all suggestive of the sonnets.[4] Like "lilies that fester,"[5] their effect depends upon a sharp opposition of acute sense impressions. The intensity of desire implied in "sense *aches* at thee" and the feeling for life behind "quicken" are set against the loathing which produced "shambles" and the "blowing" of the flies. "Blowing" is especially subtle in that it speaks of the generation of flies out of corruption whilst using a word that suggests the opening of the rosebud into mature beauty. The reminiscence of the sonnets is not accidental, for the story of *Othello* is precisely a dramatic representation of the inevitable degeneration of desire, in a world where "value" appears to have no foundation, into selfish and destructive appetite.

The whole of this part of the play shows Othello, as his personal integrity collapses, taking up Iago's attitudes and becoming impregnated with Iago's obsessions. By the end of the tragedy, this once splendid figure of a man has been reduced to a barely human state, in which broken remnants of astonished resentment grope in vain for an appearance of certainty upon which to found the action which he so intensely and so impossibly craves. As his ruin proceeds, the egoism which has always been a part of his nature comes to the fore, no longer in relation to military glory, but rather in his attitude toward his own folly. The great final speeches in which he attains a true measure of tragic stature are also merciless exposures of weakness. In the first, addressed to Desdemona, there emerges, besides a profound note of pathos, the speaker's unpreparedness to meet the situation in which he finds himself. "Had it pleased heaven," he says,

> To try me with affliction; had they rain'd
> All kinds of sores and shames on my bare head;
> Steept me in poverty to the very lips;
> Given to captivity me and my utmost hopes;
> I should have found in some place of my soul
> A drop of patience. (IV. ii)

If life, Othello seems to say, had presented to him a problem which could have been met by asserting a nobility at once true and flattering to his self-esteem, all might have been well. As he lists the forms of trial which he believes himself able to resist, we feel the speaker recovering a kind of confidence, assuring himself that in resistance too there is a sort of heroism, that the exercise of patience to the limit of endurance is not, after all, incompatible with his conception of his own moral dignity. Only at the end are we shown the true source of Othello's suffering:

> But, alas, to make me
> A fixed figure for the time of scorn
> To point his slow, unmoving finger at! (IV. ii)

To become an object of ridicule without being able to react, to assert his own "nobility"—this is the shame from which Othello feels that there is no escape, and which accompanies him to his tragic end.

That end, when it comes, adds little to what we already know of his character. Having set himself up, impossibly, as accuser, judge, confessor, and executioner in his own "cause,"[6] Othello advances to the final catastrophe with something of the quality of a sleepwalker about him. To the last, in his meditation over the sleeping Desdemona before he stifles her, we find intensity matched by coldness, sensuous feeling by a strange remoteness from living passion. Beginning with an invocation to "you *chaste* stars," he goes on to speak of a skin "whiter than *snow*" and "smooth as *monumental alabaster*"; while there is something intense but distant in the apostrophe to "thy light" which follows, and in the almost studied reference to "Promethean heat" (V. ii). Putting together these impressions, we come to feel that Othello's passion at this critical moment is, as we have felt it to be before, as cold on the surface as it is intense just below; it combines a certain monumental frigidity with a keen impression of the activity of the senses.

That the senses are present is clearly guaranteed—at this stage—by Othello's own behavior; and, indeed, the same speech proves that this is so. As he gazes upon his sleeping victim his underlying sensuality is felt in the comparison of Desdemona—once more—to the "rose" and in the keenness with which the sense of smell asserts itself in "balmy breath" and in "I'll smell it on the tree."[7] Even here, however, the note of incompleteness persists. The impression is once again of overwhelming passion unable to express itself otherwise than in cold and distant imagery: the imagery, never quite freed from the conventional, of the sonnets. Even when he is stressing the full happiness he had hoped to find in his love Othello sees perfection, not in terms of warm life, but in the chill flawlessness of a precious stone:

Nay, had she been true,
If heaven would make me such another world
Of one entire and perfect *chrysolite*,
I'ld not have sold her for it. (V. ii)

As we have seen, the strength of his passionately emotional being finds adequate expression, not in love, but in the poetry of action, untrammeled by reference to objects and needs beyond itself. In his love poetry the same intensity has habitually failed to express itself completely toward another person; but precisely because he has, in spite of this, become involved in another person's needs and committed to her his own, the moment of his awakening to reality is also the moment of his ruin.

In the last scene, in which dignity and weakness are blended in the process of awakening to the extent of his disaster, in which he kills Desdemona and falls, dead by his own hand, across her body, the nearest approach to an impartial comment is made in terms of common realism by Emilia when she calls him "dull Moor"; an accusation to which he can only answer, once the enormity of his error has come home to him, with the simplicity of truth: "O fool, fool, fool!" (V. ii) Yet, in spite of this, Othello retains to the end the simplicity which formed part of his egoism throughout, and with it a good measure of tragic dignity. His weakness and his tragedy are, indeed, closely united to the last. As T. S. Eliot noted,[8] his last speech is both a splendid expression of self-centered poetry and a final attempt at self-justification in an irrelevant pose:

> I have done the state some service, and they know't . . .
> . . . then must you speak
> Of one that loved not wisely but too well;
> Of one not easily jealous, but, being wrought,
> Perplexed in the extreme. (V. ii)

We shall recognize that this speech, as we follow it, carries us with the speaker to the culminating moment in which he kills himself, to fall, as in a final gesture of expiation, over the body of his murdered wife. And yet there is more than this. If we are not mistaken in finding here the last words of a hero of true tragic stature, we should nonetheless not allow this to blind us to other realities, those to which Othello has so painfully awakened in the course of this same scene. For who, in point of fact, has been "more easily jealous" than Othello? For all the declamatory splendor of his final words, much of what is said has nothing to do with the burden of responsibility that rests so heavily upon him. For the real point, or a great part of it, lies in the presence of Desdemona's body, killed by the speaker himself in his blindness, wantonly and unnecessarily sacrificed; and his last words are not only "poetry," but a final confession of failure. "Perplexed," by his own admission, betrayed by emotions he has never really understood, Othello's last words are a pathetic return to his original simplicity. Unable to cope effectively with the complicated business of living, he recalls his generous past and commits the "simple" act of suicide. But already the critical acid applied by Iago has destroyed the structure of his greatness.

We may say with some justification that the spectacle of Othello's fall is excessively painful. The prevailing spirit of the tragedy tends undoubtedly to destruction, so much so that it possibly lacks balance and fails to satisfy completely as a reflection of human experience. Other elements, however, also emerge from a balanced view of the play. Iago, so triumphantly in charge of his intrigue, loses control of it at the last and is faced unexpectedly, in the person of the wife whom he has consistently used and despised, with the reaction of elementary human decency.[9] "'Tis proper I obey him, but not now"; "Perchance, Iago, I will ne'er go home" (V. ii). The truth "will out," in spite of all the efforts of malignant and self-confident cunning to conceal it. It will destroy Othello, who has contributed to his destruction by his own folly, but it will also reduce Iago from his wonted command of events to a final enigmatic silence:

> Demand me nothing; what you know, you know:
> From this time forth I never will speak word. (V. ii)

In spite of all his shortcomings, we feel at the last that Othello has been connected with love and natural emotion; nor is there anything grudging about the nobility conferred upon him at his best moments. Iago, on the other hand, is felt, for all his claim to superior "intelligence," to be at once limited, mean, and evil. His attitude, repellent as it is, represents truth in so far as it answers to flaws truly present in the character of his victim; but there is no suggestion in the play that his acceptance of these flaws as final is anything other than a perverse interpretation of human reality, against which it is necessary to fight by gaining that degree of self-knowledge which Othello so conspicuously lacked. Within the unity which it imposes upon contradictions still present in its author's experience, *Othello* allows us to glimpse the decisive orientation of Shakespearean *good* and *evil* in *Macbeth.*

MACBETH

Macbeth, which represents in more ways than one a crucial stage in the development of Shakespeare's art, exhibits the conflict between reason and passion—the constant theme of the great tragedies—under aspects notably different in kind and implications from any he had hitherto attempted.[10] The play deals this time with the overthrow of harmony, not merely in an individual tragic hero (such as Othello) but in an ordered society; and the conflict is worked out in terms that are more clearly and unequivocally moral than in any of the preceding plays. The plot, reflecting this modification of purpose, turns upon a clear contrast between two completely opposed orders. Duncan and Malcolm, who both suffer at the hands of a usurper, are not bound, as Othello had been, by egoism or weakness to the evil which aims at their overthrow; rather do they stand over against Macbeth less as characters in the generally accepted sense than as "symbols" of order, loyalty, and goodness. *Macbeth* is, in the first place and above all, a play about the murder of a king; and there is a very real sense in which the center, the focal point of the conception is to be found neither in the criminal usurper nor in the wife who initially urges him to crime, but in the figure, too easily neglected in its central, normative function, of Duncan.

To say this is clearly to depart in some degree from the conceptions of dramatic character which have inspired so much past study of the play. The significance of Duncan, however we may choose to conceive it, cannot depend upon a character study carried out on conventional lines; some critics, starting from the method of analysis often associated with the name of Bradley, have even found him weak and ineffectual, which was certainly no primary part of Shakespeare's intention. Duncan's function in the play emerges rather, as we shall shortly see, from the images of light and fertility which surround his person and confer substance and consistency upon the "symbolic" value of his rule. The universal implications of this value, again, are only fully appreciated after due weight has been given to the short initial appearance of the Witches, which establishes the climate, moral as much as merely physical, within which the action is to be conducted.[11] The Witches, as a prelude to the human tragedy, introduce us to a situation in which "Fair is foul, and foul is fair" (I, i); through the calculated ambiguity of their utterance and through the elemental commotion which surrounds them, they prepare the way for the entry of evil and disintegration into a state which has been, under Duncan, positive, natural, and orderly. When the evil obscurely present in Macbeth's mind is stirred to conceive and execute the murder of Duncan, he introduces both into the Scottish realm and into his own nature a disrupting evil which must work itself out through the process it has initiated. The play, thus conceived as a harmonious dramatic construction, deals with the overthrow of the balance of royalty by Macbeth's crime, with the full development of the malignity which that overthrow implies, and, finally, with the restoration of natural order under the gracious successor of the murdered king.

Macbeth's murder of Duncan is, accordingly, in the first place a crime against the natural foundations of social and moral harmony; it is at the same time an attack by the destructive elements contemplated in Shakespeare's experience upon those which make for unity and untrammeled maturity. As we have already suggested, the positive values of the tragedy are concentrated on the "symbolic" function of Duncan's royalty and upon the poetry in which it finds expression. As king, Duncan is the head of a "single state of man" (we shall see later the full implications of this phrase of Macbeth's), whose members are bound into unity by the accepted ties of loyalty. By virtue of this position he is the source of all the benefits which flow from his person to those who surround him; receiving the free homage of his subjects, he dispenses to them all the riches and graces which are the mark of true kingship, so that the quality of his poetry is above all life-giving, fertile. The early, light-drenched scenes of the tragedy are dominated by this rich, vital relationship between service spontaneously given and abundant royal bounty. Macbeth himself, still speaking as the loyal general who has saved his country from the consequences of internal rebellion and foreign invasion, describes the subject's duty in repeated protestations of devotion that only in the light of his own later behavior become ironic;[12] in his expression of them his poetry attains, though fugitively and imperfectly, a breadth, a completeness of emotional content, that it will never recover. Duncan, in turn, replies to these professions of loyalty with an overflowing bounty expressed in terms of harvest fullness:

> I have begun to plant thee, and will labour
> To make thee full of growing,

to which the devoted Banquo replies by taking up the same image—

> There if I grow,
> The harvest is your own—

and receives from his king a final expression of abounding joy:

> My plenteous joys,
> Wanton in fullness, seek to hide themselves
> In drops of sorrow. (I. iv)

Duncan and his subjects, in short, vie with one another in the celebration of a relationship that is not one of mastery or subjection, but essentially free, expansive, life-giving. It is in accordance with the spirit of his kingship that Duncan's brief appearances before his murder are invariably invested with images of light and fertility to which are joined, at his moments of deepest feeling, the religious associations of worship in a magnificent, comprehensive impression of overflowing *grace.*

This impression, which is at this stage new in Shakespeare (we shall see something similar, expressed in a different context, in the conception of Cordelia in *King Lear*), from now on acquires growing significance in his work. It is perhaps most finely conveyed in this play at the moment in which Duncan and Banquo, when the former makes his last living appearance, pause before they enter Macbeth's castle at Inverness. The exchange between them is more than decorative in its effect:

> *Duncan:* This castle hath a pleasant seat; the air
> Nimbly and sweetly recommends itself
> Unto our gentle senses.
> *Banquo:* This guest of summer,
> The temple-haunting martlet, does approve
> By his loved mansionry that the heaven's breath
> Smells wooingly here: no jutty, frieze,
> Buttress, nor coign of vantage, but this bird
> Hath made his pendant bed and procreant cradle:
> Where they most breed and haunt, I have observed
> The air is delicate. (I. vi)

The combination of natural sweetness and supernatural "grace" is here achieved in an amplitude of reference that gathers its component images into a single triumphant effect. The "martlet"[13] that builds on the castle walls its "*pendant* bed and *procreant* cradle" (note the sense of weight, of life concentrating itself naturally in the process of birth, reflected in the sound and meaning of the adjectives) is "temple-haunting," a dweller in the shadow of sanctity; and the "loved mansionry" of its home, "loved" both as an auspicious presence and as itself the home of love, is attracted to spots where the breath of heaven "smells *wooingly*" with a sense of fulfillment that is the prelude to generation. The combination of spring with the delicate air which so "nimbly and sweetly" lends itself to senses described as "gentle," purged of all grossness and yet intensely, naturally alive, is an achievement so richly and finely compacted as to be new in Shakespeare. It marks a fresh stage in the dramatic ordering of his experience, and in the resulting liberation of its full possibilities for life and harmony. The "canker" of frustration which was still eating into Othello's love is now fully mastered, artistically worked out in the evil of Macbeth; and all the vitality and goodness so freed find expression in a new intuition of life as fertile and sanctified.

In accordance with this conception there is between Duncan and the loyal Macbeth of these early scenes a relationship rich in honor and fertile in royal bounty. As Duncan's instrument in war, Macbeth wins two arduous battles and becomes Thane of Cawdor. No sooner has he heard the prophecy of the Witches, however, than a new quality enters his meditations, expressing itself in verse of a very different kind. The verse of *Macbeth,* apart from that associated with the loyal personages of the play, is often, at a first reading, so abrupt and disjointed that some critics have felt themselves driven to look for gaps in the text. Yet the difficult passages do not look in the least like the result of omission; they are demonstrably necessary to the feeling of the tragedy. In practically every one of Macbeth's speeches there is a keen sense of discontinuity, a continual jolting of the sensibility into disorder and anarchy. Macbeth, from the time when the thought of murder first forces its way into his consciousness, moves almost continuously in a remarkable state of nervous tension, a state in which a very palpable obscurity is suddenly and unexpectedly shot through by strange revelations and terrifying illuminations of feeling. This state is fully significant only as an inversion of the rich, ordered poetry of Duncan; it is the natural consequence of his murder, a reflection of the entry of evil both into the individual and the state. The quality of this disturbance, which changes with the various stages of Macbeth's own situation, should be carefully considered.

Immediately after his first meeting with the Witches, when the thought of his crime first claims his attention, Macbeth, standing for a moment aside from his companions, speaks with typical disjointed intensity:

> This supernatural soliciting
> Cannot be ill; cannot be good: if ill,
> Why hath it given me earnest of success,
> Commencing in a truth? I am thane of Cawdor;
> If good, why do I yield to that suggestion
> Whose horrid image doth unfix my hair
> And make my seated heart knock at my ribs,
> Against the use of nature? Present fears
> Are less than horrible imaginings:
> My thought, whose murder yet is but fantastical,
> Shakes so my single state of man that function
> Is smothered in surmise, and nothing is
> But what is not. (I. iii)

Nothing quite like this following of thought in the very process of conscious formulation can be found in Shakespeare's early work; it is another development new to *Macbeth*. There is nothing accidental about the telescoping of the syntax in the last few lines; the strange juxtaposition of "thought" and "murder" conveys perfectly the actual birth of the unnatural project in the tangled chaos of ideas. Taken with the rest of the speech it conveys even more. It anticipates the whole disturbance of natural "function," of the "single state of man," which the very thought of such a crime implies; it expresses with unsurpassed nervous directness the shaking to its foundations of what has been a harmonious personality. The speech, indeed, is much more than a mere statement of the ambiguity and tension present in Macbeth's mind. It is a *physical* apprehension of ambiguity, a disordered experience expressing itself in terms of a dislocated functioning. There is a tremendous sense of heightened animal feeling about the unfixed hair and the hammering of the heart. And yet (and it is here that the moral judgment which the whole play will be concerned to enforce is implicitly revealed), keen as it is in its operation, this almost bestial sensitivity is quite meaningless. It introduces unreality even into the thought of murder, in a way which the following scenes will make apparent. When Lady Macbeth, immediately after the killing of Duncan, tries to rouse her husband to a fuller awareness of himself, she says:

> the sleeping and the dead
> Are but as pictures; 'tis the eye of childhood
> That fears a *painted* devil. (II. ii)

The terms in which this attempt to encourage the bemused Macbeth is couched themselves incorporate it into the spirit of unreality, of hideous mockery, which dominates this part of the action. Divorced from its proper place in the "use of nature," the most intense feeling has only a quality of hallucination—that is the full force of "horrible imaginings" and "fantastical." Feeling is "smothered in surmise," and the same keen senses that so effectively seconded the gracious gentleness of Duncan are directed only to a muffled fumbling among uncertainties.

The full meaning of Macbeth's first aside should now be clear. The fertile poetry of Duncan, based upon so delicate and so complete an organization of the "gentle" senses, depends upon a right ordering of the "single state of man." Harmony in the individual is balanced by harmony in the Scottish *state* under its lawful king. Macbeth's poetry, however, reflects the growth into consciousness within his mind of a willful determination to break down this "single state"; and, by means of it, Shakespeare identifies the evil of his play with the disrupting of a most harmonious experience. The result in psychological terms is presented with rare immediacy in Macbeth's early meditations upon his future course of action. It produces in him a discontinuity between the senses and the mind, between the mind and the conscience (note how the speech already quoted opens with a vain fumbling at the meaning of "good" and "ill"), and between these gaps nothing but an intense awareness of their existence. Considered in this way, *Macbeth* can be related to the whole line of development traced in the earlier plays. Its subject is still the "degree" theme of *Troilus and Cressida,* but now immeasurably enriched by a firmer grasp of personality and by a new, more mature organization of feeling. By the side of this contrast between Duncan and Macbeth, the conception behind Ulysses' discourse on "degree"[14] must strike us as sluggish and, dramatically speaking, unrealized. Here, unlike the earlier play, there is no gap between the statement of the argument and its apprehension in terms of immediate experience. Ulysses, on the whole, *tells us* about the breakdown of "degree" in abstract terms, whereas here we *feel* the personality in dissolution, striving vainly to attain, on the basis of its own illusory desires, an impression of coherence. To the gain in poetic immediacy corresponds an advance in dramatic presentation. The "single state of man," a state which depends for both the individual and the social organism on the due observance of ordered loyalty, is here replaced by a cleavage in the innermost fabric of the mind, an uncertain groping in the bottomless pit of psychological and spiritual darkness, in the first obscure glimpses of a state where fundamental values are inverted, and where "nothing is But what is not."

Darkness, indeed, is from now on Macbeth's native element. From the decisive moment in which his crime is conceived he is excluded from the light which radiates from the royal figure of Duncan, so that it is no surprise when, in the very next scene, we meet with his exclamation:

> Stars, hide your fires;
> Let not light see my black and deep desires:
> The eye wink at the hand; yet let that be,
> Which the eye fears, when it is done, to see. (I. iv)

In point of fact, Macbeth himself, already involved in obscurity, is not at this moment clear as to the true nature of these desires. The decisive part in clarifying his still confused thoughts is played by Lady Macbeth, whose first significant utterance, on receiving her husband's letters with an account of his meeting with the Witches, turns upon two closely associated ideas. The first is the recognition of his lack of clarity, expressed in her own concise definition of him as one who

> wouldst not play false,
> And yet wouldst wrongly win. (I. v)

The second is her determination to oppose to this contradiction in his nature the conviction (which she, in her own way, shares with all the great Shakespearean "villains": Iago, Edmund, Antonio) that success in action implies, as a necessary condition, the abolition of any gap in the mind of the agent between the act itself and the will whose decision alone makes action possible. It is the elimination of this gap, the equivalent on an avowedly moral level of Hamlet's rooted disinclination to carry out the duty imposed upon him, that she is determined to produce in her vacillating husband; for, as she says:

> that which rather thou dost fear to do
> Than wishest should be undone. (I. v)

By introducing this element of logic, spurious though it be, into Macbeth's uncertainty, she makes the crime possible. The relationship between the two characters, in the course of which one of them takes the initiative in bringing to the surface elements obscurely present in the mind of the other, is a characteristic feature of Shakespeare's dramatic constructions. We have already seen it in operation in the disintegration, by Iago, of Othello's heroic nobility: applied here in a different context, and to a very different purpose, it confers upon the plot a dynamic element, a sense of development essential to the complete effect.

The connection between *Macbeth* and Shakespeare's previous work becomes still clearer once it is seen that the murder of Duncan is the result of a movement of the "blood," of the deeper sources of passion exercising their potent influence upon the will. The nature of the relationship that unites husband and wife is worth careful consideration. It is implied in the words in which Lady Macbeth, having read her husband's letter, greets him upon his arrival:

> Thy letters have transported me beyond
> This ignorant present, and I feel now
> The future in the instant, (I. v)

and in the ecstatic quality of his response: "My dearest love!" It is precisely this intensity of passion which, diverted from its natural channels, is turned onto a craving for power and issues in murder. To follow the common line of interpretation and call this craving "ambition" is not enough, for ambition is an abstraction and this is something that comes, as we have seen, from the "blood," from the hidden instinctive foundations of the personality. Lady Macbeth's attitude, indeed, logical though it be once its premises are granted, involves a passionate distortion of normal humanity which balances that which she herself helps to produce in her husband. Born of a reversal of nature, its expression is consistently unnatural. Her first prayer, as her purpose takes shape, is "*Unsex* me here!" Her second —prefaced by the significant apostrophe, "Come, thick night!"—is an appeal to the darkness that makes possible the exclusion of reason and pity. From this to the expressions of forced, unnatural determination which follow—the declared willingness to kill her own child rather than fail in the course of action which her "blood"-impelled craving for power has dictated, the final conquest of her feeling that the sleeping Duncan resembled her own father—the passage is as easy as it is monstrous, inhuman. The whole crime is, in the words of Ross, from the moment of its conception to that of its final execution, "against nature still" (II. iv). The overthrow of the royal symbol of order and fruitful unity is the result of a preceding disturbance of the balance between impulse and conscience, instinctive "blood" and reasonable will; and this, in turn, naturally produces a dissociation of bodily function, an anarchy in which animal feeling works in an isolation divorced from all control, and so void of continuity and significance.

After this, the actual murder of Duncan comes as the grotesque climax of a process that has involved from the first an inversion of every natural bond and feeling. Macbeth moves toward it in a state of hallucination, still invoking the darkness in which evil thoughts have at least the illusion of free play. "Each corporal agent" in him is "bent up" (I. vii), as by a conscious, strained effort, to the deed that awaits him. Even at this stage, however, more is involved than a statement, conveyed with the greatest linguistic immediacy, of psychological disorder. The supernatural sanctions against which Macbeth has rebelled in conceiving the murder of his king make themselves felt, in a broken form indeed, because they are reflected in a mind already irretrievably shattered, but with the power to impose their validity in his own despite. The speech in which Macbeth pauses in a final attempt to take stock of his situation is at once a ruthless revelation of character and a contribution to the dominant spiritual theme:

> If it were done when 'tis done, then 'twere well
> It were done quickly; if the assassination
> Could trammel up the consequence, and catch
> With his surcease success; that but this blow
> Might be the be-all and the end-all here,
> But here, upon this bank and shoal of time,
> We'ld jump the life to come. (I. vii)

Macbeth is trying to persuade himself that the only valid reason for hanging back from the murder he is about to commit is one of expediency, the fear of rousing to retribution the public opinion which an attack on Duncan must inevitably outrage. From the first, however, the expression of his position is anything but dispassionate or clear. The succession of uneasy suppositions with which his reflections open, and the very avoidance, through the repeated use of "it," of all direct reference to the absorbing object of his meditations, show that even his efforts at logical expression are caught up in the incoherence, the broken continuity, which has dominated his thought ever since he first considered the revelation of the Witches. The breathless confounding, so superbly echoed in the sound of his words, of "a*ss*a*ss*ination" with "con*se*quence," "*s*urc*ease*" with "*suc*-*cess*," reflects a mind involved in the incoherent flow of its own ideas, while the force of "trammel" and "catch," each stressing with its direct impact a break in the rhythm of the phrase, conveys perfectly the peculiar disorganized intensity which Macbeth will bear with him to the final extinction of feeling.

Disorganization and incoherence, however, are not the only aspects of Macbeth's condition revealed by the speech. Beneath them, rising to take possession of his mind in a swelling flood of emotion, is a tide of feeling which, while reflected through the speaker's own state, derives ultimately from the outraged spiritual values of the play. The true sources of the murderer's fear are not what he declares them to be. Self-ignorance and self-deception are essential parts of his nature, and as his words bring them to light, they are seen to be connected, in his own despite, with the supernatural terrors which he has just declared his readiness to "jump":

> Besides, this Duncan
> Hath borne his faculties so meek, hath been
> So clear in his great office, that his virtues
> Will plead like angels, trumpet-tongued, against
> The deep damnation of his taking-off;
> And pity, like a naked new-born babe,
> Striding the blast, or heaven's cherubin, horsed
> Upon the sightless couriers of the air,
> Shall blow the horrid deed in every eye,
> That tears shall drown the wind. (I. vii)

To discuss the logic of this passage in terms of mixed metaphor would clearly be to miss the whole point of the speech, dramatic not less than poetic (and how, indeed, shall we separate one aspect of the total effect from another?). Macbeth's emotion grows in the course of its expression, and in a way which involves the presence of the whole in each of its stages. It passes from a consideration of the inexpediency of murdering Duncan to embrace a sense of supernatural terror which is at once, in itself, a sign of hysterical weakness, and, in the general design of the play, a reflection of the positive sanctions that dominate the entire action. His first impulse is to contrast the brutality of his projected deed with the "meekness" of his victim, the guilt he feels in himself with the "clarity" of the king he is about to kill. "Meekness" and "clarity," however, when associated with the royal office, are not merely innocent and pacific qualities. They have, by virtue of the spiritual foundation on which the royal office rests, a force that will impose itself by pleading "trumpet-tongued," with apocalyptic power, against the horror of his death; and the sense of this horror is itself fused, in Macbeth's mind, with a growing fear of the "damnation" that the intrinsic evil of his act will bring upon him. The supernatural sanctions associated with the holiness of the royal office, based themselves on a coherent, unified conception, are reflected in the weak, divided mind of the murderer in the form of a hysterical and disintegrating sense of terror.

In this way Macbeth's thoughts, still developing his reaction to Duncan's innocence and the public effect, as he foresees it, of his death, rise to the great complex image in which the speech culminates. The universal pity which he feels to be an obstacle to the carrying out of his project is now seen to combine the attributes of innocence ("a naked new-born babe") already associated with his victim, with that of a supernatural power rising, as it were, out of the depths of his own consciousness to overthrow him. The speech thus affirms the relevance of the very values it is engaged in setting aside, recognizes in its own darkness the existence of light, albeit seen through distortion and obscurity. The "new-born babe" becomes, in his distraught imagination, an avenging power "striding the blast," carrying on the sense of irresistible denunciation already conveyed in "trumpet-tongued" and finally projected as "heaven's cherubin"

horsed
Upon the sightless couriers of the air,

to make his hidden crime universally, inescapably known. Fear, not less than loyalty, testifies in its own despite to the validity of the order it is engaged in outraging. Finally, the emotion which has thus risen to its distraught climax subsides as Macbeth returns to a consideration of his own situation, isolated before the fear which now possesses him and acutely conscious of his lack of genuine motivation:

> I have no spur
> To prick the sides of my intent, but only
> Vaulting ambition, which o'erleaps itself
> And falls on the other. (I. vii)

The speech, already so rich in its development of living metaphor, now introduces a new, final comparison: that of the rider who puts an excess of energy into his effort to vault into the saddle, only to find himself, having overshot the mark, falling into vacancy. After the preceding swell of the apocalyptic vision of pity, at once produced by an accentuating a sense of moral emptiness, the speech turns brokenly to a consideration of the speaker's own state—his "I" is lamely introduced in the middle of a line—while the verses which follow are deliberately interrupted at "only" (the adverb in itself carries on a restrictive sense) and at "o'erleaps itself," to fall away with lame inconclusiveness "on the other." Few speeches, even in this most tensely conceived of plays, achieve a closer, more intimate fusion between the psychological disintegration of an individual and the overriding supernatural conception which finds harmonious expression in the innocent and a broken, incoherent reflection in the hysterical fear of the guilty.[15]

By the time the murder of Duncan has taken place it is abundantly clear that Macbeth's crime is, as we have argued, a rift in the harmony and richness of the unity "symbolized" in the royal rule and realized in the poetry associated with the dead king. Such a rift, once it has appeared, has to exhaust its destructive consequences before coherence can be restored; and in the central part of the play Macbeth's kingship, contrasted with that of Duncan as "evil" with "good," is shown as simply the working out of the negation upon which it was founded. The usurper, as he comes to realize that the crime he has committed to gain, in his wife's overweening words, "solely sovereign sway and masterdom" (I. v), has in fact failed to achieve this goal, progressively loses the illusion of freedom and plunges into a further series of unnatural actions. At the lowest point in his downward progress, he consults the Witches once more in a determination to know "by the worst means the worst"; and the Witches respond (IV. i) both by offering further false "certainties"—in the form of the various apparitions set before his eyes—and by confirming finally, through the vision of Banquo's succession, the sterility of his own line. With this revelation, and the last, useless killing of Macduff's wife and children which immediately follows (IV. ii), the central part of the action, exhausting the possibilities of evil and uniting Macbeth and the realm he has usurped in a common degradation, is logically complete. Its third and last stage will show a process of recovery in which the forces of "good," of life and ordered harmony, drawing their strength originally from the holy ruler of England, flow back like a returning tide over Scotland to sweep away Macbeth's shadow of power and to restore, in the person of Duncan's rightful heir, Malcolm, the kingship of "grace." The complete effect, as will be seen, is that of a balanced construction, each successive stage of which, linked to the preceding action by threads of imagery and the logic of events, also prepares the ground for the final resolution.

From the moment of Duncan's murder until the final overthrow of Macbeth the action turns upon a contrast between two royalties: that of the dead king, founded upon natural allegiance and rich in generous bounty, and that of his murderer, which, initiated in a reversal of "nature," can only have as its end unnatural chaos and inevitable death. The terms of the contrast are already established at the moment in which Duncan's dead body is discovered. Macduff, bursting in with the news of the discovery, stresses those aspects of it which imply the reversal of natural order and the commission of sacrilege:

> *Confusion* now hath made his masterpiece!
> Most *sacrilegious* murder hath broke ope
> *The Lord's anointed temple,* and stole thence
> *The life o' the building.* (II. iii)

On his own re-entry, a moment later, Macbeth once more expresses, in the typically heightened and unnatural spirit which reflects his distraught condition, the positive values which he has deliberately chosen to attack. Royalty truly established and freely accepted is, indeed, "the life o' the building," the foundation upon which all natural relationships in society depend; and Macbeth, in his effort to simulate a sorrow which he alone cannot feel, speaks more truly than he knows when he says:

> from this instant,
> There's nothing serious in mortality:
> All is but toys; renown and grace is dead;
> The wine of life is drawn, and the mere lees
> Is left this vault to brag of. (II. iii)

When the murderer thus surrounds the dead majesty of Duncan with images of life and "grace," he both stresses the sacramental quality, so to call it, of the victim's office (even the implications of "the wine of life" may hold a subsidiary meaning in this respect) and reveals how his own deed has left him nothing but the dregs and "toys" which will from now on dominate his utterances to the end of the tragedy. The sense that the future is, for Macbeth, as obscure as the manifestations of darkness and chaos which now surround him leads finally to the complete reversal of the "gracious" imagery of life and light which surrounded the figure of Duncan. "Dark night *strangles* the travelling lamp," the king's horses "contend against obedience," and, most powerfully of all,

> darkness does the face of earth *entomb*,
> When *living* light should *kiss* it. (II. iv)

The point of balance between the happy past and the forebodings of the future is finally expressed in Macduff's remarks to Ross:

> *Ross:* Will you to Scone?
> *Macduff:* No, cousin, I'll to Fife.
> *Ross:* Well, I will thither.
> *Macduff:* Well, may you see things well done there.—adieu,
> Lest our old robes sit easier than our new. (II. iv)

Exchanges of this kind repeatedly mark what are in effect turning points in the spiritual not less than in the surface development of the action; their use, indeed, is a typical feature of this most carefully and deliberately constructed of plays.

During the central part of the tragedy, which opens with the shift from Inverness to Forres and closes with the murder of Lady Macduff (IV. ii), the contrast between the usurper's kingship and that of his victim is fully developed in a series of balanced images. Its outstanding dramatic expression is Macbeth's banquet (III. iv), which is set, in its spirit and final outcome, against Duncan's great feast at Inverness, when he distributed "great largess" to his thanes and finally "shut up in *measureless* content" (II. i). The force of "measureless," and its connection with the infinite generosity in which the spirit of Duncan's kingship is consistently expressed, should by now be amply clear. It is significant that Macbeth should be absent from this demonstration of free loyalty and corresponding royal bounty; the action upon which his imagination has already embarked is the flaw in "the single state of man" which depends upon natural reverence for the throne. If we return to Macbeth's own banquet, which takes place just after he has advanced a step further on his empty progress only to learn that the escape of Fleance has once more meant the dropping of a link in the chain of rigidly determined acts in which he follows the illusion of freedom, we shall find the ghost of Banquo intervening to occupy the place destined for him as king at the head of his table. The apparition breaks in upon the show of loyalty and order which Macbeth seeks, by virtue of his usurped dignity, to command; and the effect of its entry is such that the whole scene is closed by Lady Macbeth's most significant words:

> You have displaced the mirth, broke the good meeting,
> With most admired disorder. (III. iv)

The use of the word "disorder" is especially revealing. It is a precise description of what Macbeth's crime has let loose upon Scotland, and also—in the personal sphere—of the effects of evil as revealed more intimately in his own person. The two disorders, individual and universal, stand in the closest connection; they develop side by side, until both reach their culminating point, in terms of the external action, in the murder of Macduff's family.

The state of intimate disorganization in which his crime has left Macbeth is closely associated, from an early stage, with the loss of the power to sleep. The darkness which he has invoked from the first conception of his crime, far from bringing with it rest, natural renewal after the exertions of the day, is associated for him with a wakefulness which the dissociation of his various faculties—the divorce between "eye" and "hand" (I. iv), consciousness and act—can only render more horrible in its effects. The sleep in which Macbeth found Duncan when he raised his hand against him is henceforth woven into the innermost fabric of his conscience; his imagination, in which he sees himself as the "murderer" of sleep itself, clutches incoherently at the healing properties of rest in words which escape his wife's more literal understanding and express the chaos which has taken possession of his mind:

> the innocent sleep,
> Sleep that knits up the ravell'd sleave of care,
> The death of each day's life, sore labour's bath,
> Balm of hurt minds, great nature's second course,
> Chief nourisher in life's feast. (II. ii)

By a process typical of this play, these words are at once a revelation of breaking coherence and, through the positive force of the images with which the speaker so disjointedly, hysterically fumbles, a contribution to the spiritual content of the tragedy. Sleep should bring repose, the renewing of the whole man in his rest; it is at once a sign of health, moral and physical, and, for those to whom it is available, a means of recovering health after exposure to the strain of daily living. Lady Macbeth, confronted at a slightly later stage with her husband's uneasiness, says to him, "You lack the season of all natures, sleep" (III. iv); the "season," the element that makes life sweet and acceptable, as to the natural taste. The full force of sleep as a Shakespearean symbol becomes increasingly clear in his last plays, in Pericles and in Leontes;[16] already in *Macbeth* it is related to seasoning and so, in a very vital way, to the natural functioning of the "gentle senses." Macbeth's words as he first contemplates the nature of his act constitute an inverted homage to the values he has willfully destroyed. By his crime he has cut himself off from all that is natural, and so his sleep, under the palpable "blanket of the dark" that henceforth envelops him, is shot through with

> the cursed thoughts that nature
> Gives way to in repose. (II. i)

This double nature of sleep, which nourishes the innocent at "life's feast" and restores the faculties of "hurt minds" at the same time that it releases, in the guilty, the subconscious images of terror present in their natures, is variously and richly related to the complex poetic structure of the tragedy.

To Macbeth, indeed, who has murdered not only a man and his kinsman, but, in the person of his king, order, unity itself, sleep can offer no refuge and no restoration. At best he can connect it, not with the renewal of vital energy, but with death, the only release from the continuation of a life the content and significance of which he has killed. In this spirit, when first alone with his wife after their crowning, he opposes his own insomnia nostalgically to the peace which his victim has found in death:

> better be with the dead,
> Whom we, to gain our peace, have sent to peace,
> Than on the torture of the mind to lie
> In restless ecstasy. Duncan is in his grave;
> After life's fitful fever he sleeps well. (III. ii)

To suggest, as Santayana once suggested,[17] that this phrase sums up Shakespeare's attitude toward life (in so far as one can be discovered) is remarkably misleading. Macbeth's state of mind can in no way be identified with the complete conception of this tragedy. Opposed to it there stands, as we have noted and shall see again in the concluding scenes, the norm and plenitude, the splendid ordering of experience achieved in the poetry of Duncan and finally confirmed in the "symbolic" function of Malcolm. Macbeth's attitude toward death cannot be identified with that of Shakespeare in this play (something like it is perhaps the most unambiguous feeling in *Hamlet*), though the dramatist no doubt felt it keenly and persistently as an element in his experience. It is rather the product of Macbeth's original crime against loyalty and order, against the harmony and continuity which makes experience valuable. In murdering Duncan, his usurper murdered the coherence of his own life, so that henceforth we expect of him (as, in reality, he expects of himself) nothing but death.

The turning point of the entire action (if a turning point can properly be spoken of in a series of events so closely and continuously related to their point of departure) is finally reached in the two scenes in which Macbeth, after returning to consult the Witches, proceeds in full disillusionment to the murder of the family of Macduff. The new approach to the Witches involves a fully conscious acceptance of anarchy; he will know the future, he says, even though the result be universal chaos, even though

> the treasure
> Of nature's germins tumble all together,
> Even till destruction sicken. (IV. i)[18]

NORTHWEST MISSOURI
STATE COLLEGE LIBRARY
MARYVILLE, MISSOURI

The reply he receives, ambiguous to the last in accordance with the nature of evil as it presents itself to its servants in this play, at once offers an illusory certainty and, in the succeeding apparitions offered to his eyes, foreshadows the future development of the action. Each of the apparitions, indeed, insinuates a double meaning, offers a fallacious confirmation to Macbeth's evil instincts at the same time that it symbolizes a stage in the birth, through tragedy and retribution, of a new positive order. The first appearance, that of the "armed Head," while warning him of the struggle that awaits him, fixes the threat to his security upon the person of Macduff; it thus confirms him in his determination to eliminate the latter, who will thereby be given an added personal motive to seek his overthrow. The following apparition, that of the "bloody Child," both strengthens Macbeth in his confidence by offering him immunity from all "of woman born" and suggests the birth in travail of an innocence in which the usurper can have no part. This birth is confirmed, and given the seal of royalty, in the final apparition of "a Child *crowned*, with a tree in his hand," offering, beyond the shadowy assurance associated with the wood at Birnam, a symbol of infant authority invested with the green of living hope and the fertility which, in this play, is the accompaniment of "grace." Seen in this way, the scene turns upon a contrast between the false certainties offered to Macbeth and the anticipated rebirth of innocence in ordered loyalty; the only unambiguous glimpse into the future conceded to the usurper is that which his insistence wrings from the Witches and which shows him the sterility of his line in contrast to the fruitful succession derived from the loyal Banquo. From this moment the murderer, now aware that his crime has been in vain, knows also that there is no retreat from its consequences, that what remains of his life is inexorably caught in the determined chain of circumstances which his own act has initiated.

The disillusionment produced in Macbeth by the revelation of the Witches henceforth dominates his whole being. The crown placed on his head has proved "fruitless," the scepter grasped by his usurping hands "barren" (the continuation, implied in its opposite, of the imagery of fertility so closely connected with Duncan is most significant), and the supernatural fears of the early scenes have hardened into the conviction that he has indeed, and vainly, surrendered "the eternal jewel" of his soul "to the common enemy of man" (III. i). The decision to murder Macduff and his family (IV. ii)

NORTHWEST MISSOURI STATE COLLEGE LIBRARY MARYVILLE, MISSOURI marks his final enslavement to the determined course of events. To "What's done is done" (III. ii), the conviction urged on him by his wife when she first becomes conscious of the futility of their common crime, he has already replied with the statement of a philosophy of illusion: "Things bad begun make strong themselves by ill" (III. ii); and this conviction, or the need for clinging to it, henceforward dominates his actions. Macbeth follows a course which he originally chose, indeed, but now no longer controls. Crime leads to further crime, until—in a moment of despairing insight—he realizes that his real wish is to retrace his steps, to recover an original state of innocence, but that, being what he has now become, he cannot do so:

I am in blood
Stepped in so far, that, should I wade no more,
Returning were as tedious as go o'er. (III. iv)

This, far from being the voice of the confident man of action, is that of the self-deluded criminal who has waked finally, but too late, to the hopeless weakness which all his actions imply.

The two scenes which thus mark the final disillusionment of Macbeth also convey the lowest point in the misery of Scotland, whose state is now so clearly contrasted with the happiness formerly enjoyed under Duncan. Her sorrows, in Macduff's phrase, "strike heaven in the face" (IV. iii), the loyal remnants have fled, and Macduff himself, with a carelessness that he admits to be unpardonable, has left his family to die at the hands of their butcher. Yet, at the very moment when this particularly gratuitous crime is carried out, Shakespeare confirms through a single speech of Ross that a further decisive stage in the action has been reached. Ross is one of those minor personages to whom Shakespeare, more especially in his later plays, gives some of the functions of a chorus; he comments upon the events which take place before him, and his speeches are often statements of fact so made that their imagery unites them to the poetic construction of the play. Ross now addresses Lady Macduff in these words:

cruel are the times, when we are traitors
And do not know ourselves; when we hold rumour
From what we fear, yet know not what we fear,
But float upon a wild and violent sea
Each way and move. I take my leave of you;

Shall not be long but I'll be here again:
Things at the worst will cease, or else climb upward
To what they were before. (IV. ii)

The conclusion clearly anticipates the course of events to follow: Macbeth's overthrow with the recovery of loyalty and the "single state of man" in the triumph of Malcolm. This scene, in fact, in spite of the horrors enacted in it, marks a point of balance in the entire development (that is, the effect so finely conveyed in the suspense of "Each way and move"), with a first suggestion of the recovery. It is worth noting, too, how the opening lines drive home the impression of evil which Macbeth's own speeches have already stressed. The essence of evil, which communicates itself from the usurper to his whole realm, lies in uncertainty, in ignorance of one's impulses, of the true causes of one's own actions. This uncertainty has reached such a degree of anarchy that it must either "cease," lead to the annihilation which Macbeth's whole career has presupposed as its end,[19] or else "climb upward" and so return to the former condition under Duncan.

This speech, and the assassinations which follow, lead to a long scene (IV. iii), the effect of which is as puzzling as anything in the play. This is the episode in which Malcolm, after "confessing" to a series of hideous faults which are not in fact even remotely connected with his character, reveals himself finally as a truly dedicated man and undertakes to place himself at the head of the movement which is to restore order and peace to his country. In terms of common realism, Malcolm's change of attitude is neither adequately motivated nor convincing, and we must surely regard it as a "symbolic" experiment, the true meaning of which lies in its relation to the preceding and the following action. Read in this way, the episode is a dramatic projection of the balance of contraries recently affirmed by Ross. The catalogue of Malcolm's "vices," in fact, is not meant to be intrinsically probable; it simply gathers up those really associated with Macbeth and is finally rounded off by an evocation of universal disorder that is connected with the usurper's previous utterances:

Nay, had I power, I should
Pour the sweet milk of concord into hell,
Uproar the universal peace, confound
All unity on earth. (IV. iii)

"Vice," thus conceived, is more than personal in its implications, just as the virtue and purity which stand against it, and which Malcolm also finally associates with his own person, is related to the sanctity of the royal line; for, as Macduff puts it,

> Thy royal father
> Was a most sainted king; the queen that bore thee,
> Oftener upon her knees than on her feet,
> Died every day she lived. (IV. iii)

This association of sanctity with penance, this deliberate spiritualizing of the idea of death, corresponds perfectly to the state of the action. While Macbeth is spreading death through his usurped kingdom, the royalty round which the forces of recovery are beginning to gather finds in awareness of mortality a prelude to the restoration of "grace" and the positive values of life. *Macbeth,* taking a stage further the presentation of the Shakespearean tragic hero, sets him against a universal moral background in what is essentially a fresh dramatic conception; the deliberate abandonment of realism in this scene corresponds to a new "symbolic" purpose, related less to the simple portrayal of the events which constitute the tragedy than to the poetic unity which, underlying it, confers upon it its true meaning. This is not to say that the combination of vestiges of "realism" with the new "symbolic" purpose is here achieved with entire success.

The last act of *Macbeth,* the logical rounding off of a process conceived from its first moment as a unity, deals with the return of the kingship of "grace." The word, which we shall meet again in the last plays (notably in *The Winter's Tale*), is used by Shakespeare to express the harmony associated with the "single state of man." It is noteworthy that in the very scene between Malcolm and Macduff which we have just considered, the loyal elements scattered by Macbeth's tyranny anticipate the access of new strength to their cause from the action of yet another holy king—Edward the Confessor of England. The Lord who converses with Lennox just before Macbeth's return to the Witches first indicates the coming reaction when he speaks of the sanctity of "the most pious Edward" and associates it openly with the restoration of natural harmony to a wounded society:

by the help of these—with Him above
To ratify the work—we may again
Give to our tables meat, sleep to our nights;
Free from our feasts and banquets bloody knives;
Do faithful homage, and receive free honours. (III. vi)

The insistence upon threads of imagery already seen to be variously significant in the play—"meat" and "sleep" as attributes of normal, healthy functioning, the disturbance of banquets by bloody visions of murder, the counterpoise of "faithful homage" and "free honours"—leads to the more explicit note of "symbolism" which underlies Malcolm's account of the curing by Edward of the "king's evil":

'Tis called the evil . . .
How he solicits heaven,
Himself best knows: but strangely-visited people,
All swoln and ulcerous, pitiful to the eye,
The mere despair of surgery, he cures,
Hanging a golden stamp about their necks,
Put on with holy prayers; and 'tis spoken,
To the succeeding royalty he leaves
The *healing benediction.* With this strange virtue
He hath a heavenly gift of prophecy,
And sundry blessings hang about his throne,
That speak him *full of grace.* (IV. iii)

The force of this is so clear that it does not need to be enlarged upon; the explicit reference to the "evil" and the final word "grace" tell us who are the "crew of wretched souls" of whom the Doctor has spoken, the nature of their infirmity and of the restoration that is approaching them. Scotland is to be healed and purified by the powers of harmony and reconciliation symbolized in "grace" and "benediction"; and the holy Edward will impart to Malcolm the spiritual strength needed for this task. By the end of the scene Malcolm can refer directly to the supernatural sanction which will bless his arms:

Macbeth
Is ripe for shaking, and the powers above
Put on their instruments; (IV. iii)

and again, recalling directly the persistent darkness that has surrounded Macbeth's rule since he himself invoked its cover for his original crime: "The night is long that never finds the day."

As Malcolm returns with this army of deliverance, the divisions implicit in evil come to the surface in his foes. In contrast to Edward's healing power, the Doctor at Dunsinane cannot cure the disharmony beneath Lady Macbeth's sleepwalking. "More needs she the divine than the physician" (V. i); the words reveal the absence of the "healing benediction" which Malcolm has triumphantly invoked. From the first, as we have seen, the sleep of the murderers has been wrapped in a darkness shot through with "cursed thoughts," pregnant with subconscious images of retribution. As such, it fails to bring relief to either Macbeth or to his wife. As one sin against "grace," conscience, and human obligation follows another, the chaotic intensity originally present in Macbeth's mind is replaced by a mere weary lack of feeling; even revulsion gives way to dead insensibility. Every student of the play has noted the nervous exhaustion which progressively overtakes Macbeth, until at the end we find that "unfix my hair" which he had uttered in his first obscure reaction to the message of the Witches[20] echoed thus:

> I have almost forgot the taste of fears;
> The time has been, my senses would have cool'd
> To hear a night-shriek, and my fell of hair
> Would at a dismal treatise rouse and stir
> As life were in't: I have supp'd full with horrors. (V. v)

The fact of Macbeth's weariness is much less important than the manner of its expression. Note how the feeling associated with the "fell of hair" is further connected with the cloyed palate and the satiated stomach, and so with a line of imagery variously related to feasting, royal munificence and the "seasoning" proper to healthy living processes, throughout the play. Even the disorganized sensibility of the animal, once so keenly felt in the deepest stirrings of the speaker's consciousness, is now played out, exhausted. The murderer continues to the last to go through the motions of action, but his deeds are divorced from all desire or feeling, however inhuman. His end, when it comes, is no more than the logical conclusion of a process which aimed at the destruction of harmonious life to replace it by anarchy and death.

In the light of these considerations, we may understand better the final scenes of the tragedy, reading into them something more than a monotonous series of battle episodes leading to a foregone conclusion. To this end, we need to avoid above all the temptation to sentimentalize Macbeth in the hour of his downfall, regarding him primarily as a brave warrior making his last stand against hopeless odds. He is indeed that, in part and up to a point; but it is more important to see him above all as a man who has freely chosen his own particular and appropriate hell and who is now faced with the undisguised consequences of his choice. Life itself has now become for Macbeth a pale and senseless succession of incidents—

> To-morrow, and to-morrow, and to-morrow . . .
>
> a tale
> Told by an idiot, full of sound and fury,
> Signifying *nothing*— (V. v)

a procession of events in front of which he is conscious only of a decline into meaningless old age and irreparable loss. As he puts it, more poignantly than ever before:

> I have lived long enough: my way of life
> Is fallen into the sear, the yellow leaf;
> And that which should accompany old age,
> As honour, love, obedience, troops of friends,
> I must not look to have; but, in their stead,
> Curses, not loud but deep, mouth-honour, breath,
> Which the poor heart would fain deny and dare not. (V. iii)

Lest we be tempted to find this principally pathetic in its intention (though it is, of course, that, and to a high degree: otherwise there would be no tragedy in the spectacle of Macbeth's fall), we should consider that every item in this catalogue of loss—"honour, love, obedience, troops of friends"—has been forfeited by the speaker from the moment when he chose to strike his fatal blow against Duncan. *Honour:* can a general claim this who has betrayed the king whose armies he once, in happier times, led to victory? *Love:* how did Macbeth reply to the bounteous generosity which was the external sign of Duncan's trust, of his kingly love for him? *Obedience:* how, but by rebellion culminating in assassination, did he follow up the hollow declarations of allegiance originally made to his royal master? *Friends:* what claim to friendship can he advance, who conceived the murder of Banquo, once his comrade in victorious and patriotic arms? Of Macbeth, in short, it has to be said that, possessing the human privilege of choice (for this, as we have seen, is a play about free will and determinism), he chose to exercise it against nature: and when he awoke, but too late, to the essential vanity of his motives, he discovered the bitter truth that certain choices, once freely and consciously entered upon, become irrevocable, end—following an inexorable law of human behavior—by excluding the possibility of further freedom. Such, without recourse to any notion of the future life, which would be foreign to Shakespeare's purposes, is Macbeth's particular and appropriate form of damnation. *Macbeth* is, perhaps, of all Shakespeare's plays, the most Dantesque in spirit. His hero, unlike Dante's personages, finds his hell exclusively in this life; but the loss to which his choices lead him at the last is surely akin to that which Adamo da Brescia, usurer and coiner of false images, expressed with equal and equally vain regret, toward the bottom of hell, when he remembered the world that he had lost—"the streams that from the green hills of the Casentino flow down into the Arno"[21]—and who said of these things, with the sad pathos of eternity: "Sempre mi stanno innanzi, e non indarno": "*Always* these things are before me, *and not in vain.*"

The final battle, seen in this light, merely confirms a process already foreshadowed, substantially complete. The seeds of chaos and death sown in the moral being of the usurper emerge to cover his fictitious rule. We hear almost at once that "The tyrant's people on both sides do fight" (V. vii), and the terrible Macbeth shrinks to something small and rather absurd as his fall becomes inevitable. In the words of Angus:

> now does he feel his title
> Hang loose about him, like a giant's robe
> Upon a dwarfish thief. (V. ii)

Before the advancing powers of healing good, evil has shrunk to insignificance. Macbeth is seen to be a puny figure dressed up in a usurped greatness, a dignity not his own, and we are ready for the final bravado flourish with which he dies after Macduff has stripped him of his false "supernatural" hopes. Such is the end of the ambiguity stated by the Witches as the opening theme of the play: "Fair is foul, and foul is fair" (I. i). The consequences of this inversion of values have been far-reaching indeed, but—for the first time in a Shakespearean tragedy—not beyond repair. The answer to it is seen in the concluding announcement of the coronation of a king who refers to "the grace of Grace" (V. viii) as his sanction, and who is the rightful successor of Duncan; a king, in short, to whom the loyalty of free men is properly due, and from whom royal bounty may again be expected to flow.

KING LEAR

The tragedies of Shakespeare's maturity, from *Macbeth* onward, are characterized by a consistent development of the dramatic "symbolism" which that play first anticipates. This symbolism, which derives originally from an extension of the function of the poetic image in the dramatic scheme, leads naturally to a new conception of plot. The image, expanding by a growing number of contacts with the surrounding verse, becomes more intimately and more variously related to the exigencies of story and character, until the very possibility of a sharp distinction between the action and the poetry through which its meaning in emotional and spiritual terms is conveyed becomes inconceivable. The plot, thus regarded less in terms of common realism than as an extension of the poetry, becomes in effect an expanded metaphor,[22] the "symbolic" reflection of an experience which the poet, following the promptings of his creative impulse, is concerned to mold into artistic form.

The story of *King Lear,* in some way the most complex and deliberately constructed of Shakespeare's great tragedies, is precisely of this kind. There is a very real sense in which the whole action of the tragedy might be described as a projection of the conflicting issues present in the mind of the central protagonist. As father, Lear produces in his daughters contrasting reactions that reflect different and contradictory facets of his own mind; as king, his willful impulses liberate forces of anarchy which nothing less than utter exhaustion can ultimately contain. From the conflict whose dual aspect is thus concentrated in one mind the various subsidiary issues of the play radiate as partial reflections of a common image, at once contributing depth and variety to the central situation and deriving from it the subsistent unity which alone can give the complete story its full meaning. In none of Shakespeare's mature plays is the correspondence between action and motive, the external event and its inner meaning, so exactly and significantly established.

Both aspects of Lear's position, the personal and the social, contribute to the unity of a tragedy whose various stages correspond, in the external action, to a closely knit development. The first stage in this development, occupying roughly the first two acts, is concerned with the entry of uncontrolled passion as a disruptive force into Lear's mind and with the consequent overthrow of ordered balance in himself, in his family, and in the state of whose unity he has been hitherto the royal guardian. In the second stage, which covers the central part of the play, personal disorder finds in the tempest to which the protagonists are exposed a symbol that at once reflects and transcends it; the elements at war, besides corresponding to the conflict in Lear's distraught person, act through the intense suffering which they impose upon him with the force of a self-revelation to become the necessary prelude to a species of rebirth. That rebirth, however, although achieved in the personal order during the third and final stage, cannot affect Lear's external fortunes. His reconciliation with Cordelia is followed almost immediately by their final defeat and death against a background of almost unrelieved disaster; the personal and social themes, hitherto so closely united, now separate to produce the concluding catastrophe, and the tragedy, after touching unprecedented heights in its treatment of the personal theme, is rounded off in a mood of Stoic acceptance.

The first stage in an understanding of *King Lear* is a proper interpretation of the opening scene. When Cordelia, in answer to her father's implied request for flattery, follows up her uncompromising "Nothing" with the equally direct assertion:

> I love your majesty
> According to my bond; nor more nor less, (I. i)

she introduces the central conception of the whole play. The "bond" to which she refers is, of course, far more than a legal obligation. Lear's fatherhood bears a "symbolic" value similar to that of Duncan's kingship in *Macbeth*. The family, like the Scottish state, is a "symbol" of ordered living. The authority of the father is balanced by the love of his children, and their devotion aspires normally to the grace of his benediction, just as Macbeth's loyalty in the early stages of his career is rewarded by Duncan's bounty.

The breaking up of this pattern of reciprocal loyalties in the opening scene is presented in terms of a conflict between "nature," the true, permanent reality of things, and the vagaries of individual temperament. Only in Cordelia are these two elements, objective "nature" and subjective impulse, truly united. For her, filial affection is a duty to be returned to the parent who has, in her own words, "begot," "bred," and "loved" her, in the form of obedience, affection, and respect. Her insistence upon the "bond," in other words, is based primarily upon a proper understanding of the constitution of things, and no rhetorical profession can strengthen it because it lies as a condition of health at the basis of human normality. Cordelia's behavior during the whole episode, far from reflecting the stubbornness of which she has so often been accused, represents a norm, a plenitude, in relation to which the imperfect or distorted motives of the other members of the family are seen in their evident partiality.

Of this partial understanding, Lear's behavior at this stage is a clear example. Old age has weakened his capacity for self-control, making him as soon as he is crossed the prey of an anger definitely rooted in the "blood." For, whereas Cordelia is, in a phrase later used of her, "queen over her passion" (IV. iii), Lear's external royalty is compatible with an intimate servitude which is the reverse of kingly. The splendid pagan imagery of the elemental fire of life and of the dark places of nature, the evocation of the orbs "from whom we do exist and cease to be" (I. i), represent the source of his anger against the "reasonable" Cordelia, represent passion in revolt against control driving the personality to destruction. The immediate and decisive effect of his curse is to reverse the position upon which Cordelia had taken her stand. In it Lear is moved to disclaim "propinquity and property of blood" (I. i), to break bonds which precede reason and order, but upon which depends the unity of the family and, in the long run, that of experience itself.

Lear's insistence, as father, upon the respect naturally due to his paternity leads, through the imperfect self-knowledge which vitiates it, to the division of his family into two parties both of which reflect contrasted aspects of the family nature simultaneously present in himself. Both Cordelia and her sisters are evidently Lear's children. The firmness with which Cordelia clings with unadorned simplicity to the position which she rightly regards as sanctioned by "nature" is as clearly hereditary as the passionate devotion of her sisters to the selfish purpose they have proposed to themselves. It is, indeed, precisely in their contrary readings of "nature"[23] that the difference between them lies. If Cordelia is able throughout to relate her behavior to a balanced and objective conception of reality, Regan and Goneril, while—unlike their father—perfectly conscious of their own motives, are entirely unaware of the existence or relevance of any universal norm to which these motives may be related. In other words, while Cordelia's quiet insistence on the "bond" may be said to represent the spirit of reasonable control which Lear's royal status should imply, in Goneril and Regan the passions which lurk in the darker recesses of his undifferentiated humanity are given independent life and logical consistency. Father and daughters, in short, are to be regarded as complementary aspects of a *single* development within the unity of the family. Lear's initial crime against his paternity is fittingly balanced by his elder daughters' disregard of all natural feeling, and this double reversal of the order of "nature" demands, once set afoot, a complete working out in terms of tragic disunity.

One other aspect of this opening scene, though scarcely stressed in its development, needs to be remembered for a complete understanding of it. Lear is not only father but king, and the bond which binds him to his children is, in a certain sense, a reflection of the more comprehensive one that embraces him to his subjects. At this stage the political theme, still strictly secondary to the personal conflict, is mainly indicated through the person of Kent. To Cordelia's interpretation of the duties which bind her to her father, in fact, corresponds Kent's devotion to truth, regarded by him as the highest expression of his loyalty to his king. His allegiance is of the kind that holds its best service to consist in honest independence of judgment:

> Think'st thou that duty should have dread to speak,
> When power to flattery bows? To plainness honour's bound,
> When majesty stoops to folly; (I. i)

but that "allegiance" itself, when directly invoked by his master, exacts obedience is, for him, a truth not open to question. Cordelia's devotion to the family "bond" and Kent's acceptance of "allegiance" are, in fact, twin aspects of the ordered sanity in which Lear's passion has opened a breach. The breaking of the more intimate relationship contains within itself the causes which, when projected against a vaster background, lead to the disruption of the social unity which provides the play with its "universe"; but both proceed from the original breach opened by Lear's passion in the fabric of natural relationships, the evil consequences of which must work themselves out, as in *Macbeth*, through sorrow, disruption, and anarchy.

Having thus set forth in the opening scene the central tragic situation, Shakespeare proceeds to provide a comment upon it in the form of a parallel story. The story of Gloucester and his two sons, Edgar and Edmund, is clearly intended to bring out the deeper implications of Lear's own behavior. Edmund, indeed, gives rational consistency to an attitude which proceeded in Lear from instinct and of the universal implications of which he was entirely unaware. Like Cordelia (and like no one else in this play), he shows from the outset a "philosophy" of his own based on a consistent reading of "nature." Reacting against "legitimacy," and therefore against the "bond," in the name of "nature," he gives a rational substance to the second of the two positions whose conflict is the theme of the tragedy. Cordelia's acceptance as supremely "natural" of the bond that unites parent to child and is, in some sense, the reflection of universal order is set against Edmund's contrary reading of "nature" in the light of his own origins. The law of "nature" is replaced, from the point of view represented by Edmund's self-conscious sufficiency, his confidence in his own intelligence and drive, by the prejudice of "legitimacy," itself a mere product of the "plague of custom," of the "curiosity of nations" (I. ii), based upon nothing tangible or living in the order of things as interpreted by the dispassionate exercise of reason. Acting upon this interpretation of reality, Edmund first reverses the normal foundations of family life and then, with the unchecked craving for power that springs from his "unprejudiced" nature, disrupts the accepted order of the state.

Behind Edmund's self-sufficiency, however, there lies a remarkable contradiction. Like Iago, his use of reason is a product of the passion which inspires him to revolt against sanctions which have, for him, no relationship to the sources of instinctive life. Edmund's "philosophy," in fact, is itself the product of the breaking of the "bond" which led originally to his begetting. A child of Gloucester's own disordered passion, traces of which survive to undo him in his senility, his destruction of the filial bonds imposed by "nature" is a consequence of the "natural" manner of his conception.

The relation of Gloucester to his two sons constitutes a study, one of several in *Lear*, of the complexity implied in the term "nature." Edmund's "natural" bastardizing destroys the still more natural relationship between the father and his trueborn son; in the same way passion, though "natural" to the full development of man, may yet wreck the harmony of his experience and destroy his peace.

The situation thus set forth in these parallel opening episodes works out its consequences, in terms of disruption and disunity, during the first part of the play. Successively rejected by Goneril and Regan, the full effects of his previous disclaimers of "propinquity and property of blood" emerge in Lear's passionate reaction against a "reason," now itself deliberately self-seeking and self-determined, but nonetheless in a very real sense the child of his own error. It is the awareness of this error, indeed, and his obstinate refusal to admit it, that account between them for the explosion of violence which now takes possession of his whole being when confronted with Goneril. Appealing to "nature," he prays that the natural fertility of his own daughter be suspended:

Into her womb convey sterility;
Dry up in her the organs of increase,
And from her derogate body never spring
A babe to honour her! (I. iv)

This curse, which proceeds from passion and calls upon "nature," the source of instinct and spontaneous feeling, is nonetheless an attack on the natural fulfillment of passion: that is the heart of Lear's tragedy. The full extent of his departure from normal feeling is apparent a little later when we find him in his incoherent rage anticipating his reception by Regan. *She*, he is certain, will show herself "kind and comfortable"; for that reason, on hearing of Goneril's behavior:

with her nails
She'll flay thy wolfish visage. (I. iv)

This development of moral unreason in Lear is a clear sign of the tragic consequences wrought by passion in his nature. Its development is paralleled in the later history of his daughters, who are, as we have already seen, impelled to follow their father in a disregard of natural feeling which will lead them eventually to turn against one another over Edmund in the following of their individual desires. "Appetite," upon which their apparently rational cruelty is grounded, makes them eventually rivals for the love of Gloucester's bastard son, and so prepares for their ruin. Once more, as in *Othello* and *Macbeth*, the evil elements in passion work themselves out to their natural conclusion, which is absolute disruption.

The encounter between Lear and Regan, which follows (II. iv), gradually works up to a climax with the appearance of Goneril and the complete agreement reached between the sisters. Toward the end of it, in the discussion after Goneril's arrival, Lear's palpable breaking down into the incoherence which precedes his madness is balanced by an equally evident growth in selfish ferocity on his daughters' part. Lear, on his side, touches with increasing frequency on images and ideas shortly to be revealed as essential to the play's deeper meaning; his utterances are a strange blend of dawning self-knowledge and willful passion which finally breaks down into helplessness. In his last speech before leaving, he brings together into one utterance the conflicting emotions which are about, in their clash, to shatter his sanity:

> O, reason not the need: our basest beggars
> Are in the poorest thing superfluous:
> Allow not nature more than nature needs,
> Man's life as cheap as beasts: thou art a lady;
> If only to go warm were gorgeous,
> Why nature needs not what thou gorgeous wear'st,
> Which scarcely keeps thee warm. (II. iv)

At this point we touch, almost for the first time, upon themes which the central part of the play, relating them to Lear's madness, will be concerned to develop. The conception of "necessity," of the difference between "true need" and that which passes for such in the accepted currency of society, has for some time been taking shape in the old man's distraught mind. Now, as his impotence comes finally home to him, it asserts itself as one of the principal themes to be exposed to the clarifying action of the coming tempest. The opening protest against the kind of "reason" which his children have just turned upon him merges immediately, with a consideration of what is "true need," into the social contrast which is one of the main features of the storm scenes. The true "nature" of man, so Lear argues, requires "superfluity," is distinguished by it from the beast, whose subjection to mere necessity is a sign of the cheapness of its life. The situation, however, contains a deep ambiguity, for the same superfluity which is a sign of his superior "nature" can easily become, in man, attachment to the "gorgeous," the merely superfluous, which leads in turn to the contrast between luxury, such as that shown by the sisters in their new pride of power, and the exposed misery of the beggar, who himself, nonetheless, is conscious of "superfluous" necessities. The "superfluity" which dignifies, humanizes the one leads, in short, to the arrogance and inhumanity of the other. The action of the tempest on Lear's consciousness, here indirectly anticipated in the references to "warmth," will be needed before he learns to attach their true value to each of these two extremes. For the moment he passes on to a prayer for "patience," itself caused by his grief and awareness of helplessness; but to this prayer is added a new desire to penetrate the obscure purposes of the "gods" which will also be met in the storm. Thereafter the speech, under the renewed pressure of emotion, breaks down into a fragmentary intensity and finally into the first sinister awareness of coming madness. "O fool, I shall go mad!" (II. iv); it is no accident that this recognition, addressed to the Fool, who is, in a sense, the mirror of his own broken consciousness, is followed immediately by the first outburst of the gathering storm.

Under the shadow of the tempest the two opposed groups finally separate themselves out. "Let us withdraw; 'twill be a storm," urges Cornwall, and Regan and her sister are not slow to invoke the justifying voice of reason in support of their interest. "The house is little"; "'Tis his own blame" (II. iv); it is all impeccably logical, and—at the same time—completely inhuman. "The king," on the other hand, we are told by Gloucester, "is in high rage." His passions, prelude to lunacy, have gained the upper hand, and Cornwall rightly understands that, in this mood, he will be the instrument of his own destruction. "'Tis best to give him way; he leads himself" (II. iv). In Regan's last comment this is developed further in words which, besides echoing the characteristically selfish moralizing of the speaker, contain a truth of the depth of which she is not herself aware:

O, sir, to wilful men
The injuries that they themselves procure
Must be their schoolmasters. (II. iv)

That these words, besides the speaker's obvious disclaimer of responsibility, have a connection with Lear's own growth in self-knowledge, his development in the tempest will show. Meanwhile, the doors are closed, and the worldly and the powerful come in, out of the "wild night" and the approaching storm; the way is clear for a development of the central situation of the whole tragedy.

The third act of *King Lear*, which covers the storm and its counterpart in human behavior, is a marvelous example of poetic elaboration for dramatic ends. At the center of it, at once the main protagonist and symbol of the spiritual state of a humanity exposed to fundamental disorder, wrenched out of its "fixed place" in the "frame of nature," stands the figure of the aged king. The intimate dovetailing of personal conflict with external convulsions has often been noted, and is indeed an essential part of the conception. The storm which has broken out in Lear's mind, the result of his treatment at the hands of his children, is admirably fused with the description of the warring elements mainly entrusted to his lips; the external storm, while exercising upon his aged physique the intolerable strain under which it finally breaks, is itself a projection of his inner state, being fused with it as a single poetic reality. Thus related to the action of the elements, Lear clearly assumes a stature that is more than purely personal, becomes man, the microcosm of the universe, exposed to a suffering to which the frame of things itself contributes, but which finds its acutest symbol in the intimate disunion which the earlier action has introduced into the family bond.

The whole act is beautifully contrived around this central situation. If Lear has himself become "unaccommodated man" (III. iv), it is clearly felt that he is unable to bear alone the whole weight of the situation for which the tragic conception has destined him. He is, therefore, by a superb piece of dramatic tact, surrounded during his exposure to the elements by a number of characters who serve, as it were, as the external buttresses of a great architectural construction[24] to take from him some of the strain to which he would otherwise, as a dramatic conception, be subjected. It is the presence of these buttresses in *Lear* that are the best measure of the play's success, speaking in terms of artistic conception, when compared with a play which suggests a certain partial coincidence of mood, *Timon of Athens*.[25] Timon, seen in terms of the greater tragedy, is too isolated in his suffering, and his denunciation of the human environment is too extensive, too generalized, to carry complete conviction.[26] The situation of Lear is different. Although he bears throughout the storm the main weight of suffering, and although his situation is, as I have suggested, a concentration of that of man in general, he is surrounded by beings who, in varying degrees, suffer with him, and who are further used, each in his appropriate way, to illuminate some aspect of his central situation. The Fool, Kent, and Edgar bear some fraction of Lear's tragic burden, show an insight into some part of its significance; and before the act ends, he is further joined by Gloucester, whose fortunes have been from the first evidently parallel to his own. The result is an intricate and progressive dovetailing of characters and situations which leads us, step by step, further and further into an understanding of the universal tragedy embodied in Lear's outraged fatherhood and shattered royalty.

Lear's first appearance in the storm shows him in the state of resentful denunciation which precedes the dawn of understanding. He calls upon the storm to execute upon "nature," upon the whole universe, the curse of sterility he has already called down upon his daughters:

> Crack nature's moulds, all germins spill at once
> That make ingrateful man! (III. ii)

The root of his indignation, however, is still self-pity, still a sense of outrage at an "unkindness," a lack of kinship, which he rightly feels to be contrary to nature, but whose relation to his own folly he does not yet grasp. The first step in bringing to light the deeper causes of his tragedy is taken through the Fool. In the relationship, during the tempest, between the king and his Fool, we have a clear case of those significant inversions of which this play is particularly fond. King and Fool, master and slave as they have so far been, now become, in the hour of Lear's helplessness, something very different; the bond between them grows ever closer and, in the inversion of Lear's mind, through which he sees himself, as it were, upside down, in reflection, we become aware of a deeper relation of contraries, that of the "wise man" and the "fool." The essence of this relationship consists in a reversal of accepted values. The supposedly wise man of the opening scenes, the Lear who was in a position to have his slave whipped and to exercise his own will without fear of contradiction, has become, as his own acts have shown, the fool, and his former creature can now offer the comments of a practical, popular wisdom upon his behavior and prospects. Yet both, like separated fragments of a single mind, have something in common. The Fool represents for "royal Lear" the voice of reality which, to his own ruin, he sought to ignore, but which was somewhere present beneath his own favorable estimate of himself; and Lear, in turn, retains for the Fool at least part of that compelling authority which draws from him, even in his master's diminished state, a loyalty which his own disillusioned rationalism can hardly justify:

> The knave turns fool that runs away;
> The fool no knave, perdy. (II. iv)

And both, in their divided unity, are bound together by common exposure to an external force that seems to pity "neither wise man nor fool" (III. ii).

The Fool, moreover, soon penetrates beyond these obvious dramatic contrasts. In so doing, he enters directly into what we may call the subconscious ground of the play, bringing out motives which throw light upon Lear's behavior but of which Lear himself, in his assumption of royal simplicity, has so far been quite unaware. The contrast between the "wise man" and the "fool" is seen in terms of a deeper conflict between controlling reason and a passion whose ultimate impulse is, as always, sexual. The Fool's own attitude to this contrast, and to the reversal of the state of "nature" which is, in this play, connected with it, is characteristically ambiguous. Already in earlier scenes[27] his reason told him that the contrast between "head" and "heart" has an aspect which may be called social, can be interpreted as one between thrift, an economic foresight which is essentially self-regarding, and thriftless improvidence; the poor man who follows the promptings of natural instinct, symbolized in the "cod-piece," before he has made due provision against an evil day, is apt to find his whole being, "head" and "heart" alike, involved in a catastrophe which his rational faculties had no part in willing:

> The cod-piece that will house
> Before the head has any,
> The head and he shall louse;
> So beggars marry many. (III. ii)

This saying reflects an ethic to which the whole of society, as pictured in *King Lear,* gives tacit assent. A more careful reading of this, one of the most significant of all his comments, will show, however, that the Fool himself does not regard his own statement as all the truth. At least part of his nature refuses to accept thrift as a supreme virtue; and so, in the second part of his rhyme, he shifts his ground deliberately, substituting the contrast between "head" and "cod-piece" by another, not less close to human nature, between "heart" and "toe," between proper feeling and its unworthy caricature in unchecked indulgence. "Head," "heart," and "cod-piece," in fact, represent a triangular relationship which replaces the more superficial one between control and indiscipline, thrift and improvidence, as a true reflection of the human situation.

The evident contradictions in human behavior, personal and social, can only be understood, in fact, by relating them to a reading of man's nature which will carry us eventually beyond the Fool's vision of reality, including it, but without being bound by its limitations. Of this vision, indeed, his own words, reaching out beyond his normal disillusioned realism, occasionally give a dim, broken indication. One of these indications occurs precisely at this point, when the Fool, on the entry of Kent, develops his point even more profoundly in the phrase "here's grace and a cod-piece; that's a wise man and a fool" (III. ii). Wisdom and folly, rather than implying a contrast between reason and passion, or still less between saving and spending, involves a deeper one, which in turn illuminates the others, between "grace," the state of harmony in accordance with a "natural" sanction, and the rebellious "cod-piece." The word "grace," full of significance in Shakespeare's later plays, here acquires something of its full meaning as expression of a supernaturally sanctioned harmony; this harmony has been broken up in Lear by the operation of a force based ultimately on the "cod-piece," on uncontrolled instinct operating outside the balanced order of "nature" and leading, among other things, to improvident poverty. The personal conflict is thus, by a further extension of significance, not only related to its social consequences but given a universal spiritual content.

The next contribution to the expanding pattern of meaning is made through Kent. With that solicitude for human frailty which is in him a natural extension of loyalty, he emphasizes the incapacity of man's "nature" to endure the action of the elements. Lear, in his reply, at once stresses the existence of a fundamental unity between the external and the inner commotion, the tempest in his mind and that which rages without, and shows signs of a breaking coherence:

> the tempest in my mind
> Doth from my senses take all feeling else
> Save what beats there. (III. iv)

"Filial ingratitude" is conceived by him in terms of a bestial struggle between the different parts of a single body:

> Is it not as this mouth should tear this hand
> For lifting food to it? (III. iv)

and from now on the imagery of beasts in conflict, of the human organism torn remorselessly apart as though by fang and claw, or by the pitiless action of the rack, will play an increasing part in the play. The "concealing continents" (III. ii) of man's nature, already invoked by Lear, are now being riven open, and the state of animal anarchy so revealed is no more than a physical projection of the "guilts" which they normally cover. Under the strain imposed upon him by this spectacle Lear's own mental coherence visibly breaks down. Threats of undetermined future actions which he is obviously in no position to carry out ("I will punish home") alternate with assertions of his capacity to endure; these in turn are related to fresh expressions of self-pity ("In such a night as this! . . . Your kind old father") and beneath these fragments of a once unified intelligence, present as a threat visibly approaching, lies the shadow of coming madness: "O that way madness lies . . . No more of that!" (III. iv)

Not all that is coming to the surface in Lear under the elemental pressure to which he is being exposed is negative. The distinctively human solicitude which is Kent's contribution to the total structure of the episode begins now to communicate itself to the aged king. After inviting the Fool to take shelter, he says: "I'll pray, and then I'll sleep" (III. iv). The content of his prayer is, in fact, new, represents the extension of his understanding to new areas of life. Its starting point is a new concern for the state of "houseless poverty" inspired in him by contemplation of the Fool. Contemplating the pitiful state of those whose "heads" are "houseless" (once more, he is taking up concepts originally broached, in his characteristically enigmatic form, by the Fool) and whose "sides" are "unfed," he is brought to a fresh awareness of his own lack of understanding:

O, I have ta'en
Too little care of this! (III. iv)

and, as a reaction against it, to introduce more specifically than ever before a concern for justice. The elemental equity already invoked in previous scenes now gives way to a more clearly moral criterion, one which may even be described as concretely social. The contemplation of misery is a "physic" for such "pomp" as Lear himself has so far taken for granted; it leads, in terms of what we may call social morality, to a desire to redress the balance of the superfluous well-being ("the superflux") of the privileged and thus—with tremendous daring—to show the heavens more just.

It is at this point that the scope of the action is still further enlarged by the entry of Edgar, in whom the state of "houseless poverty" becomes a visible reality. With his own nakedness confronted by that of Edgar, and both subjected to the remorseless pressure of the elements, Lear's rapidly awakening concern for "justice" shows signs of shading into something deeper, more universal. *King Lear* is a great tragedy precisely because it is a play about human "nature" before being a play about the abuses of government or social inequality. It is this "nature," indeed, that is now being revealed, stripped and exposed to the prevailing "cold" for our consideration. The state of "sophistication," through and beyond which Lear now sees, is more than the mere pride of position or the abuse of wealth. Both these things are, indeed, normal attributes of human nature, part of the conventional superstructure with which man seeks to hide even from himself his true character, as normal in their own way as the garments which he owes to the brute creation and with which he protects his otherwise "uncovered body" from the "extremity of the skies" (III. iv). To this state of false pretension the action of the storm has come as a corrective. It has brought those exposed to it back once more to the familiar but always forgotten truth that "unaccommodated" man is no more but such a poor, bare "forked animal" as Edgar. This pitiable object is, by his own confession, a "serving-man," at once a courtier "proud in heart and mind" (III. iv) and a slave to his own passions, who has now learned by bitter experience that it is a "*poor* heart" which betrays itself to the transitory satisfactions of the flesh only to find itself enveloped at the last—in accordance with Edgar's own repeated catch—in the prevailing cold.

The confronting of Lear with Edgar, though an important stage in the development of the main themes, is not an end in itself. It is the prelude to a still more important meeting in which the two parallel family histories with which *King Lear* is concerned are brought together and the two fathers whose behavior has set them in motion finally confronted. The Fool intervenes at this point with one of his most significant observations. The occasion is in part Lear's frenzied divesting of the "lendings" which still differentiate him from elemental humanity and in part the arrival on the scene of Gloucester newly moved to compassion. Gloucester, whose own past behavior in the begetting of Edmund is—like Lear's own—in the process of returning to him upon the whirlwind, has his own contribution to make to the general theme of passion. This is the meaning of the Fool's enigmatic greeting. Taking up the contrast, already developed by Edgar, between the brief fire of lust and the "cold" which surrounds it, he is moved to see in the entry of Gloucester with a "torch" a reflection of the fire of life blazing up briefly and ineffectively in the surrounding desolation: "Now a little fire in a wild field were like an old lecher's heart, a small spark, all the rest on's body cold" (III. iv). The "old lecher" is clearly Gloucester himself and the "little fire" the smoldering remains of the vitality which had formerly produced its "unnatural" fruit in his illegitimate child. As a prelude to his meeting with Lear, the Fool's greeting emphasizes both the common, "blood"-inspired source of their respective tragedies and the equally common helplessness with which they face it. Thus related in past behavior, they are from now on envisaged as sharers in a common tragic destiny.

Gloucester's approaching sufferings, indeed, make him at this stage a fit commentator upon Lear's fortunes. Lear's recent outburst—

'Twas this flesh begot
Those pelican daughters— (III. iv)

is fitly balanced by Gloucester's own situation with regard to his children; and, though he does not yet realize that the past sin of his own flesh is turning against him, he can already relate the disorders in man's behavior to a corruption, a flaw in the fleshly fabric of human nature:

Our flesh and blood is grown so vile, my lord,
That it doth hate what gets it, (III. iv)

and refer, in terms highly characteristic of this scene, to the son "now outlaw'd from my blood." In such utterances the "embossed carbuncle" in the "corrupted blood" to which Lear formerly referred in his denunciation of Goneril (II. iv) is visibly working its way to the surface. At the same time, however, in Gloucester as in Lear, another development is simultaneously taking place. His new realization of what human nature may imply in terms of depth of degradation brings with it, at this very point, the beginnings of a saving reaction, a return to the natural concept of "duty" which, in his own words, "cannot suffer" to obey commands themselves unnatural. Edgar, in turn, touched more closely than ever by the appearance of his own father and aware of the full meaning of the tragedy which Gloucester is still unable to relate to his own situation, can only repeat his sense of the cold that surrounds human helplessness: "Poor Tom's a-cold." Once more the external, physical situation, conveyed through the words of one of those subjected to the tragic process, corresponds to the spiritual state of which it is the unadorned reflection. It is Edgar's persistence in grasping the naked truth that prompts Lear to hail him, at this very moment, as "philosopher" and to inquire of him "the cause of thunder" (III. iv); the cause, that is, if any there be, of the pitiless intervention of nature to which all the actors in this episode are equally exposed. The elemental disorder which produces the thunder has its own psychological counterpart in the dissolution of sanity, and the scene ends with Kent referring once more to the oncoming of Lear's madness—"His wits begin to unsettle"—and Gloucester's parallel admission of the state to which the "outlawing" of Edgar has brought him: "I am almost mad myself . . . The grief hath crazed my wits" (III. iv).

These points once established, Lear, after being sheltered by Gloucester from the action of the elements, passes on to a consideration, in the most ample terms, of the nature of "justice" (III. vi). The execution of justice, indeed, is an essential part of the royal function, and Lear's torn mind when it recalls this fact is going back over the same range of responsibilities as he had once exercised to his own undoing. Now, with a complete reversal of the conventional values of society, the poor and the outcast, themselves seen as victims of an inadequate conception of justice are raised to the position of executing ministers. The naked Edgar becomes "thou robed man of justice," and the Fool, himself the living symbol of subjection to irresponsible power, his "yoke-fellow of equity"; while those who have risen by their ruthlessness to the exercise of authority, who are "gorgeously" clad, as indeed is the conventional judge in his robes, are now seen, stripped of their pretensions and with their subsistent animality exposed, as so many "she-foxes." The problem now presented, however, is not merely one of social categories. Behind the reversal of accepted standards of justice there lies a sense of the intractable, irreducible element of evil in human impulse with which justice itself has to deal. "Let them anatomize Regan; see what breeds about her heart. Is there any cause in nature that makes these hard hearts?" (III. vi) It is this question, rather than the extent of the personal disaster which has made it possible for him to pose it, that indicates the true extent of Lear's tragedy. A question less about the nature of justice or its application to any particular situation than about human nature itself, it lies at the heart both of Lear's madness and his possible redemption. It creates a state of spiritual tension so deep that the only possible transition from it is one into repose, sleep; and so it is at this point that Kent calls upon his exhausted master to "lie and rest awhile" and that the Fool, having accompanied him to the lowest point in his downward progress, now leaves him.

In the last episode of this central part of the tragedy (III. vii) the full effects of the cruelty unleashed in human nature by passion are revealed in terms of physical suffering. Gloucester, as a result of his concession to natural human feeling in sheltering Lear, is apprehended on the charge of treason, and Regan, Goneril, and Cornwall move round him with an intensity which is clearly inspired by "blood" and which reaches its culminating point in the blinding of their helpless victim. The spectacle of the suffering thus inflicted is almost intolerable, and only in relation to the vast conception of the whole tragedy, in which it forms a turning point, can its inclusion be justified. For it is no accident that the moment in which Gloucester loses his sight, the victim of a gratuitous act of evil, is also that in which the birth of his spiritual understanding is confirmed. It is immediately after his blinding that he accepts his own responsibility for the position in which he finds himself, in the light of the knowledge, newly dawned, that the true son of his own blood, whom he had believed to be a traitor, was in fact himself betrayed:

O my follies! Then Edgar was abused.
Kind gods, forgive me that, and prosper him! (III. vii)

When, at the same time, Cornwall's servant is moved to draw his sword in protest against his master's savagery, and to lay down his life in the name of common humanity and natural compassion, we must feel ourselves to be at a turning point of the entire action. These new developments are, indeed, the exteriorization of a central paradox implied in Shakespeare's use of the image of sight. Those who "see," who pride themselves on their clear-sighted appraisal of the world and its ways, find themselves betrayed by their sight, are, in fact, in a very real and tragic sense, blind; while those who have lost their eyes, or whom their self-styled "betters" may have regarded as incapable of "vision," may, in the very moment of losing them, receive a flash of moral illumination, in fact, "see." The achievement by Gloucester of this kind of "sight" at the moment of his blinding can only be compared with the growth into moral insight, into understanding of the true human situation, that accompanies Lear's collapse into madness.[28]

At this stage in the development of his tragedy, Shakespeare was faced by an artistic problem of tremendous difficulty: the problem, that is, of balancing the disruption so thoroughly traced in the first part of the play by a harmony corresponding to that achieved in *Macbeth* in the second. The blinding of Gloucester represents the lowest depth reached in terms of physical action as a result of man's subjection to the bestial elements in his nature. The end of the storm is followed by a kind of lull in the emotional development of the tragedy, in which misery seems to pass into a Stoic resignation to the worst. As Edgar puts it:

The lamentable change is from the best;
The worst returns to laughter. (IV. i)

The mood is the only possible transition from the horrors we have just witnessed, and during it we become aware of two new developments. In the first place, the passion which has up to now impelled Goneril to ingratitude and cruelty now begins to ruin her own prosperity. She reveals her love for Edmund and her contempt for her husband ("My fool usurps my body"—the physical intensity is noteworthy), while Albany, appalled by her bestiality, turns upon her in language that itself suggests the beast:

> Were't my fitness
> To let these hands *obey my blood,*
> They are apt enough to *dislocate* and *tear*
> Thy flesh and bones. (IV. ii)

It is the development of *Macbeth* repeated, but now with an even higher degree of animal intensity; evil, having destroyed the foundations of order upon natural dependence, proceeds to destroy itself.

The second development at this stage is the reappearance of Cordelia, who introduces a type of poetry which, although it scarcely springs from anything yet noted in the play, at once assumes an essential part in it. Cordelia is first introduced in the description of a Gentleman, whose words initiate a harmonizing and healing element to balance the cruelty which has so far prevailed in the tragic action:

> patience and sorrow strove
> Who should express her goodliest. You have seen
> Sunshine and rain at once; her smiles and tears
> Were like a better way; those happy smilets
> That play'd on her ripe lip seem'd not to know
> What guests were in her eyes; which parted thence
> As pearls from diamonds dropp'd. (IV. iii)

One is struck at once by the tremendous range of imagery at the poet's disposal. Cordelia's sorrow is expressed in a whole series of comparisons few of which have a plain factual connection with the scene and emotions described; "sunshine and rain," "ripe lip," "guests," "pearls," and "diamonds" are all connected with one another and with Cordelia less because of any visual image than because of the sense of value, of richness and fertility, which they impart. For the passage is moved by a presiding logic of its own. The struggle between the queen and her passions is now seen to be a strife between two emotions—"patience" and "sorrow"—equally natural and worthy, each contributing to a "goodly" expression of her nature. Her behavior, in fact, is so normal, so spontaneous a manifestation of her virtues that it reflects the balance of nature in "sunshine" and "rain," each contributing to the single harmonious effect which presents itself as a "better way," an indication of redemption; and this in turn causes us to feel no surprise when "happy smilets" make their appearance, immediately below, as indicative of Cordelia's mood. "Sunshine and rain," in turn, lead directly to the suggestion in "ripe" of the maturing crops, and "guests"—as in the first act of *Macbeth*—hints at the bounty which expresses itself in hospitality. Ripeness, again, indicates the riches implied in "pearls from diamonds dropp'd"; these are "rarities," and sorrow itself is in such a case less a tragic manifestation than a rarity enriching human nature, part of a harmony capable of being summed up in the terms of generous fulfillment already suggested in the phrase "an *ample* tear trill'd down" and of being, in the most spiritual sense, "beloved." Last of all, by a final step profoundly characteristic of Shakespeare's late verse, Cordelia's tears become "holy water" dropping from her "heavenly eyes," and the poetical transformation of natural emotion into its spiritual distillation is complete.

To the norm of harmonious completeness thus established, the broken and partial experience of Lear looks as to its fulfillment. With his wanderings over, his condition is such that it is ready to receive the "balm" of "broken sinews." The poetic expression of his suffering, indeed, is realized in Kent's account of his master's condition after his arrival at Dover:

> A sovereign shame so elbows him: his own unkindness
> That stripp'd her from his benediction, turn'd her
> To foreign casualties, gave her dear rights
> To his dog-hearted daughters: these things sting
> His mind so venomously that burning shame
> Detains him from Cordelia. (IV. iii)

The changed quality of Lear's suffering is reflected in a new type of poetry, the natural response of his chastened humanity to the possibilities of transfiguration symbolized in Cordelia. The storm, with its sense of division, of the human body physically torn apart on the rack or defenceless under the teeth of beasts of prey, is superseded by the memory of a pain which is still intense but which may be—within those limits that life imposes—the prelude to restoration. Not only is his shame "sovereign," at once the reaction of a king and his most rich and valuable emotion; not only is Lear's past "unkindness" (in the sense of neglect of kinship) opposed to the harmony implied in the "benediction" of which in the past he ruthlessly "stripp'd" his daughter and to the possibility of which he is now painfully feeling his way back; but "sting," "venomously," and "burning shame" suggest the cauterizing of a wound, as though his grief possessed a possible healing quality, were a necessary prelude to restoration. Read in conjunction with the overflowing fullness of Cordelia's emotion, the speech indicates that Shakespeare intends to balance the anarchy and cruelty of the first part of the play by a reconciliation of father and daughter in a natural and harmonious sublimation of their normal relationship.

Before the final meeting between Cordelia and the regenerated Lear, however, the play turns back once more to take up, and in a sense to summarize, its presentation of human suffering (IV. vi). The external purpose, so to call it, of the scene is to bring together Lear and Gloucester. The latter, brought to the limits of his endurance on the verge of Dover cliff (the fact that his lofty perch is imaginary, that its "dizzy" heights exist only in Edgar's imagination, emphasizes the symbolic quality of the situation), turns away from his attempted suicide with a declaration that he has learned his lesson:

> henceforth I'll bear
> Affliction till it do cry out itself
> "Enough, enough" and die. (IV. vi)

This, no doubt, is still less a positive attitude than the preliminary foundation upon which such an attitude may be built. Gloucester's words contain as yet nothing to connect him with the positive experience which will emerge from the entirely different spirit of the reconciliation scene; but the thoughts which will henceforth occupy him, "free" because liberated from the baser temptations of despair and "patient" because acceptance, even in obscurity, is the necessary prelude to understanding, have their own place in the development of the play.

The entry of Lear, which immediately follows, serves to give final expression to the anguish with which the whole tragedy has been so heavily charged. At its culminating point the reaction of the aged king to the unnatural behavior of his daughters universalizes itself, to take shape finally in an assertion of the dual nature of woman:

> Down from the waist they are centaurs,
> Though women all above:
> But to the girdle do the gods inherit,
> Beneath is all the fiends'. (IV. vi)

The light thus thrown on the dark and hidden nature of man's impulses, for which so much in the earlier action has prepared us, also illuminates Lear's own situation. It leads finally to his desire to "sweeten" his imagination when confronted with behavior which, like his own hand, "smells of mortality" (IV. vi). In his madness he is penetrating far more deeply than in his apparent sanity to the roots in universal human frailty of his own situation. His apparent obsession represents, in fact, the elimination of a mental poison, the purgation of unclean impulses from the spirit which cannot, while they are still present, receive the saving visitation of sleep. Exposing instincts which normally remain hidden under the "simperings" of affected "virtue" and the pretentious garb of current social behavior, he reveals, beyond his own infirmity and that of the society over which he formerly ruled, the true state of man by which Gloucester has been brought to blindness and himself to the condition in which we see him. If the contemplation of this state brings the speaker to the verge of moral disintegration, that is a necessary part of the complete pattern of the tragedy which must precede any conceivable restoration of harmony. The pressure of emotion at this point, besides twisting its expression into incoherent forms, is such that even the sightless Gloucester feels himself to be in the presence of a "ruin'd piece of nature" (the universal implications of Lear's state could hardly be more explicitly stated) and anticipates that, under the pressure of such concentrated emotion, the "great world" itself, of which Lear is so consistently the microcosm, will wear itself out to "nought."

With Gloucester and Lear once more united in the contemplation of the tragic experience which has brought them together, and with both, as king and courtier, subdued to an acceptance of their dimly conceived destinies, the way is at last open for a restoration of natural harmonies. The scene in which this takes place is, from the point of view of Shakespeare's capacity to unite the dramatic and poetic elements with which he is working, the most advanced in the play. It is full of the "symbolism" which from now on plays an increasing part in the poet's work, a "symbolism" which is not imposed upon the dramatic development but which springs from and completes it. Given the extraordinary freedom, the breadth of reference which everywhere characterizes the verse of this play, it is only a step further to introduce effects that are not strictly part of the development of the drama, but which the unprecedented control of the poet succeeds in welding organically into the total effect.

"Sleep" we have already found to form part of a "symbolic" effect of this kind; and Shakespeare now adds music, with its associations of harmony, and "fresh garments," suggesting the purification accomplished in Lear by the immersion of past sorrows into repose. The Doctor calls upon music at the moment of Lear's awakening, and Cordelia prays for his "restoration" in language which relates the musical symbol of harmony to the revival of unity and health in the torn and divided personality:

> O, you kind gods,
> Cure this great *breach* in his abused nature;
> The *untuned* and jarring senses, O, wind up
> Of this child-changed father! (IV. vii)[29]

By such means Lear's suffering is transformed, made into a condition of his revival. When his awakening takes place, it comes little by little, covering the bitter memories of the past by an incoming tide of fresh emotions. We can feel this most clearly of all in his first exclamation of wonder:

> Thou art a soul in bliss; but I am bound
> Upon a wheel of fire, that mine own tears
> Do scald like molten lead. (IV. vii)

This at once looks back to past experience, to the "burning shame" which, earlier in the act, had "stung" him and kept him from Cordelia,[30] and indicates a fresh spiritual development. Lear's difficulty in believing that he really sees his daughter before him indicates both the depth and the remoteness of what he has passed through; the suggested idea of resurrection ("You do me wrong to take me out of the grave") contributes to the same effect. So, in a different way, does the sense of compassion which prompts him, in the moment of his awakening, to say:

> I should e'en die with pity,
> To see another thus, (IV. vii)

and which is an echo, like the combination of shattered pathos and fresh understanding which prompts his "I am a foolish, fond old man," of the humanity he has learned in his exposure to the tempest. Lear, in other words, still suffers on the "wheel of fire" to which the consequences of his own passion and folly originally bound him, but his grief no longer springs from division, from the "embossed carbuncle" in his own "corrupted blood" which produced Regan and Goneril; it has become such that it can, for the first time and briefly, precariously, contemplate "a soul in bliss."

For the length of this scene, then, Shakespeare has succeeded in balancing the suffering of the first part of his play with an adequate harmony fulfilled in terms of external symbolism through Cordelia's prayer for "benediction" and Lear's corresponding confession of guilt:

> I know you do not love me; for your sisters
> Have, as I do remember, done me wrong:
> You have some cause, they have not. (IV. vii)

This is the central moment of reconciliation, full of significance for an understanding not only of *King Lear*, but of the whole pattern of Shakespeare's later work. The restoration of the original relationship of child to father is the resolution of the ruin caused by "blood" in the unity of the family. Two features of this development are especially worthy of note. In the first place, Lear, while still remembering his past experiences, looks back to them, as it were, across a great gap of intervening time, sees them as belonging to another world; in the second, his new state is explicitly described in terms of a spiritual rebirth. "Thou art a soul in bliss," "You are a spirit, I know": such phrases, added to the sense of a break in temporal continuity—

> it is danger
> To make him e'en go o'er the time he has lost— (IV. vii)

have a double effect. They at once stress the spiritual meaning of Lear's new state by placing it outside the temporal process and show that it is not of this world, that in this world, indeed, it may even be cruelly interrupted. The achievement of a state which is that of "souls in bliss" does not necessarily involve the end of exposure to suffering. If the spiritual life of Lear and his daughter is situated, from now onward, on a level which is not that of the political action, the passions which move that action still have to work themselves out, and even annihilate the main protagonists, in the last part of the tragedy.

In the sphere of political action and worldly success, indeed, the course of events moves to a conclusion which seems to make no concession to the glimpses of newly found intuition thus hardly won. If these have validity (and this is a question which the play seems to leave deliberately open), it is on another and apparently unrelated level. The final battle seems to leave Edmund in full and undisputed control of events. To his order that the aged king and his daughter should be removed to prison, Cordelia can only reply with her determination to "outfrown false fortune's frown" (V. iii) and with the profound moral integrity implied in her quiet "Shall we not see these daughters and these sisters?" If her attitude denotes a characteristic mastery, it is on a moral rather than on a practical level. Lear's response, equally typical of his new, "resurrected" state, is more pathetic, in a sense even more sentimental in kind. Life for him has been entirely concentrated, since his recovery, upon the reconciliation with his daughter; and prison itself, while he is with her, is the whole of his universe. In this spirit he takes up once more the theme of paternal blessing and filial forgiveness which lies at the heart of the central symbolic situation:

> When thou dost ask me blessing, I'll kneel down
> And ask of thee forgiveness, (V. iii)

and looks back, as though across the infinite distance imposed by the experience through which he has lately passed, at the "gilded butterflies" and "court news" which had once, in what seems a barely conceivable remoteness, meant so much to his headstrong nature. As Lear speaks at this point he is at once broken by his sufferings and beyond being affected by them. The speech moves from the gentle irony which enables the old man to contemplate the coming imprisonment of himself and his daughter in a spirit of tranquil acquiescence to the assertion, at once intensely moving and charged with a disturbing defiance, that

> He that parts us shall bring a brand from heaven,
> And fire us hence like foxes. (V. iii)

The whole episode creates, as it were, an island of peace, precariously isolated in a world of iron. Lear has attained, at the expense of his own broken nature, a vision of spiritual acceptance; but across it, present if no longer uniquely so, lies the shadow of the way of the world.

The reconciliation thus realized in this moment of intense feeling, indeed, is not maintained. Reunited with Cordelia under the eyes of their captors, Lear has spoken to his daughter, with a kind of ironic nostalgia, of taking upon themselves

> the mystery of things,
> As if we were God's spies; (V. iii)

but in fact, of course, neither Lear nor any other man has valid reason to pretend to so much. We have been engaged in an exploration of the human condition as it is under its tragic aspect, not working out a comforting moral doctrine of redemption through suffering; and so, such insights as have been gained in the course of the action fail to maintain themselves in the face of external pressure. The world is still hostile, almost intolerably cruel, in its treatment of the exhausted protagonists. The armies of Cordelia are defeated by Edmund, now undisputed master of the political action; and, though it is true that he finally dies in meeting the challenge of the disguised Edgar, his death does not take place until Cordelia has been hanged by his order. The whole of the final episode is set under the sign of dissolution, which is indeed the only possible outcome of sufferings so intolerably heavy and so protractedly borne. To conclude it, Lear enters for the last time "with Cordelia dead in his arms" and in a world dominated by a double sense of darkness and emotional petrifaction, which finds its persistent echo in the words of the victims ("O! you are men of stones"; "Fall and cease"; "All's cheerless, dark, and deadly"), the curtain falls. Lear, finally reconciled to his daughter in adversity, himself dies with her body in his arms, gaining in death the only relief conceivable in temporal terms from the "rack of this tough world," the course of which has proved so consistently indifferent to the spiritual intuitions which suffering itself has brought so painfully to birth. Kent, loyal to the end, anticipates in his own last words the "journey" in which he is shortly to follow his master, and Edgar is left by Albany with the mission of sustaining "the gored state" in a spirit in which exhaustion and sincerity, purged of all excessive pretensions by the contemplation of the sufferings just witnessed, join hands in a gesture of mutual sustainment.

TIMON OF ATHENS

It is tempting in some ways to think of *Timon of Athens* as a kind of appendix to *King Lear*. As such, it can hardly fail to suffer in the comparison. The direct, unvaried line of its action, concentrated on the hero's fall from greatness, must seem to lack the wealth of contrast which marks the earlier tragedy; the accumulated invective in which Timon expresses his disillusionment, his final rejection of life, must strike us, from the standpoint of the greater play, as excessive, one-sided, and monotonous. It is perhaps more useful, however, to see *Timon of Athens* as a play essentially different in kind from *Lear*. The comparative simplicity of its structure recalls certain features of the morality play, and its hero's excesses, both of generosity and disillusionment, are at least as much ironic as tragic in the impression they make upon us. Seen in this way, we can respond to a Shakespeare not engaged in repeating himself, but in contriving a new kind of dramatic action, an experiment which, though not entirely successful, is nonetheless the work of a great poet writing at the height of his unique powers.

The court in which Timon, as the action opens, exercises his "magic of bounty" (I. i) is clearly a reflection of the world, the ways of which are amply familiar to those who live in and by it. "How goes the world?" asks the poet, and receives from his fellow artist in counterfeit an answer—"It wears, sir, as it grows"—which is a commonplace of disillusioned experience. In this world both artists, creatures dedicated to the pursuit of self-advancement through flattery, are thoroughly at home. Their attitude to their respective arts is characteristically ambivalent, combines genuine appreciation of skill and civilized polish with the limiting implications of artifice cultivated as an end in itself or as a means to material advancement. The Poet praises the Painter for bringing out in his picture Timon's superhuman virtues—his "grace," his "big imagination," his "mental power"—all real and impressive human qualities by the exploitation of which, however, both artists live and which are accordingly limited by a persistent impression of artificiality; for the picture is, as the Poet also sees, "a pretty *mocking* of the life," an "*artificial* strife" which "lives" indeed "in these touches," but lives after a fashion suspiciously "livelier than life" (I. i).

In this way we are prepared for a realistic estimate of Timon's eminence, the situation in which his nature, recognized to be "good and spacious," exercises a fascination as universal as it is finally suspect. "You see," explains the Poet,

> how all conditions, how all minds,
> As well of *glib and slippery creatures* as
> Of grave and austere quality, tender down
> Their services to Lord Timon; his *large fortune,*
> Upon his *good and gracious nature* hanging,
> Subdues and properties to his love and tendance
> All sorts of hearts. (I. i)

At this point Timon's court is seen to be nothing less than a reflection of the "world," of society itself: a world dominated, as the Poet's parable goes on to stress, by the shifting vagaries of fortune, so that those who so readily follow Timon in his moment of exaltation, who are so suspiciously ready to

> Rain sacrificial whisperings in his ear,
> Make *sacred* even his stirrup, and *through him*
> *Drink the free air,* (I. i)

will follow the "shift and change" of his mood and finally abandon him in his fall. Once more this reflects not merely a particular situation, but, as the Painter's comment makes clear, a universal law of life: "'Tis common."

The presentation of Timon himself in these initial scenes is marked by a similar ambivalence. It is at once his virtue and his fault to be unaware of the precarious nature of his situation. His attitude toward those around him is marked by a true generosity, which expresses itself in images of conviviality and feasting—"We must needs dine together," he tells the Painter—and in the encouragement of young love against the Old Athenian's depreciation of "levity" in youth. In so far as these things are an expression of human solidarity we must respond to Timon's readiness to give away in bounty the "jewel" which he values for its beauty, to affirm in friendship a genuine positive of life:

I am not of that feather to shake off
My friend when he must need me; (I. i)

but we must also see these things against the play's persistent equation of art with artifice—"The painting is almost the natural man"—and the hero's own tendency to equate "bounty" with the sharing of "pleasure." The contrasted attitude of Apemantus, in whom "plain dealing" is a reflection of inverted pride and in whom a realistic estimate of flattery expresses itself through the hatred of society itself—

That there should be small love 'mongst these sweet knaves,
And all this courtesy! The strain of man's bred out
Into baboon and monkey— (I. i)

is there to balance excess with excess, the generosity that degenerates into self-indulgence with a moralizing that ultimately implies the negation of sociability itself. This is a world in which the sense of life is turned persistently to suspect ends, in which Alcibiades can give a peculiar twist to the imagery of banqueting—"I *feed* most hungerly on your sight"—in which the attendant Lords "*taste* Lord Timon's bounty" and hold that each of his apparently inexhaustible gifts will

breed the giver a return exceeding
All use of *quittance*. (I. i)

It is, of course, "gold" that so "breeds" in an unnatural parody of life, and the product will soon be shown to be, like the society which hangs upon it, finally sterile. It is a sufficient comment on Timon's celebrated "nobility"—

The *noblest* mind he carries
That e'er governed man— (I. i)

that its celebration is persistently set in the mouths of those who are clearly revealed as flatterers and timeservers.

Timon's ambiguous relation to an equivocal society finds its fitting projection in the banquet which reflects his generosity. Timon, in offering it, stresses the unilateral quality of his gesture—

there's none
Can truly say he gives, if he receives— (I. ii)[31]

and adds the more dubious conviction of the profligate when he affirms that "faults that are rich are fair." Apemantus, who is universally regarded as "unfit for society," is present to turn the prevailing imagery of banqueting and participation to opposite ends. In this he is no doubt moved by a misanthropy that is negative, life-destroying; but there is sinister meaning in his implacable vision of Timon's associates as "eating" him and in his insistent use of imagery that carries religious implications of sacrifice and betrayal:

> It grieves me to see so many dip their meat in one man's blood . . . the fellow that sits next him now, parts bread with him . . . is the readiest man to kill him. (I. ii)

We shall not, of course, underrate the sardonic element in these comments, or accept this bitter moralizing at its own estimate of superior, detached insight. Apemantus' realism clearly rests on an excess of selfishness that stands at the opposite extreme from Timon's "generosity" and represents an attitude equally tainted; his conclusion "I pray for no man but myself" (I. ii) is as limited, finally as self-stultifying, as the facile openhandedness it justly condemns. When Apemantus announces, in a mood akin to self-congratulation, that he will never "trust man on his oath or bond," it is in the last resort nothing less than humanity, in himself and others, that he is rejecting; and much the same can be said, in a different way, of Alcibiades when he grotesquely introduces into these convivialities a note of cannibalism in expressing the soldier's pleasure in his bloodletting vocation:

> *Timon:* You had rather be at a breakfast of enemies than a dinner of friends.
> *Alcibiades:* So they were bleeding-new, my lord, there's no meat like 'em. (I. ii)

In such a situation, the most unexceptionable sentiments become tinged with irony. When Timon is moved to declare that he has often wished himself "poor" so as thereby to "come nearer" his friends, the statement has to be weighed against his evident inability to see these "friends" as they really are. When he utters his conviction that generosity lies at the basis of all sociable living—"We are born to do benefits; and what better or properer can we call our own than the riches of our friends" (I. ii)—he is at once uttering a true law of life, a concept upon which the very possibility of society is ultimately founded, and reflecting with unconscious irony upon his own future. For, beneath all its surface of lavish splendor, the spirit of Timon's banquet is suspect. The masque of Cupid, offered by the host as the culmination of his feast, stresses a connection finally dubious between the "bounty" so abundantly revealed and the "five senses"—

> th' ear,
> Taste, touch, and smell, pleased from thy table rise— (I. ii)

whilst there is a note of complacency, of easy self-satisfaction, in Timon's own dismissal of what he calls his "idle banquet."

It is at this point, indeed, that ominous forebodings begin to make themselves felt. The satiated Lords rise from the table with "much *adoring*" of their host, who speaks with glib facility of "pleasures" and "fair fashion," confusing the lavish surface of social entertainment with true generosity. Apemantus foresees the future when he says that "Men shut their doors against a setting sun," and Timon's faithful steward Flavius condemns more explicitly his master's lack of foresight: "'Tis pity bounty had not eyes behind." His expressions of foreboding, and the first open reference to Timon's "debts," are momentarily drowned in the finally self-gratifying gesture of Timon himself:

> Methinks I could deal kingdoms to my friends,
> And ne'er be weary. (I. ii)

When he turns to Apemantus to reprove him for railing against "society," our reaction must be conditioned by these intimations of ruin. Timon is at once making a valid criticism of the negative, inhuman "virtue" which he feels to be the opposite of his own, and brushing aside a true warning in a spirit of final irresponsibility.

The following scenes, which show these premonitions turning into reality, have about them much of the "morality" quality so marked in this play. Timon's creditors are barely distinguished in terms of character. They are rather presented as abstract representatives of greed and selfishness, and as such contribute to the main patterns of imagery which convey the sense of the action. The First Senator, describing Timon's state in terms of fever, speaks of "raging waste" and equates his generosity with the breeding of gold:

> steal but a beggar's dog
> And give it Timon, why the dog coins gold. (II. i)

The critical intention is apparent in the sardonic phrase, and clearly answers to a truth; but the critic's own emphasis is throughout on selfishness, on "*my* needs," "*my* turn": as he concludes,

> I love and honour him,
> But must not break my back to heal his finger. (II. i)

As the creditors, like so many vultures, gather round their declining patron, the faithful Flavius expresses in realistic terms the excess and indulgence which have constituted the reverse side of his master's generosity:

> When all our offices have been oppress'd
> With riotous feeders, when our vaults have wept
> With drunken spilth of wine, when every room
> Hath blazed with lights and bray'd with minstrelsy. (II. ii)

In the light of this it is important to avoid all identification with Timon,[32] to realize that his "generosity" and the greed which feeds upon it are opposite excesses, made for one another and sharing a common disregard for proper human measure. Timon, thus reproached for prodigality, justifies himself with a certain complacency—"Unwisely, not ignobly have I given" (II. ii)—and clings to what is by now clearly his illusion of human solidarity. At bottom it is reality, both in himself and in those around him, that he is unwilling to contemplate.

It is not long, however, before reality forces itself upon him. As "policy," barefaced self-interest, asserts itself with increasing urgency among his creditors, his remaining friends stress the malady that has affected sociability itself, the turning of "nutriment" into "poison" and "disease," and return once more to the persistent sense of intimate betrayal:

> Who can call him
> His friend that dips in the same dish? (III. ii)

When Timon himself appears, it is to show that his surface "nobility" has broken down into the hysteria that expresses itself in the injunction to "Cut my heart in sums," "Tell out my blood," "Tear me" (III. iv); we are evidently faced now with the downfall of an excessive, finally a self-admiring confidence. The breakdown in Timon is seen in turn in relation to a larger flaw in society. Against the passionate and one-sided pursuit of martial honor by Alcibiades is set the frosty assertion of "justice" on the part of impotent old age in authority, the conviction—as coldly stated by a senator—that "Nothing emboldens sin so much as mercy" (III. v). In this conviction, the senators are ready to exercise brutally against Alcibiades and his protégé such authority as they have—"the law shall *bruise* him" (III. v)—only to be faced by a warrior who is ready to commit his power to the contrary position—"pity is the virtue of the law"—and to assert, but in one-sided passion, the "*noble* fury" and "fair spirit" of the friend he is determined to save. The conflict between passionate action and frigid control, overconfident youth and impotent old age in authority, is a genuine one, but it is characteristic of the society of this play that it should be pushed to destructive excess on either side. On the one hand, we have the intransigent execution of a law conceived in abstraction from human reality—"We are for law; he dies"—by those who are incapable of sharing the generous, if uncontrolled impulses of passionate youth; on the other, the revolt of passion itself, which, whilst purporting to reflect a generous reaction—

> Banish your dotage; banish usury,
> That makes the senate ugly— (III. v)

leads the speaker to turn upon his own countrymen and to let loose upon society the ruinous excesses of civil strife.

Timon's "banquet," which follows at this point (III. vi), is placed deliberately at the center of the entire action. It contains a sardonic parody of all the "sociable" feasting which, in happier days, accompanied his largess; and it culminates in a rejection of mankind which is at once justified by his betrayal and provides a confirmation of his excess, of the extent of his human failure. From now on, lust and "appetite" are obsessively joined in Timon's mind; seeing his former friends reduced to the status of beasts—"Uncover, *dogs,* and lap" (III. vi)—he thanks the "gods" for their revelation of human iniquity, and sees humanity itself deprived of its distinctive attributes. It is significant that, as the obsession with "disease" replaces his former too easy generosity, Timon falls into a phrasing which echoes the misanthropy of Apemantus:

> Of man and beast the infinite malady
> Crust you quite o'er. (III. vi)

"Man and all humanity" have become, for Timon, the object of a repudiation as excessive and one-sided as his former generosity had been. The astonished Lords are not far from the truth when they see his behavior as a collapse into insanity and point to the contradiction which has led him to swing from one extreme to its opposite: "One day he gives us diamonds, next day stones" (III. vi).

By the end of this crucial scene Timon's distinctively human, sociable career is ended. The second half of the play brings him to the fate which this unnatural detachment from his fellow men makes inevitable, and at the same time shows the public conflict worked out, beyond civil war, to a kind of restoration under Alcibiades. The great outbursts of misanthropy which mark these later scenes, and which have led to the comparison with *Lear,* need to be seen in their true ambivalence. As exposures of a corrupted and inhuman world they are true; but they are also the inevitable reverse of Timon's finally complacent prodigality. One excess leads to its opposite, and it is no accident that the main content of Timon's first long speech after the "banquet" he has just staged is an attack upon "degree," order, finally on the possibility of social existence itself. Timon, indeed, echoes the negative side of Lear's explosions of revulsion against humanity, but—we must add—can show less cause for it, less capacity to learn from an experience to which, finally, his own folly and lack of understanding have exposed him.

In view of this, we shall not underestimate the degree of negation, of sheer perverse destructiveness, which make themselves felt in Timon's tirades. To raise "slaves and fools" to a position of ministering authority amounts to a parody of Lear's corresponding investment of the Fool and Edgar[33] with the attributes of justice; the connection of ideas exists, but the final result is, in Timon, ironic in its effect, whereas in Lear compassion and understanding are present beneath the crazed inversion. Shakespeare, once more, is not repeating himself. To incite "the son of sixteen" to renounce "piety and fear" and to turn "degrees, observances, customs and laws" to their "confounding contraries," so that mere "confusion" may prevail; all this is *not,* in Shakespearean terms, to play the part of a moralist, however justly severe, but rather to indulge the hatred that represents the reverse side of Timon's "generosity," that has always been present *as a possibility* in him and that has only been clothed in the garb of a facile sociability. Like Lear at certain moments, but more obsessively and one-sidedly, Timon in his madness indulges instincts which are finally anti-social, destructive of humanity itself; but, unlike Lear, no real degree of recovery is open to him, and only annihilation, the final exhaustion of any kind of human emotion, awaits him at the last. Only to a diseased imagination, interpreting an equally diseased society, can "the unkindest beast" appear "more kinder than mankind" (IV. i); instead of seeking to read into Shakespeare's conception of Timon some kind of "personal" crisis of despair, we shall do well to follow the stages by which a finely balanced imagination works itself out in terms of irony and contrast.

This, however, does not mean that we should refuse all pity to Timon. The faithful Flavius follows his master, as Kent followed Lear, making a valid assertion of loyalty when all but loyalty has been lost; and Flavius accordingly, in a world which is made up of "wolves"—and this here because it *is* so made up, not, as elsewhere in this play, because Timon *needs* to feel it to be such—is capable of seeing the hero's situation with a measure of true compassion:

his poor self,
A dedicated beggar to the air,
With his disease of all-shunned poverty,
Walks, like contempt, alone. (IV. ii)

The servants too, who—again as in *King Lear*[34]—are more morally sensitive than their supposed betters, see Timon's end, and their own with it, in a common annihilation:

we must all part
Into this sea of air; (IV. ii)

and because their feeling for the human situation is a true one, Flavius can salute them as "fellows," describe them as "rich in sorrow, parting poor," and so assert that very fellow feeling which Timon, whom his world has rejected, is so spectacularly engaged in renouncing. This is the answer, in terms of normal human experience, to Timon's own preceding prayer, in which he begs that

as Timon grows, his hate may grow
To the whole race of mankind, high and low. (IV. i)

To fail to give due weight to this contrast is to destroy the true balance of Shakespeare's conception.

The scene which now follows (IV. iii), the longest in the play, amounts to a dissection, an exposure of Timon's attitudes in relation to a world which he has too readily accepted and which has now rejected him. As it opens, he is engaged in projecting his obsessions in an ever vaster scale upon the entire universe. "Infection," "rotten humidity," poison in his imagination the process of "breeding," of life itself. This is a product of madness and an exposure of fundamental unbalance; though it is also true, and relevant, that Timon follows the mad Lear in his penetration of merely external social distinctions—

> Raise me this beggar and deny't that lord— (IV. iii)

and in his perception of the universality of "flattery." "The learned pate ducks to the golden fool": we must feel that there is truth here, though also and side by side with it excess in the generalization that "*all* is oblique," that

> There's nothing level in our cursed natures
> But direct villainy, (IV. iii)

and in the conclusion that sociable living itself—"*All* feasts, societies, and throngs of men"—is to be "abhorred," that the only solid conclusion about life is that contained in the perverse and finally ridiculous prayer: "Destruction fang mankind." This may be, and indeed is, the working out of a state of disease, the mirror of perverse possibilities that certainly exist in life; but it cannot be, and is not intended to be, a conclusive judgment on life itself. When he rejects "gold" for "roots" Timon is finally caricaturing himself, joining his shadow Apemantus in a common excess.

At this point, appropriately, the world intrudes upon Timon as Alcibiades approaches in the company of his whores. The conjunction implies a comment on "blood," youthful passion and violent self-assertion, and Timon reacts to it by declaring himself "misanthropos," a hater of mankind. In this he is again excessive, though he sees truly the vanity of what is offered him:

> Follow thy drum;
> With man's blood paint the ground, gules, gules,
> Religious canons, civil laws are cruel:
> What then should war be? (IV. iii)

and relates the state of war to the individual's consuming passion for "this fell whore of thine." This is true and valid, if embittered, comment; but in Timon's following catalogue of diseases, and in his obsessive determination to cut himself off from his fellows, it is again a kind of inverted pride that prevails to grotesque and impossible ends. As a comment on the vanity of civil war, his conclusion,

> Make large confusion; and, thy fury spent,
> Confounded be thyself! (IV. iii)

is fair enough; but it is also the product of a crazed and resentful mind, which is in turn exposed to a culminating irony when those whom he has rejected press him for the "gold" they still hope to obtain from him. In this Alcibiades, exposing another aspect of his "heroic" pretensions, leads the way—

> Hast thou gold yet? I'll take the gold thou givest me,
> Not all thy counsel— (IV. iii)

to be joined, in sardonic echo of the warrior hero's greed, by the shrill importunities of his accompanying prostitutes: "Give us some gold, good Timon: hast thou more?" (IV. iii)

As Timon, in his increasingly crazed reaction, stresses his obsession with prostitution—"Be strong in whore"—and with the idea of disease that so persistently accompanies it, his vision of "gold" as the ultimate source of death finds an echo approaching the farcical in the demands of those who hear him: "More counsel with more money, bounteous Timon!" The crowning irony is reached when Apemantus at last joins the others and accuses Timon of imitating him:

> men report
> Thou dost affect my manners, and dost use them: (IV. iii)

two extreme, and equally unacceptable attitudes, which meet here in their common rejection of society. Apemantus, not without a certain bitter truth, finds Timon's nature "infected," ascribes his misanthropy, not to any genuine moral attitude, but to the mere shock of his "change of fortune," the exposure of his former lavishness, upon an ill-prepared mind. He advises Timon, with further appropriate irony, to assume the behavior of the "flatterers" who so gratified him in former days, and concludes with an uncomfortable truth—

> Thou gavest thine ears like tapsters that bade welcome
> To Knaves and all approachers—

and draws the bitter conclusion:

'tis most just
That thou turn rascal; hadst thou wealth again,
Rascals should have't. (IV. iii)

The culmination of irony is reached when Apemantus, rubbing the salt further into Timon's wound, stands on his dignity to reject him: "Do not assume my likeness."

Here, however, Apemantus in turn overreaches himself. His "virtue" has consistently lacked any sign of the generosity which Timon, in however inadequate a form, presented to the world. He too deserves the retort he receives: "Were I like thee, I'ld throw myself away" (IV. iii). The two, both outcasts, though for contrasted reasons, from the world, vie with one another in a finally absurd rejection. Apemantus accuses Timon of self-destruction—

Thou hast cast away thyself, being like thyself,
A madman so long, now a fool—

and bids him follow Lear in calling the "naked creatures,"

whose bare unhoused trunks,
To the conflicting elements exposed,
Answer mere nature, (IV. iii)

to "flatter" him. When Timon in turn dismisses Apemantus as a "fool," the latter replies: "I love thee better now than e'er I did"; but when his victim retorts "I hate thee worse," and denounces him as a "flatterer" of misery, he is driven to admit the perverse pleasure that "vexing" gives him. Once more the truth is evenly divided; to Apemantus' insinuation that Timon would willingly be a "courtier again," he can justly reply:

Hadst thou like us from our first swath, proceeded
The sweet degrees that this brief world affords
To such as may the passive drudges of it
Freely command, thou wouldst have plunged thyself
In general riot, melted down thy youth
In different beds of lust, and never learn'd
The icy precepts of respect, but follow'd
The sugar'd game before thee. (IV. iii)

This is at once a further true exposure of envious "virtue" and something more. In the tone of Timon's references to the "brief world" which was once at his disposal and which is now lost, to the "sugar'd game," and in the following statement that he, in happier times, "had the world as my *confectionary,*" the implicit criticism of his former attitudes is apparent. Again, when he goes on to ask

> Why shouldst thou hate men?
> They never flatter'd thee,

and adds petulantly "What hast thou given?" he touches the truth, in so far as generosity, the willingness to give, is a necessary attribute of life whose denial Apemantus' supposed "virtue" rests on; but there is an equal validity in the counteraccusation of pride which he himself invites:

> *Apemantus:* Art thou proud yet?
> *Timon:* Ay, that I am not thee.
> *Apemantus:* I, that I was
> No prodigal.
> *Timon:* I, that I am one now. (IV. iii)

Each has his measure of truth, and each, converging on the wilderness from his own point of departure, is now left with nothing but the dry "roots," the empty husk of life, to sustain him. There is truth, again, in the statement that Timon has never known "the middle of humanity." That is why he is where he now finds himself, translated from one "extremity" to its contrary; but, equally, when Apemantus declares his wish "to remain a beast with the beasts" Timon can justifiably call this a "beastly ambition" and make his appropriate comment:

> What beast couldst thou be that were not subject to a beast? and what a beast art thou already, that seest not thy loss in transformation? (IV. iii)

The confrontation ends, appropriately, in an exchange of incoherent insults—"Beast!" "Slave!" "Toad!"—delivered from positions mutually exclusive and in which the futility of excess on either side is brought to its farcical conclusion.

Even at this stage, however, Timon remains distinguished from Apemantus by the ability to turn his life-weariness into distinctive poetry. As he approaches his end, the craving for annihilation expresses itself in ways which rouse an emotional response:

Then, Timon, presently prepare thy grave;
Lie where the light foam of the sea may beat
Thy grave-stone daily; (IV. iii)

though even here he turns, immediately afterward and with his own kind of moralizing complacency, to the destructive properties of "gold" which have so long obsessed him. When Apemantus takes his leave, to be replaced by the bandits, Timon sees in the newcomers a further manifestation of the predatory instinct which, by now, he *needs* to see universally present in mankind: "You must eat men." Typically, he extends this vision to the entire universe—"each thing's a thief"—and ends on the familiar evocation of anarchy:

Love not yourselves; away,
Rob one another. (IV. iii)

To this the thieves, with their eyes on Timon's gold, reply with a caricature of reform. One declares himself almost "charmed" from his calling by Timon's eloquence; but the other, with whom the last word rests, comments more skeptically in delaying his "reformation" until such time as the state of "peace" is established.

Flavius, also returning, has the clarity of vision to see Timon as he is, "despised and ruinous," "full of decay and failing." His reaction to the spectacle, however, is one of "honest grief," true compassion and fellow feeling: an attitude which goes naturally with loyalty and which, alone in this play, can feel the tragic implications of the ruin of his master's "nobility." Timon's response is something less than adequate. When Flavius presents himself to his "dearest master" as his "honest poor servant," Timon clings to the misanthropy in which he has hitherto found a kind of compensation and refuses to recognize him or to admit the possibility of true disinterest. "I never had honest men about me, I": the repetition of "I," in a way which can be paralleled elsewhere in Shakespeare,[35] is not without meaning at this point. In spite of this, however, Flavius' tears end by appealing to Timon as a disclaimer of "flinty mankind," though he adds that more normally in the world which they have been brought to contemplate in its reality sorrow turns to the irony of laughter: "Strange times, that weep with laughing, not with weeping" (IV. iii). This "redemption" of human sorrow and fellow feeling brings with it a sense of his own past folly which even now Timon is unwilling to face. Asserting his compassion in the name of "duty and zeal," Flavius wrings from his former master the unwilling recognition of the existence of "a singly honest man," covered, however, to the last by a continued admonition to hate:

> Go, live rich and happy;
> But thus conditioned; thou shalt build from men,
> Hate all, curse all, show charity to none. (IV. iii)

On this unqualified assertion of inhumanity and ruin the scene ends.

As the final stage of the play opens, the Poet and the Painter return to recall its opening. The rumor that Timon still has gold has reached them, and inspires them to a certain worldly optimism. This leads in turn to the courtier's habitual recourse to the flattery which comes as second nature to him; for "promising is the very air o' the time" and "'tis not amiss we tender our loves to him in this supposed distress of his" (V. i). Thus moved by the expectation of renewed gain, they greet Timon with echoes of the rhetoric that, in former times, constituted life to him: only to find that bitter experience has led him to see through these fictions to a new sense of the "naked" truth, and that the word "honest," applied to these time-servers of his former eminence, now rings with supreme irony in his ears. Beneath the obsessive tone of his references to "honesty" Timon has come to see the artist who once ministered to his vanity as a fraud—"Thou counterfeit'st most lively"—and the poet as falsely "natural":

> Why, thy verse swells with stuff so fine and smooth
> That thou art even natural in thine art, (V. i)

and concludes the exchange with a bitter invitation to each to kill the "villain" who is in reality none other than himself.[36] It is significant that Flavius, in commenting on this, stresses the continued presence of an element of self-absorption in Timon's reactions:

> *he is set so only to himself*
> That nothing but himself which looks like man
> Is friendly with him. (V. i)

We shall not be following the true intention of the play unless we see that Timon's attitudes, however explicable in terms of the way in which the world has treated him, involve finally a rejection of man's true nature in the name of personal disillusionment and, with it, a negation of life itself.

Timon's attitude to his fellow citizens points in the same direction.

To the Senators who plead for Athens, and who formerly deserted him in his need, he reacts as an exaggerated and unilateral Coriolanus,[37] having only "blisters" and the "plague" to offer. There is finally more truth than he may realize in his observation that he himself is worthy "of none but such as you, and you of Timon" (V. i). The same point is made when the approach of Alcibiades is announced, threatening the city with the consequences of its sin and inhumanity, imposing the unnatural savagery of one who

> like a boar too savage, doth root up
> His country's peace; (V. i)

it is significant that in answer to the plea for aid, uttered now in the name of the familiar pieties, Timon can only confirm his indifference: "I care not!" The logical end of such an attitude, by which Timon confirms his separation from society and all the natural positives, is an acceptance of annihilation, and to this he now tends with the deepest emotion left to him:

> my long sickness
> Of health and living now begins to mend,
> And nothing brings me all things. (V. i)

From the moment of his initial disillusionment Timon has tended to see life in terms of disease, "sickness"; the end of this perversion of life is now seen to be the illusion that seeks in "nothing," the mere renunciation of continued living, the only end to which it can aspire.

This in turn is followed, again most logically, by a last invitation to suicide:

> Timon hath made his everlasting mansion
> Upon the beached verge of the salt flood: (V. i)

even the "sour words" in which he once expressed his misanthropy are played out as he stands, looking out to vacancy, from the farthest limits of his disillusionment. The resources of language itself, as a means to human communication, are exhausted—"let language end" —as "plague and infection" are called in to redress universal human faults, and absolute death is seen as the end of all: "Graves only be men's works, and death their gain" (V. i). The death wish, the natural reverse of Timon's former excess in self-centered generosity, has now taken total possession of his being.

As Timon speaks thus for the last time "hope" is "dead" in those who hear him, and Alcibiades is left to sound the trumpets of retribution against "this coward and lascivious town" (V. iv). His speech heralding the reversal of what has gone before is expressed with the sinewy strength of the best verse of *Coriolanus:*

> now the time is flush,
> When crouching marrow in the bearer strong
> Cries of itself "No more": now breathless wrong
> Shall sit and pant in your great chairs of ease,
> And pursy insolence shall break his wind
> With fear and horrid flight. (V. iv)

This is at once a reversal of Timon's negatives and an intimation of doom toward the society which brought him to them. The Senators, however, for all their manifold faults, can still offer through their spokesman a human regret which lies beyond Timon's latter comprehension. "We were not all unkind" (in the sense of lacking in *kindred,* human fellow feeling): "All have not offended" (V. iv). Even against the running tides of negation and excess, the natural instinct of sociability reasserts itself to win a measure of final recognition. The once predatory Alcibiades can accept the spirit of the First Senator's plea, urging him to become the instrument of a justice based on the drawing of necessary distinctions:

> For those that were, it is not square to take
> On those that are, revenges; crimes, like lands,
> Are not inherited. (V. iv)

There could be no more direct comment on Timon's universalizing of a hatred based finally on flaws in his own nature; and it is followed, again logically, by an affirmation of the relevance of "your public laws," as Alcibiades closes the action on a gesture of justice against which Timon's epitaph—the recalling of one who, "alive," "all living men did hate"—stands out as a manifestation of "nobility" flawed, undone by its own self-engendered excesses. In the world that now opens before Athens, "war" is to "breed" peace, the "olive" fittingly to accompany the "sword." The last word lies with a gesture of reconciliation in favor of the processes of life renewed.

XI

The Roman Tragedies

Shakespeare's major plays on Roman history span between them the supremely creative years of his dramatic career. The earliest of the three, *Julius Caesar,* was separated by no great distance in time from the two parts of *Henry IV* and *Henry V* and is concentrated, like these plays, upon the interplay of personal motives and public necessity; whilst the other two—*Antony and Cleopatra* and *Coriolanus*—belong to the dramatist's last years and combine an acute understanding of historical processes with the illuminating presence of a distinctive tragic vision. Thus variously situated in time, the plays, by bringing together into a mutually enriching unity two of the principal themes of Shakespeare's mature work—those expressed respectively in the historical chronicles and in the series of great tragedies which followed them—constitute one of the undoubted peaks of his achievement.

The historical matter of all three plays is principally derived from Plutarch's *Lives of the Noble Greeks and Romans,* as translated into English from the French of Amyot by Thomas North.[1] The fact is important for an understanding of the plays themselves; for, whereas it is, generally speaking, true that Shakespeare's acknowledged masterpieces—*Hamlet, Macbeth, King Lear*—owe little more than the barest outline of their plots to the comparatively artless narratives from which they derive, in the Roman tragedies we are conscious of dealing with what might almost be called a collaboration. It is well known that long passages from North's highly workmanlike translation were almost directly versified by Shakespeare; but a comparison of the relevant passages[2] shows that the dramatist, in following his original closely, was in fact developing his own conception, being fully himself. The style of these plays, far from reflecting a pedestrian process of versification, shows a unique combination of narrative lucidity, achieved through the easy, almost conversational use of spoken rhythms and vernacular phrases, with poetic intensities that flow effortlessly from this foundation whenever the state of the action so requires. By the side of these works, even some of the effects of the great tragedies seem to have been reached with effort, to represent a sensibility strained to the utmost in the intensity of its reaction to emotional stresses; whilst the verse of the final comedies seems at times to achieve its symbolic effects through conventions of greater and more artificial complexity.

JULIUS CAESAR

The action of *Julius Caesar* turns, in the tense simplicity of its narrative, upon an event of unique historical importance. Round this event with its varied and often contrasted significances for the Elizabethan mind,[3] Shakespeare has developed a pattern of political passions which answers to a closely knit dramatic plan. The early scenes show Caesar and his enemies converging upon the striking of a blow which has in its inevitability, in the universal concern it focuses upon itself, the quality of a tragic sacrifice. The deed itself and the action which follows from it lead, in the central episodes, to the conflict of public and personal motives involved in the clash of Brutus and Antony over the dictator's dead body. Finally, in the concluding stages, the consequences of the murder are revealed through their effect upon each of the contending parties. The conspirators, brought to see their motives in the unflattering light of reality, collapse into mutual recrimination and confessed futility; whilst, against a background of practical assertion and ruthless calculation of the odds, a new Roman order replaces that which has been destroyed.

In one sense, and in one sense only, the entire action is centered upon the murdered dictator. He disappears, it is true, at the end of the first half of the play, and his appearances before his elimination have been strangely brief and enigmatic; but the fact remains that, alive, the action turns upon him, and when he is dead his spirit remains, as Brutus unwillingly confesses,[4] persistently and implacably alive. The emphasis, however, in the presentation of the character lies elsewhere, in a notable sense of discrepancy between the figure which the dictator, obliged by the force of circumstance, presents to the world and the reality of what he in fact is. From the first, his use of the impersonal, royal style implies an effort to live self-consciously up to the requirements which his isolated and uneasy eminence imposes. "Always," in his own phrase (I. ii), "I am Caesar," and in that "always" there is a sense of danger, of living poised over a void, an imminent disaster, which, as we approach him more closely, his behavior repeatedly confirms. It is true that many of the initial intimations of weakness in Caesar—Cassius' ascription to him of physical feebleness, Casca's belittling report of his "swooning" in the market place (I. ii)—come from his enemies, and are to be understood as the product of envy: but true also that these same incidents contribute to the impression of one whom his circumstances oblige to play out a role, a course moreover in which he is largely supported by a vanity which will at the last contribute to his disaster.

The scene (II. ii) in which Caesar is persuaded, against his intimate will, to go to the Capitol is in this respect revealing. As Calpurnia, shaken by premonitions which the elements confirm, presses him to stay at home he clings obstinately to the determination which his situation has imposed upon him. "Caesar shall go forth": the dangers that threaten him are always *behind* him, out of sight, waiting to assert themselves against a man whom his position obliges to outface them:

> when they shall see
> The face of Caesar, they are vanished. (II. ii)

Upon this illusion of constancy the dictator's position, and with it the fortunes of the Roman world, depend.

Faced, indeed, by portents "beyond all use," threats to human conceptions of order and purpose, Caesar responds with what is at once the striking of an attitude and a touch of sincerity:

> What can be avoided
> Whose end is purposed by the mighty gods? (II. ii)

In the light of this implicit fatalism the renewed affirmation which follows—"Caesar shall go forth"—must seem strangely obstinate. It is followed by a further insistence upon the pose which we have come to associate with his dignity, a stressing of self-consciousness which ends by insinuating the presence of the weakness it seeks to deny:

Of all the wonders that I yet have heard,
It seems to me most strange that men should fear;
Seeing that death, a necessary end,
Will come when it will come. (II. ii)

The lines answer to that sense of fatality, of subjection to the temporal process, which is present as a factor limiting human choices in all Shakespeare's plays of this period. Against this pervasive influence, Caesar is engaged in building up an impression of consistency which began no doubt as a real reflection of greatness, but which his situation, and the destiny which covers all human actions, now imposes upon him.

Caesar is revealed, in fact, less as brave and consistent at this moment than as talking himself into consistency. Beneath this determination, however, weakness once more asserts itself. Calpurnia persuades him to a course which his own instincts have already insinuated; he acquiesces ("Mark Antony shall say I am not well"), even while clinging to the excuse that it is the frailty of others that has imposed this change of plan: "for thy humour I will stay at home." The arrival of Decius Brutus to escort him to the Senate brings to the surface the contradictions by which he is torn. Decius is to tell the senators that he "will not come to-day"; since it is false that he cannot, and that he "dare not, falser," only the bare affirmation of his will can meet the case:

The cause is in my will: I will not come;
That is enough to satisfy the senate. (II. ii)

The retort reveals the arbitrary nature of the consistency which circumstance imposes upon Caesar. It also covers an inner uncertainty; the pose has taken possession of the man, and will from now on lead him to his fate.

After Caesar's account of Calpurnia's dream and Decius' ingenious exercise in interpretation—both expressed in the heightened, almost hysterical language which surrounds conspiracy throughout —Decius drives home his point by a highly effective combination of flattery with an appeal to the dictator's unavowed love of power. The Senate have decided to confer a crown upon "mighty Caesar," and if he does not attend the session, "their minds may change." More dangerously still, Decius emphasizes the mockery which may follow if the truth were known:

It were a mock
Apt to be rendered, for some one to say
"Break up the senate till another time,
When Caesar's wife shall meet with better dreams." (II. ii)

The appeal to vanity supports that to ambition, and indifference to Calpurnia—reflected in an attitude toward her that surely stands in significant contrast to Brutus' tender treatment of Portia (II. i)—is present in both. Above all—and here Decius is careful to cover his daring with a profession of love—it will be whispered that the master of Rome is "afraid": a hint than which none is better calculated to play upon the strange complex of conflicting emotions at the dictator's heart.

With this last speech, Decius achieves his aim. The victim brushes aside all misgivings—"How foolish do your fears seem now, Calpurnia"—jokes with his enemies, and greets Antony with a manly jest. Throughout we feel a recovery of confidence, a readiness to accept willingly what has now become his fate. The emphasis on "friendship," on taking wine together, underlines the monstrous treachery afoot; only Brutus, standing aside from the main stream, "yearns" to think that appearances are "false," that "every like is not the same." From this moment, Caesar's history marches together with that of his enemies to converge at the base of Pompey's effigy.

Caesar, however, though he dominates the action by virtue of his public position, is in no sense the principal moving force of the tragedy. This is provided, in the early scenes, by Brutus, who, in seeking the clarification of his own motives, gives the action its dynamic quality. His initial reflections are already charged with implications of character:

Vexed I am
Of late with passions of some difference,
Conceptions only proper to myself,
Which give some soil perhaps to my behaviours. (I. ii)

The expression, notably reminiscent of certain utterances of Hamlet, stresses the nature, essentially inward-looking and exploratory, of his dilemma. To this Stoic theorist, tied to the contemplation of his own virtue, the "passions" present themselves as disturbing elements, shadowing the unity and self-control which he craves as the key to action. It is of the nature of his conflict to be without communication, "proper" to himself alone; and this inwardness, the product of his character and of his assumptions about life, affects him, when uneasily stirred to action, as a blot upon the harmonious personality at which he aims, a "soil" upon the fair outward presentation of himself which he so persistently craves.

It is the function of Cassius, by playing upon this desire for communication, to mold him to ends not finally his own. The peculiar relationship between the pair, and the method of its dramatic presentation, are both indicated in the query which opens his attack and in Brutus' reply:

Cassius: Tell me, good Brutus, can you see your face?
Brutus: No, Cassius: for the eye sees not itself
But by reflection, by some other things. (I. ii)[5]

Under the guise of providing, in the shape of "thoughts of great value, worthy cogitations," a "mirror" to reflect his friend's "*hidden* worthiness," Cassius will bring him to see not a reality, an objective vision of his strength and weakness, but the "shadow" of the imperfectly understood desires which will finally bring him, not to the affirmation of his ideals, but to personal and public ruin.

Beneath these assertions of friendship and plain dealing, Cassius' approach to Brutus is fraught with calculation. Those of "the best respect in Rome" look to him for redress; as they groan beneath "this age's yoke," their desire is that "*noble* Brutus"—the adjective initiates a line of flattery which, precisely because it contains truth, will be particularly insidious—understood his own wishes and motives, "had his eyes." Brutus' first reaction is honest and true to character:

Into what dangers would you lead me, Cassius,
That you would have me seek into myself
For that which is not in me? (I. ii)

It is some time before he will speak so truly again. Meanwhile, it is Cassius' mission to undermine this candid self-estimate, replacing it by a false confidence which carries no inner conviction. Taking up the image of the mirror, he turns to his own ends the need for guidance which makes his friend so pliable to his purposes:

> since you know you cannot see yourself
> So well as by reflection, I your glass
> Will modestly discover to yourself
> That of yourself which you yet know not of. (I. ii)

This is a dangerous proceeding, made the more so by the tendency, which the following exchanges reveal, for the two friends to vie with one another in setting up idealized images of themselves to minister to what is finally, beneath their poses of Roman virtue and public spirit, an intimate self-satisfaction. When Cassius denies that he is "a common laugher," "fawning" on men with the intention of later "scandalling" them, he is no doubt comparing himself, not altogether unjustly, with such as Antony and pointing to some true consequences of Caesar's exorbitant power; but, beneath the implied contrast, envy, the desire to debase what he has been unable to achieve, vitiates the judgment.

For Brutus, similarly, devotion to the public good expresses itself through assumption of that "honour" which was, more especially at this time, so variously in Shakespeare's mind:

> What is it that you would impart to me?
> If it be aught toward the general good,
> Set honour in one eye and death i' the other,
> And I will look on both indifferently. (I. ii)

Though expressed with a more "philosophic" detachment, the spirit behind these words is akin to that which prompted Hotspur to his generous but useless sacrifice;[6] and it reveals much the same tendency to replace the balance of judgment by simpler but more illusory certainties. As Brutus concludes, not without a touch of self-esteem,

> let the gods so speed me as I love
> The name of honour more than I fear death. (I. ii)

It will be, perhaps, one of the lessons of Brutus' tragedy that the "names" of things, however noble and consoling in abstraction, are no substitute for a balanced consideration of their reality. "Honour" is in the way of becoming a trap set for those who, like Brutus, fail to temper idealism with a proper measure of self-awareness.

The soliloquy in which Brutus finally arrives at his decision, and thereby makes the murder of Caesar possible, is so riddled with implicit contradictions that some students of the play[7] have judged it incomprehensible. It is, however, thoroughly in character. Brutus, not himself an evil man, is about to perform an act which will release evil impulses whose true nature he persistently fails to grasp; the discrepancy between what he is and what he does is reflected in his recognizable effort to persuade himself, against convictions intimately present in his nature, that the resolve he is about to take is necessary and just. Had he been consistently the doctrinaire republican Cassius would have him be, the admitted fact that Caesar "would be crown'd" would have been, for him if not for Shakespeare and most of his contemporaries, a sufficient reason for his elimination. Brutus, however, as the play presents him, is no such thing, but rather a man who seeks in decisive action the confirmation of his own virtue, whose purposes are imposed upon him by those who play upon inconsistencies, weak spots in his own nature; and it is part of his tragedy that he cannot forget, much as he now desires to do so, that his intended victim is a human being and his friend. This situation bears fruit in his recognition, which a convinced republican would have found irrelevant, that he has as yet no valid *personal* reason for the deed he contemplates. "To speak truth of Caesar," he admits,

> I have not known when his affections sway'd
> More than his reason. (II. i)

"I know no personal cause to spurn at him": the admission is, for a man who sincerely values friendship, personal relationships, serious enough; but since another side of Brutus' nature craves abstract consistency, the wedding of high principle to effective action, he turns this recognition into an argument for clearing himself of dubious personal motives and seeks to place the burden of justification squarely upon an appeal to the "general" good.

The argument, inevitably, is pressed home with less than complete conviction. "How that *might* change his nature, there's the question," Brutus urges upon himself, in a strangely tentative attitude, only to recognize later that

> the quarrel
> Will bear no colour for the thing he is; (II. i)

but, since a contrary necessity urges him to conceal these doubts, calls upon him to assert a certainty which he is far from feeling, emphasis must be laid on a *possible*, an unproven danger:

Fashion it thus; that what he is, augmented,
Would run to these and these extremities. (II. i)

The vagueness, the readiness to "fashion it thus" in accordance with preconceptions in which observed reality has little part to play, is highly symptomatic. Brutus, precisely because the vacillation which has characterized his reactions since the beginning covers deep inner uncertainty, speaks to himself evasively in terms of specious "philosophical" commonplace—

The abuse of greatness is when it disjoins
Remorse from power— (II. i)

lowliness is young ambition's ladder . . .

and takes refuge in an imposed ruthlessness:

think him as a serpent's egg
Which hatched would as his kind grow mischievous,
And kill him in the shell. (II. i)

The tendency to cover lack of intimate consistency with a show of impersonal brutality belongs to Brutus' peculiar brand of theoretical idealism. It is part of the presentation of human contradiction, whose exposure is so close to the spirit of this play. Brutus seeks at this moment to resolve an intimate, tragic disharmony through an act of decision foreign to his nature; the confusion revealed in his own motives, and in his attitude to the world of external realities, is one that will follow him through the contradictions of his career to the final resolution of suicide.

Confronted with the conspirators he has agreed to lead, Brutus further reveals his true nature. In presenting him to them Cassius stresses his need to live up to the conception of himself that his ancestors and his "philosophy" have laid upon him. He suggests that, unlike these ancestors, Brutus is weak, indecisive; public opinion demands of him that "opinion" of himself that every true Roman wishes to share. Brutus, in reply, urges his new associates to confirm their dedication and seeks confidence in a rhetorical declaration of his own:

do not stain
The even virtue of our enterprise,
Nor the insupressive mettle of our spirits,
To think that or our cause or our performance

> Did need an oath: when every drop of blood
> That every Roman bears, and nobly bears,
> Is guilty of a several bastardy
> If he do break the smallest particle
> Of any promise that hath pass'd from him. (II. i)

The best comment on this earnest but slightly self-conscious harangue is provided by the return, which at once follows, to practical considerations. Cassius and his friends wish to enroll the support of Cicero, whose reputation will "purchase us"—the verb is appropriately chosen—"a good opinion,"

> And buy men's voices to commend our deeds.

Since, however, it is Brutus' adhesion that all desire, it is enough for him to reject Cicero as incapable of "following" for all to agree that he should not be approached.

The basic weakness of the plot is more closely touched upon when Cassius urges that Mark Antony should die. Brutus' rejection of this advice is of very considerable interest as a further revelation of the kind of man he is. It combines an effort to be practical, revealed in the opening concession to expediency ("Our course will seem too bloody"), with failure to be so. It is finally the pose, the elevation of himself into a figure of magnanimous principle, that engages his emotions. The expression is not without a touch of the grotesque. "Let us be sacrificers, but not butchers, Caius," he urges, and follows up the plea with an unreal distinction between "the spirit of men" and their material "blood" which must so regrettably be shed:

> We all stand up against the spirit of Caesar,
> And in the spirit of men there is no blood!
> O, that we then could come by Caesar's spirit,
> And not dismember Caesar! (II. i)

The distinction no doubt answers in part to the desire to make credible Brutus' nobility in the face of the nature of the deed on which he has set himself. The difficulty, however, is turned into an asset, a revelation of character. Brutus the idealist is seen as one more example of that typical Shakespearean creation, the man who, willing an end, is ready to deceive himself concerning the means necessary to gain it. "Caesar must bleed for't," he recognizes, but covers the admission with futile and self-conscious posing:

> gentle friends,
> Let's kill him boldly, but not wrathfully:
> Let's carve him as a dish fit for the gods,
> Not hew him as a carcass fit for hounds:
> And let our hearts as subtle masters do,
> Stir up their servants to an act of rage,
> And after seem to chide 'em. (II. i)

The speech points to the presence of a variety of motives in the process of decorating brutality with strained emotional expression. Addressing his future accomplices as "gentle friends," Brutus, in admitting the fact of bloody death, embroiders it with the farfetched and finally absurd evocation of "a dish fit for the gods." The odd mixture of unpracticality and a certain unconscious cynicism is brought home forcibly in the description of the conspirators' hearts as "*subtle* masters" who, in rousing their "servant" feelings to a simulation, an "act of rage," *seem* after, for the purpose of obtaining public approval, "to chide them." "We shall be call'd purgers, not murderers": the reality, as so often occurs with men of Brutus' type, is disguised by a change of name, and this becomes the justification of a decision politically unwise, if humanly comprehensible, which will finally bring the conspiracy to ruin.

Such are the main elements which, converging, unite in the blow which strikes down Caesar in the central action of the play. The victim's last utterance, claiming the constancy of the "northern star," is the most theatrical of all his assertions of fixity. Just as his fall is about to stress his common humanity, he accentuates unnaturally the distance that separates him from other men:

> men are flesh and blood, and apprehensive;
> Yet in the number I do know but one
> That unassailable holds on his rank,
> Unshaked of motion; (III. i)

but already his own unsuspecting words—

> and that I am he
> Let me a little show it, even in this— (III. i)

amount to a plea, an appeal to the world to support him in this self-estimate. It finds its answer in the repeated stabs of Brutus and his associates, and in his fall at the foot of the effigy of Pompey, whom he himself formerly overthrew.

The fall is followed by a tense moment of silence, set against the gathering climax which has so splendidly preceded it. Immediately after this, the emotions so far concentrated upon Caesar's overpowering presence break out with the rising hysteria of libertarian sentiment. "Liberty! freedom! tyranny is dead!" cries Cinna; and even Brutus, after calling on those around him to maintain their calm, turns to a more emotional line of appeal:

Stoop, Romans, stoop,
And let us bathe our hands in Caesar's blood
Up to the elbows, and besmear our swords;
Then walk we forth, even to the market-place,
And waving our red weapons o'er our heads,
Let's all cry, "Peace, freedom, and liberty!" (III. i)

Here, if anywhere, and in the self-congratulatory exchanges that follow, a final comment on the true nature of conspiracy is unerringly made. The gap between profession and reality, the aspiration to freedom and the deed to which it has led, is remorselessly asserted in the insistence upon spilled blood: blood not, as in *Macbeth*, horrifyingly sticking to the assassin's hands, but lavish, free-flowing, answering to the strained emotions with which the murderers have sought to disguise, even from themselves, the true nature of their crime.

In this charged emotional climate, Mark Antony—first through a messenger and then in his own person—cautiously feels his way to the center of the stage. By the end of his exchange with Brutus, which culminates in a grotesque parody—"Let each man render me his bloody hand"—of the reconciliation which Caesar's assassin has so impossibly proposed, he knows that his position is stronger than he can have dared to hope. Left alone with his thoughts, his last speech in this scene is a further revelation of character. Couched in the facile rhetoric which comes so readily to him, it apostrophizes the dead Caesar as "thou bleeding piece of earth" and goes on to speak of "costly blood" and to characterize his wounds as "dumb mouths" and "ruby lips." In a world so fluent in feeling, where emotion swells in accordance with the forms of rhetoric, intensely rather than deeply, like the blood which issues from the wounds it contemplates, Antony's oratory is perfectly at home. It issues, however, in a vision of chaos. "All pity" shall be "chok'd" with "custom of fell deeds,"

And Caesar's spirit ranging for revenge,
With Ate by his side come hot from hell,
Shall in these confines with a monarch's voice
Cry "Havoc!" and let slip the dogs of war;
That this foul deed shall smell above the earth
With carrion men, groaning for burial. (III. i)

This conclusion to the first open revelation of his pent-up feelings carries with it an estimate of Antony's limitations as a moral being. His rhetoric pays itself with its own expression, represents emotional irresponsibility in one who can also calculate and use his rhetorical gifts for ends deliberately and cunningly conceived. The vision of chaos, far from appalling Antony, finally attracts him, answers to a necessity of his nature; and that is why his type of emotion, not less than Brutus' frigid assertions of principle, is to be seen less in its own right than as a fragment, a partial aspect of the unity which Caesar's death has destroyed in Rome. The end of this process is "carrion," self-destruction, death; that Antony, carried on the flow of words which reflects his emotional nature, can dwell with complacency on these dreadful realities is, by implication, an exposure of his most intimate motives.

The famous oration scene (III. ii) is too familiar to call for analysis in detail. It shows a Brutus caught in the consequences of his own act, deprived—now that the mood of exaltation which accompanied him to it has passed—of the impulse to go further. Against him is set an Antony who, in the act of affirming himself as the adventurer and theatrical orator he is, is also the instrument by which the *truth* about murder emerges to the light of day. This clash of aims and temperaments takes place before a background provided by a new element in the action: the Roman populace. The crowd has not hitherto played a decisive part in events, though its fickleness has been indicated more than once in the early scenes.[8] It now makes the voice of its appetites heard in a more direct fashion, thereby showing from still another point of view the nature of the forces which Brutus and Cassius have so irresponsibly released from their normal restraints. At the end of the scene, as the mob moves off to burn and plunder, Antony's final comment is a revealing disclaimer of responsibility. "Now let it work": the orator, resting on his laurels, looks with satisfaction on his achievement, dwells with a certain pleasure on the chaos he has let loose:

Mischief, thou art afoot,
Take thou what course thou wilt. (III. ii)

The final effect is a revelation of irresponsibility accompanied by sinister pleasure:

Fortune is merry,
And in this mood will give us anything. (III. ii)

That, later on, she will assume other moods, ultimately less congenial to the speaker, remains to be seen. Meanwhile, the grim little episode (III. iii) of the destruction of Cinna the poet for a chance coincidence of name comes effectively to announce the brutality which will from now on so frequently preside over the course of events.

The unleashing of the Roman mob brings to an end the more dynamic part of the action. The last scenes of the tragedy exhibit the consequences of Caesar's murder in a spirit of notable detachment. They show a Rome divided by covert rivalries which can only end in the elimination of all but one of its contending factions and, after that elimination, in the restoration of unity under Octavius. Apart from this resolution, the personal tragedy of Brutus is rounded off in the self-inflicted death which is its logical conclusion.

It is important to note that this dispassionate evaluation falls impartially on both parties. As the fourth act opens, Antony and a notably frigid and non-committal Octavius are seen in the company of Lepidus, contemplating the death of their relations and former friends without illusion and without feeling. The initial words of Antony, who has so recently exhibited himself in the forum as a man of sensibility, are "These many then shall die"; Octavius, typically passing from the general statement to its particular application, adds (turning to Lepidus) "Your brother too must die," and obtains his companion's assent:

Upon condition Publius shall not live,
Who is your sister's son, Mark Antony. (IV. i)

The callousness of the exchange, the readiness to write off human lives by marks on paper, is rounded off by Antony's complacent rejoinder: "He shall not live; look, with a spot I damn him." The final suggestion that the will, which Antony has so recently used to stir up mob emotion in the name of generosity, should be studied to determine "How to cut off some charge in legacies" adds a revealing touch of parsimony to the display of cynicism in action.

The world which is to replace that formerly dominated by Caesar is indeed mean, petty, and dangerous. The triumvirs are already engaged in the first stages of a ruthless struggle for power. As soon as Lepidus has been dispatched for the will, Antony refers disparagingly to him ("a slight unmeritable man"; "meet to be sent on errands") and proposes his elimination. Octavius, whose moment is still to come, bides his time ("he is a tried and valiant soldier") and is answered by Antony with a further display of cynicism. "So is my horse, Octavius"; with Lepidus thus removed from consideration, the two leaders return to discussion of the "great things" in which their own future is involved. The last words of the scene, spoken by Octavius, stress the insecurity that now surrounds the entire political future:

> some that smile have in their hearts, I fear,
> Millions of mischiefs. (IV. i)

Such is the world which has survived Caesar, and in which his avengers are fated to move.

On the other side the circumstances of Caesar's enemies, as they are shown in the process of coming to terms with their real as distinct from their rhetorical selves, answer to a conception which is, in its accepted pessimism, finally similar. In them, division and self-doubt replace the cynical maneuvers of their foes. Cassius, no longer the ardent friend of the early scenes, whom the prospect of action united (perhaps, in the last analysis, spuriously) to a colleague whom interest also demanded as his associate, now salutes that associate with distant correctness, no longer shows

> such free and friendly conference,
> As he hath used of old. (IV. ii)

Brutus' reaction is heavy with the sense of fatality. Lucilius has described "a hot friend cooling," and the process by which love begins "to sicken and decay" has its symptoms in "an enforced ceremony." The wish of Brutus to maintain "plain and simple faith" is at once moving and strangely inadequate. It springs from his most deeply held theoretical conception of life, in the absence of which his integrity, his belief in himself and in the purity of his motives, must founder; but it runs against the nature of things as determined by the course of action in which he has compromised his honesty. Against the background of advancing armies we feel already the "sinking at the trial" which, proceeding from adverse external realities, mirrors inner dejection.

The motives behind this discussion are, from the first, of some complexity. Cassius, rushing typically into the void which opens before him, complains that he has been "wrong'd"; but it is clear from his explanation that the wrong—an accusation of connivance in accepting bribes—has been inflicted in a dubious context. Brutus, indeed, having made his point in a tone of moral superiority—"You wrong'd yourself to write in such a case"—cannot refrain from rubbing salt into the wound. By accusing Cassius of "an itching palm," he rouses the impetuous self-respect of his friend to violent protest:

> You know that you are Brutus that speaks this,
> Or, by the gods, this speech were else your last; (IV. iii)

and there is a touch of insensitivity in the responding reference to "chastisement" which leaves Cassius speechless in its implication of lofty superiority. The two characters, so precariously united against Caesar, are seen to be perfectly designed to exasperate one another to the limits of endurance.

As the gap between them widens, Brutus is led to recall the integrity which inspired their actions: "Did not great Caesar bleed for justice' sake?" This thought, contrasted with the sad reality of the present, leads him to back his reproof with a further gesture toward the idealism of the past:

> What, shall one of us
> That struck the foremost man of all this world
> But for supporting robbers, shall we now
> Contaminate our fingers with base bribes,
> And sell the mighty space of our large honours
> For so much trash as may be grasped thus? (IV. iii)

The gesture is ample, noble, and yet it covers weakness. As always, Brutus is taking refuge in a satisfactory picture of himself as one who has dared, for "honour" alone, to lead and inspire a conspiracy that overthrew "the foremost man of all this world"; but where disinterest ends and egoism, the need to live up to an ennobling vision of his own motives, begins, we might be hard put to decide.

Whatever the truth about Brutus' purity of motive (and no simple judgment would be appropriate) his attitude could not be more precisely calculated to rub the raw edges of Cassius' sense of inferiority. As Brutus ceases, he describes what he has heard as a "baiting" of himself and utters the ominous warning: "I'll not endure it." His touchy self-respect has been offended, and now responds by appealing to his superior experience:

I am a soldier, I,
Older in practice, abler than yourself
To make conditions. (IV. iii)

The repetition of "I" indicates the nature of the wound inflicted upon Cassius' own type of egoism. That of Brutus, though more complex, is not less strong. It impels him, where tact would have passed over the burning issue, to exasperate his companion further by contemptuous denial. "You are not, Cassius." "I am." "I say you are not": the result is to create an ugly wrangle in which the last threads of self-respect seem likely to be swallowed up. At the culminating moment, Cassius' threatening "tempt me no further" is matched by the infuriating superiority of "Away, slight man!" and by the final insult:

Hear me, for I will speak.
Must I give way and room to your rash choler? (IV. iii)

At this moment, the realities of character which underlie the previous affirmations of constancy and devotion to principle are revealed for what they are. The rest of the scene is devoted to working them out fully, and to an attempt to cover them up in the interests of a cause already lost.

At first, however, it is not a matter of covering up, but of adding further irritation to Cassius' open wound. In this Brutus, by a trait which links curiously with his self-conscious idealism, but which is not on reflection incompatible with it, is a master. "Must I endure all this?" Cassius cries, as though demanding clemency, and receives the bitter exasperation of the insult—"All this! ay more! Fret till your proud heart break"—and the contemptuous dismissal that follows:

Go show your slaves how choleric you are,
And make your bondmen tremble! (IV. iii)

The rest of the speech, so true to the frigid egoism of the man "armed strong in honesty," rises to a final, almost sadistic determination to inflict humiliation:

> By the gods,
> You shall digest the venom of your spleen,
> Though it do split you; for from this day forth,
> I'll use you for my mirth, yea, for my laughter,
> When you are waspish. (IV. iii)

The lines are rich in inflection, in the varied revelation of character. There is pleasure in inflicting humiliation, moral callousness, and contempt, together with a bitter pleasure in true characterization in the final description of Cassius as "waspish." The fact is that the element of egoism present from the first beneath Brutus' noble façade is coming to the surface under the stress of his growing awareness of standing intolerably in a false situation. The effect of this outburst, though palliated, can never be undone; and Cassius' broken reply, "Is it come to this?" clearly involves a glance back to the idealistic unity of purpose in which Caesar's murder was carried out and which is now being revealed in so unflattering a light.

The healing of this breach and the return to at least the appearance of unity are accomplished with no small tact. The conspirators, seeing the abyss opening at their feet, draw back in horror. Both, we may feel, are moved beneath the surface of their reproaches by a sense that it is their own past, their capacity for continued belief in their moral dignity, which they are in reality placing in jeopardy; and when Cassius breaks into further reproach, self-exhibition is subtly combined with a true sense of personal betrayal. "Cassius is a-weary of the world": here it may seem that a conscious appeal to emotion prevails, but the following phrases surely strike a valid note in their criticism of Brutus' frigid moralizing:

> Hated by one he loves; braved by his brother!
> Check'd like a bondman; all his faults observed,
> Set in a notebook, learn'd, and conn'd by rote,
> To cast into my teeth. (IV. iii)

Brutus, no doubt realizing that he has gone too far, meets this outburst, which culminates in Cassius' offer of his dagger, with a genuine attempt to reduce the tension. He is, however, characteristically clumsy in his effort to adjust his words to a new mood. His phrase

"Be angry when you will, it shall have scope" sounds stiffly, rather like the humoring of a self-willed child; men such as Brutus do not easily descend from the pedestal on which their lives are based. Beneath the clumsiness, however, there is now revealed a deep unhappiness, the immediate cause of which is still being held back from us:

> O Cassius, you are yoked with a lamb,
> That carries anger as the flint bears fire,
> Who, much enforced, shows a hasty spark,
> And straight is cold again. (IV. iii)

The reference to feeling hardly struck as from a flinty surface, an innate coldness, reveals tellingly the diffidence, the emotional clumsiness, which is part of the character; and the sincerity of the revelation opens the way to a rueful, disillusioned reconciliation. The impression left by the whole exchange is one of the cooling embers of a passion doomed to extinction, but surviving, at least for the moment, the death of the original flame.

The immediate reason for Brutus' state, however, and for much that has gone before, has so far been held back by an admirable stroke of dramatic tact. It is now revealed. After calling for a bowl of wine, symbol—as it were—of harmony between friends, he meets Cassius' wondering comment "I did not think you could have been so angry" and the reproof of "Of your philosophy you make no use" with his simple revelation: "No man bears sorrow better: Portia is dead." The disclosure, followed by an admirably brief and tense exchange of phrases—

> —Portia is dead.
> —Ha, Portia!
> —She is dead— (IV. iii)

gives a center of stillness to the bitter exchanges that have gone before. From this heart of silence, Cassius' emotion speaks in a new, transformed tone: "How 'scaped I killing when I cross'd you so?" and backs it with the almost choric quality of his following exclamation: "O insupportable and touching loss!"

The revelation is rounded off with the recovery by Brutus of his Stoic mask: "Speak no more of her!" If the "philosopher" in him dictates this assertion of emotional control, the husband's affection warns him not to give voice to a feeling which, once expressed, might shatter all containing limits. The hidden cause of emotional stress having been thus revealed, the bowl of wine is brought in, and in it Brutus pledges himself to "bury all unkindness," receiving in return the fullness of Cassius' answering pledge:

> My heart is thirsty for that noble pledge.
> Fill, Lucius, till the wine o'erswell the cup;
> I cannot drink too much of Brutus' love. (IV. iii)

The reconciliation takes place under the shadow of tragedy. It cannot be a restoration of the original relationship, now irretrievably flawed by past choices; but, in spite of this, the human content is there, beyond all the purposes of political realism, and it rounds off suitably the issues so dramatically represented in what is, in some respects, the most interesting scene of the play.

The last stages of the tragedy represent the winding-up of the action in accordance with its underlying constants. The defeated Romans fall on their swords in a show of Stoic resolution, because no other choice is left open to them, and the victors turn away from the field "to part the glory of this happy day." As we follow these episodes to their conclusion, we cannot help feeling that something of the shadow of the Greek heroes in *Troilus and Cressida,* written possibly at a time not very far distant, already lies over them. Cassius commits suicide in an error caused by his own shortsightedness (as Titinius says: "Alas, thou hast misconstrued everything!"), and the cold, practical Octavius is shown on the other side as reacting against the tutelage of Antony, who has made his victory possible and whom he will soon be ready to discard. With all his flaws, which have been so uncompromisingly revealed in the course of the play, Brutus is the only character who emerges with some measure of genuine personal stature. His last farewell rises, in contrast with so much that surrounds it, to the dignity of tragic assertion. "Countrymen," he says, addressing through his remaining followers Rome and posterity:

> My heart doth joy that yet in all my life
> I found no man but he was true to me.
> I shall have glory by this losing day,
> More than Octavius and Mark Antony
> By this vile conquest shall attain unto. (V. v)

Once more it is important to avoid any simple reaction to the mood so expressed. The speech is truly noble but is also an effort made by the speaker, in the absence of more solid ground for satisfaction, to encourage himself on the threshold of the annihilation that he has, after all, brought upon himself and perhaps even obscurely come to desire.

The mood is, in any case, neither false nor triumphant, implies rather an acceptance of the end Brutus has come to see as inevitable, involved in the entire logic of his own past, and which he now approaches with a certain nostalgic craving for the dark:

Night hangs upon my eyes; my bones would rest,
That have but labour'd to attain this hour. (V. v)

In this mood of self-awareness, and snatching some crumb of comfort from the fact that Strato, the instrument of his release, is "a fellow of a good report," he dies in a mood akin to expiation:

Caesar, now be still;
I kill'd not thee with half so good a will. (V. v)

In this admission, the whole contradictory nature of the enterprise to which Brutus so perversely forced himself in the name of humanity is gathered up in the prelude to a last act of self-annihilating resolve.

When Octavius enters to wind up the action with Antony, Strato is able to turn on Messala, now a bondman to the conqueror, with an assertion of the freedom that Brutus has found in death:

Brutus only overcame himself,
And no man else hath honour by his death. (V. v)

For all his devotion, however, he is ready to follow Messala by joining the conqueror; the world of rhetorical aspiration and that of practical reality rarely run parallel. The contrast between personal integrity and the way of a world from which, we have good reason to believe, it will be increasingly exiled, is implicit in Antony's epitaph, in which he justifiably glorifies Brutus' personal qualities—

This was the noblest Roman of them all— (V. v)

without concealing the "envy" which surrounded this nobility and used its inherent flaws for ends of its own. Octavius, having made the victor's appropriate gesture of generosity, now that generosity can no longer endanger his triumph, turns away with his companion to enjoy the "glory" they have won. The results to which this sharing of the fruits of victory will lead are to be the theme for another play.

ANTONY AND CLEOPATRA

The critic of *Antony and Cleopatra* has, in offering an account of this great tragedy—for the fact of its greatness is plainly evident in purely poetic terms—to resolve a problem of approach, of the interpretation of the author's true intention. This problem has in the past produced a variety of strangely contrary solutions. Sooner or later, the critic finds himself faced by two interpretations of Shakespeare's intention in this play, each of them strongly defended and each of them arguing from elements demonstrably present in the text, whose only disadvantage is that they appear to be mutually exclusive. Is *Antony and Cleopatra,* to put the matter in other terms, a tragedy of lyrical inspiration, justifying love by presenting it as triumphant over death, or is it rather a remorseless exposure of human frailties, a presentation of spiritual possibilities dissipated through a senseless surrender to passion? Both interpretations, as we have said, can be defended; but to give each its due, to see them less as contradictory than as complementary aspects of a unified artistic creation, is as difficult as it proves, in the long run, to be necessary for a proper understanding of the play.[9]

The fact that these two readings can, in spite of their appearance of contradiction, *both* be derived from a dispassionate examination of the tragedy can be explained in the light of the past development of Shakespeare's art, as we have sought to follow it in the preceding pages, for both correspond to aspects of that development which we have already had occasion to consider. From one point of view, indeed, this tragedy is the supreme expression in Shakespeare of love as *value,* as triumphant over time through and in despite of death; from another, it exposes, again through a consideration of human relationships in love, the weakness which makes possible the downfall of the tragic hero, a weakness, moreover, which is given a *social* reference by being consistently related to the presentation of a society in the advanced stages of decay. Now all these factors, positive and negative alike, have been given expression in Shakespeare's earlier plays, and the novelty of *Antony and Cleopatra*—which is at once the last and greatest of his chronicle plays[10] and (with the exception of *Coriolanus*) his final exercise in tragedy—lies not in the fact of their presence but in the manner and complexity of their interrelation. The desire to see love as a manifestation of spiritual values derives, as we have seen,[11] from as far back at least as the sonnets, and in so far as *Antony and Cleopatra* succeeds in presenting it as such, the tragedy can be described as a positive counterpoise, given full depth and maturity, to *Troilus and Cressida.* The exposure of tragic weakness in the hero, first dramatically presented in *Othello,*[12] gathers strength through the great plays which follow and is finally related to an explicit political study, similar in kind though vastly developed in conception to that originally expressed in the later works on English history, in the Roman theme of *Coriolanus.* It is the supreme achievement, rather than the problem, of *Antony and Cleopatra* to show that these two lines of development, far from excluding one another, are in fact mutually illuminating.

The presence of these various elements, positive and negative so to call them, is admirably indicated in the short opening scene of the play, which serves, in a manner highly characteristic of the mature Shakespeare, as a kind of overture to the main action, a first brief exposition of the themes which will be developed in the course of the tragedy by relationship and contrast. The opening speech of Philo leaves us in no doubt as to the adverse estimate which we are bound, on a dispassionate, realistic view, to form of Antony's relationship to Cleopatra. His love is described as a manifestation of "dotage," which has, moreover, reached the point at which it can no longer be tolerated, at which it "overflows the measure"; his former martial virtues, through which he maintained his position of responsibility as a "triple pillar of the world"—the phrase is one which will be repeatedly echoed in the course of the political action —have been shamefully abandoned, have become, in the scathing comment of the common soldier,

> the bellows and the fan
> To cool a gipsy's lust. (I. i)

Nothing in the action to come, no poetic exaltation of the passion that animates the main protagonists, can make this first estimate irrelevant; it is part of the truth, and no later development can properly contradict it.

The entry of Antony and Cleopatra, immediately after this indignant comment, at once confirms it and introduces further themes for consideration. The first exchanges of the lovers are couched in an antiphonal form that will become familiar in the passionate personal passages of this play: emotion responds to emotion in a mutual heightening, a progressive accumulation of intensities. The effect at this point is a cunning combination of lyricism with artifice, passionate dedication with the conscious stimulation of feeling. To Cleopatra's request that Antony should tell her "how much" is his love for her, he replies, "There's beggary in the love that can be reckon'd"; and to her further statement, made as it were to dare him, to provoke further and more far-reaching expressions of devotion, that she will "set a bourn how far to be beloved," he responds with a lyrical declaration that suggests infinity, transcendence in emotion: "Then must thou needs find out new heaven, new earth." Once more this sense of superhuman value apprehended through love is one that the play will be concerned to repeat and develop. Its final relationship will be to the experience of death imposed, as a consequence of their public failure, upon both characters at the end of the tragedy; but meanwhile its emotional force must not blind us to its irrelevance in terms of common realism. The fact that the lovers who can thus address one another are in fact persons subdued to the course of events in the world is stressed by the entry of a messenger from Rome and by the manner, remarkably discordant with the spirit of what we have just heard, of his reception. Antony's gesture in thrusting aside the newcomer in order to turn again to the mistress who has enslaved him is rather petulant, self-indulgent, than noble or generous; and Cleopatra, with the intention of playing upon his dependency, is not slow to chide him with the imagined anger of his wife or with that inferiority to the "scarce-bearded Caesar" which already rankles in his uneasy conscience. The scene, in fact, by relating the political action to emotion poetically expressed, calls in the characteristic Shakespearean way for a balance in judgment which will have to be maintained throughout the play. On the one hand, Antony's readiness to turn away from outside events is given a certain weight by his first opulent gesture of triumphant love; on the other, that gesture is itself finally subjected to criticism, seen in its double nature as splendid and yet mean, a product of personal degradation. To bear *both* judgments in mind, refusing to neglect one in order to exalt the other, is to respond truly to the intention of the play.

This intention emerges further from Antony's full declaration of the emotion which moves him:

> Let Rome in Tiber melt, and the wide arch
> Of the ranged empire fall! Here is my space.
> Kingdoms are clay: our dungy earth alike
> Feeds beast as man: the nobleness of life
> Is to do thus; when such a mutual pair
> And such a twain can do't, in which I bind,
> On pain of punishment, the world to weet
> We stand up peerless. (I. i)

The expression, considered with care, introduces a number of elements which the later action will develop. The vast spaciousness of the political background, the sense that a world order, a universal structure of society, rests as upon its keystone on the individuals whose tragedy is to be presented is conveyed by reference to the "wide arch" of the "ranged empire"; and the very fact that Antony is ready to turn aside from issues so endowed with universality gives weight and a presumption of value to his emotion. By contrast with his assertion of devotion, the material nature of the outside world is stressed. Kingdoms become "clay" and, in a phrase as daring as it is relevant, the earth itself is "dungy," at once contemptible and yet, when brought to life by the transforming presence of passion, potentially fertile. Against this background, both vast and petty, equally related to "beast" and "man," the presence of intense personal emotion serves to emphasize "the *nobleness* of life," a nobility which has often concerned Shakespeare in his earlier tragedies[13] and which is here presented, for exaltation and criticism, in the story of his pair of lovers.

To what extent these will be able to maintain their worth, to justify the arrogant exaltation of themselves as "a mutual pair," fit each for the other and ready to assert their "peerless" quality before the world, time will show. Already there is a clear element of shame and indulgence, which the splendor of his rhetoric cannot conceal, in Antony's readiness to contemplate—publicly and with satisfaction—the crumbling into ruin of the arch of empire; and his display of emotion is not left at its own estimate. Having been largely produced in reaction to Cleopatra's calculated ironies, it is followed immediately by the realism of her comment:

> Excellent falsehood!
> Why did he marry Fulvia, and not love her!
> I'll seem the fool I am not; Antony
> Will be himself. (I. i)

Antony's own following words confirm this estimate. From the high-flown expression of "nobility," of transcendent emotion, we pass at a stroke to the cloying sensuality which is equally a part of his character. He exhorts her "for the love of love and her *soft* hours" to set aside the reality of the outer world, which he dismisses in terms of "conference *harsh*":

> There's not a minute of our lives should stretch
> Without some *pleasure* now. What *sport* to-night? (I. i)

The desire to fill every moment of life with its utmost content of sensation belongs, perhaps, to a certain vital element in Antony's apprehension of passion; but this vitality is qualified by the nature of the content which he foresees. *Sport* and *pleasure:* these turn out, when we pass from the universally lyrical to concrete reality, to be the true ends of Antony's devotion. The *sport* is, characteristically, obtained by neglecting the discharge of the speaker's political duties in the hearing of the Roman ambassadors; the seizing of the *pleasure* of the moment and the desire to endow it with a spurious eternity by thrusting aside all other responsibilities represent in fact the real content of Antony's generalized expressions of emotional nobility. The working out of the contrast so presented until, through a fusion of poetic and dramatic resources as comprehensive and complete as anywhere in Shakespeare, its diverse elements are shown to belong to a single range of emotion, is the true theme of *Antony and Cleopatra.*

Only a detailed analysis of the play can show Shakespeare achieving this aim by what is, in effect, a series of perfectly definable steps. The first of these concerns his use of the political action of the play, which is admirably adapted to a purpose that is no longer, as it had been in *Julius Caesar* and even, though to a lesser extent, in *Coriolanus,*[14] primarily political. The story of Antony and Cleopatra, as we have already seen in considering Antony's first speech, is set against an imperial background of far-reaching universality;

and this vastness of range is itself an important factor in the play. The story of the lovers is influenced by events significant for the entire civilized world, and the poetry of the play deliberately and repeatedly stresses a sense of vast issues and tremendous dominions. Antony himself, as we have seen, is not only an infatuated lover but a "triple pillar of the world." Even the attendant who bears off the drunken Lepidus after the feast at which the triumvirs meet (II. vii) carries upon his shoulders "the third part of the world"; and Octavia tells Antony that a quarrel between himself and Caesar would be

> As if the world should cleave, and that slain men
> Should solder up the rift. (III. iv)

This emphasis on the world background of the tragedy can be related to Antony's own behavior in either of two ways, each of which was anticipated in the opening scene and will assume its relevant place in the total effect. On the one hand, as Philo from the first asserted, the thrusting aside of responsibilities so great is at once an act of folly and a grave repudiation of duty; on the other, if Antony, although at times aware of this aspect of his conduct, is nonetheless repeatedly moved to confirm it, then we may think that the measure of his passion must be correspondingly universal, endowed with value in its own sight. The first estimate will be consistently confirmed by the comments of those who surround Antony and by the development of his tragedy; the second will find expression mainly in the lyricism of his own utterances and in the corresponding intensity of Cleopatra, but will loom increasingly larger as the confirmation of his own failure in action is brought home by the course of events.

Our attitude toward this failure, indeed, is most subtly affected by the way in which Shakespeare has chosen to portray the political action of the play. For the world of the triumvirs, vast as it is and correspondingly opulent, is steeped in meanness and treachery. The presentation of it is full of touches which recall the realism of *Henry IV;* there is a good deal of the less admirable side of Prince Hal's character (though little, we must add, of Henry V's sense of the tragic burden of the royal vocation) in Caesar's controlled, ungenerous dedication to the pursuit of a power in itself necessarily and responsibly exercised; and Antony's own political folly, the reverse of Caesar's impressive command of the public situation, is not exempt from a note of hard calculation which his incapacity to calculate successfully does not make any more attractive. The expression of the play, indeed, lays continual stress upon the intrigue which, in Rome, takes the place of Egyptian corruption. Antony's account of the state of the Roman world near the beginning of the action is no more than typical:

Our Italy
Shines o'er with civil swords: Sextus Pompeius
Makes his approaches to the port of Rome:
Equality of two domestic powers
Breeds scrupulous faction: the hated, grown to strength,
Are newly grown to love: the condemn'd Pompey,
Rich in his father's honour, creeps apace
Into the hearts of such as have not thrived
Upon the present state, whose numbers threaten;
And quietness, grown sick of rest, would purge
By any desperate change. (I. iii)

It would be hard to find a better example of the way in which what can easily be read as no more than a straightforward piece of exposition is in fact charged with a linguistic vitality that relates it variously to the deeper issues of the play. Rome is in a dangerous state of "equality," poised between two powers which, uncertain of the future and unable to trust one another in the present, "breed" (the verb, with its sense of organic growth, has a quality of its own) a "scrupulous," calculating "faction." Pompey, in turn, the common enemy of Caesar and Antony, is "rich" only in his father's reputation; thus speciously endowed, he "creeps" by a process of stealthy treachery into the hearts of those who have not made their fortunes, "thrived" in the "present state" of deceptive peace. These as a result grow (through the "breeding" process already defined, we might say) into a threatening condition, and the result of the whole development is summed up in one of those images of dislocated organic function by which Shakespeare, from *Henry IV* at least onward, has habitually chosen to express the implications of civil strife. The discontented elements in Rome are "sick": "sick" in themselves, because domestic war is the symptom of political disorder, and "sick" too of the false state of "rest," or stagnation, by which other interests in turn prosper. The end of this sickness here, as ever, is a "purge," but one scarcely less uncertain, "desperate" in its possible consequences, than that the desire for which had inspired Northumberland and his fellow conspirators to action in the Second Part of *Henry IV*.[15]

There are two scenes in the first, the predominantly "political" part of the play, which particularly illuminate Shakespeare's presentation of the Roman world. The first is the episode (II. ii) in which Antony and Octavius, brought together for an attempted settlement of their differences, first eye one another in mutual distrust like two hard-faced gamesters, each jealous of what he is pleased to regard as his reputation and each equally distrustful of the trick which he feels his fellow "pillar of the world" may have up his sleeve, and are finally persuaded by the calculating go-between Agrippa to build a sham agreement on the sacrifice by Caesar of his own helpless sister Octavia. The successive stages of this shameful proceeding are indeed beautifully indicated. To Caesar's frigid greeting, "Welcome to Rome," Antony replies with an equally distant "Thank you," and to his further laconic invitation "Sit," with the corresponding show of wary courtesy: "Sit, sir." These preliminaries over, the true discussion is opened by Antony with a phrase that shows, in its deliberate churlishness, his determination to be the first to take offense:

> I learn, you take things ill which are not so,
> Or being, concern you not. (II. ii)

If, after a considerable amount of further recrimination, in which Caesar's thin-lipped, efficient disdain and Antony's libertine carelessness display themselves to the worst possible advantage, the trend of the discussion changes, it is because of one of those sudden, theatrical changes of mood for which Antony's behavior is notable throughout. Caesar's accusation of perjury prompts a facile gesture to "honour"—

> The honour is sacred which he talks on now—

and this in turn leads to a show of self-excuse which reflects yet another facet of Antony's shifting personality. His oath to come to Caesar's aid has been, in his view, "neglected" rather than denied; negligence, indeed, has always been an outstanding feature of his character, and the excuse is, not for the first time, that of the weak man who ascribes his own failing to the machinations of others:

> when *poison'd* hours had bound me up
> From mine own knowledge. (II. ii)

The "poison," indeed, has worked more deeply than Antony knows. His infatuation for Cleopatra, which he is now turning with singular meanness into an excuse for his own indignity, is at least as much the product as the cause of his self-betrayal.

Having thus shifted the fault, to his own satisfaction, upon Fulvia, upon Cleopatra, upon anyone but himself, Antony's "honour" is satisfied and he is ready to come to terms. Around him are the helpless tool Lepidus, always disposed to find "nobility" in the words of the shabby cutthroats who surround him, and Agrippa, ready as a courtier should always be to whisper his supremely cynical suggestions into his master's ear:

> Thou hast a sister by the mother's side,
> Admired Octavia: great Mark Antony
> Is now a widower. (II. ii)

Thus seconded, and with the ground so prepared, the most dishonorable project cannot but prevail. It is, indeed, insinuated before it is openly proposed, and the jibe implied by Agrippa when he describes Antony as a "widower" is sufficient to produce in him, after Caesar's ironic reference to Cleopatra, the parody of "honour" contained in his "I am not married, Caesar": a false dignity which fittingly crowns a false situation and leads to a transaction as cynical as it is clearly destined to be impermanent. The degradation implied in Antony's relationship to the political action which surrounds him will find no expression more complete than this most specious and sordid of reconciliations.

Even more subtle, more beautifully constructed, is the great drunken scene (II. vii) which celebrates this agreement, with its contrast between the witless conviviality of the triumvirs and the "quick-sands" of sober treachery represented by Menas and turned aside by Pompey less through honesty than through weakness. The opening remark of the servant—"Some o' their plants are ill-rooted already; the least wind i' the world will blow them down" (II. vii)—refers as much to the farce of reconciliation now being enacted as to the business the speaker has in hand, and the further comment on the position of Lepidus—

> To be called into a huge sphere, and not to be seen to move in't, are the holes where eyes should be, which pitifully disaster the cheeks— (II. vii)

adds its own contribution to the note of hollowness, at once grotesque and sinister, which the whole episode is intended to convey. The following conversation between Lepidus and Antony, taking us further at each moment from common reality, leads up to its culminating phrase in Antony's

> These quick-sands, Lepidus,
> Keep off them, for you sink, (II. vii)

and thence to the return of sober calculation in Menas' blunt offer to Pompey which so effectively follows it: "Wilt thou be lord of all the world?" The offer, of course, is rejected by Pompey, though with something less than conviction; but the moral tone of the episode has been established and the following descent into dissipation proceeds, as Lepidus, "the third part of the world," is carried away, in the spirit of Menas' revealing observation to Enobarbus:

> The third part then is drink: would it were all,
> That it might go on wheels. (II. vii)

The construction of the whole scene, which turns upon a superb counterpointing of the related motives of drunken folly and treachery, is far beyond the type of political realism formerly exhibited in *Henry IV*, but the inspiration is still demonstrably related to that of the earlier play.

Shakespeare's mature experience, therefore, moves him to present his characters in a world in which imperial pretensions, themselves laden with falsity, are associated through their poetical expression with the presence of overripeness and luxury in individual experience. "Rest," as we have seen in Antony's account of the social significance, so to call it, of Pompey's rebellion, is the state of stagnation produced by opulence which inevitably leads to the purge of civil war. When the messenger, in the following scene (I. iv), brings Caesar news that "flush youth revolt," he is relating imperial disorder further to bodily surfeit and its consequences; his words underline those of Octavius which immediately precede them:

> This *common* body,
> Like to a vagabond flag upon the stream,
> Goes to and back, lackeying the varying tide,
> To *rot* itself with motion. (I. iv)

Such a speech has its own function in the play, pointing to a tightening in poetic terms of the bond which unites the political, the "Roman" action, to the "Egyptian" fortunes of the tragic protagonists. The passion of Antony and Cleopatra, whatever may be said further of it, shares the weakness, the corruption of the world in which it grows to expression. One scarcely needs, in establishing this point, to feel the Elizabethan association of "common" with sexual promiscuity; the link which binds the use of "rot" to the images of decay associated more than once with Cleopatra[16] is enough to show how Shakespeare, through the continuous stressing of imagery invoking disorder and physical corruption, connects the universal situation of his play with the particular tragedy of mature love with which it is primarily concerned.

The decadence thus shown, and poetically integrated into the spirit of the play, in the public affairs of the Roman world is balanced, where more intimate relations are concerned, by a corresponding effect in the expression of the love of Antony and Cleopatra with its consistently Egyptian setting; indeed, the connection which underlies these contrasted realities, presented dramatically in terms of character and poetically by continuity in the use of imagery, is one of the principal keys to the total effect. Antony's advancing years are repeatedly stressed, and Caesar's exposures of his vices are too full of individuality in phrasing, too closely related to the characteristic overripeness of the play, for them to be taken at less than their full value:

he fishes, drinks and wastes
The lamps of night in revel. (I. iv)

Nor are we allowed to overlook the disintegration which falls upon Antony in adversity. The qualities of self-deception, and the weakness which has led him repeatedly to place responsibility for his own actions in the hands of others, bear fruit in the hour of defeat in reactions which are almost invariably illogical and at times tinged with hysterical cruelty. In such a mood he finds consolation for his state in ordering the messenger of Octavius to be whipped until "he whine aloud for mercy" (III. xiii). The futile viciousness revealed by this action is an essential part of Antony's nature. His relations with Cleopatra, whatever else they may be, are ruthlessly presented in terms of a weakness which the experience of disaster amply confirms. Every meeting between them, from the opening which we have already considered, is the exposure of an aging libertine and a decaying queen; though it is the peculiar triumph of this tragedy that the most important meetings, being that, are also a great deal more. Shakespeare did not write a great play by ignoring Antony's failings or the presence of a corresponding corruption in Cleopatra; rather, while giving full weight to the weaknesses, he assimilates them into a poetic mood in which other elements, positive and triumphant in their associations, contribute to the total effect. Antony's love asserts itself at the play's supreme poetic moments in spite of his continual awareness that Cleopatra is "a whore of Egypt" and the discarded mistress of Julius Caesar, in spite of the fact that his is the infatuation of an aging soldier for a woman who has already served the pleasure of many men. It is the play's achievement to leave room for *both* estimates of the personal tragedy, the realistic as well as the lyrical; and if each has to be continually balanced against its opposite, so that the total impression can never, even at the last, rest upon one to the exclusion of the other, full understanding of what is intended depends upon an appreciation of the poetic quality so marvelously, richly present throughout the play. The gap between what is clearly, from one point of view, a sordid infatuation, and the triumphant feeling which undoubtedly, though never exclusively, prevails in the final scenes is bridged by a wonderful modification of connected imagery. Rottenness becomes the ground for fertility, opulence becomes royalty, infatuation turns into transcendent passion, all by means of an *organic* process which ignores none of its own earlier stages, which, while never denying the validity of the realistic estimates of the situation which accompany it to the last, integrates these in the more ample unity of its creative purpose.

This poetic effect, in turn, can be seen as firmly anchored, still in the case of Antony, on the reading of character. In the moment of his supreme degradation, just after he has vented his vain resentment on Caesar's emissary and accused Cleopatra of betraying him, he is capable of a clear-eyed statement of the hardening of the moral vision which accompanies the persistent surrender to the compulsions of appetite:

> when we in our viciousness grow hard—
> O misery on't!—the wise gods seal our eyes;
> In our own filth drop our clear judgements: make us
> Adore our errors; laugh at's while we strut
> To our confusion. (III. xiii)

Antony, seeking to console himself, to place elsewhere the responsibility for his disaster, is driven in his own despite to a very clear comment on his condition. He is, indeed, one who has grown "hard" in his "viciousness," lost sensibility by his submission to "appetite"; and the result has been to close his eyes, as though by a dispensation of fate, cruel but just, appropriate to the nature of his choices, to moral realities. The "judgement" which should have been his distinctive quality as a man, a purposeful reasoning being, has been dropped into "filth" of his own creation; the consequence of his "errors" has been to reduce him to an absurd figure "strutting"[17] in a caricature of self-approbation to his final confusion. The stroke which brings this moment of intimate revelation out of hysteria and attempted self-deception is one of the most revealing in the play.

In Antony, however, realism of this kind is still compatible with a sense of personal tragedy. At a later stage in his downfall, as his last moments of illusory triumph in battle fade away, he is capable of uttering, beyond the sentimental heroic gestures which are also part of his nature, a remorseless exposure of tragic weakness, of a personality dissolving in the contemplation of its own contradictions:

> All come to this? The hearts
> That spaniell'd me at heels, to whom I gave
> Their wishes, do discandy, melt their sweets
> On blossoming Caesar; and this pine is bark'd
> That overtopped them all. Betrayed I am.
> O, this false soul of Egypt! this grave charm,
> Whose eye beck'd forth my wars and call'd them home,
> Whose bosom was my crownet, my chief end,
> Like a right gipsy hath at false and loose
> Beguiled me to the very heart of loss. (IV. xii)

The sense of dissolution makes itself felt first through the contemplation of those who have abandoned Antony's failing fortunes; those who formerly followed him with dog-like servility in return for his generosity now "discandy," "*melt* their sweets," with cloying insistence, on the growing fortunes of "blossoming Caesar." By contrast the "pine" that was Antony, who formerly "overtopped them all" (and here we look forward to Cleopatra's image of "the soldier's pole"[18]), is "bark'd," stripped of its trappings of nobility and honor. This leads Antony to express his sense that he has been betrayed, that the "grave charm," the superstitious amulet that Cleopatra has been to him, has become his "false soul": "soul" in recalling her former inspiration, and "false" on account of the ruin to which his infatuation has led him. Even at this moment, Antony confesses to her magnetism and his own subjugation. It has been his tragedy to place his manhood in the hands of one who at once inspired his wars and irrationally, illogically "call'd them home." Upon her, abandoning all sense of his male responsibilities, he rested, her bosom his "crownet," her love his impossibly exclusive end; and the result has been a betrayal, the "beguiling" of his manhood into what he now sees—in a phrase that wonderfully combines haunting emotion with the sense of intimate failure—to be "the heart of loss."

It is because his moral being is flawed by this double vision that Antony falls; but it is also on account of it that he rises, at his best moments, to genuine tragic stature. The starting point of this poetic "redemption" (if we may so call it without unduly simplifying the complete effect) is the very rottenness we have observed in the world around him. The overripeness of that world is variously related to the personal tragic theme; if it is a fitting background to the story of mature passion, which indeed springs from and reflects it, it also lends point to Antony's assertion of the supremacy of his personal feeling. Antony undoubtedly gambled away his dignity as "a triple pillar of the world," but the corruption and treachery of that world in part redeems his folly and justifies the contempt which at certain moments he expresses for it. To assert, however, that Shakespeare was content to make this contrast after the manner of the seeker after moral axioms (*All for Love, or The World Well Lost:* axioms based indeed on a strangely indulgent morality) is vastly to underestimate his achievement. The play, as we have said, relates the rottenness of their world *poetically* to the individual fortunes of the protagonists; the love imagery springs from the overripeness, sharing its decay and yet exacting from it something not entirely limited to it. The presence of this further element, incommensurate with the realistic presentation of the tragedy but not contradictory to it, is most clearly grasped not in Antony (who may be said to receive it through participation), but in the more vital and complex poetry given, at her moments of supreme emotion, to Cleopatra.

Cleopatra's relationship to Antony is one in which complexity and falsehood, stressed from the first, are interwoven with other elements. As Antony, when he announces initially his decision to leave her to return to Rome and his public duties, interposes his efforts to justify himself—"Cleopatra," "Most sweet queen"—her emotion responds to his own and soars finally into what is, while it lasts, an intuition of permanent value:

> Nay, pray you, seek no colour for your going,
> But bid farewell, and go: when you sued staying,
> Then was the time for words; no going then;
> Eternity was in our lips and eyes,
> Bliss in our brows bent, none our parts so poor
> But was a race of heaven. (I. iii)

The supreme statement of mutual dedication is made to rest, for its force and poignancy, upon a foundation of accepted parting. Like Antony, Cleopatra needs to have her emotions stimulated, brought to a pitch by what is in the last analysis a contemplation of their lack of solid foundation. "Bid farewell, and go," she says, and we know that she means the opposite; and yet the power of what follows forbids us to see in her gesture merely a stratagem, obliges us to regard it as a trick indeed, but as a trick based finally on a measure of truth. In the world of time parting is the order of the day; but there has been for these lovers a time when "eternity" at least *seemed* at their command, "was in our lips and eyes," and when the "bliss" reflected in their mutual gaze had a transforming quality, appeared to raise ordinary human attraction to an intuition of superhuman perfection:

> none our parts so poor
> But was a race of heaven.

Belief in Antony's integrity, so dubious to the dispassionate eye of common sense, is made to rest on the validity of an experience which can only be held in a moment of emotional intensity and in reaction against what Cleopatra knows, even as she speaks, to be reality. While it lasts, and so far alone, the "parts" of the lovers, the attributes of their physical presence, are transformed, rendered heavenly to the eyes of the imagination; and to maintain that vision is the aim, impossible but now necessary (because for it all else has been sacrificed), of life. Antony has chosen this life with Cleopatra, and by the constancy of his devotion to it he can fairly, if not exclusively, be judged. This constancy may be, is indeed, incommensurate with his other, public responsibilities; but the choice has been made and cannot now, without an acute sense of loss, be renounced.

This does not mean, of course, that Cleopatra is exempted from the realistic judgment which falls, at one time or another, on all the characters in this play. We have seen already that Shakespeare insists on her ripe maturity, on her dubious past, on the corruption undoubtedly represented by her person. This, however, is not all. Cleopatra, like Antony, is to be judged not only through her own words but through the reaction of those who surround her. Even Enobarbus' famous account of her meeting with Mark Antony at Cydnus (II. ii) is at least as much an exposure as a glorification. The beauty unquestionably conveyed by his description is, like so much else in this play, deliberately overripe, artificially opulent in its effect. The poop of Cleopatra's barge was "beaten gold," the oars "silver," and she herself lay in a pavilion "cloth-of-gold of tissue"; surrounded by "pretty dimpled boys, like smiling Cupids," her own person was an elaboration, wrought less by nature than by conscious artifice, on what is already conceived as a work of art:

> O'er-picturing that Venus where we see
> The fancy outwork nature. (II. ii)[19]

On this vessel, indeed, nature has no place, and genuine feeling correspondingly little; its sails are "purple" (the color itself is, in a boat, unnatural) and so "perfumed" that the very winds, sharing in the prevailing tone, are "love-sick" with them. The smiling boy-Cupids and the "gentlewomen, like the Nereides," belong, as do their rhythmic motions, to a world of elaborate decoration from which Cleopatra herself was not freed until she became involved in the popular acclaim—

> The city cast
> Her people out upon her—

and until we hear of her a little later, again through Enobarbus, as able to

> Hop forty paces through the public street;
> And having lost her breath, she spoke and panted,
> That she did make defect perfection,
> And, breathless, power breathe forth. (II. ii)

The presence of these two contrasted elements in the description corresponds to the essential diversity of the character. Cleopatra, though the creature of the world which surrounds her, can at times emerge from it, impose upon her surroundings a vitality which is not the less astonishing for retaining to the last its connection with the environment it transcends. This combination of "nature" with artifice, vitality with corruption, in a single, infinitely complex creation, is at once the essence of her personality and the key to the conflicting estimates which her relations to Antony inspire in the course of the tragedy.

The manner in which much of Cleopatra's poetry derives from the idea of Eygpt, of the overflowing fertility of the Nile, is especially significant in this respect, for in Egypt, and more particularly in its sacred river, the ideas of corruption and natural growth are most closely interwoven. Her love is, in the words of Antony's promise, "the *fire* that *quickens* Nilus' slime" (I. iii), a living fertility, expressed in terms of fire, that grows by a continuous process of nature out of the corruption of "slime." The play is full of this balance between decay and fruitfulness; in her declining fortunes Cleopatra describes herself as "the blown rose" (III. xiii), combining beauty and decline in a complex unity of sensation. So assured is Shakespeare's mastery that he can impart dignity even to Cleopatra's relations with Julius Caesar. In those days, she says, she was "a morsel for a monarch" (I. v), and the "monarch" redeems, at least in part and while the emotional spell of her utterance is maintained, the indignity of having been a "cold" scrap upon "dead Caesar's trencher" (III. xiii). But perhaps the most complex example of Cleopatra's conversion of slime into fertility is her speech to Antony immediately after the whipping and dismissal of Thyreus:

> as it determines, so
> Dissolve my life! The next Caesarion smite!
> Till by degrees the memory of my womb,
> Together with my brave Egyptians all,
> By the discandying of this pelleted storm
> Lie graveless, till the flies and gnats of Nile
> Have buried them for prey. (III. xiii)

The proper reading of this speech brings us very close to the spirit in which this tragedy is conceived. The astonishing poetic power involved is not open to question, nor is the fact that it contributes, within certain limits, to an assertion of constancy in the face of death: but the emphasis is at least equally on decay, and the emotional compensation offered to Antony is significantly couched in terms of dissolution. Dissolution, indeed, the "melting" of a personality into its component elements of corruption, has been the essence of the entire episode, and here Cleopatra is engaged in turning it into her own kind, at once intense and equivocal, of poetry. "Discandying" imparts a sense of melting sweetness to corruption, and "dissolve," whilst presenting the end of the corrupt process itself, gives it an ease and inevitability which looks forward to the final aspic scene; and "the memory of my womb" again suggests the full fertility associated with the speaker's desires, the reflection of a certain richness of life (real or fictitious?) which seems to blend with its foreseen conclusion, the decay so vividly implied in "the flies and gnats of Nile." Within these variations, at once hauntingly lyrical and ruthless, the speech contains the whole range of an emotion particularly relevant to this stage, combining disenchantment with a first, flushed anticipation of the conclusion, of the play's development.

These complexities, indeed, have one principal aim—to evolve a certain tragic greatness for Cleopatra's passion out of its very stressed imperfections, out of the impermanence of the flesh and the corrupt world with which it is organically connected. As the story proceeds, Antony is subjected to a similar development, making him, without evading or in any way minimizing his weaknesses, fit for an end in which *value* and therefore true tragedy have a part to play. From the first, certain moments of generosity and bravery, fragments which might, under different circumstances and without the accompanying weakness, have made him a complete man, are brought out in him by contrast with Caesar's calculating self-control and the treachery of the surrounding world. Even the folly and shame of his renunciation of practical affairs is to some degree compensated by the splendid assertion of his love; "kingdoms are clay" for him, as we have seen, and the only value of the clay is to be at certain moments a ground in which the fertility of love may take root. In accordance with this intention the decline of Antony's fortunes is balanced by a series of devices which, while they do not free him from responsibility for his fate, set him apart from the increasingly disreputable issues which so persistently shadow the public conduct of the Roman world; that issues so great, so imperial in their scope can come, even if only for certain moments, to be felt as trivial is in itself a measure of the quality of his passion. The evolution of his fortunes balances a similar development in Cleopatra until, after their defeat, they are ready for the great meeting on the monument (IV. xv), in which irony and criticism are against all probability dissolved (the word is appropriate) into transcendent poetry.

It will be seen that the total effect of the tragedy is one of no small complexity. How far this is so is amply confirmed in the final scenes. Antony's death is a natural consequence of political folly and personal infatuation. We are not allowed to forget that its immediate cause is a miscarriage of Cleopatra's ingenuity, which leads her to announce falsely her own death and so drives him to despair; to the last Antony is involved in subterfuges and deceptions which spring logically from the nature of his passion. But just as "slime" was converted into the memory of fertility, just as the folly of renouncing the "ranged empire" was to some degree balanced by the rottenness of that empire, so does death, which is the consequence of Antony's prodigality, bring with it a certain liberation from triviality and an opening of the way to the poetic assertion of a truly tragic emotion. We can feel this liberation in the very movement of the blank verse, in which "labour" and its opposite are marvelously fused in what is simultaneously weakness, a renunciation of all effort in the light of admitted failure, and an intuition of peace:

> now all labour
> Mars what it does; yea, very force entangles
> Itself with strength. (IV. xiv)

A little further on, death is explicitly associated with love:

> I will be
> A *bridegroom* in my death, and run into't
> *As to a lover's bed.* (IV. xiv)

In the face of death the contrary judgments which this tragedy invites are maintained and marvelously fused. Not for the first time in Shakespeare the tragic hero, as he approaches the moment of resolution, incorporates expressions that proceed from the weakness, the self-indulgence that is destroying him, into an effect that transcends them. Antony's suicide, indeed, becomes thus an integral part of the final lyrical assertion of emotional *value* and therefore, up to a point, of life. It looks forward to its counterpart in the poetry of Cleopatra's death, in which "baser life" is finally transmuted into imagery of fire, air, and immortality.

The spirit of the great scene on Cleopatra's monument (IV. xv) is thus prepared for by what has gone before. Its poetry is marked by the extraordinary range of imagery which characterizes the play, and which implies an equally extraordinary power of fusing it into a single and continuous effect. Shakespeare himself could not have written this at any previous point in his career:

> O, see, my women,
> The crown o' the earth doth melt. My lord!
> O, withered is the garland of the war,
> The soldier's pole is fall'n; young boys and girls
> Are level now with men; the odds is gone,
> And there is nothing left remarkable
> Beneath the visiting moon. (IV. xv)

One has only to attempt to separate a few of the images in this "knot intrinsicate" (V. ii) of poetry to realize the extent of the poet's control. "The crown o' the earth" carries on naturally enough the tone of transcendent royalty with which Cleopatra has emphasized Antony's greatness and the depth of her love and grief. The verb "melt," so repeatedly used in this play and with such a varied range of associations, from deliquescence to spiritualization, is not *factually* related to "crown"; it has been chosen because it removes the sense of harshness from Antony's death by suggesting a natural, gentle dissolution into purest air (there is to be a similar feeling about Cleopatra's own death—"As sweet as balm, as soft as air, as gentle") and so prepares for the sense of triumph associated with her grief. "The soldier's pole" is probably the standard of war; but "pole," taken together with "crown" and the following "boys and girls," bears a complex suggestion of May Day, when love and the renewed life of spring meet in triumph. If we set these joyful associations against the corresponding depths of desolation, we shall feel something of the tremendous emotional range covered by the episode. The final reference to the "visiting moon" lends further point to this relation of joy to death and sorrow. The fact that after Antony's death there is left nothing "remarkable" beneath the moon not only suggests the extent of Cleopatra's loss but also implies that their union, while it lasted, reduced all earthly things to a dull uniformity. The whole passage is built upon a breadth of imagery which does not yield in complexity to the greatest ambiguities of the sonnets which treat equally of love; but, unlike them, its variety is subdued to a harmony which regards both desolation and triumph as integral parts of a complete mood. The poetry which sublimates emotion in *Antony and Cleopatra*—and it is not suggested that the mood thus expressed is permanent or covers the whole meaning of the tragedy—no longer turns, like that of even the later tragedies, upon a cleavage between "good" and "evil" within the unity of experience. It depends rather, while it lasts, upon a perfect continuity between the "flesh," with its associations of earth and death, and the justification of passion in terms of emotional value and intensity. This continuity is in no way vague or sentimental, but is splendidly realized in a harmonious scale of related imagery; this scale is most completely expressed in Cleopatra's final speeches.

Cleopatra's death is preceded by a successive loosening of the bonds which have so far tied her to the political action. The loosening is, characteristically, gradually achieved. Her last negotiations with Caesar are marked, deliberately, by calculation and even fear; she seeks to obtain from him what she can, and is even detected in a stratagem to set aside material provision for her future purposes. The true direction of the scene, however, is set from the first deathward; and death itself is indicated, in its very first speech, in a manner as complex as it is intensely poetical:

> it is great
> To do that thing that ends all other deeds;
> Which shackles accidents and bolts up change;
> Which sleeps and never palates more the dug,
> The beggar's nurse and Caesar's. (V. ii)

Once more we are in the presence of the astounding breadth of reference which is typical of the imagery of this play; and once more each element in it contributes, beyond itself, to the total effect of the tragedy. That the intention of suicide is, at this moment and in the mind of this speaker (the reservation is important, for other judgments are possible and relevant), nobly conceived is beyond doubt; it is "great" precisely in that it ends Cleopatra's slavery to the world of contingencies, that—in the splendid emphasis of her own phrase—"It *shackles* accidents and *bolts up* change." The prisoner of her fate, in other words, now aims to take her own fate captive. She does so, moreover, by an act which she conceives to be gentle as "sleep," a sleep differentiated only by its eternity from that shown, in all times and conditions, by the baby at rest on its mother's breast. Only—it is essential to remember, lest the beauty of the image induces in us a mood of surrender, of unqualified acceptance which is foreign to the total intention—the baby will, in due course, turn out to be the aspic, whose "biting," in the words of the Clown, who combines realism with fascination, is "immortal" (V. ii), and the sleep, though associated with images of peace and fulfillment, will be that of death.

The next stage in Cleopatra's progress lies in her exaltation, through memory, of the Antony whom she has lost in life. Once more the breadth of reference is only paralleled by the poetic power which can fuse impressions so diverse into a single, unstrained effect:

For his bounty,
There was no winter in't; an autumn 'twas
That grew the more by reaping: his delights
Were dolphin-like; they show'd his back above
The element they lived in: in his livery
Walk'd crowns and crownets; realms and islands were
As plates dropp'd from his pocket. (V. ii)

That such an apostrophe can be accepted as natural, unstrained, and that images so diversely and intensely conceived can be gathered together to produce one impression, is a sign that we are dealing with emotion of no common depth: that Dolabella explicitly denies that it corresponds to reality[20] warns us, at the same time, against making exclusive claims upon its relevance to the whole conception. Cleopatra is living in a world which is the projection of her own feelings. That world, while it lasts, is splendidly valid, vital in its projection; but only death, which is the end of vitality, can prevent an awakening from it. For that reason, if for no other, Cleopatra is resolved to die.

Her last great speech opens significantly with an assertion of "immortal longings." The reference to immortality is in full contrast to the impression of "dungy earth," from which her love sprang and in virtue of which Antony's fall and her death were both inevitable. Yet the "immortality" so evoked has a content of "nobility" which memory supplies; it is simply the highest assertion of her love for the dead and infinitely exalted Antony, whom she can now call for the first time in the play, precisely because he is dead, "Husband!" In the light of this association of love and immortality, death assumes a fresh poetic function. It becomes a dissolution, a purging of all the earthly elements upon which love had been based:

> I am fire and air; my other elements
> I give to baser life. (V. ii)

On the edge of death the sense of dissolution acquires a further significance; only the purest elements of feeling remain in Cleopatra—and those, by a paradox particularly meaningful at this moment, which are most fully, most intensely alive. From a great distance, as it seems, we are reminded of the other elements of "baser life," the earth and fertile slime from which love sprang, with which its degradation was associated, and in virtue of which defeat and death were inevitable; but defeat and death themselves have now become subdued, at least in the speaker's exaltation, to the "immortal longings" which they themselves brought into being, and the adverse fortunes of the world are dismissed as

> The luck of Caesar, which the gods give men
> To excuse their after wrath. (V. ii)

In spite of this note of transcendence, however, the firm foundation on the senses of the imagery by which the speech achieves its purpose is essential to the full effect. It conveys no abstract triumph imposed upon what has gone before. The elements of "fire and air" represent a continual refining process from the comparative earthliness of the opening, and the effect of Cleopatra's longing is reinforced by the keenly sensed reference to "the juice of Egypt's grape," suggesting all that is most alive and delicate in the activity of the senses.

This impression of continuity balanced by infinite remoteness is a principal key to the development of *Antony and Cleopatra,* in which self-indulgence and valid emotion are bound together in the death which is their common end. Shakespeare has so refined, so intensified his love poetry by a progressive distillation of sensible experience that it is able to assimilate the apparently incompatible fact of death, which is simultaneously release and the reflection, on the plane of common realism, of moral failure:

> The stroke of death is as a lover's pinch
> Which hurts and is desired. (V. ii)

"Hurts" and "desired," which seem so contradictory, reinforce one another in a splendid balance of sensations; the pain implied in "hurts" is so delicately, so intensely felt that it becomes fused with the keenness of the lover's desire. An emotion originally sensuous, unashamedly physical in kind, has become, besides that, something more, a taking up of the sensible into a world that shadows permanence: a gesture which originated in rhetoric and deception, and which retains its connection with these base realities, has become assumed into tragic validity. The death which is the supreme proof of failure, to which everything in this equivocal relationship has tended, becomes an untying of "this knot intrinsicate" of body and soul, of infinite desires hitherto subject to adverse and earthly circumstance.

It remains only for the entry of Caesar's envoy, bringing back the external, the real world, to break against the final confidence of Charmian's defiant farewell:

> It is well done, and fitting for a princess
> Descended of so many royal kings. (V. ii)

Caesar himself, when he arrives, can only utter one of those fitting epitaphs in which he specializes, and follow it by the profounder reflection:

> she looks like sleep,
> As she would catch another Antony
> In her strong toil of grace. (V. ii)

In this last phrase, something very like the spirit which animates the entire presentation of Cleopatra finds its summary. For Antony, her fascination has been a "toil," a snare which he had accepted for both of them once he had fallen victim to her enchantment, and which led to their common downfall; but it was also a toil of "grace," in which beauty and, at the supreme moment of dedication in death, a certain fitness have made themselves apparent.

The whole development of the play has been tending to this point. The balancing of the generosity which Antony's folly sometimes implies against Caesar's successful meanness, the gradual ascent of the love imagery from earth and "slime" to "fire and air," are all part of one great process which now needs death to complete it. For death, which had seemed in the sonnets and early tragedies to be incontrovertible evidence of the subjection of love and human values to time, now becomes by virtue of Shakespeare's poetic achievement an instrument of release, the necessary condition of an experience which, although dependent upon time and circumstance, is by virtue of its *value* and intensity incommensurate with them—that is, "immortal." This effect, moreover, is achieved at the same time that death is seen, from another point of view, as the natural end of a line of conduct in which folly and self-indulgence have consistently predominated. The emotions of Antony and Cleopatra, like their weaknesses, are built upon "dungy earth," upon "Nilus' slime," and so upon time which these elements by their nature imply; but, just as earth and slime are quickened into fire and air, while retaining their sensible qualities as constituent parts of the final experience, so time itself, in which this tragedy of waste and vanity was nurtured, becomes simultaneously a necessary element in the creation of "immortality."

CORIOLANUS

It would be hard to imagine a greater gulf than that separating the world of *Coriolanus* from the one of *Antony and Cleopatra.* The poetry of the latter play takes in with effortless ease the fortunes of a world in conflict; the former achieves its effects through intense concentration upon the familiar and the material.[21] Its prevailing imagery is rigid and unadorned, more appropriate to a village or a country town than to a capital of historical significance. The aristocratic ladies of Rome sit at home upon their "stools"[22] and the people carry "bats and clubs"[23] to their riots; the action abounds in references to simple pastimes, such as "bowls,"[24] or turns upon disputes over the immediate necessities of life, "corn," "coal," and "bread."[25] To a great extent the difference is imposed by history; whereas the world providing the background to Antony's fall concerned an empire that spanned the known world, the one conditioning the tragedy of Coriolanus is concentrated within the limits of a city and its immediate surroundings and reflects the tension between its classes, the threat to its indispensable unity.

This tension, this threat, marks the struggle for power in a world at once restricted and pitiless. The sense of this struggle is conveyed almost immediately by the patrician Menenius when, in rebuking the citizenry for their rebellion against constituted authority, he embarks upon a fable which reveals more than he can himself realize of the true situation in Rome. The central image of the fable, derived from Plutarch, but considerably developed, is that of the functioning of the human body in its related parts:

> There was a time when all the body's members
> Rebell'd against the belly: thus accused it:
> That only like a gulf it did remain
> I' the midst of the body, idle and unactive,
> Still cupboarding the viand, never bearing
> Like labour with the rest; where the other instruments
> Did see and hear, devise, instruct, walk, feel,
> And, mutually participate, did minister
> Unto the appetite and affection common
> Of the whole body. (I. i)

The wording of the parable tends to the transformation of a political commonplace, a theoretical vindication of natural "degree," into a criticism, not of this attitude or that, but of Roman society itself. The impression of a general obstruction of all vital activity communicates itself through the unhealthy stagnation of "idle and unactive," the coarseness of "cupboarding." These effects are set against the very noticeable livening of the verse when Menenius turns to the "other instruments," the senses and active faculties of the body which represent, however, not the class he is defending but its enemies. These contrasted elements, thus concentrated, in a manner profoundly typical of the play, upon images of food and digestion, answer to the real state of the Roman polity. Stagnation and mutual distrust, mirroring the ruthlessness of contrary appetites for power, are the principal images by which we are introduced to the public issues of *Coriolanus*.

It does not follow that our sympathies are to lie, as Menenius intends, solely with the patricians. He criticizes justly the failure of the populace to recognize the part played by their superiors in the social organism; but there is a sense in which the figure he uses to illustrate his point turns the argument against his own thesis. The patricians are presented in the likeness of the "belly"; and though this was indispensable to the proper functioning of the body it was also, in the view of its detractors, "idle and unactive," self-satisfied and complacent in the security of its central position. In this connection we should not overlook that brilliant stroke,

> with a kind of smile,
> Which ne'er come from the lungs, but even thus, (I. i)

where the fine balance between the ironic and the self-contented implies so much more than the patrician speaker realizes. By making the belly speak "tauntingly" against the "mutinous" members, Menenius asserts the invincible self-satisfaction which has already made itself felt in the assumption of infallibility—

> Confess yourselves wondrous malicious,
> Or be accused of folly— (I. i)

with which he embarks upon his reproof. Thinking of the motives of those who dare to challenge the authority of his own class in terms of sterile "malice," he fails to penetrate to the causes of a dislocation deeper than any partial vision can adequately compass.

So much is confirmed by the force of the Citizen's rejoinder. His vigorous defense of the superior organs—the "kingly-crowned head," "the vigilant eye," "the tongue our trumpeter" (I. i)—has little indeed to do with the reality he is defending; but it cuts across the complacency of the patrician rebuke with a force that the patronizing interruption—"Fore me, this fellow speaks!"—cannot diminish. The total effect of the fable is to convey, through and beyond Menenius' justification of privilege, the condition of the social organism from which the hero's tragedy will spring. We are shown, indeed, a populace incapable of discerning its true good, confirming by its shortsighted behavior its need for the guidance which only a class recognized to be superior can give it; but we are shown also a patrician caste unreasonably contemptuous of the rest of society, who have forfeited much of their claim to superiority by their attitude toward those upon whose existence and effort their own well-being, in the last analysis, depends. Both the factions thus confronted in sterile obstinacy are set in an iron framework which permits no real contact or community of purpose, nothing but ruthless repression countered by outbursts of animal discontent. So situated toward one another, they cannot fail to come to blows. "Rome and her rats are at the point of battle": Menenius describes the situation in one relevant way, but other possible interpretations suggest that there can be no final victory in this struggle, that the contending factions are involved in a common disaster which their mutual obstinacy has brought upon the city.

Menenius' first speech in verse, preluding his fable, reflects his assumption that the position by which his own class stands to benefit belongs to the natural and unalterable nature of things. His habitual kindliness, which allows him to show himself benignly human toward those whom he assumes to be his inferiors, should not blind us to the iron beneath his words. He takes it for granted that it is the duty of himself and his like to exercise "charitable care" over the people; but his concept of "charity," kindly and condescending so long as it is unquestioned, is compatible with the denial of responsibility when "charity" is not enough:

For your wants,
Your suffering in this dearth, you may as well
Strike at the heaven with your staves as lift them
Against the Roman state; whose course will on
The way it takes, cracking ten thousand curbs
Of more strong link asunder than can ever
Appear in your impediment. For the dearth,
The gods, not the patricians make it, and
Your knees to them, not arms, must help. (I. i)

The effect is more searching in its revelation of complacency than may at once appear. Rhythm and expression combine to embody the irresistible motion of an impersonal and overbearing force with which the speaker finally feels himself identified. The effect of the division in the earlier part of the speech between "cracking" and "asunder," both words which carry a strong sense of violent physical separation, is to convey an impression of ruthless dedication to an indifferent fatality. The emotional impetus so generated is then brought to a sudden curb after "impediment": the long period comes to an emphatic pause in the middle of its implacable development and Menenius, turned from the bland counselor into the mouthpiece of an unrelenting social destiny, throws upon the "gods" the responsibility for a catastrophe which no thought of human solidarity is allowed to mitigate.

NORTHWEST MISSOURI
STATE COLLEGE LIBRARY
MARYVILLE, MISSOURI

The speech, indeed, strikes for the first time a note which will be almost obsessively present in the following development. Its spirit emerges perhaps most clearly from the phrase "strike at the heaven with your staves," with which Menenius dismisses the protests of the citizens and the efficacy of their "*stiff* bats and clubs." These phrases, and others of a like nature scattered through the play, answer to the peculiar sensation of hardness with which its conflicting attitudes are presented. The rough implements of the people and the iron weapons of their masters threaten one another in a closed and indifferent universe; the "heavens" remain stonily impenetrable, so that the "stiff" weapons can almost be heard to clang when raised, not so much against injustice as against the imposition of an impersonal fatality. This sense of hard hostility answers to an order in which patricians and people are out of contact, hostile and exclusive in positions which seem to have been imposed upon them by the nature of things. If Menenius is right to stress this fatality—

> You are transported by calamity
> Thither where more attends you— (I. i)

the fact remains that the prospect of "calamity" rouses no real echo of sympathy in his mind. When he blandly asserts that his fellow patricians care for the people like "fathers," he lays himself open to a retort which the facts of the situation in no small measure confirm:

> They ne'er cared for us yet: suffer us to famish, and their storehouses crammed with grain; . . . repeal daily any wholesome edict established against the rich, and provide more piercing statutes daily, to chain up and restrain the poor. (I. i)

Envy and blind resentment no doubt play their part in the Citizen's accusation of patrician egoism; but the concluding answer to so much complacent paternalism is, as far as it goes, blunt and effective: "If the war eat us not up, they will, and there's all the love they bear us."

Into the caldron of dissension thus ominously overflowing the most disconcerting and incongruous of all Shakespeare's heroes plunges with a characteristic outburst of uncontrolled and misdirected energy:

> What's the matter, you dissentious rogues,
> That, rubbing the poor itch of your opinion,
> Make yourselves scabs? (I. i)

The long speech thus introduced is an unconscious self-revelation, alternating the slow and weighty amplitude proper to the speaker's martial dignity with descents into an explosive directness which tells its own tale of imperfect control. The most striking effect is one of intense contradiction—

> Your virtue is
> To make him worthy whose offence subdues him
> And curse that justice did it.
>
> . . . your affections are
> A sick man's appetite, who desires most that
> Which would increase his evil— (I. i)[26]

a chafing of contrary sensations, as spontaneous in impulse as they are labored, unnaturally hard in expression, which rises to the crowning denunciation:

> He that depends
> Upon your favours swims with fins of lead
> And hews down oaks with rushes. (I. i)

The plain but ponderous images fall like sword strokes, deadly, forceful, metallic, upon the abuses which they repudiate; but the periods in which they are embedded break habitually in the middle of their rhythmic structure, fail to cohere in a cumulative impression of life. The general sense is of a violent torrent of energy concentrated upon a narrow range of ideas and prejudices, deriving finally from an irreparable lack of spontaneity in the intimate relationships which have made the speaker what he is.

The full significance of this attitude will only emerge as the tragedy progresses. In the meantime Coriolanus, convinced by breeding and temperament that to defer to his natural inferiors is to "flatter beneath abhorring," asserts in its most extreme form the patrician claim to unlimited authority:

> You cry against the noble senate, who,
> Under the gods, keep you in awe, which else
> Would feed on one another. (I. i)

The claim is one which the facts in part justify, but which is in danger of being turned into a brutal imposition. So much is clear when Marcius winds up his tirade with a ruthless assertion of force which amounts to a caricature of true valor:

> Would the nobility lay aside their ruth,
> And let me use my sword, I'ld make a quarry
> With thousands of these quarter'd slaves, as high
> As I could pick my lance. (I. i)

Here, at least, the strength of emotion, hitherto half strangled by its own indignation, issues in an image close to the speaker's heart; but, though it is clear that the people against whom this anger is directed are weak, worthless, and brutal in many of their reactions, this truth cannot lend validity to what remains a barbarous perversion of traditional heroic values.

This initial confrontation does not lead immediately to disaster. Rome's need of its warrior hero is stressed by news of the Volscian rising, which he welcomes as offering the authorities an opportunity to "vent" the "musty superfluity" of the state into a foreign adventure. But before Marcius is set in motion on the first, ascendant stage of his career, we are offered a revealing glimpse of his family circle, and more particularly of the mother whose demands upon him will determine the course of his tragedy. The First Citizen has already linked these demands to his martial prowess when he has said, in explanation of his service to Rome, that "he did it to please his mother and to be partly proud" (I. i). This pride proceeds from a strange mixture of solicitude and ruthlessness, possession and renunciation in Volumnia's own nature. Remembering "the only son of her womb" as "a tender-bodied child," the repository of all her affection, whom "for a day of kings' entreaties" she would not "sell an hour from her beholding," she can yet recall how she found herself "considering how honour would become such a person" and how she directed his youth to a stern and fanatical conception of duty. Fearing that her son might "picture-like hang by the wall," she willed that he should "seek danger where he was likely to find fame"; and, as she dwells on this decision, her thoughts rise to a severe exaltation of the sacrifice which she imposed upon her affection and which she is now determined to assert as freely and responsibly taken. "To a cruel war *I sent him:* from whence he returned, his brows bound with oak" (I. iii). Seen in this way, the hero's glory becomes the reflection of his mother's purpose, a compensation for the sacrifice which sent him forth, in despite of a mother's natural attachment, to affirm in dedication to "honour" the exalted destiny she has chosen for him.

Before long, and in the course of the same scene, this concentration rises to a ruthlessly masculine participation in her son's achievements. Her ideal, to which he will amply correspond, ceases to be human, becomes the exaltation of an engine impersonally dedicated to destruction. Marcius will "pluck Aufidius down by the hair," be shunned by his enemies as children "fly from a bear"; as she imagines him defying the Volscians it is as if she were herself engaged in the bloody work, sharing in its ruthless fascination. The picture of her victorious son—

> his bloody brow
> With his mail'd hand then wiping, forth he goes
> Like to a harvest-man that's task'd to mow
> Or all, or lose his hire— (I. iii)

balancing against a touch of spontaneous poetry the grim aspect of the warrior bathed in blood, is not allowed to deflect her from the dedication which her nature so insistently demands. When Virgilia, with wifely concern, pleads "no blood," her answer is ferociously concentrated on the idea which entirely possesses her. "Away, you fool": the repudiation ends in a glorification of bloodshed more fantastic and inhuman than all that has gone before:

> the breasts of Hecuba,
> When she did suckle Hector, look'd not lovelier
> Than Hector's sword when it spit forth blood
> At Grecian sword, contemning. (I. iii)

Even at this moment of supreme dedication to her martial ideal, the thought of maternity lingers on as an obsessive presence in the mother's mind. Sacrificed to the masculine cult of "honour," its survival emphasizes the moral incompleteness which will bring her son to ruin.

These narrow and perverse intensities are not allowed to pass without implicit comment. This is provided by Volumnia's picture of her grandson in the nursery:

> O' my word, the father's son; I'll swear, 'tis a very pretty boy.
> O' my troth, I looked upon him o' Wednesday half an hour together;

> has such a confirm'd countenance. I saw him run after a gilded butterfly; and when he caught it, he let it go again; and after it again; and over and over he comes, and up again; catched it again: or whether his fall enraged him, or how 'twas, he did so set his teeth, and tear it; O, I warrant, how he mammocked it! (I. iii)

There could be no better comment on the deadly lack of feeling which has surrounded Marcius from birth and of which his child, in turn, partakes; the boy is, after all, "the father's son." To complete the effect we need only the crushing, if unconscious, irony implied in Valeria's observation, "Indeed, la, 'tis a noble child." The entire episode, with its glimpse of the father's narrow and inhuman concentration mirrored in the precocious savagery of his child, makes a revealing introduction to the episodes of war which follow.

All this, however, acutely and finely observed as it is, is only one side of the picture which this strangely inconsistent hero presents. On the other, and not less real, we are made to feel in this same exclusive family circle the reality of an affection so intense, so concentrated, that it binds the son irrevocably to his mother, making him indeed a hero and the savior of his city, but finally, in its one-sided possessiveness, leading to his ruin. Subject from birth to the relentless pressure of his mother's affection, Coriolanus has grown into a man at once capable of the deepest feeling and unable to give it free expression, even at times ashamed of what he feels: the man who at one moment can salute his wife, on his return from the hazards of war, with a marvelous, shy tenderness—

> My gracious silence, hail!
> Would'st thou have laugh'd had I come coffin'd home,
> That weep'st to see me triumph? Ah, my dear,
> Such eyes the widows in Corioli wear,
> And mothers that lack sons— (II. i)

and who, at another, thrusts aside his own heroic deeds, bashfully and awkwardly, as scarcely worthy of mention or recall: in other words, at once a hero, an inexorable fighting machine, and a childishly naïve and undeveloped human being. The play is consistent in presenting Coriolanus under both these aspects. As a warrior, neither material rewards nor normal pity can make him other than a superb but inhuman engine of war placed at his country's service;

as a son, his intimate resolution is helpless before his mother's successive demands upon him, and he is brought to isolation and disaster by following the strain of natural sensibility which lies present in the deepest recesses of his nature, but which he has never really been brought to consider or to understand.

This combination of nobility and weakness is fully revealed in its true nature when Coriolanus returns to Rome to celebrate his victory at Corioli. The victory has been won in the name of his city's aristocracy, the ruling patrician class to which he is so proudly conscious of belonging, and in the pursuit of personal rivalry with Tullus Aufidius. The common soldiery whom he regards with contempt as the "musty" raw material for slaughter have had no share in his exploits: so much so that, when he rallies them on the field of battle, they watch him go, as they think, to meet his fate behind the closing gates of the enemy city to the accompaniment of an indifferent comment: "To the pot, I warrant him" (I. iv). Now, as he receives the offer of supreme authority in Rome, the virtues which have made him a hero are balanced against his lack of flexibility and human understanding, both wonderfully present in the great eulogy with which Cominius, his peer and colleague, proposes him for the supreme office. The speech underlines by its weight and gravity a decisive turning point in the action. At this dangerous moment in the hero's career, when his triumph and his ruin stand face to face, it stresses the energy, the splendor of superabundant power, made manifest in his victorious campaign. This impression of life is conveyed not only in the triumphant image which mirrored his youthful rise to glory—"he waxed like a sea"—but in the intensity which records in terms of vivid sensation his inexhaustible response to the challenge of danger:

> the din of war 'gan pierce
> His ready sense; then straight his doubled spirit
> Re-quickened what in flesh was fatigate. (II. ii)

This magnificent rousing of the spirit to the sounds of conflict carries us back to the nostalgia felt by Othello for "the spirit-stirring drum, the ear-piercing fife";[27] both passages convey, in their respective evocations of what is, for each of these heroes, life and fulfillment, a sense of the imagination reaching out to the confines of sensual intensity. The exaltation of the warrior as he advances toward his goal, the crowning of triumph with the "garland" of victory, impresses itself through a fine keenness of sensation, this play's parallel to that which, at certain moments, transfigures the utterances of passion in *Antony and Cleopatra.*

Just, however, as *Antony and Cleopatra* does not finally invite to uncritical romantic surrender, so the celebration of the soldierly virtues in *Coriolanus* is balanced by a contrary impression. Side by side with its superb sense of vital energy, Cominius' speech asserts the presence of a dead heaviness, an almost grotesque insensibility. The expansive splendor of "he waxed like a sea" is immediately qualified by the ponderous, dead impact of

> in the brunt of seventeen battles since,
> He *lurch'd* all swords of the garland; (II. ii)

even as the hero attained with manhood the complete martial assertion of his being, the power so revealed converted itself into a heavy indifference to life. From the comparison, at once splendid and sinister, of the warrior to a "vessel under sail," bearing down upon the lives which he regards as "weeds," we pass to the evocation of his sword as "death's stamp," invested with the destructive weight of a battering-ram. As the eulogy draws to its close, its object is converted into a mechanical instrument of carnage, indifferent to the ruin he has caused:

> from face to foot
> He was a thing of blood, whose every motion
> Was timed with dying cries. (II. ii)

The impression of inhumanity is further reinforced by the irresistible impact with which the hero "with a sudden reinforcement" *struck* Corioli "like a planet"; the effect is to make Coriolanus no longer a mere soldier but an instrument of "shunless destiny" launched against "the *mortal* gates of the city." In the word "mortal" is contained not only a sense of the frailty of those who sought to bar his progress, but the protest of downtrodden life against the power which began as an affirmation of vital energy and is now revealed in ruthless dedication to destruction. Then, to balance the effect yet again, the machine quickens in response to new perils in the lines about "the din of war" and the effect of "re-quickening" to which it leads: a revival followed, however, by the renewed callousness of

> he did
> Run reeking o'er the lives of men, as if
> 'Twere a perpetual spoil; (II. ii)

until we are left, as Cominius bows to the acclamation which greets his close, with a final picture of Coriolanus pausing to "pant" like a hot-blooded bull after his orgy of carnage.

On the tide of emotion which the speech rouses, Coriolanus is lifted to the culmination of his public glory. If he fails to remain there it is because his true enemy lies finally, not in those around him, but in himself. The prospect of addressing himself to the people produces in him a deep-seated, almost physical repugnance associated with the fear of finding himself "naked," intimately exposed in his hidden weakness. In this reaction the tribunes see an opportunity which they hasten to press home. The people "*must* have their voices"; they will never "bate one jot" of the "ceremony" which they know to be their due. The growing rift is healed for the moment by Menenius and the hero is left to "blush" boyishly and to express an unwillingness to "brag" which, however creditable in itself, answers to motives deeper than he can readily understand. The entire situation is already variously and impossibly fragile. The demagogic demands of the tribunes are balanced by an unreasoning obstinacy in the warrior, who is being compelled, against every instinct of his stubborn nature, to exhibit his most intimate feelings to further ends which others have imposed upon him.

In this situation the final triumph of the hero's enemies is assured. Before they finally achieve their end, however, Coriolanus, feeling himself lost, at sea in a world too complicated for his understanding, turns, as he has always been accustomed to turn, to his mother, seeking from her a confirmation of what he regards as his sacred integrity, his belief in himself: only to find himself *there*, in the very place where all his confidence has rested, inexplicably betrayed. For it is indeed Volumnia who now strikes the decisive blow at his consistency by calling him "too absolute"—as if he could be so in his own esteem—and by wrapping her counsel in what must strike him, being what he is, as a deep moral ambiguity. In war, she urges, it is in accordance with "honour" to seem "the same you are not" and to shape "policy" accordingly; why then should it be "less or worse" to do precisely this in an emergency of peace? From this opening, which he can only receive in bewilderment ("Why force you this?"), she goes on to urge him to dissimulation:

> now it lies on you to speak
> To the people; not by your own instruction,
> Nor by the matter which your heart prompts you,
> But with such words that are but rooted in
> Your tongue, though but bastards and syllables
> Of no allowance to your bosom's truth. (III. ii)

The wording of this advice is calculated to bring home to Coriolanus the moral monstrosity, as it must seem to him, which it implies. To tell such a man that he must speak, not from the "heart," according to the dictates of that "honour" which is life to him, but according to the promptings of expediency is to run counter to the self-respect, the narrow but absorbing sense of fitness, for which he has been taught to live. Most shocking of all is the assumption that dissembling is an acceptable and even a necessary part of the warrior's occupation:

> Now, this no more dishonours you at all
> Than to take in a town with gentle words,
> Which else would put you to your fortune and
> The hazard of much blood. (III. ii)

The one-sidedness, the artificial simplicity, of the hero's attitude to his martial profession could hardly be more devastatingly exposed. When his mother tells him,

> I would dissemble with my nature, where
> My fortunes and my friends at stake required
> I should do so in honour, (III. ii)

the notions of "honour" and "dissembling," hitherto so clearly separated in his mind, are presented to him as intolerably mingled, have become pointers to disorientation and inner doubt.

The manner in which Volumnia goes on to depict the piece of play acting she is urging upon her son can only add to his shame. His "bonnet" is to be stretched out in supplication, his knee to be seen "bussing the stones"; the "waving" of his head must correct the impulse of the "stout heart," which is to become

humble as the ripest mulberry
That will not hold the handling. (III. ii)

Worst of all, the hero is to prostitute his soldiership, declaring himself the servant of the people and exhibiting himself as tongue-tied and unapt of speech:

being bred in broils,
Hast not the soft way which, thou dost confess,
Were fit for thee to use, as they to claim,
In asking their good loves. (III. ii)

By the end of this harangue, Coriolanus is a hero shattered in his inner integrity, exposed to the play of forces which can have for him no intimate reality. It is supremely ironic that Volumnia, having achieved her purpose by tying up her son in doubt and self-mistrust, should claim at the last to have left him free: "Do thy will." In fact, his will is now for his friends and, above all, for her to dispose of. As he goes to meet the populace, with the words "honour" and "mildly" ringing inarticulate and clashing changes in his stunned thought, we know that they have prevailed. The consequences of their victory for Rome and for himself will emerge in the remaining course of the tragedy.

In the immediate event we are shown the hero, puzzled and without conviction, struggling to apply in the world the lesson he has so incomprehensibly been forced to learn. He tries to woo the people, to show them the wounds which his mother has so frequently exalted as a sign of honor—"He is wounded: I thank the gods for it" (II. i)—and which are now so strangely to become a public spectacle. Inevitably this attempt to reverse his entire being cannot have lasting effects. Emotion wells up in him as he faces the mob who have been roused against him, and he ends by repudiating violently the role that has been forced upon him. As a result he is condemned first to death and then to banishment, uprooted from his family and his country and the values which have hitherto sustained him, left a man at sea, adrift, with only passionate devotion to an unnatural and impossible revenge to sustain him. Consistency, truth to his narrow but absorbing conception of himself and his honor, is perhaps the virtue he has most highly prized in life. It has now become a virtue which, in Rome, he can no longer practice, having become in his own phrase, at once darkly tragic and finally self-dramatizing,

> a lonely dragon, that his fen
> Makes fear'd and talk'd of, more than seen; (IV. i)

and so it now becomes his fate, in the very act of unnaturally stressing this same consistency, to follow his avenging purpose into the camp of his former enemy.

Coriolanus' approach to Aufidius shows him aware of the equivocal situation which his presence in Antium implies. Having cut himself off from Rome, exiled himself to what he bitterly describes as "the city of kites and crows," he recognizes that he has made himself acceptable to none:

> I have deserved no better entertainment,
> In being Coriolanus. (IV. v)

The sense of his untenable position leads him, as though in compensation, to an attitude of defiance. Stressing the "hurt and mischief" which he has done to the Volscians, he proudly recalls

> The extreme dangers and the drops of blood
> Shed for my thankless country; (IV. v)

all this, he insists, gained for him in Rome the surname which must be most galling to those to whom he now offers his services. These glories, however, belong to the past. In the present, "only that name remains"; dedicated to a purpose of negation and destruction, he ends by taking refuge from his sense of his own vanity in an empty caricature of purpose:

> I will fight
> Against my canker'd country with the spleen
> Of all the under fiends. (IV. v)

Whatever voice speaks here, it is not that of heroism or firm consistency. The true spirit of his resolution is contained in Coriolanus' admission that, if his offer is not accepted, he is "longer to live most weary": moved by the sense of vanity which now dogs his career, he offers his throat to be cut by his rival even as, with a remnant of his native pride, he stresses yet again the harm he has done to the enemy into whose hands he is delivering himself.

If Coriolanus shows himself lost in a world of ill-considered perplexities, Aufidius' reply is notably and, in view of his normal attitudes, strangely romantic in tone:

> Let me twine
> Mine arms about that body, where against
> My grained ash an hundred times hath broke,
> And scarr'd the moon with splinters: here I clip
> The anvil of my sword, and do contest
> As hotly and as nobly with thy love
> As ever in ambitious strength I did
> Contend against thy valour. Know thou first,
> I loved the maid I married; never man
> Sigh'd truer breath; but that I see thee here,
> Thou noble thing! more dances my rapt heart
> Than when I first my wedded mistress saw
> Bestride my threshold. (IV. v)

It may seem curious that Aufidius, habitually moved by envy and emulation, should give fine expression to the ecstatic values of war just as Coriolanus is finally renouncing them. The inconsistency, however, is true to the tragic conception, in which contradiction plays an essential part. Aufidius, who welcomes his former enemy so generously, who feels bound to him in an emotional relationship which he expressly declares to be in some sense akin to love, will not on that account be less ready to take advantage of his weakness. Heroism and consuming jealousy live together in his nature: in much the same way, Coriolanus himself is divided between heroic integrity and an intimate sense of failure.

The later stages of Aufidius' welcome notably modify the opening lyricism. The romantic values of war are replaced by the memory of tough physical rivalry—

> I had purpose
> Once more to hew thy target from thy brawn— (IV. v)

and by the recalling of a dream in which he has seen himself and his rival "Unbuckling helms, fisting each other's throat," intimately engrossed by the clash of armed bodies in ruthless conflict. After this transition, the speech ends on a combination of offered friendship and careful calculation. Aufidius confers upon Coriolanus the leadership of his own "revenges," not simply out of deference to his soldiership, but because he is "best experienced" to know "his country's strength and weakness" and so to bring about its ruin.

Upon these conditions he declares himself ready to greet his one-time opponent as "more a friend than e'er an enemy"; but there is an undertone in the rounding-off of his welcoming gesture—"Yet, Marcius, that was much"—which suggests that this strange coincidence, though acceptable while it serves the turn of the moment, must not be expected to last.

Having taken his grotesque resolution, Coriolanus advances upon Rome in a progress of which the absolute and unnatural ruthlessness is stressed. Cominius returns from him with his mind dominated by the pervasive image of consuming fire:

> I tell you, he does sit in gold, his eye
> Red as 'twould burn Rome; and his injury
> The gaoler to his pity. (V. i)[28]

Menenius, speaking before the news of Volumnia's successful mission has reached the city, describes most vividly the hard inflexibility which has so recently impressed him at their meeting:

> The tartness of his face sours ripe grapes: when he walks, he moves like an engine, and the ground shrinks before his treading: he is able to pierce a corslet with his eye; talks like a knell, and his hum is a battery. He sits in his state, as a thing made for Alexander . . . He wants nothing of a god but eternity and a heaven to throne in. (V. iv)

The emphasis rests, as so often before, on bitter and implacable determination. When Menenius sums up his impression by saying that, except for "eternity," Coriolanus lacks none of the attributes of divinity, the tribune Sicinius—speaking for once profoundly—adds by way of comment, "Yes, mercy, if you report him truly," only to find confirmation in the patrician's rejoinder: "there is no more mercy in him than there is milk in a male tiger" (V. iv). We are reminded once again of the element of arrogant presumption that has been stressed in Coriolanus from the first, and to which the other tribune, Brutus, referred at an earlier stage when he said:

> You speak of the people,
> As if you were a god to punish, not
> A man of their infirmity. (III. i)

But the element of weakness which was then only implicit in his attitudes is now on the point of coming to the surface to destroy him. Coriolanus needs to stress his inhuman dedication precisely because the emphasis covers an emptiness, a lack of true belief in himself. He seems in the eyes of his former friends to be consistent, fully dedicated to his avenging purpose; but at the crucial moment, and when the Romans have lost all hope, the submerged side of his strangely divided nature asserts itself to bring about his ruin.

The final confrontation between the hero and his family (V. iii) is beyond doubt one of Shakespeare's most moving and eloquent creations. Coriolanus, bracing himself instinctively to meet the challenge which it implies, calls on his Volscian allies to witness what he intends to be a demonstration of his firmness; but when Volumnia actually stands before him, with his wife and child, a notable admission of natural feeling escapes his lips—

> I melt, and am not
> Of stronger earth than others— (V. iii)

before he takes refuge in further emphatic denials of instinct and family alike. The expression of these is, indeed, revealing. Coriolanus seeks, by sheer emphasis of assertion, to return to the simplicity of purpose which his being craves. Let the Volscians, whom he has so often defeated in his country's service, "plough Rome" and "harrow Italy." To "obey instinct" by accepting the validity of the intimate emotion he has just allowed himself to reveal is—so he seeks to persuade himself—to confess himself a "gosling," incapable of asserting integrity of will in his new situation. Self-depreciation here is a cover for doubt and inner contradiction. To smother the powerful voice of "instinct" Coriolanus needs to postulate the impossible, to assert that a man may be "author of himself" and "know no other kin." The effect is to make him a renegade, not only to his city and to the family which has bred him, but—in a sense deeper than he can fully understand—to his own being.

When he ceases to speak, enough has been said to show where the hero's resolution will be vulnerable. The first indication of what is to come is a recognition of the clumsiness with which, like a "dull actor" who has forgotten his lines, he moves toward the exposure of his "full disgrace." The admission leads naturally to a more personal expression of the emotions which, do what he will to smother them, remain so close to his heart. "Best of my flesh," he salutes his wife, and goes on to beg forgiveness for the "tyranny" which his attitude toward her implies; but, once feeling has thus forced its way to the surface, he makes yet again to cover it, pleads to be allowed to maintain the fiction he has chosen to present to the world:

> do not say,
> For that, "Forgive our Romans." (V. iii)

The plea, however, is already advanced in the name of a lost cause, and the emotion he seeks to repudiate finds issue in a further lyrical outburst which gains enormously by contrast with Virgilia's reticence and his own assertions of iron sufficiency:

> O, a kiss
> Long as my exile, sweet as my revenge!
> Now, by the jealous queen of heaven, that kiss
> I carried from thee, dear, and my true lip
> Hath virgin'd it e'er since. (V. iii)

Beneath the depth of feeling, the sense of a return, through emotions so long and so perversely excluded, to the natural foundations of the speaker's being, there lies a further revelation of character. The emphasis on virgin purity answers to an essential simplicity of nature: the simplicity which underlies, on its more positive side, the code of martial "honour" for which he has lived and which he cannot, without involving himself in ruin, sever from its intimate inspiration. Because the simplicity is true, Coriolanus' downfall must affect us as truly tragic; because his own perverse choices have led him to deny it, a pitiless element of irony shadows his end.

Once so much has been admitted, the gesture of natural submission at once imposes itself:

> sink, my knee, i' the earth;
> Of thy deep duty more impression show
> Than that of common sons. (V. iii)

There could be no better comment on the determination, so recently asserted, to show himself "author" of his own decisions, autonomous, released from the ties of nature. As the hero's knee bends, a frame of tense and self-imposed rigidity bows to the reality it has sought to evade, even while it seeks, in a vestige of obstinate pride, to assert its devotion in terms more absolute than those afforded to the rest of men. The emphasis cannot conceal the reality of the transformation which is taking place under our eyes. Nature, so long and so vainly denied, has begun to reassert herself. The way is open for Volumnia to press her plea and to compass, through her very success, the downfall which her son's choices have from the first implied.

It is highly significant that Coriolanus should have gone so far in admission before his mother has really had occasion to marshal the full force of her arguments. In her marvelously eloquent reply she pleads, in fact, for all the pieties that she has instilled into him, which have made him what he is, and which he has so unnaturally been brought to deny. Her plea gains its end because, as we have already been shown, there is nothing true, nothing but inner emptiness, beneath the resolution that the exile has sought to oppose to it. As she ceases, he is left "silent," holding her by the hand and contemplating the sorry spectacle of his shattered integrity. When at last he speaks, the effect is overwhelming in its recognition of personal disaster. "O mother, mother," he exclaims, "What have you done?" (V. iii) The question comes from one bewildered, conscious not of a true resolution to his conflicting loyalties, but of obscurely threatening deities who look down upon an "unnatural scene" and "laugh" at what they see. The sardonic note which has throughout lent the scene a distinctive quality finds issue at this point in a vision of life, as it presents itself to the hero, finally desolate and meaningless:

O my mother, mother! O!
You have won a happy victory to Rome;
But, for your son, believe it, O, believe it,
Most dangerously you have with him prevail'd,
If not most mortal to him. (V. iii)

At this moment, if anywhere, we are face to face with the tragic contradiction on which the entire action has rested. Coriolanus' submission, made under the eyes of a withdrawn and notably noncommittal Aufidius, represents an affirmation of natural feeling, but one made in vacancy, which answers to the pathetic crumbling of an impossible purpose with nothing real or consistent to take its place. He has spared Rome, but cannot in the nature of things return to it. The patriot is left without a country to serve, the son, having chosen a course which is now seen as in turn enslaving him, is debarred from accompanying his mother. Uprooted, with a strange, almost adolescent gesture of clumsiness, he turns away for the last time from the women and the child before him: turns away to what he knows already to be his ruin.

The ruin, indeed, is not long in coming. In the city he has left forever, a new mood of "merriment," of relief from tension, makes itself felt in a poetic transformation which bursts the iron bonds that have habitually restrained imagination in the public scenes of the play. The messenger is as certain of the truth of his tidings of peace as he is that "the sun is fire," and he follows up his assertion with a most graphic picture of the returning tide—

> Ne'er through an arch so hurried the blown tide— (V. iv)

as the "recomforted" swarm in jubilation through the city gates. "All together," as the stage direction has it,

> The trumpets, sackbuts, psalteries and fifes,
> Tabors and cymbals and the shouting Romans
> Make the sun dance. (V. iv)

The restoration of peace, however, though it restores Roman society to sane unity and produces these manifestations of life and joy, is powerless to ward off the hero's own fate. Aufidius, who no longer has any use for his former enemy, finds it easy to accuse him of betraying his new masters. Returning to Corioli, which he had once conquered in the name of Rome, Coriolanus is taken unawares, surrounded and stabbed ignominiously to death. His reaction, somewhat like that of Othello before him,[29] is a last pathetic glance back to the days of his glory: the days when he had been a triumphant warrior in the service of Rome, and before division had become the substance of his soul:

> If you have writ your annals true, 'tis there,
> That like an eagle in a dove-cot, I
> Flutter'd your Volscians in Corioli;
> Alone I did it. (V. vi)

"Alone": perhaps here, in the turning into a heroic virtue of what is in fact a weakness, the isolation from his fellow men which birth and prejudice have combined to impose upon him, lies in great part the key to Coriolanus' tragedy. Both the angry scolding and the attempt to reaffirm a lost dignity represent some aspects of the truth about this strangely divided, inopportune hero; and since these aspects do not harmonize, since he cannot now hope to recover the shattered simplicity which he abjured when he turned his back on his city and his family, the tide of vengeance flows over him with the repeated clamor of "Kill!" and Aufidius, in a last gesture of gratuitous brutality, "stands on his body" in triumph.

XII

The Final Romances

The two great Roman tragedies of Shakespeare's last years do not represent the last stage in his dramatic development. They were followed by a series of plays—*Pericles, Cymbeline, The Winter's Tale,* and *The Tempest*—which are clearly related in theme and represent an effort to give, through the extension of conventions familiar in the earlier comedies, artistic form to a new "symbolic" purpose. Of these romances *Pericles* and *Cymbeline* seem to be, each in its very different way, frankly experimental; the first appears to contain passages not from Shakespeare's pen, and the latter suggests an effort to adapt current forms of romantic comedy to express the intensely individual vision which is clearly present in the whole series. *The Winter's Tale* and *The Tempest* are, on the other hand, finished masterpieces that can stand comparison with the best of Shakespeare's writing.

That the whole series forms a close artistic unity is clearly revealed in the pattern discernible in the respective plots of the plays. At the heart of each lies the conception of an organic relationship between breakdown and reconciliation, between the divisions created in the most intimate human bonds by the action of time and passion and the final healing of these divisions. Near the opening of each play—even in *Cymbeline,* where the central theme is partially obscured—a father loses his offspring through the effect of his own passion-driven folly; the main action is devoted to the sufferings and remorse which follow from their mutual estrangement, and at the end of each play, the lost child (normally a daughter whose name has evident symbolic associations: Marina Perdita, Miranda) is restored to her father's blessing and becomes the instrument of a reconciliation which in turn throws a light of its own upon some of the principal themes—more particularly those of the individual's relation to society, and of the relationship between untutored "nature" and civilized "nurture"—with which Shakespeare's earlier work is consistently engaged. In these final romances the harmonizing theme first attempted in *King Lear*[1] and there broken, after the brief restoration of the aged king to Cordelia, by the prevailing tragic development produces a conception of drama largely removed from common realism and scarcely paralleled in English literature.

PERICLES, PRINCE OF TYRE

Pericles is, by the common consent of criticism, a problematic play. A late arrival to the accepted canon,[2] it is clearly in some sense a stratified construction, in which passages in Shakespeare's latest manner are superimposed upon others relatively crude and undeveloped. Whatever explanation these inequalities may bear, however, it seems likely that the play represents an early approach to the conception of drama which later produced *The Winter's Tale* and *The Tempest.* Conceived as an experiment in poetic symbolism, it shows the basic conceptions of the last comedies, still in the process of formation, striving to impose artistic unity upon an imperfect theme; and it is this fact, rather than the uncertain authorship of disputed passages, that constitutes the primary interest of the play.[3]

If this be a true account, we can regard Pericles, when the play opens, as embarked upon a pilgrimage in search of true happiness. His appeal before Antiochus (I. i) is to the "gods that made me man and sway in love," who have inflamed in his breast the desire "to taste the fruit of yon celestial tree," and his reaction to the king's ambiguous warning is an affirmation of deepened moral understanding:

> Antiochus, I thank thee, who hath taught
> My frail mortality to know itself. (I. i)

Driven by the discovery of hidden evil to abandon his first dream of felicity, Pericles is exposed to a succession of experiences which, crudely expressed as they often are, can be interpreted as representing various stages in moral growth. The anger of the tyrant obliges him to leave his kingdom, exposing him first to penury and then to a storm which, as in so many of Shakespeare's later plays,[4] reflects the hero's subjection to tragedy. In the storm, and through the action of three Fishermen, he recovers the armor bequeathed to him by his father, an incident (II. i) itself capable of bearing a symbolic interpretation; and, once more clothed in it as his defense, he wins in tournament the hand of Thaisa, daughter of Simonides of Pentapolis. With the consummation of their marriage the first part of a play so far remarkably uneven, not to say imperfect, is complete.

The rest of the tragedy brings us, beyond all reasonable doubt, into contact with Shakespeare's first attempt to develop the theme of symbolic reconciliation in the manner of his final romances. With Pericles exposed to a storm at sea which he ascribes to the will of the "gods" (III. i), and with the death in childbirth of his wife, the true sense of the action at last begins to emerge. Thaisa, dying through exposure to the elements, bequeaths her husband a living continuation of herself ("this piece of your dead queen"), and Pericles hails the event in words in which stress and calm, tragedy and following peace, are blended:

> Now, mild may be thy life!
> For a more blustrous birth had never babe:
> Quiet and gentle thy conditions! for
> Thou art the rudeliest welcome to this world
> That ever was prince's child. Happy what follows!
> Thou hast as chiding a nativity
> As fire, air, water, earth and heaven can make,
> To herald thee from the womb. (III. i)

The balance of contrasted images here is at once unmistakably Shakespearean, a product of the same imagination as that which conceived Cordelia's regal grief,[5] and an indication of the point reached at this stage in the symbolic pattern. Pericles prays that the "mildness" of his daughter's life may compensate for the unprecedented "blustrous" condition of her birth, the future hope of a "quiet and gentle" environment for the "rudeliest welcome" to the world which she has undergone at the moment of her begetting. Behind the more superficial aspects of this prayer for peace lies the characteristic Shakespearean intuition of subsistent continuity, the sense that birth and death, tempest and following calm, are in reality related aspects of a single process to which the elements themselves are, in their universal presence, witnesses. Thus imaginatively supported and given poetic substance, the episode, which at once looks back to the sufferings of Pericles in his pilgrimage (of which it is the consummation) and anticipates the birth of a new and deeper understanding, becomes the pivot of the whole action.

Before the compensating development of the future can receive its dramatic expression, however, the death so recently announced needs to be introduced more fully into the symbolic pattern. The dialogue with the sailors by which this is achieved is set against a background of tempest evoked in prose that clearly anticipates the similar scene in *The Winter's Tale;*[6] whilst Pericles, responding to external pressure with a corresponding growth in moral insight, combines the patience expressed in

> Courage enough: I do not fear the flaw;
> It hath done to me the worst (III. i)[7]

with tender concern for the well-being of this "fresh, new sea-farer." Death and birth, the old and the new, are seen to be more closely connected than ever in a single process. When, as a final tribute to the storm, the sailors insist that the "ship be cleared of the dead," the symbolic action is taken a step further; for the burial of his wife at sea is not only a sacrifice on the part of the prince, but is seen to imply the elimination of death as prologue to its poetic transformation. The shift of emphasis begins to make itself felt in Pericles' dispositions for the funeral. Thaisa's death, though the result of the "terrible child-bed" to which she has been exposed, has found issue in a new life; and so even her burial, conceived as the sacrifice of her corpse to the "unfriendly elements," becomes subject to a process of mutation reflected in the motion and texture of the verse:

> nor have I time
> To give thee hallow'd to thy grave, but straight
> Must cast thee, scarcely coffin'd, in the ooze;
> Where, for a monument upon thy bones,

And aye-remaining lamps, the belching whale
And humming water must o'erwhelm thy corpse,
Lying with simple shells. (III. i)

This deliberately poetic recalling of the body's consignment to the sea, destroyer and preserver, aims at giving the idea of death a transforming quality of remoteness, at making it, in the words of Ariel in *The Tempest*,[8] "suffer a sea-change" to which the supporting indication of expanding moral understanding will give the necessary substance. The imaginative quality conveyed in the use of "ooze" to indicate the sea,[9] in the transmuting musicality of "*humming* water" and "*aye-remaining* lamps," is a fit introduction to the burial of Thaisa with her "casket and jewels," whilst the mention of the "satin coffer" and the rich "spices" by which her body is preserved from the temporal action of the elements and disposed for the coming resurrection contributes to the creation of a subtle effect of harmony which will be taken up into the final scenes of reconciliation.

The following scene (III. ii) transports the action to Cerimon's house at Ephesus. Cerimon occupies in *Pericles* a position intermediate between that of the physicians who ministered to spiritual infirmities in *Macbeth* and *King Lear* and that of Prospero in *The Tempest,* whose studies give him power over nature and an insight into the true character of things. His studies are as much spiritually as medically conceived. They concern the "*blest* infusions" that dwell in the properties of nature and tend to the cure of deep-seated "disturbances"; they proceed, in fact, from a contemplative depth that recalls that of Prospero and aims at restoring the broken moral harmony of human nature.

To the figure thus conceived the coffin of Thaisa, recovered in accordance with the prevailing symbolic design from the sea, is brought in. Her resurrection is, as in the parallel case of Lear,[10] a gradual process, during which the returning tide of life is first hailed by the bystanders in terms of the manifestations of renascent nature—

see how she 'gins to blow
Into life's flower again— (III. ii)

and at last confirmed in the reopening of her eyes to the light. Her revival is greeted by Cerimon with fresh intimations of value and beauty:

She is alive; behold
Her eyelids, cases to those heavenly jewels
Which Pericles hath lost,
Begin to part their fringes of bright gold;
The diamonds of a most praised water
Do appear, to make the world twice rich. Live,
And make us weep to hear your fate, fair creature,
Rare as you seem to be. (III. ii)

In this speech, a new, transhumanizing element (so to call it) enters the verse, giving its full symbolic quality to what has now become a poetry of resurrection. This is perhaps the first time in Shakespeare that the full range of his mature poetry is lent to an effect so deliberately remote, so charged with a quality that can truly be described as supernatural, and yet so free from any suggestion of abstraction or strain. Thaisa, once "lost" to Pericles in her death, is again *alive,* and the first sign of her restoration is a renewal of value by which her very physical attributes are transformed. Her eyelids have become "cases" to the "heavenly jewels" of her eyes, jewels which were formerly the most valued treasures of Pericles and which their loss has made doubly precious to him. The lashes on these lids have become transmuted into "fringes of bright gold" and the eyes themselves "diamonds of a most praised water," whose influence in their resurrected beauty is able to enrich, even more than in her first life, the world which had already celebrated their loveliness. The beauty of Thaisa, thus exalted above common realism, is of a "rarity" that has now only to wait for the final reconciliation to Pericles to exercise its power as the key to a new life.

The time for this reconciliation, however, is still distant. The next scene (III. iii) shows Pericles resigned to his irreparable loss:

We cannot but obey
The powers above us. (III. iii)

The need for acceptance, conformity to ends still only dimly apprehended in the course of exposure to tragic experience, is an essential part of the conception on which each of Shakespeare's last plays is built. Such resignation, however, is not final. Already, in the stress of the very tempest that robbed him of Thaisa, his daughter Marina, herself symbolically named, has been born. Pericles now leaves her in the hands of Cleon, so that she may receive from him "princely training" and "be manner'd as she is born," stand out by her possession of the civilized virtues in a society whose courtly spirit has already been indicated (I. iv) and whose shortcomings will soon be revealed. The act concludes (III. iv) with Thaisa learning from Cerimon of her situation and balancing Pericles' vow to leave his hair uncut until his daughter's marriage by assuming a "vestal livery" in the temple of Diana. With this pair of resolutions duly adopted, and waiting upon the future development of events, this central stage in the play, poised between past tragedy and future reconciliation, is brought to a close.

Most of the action of *Pericles* covered by the fourth act shows a partial decline in emotional tension and poetic mastery. The reasons for this are not easy to define. It could be argued that the greater part of the action at this point belongs to an earlier version of the play, perhaps only occasionally touched by Shakespeare to bring his material into a minimum of concordance with his general purpose. The argument, however, would need to be advanced with caution. The contrast between Marina's purity and the trials to which she is subjected in the brothel is excessively facile and sentimental, but its spirit, and some of its phrasing, can be paralleled in earlier plays. The first exchange between Pander and Boult (IV. ii) and the final discussion between the latter and Marina (IV. vi) recall, at times closely, the scenes in *Measure for Measure*[11] which present social dissolution as a background to the central conflict. Like the prostitutes of Vienna, the "unwholesome wenches," "pitifully sodden" (IV. ii) of the Mytilene brothel are conceived as victims, subject to creatures conscious of the iniquity of their trade ("the sore terms we stand upon with the gods") but powerless to react against adverse circumstances;[12] the physical infirmities which accompany the exercise of their "profession" are as much morally as bodily significant, symptoms of a process of social disintegration to which the universal force of "appetite" subjects them and against which only the consistent purity of Marina stands out in flawless integrity. The weakness of these scenes, indeed, lies precisely in the excessive clarity of the contrast. Marina, unlike Isabella, does not answer to the realistic conception of drama which still prevails in the presentation of her background. Her motives are not analyzed, and still less subjected to the possibility of conflict; they are inflexibly simple, self-consistent, and therefore, in terms of the dramatic objectivity with which Boult, Pander, and their like are presented, artistically incompatible. The fault lies in the attempt to adapt the realism of Shakespeare's earlier manner to symbolic purposes still in the process of elaboration; but the presence of this inconsistency does not alter the fact that the whole episode is conceived as a necessary stage in the development of the action to which it belongs.

In the concluding episodes, which bring the principal strands of the play together in a harmonious close, the main symbolic line is once more taken up in full poetic mastery. Pericles appears on board ship, curtained from the sight of onlookers and so cut off, in a sense, from a world he has decided in his sorrow to abandon. Marina, still unaware that she is in her father's presence, goes in to him to exercise her healing gifts. She begins by singing to Pericles, for "music" is here, as always, the prelude to restoration. The effect upon him is not immediate; but when she invokes her subjection to a "grief" equal to his own and refers to her noble but "forgotten" parentage, Pericles is moved to break his silence with words which in their halting incoherence record the first tentative groping toward a restored life. Thus we are brought, step by step, to the presentation of the central symbolic situation, when Pericles finally brings himself to ask Marina

> What countrywoman?
> Here of these shores?

and meets with a reply in which fact and symbol are blended:

> No, nor of any shores:
> Yet I was mortally brought forth. (V. i)

From now on, Marina clearly fulfills a double function. She is at once "mortal," the issue of Pericles' own flesh and blood, and the instrument of entry into a new, transfigured life; the conditions of her birth both link her to "mortality," and so to the strain and suffering symbolized in her past subjection to the elements, and exalt her to the spiritual freedom of a fresh creation. Through her, past and present, death and life, temporal servitude and spiritual freedom are fused in a single organic process tending to the affirmation of a new state of being.

The gateway to this new state is, as Pericles now realizes, the "grief" imposed upon him by his tragic past and accepted as the necessary condition of moral growth. As this truth comes home to him, he breaks into renewed speech and finally salutes her in terms that carry a step further the spirit of poetic symbolism in which all this part of the play is steeped:

> I am great with woe, and shall deliver weeping.
> My dearest wife was like this maid, and such a one
> My daughter might have been: my queen's square brows;
> Her stature to an inch; as wand-like straight;
> As silver-voic'd; her eyes as jewel-like,
> And cas'd as richly; in pace another Juno;
> Who starves the ears she feeds, and makes them hungry,
> The more she gives them speech. (V. i)

Pericles' opening words indicate that his past grief has been, spiritually speaking, fertile and introduce once more the birth theme with which so much of the play is steeped. The physical birth in the tempest is, in fact, at last opening into its counterpart in the spiritual order. What is in process of being born, under the revival of poignant past memories, is now expressed as a new vision of humanity restored to a stature almost divine. In the healing figure of Marina are reborn the "square brows" of Thaisa, her perfect carriage, her "silver voice" and "jewel-like" eyes (the epithets, with their indication of infinite riches, recall those formerly used to indicate the quality of Cordelia's royal grief[13]), and, above all, the "pace" of Juno, the queen of the gods; and to round off the transforming splendor of the description, her utterance is such that it gives nourishment without surfeit (she "starves the ears she feeds") and, as it nourishes her hearers, makes them "hungry" for further speech. Almost all the recurrent themes of Shakespeare's symbolic imagery are here gathered together into a vision of life reborn, exalted in "grace."

To the spectacle thus miraculously presented to his eyes Pericles responds by an exercise of faith. He calls upon Marina to tell her story, promising to believe even what still seems impossible; for the truth of the words she speaks is guaranteed, for him, by the echo they call forth from the depth of his past experience, and, as he puts it,

> thou look'st
> Like one I lov'd indeed. (V. i)

As Marina replies, and the tide of memory flows back in a process which reminds us even more strongly than what has gone before of the gradual restoration to life of Hermione in *The Winter's Tale*,[14] his desires convert themselves step by step into reality. First she tells him that her name is Marina, then that her father was a king; and when he feels himself, as it were, mocked by this miraculous rehearsal of his abandoned hopes, she comes finally to the full revelation:

Pericles: Where were you born?
And wherefore call'd Marina?
Marina: Call'd Marina,
For I was born at sea. (V. i)

By this declaration of her origins, Marina finally assumes her full place in the symbolic pattern. Connected by her birth "at sea" with the tempest that bore Pericles apart from Thaisa and confirmed their separation in her supposed death, Marina, having passed unscathed through the trials to which her separation from her father exposed her, now returns as the harbinger of harmony restored. With the response aroused in Pericles by the contemplation of her transfigured humanity, the necessary conditions for the final reconciliation are at last established.

In complete possession of a truth which gives meaning to his own past, and after receiving the confirmation of Lysistratus, Pericles at last gives expression to the rebirth in himself of natural emotion. The stages of his final awakening are conveyed with an exquisite tenderness. As Lear, when restored to Cordelia, called for a pin to put himself to the test in order to discover whether he was in fact alive,[15] so Pericles calls upon Helicanus to "strike him," give him a "gash,"

Lest this great sea of joys rushing upon me
O'erbear the shores of my mortality,
And drown me with their sweetness. (V. i)

At this point and after Marina's recent declaration, the references to the "sea" and to "mortality" are more than ever relevant. Their emotional content has now been finally transformed; for the sea to which Pericles' wife and child were exposed, and which has so far served as a symbol of tragic suffering, has now become a "sea of joys" which threatens to overthrow his weak "mortality" and to cause a death conceived in terms of "sweetness." Against this background, Pericles calls Marina to himself in words which express the symbolic kernel of the whole play:

O, come hither,
Thou that beget'st him that did thee beget;
Thou that wast born at sea, buried at Tarsus,
And found at sea again. (V. i)

What is here asserted, under the guise of the play's poetic symbolism, is nothing less than a concept of spiritual resurrection. Its instrument is Pericles' own child, formerly begotten as the fruit of a marriage that was itself the result of search in pilgrimage, and now, in the moral sphere, the instrument of his rebirth. Marina, recently described in terms that confer a certain status of divinity upon the human, has brought her father the intuition of a new and deeper life; and this she has been able to do as a result of her own experience, the pattern of which involved her birth in tempest, her "death" and burial, her exposure to human malevolence, and finally her triumphant resurrection—once more at sea—as symbol of a reintegrated and regenerated humanity.

Having declared this truth, Pericles calls upon those around him to give thanks to the "holy gods" whose provident action has shaped his story. He also recalls, through Marina, her mother and his "lost" wife who, in his daughter's words,

did end
The minute I began. (V. i)

In this mood of enlightened conformity, Pericles is ready to acknowledge his child and to assume—in clear symbolic reference to his new state—"fresh garments"; once more there is an obvious parallel with the reawakening of Lear.[16] Like Lear again, his first gesture on being restored to his position as father is to respond to Marina's kneeling to him by embracing her and giving her his blessing; and finally, as a background to restored harmony, his speech becomes penetrated by the "music of the spheres" which fills her enraptured imagination. This "heavenly music," in turn, brings Pericles the sleep which is the necessary prelude to lasting restoration.

The last scene (V. iii) brings the chief protagonists together before the altar of Diana at Ephesus; the final reconciliation of Pericles with his wife takes place in the presence of the "gods" to whom she has, in the intervening years, dedicated herself. Pericles begins by recalling the death of Thaisa "in childbed" and the bringing forth of their "maid-child"; the self-dedication of Marina to Diana is also referred to, as are the "better stars" which have preserved her from adverse "fortunes" and restored her finally to her father's care. Hearing her own story thus repeated, Thaisa faints, and Cerimon, taking up the prevailing symbolic imagery, describes how he found her "early in blustering morn" upon the shore with "rich jewels" in her coffin, and how, having restored her, he placed her in the holy temple. Thaisa's recovery from her swoon is also, and simultaneously, the awakening into a new condition. Like Pericles before her, she gropes her way toward the truth, leaning for enlightenment upon her obscure understanding of the symbolic situation by which birth and death, united in common exposure to adversity, are seen as related aspects of a single process issuing in a new life:

> did you not name a tempest,
> A birth, and death? (V. iii)[17]

With this, and the showing of the ring given her as symbol of union by Pericles' father, her husband is convinced. In the light of the harmony thus restored, his "past miseries" are seen as "sports," and his happiness is such that only in terms of death can its absolute, *final* quality find expression:

> O, come, be *buried*,
> A second time within these arms. (V. i)[18]

Marina, in turn, feels her heart leap "to be gone into my mother's bosom," kneels, and is presented by Pericles to her mother with the pregnant simplicity of "Flesh of thy flesh, Thaisa." It is significant, indeed, of the play's intention that, even in this moment of achieved spiritual harmony, physical normality is given its full and essential part. The central balance of filial prayer and answering paternal benediction having thus been established, the healing function of Cerimon ("through whom the gods have shown their power") is given its proper spiritual context, and Helicanus for the last time affirms his loyalty. With the concluding betrothal of Marina to Cerimon, the pattern of reconciliation in *Pericles* is finally complete.

CYMBELINE

The second play of this period, *Cymbeline,* though without the disconcerting crudities of the early scenes of *Pericles,* is in some ways a less immediately striking piece. More closely connected with the fashionable dramatic convention of the moment, which called for sentiment and a glorification of the simple life on lines popularized by John Fletcher, it nonetheless shows Shakespeare attempting—with partial success—to use these conventions for his own purposes. The theme of loss and reconciliation, though less clearly defined than in *Pericles,* is present in the new story. Cymbeline loses his children, Guiderius and Arviragus, whose place at court falls to Cloten through the machinations of his twice-married queen; they are exposed for long years to the simplicities, crude but noble, of the primitive life under the charge of the banished Belarius, and finally return to their father's embrace. Thus restored to civilized life, they bring with them the virtues of barbaric honesty which are henceforth to be integrated into the order of true courtliness.

This order is introduced into the play, and related in turn to the master-theme of loss and gain, through yet another story of division and exposure to trial, that of Imogen and Posthumus. In the treatment of this second action, which derives equally with the first from Cymbeline's primary error of judgment in his second marriage, Shakespeare's language comes to life in a way that distinguishes the play decisively from the sentimental conceptions of Fletcher. The clash of loyalties occasioned by Imogen's forced betrothal to Cloten is given a definite universality of context in the opening words of the play:

> our bloods
> No more obey the heavens than our courtiers
> Still seem as does the king. (I. i)

Against the background of concord which relates the observation of courtly "degree" to the operation of the "heavens," the arbitrary act of the monarch produces in his subjects an underlying sense of profound disquiet. First indicated, perhaps, indirectly in "seem," it is openly expressed a little later in the First Gentleman's assertion that

> not a courtier,
> Although they wear their faces to the bent
> Of the king's looks, hath a heart that is not
> Glad at the thing they scowl at. (I. i)

The linguistic quality of this passage, with its suggestion in "wear their faces"[19] of the masking of true sentiment and the conflict of natural feeling and duty implied in the contrast between "glad" and "scowl at," indicates the prevailing state of moral dislocation. This uneasiness, implying a disturbance of the bond which binds individual conduct to the functioning of the cosmic order, has its part to play in the complete conception. The return to normality through the integration of natural simplicity and true courtly virtue, and the subordination of both to a higher loyalty, is the true theme of *Cymbeline.*

In accordance with this general plan, Imogen's repudiation of the uncouth pretensions of Cloten, whose supposed courtliness can only be acceptable to Cymbeline's passion-distorted vision, implies her choice of a superior conception of humanity, at once natural and deeply civilized. This conception inspires the opening description of Posthumus, whom the king formerly endowed with

> all the learnings that his time
> Could make him the receiver of; which he took,
> As we do air, fast as 'twas minister'd;
> And in's spring became a harvest; liv'd in court—
> Which rare it is to do—most prais'd, most lov'd;
> A sample to the youngest; to the more mature
> A glass that feated them; and to the graver
> A child that guided dotards. (I. i)

The virtues thus celebrated in Posthumus are those of true courtliness, fostered by a "learning" imbibed as naturally as air and proceeding, in the normal course of youthful development, to its spontaneous "harvest." In a world in which true virtue is indeed rare, he has become an example to all ages and conditions, a mirror of the finer human qualities which Imogen, in loving him, has appreciated at their proper worth.

The "rarity" of this example is emphasized first by contrast with the aristocratic pretensions of Cloten—a court parody of the truly "natural" man, enslaved to the prompting of his own passions—and later by the success which attends the cynical intrigues of Iachimo. The arrival of Posthumus in Rome (I. iv) introduces the convention of Italianate court cynicism, which is allowed to play with critical detachment, or the appearance of it, upon the values incarnated in Posthumus' idealization of Imogen. Iachimo's attitude of negation should not obscure his part in expanding the moral content of the action. He sees Posthumus' virtues not as illuminating social existence, as the crown of human living, but as conditioned by it, tainted by its inescapable hollowness. His devotion to Imogen becomes from this new standpoint a proof of imperfection; for, to a critical eye, it seems to imply that "he must be weighed rather by her value than his own," whilst the very "approbation" of those that welcomed the match can be explained in terms of a desire to "fortify" the weak judgment of Imogen, "which else an easy battery might lay flat, for taking a beggar without less quality." The intricate verbal pattern thus woven round the central situation has, beyond its obvious purpose as a reflection of sophisticated "Italianate" cynicism, a strictly analytic content. To Iachimo, absolute "value" of the kind postulated in love by Imogen and Posthumus is inconceivable. His intelligence, acute in its limitations, plays upon such "value" and the virtue which is its moral expression, reducing both to a mixture of sentiment and interest; and if his attitude is rootedly negative, if such a phrase as "how *creeps* acquaintance" clearly reflects a tendency toward systematic debasement, undervaluation, it is nonetheless true that his position needs to be taken into account, first isolated in its expression and then assimilated, through the positive reaction it will eventually produce, into the final pattern.

To this clash of contrary attitudes to "value," the symbol of the ring serves as a point of focus. Posthumus is ready to defend his belief in his mistress' virtue in terms of tangible worth, and Iachimo uses this readiness to insinuate that the two concepts of value, the moral and the material, are in fact identical, that the one is only to be conceived in terms of the other. In this he is helped, if not justified, by a strain of romantic rashness in Posthumus, which is indicated in his preparatory exchange with the Frenchman. What strikes the latter, in remarking upon an incident in Posthumus' earlier career, as a disparity between the "mortal purpose" of a challenge and the "trivial" nature of its cause, is at once acknowledged by him to have been the product of impulse in a "young traveller" and confirmed by what he now considers to be his "minded judgement." The distinction both affirms a valid principle—for Posthumus' adoration of his mistress is clearly intended to be ratified by his mature evaluation—and indicates a possible danger; for, although it is undoubtedly true, as he asserts later, that there is a fundamental difference between "what may be sold or given" and what is "only the gift of the gods," the assumption that the two values are connected, that the one may properly be discussed in terms of the other, is perhaps a little too easily made. Certainly it gives Iachimo his opening. To Posthumus' sweeping assertion that his jewel and the object of his love stand alike unparalleled in his estimation—"I praised her as I rated her: so do I my stone"—the answer inspired by his rooted relativity is, as far as it goes, indisputable: "I have not seen the most precious diamond that is, nor you the lady." The attempt, whether successful or not, to turn romantic commonplace to the ends of moral analysis is undoubtedly present. The romantic love of Posthumus, far from being a final and sufficient relationship, needs to be subjected to a destructive process which will eventually bring it to full maturity. "She your jewel" and "this your jewel," thus brought together in the subtleties of court conversation, represent a knot of contrasted interpretations of value which the play, in so far as it is consistent with its deeper purposes (which is only in part), will be concerned to unravel.

With the two conceptions of "value"—the romantic and the critical, so to call them—thus contrasted, the rest of the first stage in the development of the play deals with the undermining of the former by the latter. To Iachimo, apparently dispassionate but in reality enslaved to his own sensuality,[20] pure virtue is inconceivable. In his attack upon Imogen, the overflow of physical imagery, product of

> the cloyed will,
> That satiate yet unsatisfied desire, that tub
> Both filled and running, (I. vi)

is at once intense and deeply repellent; this is a speaker to whose cynical intelligence passion seems sterile, even disgusting, but to whom no limiting conception of value is conceivable as a check to the senseless operations of desire. It is his resentment against the physical embodiment of such a conception in Imogen that causes him to intrigue against her chastity. She repels, easily enough, his direct assault, but is powerless to meet the guile by which he steals from her in sleep the "proof" of his conquest: powerless, above all, to overcome a plot which owes its success, finally, to the gullible complacency of her lover.

From this point, it is natural to pass to the scene (II. ii) in which the "temple" itself is finally subjected to direct siege by the furtive entry of Iachimo into Imogen's bedchamber. The assault upon her honor is characteristically wrapped, for Iachimo, in a pervading sense of decoration. Her eyes are "lights"

> canopied
> Under those windows, white and azure, laced
> With blue of heaven's own tinct: (II. ii)

the sleep in which she lies is "ape of death" and her sense

> a monument
> Thus in a chapel lying! (II. ii)

The introduction of a literary parallel with the "tale of Tereus," and the reference to the open book by Imogen's side, contribute to the same effect. They convey a sense of artificiality and opulence which correspond to a contrived quality of feeling. Iachimo's sensuality, which habitually dwells, for all its appearance of intensity, on the surface of things, is as much at home in this elaboration as Imogen's virtue is obscured, in a sense stifled by it; the liberation of her integrity by removal to another environment, as well as the awakening of her lover from the artificial dream which has led him to confuse the reality of love with its material symbol and to allow love itself to become involved in a cynical and irresponsible game of hazard, are essential features of the full development of the play.

At this point, and as a result of their common expulsion from the so-called civilized world, the story of the two lovers, transferred to Milford Haven, meets that of the lost sons of Cymbeline in a common exposure to "nature." They, in their discussion with Belarius (III. iii), balance a realization of the advantages of the simple life against their sense of its limitations. On the one hand,

> Haply this life is best,
> If quiet life be best;

on the other, Arviragus acknowledges his state to be "beastly" and feels its limitations as a prison:

> our cage
> We make a quire, as doth the prison'd bird,
> And sing our bondage freely. (III. iii)

Simplicity has limitations of its own, freedom under conditions of primitive life involves the "bondage" of the higher, specifically civilized faculties. These will only be awakened in Cymbeline's sons when they are restored to free loyalty and to a proper relationship with the father they have lost.

The scene (IV. ii) which brings Imogen and her brothers at last together is clearly intended, in its length and elaboration, to be of central importance. Through her exposure to tragic circumstance Imogen is learning how far beneath the surface appearances of courtliness lie the true sources of a "nobility" which "nature" possesses indeed, but which needs to be confirmed and deepened before being assumed into a more ample, civilized order; and through this development, she will attain to a true brotherly relationship as well as to the confirmation of her love for Posthumus. Meanwhile, it is precisely the failure of the merely sociable to sustain her that is stressed in her attitude:

> society is no comfort
> To one not sociable. (IV. ii)

The whole episode rests on an atmosphere of moral commonplace to which the development of the action and its poetic unfolding are meant to contribute a distinctive life. "Nature," following Belarius' aside, "hath meal and bran, contempt and grace," and Imogen's sojourn in his cave will lead to a more discerning separation of the one from the other.

The entry of Cloten and the threats with which he approaches Guiderius revive once more the theme of true nobility as the gift of "nature," in opposition to its appearance, symbolized in the possession of gorgeous clothes. "Natural" nobility may not be the crown of human virtue; but, when confronted with Cloten, it is seen to be in a very true sense its foundation. Cloten demands to be recognized by his possession of surface splendor—"know'st me not by my clothes"—before seeking to intimidate his opponent by declaring himself "son to the queen"; Guiderius replies by stressing the need for correspondence between inner worth and the pretensions of origin:

I am sorry for't; not seeming
So worthy as thy birth. (IV. ii)

The fight which follows, leading to the elimination of Cloten, serves as a decisive evaluation of his claim to nobility.

The final removal of Cloten is followed by the playing of the "solemn music" which announces Imogen's "death," and with it the opening of one of the most deliberately worked passages in the play. The phrasing is from the first pervasively sentimental. Personal emotion is set in an elaborate decorative framework, sound and image combining to give feeling a sense of remoteness on the basis of which the desired effect of acceptance may be achieved. Such is the purpose which underlies Belarius' grave apostrophe to sadness—

O melancholy!
Who ever yet could sound thy bottom? find
The ooze, to show what coast thy sluggish crare
Might easiliest harbour in?— (IV. ii)[21]

and such too the intention of Guiderius' following invocation:

With female fairies will his tomb be haunted,
And worms will not come to thee.

The tone of such passages presents a critical puzzle highly characteristic of *Cymbeline*. Their beauty cannot fail to strike us less as a new creation than as an evasion of true tragic feeling; unlike the best of Shakespeare's mature verse, their aim is primarily decorative, their relation to the situation described tenuous and remote. Were it not for the presence of similar passages in more successful plays of this period, such as *The Winter's Tale* and *The Tempest,* we might pass these off as imitations of the fashionable sentimentality of Fletcher. There is no reason, indeed, to prevent us from supposing that an influence of this kind exists; but, in view of the later successes, we shall probably do better to regard these speeches as a first attempt to elaborate a type of poetry which, if not convincing in isolation, will later be an essential element in a fuller and more various effect. It is part of the technique of the last plays to absorb direct emotion into a more complex poetic harmony, and this seems to be Shakespeare's intention here in his handling of the romantic conventions; except that in this part of *Cymbeline* the prevailing tone seems to be still that of a sentimentality which is its own justification, rather than that of a harmony in which tougher and more realistic states of feeling can find their context in reconciliation.

The impression of an incomplete security of purpose is heightened in the two central passages of the burial episode: Arviragus' catalogue of flowers and the famous dirge over Fidele's "body." The delicacy of feeling of the first strikes an unmistakable note:

> With fairest flowers,
> While summer lasts, and I live here, Fidele,
> I'll sweeten thy sad grave: thou shalt not lack
> The flower that's like thy face, pale primrose, nor
> The azured harebell, like thy veins; no, nor
> The leaf of eglantine, whom not to slander,
> Out-sweeten'd not thy breath. (IV. ii)

The whole passage turns on a romantic balance of beauty and subsistent melancholy. The "sweetening" effects of the "fairest flowers" promised by the speaker are set against a sense of temporal impermanence—"While summer lasts"—and of the sadness associated with the grave; and, as counterparts to the emotional background thus created, the flowers—"*pale* primrose" and the "azured harebell"—are evoked to produce a sense of personality dissolved, poetically transmuted in death. The beauty of the passage has obvious points of contact with Perdita's more perfect flower speech in *The Winter's Tale*.[22] It leaves us with a sense of evasion, even of dissatisfaction, to which Guiderius himself gives expression when he makes his realistic comment:

> Prithee, have done;
> And do not play in wench-like words with that
> Which is so serious. (IV. ii)

Throughout this part of *Cymbeline* there are signs of a certain effort to balance, in the utterances of the two brothers, contrasted attitudes to tragic experience. Arviragus proposes to express tragedy in song, transmuting feeling into harmonious dirges, whereas Guiderius says: "I cannot sing: I'll weep, and word it with thee," stressing the necessity for concordance between feeling and its expression:

> For notes of sorrow out of tune are worse
> Than priests and fanes that lie.

If the voice of "nature" clearly speaks here, condemning the fictions of courtly life and modifying his brother's more decorative attitude,

Belarius, recalling Cloten's end, reminds us that differences in rank have in the world their proper relevance:

> though mean and mighty, rotting
> Together, have one dust, yet reverence,
> That angel of the world, doth make distinction
> Of place 'tween high and low. (IV. ii)

Guiderius' reaction, again characteristically blunt, speaks with the voice of "nature":

> Thersites' body is as good as Ajax',
> When neither are alive; (IV. ii)

but the following dirge envelops the whole in a quality of poetic remoteness, evoking indeed the elements of a tragic experience, but seeing them as it were from afar. The feeling behind the reference to the "completed worldly task" and the following catalogue is evidently a residue of elements present in the tragedies; but the mellow sensation behind "golden," which is repeated elsewhere in the play,[23] combines significantly with a feeling for youth and innocence which has already been present in the early part of the scene and lends a note of peaceful "consummation" to the whole.

This, however, is not the last word. When Imogen wakes, after the departure of Belarius and his "sons," her first words give a moral quality to the rites we have just witnessed:

> These flowers are like the pleasures of the world;
> This bloody man the care on't. (IV. ii)

The speech thus introduced, however, leaves us yet again with a sense of imperfect concordance between action and expression. Imogen's statement that she has awakened from the dream of simple life in which she was a "cave-keeper" aims at a universality of human reference which recalls, for a moment and imperfectly, the phrasing of *King Lear:*

> 'Twas but a bolt of nothing, shot at nothing,
> Which the brain makes of fumes: our very eyes
> Are sometimes like our judgements, blind. (IV. ii)

The feeling, however, is not sustained. When Imogen passes from general moral statements to face her particular tragedy—the death, as she believes, of Posthumus—her words slip into an incoherence which is justified by the situation but adds little to its poetic development:

> Damn'd Pisanio
> Hath with his forged letters—damned Pisanio—
> From this most bravest vessel of the world
> Struck the main-top. (IV. ii)

This is rather a normal, ample gesture of Elizabethan verse drama than a contribution to the poetic integration of the main theme. It gives way to the entry of the Roman Lucio and the carrying of the plot a stage further by the incorporation of Imogen, disguised as Fidele, into the Roman army. The episode at Milford has played its part in the development of the general theme; what follows is the incorporation of the values there expressed into a wider range of action and, more particularly, the assimilation of "natural" virtue through patriotic dedication and further exposure to death into a more ample field of harmony.

The last act of *Cymbeline,* whilst maintaining the inequalities so typical of the play as a whole, has some of its most interesting effects to offer. The main symbolic structure leading to the final reconciliation is clear enough, as is the aim of absorbing personal vicissitudes into a more universal inclusiveness. To this conception the "death" of Imogen already belongs. It implies, as we have seen, a certain liberation, and to it now corresponds the captivity of Posthumus and the tone of his meditations in prison:

> Most welcome, bondage; for thou art a way,
> I think, to liberty. (V. iv)

Both attitudes, in so far as they reflect a mood of tempered acceptance, are proper preludes to the battle in which Posthumus and the sons of Cymbeline find their natural place fighting against the foreign invader in the orbit of patriotism. Patriotism, however, is not the last word. The Britons, though they defeat the Roman invader, are finally absorbed into an order more than patriotic, and accept the payment of tribute, which is the sign of a unity that surpasses the national. The play ends, not on a note of victory, but on one of reconciliation, coupled with an ample gesture of thanksgiving. To the Soothsayer's declaration of the relevance of supernatural purpose—

> The fingers of the powers above do tune
> The harmony of this peace—

Cymbeline, restored to true self-knowledge and to his position as royal symbol of unity, replies with a gesture of forgiveness and a final offering of thanks:

> Laud we the gods;
> And let our crooked smokes climb to their nostrils
> From our blest altars. (V. v)

In no part of the play, perhaps, is the link which binds it to the development of the final Shakespearean conception so fully realized.

The sense of having reached a new and decisive stage in the action is brought home to us as a suitably chastened Posthumus, for some time past displaced by Imogen and the sons of Cymbeline, is reintroduced in his disguise. The description of the battle, as placed in his mouth, is, to the most cursory reading, intensely alive in its free, supple adaptation of the resources of speech to the blank verse construction. Against the suggestion of divine control, indicated in "the heavens fought," the speaker builds up a fine impression of vast and powerful action. The first lines stress the magnitude of the British defeat, transforming it into a tide of adversity by which they are carried, their wings "destitute," their army "broken," "all flying" toward the "strait lane" which is to be the focal point of the whole episode. Against this helplessness, and balancing the British dejection with the corresponding confidence of victory, the Roman enemy is evoked in all his exaltation, "full-hearted," "lolling the tongue with slaughtering." The sense of an irresistible tide is wonderfully conveyed, at the peak of the Roman success, by the carry-over of the blank verse rhythm in the description of the victims—

> struck down
> Some mortally, some slightly touched, some falling
> Merely through fear;

and this, in turn, culminates once more in the "strait pass," where the critical moment is beautifully indicated in the complex final reference to

> cowards living
> To die with lengthened shame. (V. iii)

By this culminating phrase, the action is carried to its decisive turning point in the "lane," and with it to the affirmation that life dishonorably saved is a form of death which calls for redemption by a reaction on the moral as well as the military level.

The reaction, indeed, is given substance in the second part of Posthumus' description. After the short question interposed by the Lord, his account proceeds to a decisive reversal of the original ebbing rhythm. It opens with a more detailed description of the crucial "lane," of the "ancient soldier," and of the two "striplings" who stood in its defense. In their reported words to the routed British troops, the verse for the first time ceases to ebb, reflects in its change of movement a repeated emphasis on the idea implied in the thrice-repeated call to "stand":

> To darkness fleet souls that fly backwards. Stand;
> Or we are Romans, and will give you that
> Like beasts which you shun beastly, and may save
> But to look back in frown: stand, stand! (V. iii)

The pattern of words and rhythms at this point responds admirably to the purpose in hand. The first line flows naturally to its culmination in "backwards," and then balances it in the single, isolated syllable of command. The threat of the very death which the soldiers are seeking "beastly" to escape, but which will come upon them "like beasts," emphasizes the balance of physical situation and decisive moral choice; and, in the light of this, the earlier "backwards" is balanced by a "back" that implies the opposite of flight and leads finally to the firmness of "stand, stand." The accumulation of phrases, in other words, whilst recalling that of the early part of the speech, is now built up round the idea of resistance and leads finally to the reversal implied in "Part shame, *part spirit renewed.*"

From this moment, the rhythm of recovery makes itself felt irresistibly to the end of the description:

> Then began
> A stop i' the chaser, a retire; anon
> A rout, confusion thick: forthwith they fly
> Chickens, the way which they stoop'd eagles; slaves,
> The strides they victors made: and now our cowards,
> Like fragments in hard voyages, became
> The life o' the need: having found the back-door open
> Of the unguarded hearts, heavens, how they wound!

> Some slain before, some dying, some their friends
> O'erborne i' the former wave: ten chased by one
> Are now each one the slaughter-man of twenty;
> Those that would die or ere resist are grown
> The mortal bugs o' the field. (V. iii)

At this point, and henceforth, the reversal of the previous ebb is decisive. The verse grows from the opening check implied in "stop," in which the reversal of the retreat is finally concentrated, through the "retire" of the pursuer to the accumulated effect of "rout" and "confusion thick." Confusion itself, indeed, is here given controlled expression, subordinated to the development of a coherent artistic purpose. The beautifully telescoped syntax of the reference to

> Chickens, the way which they stoop'd eagles; slaves,
> The strides they victors made,

at once adds breathless immediacy to the change of fortunes and relates it to the new rhythmic development of the whole; intensity and the breathlessness of the moment are combined in a single comprehensive effect. To this splendid rhythmic control answers an equal vigor and immediacy of speech, conveyed in phrases such as "fragments in hard voyages" and "the life o' the need," as well as in the grotesque power of

> having found the back-door open
> Of the unguarded hearts.

With language and verse movement thus fused in a single, forward-flowing impression, the way is open for a full expression of the rhythm of recovery, and the speech attains complete freedom of movement in the cumulative power of the final lines. "A narrow lane, an old man, and two boys." The central situation, further invested by the Lord's wondering comment with a symbolic overtone of its own, has become the point of departure for a process by which rout has been turned into recovery, confusion into restored harmony.

Posthumus, however, before he can take his place in this movement, must pass through the shadow of death and imprisonment. In the scene which follows (V. iv), he declares himself more "fettered" by the accusations of his own conscience than by the external fact of his imprisonment. The "penitent instrument" of his reflections is coupled with a sense of the "mercy" of the "gods" and of his own mortal dependence:

For Imogen's dear life take mine; and though
'Tis not so dear, yet 'tis a life; you coin'd it:
'Tween man and man, they weigh not every stamp;
Though light, take pieces for the figure's sake:
You rather mine, being yours; and so, great powers,
If you will take this audit, take this life,
And cancel these cold bonds. (V. iv)

What is being stated here is something very like an adaptation to the circumstances of the Christian view of atonement. Springing from the deep sense of mortality which Shakespeare shares with other writers of the age, the argument proceeds, after admitting the inequality between the "value" of Imogen, murdered as an indirect consequence of the speaker's own behavior, and his repentance, to stress their common dependence on the "gods" in restoration of the balance. His life, though less "dear" than Imogen's, has been equally "coined" by the "gods," and in their common dependence at least there is an implication of equality. "'Tween man and man, they weigh not every stamp"; in their common need for mercy, at least, men are equal, and the processes of divine forgiveness can properly ignore the discriminations and evaluations of relative guilt which are a necessary part of the "cold bonds" of human justice.

The peculiar vision which appears to Posthumus in his following dream, though it falls naturally into place at this point as a supernatural intervention, is one of the puzzles of the play. The verse, taken as a whole, is poor enough to make the theory of interpolation plausible, and yet there is no denying that the episode, like so much in the early part of *Pericles* and like the masque in *The Tempest,* is firmly integrated into the structure of the play. Whatever may be thought of its expression, there can be little doubt, in particular, that the words of Sicilius immediately after Jupiter's withdrawal are impregnated with a sense of supernatural "grace" that is entirely in line with the spirit of these final romances:

He came in thunder; his celestial breath
Was sulphurous to smell: the holy eagle
Stoop'd, as to foot us: his ascension is
More sweet than our blest fields: his royal bird
Prunes the immortal wing and cloys his beak,
As when his god is pleased. (V. iv)

The feeling conveyed in "*celestial* breath," "*holy* eagle," and "*sweet* ascension," in "*blest* fields" and "*immortal* wing" is, cumulatively speaking, unmistakable. It belongs to the imagination that put into the mouth of Banquo the description of Macbeth's castle at Inverness[24] or evoked, in *The Winter's Tale,* the holiness of the "sacrifice" to the oracle in Delphos in terms of "sweet air," "delicate climate," fertility, and the "celestial" quality—"ceremonious, solemn, and unearthly"—of the offering.[25] Royalty, holiness, and immortality are fused in an impression of transforming "grace" which will, in due course, be taken up in the splendid, sun-drenched vision which rounds off the concluding scene.

The full implications of this complex scene are still, however, to be completed. Posthumus in prison is in a state of trial, balancing appearance and substance against the sense of imminent death; and, accordingly, it is proper that the revelation enigmatically offered comes to him not as enlightenment but as puzzlement and obscurity, a further instance of the apparently inconsequent fabric that goes to make up the dream of living:

> 'Tis still a dream; or else such stuff as madmen
> Tongue, and brain not: either both, or nothing:
> Or senseless speaking, or a speaking such
> As sense cannot untie. Be what it is,
> The action of my life is like it. (V. iv)

Just as Prospero's famous vision of the dream fabric of our experienced world[26] proceeds from his "beating brain," is set against the brutality of Caliban's design upon him in a way that forces actuality upon us, so here the vivid energy of phrasing corresponds to the felt pressure of reality. Of that pressure, Posthumus' imprisonment and impending death are the external impression. The moment has come for self-examination, for the unraveling of complex and contradictory themes; the final resolution indicated in Jupiter's words—

> Whom best I love I cross; to make my gift,
> The more delay'd, delighted— (V. iv)

is still bound up with fantasy and dream.

The final grave prose dialogue with the Gaoler rounds off this fine scene in a most fitting manner. The elements that go to make up the Gaoler's "philosophic" attitude are, of course, Elizabethan commonplaces, used as such by many inferior writers; a phrase like "he that sleeps fears not the tooth-ache" bears an air of self-conscious truism that can easily be paralleled among Shakespeare's lesser contemporaries. What really matters, however, is the delicate and deeply individual balancing of contrary attitudes, the setting of death conceived as liberation—an emotion itself deeply, genuinely felt—against an equal sense of the uncertainty which the contemplation of mortality inspires: "look you, sir, you know not which way you shall go." The Gaoler hesitates between the conceptions of death as release, as implying freedom from the burden of life, and as obscurity, entry into the unknowable; and to this Posthumus opposes a feeling akin to religious conviction, which naturally accompanies the distinctively moral outlook which characterizes his utterances throughout this part of the play: "there are none want eyes to direct them the way I am going, but such as wink and will not use them." The tone of the dialogue, however, remains one of balance, of poised alternatives. Posthumus' mood of religious acceptance is set against the Gaoler's skepticism, expressed above all in his clear statement of the alternatives that face the prisoner:

> you must either be directed by some that take upon them to know, or take upon yourself that which I am sure you do not know, or jump the after-enquiry on your own peril. (V. iv)

The alternatives as here stated are an acceptance of spiritual authority, itself given a certain sense of pretension in "some that *take upon them* to know," an admission of the helplessness of individual judgment ("take upon yourself that which *I am sure you do not know*"), or a plunge into the unknowable that recalls, in its expression, Macbeth's frustrated impulse to "jump the life to come."[27] All these are, in the Gaoler's eyes, equally confessions of impotence, for the only certainty is, in his own terms, "how you shall speed in your journey's end, I think you'll never return to tell one." In this balance of opposing attitudes, none accepted as final but each serving to add immediacy to its fellow, the genuine Shakespearean note makes itself unmistakably felt.

The final scene uses the familiar mechanism of romantic reconciliation for symbolic ends of its own, working through successive stages to a final inclusive effect. The first stage is to bring Belarius and his charges before Cymbeline, who is still unaware of his true relationship to them, so that they may receive the knighthood conferred by his royal "grace"; the second disposes of the queen and her machinations through her suicide, in which, having been "cruel to the world," she concludes "most cruel to herself." These, however, are no more than preliminaries. The entry of the Roman prisoners opens the way for Cymbeline to demand of Iachimo, with Imogen's prompting, an account of the diamond he wears upon his finger. The confession leads to the self-revelation of Posthumus and to his admission of a guilt that amounts, in his own eyes, to sacrilege:

> it is I
> That all the abhorred things o' the earth amend
> By being worse than they. I am Posthumus
> That kill'd thy daughter. (V. v)

Finally, in his hysterical remorse, he strikes "Fidele," and her fall is the occasion for Pisanio to declare the true identity of the victim. It is at this point that the spirit of the episode comes to life in Cymbeline's charged phrase:

> If this be so, the gods do mean to strike me
> To death with mortal joy. (V. v)

The balance thus asserted between life and death, joy and mortality, is clearly akin to the mood of the final scenes of *Pericles*.[28] It raises the tone to one of spiritual integration, in which sorrow, neither forgotten nor set aside, is transmuted into an element of deeper joy. With the mystery of her "death" finally revealed, the way is open for Posthumus and Imogen to be reconciled, in lines pregnant with symbolic meaning and unmistakably belonging to the spirit of Shakespeare's last romances. "I was dead," says Imogen, and her words, beyond the mere recalling of a past event, bear a distinctive quality of marvel that itself implies the integration of the action on the symbolical level. In the light of her following question—

> Why did you throw your wedded lady from you?—

Posthumus' intense, broken exclamation, "My queen, my life, my wife," combining the personal and familiar with the vivifying and the regally transcendent, is given its proper counterpart, and the embrace of the lovers surrounded by intimations of a harmony more than merely personal:

> Hang there like fruit, my soul,
> Till the tree die! (V. v)

The feeling, in fact, is so fine, so precious, that it can only be described in terms of "soul," and by relating the spiritual suggestion to an evocation of the rich fertility of nature. Cymbeline, in turn, responds with words that stress the closeness and value of the reconciliation which has just flooded him with a rebirth of emotions long presumed dead; again, like Pericles, he salutes his daughter as "my flesh, my child,"[29] and the strength of his feeling is such that he senses himself reduced to the state of a "dullard" by his incapacity to express it. Finally, the reconciliation assumes its proper external form. Imogen, kneeling, requests the "blessing" of her father, the tears of whose mingled happiness and grief become, in his own mind, "holy water," a transformation of mortal sorrow into spiritual joy. In the light of these discoveries, the queen and her machinations have become "naught," the unwitting cause of the miracle taking place before his eyes:

> long of her it was
> That we meet here so strangely. (V. v)

The pattern of plot, thus filled out with a corresponding harmony of poetic imagery, assumes its complete, balanced form.

The spirit of restored unity which dominates the conclusion needs, however, to be further confirmed by Cymbeline's recognition of his lost sons. Belarius prepares the way by invoking upon his charges, even as he delivers them to their father, "the benediction of the covering heavens"; the notions of benediction and reconciliation are, as ever, closely connected, and Cymbeline's answering expression of grief at the very moment when the way is clear for him to return to felicity—"Thou weep'st, and speak'st"—is also significant. The convenient recalling of the mole on Guiderius' neck belongs, of course, to the external commonplaces of romance; but it is followed by an intensification of the idea of recovered paternity in Cymbeline's exclamation:

> O, what am I?
> A mother to the birth of three? Ne'er mother
> Rejoiced deliverance more. (V. v)

The lines clearly contain the various elements that contribute to the final emotional transformation of Cymbeline's grief. Birth, and a certain rediscovery of the self, are indicated; so are the pangs of "deliverance" by which sorrow finds relief in compensating joy. In the light of this intensified feeling, the paternal blessing falls naturally into place—"Blest pray you be"—and is in turn associated with the restoration of natural order:

> That, after this strange parting from your orbs,
> You may reign in them now. (V. v)

The completing dialogue with Imogen:—

> *Cymbeline:* Thou hast lost by this a kingdom.
> *Imogen:* No, my lord;
> I have got two worlds by it— (V. v)

with its characteristic sense of overtone, of a poetic content that surpasses its occasion, combines with a stressing of the sanctity of intimate family relationships—

> O, my gentle brothers . . .
> you call'd me brother,
> When I was but your sister; I you brothers,
> When you were so indeed— (V. v)

to produce at least a verbal sense of latent significance springing through to the surface; later plays will wed this sense more closely to a relevant plot, but the poetic conditions for the full development are clearly present, at least in potentiality. How far they can be taken will be seen in *The Winter's Tale* and *The Tempest.*

The development of the action is now ready for completion. Cymbeline, once more king over himself and the realm he has seen victorious, points the way to a final act of religious affirmation, in which the consummation of marriage between Imogen and Posthumus will be one with the rendering of thanks for victory achieved:

> Let's quit this ground,
> And smoke the temple with our sacrifices. (V. v)

Once more, the ideas of sacrifice and worship anticipate a fuller development in *The Winter's Tale.*[30] With Iachimo's confession of guilt and the forgiving gesture of Posthumus the way is open for an act of religious integration which will give its justification to the "gracious season" into which the action has at last entered. To confirm this conclusion on the "political" level, victorious Britain, through its king, acknowledges its "wonted tribute" to the universal empire of Rome, reintegrates itself in bonds of peace and equality to a conception vaster even than its own vindicated patriotism; and finally both states are united in subjection to a spiritual vision, full of mellow, "golden" richness, which is itself expressed in Shakespeare's best manner:

> The fingers of the powers above do tune
> The harmony of this peace. (V. v)

"Harmony," indeed, on a scale of ever-increasing spaciousness, is the keynote of this conclusion. "The Roman eagle," lessening herself, is gathered into the "beams of the sun," vanishes, is absorbed into a greater union; and the final reference, sustained by verse at once free, ample, and superbly concise, is to sacrifice and the praise of the "gods." In this final vision of consecration to a unifying purpose, the personal issues of the play, the love of Imogen for Posthumus maintained through trials and separation, and the integration of natural simplicity to the graces of civilized order, find in subjection to a universal unity, through the figure of Cymbeline as father and king, their proper culmination.

THE WINTER'S TALE

The plot of *The Winter's Tale* is a perfect example of the symbolic technique perfected by Shakespeare in his last plays. It is a story of the division created in love and friendship by the passage of time and by the action of "blood," and of the healing of these divisions through penitence and renewed personal devotion. The play's successive stages coincide with the development of the plot. This opens with a statement by Leontes' counselor, Camillo, of the close friendship which has since childhood bound together Leontes and Polixenes, kings, respectively, of Sicily and Bohemia. Camillo's prose, however, not only prepares for the facts of the story but also proceeds to develop the obscurities which underlie them. Beneath the closeness of their intimacy, as yet unrealized but implicitly present, lie hidden seeds of division:

> Sicilia cannot show himself over-kind to Bohemia. They were trained together in their childhoods; and there rooted betwixt them then such an affection, which cannot choose but branch now. Since their

> more mature dignities and royal necessities made separation of their society, their encounters, though not personal, have been royally attornied with interchange of gifts, letters, loving embassies; that they have seemed to be together, though absent; shook hands, as over a vast; and embraced, as it were, from the ends of opposed winds. (I. i)

As a mere exposition of fact, this would be elaborate to a fault. It is, however, more than that. The force of the passage lies in the combination under one set of images of two processes apparently contradictory—that of natural, unified development existing side by side with that of spreading division. The word "branch" can imply either the natural unity of living growth from a central trunk or a spreading division within that growth. If the affection that unites the kings is such that "it cannot choose but branch," this may mean either that it must continue to grow and bear fruit or that it must inevitably separate and break down as it grows. In other words, this friendship, though rooted and natural in its origins, bears within itself the possibility of future disunion. The concluding lines stress the same idea, and the reference to "opposed winds" further anticipates not only the emotional storm in which the present unity is shortly to be tested but also the actual tempest in which Leontes' daughter Perdita is lost and found, and which is to play a decisive part in the whole construction.

The opening scene, then, suggests how the plot will develop. There will be a conflict between Leontes and Polixenes, a conflict caused by Leontes' jealous conviction that Polixenes has usurped the affections of his wife Hermione. The first movement will be the breakup, already anticipated, of happy human relationships by the folly of Leontes; the exact nature of this breakup needs careful study. Since Shakespeare, as usual, develops at the same time both his plot and its implications, we are soon given a further key passage:

Polixenes: We were, fair queen,
Two lads that thought there was no more behind,
But such a day to-morrow as to-day,
And to be boy eternal.
Hermione: Was not my lord
The verier wag o' the two?

Polixenes: We were as twinn'd lambs that did frisk i' the sun,
And bleat the one at the other: what we changed
Was innocence for innocence; we knew not
The doctrine of ill-doing, nor dreamed
That any did. Had we pursued that life,
And our weak spirits ne'er been higher rear'd
With stronger blood, we should have answer'd heaven
Boldly "not guilty," the imposition clear'd
Hereditary ours. (I. ii)

The importance of youth and springtime in this play is sufficiently obvious, and this passage first shows the reason for it. Shakespeare is using this description to point a contrast between spontaneous human emotion and the continual pressure of time—a friction clearly connected with the "metaphysical" ambiguity we have already considered in certain of the sonnets.[31] Time, in brief, which brings friendships to maturity also destroys them, just as, in the earlier works, it destroyed the love which developed with it. But Polixenes' speech adds something which is new in *The Winter's Tale*—the connection of this friction with sin, "the doctrine of ill-doing." The action of time, as seen at this stage in the play, is a corrupting action; experience, as it enters into the life of innocence, destroys the foundations of spontaneous friendship. The youthful freshness which is set against this deterioration is coupled with an ominous ignorance of "ill-doing." Its beauty is nostalgic and pathetically defenseless ("Temptations have since then been born to's," as Polixenes puts it), an easy prey to the inevitable action of the "sneaping winds" whose imminence has already been suggested.

Polixenes' account, however, takes us even further than this. The cause of Leontes' quarrel with his friend is, significantly enough, jealousy, the conviction that he has betrayed him with Hermione, who is known to be with child. Polixenes' introduction of the idea of "blood," coupled with the birth of this obsession in Leontes, gives the "idyllic" content of the speech a fresh meaning by relating it to the problems raised by the nature of sexual passion. "Blood," in fact, and the action of time are here fused into a single intuition; that is what is behind the contrast between "stronger blood" and "weak spirits." The friendship between the two kings has rested so far on the youthful state of innocence; based on a sentimental ignoring of the reality of the temporal process, it has assumed with pathetic simplicity that it was possible to remain "boy eternal." The realities of human nature, however, make this impossible. Boyhood is necessarily a state of transition. The development of the sensual life, "stronger" than the innocence which preceded it, is necessary to complete maturity of the spirit. Without it, the ideal of eternal youth and pastoral innocence is "weak," though lovely. It is an ideal which at once depends upon its illusory timelessness and is vitiated by it; the continual action of time, here equated with the growth of a man into sexual maturity, gives the necessary fullness of the "blood" to human experience, but also destroys it by exposure to the impersonal laws of mutability. The sensual life of man, while giving substance to his development, implies the subjection of his ideal innocence to the capacity for evil. Only through a conscious reaction to tragedy, and the consequent acceptance of deeper experience, can this idyllic state of childhood grow into an independent, conscious maturity.

For the moment, however, this harmonious development is no more than a remote possibility. Meanwhile, the capacity for sensual passion which time imposes upon man bears a double interpretation. It may be good, if it leads to its natural fulfillment in the creative unity of the family, or evil and destructive, in the form of egoism and its consequences, jealousies overcoming all restraint of reason. In Leontes it is the evil impulse which first comes to the surface, destroying his friendship with Polixenes and leading him to turn upon Hermione with an animal intensity of feeling. That his jealousy, so often dismissed as the product of a dreary obsession, is in fact the moving force in this, the first stage in the development of the play, should by now be clear. The power of the verse in which it finds expression is, indeed, a sufficient guarantee of this:

> Too hot, too hot!
> To mingle friendship far is mingling bloods.
> I have *tremor cordis* on me: my heart dances;
> But not for joy; not joy . . .
>
> But to be paddling palms and pinching fingers,
> As now they are . . .
>
> They're here with me already; whispering, rounding
> "Sicilia is a so-forth": 'tis far gone
> When I shall gust it last. (I. ii)

Shakespeare's rhythms were never more impressive, never more delicately adjusted to the breaks in an overwrought consciousness, never more vivid in their ultra-sensual repulsion from the physical. This is apparent in the superbly palated "gust," allying Leontes' loathing to the offending of a highly sensitive taste. *Troilus and Cressida* abounds in such imagery, though the adaptation to the dramatic ends proposed is there less completely realized. The delicately broken line—"I have *tremor cordis* on me; my heart dances"—could, again, only have come from Shakespeare at the height of his power. Leontes plays his part in the play at this stage as the "embossed carbuncle"—to echo *King Lear*[32]—in the organism of human relationships, as one by-product, perversely and destructively dynamic, of that organism's growth through rising "blood" to maturity.

It is significant that, having reached this stage, Leontes declares himself ready to invert reality itself in the following of his released instincts. "Affection," he affirms, makes "possible things not so held," truth is confounded with dreams, and the unreal is "coactive" with reality to the "infection" of his peace of mind:

> Should all despair
> That have revolted wives, the tenth of mankind
> Would hang themselves. Physic for't there's none;
> It is a bawdy planet, that will strike
> Where 'tis predominant. (I. ii)

With the universalizing of his own infirm obsession into a not very impressive piece of Elizabethan commonplace, the infection of Leontes' mind is substantially complete. In the following exchange with Camillo his concern is not so much to discover the truth as to confirm what he holds in his own mind to be certain. In his perversity, indeed, and not unlike Othello before him, he craves for this confirmation as an alternative to the sense of chaos which is one of the accompaniments of unleashed passion; for, "if this be nothing,"

> Why, then, the world and all that's in't is nothing;
> The covering sky is nothing; Bohemia nothing;
> My wife is nothing; nor nothing have these nothings,
> If this be nothing. (I. ii)[33]

The whole of Leontes' behavior has now become a frenzied building-up of supposed certainties on "nothing," on the baselessness of an irrational emotion followed to the limits of self-centered impulse. The consequences of this development, as they affect the world beyond him, soon make themselves felt in the choice offered to Camillo. To the loyal courtier it is clear that his master is of a "diseased opinion" and, as such, intensely dangerous; but the only effect of his protest is to provoke the accusation of lying and the command, based on royal authority, to poison Polixenes. Thus placed in a position where loyalties clash, Camillo's final comment stresses at once the irrationality of his master's behavior, "in rebellion with himself" (I. ii), and its extension implied in the determination to have "all that are his so too." As always, the introduction of passionate division in the mind of a king is followed by a split in the fabric of society, whose unity is only conceivable under a royal guarantee.

A full understanding of Leontes' position is furthered by referring to the contrasts of feeling in Polixenes when he becomes aware of Leontes' suspicions:

> O, then my best blood turn
> To an infected jelly, and my name
> Be yoked with his that did betray the Best!
> Turn then my freshest reputation to
> A savour that may strike the dullest nostril
> Where I arrive, and my approach be shunn'd,
> Nay, hated too, worse than the great'st infection
> That e'er was heard or read. (I. ii)

The sensitive quality of these lines, based on a delicate balancing of opposed impressions, is notable. On the one hand, there is an insistence upon "infection" allied to the odor of decay; on the other, freshness is associated with the idea of boundless value twice stressed, and given a specifically religious sanction in the use of "best." This peculiar quality of "freshness," with its persistent symbolic overtones, is as familiar in the great tragedies as the notion of contagious infirmity set against it. Lear, awakening from his madness, was dressed in "fresh garments,"[34] and in *Macbeth* infection plays an important part in the account given of the "healing benediction" of the English king,[35] in the Doctor's work at Dunsinane, and in the diseased disorder of the murderer's mind. The contrast, in fact, implies that Shakespeare is once more using his unrivaled control of sensual imagery to set forth, through Leontes' jealousy and its effects, a contrast between the good and evil elements of experience, between the fullness of maturity crowned by "grace" and the vicious and disintegrating savagery of uncontrolled "blood."

The mention of "grace" reminds us that the behavior of Leontes throughout this scene, and indeed in the whole play, is only fully comprehensible in a context provided by the concept of family unity. Of that concept, in its full moral significance, Hermione is the gracious symbol. "Grace" is a word to note in Shakespeare's later plays. We have already found it in *Macbeth*[36] applied to Malcolm's restoration of just kingship and to the sanctity and healing powers of Edward the Confessor. Cleopatra's triumphant beauty on her throne was described as her "strong toil of grace,"[37] and the last plays are full of the word. Its implications, which shift and develop in the intricate pattern of the plays, are hard to define. In *The Winter's Tale* Shakespeare seems to reinforce the Christian associations already acquired in *Macbeth* with a deeply personal intuition of natural fertility, fulfilled in the intimate unity of the family. The play, indeed, contains a profound and highly individual effort to bring the impasse suggested by his exploration of the part played by "blood" in human experience—a part at once destructive and potentially maturing—into relation with feelings which imply the understanding of a positive spiritual conception. Only so can we read the poetry of Hermione. From her earliest appearance she is deliberately surrounded with religious associations and intimations of value. Polixenes addresses her at the outset as "most *sacred* lady" (I. ii), and backs the apostrophe with a further reference to "your *precious* self." Value and spiritual perfection are, indeed, closely associated with her in the eyes of those who surround her, and it is not long before her own words bring the idea of "grace" still more intimately before us:

> My last good deed was to entreat his stay:
> What was my first? it has an elder sister,
> Or I mistake you: O, would her name were Grace! (I. ii)

And when Leontes has replied, she comments, "'Tis Grace indeed." In her trials too, the same note is stressed—

> this action I now go on
> Is for my better grace— (II. i)

in which the idea of purification behind Lear's sufferings is repeated with a much more explicit sense of religious values.

This, however, is only a part of Hermione's significance; the rest of it lies in her relationship to Leontes and in her child. Leontes' jealousy, as its true nature finds confirmation in his mounting brutality, is much more than criminal shortsightedness. It is a sensual repudiation by the uncontrolled "blood" of a right sexual relationship, of natural fertility consecrated, given its proper spiritual context in the bond of marriage. In his insults Leontes stresses brutally the fact that his wife is with child:

> let her sport herself
> With that she's big with; for 'tis Polixenes
> Has made thee swell thus. (II. i)

His words echo, in the form of perverted brutality, the conversation between Hermione's ladies at the beginning of the scene, words which give a rich and natural quality to her state:

> *First Lady:* The queen your mother rounds apace; we shall
> Present our services to a fine new prince
> One of these days . . .
> *Second Lady:* She is spread of late
> Into a goodly bulk: good time encounter her! (II. i)

The "rounding" of the queen is here envisaged as part of a natural, beneficent process, "goodly" and destined, in "good time," to find its proper fulfillment in maternity. The unsoftened harshness of Leontes' use of "big" and "swell," with their implication of the grotesque and the deformed, appear in the light of this contrast as a deliberate inversion of nature which will produce its own fruit in the disruption of normal human relationships.

That disruption, indeed, follows logically from the nature of Leontes' sin, now bearing fruit in action. His is more than a personal offense: it is against "nature," and so against the "grace" for which Hermione in her simple integrity stands. The perverted keenness of his senses, at once sharpened and debased by the action of "blood," have become a spiritual "infection." It is the essence of Leontes' tragedy that, having raised an irrational and indeed unnatural impulse to the status of certain knowledge, he makes it the foundation of his whole being. Regarding his suspicion, with unconscious irony, as "just censure" and a "true opinion," he follows Othello in craving for lesser knowledge and in regarding himself as less "blest" than "accursed" by what he believes he knows. His knowledge, indeed, as it emerges through the powerful expression of his disillusionment, is "infected." It leads to abhorrence, to a sense of nausea which characterizes the whole of his utterance in the early stages of the play:

> There may be in the cup
> A spider steep'd, and one may drink, depart,
> And yet partake no venom; for his knowledge
> Is not infected; but if one present
> The abhorr'd ingredient to his eye, make known
> How he hath drunk, he cracks his gorge, his sides,
> With violent hefts. I have drunk, and seen the spider. (II. i)

Like Othello again, he rests the entire foundation of his being upon the assertion as truth of his error, in words which clearly convey the universal implications of his disorder:

> if I mistake
> In those foundations which I build upon,
> The centre is not big enough to bear
> A school-boy's top. (II. i)

The whole of Leontes' subsequent progress, from this moment to that in which he finally awakens to his folly, is contained in this image. Upon the central point of his illusory certainty his mind revolves in an ever-increasing rhythm of lunacy to the final collapse. Before that collapse is complete, he has dragged the whole of his world with him into ruin. Because of the "infection" in his spirit Hermione suffers, the natural human relationship which binds him to Polixenes is rudely broken, the young prince Mamillius dies out of the course of nature, and the winter of the gods' displeasure rests upon them all. The first stage of the play's development is complete with the withdrawal and supposed death of Hermione. The rest of it is to show how "grace" can spring from the jarrings and maladjustments of "blood," the summer of right human relationship out of the winter of disorder and penance.

The turning point of *The Winter's Tale* is not so much the long, central gap of sixteen years as the scene (III. iii) in which Antigonus leaves Hermione's child, banished by order of Leontes, on the desert shore of Bohemia, where it is found and cherished by shepherds. Before this, at the very point where the consequences of Leontes' passionate impulses are becoming apparent, the action shifts for a moment to an entirely different plane, indicates in passing the positive spiritual forces which are already, at this apparently unpropitious moment, in charge of the action. Such is the meaning of the short dialogue between Cleomenes and Dion (III. i) on their return to Sicily with the gods' vindication of Hermione's innocence. Placed at this particular moment, before the full tragedy has been unfolded, the peculiar "freshness" which invests Cleomenes' account of Delphos is doubly significant:

> The climate's delicate, the air most sweet,
> Fertile the isle, the temple much surpassing
> The common praise it bears. (III. i)

We are immediately reminded of Banquo's description of Macbeth's castle,[38] similarly placed to point a contrast with the growing darkness of the surrounding action. There too the air was "delicate," and the impression of holiness associated with the king's arrival was reflected in images of fertility and the nimble sweetness of the senses. This is poetry, indeed, in which exquisite sensual refinement appears as the tangible manifestation of a hallowed state. Associated in Dion's reply with the "celestial habits" and "reverence" of the priests and the spiritual quality, "ceremonious, solemn, and unearthly," of the sacrifice, it becomes the prelude to a return journey which is "rare, pleasant, speedy," filled to the brim with a pervading impression of the supernatural (an impression, however, which is itself conveyed through the continuous, intense operation of the senses), and leads to a taking up of the key word of the play in the final prayer, "*gracious* be the issue."

This scene, however, for all its beauty, is no more than a prelude to the introduction into the action of Perdita. The first "movement" of the play is closed by the series of calamities which concluded Hermione's trial, ending in Leontes' broken confession of guilt:

> Apollo's angry; and the heavens themselves
> Do strike at my injustice,

and the gesture of acceptance which follows it:

> Come and lead me
> To these sorrows. (III. ii)

The next scene (III. iii) which, short as it is, may be said to constitute the second "movement" of the play, links the past and future action in the person of Perdita, looking back to the folly of Leontes at the same time that it anticipates the final resolution. The singularly beautiful prose in which the storm and shipwreck are evoked strikes a new note, which can, however, be paralleled in other plays of this period, notably in *Pericles* and *The Tempest.* The disturbed skies and the angry sea carry on the impression of the divine displeasure ("The heavens with what we have in hand are angry," as the Mariner puts it), and create a background for the central remark of the whole scene: "thou mettest with things dying, I with things newborn." This scarcely needs the parallel from *Pericles*—

did you not name a tempest,
A birth and death?— (V. iii)

to give it point. The implication of the two phrases is indeed the same. Out of storm and tempest, themselves connected in the symbolic scheme with the results of human folly, is born a new life, destined to grow in the course of time into the harmony of "grace" and to lead to final reconciliation. From this moment, Hermione's child is connected with the general theme of "grace" and fertility born out of passion and jealousy. The child is the product of that "mingling of bloods" which, misinterpreted in the light of his obsession, so repelled Leontes and jarred upon his peace; but it is also the outcome of that natural human fertility which is the soil of "grace" itself, so that it looks not only back to the decisions of the past but forward to the reconciliation of the future.

In this way we are led up, in what we may agree to call the third "movement," to the great pastoral scene (IV. iv) which is by no means a simple, almost naïve contrast to the preceding bitterness, but an artistically logical development of the situation. The closely woven strands of feeling that run through the apparent simplicity of this episode have already been foreshadowed in Polixenes' account of his youthful friendship with Leontes; they are now further developed in the dialogue upon the flowers between himself and Perdita. The pastoral convention has never been put to more individual use than in Perdita's speech:

Sir, the year growing ancient,
Not yet on summer's death, nor on the birth
Of trembling winter, the fairest flowers o' the season
Are our carnations and streak'd gillyvors,
Which some call nature's bastards: of that kind
Our rustic garden's barren; and I care not
To get slips of them. (IV. iv)

A reader aware of the possibilities of Shakespearean language will not pass by the beautiful linking of summer and winter, birth and death, into continuity. "Death" is joined to "summer" and "birth" and "trembling" are given to "winter" so as to suggest that the passage of the seasons is only part of one inseparable process; and, since we know that the relations of birth and death are central to the play, we now realize that the various developments of *The Winter's Tale* are, like the cycle of the seasons, a necessary and connected whole. The contrast of the two seasons, moreover, has a further meaning. Summer is linked with the flowering of youth into the love of Florizel and Perdita, Bohemia's son and Sicilia's banished daughter, while "winter" reminds us that the age of their parents will before the end of this same scene once more affect their children's relationship. It is, indeed, a winter of lust and egotism, which implies the vain barrenness of jealous, impotent age[39] in contrast to the fair summer of youth. The coming brutality of Polixenes in separating the lovers, and especially in his ferocious attack on Perdita's beauty ("I'll have thy beauty scratched with briars"), is an exact complement to Leontes' earlier sin; it proceeds from the same impotence of aging blood, the same failure to see in the youth before it a normal, natural fulfillment by succession. By the time Camillo has brought them together, *both* his masters will have had cause to regret the importunities of passion. At present, however, the play has only reached a stage midway between the winter of disordered passion and the full summer of "grace." Perdita's speech goes on to make this clear. Between the two terminal seasons, so to call them, of winter and summer, unregenerate "nature" and the fullness of "grace," there are flowers which have a certain beauty of their own, but a beauty imperfect and, as it were, alloyed, like that of human passion unconsummated by "grace." These flowers are "*carn*ations," in which the *carn*-stem has a clear connection with the flesh, and "streak'd gillyvors," "bastards" between crude nature and the realm of "grace."

It is important to catch these associations; but more striking still is Perdita's attitude toward these flowers in the dialogue which follows. Polixenes greatly extends the scope of the discussion when he points out that the "streak'd" process is, after all, engrained in nature; in the same way the action of "blood," though capable of producing the disruption of harmony and natural relationship, is essential to a full growth into maturity:

over that art
Which you say adds to nature, is an art
That nature makes. You see, sweet maid, we marry
A gentler scion to the wildest stock,
And make conceive a bark of baser kind
By bud of nobler race; this is an art
Which does mend nature, change it rather, but
The art itself is nature. (IV. iv)

To Perdita's conception of "art" as an addition to "nature," and therefore, from the standpoint of her absolute simplicity, as a deformation of it, Polixenes opposes another of "art" as completing "nature," based on it indeed but as its crown and perfection. The conception is clearly capable of expression in social terms, and Polixenes, in what follows, proceeds to make this relation explicit by discussing the process of grafting in terms of marriage; the union, in this case, of "the wildest stock" (in other words, "nature," or, in human terms, "blood," unregenerate humanity) to a "gentler scion," the product of civilized urbanity, of "nature" in its complete, fulfilled sense, which is "grace." The "bark of *baser* kind"—the adjective is now clearly indicative of the lack of the civilized graces—is made to "conceive" by "a bud of *nobler* race": the idea of birth following on marriage thus acquires a new and wider meaning, becomes a completion, itself natural, of "nature," an assumption by normal humanity of the crowning qualities, social and spiritual, of "grace."

To Polixenes' attempt, on the strength of this argument, to dissuade her from excluding these flowers, Perdita, however, turns away with an extreme repulsion which is most significant:

I'll not put
The dibble in earth to set one slip of them;
No more than were I painted I would wish
This youth to say 'twere well, and only therefore
Desire to breed by me. (IV. iv)

The introduction of the familiar Elizabethan horror of being "painted," together with the force of "breed," shatters pretty thoroughly any suggestion that this scene is exclusively concerned with a state of idyllic make-believe. Clearly the innocent poetry so far given to Florizel and Perdita is no sufficient resolution of the great disunities developed in the early part of the play, and the brief moment of pastoral felicity is, in fact, broken by the open intervention of Polixenes. Only when the action has been decisively raised from the pastoral level will a final integration become conceivable.

The impression so far conveyed is, indeed, confirmed by the presence of a certain pathetic weakness, a kind of wilting from life, in the great list of flowers presented to Florizel which immediately follows. The emphasis on "virgin branches" and "maidenheads" is full of meaning in the light of the intense reaction against unregenerate passion which preceded it; still more so is the contrast with "hot lavender"—the epithet is full of associations with "blood"—and the other flowers given to men of middle age. Above all, there is the feeling behind the lines:

> pale primroses,
> That die unmarried, ere they can behold
> Bright Phoebus in his strength, a malady
> Most incident to maids. (IV. iv)

The beauty of these lines is devoid of strength, even clings pathetically to its own lack of vigor. The final reconciliation will be far less precarious. The spring-like beauty of this episode will have to be intensified and reinforced by the deep penitence of Leontes. Only thus can the idyllic pastoral be given sufficient substance to balance the harshness of the early scenes; and only so can a feeling for innocent beauty be raised to the level of Shakespeare's unique sensation of the fertility and maturity of "grace."

Meanwhile the vitality which, in spite of what we have said about certain elements in her flower speech, underlies Perdita's love for Florizel is indicated by the reference to the royal flowers—"bold oxlips" and "the crown imperial"—with which she rounds off her apostrophe, and by the intense feeling for life which emerges from her final turning to her lover:

> *Perdita:* O, these I lack,
> To make you garlands of; and my sweet friend,
> To strew him o'er and o'er.
> *Florizel:* What, like a corse?
> *Perdita:* No, like a bank for love to lie and play on;
> Not like a corse; or if, not to be buried,
> But quick and in mine arms. (IV. iv)

The previous references to "maladies" and unconsummated fading find their natural climax in Florizel's pathetically romantic evocation of the idea of death; but equally natural, equally a part of the beautifully balanced effect, is the spontaneous warmth and confidence of Perdita's reply. The consummation of their mutual love is *not* to lie in death, but in a reaction toward life. Florizel is not to be "buried" by the flowers which she will bestow on him, but these are to be a sign of the vitality which is to deliver him "quick" into her arms. The powerful strength of Perdita's youthful emotion has already, at this moment, laid the foundations for the final consummation, and the reference, which follows, to "Whitsun pastorals" is far more than a piece of decorative folklore. It introduces, deliberately and at this most fitting moment, the theme of the Holy Spirit to stress the note of "grace" (for Whitsun is, in the Christian cycle which conditions, however indirectly, the deeper purposes of *The Winter's Tale,* the feast of the descent of the Holy Spirit, harbinger of grace) as a crown to that of spring and love with which this part of the play is concerned.

These utterances of Perdita are balanced, immediately below, by the quality of Florizel's reply, which can be said to gather up in a most immediate form some of the basic sensations of the play:

What you do
Still betters what is done. When you speak, sweet,
I'd have you do it ever: when you sing,
I'd have you buy and sell so, so give alms,
Pray so; and for the ordering your affairs,
To sing them too: when you do dance, I wish you
A wave o' the sea, that you might ever do
Nothing but that; move still, still so,
And own no other function; each your doing,
So singular in each particular,
Crowns what you are doing in the present deeds
That all your acts are queens. (IV. iv)

The most striking quality of this passage is the sensation it conveys of balance, of a continual relationship between motion and stillness. The verse is carefully constructed to reproduce this sensation, this balance, in terms of the rise and fall of the speaking voice. Consider the effect of the double "so" in the fourth line, the first bringing the movement of the speech to its height and the second deliberately leading from that height, while a third "so" in the next line binds the central idea to those which follow; a little further on there is another "so," again associated with two balanced phrases, bringing out still further the relationship of motion to stillness, the unity of experience to the incessant flow of its material. The same effect is obtained by the choice of echoing sounds in "singular" and "particular." Still more important is the final association of "*present* deeds" with "*all* your acts"; every action of Perdita's involves all her perfections and is a complete expression of her natural queenliness. And this, in turn, connects her with the central image of the whole speech—that of the wave which is always in motion and yet is ever the same. This image, like the speech of which it forms a part, is much more than a beautiful piece of decorative poetry. It is rather the particular expression of a theme vital to the play, and indeed to all Shakespeare's mature plays—the relation between the values of human life, which postulate timelessness, and the impersonal "devouring" action of time which wears these values ceaselessly away. The wave image conveys perfectly the necessary relation between the mutability of life and the infinite value of human experience which it conditions but which is finally incommensurate with it. When this intuition and that of Perdita in the expression of her love have been gathered up into the wider framework of penitence and reconciliation, the full scope of *The Winter's Tale* will be finally clear.

The expression of this integration is the work of the last act. This opens with a return to Leontes, who is introduced, through the words of Cleomenes, at the moment when the "saint-like sorrow" which has prevailed in him since the revelation of Hermione's innocence is ready to be crowned by reconciliation to the divine powers he has offended. The years since his last appearance have been passed in a sorrow that now appears to Cleomenes as a prelude to sanctity. His faults have been "redeem'd," and the time has come when he can be called upon, without undue levity, to "forget" his past, to accept by reassuming his royal functions the forgiveness which the "heavens" are now ready to grant him.

Leontes, however, cannot immediately accept the invitation of his courtiers. For him, if not for those around him, the consequences of his sin are still alive, and their memory makes it impossible for him to act as a free man:

Whilst I remember
Her and her virtues, I cannot forget
My blemishes in them; and so still think of
The wrong I did myself: which was so much,
That heirless it hath made my kingdom, and
Destroy'd the sweet'st companion that e'er man
Bred his hopes out of. (V. i)

The rhythmic construction of this speech, with its break at the crucial words "the wrong I did myself," stresses the enunciation of its most important points. In the first part, the weight of memory in Leontes leads him to recall the perfections of Hermione and to weigh them against the magnitude of his faults. These have been so great ("so much": the poignancy of the simple expression is stressed by its place at the end of a rhythmic unit) that they have left his kingdom "heirless" and "destroy'd" (once again the break after the inconclusive "and" of the preceding line adds power to a word itself loaded with tragic meaning) the "sweet'st" companion

that e'er man
Bred his hopes out of.

The sharp bitterness of "destroy'd" is balanced by the intense pathos of "sweet'st" and leads up to the final evocation, in "bred," of fertility as the tangible expression of the deepest "hopes" of paternity. The speech, in fact, is calculated to bring out the two emotions which now prevail in Leontes; they give new depth to the preliminary utterance of Cleomenes, which they extend without, however, contradicting. The first of these is his "saint-like sorrow," a repentance for past sins kept alive in him by the unfailing memory of Hermione, and the second is his desire for an heir to be the fulfillment, as king and father alike, of which his sin has deprived him. It is here, however, that the past more especially lives on in the present as a limiting, restraining influence. A new son for Leontes can only be born from Hermione, whom he believes to be dead and can only therefore be the daughter whom, in his past folly, he condemned to die.

The other side of the picture, however, though Leontes cannot yet accept it, is nonetheless relevant. For his other courtly adviser, Dion, he is king as well as husband, and his duty to the state justifies a line of conduct which, as an individual, he might not be required to follow. The speech, indeed, has a meaning far beyond its value in developing the argument:

What were more holy
Than to rejoice the former queen is well?
What holier than, for royalty's repair,
For present comfort and for future good,
To bless the bed of majesty again
With a sweet fellow to't? (V. i)

The desire for an heir is thus taken out of the purely personal sphere, acquires a fresh universality in relation to the traditional conception of royalty in its social function. Dion's words, moreover, stress the note of sanctity ("holy," "holier"), and add to it the emphasis on human fertility which preceded it, thus extending decisively the scope of an emotion which, on the purely personal plane, could hardly compensate the preceding tragedy. We now begin to see how the pattern of the play is to be completed. Penitence and devotion, kept alive in Leontes by his memory and by Paulina's stressing of his responsibility for his loss, can be raised to the level of sanctity, and the functions of "blood," no longer the cause of jealousies and divisions which have exhausted their tragic consequences with the passage of time, can now become a source of life to the unified and gracious personality.

The necessary prelude to reconciliation, meanwhile, is a further projection of the past into the present, a poignant deepening of Leontes' love for Hermione. This is apparent when he says of her:

I might have look'd upon my queen's full eyes;
Have taken treasure from her lips, (V. i)

and when Paulina takes up and emphasizes the sensation of spiritual wealth in her reply:

And left them
More rich for what they yielded,

the lover's gift of himself in emotional fullness becomes, typically, a cause of deeper enrichment. Again, when Leontes abjures all other loves as he remembers the eyes of his former queen—

Stars, stars,
And all eyes else dead coals!—

the intensity of his emotion suggests how the sense of the constant pressure of time is in the process of being overcome. The answer, of course, is not that of the philosopher but of the artist. It consists in opposing to the action of time, sensibly apprehended, the value of Leontes' experience, intensifying it as a sensation of boundless wealth, until time itself is felt to be only a necessary element in the creation of this rich intuition. Time, as at certain moments in *Antony and Cleopatra,* has become irrelevant; in *The Winter's Tale* it has simply served to shape the fullness of "grace." Only, whereas in *Antony* the achievement of transcendent, vital justification is purely personal, balanced against aspects of corruption and egoism which threaten it continuously with collapse, here we are moving in a world less limited, more symbolic and universal in its implications. The restored fulfillment of Leontes' love is to take place against a background more ample than anything in that love itself. The past, far from being forgotten, will need to live again in the present as a formative influence, individual feeling will find its proper context in the social obligations of the king, and both will be subject together to a common dedication to the ends of "grace." There could be no better indication of the essential novelty of Shakespeare's purpose in these, the last plays of his full maturity.

The transformation toward which the whole action has been pointing is completed, given visible dramatic expression, in the final scene (V. iii). In it the Shakespearean experience, different in kind and quality from anything else in English poetry, reaches a complete integration. The fetters of the plot are dissolved; or rather the plot itself, conceived as an extension of the poetic development, is at last finally assimilated to the interplay of imagery. The words of the reconciled parties at the foot of Hermione's "statue" are as significant in their sequence as in their sense; they proceed by an antiphonal building up toward the final inclusive harmony. This sequence is given continuity, dramatic projection, by the process of Leontes' slow awakening to the fact that Hermione herself is before him, and by the almost imperceptible stages of her coming to life, which itself corresponds to the definitive birth of the new "grace" out of the long winter of his penance. In this final scene plot at last assumes its full status as the crown of an intricate development of poetic resources. Technique becomes the free and adequate instrument of experience, and the development of imagery through which we have tried to trace the various stages of the Shakespearean pattern is logically complete.

Compared with this general impression, irresistibly conveyed by the very movement of the action toward its conclusion, the analysis of detail becomes of secondary importance. Leontes' first reaction to the "dead likeness" of his queen, presented to him by Paulina as a work of art which excels art, is one of "silence" and "wonder." His first words, recalling his past treatment of Hermione, are a request that she should "chide" him; his second utterance contrasts his sense of sin explicitly with the perfection he remembers, and associates his memory of that perfection with a new birth:

for she was as tender
As infancy and grace. (V. iii)

It is, indeed, a rebirth whose successive stages we are now witnessing, a rebirth the impression of which is strengthened in Leontes by his acute sense of the passage of time; for the Hermione he sees is "wrinkled" as the wife of his memories never was, and Paulina has to explain that this is due to the artist's skill in taking into account the years which have passed since her "death." The relation of the time theme to those of rebirth and reconciliation is thus retained to the last as necessary to the complete effect.

The revelation of the restored image, as he believes it to be, of his "dead" wife inspires Leontes initially to a mood of profound disquiet. The sight is now as "piercing" to his soul, as full of memories of the follies he has committed, as her life, by himself destroyed, might have been to his "good comfort." In Perdita, on the other hand, the vision produces the first move toward reconciliation. She kneels and, like all the children of these plays in like situation, implores her parent's "blessing." Her prayer, moreover, is addressed to her "that ended when I but began," binding together—as in *Pericles*—mother and daughter in the single process of re-created life which the play aims at conveying. It is, in fact, the triumph of this continuity, a triumph as natural and inevitable as life itself, that we are witnessing. When Leontes is "transported" by the contrary emotions which assail him, when, in spite of the grief which the sight of the "statue" has roused in him, he begs that the deceptive life-likeness, as he still considers it, may not be taken from him—

Make me to think so twenty years together—

and echoes the idea so emphatically in his exclamation, "No, not these twenty years," he is once more suggesting that time can stand still as he contemplates the image of his love. This can only be justified by the power of the poetic process, which shows that this conception of love is one of life and value, incommensurate with time, which has now become only a condition of it. It is not an accident that Hermione's slow reawakening—slow both to ease the intolerable burden to Leontes' own senses and to reflect the successive stages of his full restoration to reality—is from now on surrounded by symbols explicitly religious. The "statue" is said to be placed in a "chapel," and the war between Leontes' contradictory feelings is envisaged as one in which good and evil spirits are at odds for possession of his soul. Above all, and most explicitly, Paulina stresses that as a prelude to Hermione's "descending,"

> It is required
> You do awake your faith; (V. iii)

and her final call removes any doubt as to the true scope of the "resurrection" we are about to witness:

> 'Tis time; descend; be stone no more; approach;
> Strike all that look upon with marvel. Come,
> I'll fill your grave up; stir, nay, come away,
> *Bequeath to death your numbness, for from him*
> *Dear life redeems you.* (V. iii)

The first line, broken into short phrases, intense, insistent, is as much the evocation to a descending spirit as a call to Hermione to leave her pedestal. Her restoration to Leontes is to be hailed as a "marvel" of more than physical content, as the miracle of life spiritually reborn. The sense of temporal impermanence overcome is indeed present in the reference to the filling up of the grave, the returning of former "numbness" to death, and, above all, in the assertion of the redemption by "dear life" from the bonds of mortality.

With Leontes and Hermione finally embraced, it only remains for the play to be rounded off by the gesture, typical of these comedies, by which the family unity is finally restored and in which the father bestows his blessing. First Paulina restores Perdita to her mother, laying emphasis on the symbolic meaning carried by her name:

> kneel
> And pray your mother's blessing. Turn, good lady;
> Our Perdita is found; (V. iii)

and secondly, Hermione, in terms equally familiar, makes it her first act in her restored state to beseech the gods to "look down" and pour their "graces" upon her daughter's head. With the marrying of Paulina to Camillo, ratified by "us, a pair of kings," Leontes and Polixenes newly rejoined in amity, the pattern of reconciliation is finally complete. It would be hard to find, even in Shakespeare, a more profound purpose more consistently carried out to its proper artistic conclusion.

THE TEMPEST

Whether *The Tempest,* which we may assume to have been written almost immediately after *The Winter's Tale,* is or is not a more satisfactory play is a question about which opinion may reasonably differ. What seems certain is that it represents a further and logical development in the "symbolic" technique evolved in the series of Shakespeare's last comedies. We might define this development by saying that, whereas *The Winter's Tale* is still concerned with the evolution of experience toward its completely adequate symbolic representation, *The Tempest* assumes that this consummation has already been achieved, so that the various characters and situations exist from the first entirely in terms of their "symbolic" function. The sense of motion and development which is so prominent in the earlier comedy is no longer a primary feature of *The Tempest.* Its absence, although we may agree that it makes the play poorer in a certain human content, was the inevitable consequence of a great artist's inability to repeat himself; for *The Tempest* is, whether we prefer it or not, the logical conclusion of the integrating process that produced *The Winter's Tale,* and consequently of Shakespeare's art.

The main outline of the "symbolic" pattern of the play follows familiar lines. We should never forget, in this respect, that it is called *The Tempest,* and that it opens in a storm at sea. As in *The Winter's Tale,* the storm and the calm which follows it are related respectively to the tragedy caused by human passion and the reconciliation which, after an acceptance of the suffering implicit in that tragedy, follows upon repentance in its aftermath. At the center of the action, formerly victim of the storm roused by unleashed human egoism, but now as much its master as he is in control of the physical tempest he has raised to bring his enemies to the stage upon which their destinies are to be decided, stands the enigmatic figure of Prospero. At once the victim and the master of circumstances—and it is perhaps this double aspect of his nature which has proved, for many, the stumbling block in the way of a full acceptance of the play—Prospero emerges increasingly as the plot takes shape as the instrument of judgment. Through his actions, and those of Ariel, the different motives which prevail in his former enemies are brought to the surface, evaluated, and finally judged. In the process of judgment, the meeting of Prospero's daughter with the son of Alonso provides a symbolic ground for reconciliation in the familiar Shakespearean manner. Only after the final restoration of harmony has taken place on the island does Prospero, with his associates, return to resume his place in the human society from which envy and ambition had originally driven him.

With Prospero's opening exposition to Miranda (I. ii) the symbolic design of the play begins to take shape. His aim is to bring her, by recalling her forgotten past, to an understanding of her present position, not only as an exile on the island, but as a human being on the threshold of her moral maturity. Although this understanding comes, in the nature of things, gradually, the tone and phrasing of Prospero's first speech are significant:

> There's no harm done . . .
>   No harm.
> I have done nothing but in care of thee,
> Of thee, my dear one, thee my daughter, who
> Art ignorant of what thou art, naught knowing
> Of whence I am; nor that I am more better
> Than Prospero, master of a full poor cell,
> And thy no greater father.   (I. ii)

Prospero's confidence contrasts with the compassionate fear which is Miranda's instinctive emotion. This fear, natural, human as it is, springs from her ignorance. It is a product of the same inexperience which has just led her to imagine "some noble creature" upon Alonso's ship and to live throughout with visions of a "brave new world" and of the ennobled humanity that is to live in it. Prospero does not disapprove of these visions, or of the "virtue of compassion" which he has deliberately roused to expression in his daughter.

Eventually he will endorse her feelings, give them their proper place in his own comprehensive view of spiritual reality; but, before this can be done, they need to be reconciled to a fuller experience of the possibilities of human nature. It is the story of Florizel and Perdita over again. As their full happiness involved, as a preliminary condition, the breaking-up of the rustic paradise in which they first met, so must Miranda leave behind her the "ignorance" of her own nature, come to know "what she is" in a way that can never be achieved in the isolation of her life on the island.

In the telling of the story which follows, Miranda is, as it were, awakened gradually into maturity. More properly speaking, as he penetrates the veil which shrouds for her "the dark backward and abysm of time" (I. ii), Prospero makes her aware, in terms of her own past, of the knot of mingled motives which constitute the behavior of men in society. In the course of this exposition her state is closely and variously related to the main conception; for the successive stages by which her mature judgment emerges from the dream in which it has so far been enveloped corresponds to the development which, by bringing together Prospero and his former enemies, is to restore both to a full participation in civilized life. Dream and reality, sentimental idealization and mature judgment, are in fact integrated by participation in the successive stages of a single action.

Remembering previous plays, we are not surprised to find as we follow the story of Prospero's expulsion from Milan that evil in *The Tempest* has two aspects—personal and social—which stand in the closest connection with one another. Throughout the tragedies the first consequence of evil is anarchy, and its starting point the overthrow of "degree" by the dominating force of passion. "Degree," in turn, is associated in ever-increasing measure with the human institutions, the family and the body politic, in which personal "value" receives, as it were, an external projection, a sanction in the objective order of reality. In the story of Prospero's banishment evil strikes both at the roots of social stability—for, as head of the state, he was the guarantor of that "degree" by which alone societies can prosper—and at the unity of the family to overthrow the natural order of things. In casting Prospero with his daughter on the open sea, Antonio transgressed both against the Duke of Milan and his own brother.

His first crime in the social-political order—so to call it—is deliberately related to the character of his victim. Like the Duke in *Measure for Measure*, Prospero lived "retired," withdrawn from the world and devoted to contemplation and the "liberal" arts:

> I, thus neglecting worldly ends, all dedicated
> To closeness and the bettering of my mind
> With that which, but by being so retired,
> O'erprized all popular rate; (I. ii)

and, like him again, he delegated his whole power to another. In so doing, both opened the way for evil to enter their respective dominions. Prospero is quite explicit about this when he tells Miranda that his own "closeness," his "neglect" of the ends of government,

> in my false brother
> Awak'd an evil nature; and my trust,
> Like a good parent, did beget of him
> A falsehood in its contrary, as great
> As my trust was, which had indeed no limit,
> A confidence sans bound. (I. ii)

Prospero, of course, is more secure than the earlier Duke in his mastery. His apprenticeship to experience has already been served before *The Tempest* opens, whereas the Duke, conceived before the process of deepening insight shadowed in the great tragedies had taken place, is still involved in his own search for clarification.[40] But the position of both is, at bottom, similar. Both begin by consecrating themselves to an ideal of purely personal perfection, and both in so doing neglect not only social duties but also an instrument, when properly considered, for the attainment of that perfection itself. In the case of Prospero, however, the corruption which brings him suffering and loss springs from his own family.

At this point the political is replaced by the presentation of the family theme. Prospero's own brother becomes

> The ivy which has hid my princely trunk,
> And suck'd my verdure out on't. (I. ii)

Perhaps only the very intimacy of the ties which bind a man to his brother enables Antonio to assume a part so completely contrary to Prospero's own; the man of the world is, as it were, the enemy of the contemplative precisely because of the unity of blood that joins them. To Antonio's crime against the state is added at all events a crime against the bond of unity in the family which Prospero feels even more deeply:

> I prithee, mark me, that a brother should
> Be so perfidious. (I. ii)

The two crimes are, in fact, one, a descent into anarchy prompted by personal selfishness which is, in the Shakespearean outlook of the great plays, the supreme cause of tragedy. But Prospero's past retirement has unwittingly helped to bring these crimes about; and so only now, after exposure to the tempestuous seas and years of confinement on "a most desolate isle"—desolate, in spite of all the graces with which his wisdom has endowed it, because deprived of human society—is he in a position to assume with authority his vocation of judgment.

Beyond judgment, however, Prospero has yet another purpose—reconciliation. It is here that the process of Miranda's "education" links up with the more general "symbolic" theme. The instrument of reconciliation, as in *The Winter's Tale*, is to be the love spontaneously born in the children of the very fathers whose friendship envy and hatred have destroyed; and so Miranda, now instructed into the secret of her own past, is led to see Ferdinand. Moved still by innocence, she greets him at once as something supernatural, the representative of a humanity exalted, in her view, to something above the normal condition of man:

> I might call him
> *A thing divine*, for nothing natural
> I ever saw so *noble*. (I. ii)

The idea of *nobility* exalted to something like a state of divinity is essential to Shakespeare's purpose. It is, indeed, the conclusion toward which Prospero himself is moving; but the moment for asserting it has not yet come, and so he interrupts his daughter's ecstasy, breaks off the developing love, to which Ferdinand has immediately responded, with what seems unnecessary brutality. For the fact is that Miranda's idealization, her divinization of Ferdinand, based though it is upon sound instincts, is premature. She greets Ferdinand as a god simply because she has seen nothing like him before; and yet, as Prospero is quick to remind her, she has seen no other man than himself and Caliban. The behavior of the men who have been cast ashore on the island by Prospero's providential storm—many of them presumably not much less "god-like" than Ferdinand to an inexperienced gaze—will show how dangerous are her simple assumptions. Their behavior calls for consideration in the main body of the play. Only after Prospero's former enemies have done their worst and been, in turn, dominated by the superior power and insight of the man upon whose wronging their temporal good fortune has so far depended will he be able to unite his daughter convincingly to Ferdinand in terms that are little short of god-like. But the divinity—such as it is—will then be founded upon a true experience of human nature and will express a spiritual reality, not merely a sentimental intuition; and this experience will have been obtained in the process of passing judgment on all the characters in the play.

It is to pass judgment, as a prelude to reconciliation, that Prospero has caused all those concerned in his former banishment to be cast ashore on the island. From their first appearance there (II. ii) he subjects them to what is, in effect, an analysis of their respective guilts. Of all the newcomers, Alonso, the King of Naples, comes best out of the test.[41] Having lost, as he thinks, his son and feeling that his journey to Tunis has been the cause of the disaster in which he and his companions have been involved, he refuses to be comforted. It is, indeed, the very inconsolable quality of his sorrow that shows him to be capable of repentance; and Shakespeare no doubt intends to emphasize this when he makes him capable of receiving the visitation of sleep. Alonso, in short, is morally sensitive, and so his response to Ariel's music is a positive one:

I wish mine eyes
Would, with themselves, shut up my thoughts. I find
They are inclined to do so. (II. i)

So Alonso sleeps, and his sleep is a sign that he will, when the time comes and his understanding has been completed, find his place in the final pattern of reconciliation.

The next stage in the analysis concerns Antonio and Sebastian. Their first appearance marks them out, in the repartee to which they subject Gonzalo's efforts to cheer Alonso, as cynics of the familiar Shakespearean type, their intelligence applied exclusively to purposes of destruction and self-assertion. Taken in itself, their cynicism does not seem of great moment, but we are soon shown that it is the prelude to greater crimes. As soon as Alonso succumbs to sleep Prospero's "nimble"-spirited enemy feels himself once more moved by the desire for power:

> methinks I see it in thy face,
> What thou should'st be: the occasion speaks thee, and
> My strong imagination sees a crown
> Dropping upon thy head. (II. i)

This strikes a note familiar in earlier plays. Lady Macbeth, after crowning her husband in her thoughts, played in the murder of Duncan very much the part played by Antonio in the plot to dispose of Alonso. His motive power, like that of Iago and Edmund, is a peculiarly self-sufficient conception of fortune:

> Noble Sebastian,
> Thou lettst thy fortune sleep—die, rather, wink'st
> Whiles thou art waking. (II. i)

The new twist thus given to the prevailing sleep image is deeply characteristic of the speaker. To act is to be awake, to seize the chance for self-assertion which fortune has offered; to hesitate, on the other hand, is to "wink," to sleep beneath the appearance of watchfulness. This is the "philosophy" which, carried to its logical conclusion, formerly led Antonio to play the chief part in his brother's banishment and which now, energetically communicated to Sebastian, leads his weaker associate to contemplate a similar betrayal of Alonso.

The nature of Antonio's domination over Sebastian is most clearly revealed in his reply to the latter's tentative expression of doubt. "But for your conscience?" The very word, as indicating any reality, is meaningless to him:

> Ay, sir, where lies that? if it were a kibe,
> 'Twould put me to my slipper: but I feel not
> This deity in my bosom: twenty consciences,
> That stand 'twixt me and Milan, candied be they,
> And melt ere they molest. (II. i)

The opening image, with its comparison of conscience to a purely physical inconvenience, is pure Iago. So is the sneering reference to "deity," a word which can mean nothing to Antonio but a sentimental illusion intervening between a man and the furthering of those selfish ends in the attainment of which alone he feels his manhood. The sense of sentimental unreality is driven home by the references, common in Shakespeare and everywhere expressive of loathing, to "candied" and "melt";[42] the stomach of the practical man of action is turned by these finicky attempts to restrict his progress. The speech continues in the same strain:

> Here lies your brother,
> No better than the earth he lies upon,
> If he were that which now he's like (that's dead)
> Whom I, with this obedient steel, three inches of it,
> Can lay to bed for ever; whiles you, doing thus,
> To the perpetual wink for aye might put
> This ancient morsel, this Sir Prudence, who
> Should not upbraid our course. For all the rest,
> They'll take suggestion as a cat laps milk;
> They'll tell the clock to any business that
> We say befits the hour. (II. i)

No one can deny Antonio's brilliance as a speaker. His words reflect an intense destructive energy, to which the intelligence is bound in faithful service. Behind them lies a deep-seated pessimism, the conviction that a dead man is "no better than the earth he lies upon" and that only three inches of "obedient" steel lie between his victim and extinction. If this be so, if there be no moral sanction governing our acts and if conscience be a mere "kibe," an inconvenient "deity" which a moment's reasoning can put securely to sleep, then the murder of a man who stands between him and power is the most natural thing in the world: so natural that he can discuss that man's death in terms of putting him "to bed for ever." As for Gonzalo and those who, like him, still feel conscience as a living thing, they are brushed aside in the contemptuous "ancient morsel," "Sir Prudence," and in the brilliant, scornful comparison implicit in "They'll take suggestion as a cat laps milk." The whole thing, given the will, the determination to act, is simplicity itself.

Sebastian has nothing to oppose to this conviction of anarchy. He yields at once, and as he yields Shakespeare is careful to remind us of Antonio's other crime:

> Thy case, dear friend,
> Shall be my precedent; as thou gott'st Milan,
> I'll come by Naples. Draw thy sword; one stroke
> Shall free thee from the tribute which thou payest,
> And I the king shall love thee. (II. i)

The last words show how fully Sebastian has succumbed to the spirit of Antonio. "One stroke," one simple action, is sufficient to cut through all the obstacles which antiquated ties of conscience and custom put in the way of the plotters; and in a world in which only the blow really counts, the decisive stroke backed by the will resolved to achieve its ends, everything is simple. The blow when struck, moreover, is to free Antonio from "tribute," from the material pledge of that natural allegiance on which all order finally depends. It is all simple, so simple that it leads fatally to destruction: a destruction logically implied in the act itself even before it is condemned by Prospero and judged by the standards of the moral law which upholds him and which he in turn, within his limited sphere, upholds.

In the same scene Shakespeare takes his analysis of the situation on the island a step further by relating it to a personal interpretation of the doctrine of man's original innocence.[43] In landing upon the island Alonso and his followers are placed in the possession of virgin soil. Here, according to Gonzalo, is their opportunity to organize a community untainted by competition or the shadow of ambition, an Arcadian anarchy founded upon the free following of instinct. His remarks, with the accompanying comments of Antonio and Sebastian, are full of interest:

Gonzalo: Had I plantation of this isle, my lord—
Antonio: He'd sow it with nettle-seed.
Sebastian: Or docks or mallows.
Gonzalo: And were the king on't, what would I do?
Sebastian: 'Scape being drunk for want of wine.
Gonzalo: I' the commonwealth I would by contraries
Execute all things; for no kind of traffic
Would I admit; no name of magistrate,
Letters should not be known; riches, poverty,
And use of service, none . . .
No occupation, all men idle, all;
And women too, but innocent and pure;
No sovereignty:—
Sebastian: Yet he would be king on't.
Antonio: The latter end of his commonwealth forgets the beginning. (II. i)

The dispassionate, academic catalogue reflects the unreality of the whole dream. The sources of human misery are to be excluded, according to Gonzalo, from the commonwealth; but with them, as soon appears, every distinctive quality of human life. The state of innocence is also necessarily the state of inexperience:

> All things in common nature should produce
> *Without sweat or endeavour;* treason, felony,
> Sword, pike, knife, gun, or need of any engine
> Would I not have; but nature should bring forth
> Of its own kind, all foison, all abundance,
> To feed my innocent people. (II. i)

All this is to come about, according to Gonzalo's dream, "without sweat or endeavour"; but also, we must add, without the salutary experience of effort from which is born, often slowly and painfully, the capacity to distinguish between good and evil which is the foundation of the moral life. The inadequacy of Gonzalo's simplicity, already implied in the flat, abstract tone of his speech, is confirmed once more by the comments of Antonio and Sebastian:

> *Sebastian:* No marrying 'mong his subjects?
> *Antonio:* None, man, all idle; whores and knaves. (II. i)

Gonzalo's commonwealth is founded upon an amorality which leaves place for "nettle-seed," "docks," and "mallows" to take possession of the ground. The fact that men like Antonio and Sebastian exist proves that some kind of cultivation of the human terrain is necessary.[44] The state of nature is one which man must in the course of things outgrow; the crucial problem is whether this development will be toward good, in the acceptance of some adequate moral standard (sanctioned, in this play, by the Destiny which upholds Prospero) or toward the anarchy of unlimited personal desires.

At this point, with the problem of the state of nature before us, it is time to consider Caliban. For Caliban, half man and half beast, represents the real state of nature far more truly than any of Gonzalo's courtly theorizings, and in his relations with Prospero the connection between "nature" and the moral, civilized state is far more profoundly considered. Finding him already on the island, Prospero tried from the first to incorporate him into the new civilized order of moral realities; and Caliban himself at once admits this and turns the admission into a formidable indictment of the whole civilizing process which began by flattering him and finally became his tyrant:

When thou camest first,
Thou strok'st me, and made much of me; would'st give me
Water with berries in't; and teach me how
To name the bigger light, and how the less,
That burn by day and night; and then I lov'd thee,
And show'd thee all the qualities o' the isle,
The fresh springs, brine-pits, barren place and fertile:
Cursed be I that did so! All the charms
Of Sycorax, toads, beetles, bats, light on you!
For I am all the subjects that you have,
Which first was mine own king. (I. ii)

From this we may learn more than one thing fundamental to the play. In the first place, the poetry we admire in Caliban was given to him, at least in part, by Prospero; the instinctive appreciation was, if we like, his own, but the gift of expression, essentially a social, a civilizing gift, came to him from Prospero. The burden of Caliban's grievance is that Prospero has deprived him of his freedom, subjected his physical individuality to the pre-eminence of spiritual rule; and he goes on to accuse his master of keeping him in prison who had originally been master of the island. Prospero's answer once more shows the problem in all its complexity:

I have used thee,
Filth as thou art, with human care, and lodg'd thee
In mine own cell, till thou didst seek to violate
The honour of my child. (I. ii)

The intensity of Prospero's reaction ("*Filth* as thou art") is a clear indication of the gravity of the issues involved, and of the tension which so persistently underlies the moralizing harmonies of this play. Caliban, who is necessary to Prospero, whose animal instincts are a true part of human nature (for Prospero, who thus declares his contempt for him, is dependent on him for his services), is yet recalcitrant to all restraint or discipline. Regarding himself as rightful owner of the island, he echoes, in his own way, Antonio by the assertion of his right to enjoy all that appeals to his passions as desirable; so that when Prospero gave him liberty and the use of his own cell, he used this liberty to attack his master's dearest possession in the person of his daughter.

The deficiencies of Caliban's natural anarchism, thus indicated by Prospero, are further brought out by his meeting with Stephano and Trinculo. The arrival on the island of men from the outer world of "civilization" is fatal to the natural creature, who escapes from the bondage of Prospero only to fall into that, infinitely more degrading, of the basest camp followers of a supposedly civilized society. Caliban is, of course, in many ways greatly superior to Stephano and Trinculo. The poetry which marks the simplicity of his response to nature is enough to ensure that; but, divorced as he is from spiritual judgment and seeking only the anarchic freedom of his desires, he falls into a slavery which the superiority of his expression, being so incongruous, so divorced from the reality of his behavior in the play, only serves to make more grotesque. Seduced by the "celestial" liquor which Stephano gives him, he offers to serve him as a god:

> I prithee, be my god.
>
> That's a brave god and bears celestial liquor;
> I'll kneel to him.
>
> I'll kiss thy foot; I'll swear myself thy subject. (II. ii)

His aim in doing so is to free himself from service—"I'll bear him no more sticks, but follow thee" (II. ii)—but in following the freedom thus offered him by his fallacious instincts, he goes out drunk, crying "Freedom, hey-day," indeed, but reduced in reality to a slavery far more degrading than any to which he had been subjected before.

At this point the development of the situation on the island is substantially complete. Two plots—one against Alonso and another against Prospero himself—have been fully launched, and the original seclusion of Prospero's domain has been most effectively shattered by the entry of human passion and sin. Yet Prospero, in spite of all, maintains the threads in his hands and it is precisely at this moment that he chooses to indicate, through the instrument of his purposes, the moral resolution at which he aims. Ariel's great speech addressed to Alonso and his companions just before he deprives them of the enchanted banquet that has just been set before them is, in fact, nothing less than the turning point of the whole play:

> You are three men of sin, whom Destiny,
> That hath to instrument this lower world,
> And what is in't, the never-surfeited sea
> Hath caused to belch up you; and, on this island

Where man doth not inhabit, you 'mongst men
Being most unfit to live . . .
But remember
(For that's my business to you) that you three
From Milan did supplant good Prospero,
Expos'd unto the sea (which hath requit it)
Him and his innocent child: for which foul deed,
The powers delaying, not forgetting, have
Incens'd the seas and shores, yea, all the creatures,
Against your peace. Thee of thy son, Alonso,
They have bereft; and do pronounce by me
Lingering perdition (worse than any death
Can be at once) shall step by step attend
You and your ways, whose wraths to guard you from,
Which here, in this most desolate isle, else falls
Upon your heads, is nothing but heart's sorrow
And a clear life ensuing. (III. iii)

Here at last is an explicit statement of what *The Tempest* is about. The speech is introduced with a degree of pageantry and circumstance that makes it stand out with great dramatic force from the general action. Ariel—generally the "gentle Ariel" of Prospero's preference—is brought onto the stage in the form of a harpy to the accompaniment of thunder and lightning. He causes the banquet to vanish, and then, left face to face with those he has come to judge, he speaks. His words have a weighted simplicity that underlines their unique seriousness. The effect is obtained by means so direct that they barely call for analysis. Partly by the persistent use of heavy vocalic stresses, partly by the emphatic use of pauses in the middle and at the end of lines, partly by the significant insertion of parenthetic pauses into long unfolding sentences, the speech attains a measured magnificence unsurpassed in its kind anywhere in Shakespeare. Unsurpassed because, perhaps for the first time in his work, the voice of Destiny delivers itself in judgment. "I and my followers," says Ariel, "are ministers of Fate." As such he speaks, and, by so speaking, brings out the full meaning of the play.

The most important feature of the speech, indeed, is its affirmation, of Destiny. This affirmation is, in its unequivocal expression, unique in Shakespeare's work. Much of the symbolism of the later plays—the use, for example, of the associations of "grace" in relation to fertility—has religious implications; but nowhere, not even in *The Winter's Tale,* with its still rather misty references to "the gods," is

Destiny so *personally* conceived or conceded such power in the working out of human affairs. Destiny, says Ariel, "hath to instrument the lower world." "Delaying, not forgetting," it watches over the whole story and brings the characters concerned in it, with absolute foreknowledge, to the conclusions willed by absolute justice. All this, however it may have been foreshadowed in earlier works, is substantially new, but at the same time inevitable. For all Shakespeare's symbolism, with the harmonizing purpose which underlies it, moves toward the presentation of the problems, moral and artistic, involved in this final acceptance of the reality of Destiny. Without that acceptance the intuition of "grace" is only an insubstantial dream, a tenuous harmony woven out of elements that have no more permanence than that of a personal mood; with it, possibly, the author lays himself open to the charge of going beyond his experience, of introducing an element of discontinuity into what had been so far the harmonious pattern of his work. Needless to say, it was not part of the artist's purpose to substantiate this objective conception of Destiny by argument; but it was his aim, inevitable and necessary given the general direction of his previous writing, to place it in the center of his play, to allow the symbolic web of experiences to form around it and to see if it would, in the last analysis, fit. For this reason we are justified in seeing Shakespeare's last great romance not simply as one more exercise in his final manner, but, beyond this and most remarkably of all, as a new kind of play.

The keynote of the whole action, as Ariel now emphasizes it, is indeed *judgment.* Only when the good and evil in human nature have been understood and separated will the final reconciliation take place. For this end—and really for this end alone—the various actors in the forgotten story of Naples and Milan have been brought together through the providential action of the storm upon this "most desolate isle," "where man doth not inhabit." "Desolate" surely because the work of purgation about to be accomplished needs to be accompanied by abstinence and a certain asceticism; and desolate too because it is not a place upon which men are to live their full, civilized lives—after the final reconciliation it is left by all, including those whose nature debars them from playing a part in the "brave new world" of beings at once spiritualized and social to which they are being offered entry—but on which they are to achieve moral understanding and learn to accept the judgment passed on them. Unless their sojourn on the island has shown them the need for "heart's sorrow" and a "clear life" to follow, their doom is certain. For it is in the nature of unbridled passion, as Shakespeare had presented it in the great series of tragedies from *Othello* to *Timon of Athens,* to lead its victims to self-destruction; and *The Tempest,* with its insistence upon ideas of penance and amendment that can only follow from acceptance of a personal, spiritual conception of Destiny, is conceived as nothing less than a counterpoise to this process of tragic ruin.

The work of drawing to their appointed conclusion, after Ariel's intervention, the symbolic threads of *The Tempest* has several stages. The first is to consummate the union of Miranda and Ferdinand; for upon the union of the children, in *The Tempest* as in *The Winter's Tale,* the reconciliation of the parents, and of all the characters, depends. Their love, indeed, as it unfolds under the eyes of Prospero, brings both the lovers to a new and intenser life. Miranda becomes "precious creature," "perfect," "peerless"; whilst she, in turn, says all of Ferdinand when she says

> I would not wish
> Any companion in the world but you;
> Nor can imagination form a shape,
> Besides yourself, to like of. (III. i)

Moved by such love for one another, both are ready for Prospero's blessing upon their union. He gives it, still invisible, in lines pregnant with fertility and "grace" which are most splendidly interwoven with those of the lovers:

> *Ferdinand:* I,
> Beyond all limit of what else i' the world,
> Do love, prize, honour you.
> *Miranda:* I am a fool
> To weep at what I am glad of.
> *Prospero:* Fair encounter
> Of two most rare affections! Heavens rain grace
> On that which breeds between them.
> *Ferdinand:* Wherefore weep you?
> *Miranda:* At mine unworthiness, that dare not offer
> What I desire to give; and much less take
> What I shall die to want. But this is trifling,
> And all the more it seeks to hide itself,
> The bigger bulk it shows. (III. i)

Once again the parallels with other Shakespearean utterances are numerous and significant. All the symbolic imagery of the last plays is here: the "grace" which blesses union and expresses itself in fertility and a grief which is itself life-giving. Miranda's love opens to expression like the child growing in the mother's womb. Her grief becomes something rich and infinitely precious, itself of redeeming quality; and her father, who has given Ferdinand "a third" of his own life, lays by his gift the foundations of reconciliation in the eyes of Destiny:

> here, afore heaven,
> I ratify this my rich gift. (IV. i)

The rather perfunctory masque, which follows this decisive gesture, is by comparison with what has gone before a little disappointing. The best of it, and the most germane to the general purpose, is the song shared between them by the spirits representing Juno and Ceres, where the note of fruitfulness is least artificially expressed, and where the season of birth and that of autumnal fulfillment is bound together in a manner that reminds us of a similar union in *The Winter's Tale:*[45]

> Spring come to you at the farthest
> In the very end of harvest. (IV. i)

As a whole, however, it is hard to deny that this interlude, like its not altogether dissimilar predecessor in *Cymbeline,*[46] belongs more to the structural unity of the play than to its intimate poetic sensibility. As such, we may pass over it to the other issues which await Prospero.

For, in spite of these notes of reconciliation and redeeming love, the presence of passion still makes itself uneasily felt. Prospero, indeed, never forgets the somber background of these idyllic exchanges. His preoccupation with it has been present from the first in a notable irritability which contrasts, at times strongly, with his prevailing serenity; and now even as he is bringing Ferdinand and Miranda finally together, it comes out in a warning which strikes us at first as almost cryptically out of place. A wintry tone, compatible with his age if not with the pervading beneficence of his purpose, appears to take possession of his words in a mood closely related to the sense of weariness and disillusionment which the contemplation of human behavior, on the island and off it, seems to awaken in him:

> Look thou be true; do not give dalliance
> Too much the rein: the strongest oaths are straw
> To the fire i' the blood; be more abstemious . . . (IV. i)

The fact is that Prospero has good reason to remember the evil effects of passion. The forces of evil are still at work around him. He has brought them there himself for the final and decisive conflict. As we already know from Ariel's speech, he is called upon to judge as well as to reconcile; and as soon as the marriage "ceremony" is over his other cares press back on his mind:

> I had forgot that foul conspiracy
> Of the beast Caliban and his confederates
> Against my life. (IV. i)

The thought, as Ferdinand observes, moves Prospero deeply, and in the shadow of it he makes his famous reflections on the insubstantiality of human affairs. The spirit in which these are spoken is manifest in the concluding lines:

> Sir, I am vexed;
> Bear with my weakness, my old brain is troubled;
> Be not disturbed with my infirmity;
> If you be pleas'd, retire into my cell,
> And there repose; a turn or two I'll walk,
> To still my beating mind. (IV. i)

It is a mood very akin to pessimism that the thought of Caliban's plot arouses in Prospero. We feel him steeling himself to meet it, to overcome evil in accordance with the moral conception of which he is the instrument. The note of age, and that of a certain impotence which, albeit momentarily, it inspires in Prospero, is the equivalent in this play of the disillusioned resentment of Polixenes in the pastoral scene of *The Winter's Tale*.[47] Both are characteristic of the last plays and to ignore them is to convey something less than the total impression which they should properly make.

There is, indeed, a deep sense of tension and impending conflict in Prospero's following greeting to Ariel: "We must prepare to meet with Caliban." With Caliban, be it noted, rather than with his fellow conspirators. They, when the time comes, will be easily led from their purposes by the prospect of trumpery spoils. Caliban is more formidable, because his evil is rooted in an animal nature which it seems that no amount of civilized attention can change. He is an original inhabitant of the isle as Prospero found it; and his is the irreducible element of bestiality in unredeemed human nature:

> A devil, a born devil, on whose nature
> Nurture can never stick; on whom my pains,
> Humanely taken, all, all lost, quite lost;
> And as with age his body uglier grows,
> So his mind cankers. (IV. i)

The lines are pregnant with the rotting, cankering effect of evil on man's being, driven home by the contrast between "nature" and "nurture," between inherent savagery and the civilizing sense implied in "humanely." All Prospero's efforts to regenerate Caliban have failed, and when he actually comes in, driven by Ariel with his fellow conspirators, he alone shows himself obdurate in his purposes. While his companions are carried away by the hope of easy loot, he remains firm in his murderous intention: "Let it alone, thou fool, it is but trash" (IV. i). Stephano and Trinculo have corrupted him indeed in so far as they have added to his original nature a ridiculous deification of the vices of civilization symbolized in the figure of the bottle-bearing god; but the evil was in him before their arrival, since he was—after all—the heir of Sycorax, against whom Prospero had struggled to purify the island. The purpose of Caliban is to achieve liberty, to destroy civilized restraints and live a life of anarchic, passion-directed freedom; the existence of this purpose is not affected, though the possibility of attaining it is, by his willingness to become, in the very hour of his apparent liberation from Prospero, the servant of Stephano:

> Do that good mischief which may make this island
> Thine own for ever, and I, thy Caliban,
> For aye thy foot-licker. (IV. i)

Yet this amounts to an admission that the liberty desired by Caliban is unattainable, that his freedom from Prospero's direction can only be bought at the price of slavery to something infinitely lower and more degrading; and, in fact, with the help of Ariel, they are all three—Caliban, Stephano, and Trinculo—easily defeated.

With their defeat the way is clear for a building-up of the final resolution. To Ariel's picture of the penitent state in which he has left Alonso and his companions Prospero responds, as the last scene (V. i) opens, by a declaration of his intention to forgive:

> Though with their high wrongs I am struck to the quick,
> Yet with my nobler reason 'gainst my fury
> Do I take part; the rarer action is
> In virtue than in vengeance; they being penitent,
> The sole drift of my purpose doth extend
> Not a frown further. (V. i)

The wording of the speech is worth pausing over. The victory of compassion over retribution is now a victory of the "nobler reason" over passionate fury. Reason and nobility have been closely associated through all Shakespeare's tragic period. For Hamlet it was the use of reason that distinguished man from the beast, made him, however precariously, "the paragon of animals";[48] and it is just because reason did not lead him to realize this ideal in action that he was plunged into tragedy. Now, in *The Tempest,* the nobility of reason is finally asserted in an act of compassion which transcends the exercise of reasonable justice itself. In Ariel's great speech, as we have seen, the reality of retribution is stated. Now, once it has been affirmed, it gives way to the higher, still more "reasonable" (because "nobler") virtue of compassion; and the bond between them, the thing that makes the transition possible, is simply the reasoned admission of guilt on the part of those whom Destiny has punished. To their reason, which has at last ennobled itself by acceptance, only a similar nobility in forgiveness can fitly respond. When it does so, in the words of Prospero, the pattern of the play is to all intents and purposes ready for completion. The illusion which he has been concerned to build up on the island, the state of dream-like suspension from self-awareness in which each offending or meritorious instinct has been released as though in sleep, is now ready to be broken, the sway of magic to give way to the return of conscious reality.

The moment of resolution, indeed, heralded by the return of Ariel, is at hand. Alonso and his companions are brought in, spellbound, and Prospero's first action is to restore them to their full reason. The instrument of restoration is music, to the notes of which they wake, recover their being, or—more accurately—are transformed into a new life:

> The charm dissolves apace,
> And as the morning steals upon the night,
> Melting the darkness, so their rising senses
> Begin to chase the ignorant fumes that mantle
> Their clearer reason . . .
> Their understanding
> Begins to swell, and the approaching tide
> Will shortly fill the reasonable shore
> Which now lies foul and muddy. (V. i)

Once more the symbolic purpose is clear enough. The restoration to normality of Alonso and his followers is at the same time a triumph of the dawning reason over the night of passion-inspired sensuality. The "approaching tide" of life, purified and re-created, fills the "reasonable shore" and heralds the arrival of a new, more gracious humanity.

The final reconciliation, which follows Prospero's rebuke to Antonio and Sebastian, is completely typical of Shakespeare's latest manner. Upon its poetic quality depends the success of the symbolic purpose. For, realistically considered, the whole action of these last scenes—Alonso's repentance, Prospero's "loss" of his daughter to counterbalance the supposed loss of Ferdinand at sea—is thin and inadequate. But the details of the plot here have no more importance than that which attaches to them as the necessary thread of incident upon which is based the choreography of a great ballet; and indeed the whole of the last scene of the play is really conceived as a formal ballet in which words replace visual images as the main artistic medium. The crucial passage opens with a recognition by Ferdinand of the part played throughout by the sea as the minister of Destiny:

> Though the sea threaten, they are merciful;
> I have curs'd them without cause. (V. i)

The tragedy and suffering caused by human sinfulness have turned, in other words, into the instruments of reconciliation, the gateway to a richer and fuller life. The entry into this life is symbolized, as usual, by the mutual act of blessing and forgiveness by which fathers and children are reconciled. Ferdinand kneels for blessing and is joined to Miranda. In their words the intuition of a reconciled, redeemed state is at last given clear poetic expression:

Alonso: Now all the blessings
Of a glad father compass thee about!
Miranda: O, wonder!
How many goodly creatures are there here!
How beauteous mankind is! O, brave new world,
That has such people in't! (V. i)

The vision of a new humanity, already glimpsed by Miranda in her innocent compassion when she first saw Ferdinand, and now deepened by the trials to which Prospero has put her, here reaches its full expression; and in the lines which follow immediately after, Ferdinand recognizes both that this bride has been given him by "immortal Providence" and that he has received from Prospero nothing less than a "second life." In that second life his fellows—those who have shown a proper disposition—naturally participate. As the children are finally joined the two fathers are also brought together, Alonso craving pardon and Prospero granting forgiveness, both with the blessing of the divine grace:

Alonso: O, how oddly will it sound that I
Must ask my child forgiveness!
Prospero: There, sir, stop,
Let us not burthen our remembrances with
A heaviness that's gone.
Gonzalo: I have inly wept,
Or should have spoke ere this. Look down, you gods,
And on this couple drop a blessed crown!
For it is you that have chalked forth the way
Which brought us hither. (V. i)

In the light of earlier plays this is not difficult to interpret. Alonso, like Lear, like Leontes, has come through penitence to realize his errors and to ask his child forgiveness; and Prospero replies that the time has come to cast off the burden of past memories and to look forward to a harmony that long and often bitter experience has gained. Apart from them both, the faithful Gonzalo is given for a moment a dignity that he has not so far reached in the play, a dignity that makes him at this stage—rather even than Prospero—the mouthpiece of Destiny. In his words the gods are invoked to "crown" the newborn vision of humanity with a symbol of royalty: the "gods" who have unwound the whole plot and brought it at last to its harmonious conclusion. The crown that they bestow is, in effect, a sign of the "second," the redeemed and "reasonable" life which has been given the protagonists of the play through their experiences on the island. As Gonzalo puts it:

> In one voyage
> Did Claribel her husband find at Tunis,
> And Ferdinand, her brother, found a wife
> *Where he himself was lost;* Prospero his dukedom
> In a poor isle: *and all of us ourselves,*
> *Where no man was his own.* (V. i)

In the light of these lines the whole action—the loss no less than the finding, the separations no less than the reunions—is clearly seen to be a closely woven texture of symbolic elements. Recognized as such, it grows vastly into a significance that rounds off our understanding of the whole play. For it is at this point, if anywhere, that the pattern of *The Tempest*—and with it the whole pattern initiated in the historical plays and carried through the tragedies to these last symbolic comedies—is substantially complete.

NOTES

INTRODUCTION

1. First published in 1904.
2. The stock example is provided by Charles Lamb's famous observations on the stage impression produced by *King Lear.*
3. Granville-Barker's *Prefaces to Shakespeare* were published in five series from 1927 to 1947.
4. See Chapter VII below.
5. *Shakespeare's Imagery and What It Tells Us* (Cambridge, 1935).
6. Published in 1932.
7. *A Midsummer Night's Dream,* I. ii:

   The raging rocks
   And shivering shocks
   Shall break the locks
   Of prison-gates;
   And Phibbus' car
   Shall shine from far,
   And make and mar
   The foolish Fates.

   Professor Wilson Knight comments on this as follows: "The sombre plays were plays of tempest and earthquake, and yet their shattering violence itself cleaves that confining pain, breaks it as a shell, bursting the 'prison-gates' of mortality to disclose a newer life in *Antony and Cleopatra* and *Pericles.* In *Antony and Cleopatra* 'Phibbus' car' rises, dispelling the murk of *Macbeth* and the mists of *Lear,* and does indeed mysteriously 'make and mar' the fates, which are, in that vision, by themselves 'foolish.'"
8. The title of my original essay was "*An* Approach to Shakespeare," not—as a choleric critic once stated—"*The* Approach to Shakespeare."
9. These phrases are taken from the original 1938 edition of my essay. They were only slightly amended in the reprint and expansion of 1956.
10. This quotation represents the thought of the 1938 essay as slightly amended, for greater clarity, in 1956.

11. Once again the argument developed in this passage, though valid in its general aim, now strikes me as less than complete. In particular it seems to suggest a serious undervaluation of the originality and power of Shakespeare's early work: an undervaluation which I hope that the account of these plays in the pages that follow will serve to correct.
12. I am referring here, of course, to the Globe playhouse. The theater at Blackfriars, for which the last romances were written, was different in kind, and the difference is no doubt reflected in the plays themselves; but the difference does not affect the general line of the argument here put forward.

PART I

I

THE EARLY CHRONICLE PLAYS

1. Notably the productions by Peter Hall and John Barton at Stratford-on-Avon in 1964.
2. Professor Dover Wilson, following earlier students of the *Henry VI* plays, has been a chief defender of the view that these represent the reshaping for performance by Shakespeare's own company of plays written at least in part by other hands; but more recent investigation, following Peter Alexander's important study, *Shakespeare's Henry VI and Richard III* (Cambridge, 1929), has tended to give Shakespeare greater credit for originality in his early writings.
3. Compare the spirit of Hotspur's last words:

   . . . thought's the slave of life, and life time's fool;
   And time, that takes survey of all the world,
   Must have a stop. (*Henry IV*—Part I, V. iv)
4. *Henry V*, III. iii. See p. 247 below.
5. *Henry V*, V. ii.
6. *Troilus and Cressida*, passim.
7. See pp. 27–42 below.
8. Compare Richard II on Bolingbroke,

   Ourself and Bushy, Bagot here and Green
   Observed his courtship to the common people;
   How he did seem to dive into their hearts
   With humble and familiar courtesy. (*Richard II*, I. iv)
9. Act III, sc. i.
10. *Julius Caesar*, III. ii.
11. Act I, sc. ii. See p. 9 above.
12. Compare *Macbeth:* "Things bad begun make strong themselves by ill" (III. ii).
13. The phrase is used of Savonarola in *The Prince*, Chapter VI.
14. Compare the opening speech of *Richard III*. See p. 27 below.
15. See *Henry VI*—Part II, V. i, and p. 15 above.
16. A similar deal, described with immensely greater mastery, joins Caesar's sister Octavia to Antony in one of Shakespeare's finest exposures of political realism (*Antony and Cleopatra*, II. ii).
17. *Henry IV*—Part II, IV. ii. See p. 232 below.
18. See p. 22 above.

19. *The Tempest,* I. ii.
20. See p. 26 above: "I am myself alone."
21. See p. 30 above.
22. Compare, for the phrasing, *Macbeth,* III. iv:

    I am in blood
    Stepp'd in so far that, should I wade no more,
    Returning were as tedious as go o'er.

23. Compare Macbeth's exchanges with Seyton and the Servant (V. iii).
24. *Macbeth,* V. vii.
25. Compare Macbeth's efforts to escape consideration of his true state in action, especially in V. iii, v.
26. Compare Clifford in *Henry VI*—Part III:

    The foe is merciless, and will not pity;
    For at their hands I have deserved no pity. (II. vi)

    See p. 21 above.
27. *Dr. Faustus,* the last speech.
28. Compare the attitude of Clarence's murderer, quoted on p. 33 above.
29. Compare once more the spirit of Macbeth's final show of resolution:

    Ring the alarum-bell! Blow, wind! come, wrack!
    At least we'll die with harness on our back. (V. v)

30. Compare, for the vivid phrase, Biron's protest against the penance imposed on him by Rosaline:

    To move wild laughter in the throat of death?
    It cannot be; it is impossible. (*Love's Labour's Lost,* V. ii)

II

TITUS ANDRONICUS

1. Published respectively in 1593 and 1594.
2. *Macbeth,* III. ii:

    Duncan is in his grave;
    After life's fitful fever he sleeps well;
    Treason has done his worst: nor steel, nor poison,
    Malice domestic, foreign levy, nothing,
    Can touch him further.

3. Compare *Richard III,* I. ii:

    Was ever woman in this humour woo'd?
    Was ever woman in this humour won?

4. For *As You Like It,* see pp. 279–301 below.
5. *The Winter's Tale,* IV. iv.

6. *A Midsummer Night's Dream,* IV. i. See p. 143 below.
7. Compare Albany in *King Lear,* IV. ii: "Tigers, not daughters, what have you perform'd?"
8. "When did the tiger's young ones teach the dam?" (*Titus Andronicus,* II. iii)
9. Compare *Timon of Athens,* V. i:

   Timon hath made his everlasting mansion
   Upon the beached verge of the salt flood,

   and the lines which follow.
10. Compare Lear's

    the small gilded fly
    Does lecher in my sight. (*King Lear,* IV. vi)
11. Aaron has already called the woods "Ruthless, dreadful, deaf, and dull" (II. i). See p. 47 above.

III

THE EARLY COMEDIES

1. The main argument of this chapter has been outlined in my essay on Shakespeare's early comedies, published in the *Writers and their Work* series (London, 1960).
2. The *Menaechmi* and the *Amphitruo.*
3. See pp. 65–72 below.
4. See p. 59 above.
5. For examples and a discussion of the theme of time in the sonnets see pp. 97–100 below.
6. Gascoyne's translation of Ariosto's play was first published, under the title of *Supposes,* in 1566.
7. *Induction,* ii.
8. Act II, sc. i.
9. Act IV, sc. ii.
10. *Richard III,* V. iii. See p. 39 above.
11. See pp. 305–6 below.
12. Compare, for one example among many of similar imagery, *Antony and Cleopatra,* IV. xii:

    All come to this? The hearts
    That spaniell'd me at heels, to whom I gave
    Their wishes, do discandy, melt their sweets
    On blossoming Caesar.

13. Compare, more especially, the spirit of the exchanges between Pompey and the judge Escalus in *Measure for Measure,* II. i.
14. See p. 169 below.
15. See p. 79 above.
16. *A Midsummer Night's Dream,* V. i. See p. 146 below.

IV

THE SONNETS

1. See Leslie Hotson's book, *Shakespeare's Sonnets Dated* (1949). Hotson's arguments have, however, been strongly contested.
2. Among many examples of this device, we may quote these from the Prologues to *Henry V:* "the *invisible and creeping* wind" (Act III): "the *quick forge and working-house* of thought" (Act V). Many other examples could be found in the plays, and very notably in *Hamlet.*
3. Compare Angelo's

   it is I
   That, lying by the violet in the sun,
   Do as the carrion does, not as the flower,
   Corrupt with virtuous season. (*Measure for Measure,* II. ii)
4. Compare Lucio in *Measure for Measure,* I. iv:

   Your brother and his lover have embraced:
   As those that feed grow full; as blossoming time,
   That from the seedness the bare fallow brings
   To teeming foison; even so her plenteous womb
   Expresseth his full tilth and husbandry.
5. Sonnet IV.
6. Sonnet IV.
7. *The Merchant of Venice,* II, ix. See p. 182 below.
8. For example, in *The Two Gentlemen of Verona.* See p. 75 above.
9. Sonnet LXV.
10. The fact that "devouring time" is a translation of this classical commonplace does not, of course, invalidate the point here made. It is the relationship between the two elements in the complete concept —"devouring time" and the "lion," respectively—that produces the poetic effect, which is not in any way modified by the origin of the elements which compose it.
11. This aspect of the sonnets has been well studied by L. C. Knights in his essay published in *Explorations* (London, 1946).

12. See pp. 104–30 below.
13. For this play, see pp. 324–40.
14. Notably the so-called "problem" plays, including for this purpose *Hamlet.*

V

FROM *ROMEO AND JULIET* TO *RICHARD II*

1. See pp. 91–101 above.
2. Sonnet CXVI. See p. 99 above.
3. Compare the treatment of the same theme in the sonnets quoted on p. 96.
4. Compare *A Midsummer Night's Dream,* I. i:

    Or, if there were a sympathy in choice,
    War, death, or sickness did lay siege to it,
    Making it momentary as a sound,
    Swift as a shadow, short as any dream;
    Brief as the lightning in the collied night,
    That, in a spleen, unfolds both heaven and earth,
    And ere a man hath power to say "Behold!"
    The jaws of darkness do devour it up:
    So quick bright things come to confusion,

   and p. 134 below.
5. It is interesting to compare these two lines, stylistically, to those, at least equally famous, from *Hamlet:*

    But look, the morn, in russet mantle clad,
    Walks o'er the dew of yon high eastern hill. (*Hamlet,* I. i)

6. It is hardly necessary to point out the relationship between these themes and those raised by the resolution of Navarre and his companions in *Love's Labour's Lost.* See pp. 78–89 above.
7. We have had occasion to note Shakespeare's concern with "doting," as a one-sided and self-centered perversion of true love, in relation to *The Comedy of Errors* and *The Two Gentlemen of Verona.* See pp. 61 and 75–76 above.
8. See *Romeo and Juliet,* II. ii, quoted on p. 113 above.
9. The poetry of Puck has a good deal in common with that of the Mercutio of the "Queen Mab" speech. See *Romeo and Juliet,* I. iii, and p. 107 above.
10. Compare *The Two Gentlemen of Verona,* IV. ii, quoted on p. 76 above.

NORTHWEST MISSOURI
STATE COLLEGE LIBRARY
MARYVILLE, MISSOURI

11. The relevance to this of Helena's "blind Cupid" speech (I. i), quoted on p. 135, is obvious.
12. There is some anticipation here of Touchstone's attitude to the Forest of Arden (*As You Like It,* II. iv), quoted on p. 287 below.
13. We are reminded of the repeatedly expressed determination of Antipholus of Syracuse, in *The Comedy of Errors,* to escape from the "madness" which surrounds him in Ephesus. See p. 63 above.
14. See p. 62 above.
15. See p. 76 above.
16. The implications of poetry of this kind in Shakespeare's final romances are discussed in my book *Shakespeare: The Last Phase* (2nd Edition, London, 1964).
17. St. Paul's *First Epistle to the Corinthians,* II. ix.
18. See pp. 85–86 above.
19. They can be compared, in spirit and purpose, to those of the song which marks the entry of the god Hymen, with Rosalind and Celia, at the end of *As You Like It.* See p. 295 below.
20. The later plays in the series are discussed in Chapter VII.
21. See pp. 242–55 below.
22. *Henry VI,* Part III, II. v. See p. 20 above.
23. See, more especially, pp. 118–19 above.
24. Compare *Hamlet,* I. ii:

    I know not "seems" . . .
    . . . I have that within which passeth show;
    These but the trappings and the suits of woe.

25. See Chapter VII.
26. A more exhaustive account of *Richard II* is given in my book *Shakespeare: From "Richard II" to "Henry V"* (Stanford and London, 1957)

VI

KING JOHN AND *THE MERCHANT OF VENICE*

1. *Richard III,* V. iii. See p. 39 above.
2. *King Lear,* I. ii.
3. This, perhaps, is not altogether different from the attitude of Prince Hal, in *Henry IV*—Part I, who is ready to draw his own lesson from proximity with dissolution and to wait for the suitable moment to declare his reformation to its best effect. See pp. 195–96 below. In saying this, I am not implying that Hal and the Bastard are similar

creations: rather, that a common political vocation, exercised to patriotic ends in times not altogether dissimilar, produces results that show some affinity.

4. There is an obvious parallel between the situation of Arthur in this play and that of Henry VI in the chronicles devoted to his reign. See, especially, the remarks on Machiavelli's "unarmed prophet" on p. 21.
5. The exploitation, in such passages as these, of a consciously "theatrical" element is one of the most interesting features of the rhetoric of this play.
6. The last and most distinguished example is the deal between Antony and Octavius over Octavia (*Antony and Cleopatra,* II. ii).
7. Here again the terms in which the problem is presented, if not the problem itself, are of some significance to the very different character and situation of Prince Hal.
8. John Bale's morality play on King John can be dated, in its final version, to 1561.
9. *Henry IV*—Part I, I. i. See p. 192–93 below.
10. *Henry IV*—Part I, V. i.
11. See pp. 302–3 below.
12. *The Taming of the Shrew,* V. ii. See p. 71 above.
13. Written in or about 1590.
14. For *Henry V,* see the debate with Williams and Bates before Agincourt (IV. i, and pp. 249–51 below); for *Hamlet,* the exchange with Polonius concerning the players: "use every man after his desert, and who shall 'scape whipping" (II. ii); and for *Measure for Measure,* the double confrontation of Isabella and Angelo (II. ii, iv), and especially:

    Alas, alas!
    Why, all the souls that were were forfeit once;
    And he that might the vantage best have took
    Found out the remedy. How would you be,
    If he, which is the top of judgement, should
    But judge you as you are? (II. ii)

15. This account of *The Merchant of Venice* rewrites and slightly expands the section devoted to the play in my essay on *Shakespeare's Early Comedies* (*Writers and their Work* series, London, 1960).

VII

HENRY IV—PARTS I AND II, AND *HENRY V*

1. We may suppose that some three years separate *Richard II,* which must have been written round 1595, from the three later plays.
2. Shakespeare made considerable use of such works as Hall's *Chronicle,* published in 1548, and Holinshed's, first published in 1577.
3. The argument developed in this chapter has been worked out, in considerably greater length and detail, in my book on these plays: *Shakespeare: From "Richard II" to "Henry V"* (Stanford and London, 1957).
4. See p. 165 above.
5. *Henry IV*—Part II, IV. v.
6. Compare, in this same opening scene, Henry's words to Westmoreland:

   Yea, there thou makest me sad and makest me sin
   In envy that my Lord Northumberland
   Should be the father to so blest a son, . . .
   Whilst I, by looking on the praise of him,
   See riot and dishonour stain the brow
   Of my young Harry. (I. i)
7. Compare the words spoken by Hotspur at the moment of death. See p. 217 below.
8. These elements have been well studied by J. Dover Wilson in *The Fortunes of Falstaff* (Cambridge, 1943).
9. See references as far apart as Richard II's hostile description of his rival's "courtship to the common people" (*Richard II,* I. iv) and Henry's own account to his son, quoted on p. 207 below, of his "politic" wooing of public opinion.
10. It is noteworthy that even Henry V, on the eve of Agincourt, is unable to throw off entirely this sense of impending retribution for sins committed in the past:

    Not to-day, O Lord,
    O, not to-day, think not upon the fault
    My father made in compassing the crown!

    which, after listing some acts of reparation, leads to the desolate conclusion:

More will I do;
Though all that I can do is nothing worth,
Since that my penitence comes after all,
Imploring pardon. (IV. i)

Claudius, on his knees in *Hamlet* (III. iii), could well have spoken in this way, which does not mean of course that his fault is equal or that he is the same kind of character.

11. See p. 247 below.
12. Compare, again, Henry V's reaction to the Dauphin's gibe, quoted on p. 244 below.
13. "I am not yet of Percy's mind, the Hotspur of the north; he that kills me some six or seven dozen of Scots at a breakfast, washes his hands, and says to his wife "Fie upon this quiet life! I want work" (*Henry IV*—Part I, II. iv).
14. Compare Aufidius:

Let me twine
Mine arms about that body, where against
My grained ash an hundred times hath broke,
And scarr'd the moon with splinters. (*Coriolanus,* IV. v)

15. See pp. 97–100 above.
16. Professor J. Dover Wilson, in his studies already referred to, has argued that the two plays are to be regarded as forming a single dramatic unit. His arguments, however, have been strongly contested by other scholars.
17. The discussions between Agamemnon, Ulysses, and Nestor (*Troilus and Cressida,* I. iii) are notably similar in conception.
18. Numerous examples of this type of imagery may be found in the Sonnets.
19. I have discussed this aspect of *Troilus and Cressida* on pp. 331–40.
20. *Henry IV*—Part I, V. iv. See p. 217 above.
21. Something like an approach to it is contained in the Prince's parody of his father (*Part I,* II. iv. See p. 203 above); but Falstaff's reaction and the final disposition of sympathy are there very different.
22. *Part I,* I. ii. See p. 196 above.
23. *Part I,* II. iv.
24. *Part I,* II. iv.
25. This carries us forward, by its phrasing, to Troilus': "This is the monstruosity in love, lady, that the will is infinite and the execution confined, that the desire is boundless and the act a slave to limit" (*Troilus and Cressida,* III. ii). The echo is striking testimony to the continuity of Shakespeare's thought in the plays of this period.
26. See *Richard II,* V. i.
27. *Part I,* IV. ii.

28. *Part I,* V. iii.
29. Compare Henry's references to "rank diseases" (III. i), quoted on p. 229 above.
30. Compare Northumberland's reception of the news of Shrewsbury, quoted on p. 220 above.
31. See, more especially, pp. 242–55 below.
32. *Part II,* V. iv.
33. See pp. 243–44 above.
34. See, especially, Sonnet XCIV: "They that have power to hurt, and will do none."
35. See pp. 363–82.
36. Compare

    Now we are well resolved; and, by God's help,
    And yours, the noble sinews of our power,
    France being ours, we'll bend it to our awe,
    Or break it all to pieces. (I. ii)

37. Compare *Coriolanus,* II. ii, and especially the feeling behind such a phrase as:

    with a sudden re-inforcement struck
    Corioli like a planet.

38. The conception has, of course, a traditional foundation of which Shakespeare was well aware and which is closely connected with the medieval view of monarchy; but the use made of it in this play also connects it with other, more "modern" reflections upon the nature and implications of princely authority.
39. *Hamlet,* III. i.
40. *Hamlet,* I. ii.
41. Theobald's famous emendation has, of course, its difficulties; but in the absence of an alternative which shall appeal both to sense and the poetic instinct we may perhaps be allowed to retain it.

VIII

THE GREAT COMEDIES

1. For the use of similar imagery in the sonnets, compare Sonnet XCV:

    How sweet and lovely dost thou make the shame
    Which, like a canker in the fragrant rose,
    Doth spot the beauty in thy budding name!

2. See pp. 70–72 above.
3. *Othello,* III. iii.

4. See p. 80 above.
5. See p. 144 above.
6. Act III, sc. iii.
7. *The Winter's Tale,* I. ii.
8. *The Winter's Tale,* V. iii.
9. For a mature Shakespearean statement of the relationship between *nature* and *art,* compare Polixenes to Perdita:

   nature is made better by no mean,
   But nature makes that mean: so, over that art
   Which you say adds to nature, is an art
   That nature makes. You see, sweet maid, we marry
   A gentler scion to the wildest stock,
   And make conceive a bark of baser kind
   By bud of nobler race: this is an art
   Which does mend nature, change it rather, but
   The art itself is nature. (*The Winter's Tale,* IV. iv)

   See also pp. 600–5.
10. Compare Edmund to Gloucester in *King Lear,* I. ii.
11. Act III, sc. ii.
12. Compare Polixenes' remarks on "innocence" and "the doctrine of ill-doing" (*Winter's Tale,* I. ii). I have discussed this on pp. 591–93.
13. Act II. sc. i.
14. The words are Duke Senior's, from Act II, sc. i.
15. For this attitude to the forest we can look back as far as *Titus Andronicus,* where Aaron describes the woods, scarcely less conventionally conceived, as "ruthless, dreadful, deaf, and dull." See p. 47 above.
16. Act III, sc. iii.
17. Act V. sc. iv.
18. Compare Prospero in *The Tempest:*

   the rarer action is
   In virtue than in vengeance. (V. i)
19. Compare the "fresh garments" with which Lear is clothed on his awakening (*King Lear,* IV. vii).
20. Jacques' description of the soldier may remind us in spirit of Hamlet's reflections on Fortinbras and his men,

   Whose spirit with divine ambition *puff'd*
   Makes mouths at the invisible event,
   Exposing what is mortal and unsure
   To all that fortune, death and danger dare,
   Even for an egg-shell. (*Hamlet,* IV. iv)

21. Compare, for a more extreme statement of this kind of attitude to love, Troilus' appeal to Pandarus:

    give me swift transportance to those fields
    Where I may *wallow in the lily-beds*
    Proposed for the deserver. (*Troilus and Cressida,* III. ii)

22. For expressions of similar sentiments in the sonnets, see p. 96 above.
23. It is scarcely necessary to stress the value, symbolic in kind, given to rings and their exchange in the development of Shakespeare's "romantic" plots. We have already touched upon a slight example from *The Merchant of Venice* (see p. 190 above), and the bracelet stolen by Iachimo from Imogen to "prove" her infidelity to Posthumus (*Cymbeline,* II. ii) is a device similar in kind.
24. See p. 63 above.
25. Jonson's play may be dated to 1599.
26. Compare Pericles' question to Marina restored:

    What countrywoman?
    Here of these shores? (*Pericles,* V. i)

27. For the various overtones associated with the Shakespearean use of the adjective "golden," implying at once the ideally remote and the precious, compare the reference to "the *golden* world" of Arden (*As You Like It,* I. i; see p. 283 above), and the refrain from the song in *Cymbeline:*

    Golden lads and girls all must,
    Like chimney-sweepers, come to dust. (*Cymbeline,* IV. ii)

PART II

IX

THE PROBLEM PLAYS

1. These plays have been discussed in the first part of this study. See Chapter VII, pp. 191–257.
2. See Chapter IV.
3. Sonnet XCIV. See p. 93.
4. See pp. 363–82 below.
5. The relation of this to *Hamlet*, and in particular to the soliloquy "How all occasions do inform against me" (IV. iv) is worth consideration. See also pp. 358–60 below.
6. Compare *Hamlet*, III. ii.

   blest are those
   Whose blood and judgement are so well commingled
   That they are not a pipe for fortune's finger
   To sound what stop she please.
7. This point of view was restated some years ago by Bertram Joseph in his study *Conscience and the King* (London, 1953).
8. Professor Wilson Knight, in his important studies of the play in *The Wheel of Fire* (London, 1930), is occasionally led by his desire to stress the elements of perversity and corruption in the hero to underestimate the sinister implications of Claudius' rule.
9. "Sullied" is actually accepted as a true reading of the text by Dover Wilson and other editors of the play, but it seems scarcely necessary to go so far. It is the presence of both *senses*, rather than the choice of one, that concerns us here.
10. Hamlet will use this comparison again. See his speech to his mother (III. iv), quoted on p. 355 below.
11. Notably T. S. Eliot, who partly followed J. M. Robertson's *Problem of Hamlet* in his well-known essay on the play (*Selected Essays*, London, 1932, pp. 140–46).
12. The phrase belongs to a later stage in the play (V. ii), but it could be used of all the lesser characters whose manipulation by Claudius has, up to the play scene and beyond it, blunted the full force of the central conflict.
13. The comparison with Hyperion has been used by Hamlet before, and to much the same effect:

So excellent a king, that was to this,
Hyperion to a satyr. (I. ii)

14. By Marcellus in the opening scene: "The nights are *wholesome*, then no planets strike" (I. i).
15. See Part I, Chapter VII passim, and especially pp. 215–19.
16. Compare the use of the same adjective to express Hamlet's distaste in the phrase "things rank and *gross* in nature" from his first soliloquy (I. ii).
17. Since the above account of Hamlet was originally published, I have been glad to find not a few of its ideas confirmed, from a different standpoint, in a most suggestive study of the play by Francis Fergusson (*The Idea of a Theater*, New York, 1953, pp. 109–53).
18. *Measure for Measure*, I. iii. The textual reading of this line has been questioned on the ground of obscurity, and "wills" or "steeds" are possible alternatives to "weeds"; but the more unexpected word is not necessarily foreign to Shakespeare's intention.
19. "Success," of course, could carry for an Elizabethan mind a sense different from that with which we are today familiar. "Certain word of my success" is likely to mean primarily something like "firm news of the way things go"; but there is surely in Isabella's words at least a touch of impulsive confidence which is true to her character and which the suggestion of a subsidiary and more modern sense in "success" may be held to confirm.
20. R. W. Chambers in his essay on the play published in *Man's Unconquerable Mind* (London, 1939) argues strongly for an opposite conclusion; but his plea for an absolutely and simply virtuous Isabella, eloquent as it is and partially justified as a protest against more cynical interpretations, reads with a strange naïveté in relation to what the play actually seems to offer.
21. The points of resemblance between Vincentio and Prospero were perhaps first noted by G. Wilson Knight in his fine essay on "*Measure for Measure* and the Gospels" in *The Wheel of Fire* (London, 1930). Many later writers have followed him.
22. See p. 365 above.
23. See our discussion of *As You Like It* in the first part of this study, pp. 279–301.
24. See *Hamlet*, I. ii.
25. It is interesting to note that the Countess' advice to Bertram reminds us, at certain moments, of Polonius' parting injunctions to Laertes (*Hamlet*, I. iii).
26. Rosalind and Viola are the most notable examples of this resourcefulness and just confidence in Shakespeare's comic heroines.
27. See the discussion, in the first part of this study, of comedies as far

apart as *The Two Gentlemen of Verona* (pp. 72–78) and *Twelfth Night* (pp. 301–20).

28. For Touchstone see, especially, pp. 292–93 in the first part.
29. Compare Falstaff's liking of himself, in his "withered" state, to "an old apple-john" (*Henry IV*–Part I, III. iii).
30. Notably V. ii, with its emphasis on "admiration" and "wonder," its talk of "a world ransomed, or one destroyed."
31. See *The Merchant of Venice,* III. ii. and p. 182 in the first part.
32. Parolles' plea in the moment of his exposure–"Let me live"–could be seen as an echo, transposed into a more cynical key, of Falstaff's more exuberant "Give me life" (*Henry IV*–Part I, V. iii) when confronted with the lifeless remains of Sir Walter Blunt.
33. For the implications of this word in Shakespeare's early comedies see Chapter III of the first part, and the discussion of *A Midsummer Night's Dream* in Chapter V.
34. Lucio uses the word of himself in *Measure for Measure,* IV. iii, but it could appropriately be used also of Parolles in his relation to Bertram.

X

THE MATURE TRAGEDIES

1. *Troilus and Cressida,* II. ii. See p. 334 above.
2. See the relevant sections of Chapter IV below.
3. This point of view, which later students of the play have sometimes echoed, was first vigorously advanced by Thomas Rymer in *The Tragedies of the Last Age,* as long ago as 1678.
4. See Chapter IV in the first part of this study.
5. Sonnet XCIV.
6. There is an excellent discussion of this aspect of Othello's behavior in the final scene in R. B. Heilman's *Magic in the Web* (Lexington, 1956).
7. It is useful to recall at this point the frequency with which the rose is associated, in the sonnets, with the "canker" of faithlessness:

   How sweet and lovely dost thou make the shame
   Which, like a canker in the fragrant rose,
   Doth spot the beauty of thy budding name. (Sonnet XCV)

   "Fragrant" here, incidentally, can be associated in its effect with "balmy breath" in the speech under consideration. There are other parallels earlier in the play; Othello, in accusing Desdemona, has addressed her as "rose-lipp'd cherubin" and subsequently as a "weed" so lovely "that the sense aches at thee" (IV. ii).

8. In his essay on "Shakespeare and the Stoicism of Seneca" (*Selected Essays*, London, 1932, pp. 130–31).

9. A somewhat similar part is played in *King Lear*, III. vii, by the servant who protests against the gratuitous savagery of Gloucester's blinding and who wounds Cornwall to the accompaniment of Regan's contemptuous exclamation: "A peasant stand up thus!"

10. The play may have been written immediately after, rather than before, *King Lear*, but the argument here advanced is not seriously affected by either alternative.

11. On this, as on other points connected with the play, it is still worth consulting Professor L. C. Knights' essay "How Many Children Had Lady Macbeth?" originally published in 1933 and reprinted in *Explorations* (London, 1946).

12. For example:

    The service and the loyalty I owe,
    In doing it, pays itself. Your highness' part
    Is to receive our duties: and our duties
    Are to your throne and state, children and servants;
    Which do but what they should, by doing everything
    Safe toward your love and honour. (I. iv)

13. It has been noted that the "martlet" can also represent, in the language of Elizabethan low life, the gulled and gullible dupe, the victim of deception. To the extent to which Duncan is unfitted, in a world in which confusion and treachery abound, and in which—as he himself confesses—

    There's no art
    To find the mind's construction in the face, (I. iv)

    to deal with the malignity of human motives, this aspect of his trust is relevant and important. It cannot, however, invalidate the positive content of the description as a whole.

14. *Troilus and Cressida*, I. iii. See pp. 339–40 above.

15. F. R. Leavis has an interesting analysis of this speech in an essay published in *Scrutiny*, March 1941, pp. 316–19.

16. See Chapter IV below.

17. In an essay published in *Three Philosophical Poets* (Harvard, 1927).

18. It is perhaps worth noting the presence of similar phrasing in *King Lear:*

    Crack nature's moulds, all germins spill at once
    That make ungrateful man. (III. ii)

19. He has accepted it himself, as we have seen, at the moment which preceded his last meeting with the Witches. See pp. 440–41 above.

20. I, iii. See p. 427 above.

21. Li ruscelletti che de' verdi colli
del Casentin discendon giuso in Arno,
facendo i lor canali freddi a molli. (*Inferno* XXX, 64–66).

22. Professor Wilson Knight was the first student of Shakespeare to use the phrase "an expanded metaphor" to describe the effect made by a given play. The phrase, like others which he originated, has since achieved considerable popularity.

23. An admirable discussion of the various uses of the word "nature" in *King Lear*, and of their importance for an understanding of the play, is to be found in John F. Danby's book *Shakespeare's Doctrine of Nature: A Study of King Lear* (London, 1949).

24. I owe this comparison to H. Granville-Barker's study of the tragedy (*Prefaces to Shakespeare*, Series I, 1927).

25. *Timon*, however, is more profitably approached as a play different in aim and spirit from *Lear*. See pp. 474–90 below.

26. It must be added that Timon's misanthropy differs from Lear's rejection of humanity in being much more a manifestation of *excess* and in being at least as much satirically as tragically conceived.

27. Notably I. iv.

28. Shakespeare's use of the imagery of sight in this play has been well studied by Robert B. Heilman in *This Great Stage: Image and Structure in King Lear* (Louisiana State University Press, 1948).

29. It is worth noting that, in her appeal to "gods" expressly addressed as "kind," Cordelia is echoing the words of Gloucester at an equally decisive moment in his development: "*Kind gods*, forgive me that, and prosper him" (III. vii). This play's attitude to its dimly conceived "gods" is a matter for endless debate, and no facile conclusion is acceptable; but upon our reaction to the challenge which the very use of the adjective in such contexts imposes our final understanding of the play will undoubtedly depend.

30. See p. 467 above.

31. On the necessity of "giving" as a law of love, and therefore of life, see our discussion of Shakespeare's comedies in the first part of this study.

32. Professor Wilson Knight, in his long and often valuable study of the play in *The Wheel of Fire* (London, 1930), seems to me to err notably in this direction.

33. See *King Lear*, III. vi, and pp. 463–64 above.

34. Most notably on the occasion of Gloucester's blinding. See *King Lear*, III. vii, and p. 465 above.

35. Compare "And I am Brutus, Marcus Brutus, I" (*Julius Caesar*, V.

iv). It would be unsafe to assume here that Shakespeare is simply filling out his line to the necessary length.

36. Compare, for this device, *Titus Andronicus,* V. ii:

    Look round about the wicked streets of Rome,
    And when thou find'st a man that's like thyself,
    Good Murder, stab him: he's a murderer.

37. Compare, for one example among many, the tone of Caius Marcius' violent eruption into his tragedy, quoted on p. 541 below.

XI

THE ROMAN TRAGEDIES

1. North's translation was first published in 1579, and there were further editions during Shakespeare's lifetime in 1595, 1603, and 1612.
2. The material for such a comparison can be found conveniently assembled in Kenneth Muir's *Shakespeare's Sources,* Vol. I (London, 1956).
3. See, for an account of these significances, Professor T. J. B. Spencer's essay, "Shakespeare and the Elizabethan Romans," published in *Shakespeare Survey 10* (Cambridge, 1957).
4. O Julius Caesar, thou art mighty yet!
   Thy spirit walks abroad, and turns our swords
   In our own proper entrails. (V. iii)
5. Compare, for an elaboration of this idea, which is closely related to Shakespeare's dramatic method in presenting character in action, Achilles' speech in *Troilus and Cressida:*

   The beauty that is borne here in the face
   The bearer knows not, but commends itself
   To other's eyes: nor doth the eye itself,
   That most pure spirit of sense, behold itself,
   Not going from itself; but eye to eye opposed
   Salutes each other with each other's form:
   For speculation turns not to itself,
   Till it hath travell'd and is mirror'd there
   Where it may see itself. (III. iii)
6. Compare Hotspur's outburst to Worcester:

   Send danger from the east unto the west,
   So honour cross it from the north to south,
   And let them grapple. (*Henry IV*—Part I, I. iii)
7. Coleridge gave classical expression to this point of view in his study of the play.
8. Most notably by Casca in I. iii.

9. An interesting study of *Antony and Cleopatra,* included in J. F. Danby's collection of essays *Poets on Fortune's Hill* (London, 1952), is worth consulting, but should be balanced by a reading of Wilson Knight's argument in *The Imperial Theme.* Neither seems to me to offer a completely satisfactory answer to the challenge represented by the play, which is possibly the supreme test of balanced Shakespearean criticism.
10. *Henry VIII* is, of course, later, but it is at least doubtful whether this was entirely Shakespeare's play.
11. See Chapter IV in the first part of this study.
12. See pp. 400–22 above.
13. Most notably, perhaps, in *Hamlet.* See p. 350 above.
14. Here, and elsewhere in discussing the Roman plays, I am aware that *Antony and Cleopatra* may well have been written *before Coriolanus.* Doubt on this point does not affect the substance of the argument.
15. See Chapter VII in the first part of this study, and especially pp. 229 and 231.
16. See, more particularly, Cleopatra's speech in III. xiii, quoted on p. 528 below.
17. Compare, for the spirit of this, Macbeth's famous

    Life's but a walking shadow, a poor player
    That *struts* and frets his hour upon the stage
    And then is heard no more. (*Macbeth,* V. v)

18. See IV. xv and p. 531 below.
19. The relation of "nature" to artifice is one which increasingly interested Shakespeare in his later plays. Parallels to the spirit of this description can be found in *Cymbeline,* and notably in Iachimo's account of Imogen's bedchamber (*Cymbeline,* II. ii). See p. 575 below.
20. *Cleopatra:* Think you there was, or might be, such a man
    As this I dreamed of?
    Dolabella: Gentle madam, no. (V. ii)
21. This aspect of the poetry of *Coriolanus* has been well brought out by G. Wilson Knight in *The Imperial Theme* (Oxford, 1930).
22. Stage direction to I. iii.
23. I. i.
24. V. ii.
25. I. i, and passim.
26. Compare, for the conception,

    Our natures do pursue,
    Like rats that ravin down their proper bane,
    A thirsty evil; and when we drink we die.
    (*Measure for Measure,* I. ii)

27. *Othello,* III. iii.

28. The idea of "burning" becomes almost obsessively related to Coriolanus' revenge as he approaches Rome in the closing scenes of the play. The point is well made by A. C. Bradley in his lecture on the play (*Oxford Lectures on Poetry,* London, 1909).
29. See pp. 421–22 above.

XII

THE FINAL ROMANCES

1. See, more particularly, pp. 469–73 above.
2. The play was first printed with the rest of Shakespeare's work in the Third Folio, 1664.
3. It is of interest to note that a theory to account for the textual problems presented by the play, put forward by Philip Edwards ("An Approach to the Problems of *Pericles,*" in *Shakespeare Survey* 5), would coincide with the argument here developed on non-textual grounds. Edwards holds that the 1609 Quarto is a debased text reconstructed by two reporters, "the first responsible for the first two acts, the second for the last three." From this he goes on to state that "the problem that has to be solved is whether the different aptitudes of the two reporters are the *sole* cause of the difference in literary value between the two halves of the play, whether, in fact, the original play of *Pericles* was all of one standard, all by one author, and that the first reporter, in his crude attempts to rebuild a verse structure . . . has perverted language such as is found in the later acts."
4. *King Lear* is the obvious example, but *The Winter's Tale* and *The Tempest* are also relevant. The most complete discussion of the whole subject is to be found in G. Wilson Knight's *Shakespearian Tempest* (London, 1932).
5. See p. 466 above.
6. *The Winter's Tale,* III. iii. See p. 600 below.
7. It is perhaps worth recalling Edgar's similar acceptance of "the worst" as a turning point or prelude to moral reaction in *King Lear,* IV. i. See p. 465 above.
8. *The Tempest,* I. ii.
9. Compare Alonso's use of the word: "Therefore my son i' the *ooze* is bedded" (*The Tempest,* III. iii) for a somewhat similar effect.
10. *King Lear,* IV. vii. See pp. 469–71 above.
11. See pp. 366–67 above.

12. Note, for example, the implications of Boult's remark: "What would you have me do? go to the wars, would you? where a man may serve seven years for the loss of a leg, and not have money enough i' the end to buy him a wooden one?" (*Pericles,* IV. vi). We are also reminded of the end foreseen by Pistol in the final scenes of *Henry V.*
13. See, again, p. 466 above.
14. *The Winter's Tale,* V. iii. See pp. 608–11 below.
15. *King Lear,* IV. vii.
16. See p. 470 above.
17. Compare *The Winter's Tale:* "thou mettest with things dying, I with things newborn" (III. iii).
18. Compare, for this juxtaposition of love and the grave, Perdita's words to Florizel:

    What, like a corse?
    No, like a bank for love to lie and play on;
    Not like a corse; or if, not to be buried,
    But quick and in mine arms. (*The Winter's Tale,* IV. i)

19. For another instance of Shakespeare's interest in the connection, liable to various degrees of ambiguity, between "face" and feeling, appearance and reality, we might quote Sonnet XCIV: "They are the lords and owners of their faces."
20. In this attitude, Iachimo is in the line of the great Shakespearean "villains": Angelo, Iago, Edmund, and Antonio.
21. It is just worth recalling other appearances of the word "ooze," with a similar suggestion of nostalgic melancholy and remoteness, in *Pericles* and *The Tempest.* See pp. 562–63 below.
22. *The Winter's Tale,* IV. iv. See p. 603 below.
23. In the final scene. See pp. 589–90 below.
24. *Macbeth,* I. vi. See pp. 425–26 above.
25. *The Winter's Tale,* III. i. See p. 599 below.
26. *The Tempest,* IV. i.
27. *Macbeth,* I. vii.
28. See pp. 566–70 above.
29. Compare *Pericles,* V. iii: "Look who kneels here! Flesh of thy flesh, Thaisa."
30. See p. 599 below.
31. In Chapter IV of the first part of this study.
32. *King Lear,* II. iv.
33. Compare, for Leontes' attitude at this point, Othello's outburst:

    Perdition catch my soul,
    But I do love thee! and when I love thee not,
    Chaos is come again. (*Othello,* III. iii)

    See p. 413 above.

34. *King Lear,* IV. vii.
35. *Macbeth,* IV. iii.
36. *Macbeth,* V. viii. See p. 448 above.
37. *Antony and Cleopatra,* V. ii.
38. *Macbeth,* I. vi.
39. Leontes and Polixenes are not, perhaps, to be considered old on a strict count of years, but their attitudes at this stage in the play bear all the marks that so frequently accompany old age and experience, when divorced from true understanding, in Shakespeare's plays.
40. "One that, *above all other strifes,* contended especially *to know himself*" (*Measure for Measure,* III. ii). See p. 376 above.
41. Excluding, of course, Gonzalo, who cannot be said to develop in the course of the action.
42. For a similarly close association of these two verbs, see Antony's speech in *Antony and Cleopatra,* IV. xii, quoted on p. 524 above.
43. Here, of course, Shakespeare is returning to themes touched upon in his earlier comedies, and especially in *As You Like It.* See our discussion of the implications of the Forest of Arden, and of Duke Senior's retreat to it, in the first part of this study.
44. A similar point is made by Polixenes in *The Winter's Tale,* I. ii. See p. 602 above.
45. Sir, the year growing ancient,
    Not yet on summer's death, nor on the birth
    Of trembling winter . . . (*The Winter's Tale,* IV. iv)

    See p. 600 above.
46. *Cymbeline,* V. iv.
47. See p. 601 above.
48. *Hamlet,* II. ii.

INDEX